Lecture Notes in Computer Science 1824

Edited by G. Goos, J. Hartmanis and J. van Leeuwen

Springer
Berlin
Heidelberg
New York
Barcelona
Hong Kong
London
Milan
Paris
Singapore
Tokyo

Jens Palsberg (Ed.)

Static Analysis

7th International Symposium, SAS 2000
Santa Barbara, CA, USA, June 29 - July 1, 2000
Proceedings

 Springer

Series Editors

Gerhard Goos, Karlsruhe University, Germany
Juris Hartmanis, Cornell University, NY, USA
Jan van Leeuwen, Utrecht University, The Netherlands

Volume Editor

Jens Palsberg
Purdue University, Department of Computer Science
West Lafayette, IN 47907, USA
E-mail: palsberg@cs.purdue.edu

Cataloging-in-Publication Data applied for

Die Deutsche Bibliothek - CIP-Einheitsaufnahme

Static analysis : 7th international symposium ; proceedings / SAS
2000, Santa Barbara, CA, USA, June 29 - July 1, 2000. Jens Palsberg
(ed.). - Berlin ; Heidelberg ; New York ; Barcelona ; Hong Kong ;
London ; Milan ; Paris ; Singapore ; Tokyo : Springer, 2000
  (Lecture notes in computer science ; Vol. 1824)
  ISBN 3-540-67668-6

CR Subject Classification (1998): D.1, D.2.8, D.3.2-3, F.3.1-2, F.4.2

ISSN 0302-9743
ISBN 3-540-67668-6 Springer-Verlag Berlin Heidelberg New York

Springer-Verlag is a company in the BertelsmannSpringer publishing group.
© Springer-Verlag Berlin Heidelberg 2000
Printed in Germany

Typesetting: Camera-ready by author
Printed on acid-free paper   SPIN: 10721137   06/3142   5 4 3 2 1 0

Preface

Static Analysis is a research area aimed at developing principles and tools for high-performance implementation and verification of programming languages. The series of Static Analysis Symposia is a forum for presentation and discussion of advances in the area.

This volume contains the papers presented at the Seventh International Static Analysis Symposium (SAS 2000) which was held on June 29–July 1, 2000 at the University of California, Santa Barbara. Previous symposia were held in Venice, Pisa, Paris, Aachen, Glasgow, and Namur.

The program committee met at Purdue University in March 2000 and selected 20 papers from 52 submissions on the basis of four reviews per paper. The program committee members were not allowed to author or co-author a submission. In addition to the 20 contributed papers, this volume contains two invited papers by Daniel Jackson and Andreas Podelski. At the symposium, there was also an invited talk by Matthias Felleisen and a tutorial by Roy Dz-ching Ju.

Special thanks to Wanjun Wang for helping me from start to finish.

April 2000   Jens Palsberg

General Chair

David Schmidt   Kansas State University, USA

Program Committee

Patrick Cousot   École Normale Supérieure, Paris
Gilberto Filé   Padova University, Italy
Roberto Giacobazzi   Università di Verona, Italy
C. Barry Jay   University of Technology, Sydney
Thomas Jensen   IRISA/CNRS, France
Neil D. Jones   DIKU, Denmark
Jens Palsberg (chair)   Purdue University, USA
David Sands   Chalmers University of Technology, Sweden
David Schmidt   Kansas State University, USA
Scott Smith   Johns Hopkins University, USA
Bernhard Steffen   University of Dortmund, Germany
Pascal Van Hentenryck   Brown University, USA
Joe Wells   Heriot-Watt University, Edinburgh, Scotland

The program committee thanks the following people for their assistance in evaluating the submissions:

Torben Amtoft   Kevin Hammond   Corrado Priami
Roberto Bagnara   John Hatcliff   Elisa Quintarelli
Frederic Besson   Sebastian Hunt   Francesco Ranzato
Bruno Blanchet   Michael Huth   Laura Ricci
Chiara Bodei   Fairouz Kamareddine   Olivier Ridoux
Michele Bugliesi   Gabriele Keller   Oliver Rüthing
Jan Cederquist   Andy M. King   Andrei Sabelfeld
Mike Codish   Jens Knoop   Davide Sangiorgi
Agostino Cortesi   Cosimo Laneve   Francesca Scozzari
Mads Dam   Francesca Levi   Helmut Seidl
Dennis Dams   Hans-Wolfgang Loidl   Christian Skalka
Giorgio Delzanno   Renaud Marlet   Ugo Solitro
Marc Eluard   Damien Massé   Harald Sondergaard
Moreno Falaschi   Laurent Michel   Fausto Spoto
Riccardo Focardi   Markus Müller-Olm   Allen Stoughton
Pascal Fradet   Oliver Niese   Jean-Pierre Talpin
Rajiv Gupta   Thomas Noll   Phil Trinder
Jörgen Gustavsson   Corina Pasareanu   Tiejun Wang
Christian Haack   Detlef Plump

Table of Contents

Invited Papers

Contributed Papers

Enforcing Design Constraints with Object Logic

Daniel Jackson
Laboratory for Computer Science
Massachusetts Institute of Technology
dnj@lcs.mit.edu

Abstract. Design constraints express essential behavioural properties of a software system. Two key elements of a scheme for enforcing design constraints are presented: a logic for describing the constraints, and an analysis that can be used both to explore the constraints in isolation (and thus gain confidence in their correctness), and to check that they are obeyed by an implementation. Examples of applications of the logic and its analysis at various levels of abstraction are given, from high-level designs to finding bugs in code. The challenge of bridging several levels, and checking code against abstract design constraints, is illustrated with a scenario from an air-traffic control system.

Introduction

Implementations often violate their design constraints, and consequently behave in a way that could not be predicted from the design alone. Safety problems aside, this seriously diminishes the value of the design, since it can no longer be used as a surrogate for reasoning about the system and its interactions with its environment. Unfortunately, design constraints tend to be non-local, involving relationships between objects from different modules. It is thus easy to break design constraints inadvertently during maintenance, and hard to check them, or to determine which constraint has been violated when a failure occurs.

One way to enforce design constraints is by static analysis of code. Given a design constraint and an implementation, the analysis determines whether the constraint is obeyed. Ideally, it also identifies, if the constraint is found not to be obeyed, which parts of the code are relevant, and what runtime scenarios might cause the violation.

Such an approach has two key elements: the language for the design contraints themselves, and the analysis mechanism by which the constraints are checked. In this paper, we describe a design constraint language called Alloy, and a mechanism that can be used both to check conformance of code, and to analyze the constraints in isolation.

Alloy is a first-order logic of sets and relations. We call it an 'object logic' because its operators were chosen to make it easy to write constraints on configurations of objects. The notion of object is completely abstract, so that it can be applied both to the conceptual entities of a system's domain and to their realization in the code as data structures in heap. The analysis mechanism is based on constraint satisfaction, and involves translation to a boolean formula and then the application of an off-the-shelf SAT solver.

The purpose of this paper is to illustrate the use of Alloy and its analysis in a number of small case studies at different levels of abstraction, and to articulate some of the challenges of checking design conformance. So far, we have used Alloy to express and analyze high-level designs, and to find bugs in low-level code. We have yet to connect the two levels.

Our paper is organized as follows. In Section 1, we explain the rationale behind our approach, arguing in particular for static analysis rather than a synthetic approach in which

J. Palsberg (Ed.): SAS 2000, LNCS 1824, pp. 1-21, 2000.

conformance is obtained by construction. Section 2 gives an outline of Alloy, by formally defining a kernel into which any Alloy constraint can be translated. Section 3 illustrates Alloy first with some toy examples, and then three applications demonstrating its use at different levels of abstraction. Section 4 describes how constraint satisfaction, which lies at the core of the Alloy analyzer, is used to perform a variety of analyses. Section 5 describes some preliminary experience in applying the ideas of design conformance to an air-traffic control system. The paper closes with a discussion of related work, and a brief mention of an alternative approach to analyzing code.

1   Rationale

Industrialized economies are rapidly becoming dependent on a complex software infrastructure. All kinds of activities, from transportation to energy distribution, rely increasingly on the correct working of software systems that are largely invisible – except when they fail. This has created a renewed interest in development method, a field that for many lost its appeal in the face of a spectacularly successful PC industry that at times seemed to do just fine without it.

As the architecture of our computing infrastructure comes to resemble the early centralized systems more than the free-standing personal computers of the 1980's, so our attitude to software is again emphasizing safety and reliability, themes that became unfashionable in a period in which time-to-market was the only important metric. 'We have become dangerously dependent on large software systems whose behavior is not well understood and which often fail in unpredicted ways' according to a recent presidential advisory committee [20]. This as predicted thirty years ago, at the conference that gave software engineering its name (and at which the term 'software crisis' was coined) [19]. As Dijkstra put it then: 'The dissemination of knowledge is of obvious value – the massive dissemination of error-loaded software is frightening'.

To meet this challenge, the way software is produced must change. Software systems will need to be *designed*, with a clear articulation both of the properties they will guarantee and of the assumptions they make about the environment in which they operate. Although almost any design work in advance of coding is useful, the greatest benefits will come if there is a mechanism to *enforce design constraints* – ie, to ensure that the implementation conforms to the design – not just at the start, but continuously, as the system evolves.

1.1 What is a Design Constraint?

A design constraint is a property of the internal workings of a software system that is essential to the system's correct operation. Here we focus on an especially important and pervasive class of constraints: invariants on the system state.

Given that a design constraint describes behaviour and not syntactic structure, one might wonder why we do not use the term 'specification constraint' instead. The term 'specification' is usually restricted to behaviour observed at an external interface; design constraints are not restricted in this way, and may talk about internal behaviour. Put another way, specifications are end-to-end, but design constraints can take a bird's eye view of the internal workings of the system, and constrain events and states that may never be directly observable from outside.

In the air-traffic control system that we discuss below (in Section 5), aircraft are classified internally into *active* aircraft, for which radar signals are being received, and *inactive* aircraft, for which flight plans but no radar signals are available. Aircraft are *assigned* to processes that compute their trajectories; these processes may die or become disconnected. The system maintains a queue of aircraft *waiting* to be assigned. A crucial design constraint says that every active aircraft is either waiting or has been assigned to a live process. If this constraint does not hold, aircraft may be lost, and the air-traffic controller may be unaware of aircraft within the airspace – clearly a source of potential catastrophe.

Although the notions of active, inactive and waiting aircraft, of connected and disconnected processes, and of assignment of aircraft to processes, etc, can all be interpreted intuitively by the user of the system, it would have been possible to design the system without them. A specification would be confined to the events and states the user can directly observe: the radar inputs, the trajectories displayed, and so on.

Of course, ideally we would like to check specification properties. But this seems infeasible. It would require end-to-end reasoning involving a long causal chain. It would have to account, for example, for failures of the display driver on the controller's screen. Moreover, it is not clear that specification constraints are even expressible. Design constraints, on the other hand, are easily expressed, and checking that code conforms to them seems within reach.

1.2 Synthesis vs. Analysis

Roughly speaking, a mechanism to enforce design constraints falls into one of two categories. *Synthetic mechanisms* achieve conformance by construction, for example by generating code from designs. *Analytic mechanisms* give more leeway to developers, but apply methods and tools to expose flaws in the code after its production, forcing the developer to bring it into alignment with the design.

The key advantage of an analytic approach is that it can be *lightweight* [9]. One can characterize essential properties of a system with very succinct design constraints. Even for a system consisting of millions of lines of code, there are useful constraints that can be expressed in tens of lines of Alloy. Back of the envelope sketches are equally terse, but are not amenable to any form of analysis or tool support. If we burden our designs with a desire to generate code from them, this succinctness must go.

Advocates of code generation will argue the advantage of having a single representation of the system, and of the savings in not having to write code by hand. For domain-specific applications this has appeal, but we believe it in general to be misguided:

· The extra effort invested in programming is not wasted. The value in methods that employ additional representations is due largely to redundancy: in short, a better system results when it has been described from two orthogonal viewpoints. If code is generated automatically from designs, any errors in the design are likely to be carried over directly; even if there is some room left for the developer, the benefits of an orthogonal view are likely to be lost.

· Unlike code, representations that are not required to be executable can accommodate multiple viewpoints. The intended behaviour of a software system is most easily expressed with conjunction: as a collection of constraints that must be satisfied simultaneously. Synthetic approaches demand a monolithic and usually sequential description, so that the design comes to look like a program, begging the question of what properties *it* should conform to. New ideas about combining different viewpoints at the code level seem promising, but it is not clear to what extent they may applied at more abstract levels [6,17].

· A design from which code is to be generated must embody a full description of the intended behaviour. In many cases code itself may be the most succinct representation. Some sobering experiences with formal specification have led us to be less confident that specifications are necessarily shorter and simpler than the code they describe. It is not at all clear, for example, that one could construct a specification of an entire word processor that is any less complex than its implementation.

Finally, for legacy code, analysis is the only option.

1.3 Desiderata

An analytic approach has two key elements: the constraint language and the analysis mechanism used to determine conformance. In this paper, we propose one combination of language and mechanism, but we view this as just one possibility. For different aspects of a system's behaviour, different constraint languages will be appropriate. Our language is aimed at the structural aspect, and would be complemented by an approach that addressed temporal issues. Nevertheless, there are some basic criteria that all approaches must satisfy:

· *Expressiveness*. The language must be expressive enough to capture the essential design constraints. Type annotations, the most successful example to date of checkable constraints, are too weak. For example, with types we might be able to say that no object in a class A can contain an object in a class B, but we cannot express the 'caching constraint' that whenever an object in class A contains an object in class B, there is another object in class C that also contains the object.

· *Tractability*. A constraint language that is sufficiently expressive is unlikely to be decidable, but it must be tractable: that is, amenable to fully automatic analysis for the size of problem that arises in practice.

· *Accuracy, soundness and predictability*. Conventional criteria for judging analyses were developed in the context of optimizing compilers. In the context of tools for software developers, where spurious bug reports may be as bad as spurious proofs of correctness, terms such as 'conservative' and 'false positive' are confusing. So let us say instead that an analysis gives a *correct* answer in response to a query about whether a design constraint holds either if (1) it says 'yes' and the constraint indeed holds (for all executions), or (2) it says 'no' and the constraint does not hold (for some execution). An important pragmatic metric, which we might call *accuracy*, is simply this: of 100 queries that arise in practice, for how many does the analysis give a correct answer? By this metric, a conservative analysis that rarely succeeds in showing a valid constraint to hold, but which never misses a failure, might rate more poorly than an analysis that is neither conservative nor complete.

In addition to being accurate, we might want some notion of soundness: that every 'yes' or 'no' answer is correct (ie, that proofs or counterexamples can be trusted); or that both 'yes' and 'no' answers are correct, in which case there will be 'maybe' answers too. Finally, if the developer can to some degree predict failures of analysis, incorrect results are more palatable. In particular, small, semantics-preserving changes to the syntax of the code should not affect the outcome.

· *Incrementality*. It must be possible to construct and check constraints incrementally. A common scenario will be to check a basic constraint first, and then refine it to perform a more exacting check. Completeness requirements on the constraints being checked – in the worst case that they form some kind of abstract program with a structural correspondence to the implementation – are undesirable. Moreover, it should be possible to obtain more refined checks by adding constraints, without retracting old ones. The constraint language should therefore be *declarative*, allowing constraints to be formed with logical conjunction. Incrementality with respect to code construction is important too, and argues for a static rather than a dynamic analysis, so that modules can be checked before the modules on which they depend have been written.

2 The Alloy Language

Alloy is a constraint specification language based on a simple logic. Here we present the logic alone; the full language adds a variety of convenient shorthands and structuring mechanisms [10]. The logic is defined in Figure 1, with an abstract syntax (on the left) and a semantics (on the right). Most of its features are standard, so we focus here on its novelties: the treatment of scalars as singleton sets, and the dot operator used to form 'navigation expressions'.

2.1 Syntax

The syntax is mostly standard, with ASCII characters in place of conventional mathematical symbols. The logic is strongly typed, and a formula is accompanied by declarations of the set and relation variables; we call the combination of a formula and its declarations a *constraint*. Each declaration associates a type with a variable. There are three kinds of type:

· the *set* type T, denoting sets of atoms drawn from T;

· the *relation* type $S \rightarrow T$, denoting relations from S to T;

· the *function* type $T \Rightarrow t$, denoting functions from atoms of T to values of type t.

Types are constructed from basic types that denote disjoint sets of atoms. We use upper case names for basic types and lower case names for arbitrary types. So in the type $T \Rightarrow t$, the index type T must be a basic type but t may be a set type, relation type or another function type.

Functions correspond to predicates of arity greater than two. The predicate *Rides* (r,j,h) (not directly expressible in Alloy) that holds when jockey j rides horse h in race r, for example, might be declared as a function

 Rides : Race => Jockey -> Horse

and, for a given race r, the expression *Rides*[r] would then denote a relation mapping jockeys to their horses in that race. Functions retain the binary flavour of the logic: they fit naturally into diagrams, lead to simpler expression syntax, and can accommodate multiplicity markings. In the full language, the question marks in

 Rides : Race => Jockey? -> Horse?

indicate that, in each race, a jockey rides at most one horse and a horse is ridden by at most one jockey.

Sets, relations and functions allow the heap of an executing object-oriented program to be modelled straightforwardly. Sets model not only classes and subclasses, but also collections of objects with particularly properties: such a set may contain objects in several classes, and may change dynamically due to mutation of objects as well as creation and destruction. A field in a class A of type B is modelled as a relation from A to B. Since object references can always be encoded with relations, functions are not strictly necessary, but

constraint ::= decl* formula
decl ::= var : typexpr
typexpr ::=
    type | type -> type | type => typexpr

formula ::=
  expr in expr   subset
  | ! formula   negation
  | formula && formula   conjunction
  | formula || formula   disjunction
  | all v : type | formula   universal
  | some v : type | formula   existential

expr ::=
  | expr + expr   union
  | expr & expr   intersection
  | expr - expr   difference
  | expr . expr   navigation
  | ~ expr   transpose
  | + expr   closure
  | {v : t | formula}   comprehension
  | expr [var]   application
  | var   variable

M : formula → env → boolean
X : expr → env → value
env = (var + type) → value
value = $\mathbb{P}$ (atom × atom) + (atom → value)

M [a in b] e = X[a] e ⊆ X[b] e
M [! F] e = ¬ M [F] e
M [F && G] e = M [F] e ∧ M [G] e
M [F || G] e = M [F] e ∨ M [G] e
M [all v: t | F] e = ∧ {M[F](e ⊕ v ↦ {c}) | c ∈ e(t)}
M [some v: t | F] e = ∨ {M[F](e ⊕ v ↦ {c}) | c ∈ e(t)}

X [a + b] e = X[a]e ∪ X[b]e
X [a & b] e = X[a]e ∩ X[b]e
X [a - b] e = X[a]e \ X[b]e
X [a . b] e = {(x,z) | ∃y. (y,z) ∈ X[a]e ∧ (y,x) ∈ X[b]e}
X [~a] e = {(x,y) | (y,x) ∈ X[a]e}
X [+a] e = smallest r such that r ; r ⊆ r ∧ X[a]e ⊆ r
X [{v: t | F}] e = {c ∈ e(t) | M[F](e ⊕ v ↦ {c})}
X [a[v]] e= X[a]e (c) where {(c,unit)} = e(v)
X [v] e = e(v)

Figure 1: Syntax and semantics of the Alloy logic

they are convenient. A table in a class *A* that maps keys of type *K* to values of type *V* may be modelled as a function

    table: A => K -> V

There are no scalar types: a scalar is represented as a set with a single element. This allows navigation expressions to be written uniformly, without the need to convert back and forth between scalars and sets, sidesteps the partial function problem, and simplifies the semantics of the analysis (and its implementation).

Formulas have a conventional syntax. There is only one elementary formula, stating that one expression is a subset of another; an equality of two expressions is written as a pair of inequalities, one in each direction. In quantified formulas, the variable is declared to have basic type, and is interpreted as being bound to singleton subsets of the type.

Expressions are formed using the standard set operators (union, intersection and difference), the unary relational operators (transpose and transitive closure), and the dot operator, used to form navigation expressions. The unary operators are prefixes, to make parsing easy.

Set comprehension has the standard form. Set and relation variables are expressions, but function variables, and functions in general, are not. Ensuring that functions can only be applied to variables guarantees that an expression involving a function is always well defined, since the function's argument will denote a singleton set.

2.2 Type System

We treat sets semantically as degenerate relations, viewing the set $\{e_1, e_2, \ldots\}$ as the relation $\{(e_1, unit), (e_2, unit), \ldots\}$ where *unit* is a special atom that is the sole member of a special type *Unit*. This allows the set operators to be applied equally to sets and relations.

2.3 Semantics

The meaning of the logic is given in a denotational style. There are two meaning functions: M, which interprets a formula as true or false, and X, which interprets an expression as a value. Values are either binary relations over atoms, or functions from atoms to values. Interpretation is always in the context of an environment that binds variables and basic types to values, so each meaning function takes both a syntactic object and an environment as arguments.

Each definition defines the meaning of an expression or formula in terms of its constituents. For example, the elementary formula *a in b* is true in the environment e when $X[a]e$, the relation denoted by a in e, is a subset of $X[b]e$, the relation denoted by b in e. The quantified formula *all v: t | F* is true in e when F is true in every environment obtained by adding to e a binding of v to the singleton set $\{c\}$, where c is a member of the set denoted by the type t in e.

The dot operator is a form of relational composition. When s is a set and r is a relation, *s.r* denotes the image of s under r. Combining this with the treatment of scalars as singleton sets results in a uniform syntax for navigation expressions. For example, if p is a person, *p.mother* will denote p's mother; *p.parents* will denote the set of p's parents; *p.parents.brother* will denote p's uncles; etc. (The definition still makes sense if neither argument is a set: ~q.p will be the composition of two relations p and q, and ~t.~s the cross product of sets s and t.)

The meaning of a constraint is the collection of well-formed environments in which its formula evaluates to true. An environment is well-formed if: (1) it assigns values to the variables and basic types appearing in the constraint's declarations, and (2) it is well-typed—namely that it assigns to each variable an appropriate value given the variable's type. For example, if a variable v has type $S \rightarrow T$ in an environment e, then $e(v)$, the value assigned to v in e, must be a relation from the set denoted by S to the set denoted by T.

2.4 Shorthands

The full language provides a variety of shorthands and structuring mechanisms. We mention a few briefly to give the flavour of the language and to make the examples below intelligible:

· *Implicit types.* Alloy does not actually require type declarations as shown in Figure 1. Instead, one declares *domains*, sets that form the coarsest classification of objects. Each domain has a basic type implicitly associated with it; this type represents the set of objects that might exist and is thus unchanging; the domain represents the objects that exist, and may change over time. When declaring a relation, the left and right sides are sets that have also been declared, and not basic types. So, for example, in a graphical user interface we might declare a domain *Window* with a subset *Visible* representing those windows that are showing; the declaration

occludes: Visible -> Visible

implictly types the relation *occludes* and also states that it relates only windows that are showing.

· *Multiplicities.* The symbols + (one or more), ! (exactly one) and ? (zero or one) are used in declarations to constrain sets and relations. The declaration

> r: S m -> T n

where *m* and *n* are multiplicity symbols, makes *r* a relation from *S* to *T* that maps each *S* to *n* atoms of *T*, and maps *m* atoms of *S* to each *T*. Similarly, the declaration

> S : T m

makes *S* a set of m atoms drawn from the set *T*. Omission of a multiplicity symbol implies no constraint.

· *Quantifier shorthands.* The usual shorthands are available for quantifiers, such as quantifying over several variables at once, and bounding their values with expressions. Alloy provides some extra quantifier symbols, *no*, *sole* and *one*, for saying that there are no values, at most one value, and exactly one value that satisfy the formula. Instead of using set constants, Alloy allows quantifiers to be applied to expressions. The formula *Q e*, where *Q* is any quantifier and *e* is a set-valued expression, is short for

> Q v | v in e

so *some e*, *no e*, *sole e*, and *one e* say respectively that the set *e* is non-empty, empty, containing at most one element, and containing exactly one element.

· *Paragraphs.* An Alloy description is divided into paragraphs for modularity, and to distinguish different kinds of constraint. An invariant (introduced by the keyword *inv*) gives a constraint that is intended to hold at all times. A definition (*def*) defines one set or relation or function in terms of others; defined variables can in principle always be eliminated in favour of more complex constraints. An assertion (*assert*) is a putative theorem to be checked. A condition (*cond*) is a constraint that, unlike an invariant, is not expected always to hold, but can be quoted in other paragraphs.

3   Examples

Paul Simon wrote in a 1973 song: 'One man's ceiling is another man's floor'. Had he been more inclined to precision, he might instead have written:

> model FloorsAndCeilings {
> domain {Man, Platform}
> state {ceiling, floor : Man -> Platform!}
> inv {all m: Man | some n: Man - m | m.ceiling = n.floor}
> assert {all m: Man | some n: Man - m | m.floor = n.ceiling}
> }

There are two domains: *Man*, the set of all men, and *Platform*, the set of all platforms, each being a ceiling or a floor depending on a man's perspective. The relations *ceiling* and *floor* map each man to exactly one platform; the declarations themselves thus include, implicitly, the constraint that each man has exactly one ceiling and one floor. The invariant says that for every man *m*, there is a man *n* distinct from *m* whose floor is *m*'s ceiling.

Since Alloy is always interpreted over finite domains, there cannot be an infinite skyscraper, and this must imply a cycle in the chain of floors and ceilings. We might wonder whether this implies that 'One man's floor is another man's ceiling'. This assertion is invalid, as Alloy's analyzer will demonstrate by displaying a counterexample:

```
Domains:
  Man = {M0,M1,M2}
  Platform = {P0,P1,P2}
Relations:
  ceiling = {M0 -> P0, M1 -> P2, M2 -> P2}
  floor = {M0 -> P2, M1 -> P0, M2 -> P1}
Skolem constants:
  m = M2
```

The Skolem constant is a witness to the refutation of the assertion: the man *M2* has a floor *P1* that is not the ceiling of another man.

Formalizing a statement from a different song, 'Everybody loves my baby, but my baby loves only me', we get:

```
model Baby {
domain {Person}
state {me, baby : Person!}
  loves : Person -> Person}
inv { (all p : Person | baby in p.loves) && baby.loves = me}
assert {baby = me}
}
```

There are two scalars (ie, singleton sets), *me* and *baby*, and a relation *loves* that maps each person to the set of persons he or she loves. The statement is expressed as a conjunction, that for every person *p*, the set of persons loved by *p* includes *baby*, and that the set of persons *baby* loves is exactly the singleton set *me*. The assertion records David Gries's observation that 'I am my baby' must follow. In this case, the assertion is valid and Alloy's analyzer finds no counterexamples.

We now move to some more practical examples, illustrating in outline how Alloy has been used at different levels of abstraction. First, we discuss how we used it to explore a problem in Microsoft COM. Here, the components of the Alloy description do not directly map to the state of the system: one component, for example, represents the relationship between COM interfaces that is implicit in the query interface method. Second, we look at how Alloy was used to check properties of an intentional naming scheme. In this case, there was a direct correspondence between the model and the realization of the lookup algorithm in code. Most of our experience with Alloy has been at the level of one of these descriptions. In the third example, we report on some recent work in which we used Alloy to specify the behaviour of procedures and find bugs in their implementations.

3.1 Exploring Queries in COM

In attempting to use Microsoft COM to implement a novel component architecture, Sullivan and his colleagues came across an interesting anomaly [24]. COM allows one component to aggregate other components, with the outer component passing off one or more services of inner components as its own, thus avoiding the cost of explicitly delegating service requests from outer to inner. Surprisingly, the rules of COM require in such a situation that every service of an inner component be visible through the outer component: in other words, hiding is compromised. Since this is clearly not the intent of the designers of COM, the published rules of COM must be amended. It turns out to be sufficient to weaken the rules for inner components.

Sullivan explored this problem by formalizing the published rules of COM in the Z formal specification language [23]. He then proved, by hand, a theorem stating that, whenever aggregation is present, hiding is lost. By introducing a distinction between 'legal' and 'illegal' components, he was able to qualify this theorem so that it applies only when the inner components are legal.

In a subsequent collaboration, we translated the Z model to Alloy so we could apply our automatic analysis [13]. With the support of the Alloy analyzer, we explored various reformulations of the model, and in the process were able to reduce it to about a third of its original size. At the same time, we checked a variety of assertions that we believed to hold, many of which turned out to be invalid.

This case study illustrates the importance of analysis of constraints in their own right. The issue here was not conformance of an implementation to a design, but rather the formulation of the essential design constraints. With an automatic analysis tool at hand, we were able to make more daring and radical changes to the constraints than we could ever have considered without tools.

A simplified version of the Alloy description is shown in Figure 2. There are three domains: *Component*, the set of COM components in the configuration in question; *Interface*, the set of interfaces or services these components provide; and *IID*, the set of interface identifiers or IID's. The *interfaces* relation maps each component to the interfaces it provides. The *iids* relation maps each interface to its identifiers; these may be thought of as the types of the interface (there being more than one because the types are arranged in a hierarchy).

The function qi models the 'query interface' mechanism. For each interface i, there is a relation $qi[i]$ (implemented in the code as a method) that maps identifiers to interfaces. This mechanism is the essence of COM, since it allows interfaces to negotiate dynamically, and work together when their composition was not anticipated in advance. At runtime, to use a particular service of a COM component, one gets a handle on an interface and then queries it with the IID of the service of interest. If the component offers the service, an interface providing that service will be returned.

Two auxiliary relations are defined: *reaches*, which maps an interface to all the interfaces it reaches via a query; and *iids_known*, which associates with an interface the set of IID's for which a query will return successfully.

The invariants capture the standard rules of COM. The first two are as expected: that a query, if successful, returns an interface with the requested IID(*QueriesSound*) and belonging to the same component (*QueriesLocal*). The third (*Identity*) summarizes the notion of identity in COM: that there is a global IID which, for any interface, returns a particular interface of the component (whose pointer value may be used to test identity of components). The remaining 3 invariants capture more subtle rules about queries, for example that if a query from an interface i might lead to an interface j, then any query on j using an IID provided by some interface of i must succeed (*Symmetry*).

Finally, the assertion expresses in more general terms the problem with aggregation: that if any two components share an interface, they must provide the same IID's.

```
model COM {
domain {Component, Interface, IID}
state {
      interfaces : Component + -> Interface
      iids, iids_known : Interface -> IID+
      qi : Interface => IID -> Interface?
      reaches: Interface -> Interface
      }
def reaches {all i | i.reaches = IID.qi[i]}
def iids_known {all i | i.iids_known = {x | some x.qi[i]}
inv QueriesSound {all i | all x: i.iids_known | x in x.qi[i].iids}
inv QueriesLocal {all c | all j : c.interfaces | all x: IID | x.qi[j] in c.interfaces}
inv Identity {some Unknown |all c | some j: c.interfaces | all i: c.interfaces | j = Unknown.qi[i]}
inv Reflexivity {all i | i.iids in i.iids_known}
inv Symmetry {all i, j | j in i.reaches -> i.iids in j.iids_known}
inv Transitivity {all i, j | j in i.reaches -> j.iids_known in i.iids_known}

assert NoHiding {
      all c, d | some (c.interfaces & d.interfaces) ->  c.interfaces.iids = d.interfaces.iids }
      }
}
```

Figure 2: Simplified version of COM constraints

3.2 Checking an Intentional Naming Scheme

An intentional naming scheme allows objects to be looked up by their specifications rather than their identities or locations. A recent framework supporting this idea [1] allows queries called 'name specifiers' in the form of trees of alternating attributes and values. These are presented to a name resolver whose database, called a 'name tree', is similarly structured, but which also contains 'name records' returned as the results of queries.

We used Alloy to check the correctness of a lookup algorithm that had been previously specified in pseudocode and implemented in Java [16]. The Alloy description was about 50 lines long, with an additional 30 lines of assertions expressing the anticipated properties to be checked. The code of the algorithm is roughly 1400 lines of Java, with an additional 900 lines of testing code. The Alloy analysis revealed that the algorithm returns the wrong results in a number of important but tricky cases, and that a key claim made about the algorithm (to do with the role of wildcards) is invalid.

This case study illustrates the value of partial modelling. Our description included only one crucial operation – *lookup* – and summarized the others as invariants on the name tree. To analyze the possible *lookup* scenarios, it was not necessary to write an abstract program that generates different prestates for *lookup* by executing operations that mutate the name tree. Instead, the analysis considered all lookup scenarios (within a bounded scope) that began in states satisfying the given invariants.

The case study also supports the *small scope hypothesis*, discussed below, that subtle errors can be detected by considering only small cases. All of the bugs that we found could be illustrated with name trees and name specifiers involving at most 3 attributes, 3 values and 3 objects.

3.3 Finding Bugs in Code

Our third case study illustrates how Alloy can be used at a lower level, to check code [14]. We took a suite of list-manipulating procedures that have been used to evaluate shape analyses [5]. Each procedure was specified by an Alloy constraint; we then used the Alloy analyzer to check that the body of the procedure satisfied the constraint. If the constraint was not found to be satisfied, a counterexample was generated that corresponds to a bad execution of the procedure.

These constraints involved, for the most part, simple set inclusions. For example, we specified for *delete*, a procedure that deletes an element from a list, that the set of list cells reachable from the result afterwards is a subset of the set of cells reachable from the argument, and for *merge* that the set of cells in the result is the union of the sets of cells in each argument. We also specified some more detailed properties, for example that the final list returned by *merge* preserves the order of cells as they appeared in the argument lists.

In addition to checking user-defined properties, we analyzed the procedures for anomalies by asserting constraints that might be generated automatically. For example, we checked for null pointer dereferences, and creation of cyclic structures. Our analysis found the bugs that had been previously found (although we did not consider memory leakage issues which one the papers had addressed), and found one anomaly which had not been identified before.

This experience again supported the small scope hypothesis; in fact, all bugs were found by considering only two list cells. It also supported a related observation, previously made by the developers of the ESC tool [4], that very few loop iterations are required to catch a high proportion of bugs. In this case, considering at most one iteration sufficed.

The analyses took roughly this form:

```
model Merge {
domain {Cell}
state {List: Cell
    next: List -> List?
    ...}
cond Merge {...}
assert {
    Merge -> result.*next' = p.*next + q.*next
    }
}
```

There is a single domain, *Cell*, representing the set of all heap cells. The state consists of *List*, the set of cells that are objects belonging to a class *List*, and a relation *next* modelling a field of this class. This relation maps each *List* object to another *List* object, or does not map it (modelling a null value in the heap). Were we translating a language without compile-time typing, we would have declared the right-hand side of *next* to be *Cell* instead of *List*, admitting the possibility that a *List* object points incorrectly to an object of a different class. The condition *Merge* holds the translation of the body of the *merge* procedure. Finally the assertion shown here expresses the set inclusion property, that the cells reachable from the result in the poststate must be the union of those reachable from the arguments *p* and *q* in the prestate. Alloy uses Z's convention of referring to values in the poststate with a fresh variable whose name is obtained by primig the name of the prestate variable.

4 Analysis

Alloy's analyzer is a constraint solver [12]. It reduces a variety of analysis questions to the problem of finding a model of a relational formula: that is, an assignment of values to the sets, relations and functions for which the formula evaluates to true. The analysis is based on a translation to a boolean satisfaction problem, and gains its power by exploiting state-of-the-art SAT solvers.

The details of the analysis are explained elsewhere [15]. Here, we describe the analysis from the user's point of view: what it does conceptually, and what guarantees it makes. This allows us to focus on the encoding of various design questions as analysis problems, and in particular on how the same analysis mechanism can be used both to explore constraints in isolation and to check conformance of code to constraints.

Earlier (in Section 2.3), we described how a formula evaluates to *true* or *false* in the context of an environment. The environments for which the formula is true are the *models* of the formula. To avoid that term's many overloadings, we often call them *instances* or *solutions* instead. If a formula has at least one model, it is said to be *consistent*; when every well-formed environment is a model, the formula is *valid*. The negation of a valid formula is inconsistent, so to check an assertion, we look for a model to its negation; if one is found, it is a *counterexample*.

Since the logic is undecidable, it is impossible to determine automatically whether a formula is valid or consistent. We therefore limit our analysis to a finite *scope* that bounds the sizes of the carrier sets of the basic types. We say that a model is *within a scope of k* if it assigns to each type a set consisting of no more than k elements. Clearly, if we succeed in finding a model to a formula, we have demonstrated that it is consistent. Failure to find a model within a given scope, however, does not prove that the formula is inconsistent. In practice, however, experience suggests that many errors can be found by considering only a small scope (eg, at most 3 elements of each type). This *small scope hypothesis* is purely empirical of course, since the language is undecidable, so for any scope there is a formula whose smallest model occurs in a scope one larger.

When our analysis is used to check that an implementation satisfies a design constraint, failure to find a counterexample does not therefore imply that the constraint holds. Moreover, it seems likely that often the encoding of the implementation will involve some abstraction, so a counterexample may be spurious. Our hope is that the analysis, although unsound, will turn out to be accurate, as it appears to be when applied to designs in isolation.

The analysis is quite efficient. Valid assertions take longer to check, since the tool must exhaust the entire space. In the three case studies describe above, most analyses were completed in less than 10 seconds (running the tool on a modestly equipped PC). It is hard to measure the size of the space searched, but, roughly speaking, a scope of 3 (the default), usually corresponds to a state that can be encoded with a few hundred bits, which gives roughly 10^{60} cases.

4.1 Analyzing Designs

A wide variety of analysis questions can be reduced to satisfaction problems. Here are some examples of the kinds of question we have posed to our analysis tool, and which the Alloy language has been designed to express:

· *Consistency.* In any declarative description, conjunction brings a risk of inconsistency. To mitigate it, we perform consistency checks, asking our tool to provide configurations satisfying an invariant, often with an additional condition. In our COM study, for example, we checked that the rules we had formulated admitted the possibility of aggregations of two components at once, and of aggregations of aggregations. The same strategy is applied to descriptions of operations. Having formulated a specification of a procedure, for example, it is important to check that there is at least some execution that satisfies it. In all these cases, the analysis is presented with the invariant or operation to be checked, and if it finds a model, consistency is established.

· *Consequences.* Having specified some constraints, it is wise to check that they have the intended meaning by formulating some additional, weaker constraints that are expected to follow. These questions are expressed in Alloy as assertions of the form

$X \rightarrow Y$

where X is the invariant or operation as specified, and Y is the consequence. The tool negates the assertion, and looks for a model of

$X \mathbin{\&\&} !Y$

A solution to this formula is now a counterexample that demonstrates that the constraint does not have the intended consequence. When X is an operation, Y may be a constraint on the pre- or the poststate alone, or may be another operation, in which case the assertion is a simple form of refinement theorem. Data refinement can be checked too, by formulating an abstraction function as a constraint A and then checking

$OpC \mathbin{\&\&} A \rightarrow OpA$

where OpC is the concrete operation and OpA is the abstract operation.

· *Comparisons.* Another useful way to check that a constraint has been formulated correctly is to compare it to a variant. Given a constraint C and a variant Cv, we assert

$C \leftrightarrow Cv$

and the analysis generates instances that satisfy one but not the other.

· *Preservation of invariants.* To check that every reachable state of a system satisfies an invariant, we use the standard inductive strategy of showing that the invariant I is established in the initial state

$Init \rightarrow I$

and preserved by each operation

$Op \mathbin{\&\&} I \rightarrow I'$

It is instructive to see some examples of analyses that would be desirable, but which are impossible (at least by our current mechanism) because they would require finding a model of a formula that cannot be expressed in first-order logic:

· *Liveness assertions.* As we saw above, the simple liveness assertion that an operation has some executions can be checked. It would be nice to be able to analyze preconditions more directly. For example, given an operation *Op*, we might want to check that it has an execution from every state that satisfies *Pre*. In languages such as VDM in which the precondition *Pre* is specified separately, this criterion is called 'implementability'; in Z, where preconditions are implicit, this criterion states that the implicit precondition is no stronger than *Pre*. Let us suppose the operation involves a state with a single relation component *R*. The check will then have the form

   Pre -> some R' | Op

where *R'* denotes the value of *R* in the poststate. The quantifier is second-order, since its variable is a relation and not a scalar.

·   *General Refinements.* To relieve the developer of the burden of providing an abstraction function, we might want to check refinement assertions similar to

   OpC && A -> OpA

but with the abstraction function *A* represented not as a formula, but explicitly as a relation. This goes beyond first-order logic in two ways: it requires a higher-order relation that maps, for example, relations (in the concrete state) to relations (in the abstract state), and, even worse, requires a quantifier over such relations!

4.2 Analyzing Implementations

To check conformance of a procedure's implementation to its specification, we extract from the procedure's body a formula *Code* that describes its behaviour. The procedure's behaviour can be specified with a constraint of the form *Pre -> Post*, for a precondition *Pre* that mentions only prestates, and a postcondition *Post*, which may mention both pre- and post-states. The check may then be formulated as an assertion

   Code -> Pre -> Post

and its counterexamples will be executions of the procedure that start in a state satisfying the precondition but end in a state violating the postcondition.

In extracting the formula from the code, we simply translate each elementary program statement into a constraint. For example, the statement

   x.f = y

which sets the field *f* of object *x* to point to object *y* becomes

   x.f' = y

where the dot is now Alloy's navigation operator, and the equals sign is an equality on set expressions. To this formula we must conjoin a frame condition

   all o | o != x -> o.f' = o.f

which says that the relation *f* changes at most at *x*.

As in Z, we can define a logical operator that mimics sequential composition. If *S* and *T* are operation formulas in which the prestates are referred to as *x*, *y*, *z* etc, and the poststates as *x'*, *y'*, *z'*, then the composition *S ; T* is short for the formula

   some x0, y0, z0 | S [x0/x', y0/y', z0/z'] && T [x0/x, y0/y, z0/z]

where *S [x0/x', y0/y', z0/z']* is the formula *S* with *x0* substituted for *x'*, *y0* for *y'*, and *z0* for *z'*. Suppose now that we have a procedure whose body consists of two statements *S* and *T* that have been translated and combined in this manner. The assertion that the procedure conforms to its constraint will be

some x0, y0, z0 | S [x0/x', y0/y', z0/z'] && T [x0/x, y0/y, z0/z] -> Pre -> Post

Although this formula appears to be second-order, after negation, the existential quantifier can be skolemized away, giving a formula of the form

Pre && SS && TT && ! Post

where *Pre* mentions only the prestate, *SS* relates the prestate to an intermediate state, *TT* relates the intermediate state to the poststate, and *Post* mentions prestate and poststate, but not the intermediate state. A model of this formula will give values to all three states: it will be a *trace* of the procedure that starts in a valid prestate but ends in a bad poststate.

If-statements are handled by conjoining the condition to the appropriate branch, so

if (C) then {S} else {T}

becomes

C && S || !C && T

Loops are unrolled at most a few times, and then treated as if-statements. One unrolling of

while (C) {S}

for example, gives

!C && SKIP || C && S && !C'

In the experiments we have performed so far [14], we do not construct formulas compositionally in the style this explanation suggests. Instead, we create labels for state components at the points in the code at which they appear, generate a graph representing the possible paths through the code for some maximum number of loop unrollings, and then construct the formula using conjunction along paths and disjunction to merge branches. This strategy gives more control over the naming of intermediate states, enables various optimizations, and makes it easier to handle jumps and exceptions.

5   Scenario

The case studies that we have described so far show how our logic and analysis can be applied at different levels of abstraction, but do not involve checking low-level code against high-level design constraints. Our ambition is to bridge the gap between these levels, using, as a starting point, the language and analysis we have developed. In this section, we describe a scenario that illustrates more concretely what a design constraint is and how an implementation might violate it. The scenario comes from a recent project in which we redesigned and reimplemented the central component of CTAS, a new air-traffic control system deployed in several US airports [11].

The Center/TRACON Automation System (CTAS) helps controllers manage air-traffic flow at large airports. It receives as input the location, velocity, and flight plans of all aircraft near an airport, along with weather data, information about available runways and standard landing patterns, and controller commands. It combines this information with aerodynamic models of specific aircraft types to make accurate predictions of aircraft trajectories as much as forty minutes in advance. This information is fed into dynamic planning algorithms that suggest a landing sequence to optimize usage of landing slots.

The Communications Manager (CM) is the central component of CTAS. It acts as a message switch between sources of data (from the radar systems and host computers), algorithmic processes (that compute trajectories and juggle landing slots), and graphical user interfaces. It also maintains a database of aircraft information. The CM is the 'main' process responsible for initializing most of the other processes and terminating them when they appear to be misbehaving. When an algorithmic process dies, a new one is restarted and the CM connects to it, but if the CM dies, the system dies with it.

An essential aspect of the CM's functionality is the allocation of aircraft amongst algorithmic processes known as Route Analyzers (RA's). As aircraft become active – that is, radar signals are received showing them to be within the airspace – they are assigned to RA's for analysis. If an RA fails, its load must be transferred to other RA's. The CM periodically balances the load, redistributing aircraft amongst RA's.

This aspect of the state can be expressed like this:

```
model Allocation {
domain {Aircraft, Process}
state {Waiting, Assigned, Active : Aircraft
    Analyzer, Connected : Process
    analyzer (~load) : Assigned -> Analyzer!
    }
inv NoLostAircraft {Active in Waiting + Assigned}
inv AnalyzersLive {Assigned.analyzer in Connected}
}
```

The state consists of two domains, *Aircraft* and *Process*, some sets classifying these domains, and a relation *analyzer* (with transpose *load*) that maps each aircraft to the process to which it has been assigned. The sets classifying *Aircraft* are: *Waiting*, the aircraft that are in a queue waiting to be assigned; *Assigned*, the aircraft that are currently assigned to processes; and *Active*, the aircraft for which radar signals are being received. The sets classifying *Process* are: *Analyzer*, those processes that are RA's; and *Connected*, the processes that are live and connected to the CM.

There are two crucial design constraints. *NoLostAircraft* says that every active aircraft is either waiting to be assigned or is assigned. *AnalyzersLive* says that any analyzer that some aircraft is assigned to is actually connected.

A significant part of the code of the CM is concerned with maintaining these invariants. As aircraft become active, they are placed in the waiting queue. At some point, aircraft are taken from the queue and distributed amongst RA's. When aircraft become inactive (usually because they have landed), they are unassigned. The load is rebalanced periodically. When the CM detects that an RA has died, it redistributes its load amongst the other RA's.

We checked these constraints by hand against two versions of the system: the original version, written in C, and our reimplementation in Java. We found no violations in the C code, although we did discover that expected representation invariants associated with the abstract properties are not preserved. In the Java code, which we had written ourselves (and which fortunately is not deployed in any airport!), we found a serious violation of one of the constraints.

Of course, no invariant that a system actively maintains can be true continuously, since it must at least be violated during the operations that reestablish it. So we had to identify points in the code at which the invariants were expected to hold. In addition, we had to relate the sets and relations of the abstract model to the concrete representations of the code. In the Java code, for example, the *Waiting* set is realized as a vector of aircraft objects and the *analyzer* relation is realized as a hash table from aircraft identifiers to proxy client objects that encapsulate communication with RA's.

The offending code was found in the method that is executed when an RA has died:

```
public void delRA (Client ra) throws ClientClosedException {
  RAs.removeElement (ra);
  RALoads.remove (ra);
  Enumeration e = acidRAs.keys ();
  while (e.hasMoreElements ()) {
    AircraftId acid = (AircraftId) e.nextElement ();
    Client acidRA = (Client) acidRAs.get (acid);
    if (acidRA.equals (ra)) {
      assignAcidToRA (acid, findLeastLoadedRA ())}
  }
}
```

The code is simple (but wrong). It first removes the RA from the vector of connected RA's and removes the record of its load. It then iterates through all the aircraft that are assigned to RA's, and when it finds one that is assigned to the RA that has just gone down, reassigns it to the least loaded RA, determined by a call to an auxiliary procedure.

The problem arises when the RA that has died is the last connected RA. In this case, the aircraft assigned to it should be transferred to the waiting queue to be subsequently reassigned when an RA is brought up again. Instead, the procedure *findLeastLoadedRA* throws an exception, and the aircraft are left in limbo, assigned to a dead RA.

We are now investigating how this analysis might be performed automatically. Our CTAS redesign made only half-hearted use of object models and design constraints, so we are now revisiting it, capturing essential design constraints in Alloy and examining the code to see what checking conformance would involve. So far, our observations support the arguments we have made in this paper:

·   There are essential design constraints that can be expressed in a few lines of Alloy on which the integrity of the entire system depends. A full description of required behaviour would be enormous, but the integrity of the system rests on a few simple properties. Partiality is key; although the code is concerned with exactly how aircraft are distributed amongst RA's in order to balance load, the design constraint addresses only the fundamental question of whether they are assigned to processes that are connected.

·   There seems to be no fundamental obstacle to checking conformance of code to constraints. The relationship between the abstract sets and relations of the constraints, and the structures of the code, is relatively straightforward. A small repertoire of representations seems to cover most cases: in our CTAS code, for example, every relation is implemented as a field of an object, with a vector of tuples, or with a hash table.

·   Although design constraints are simple to express, implementations often violate them. Our CTAS implementation was intended to demonstrate the plausibility of our redesign. Had correctness been a focus, we might not have made the error described here. Our code, however, is less than 20,000 lines long. In a larger system with a greater division of responsibility, such errors are easier to make and harder to detect without tools.

6   Related Work

Model checking. The success of state exploration techniques in hardware has led to a variety of attempts to apply similar ideas to software. The Bandera project [2] aims to extract state machines from code that can then be analyzed with standard model checkers; a prototype tool includes static analyses, such as slicing, for reducing the size of the extracted machine, and a notion of specification patterns that allows the developer to express constraints using standard templates, from which formulas in various temporal logics can be automatically generated. The Java Pathfinder tool [7] takes a more direct approach, and translates Java directly into Promela, the input language of the SPIN [8] model checker. A fundamental difference between these approaches and ours is that they focus on temporal properties – namely the sequencing of events – rather than on structural relationships between objects.

Most model checkers (with the exception of process algebra checkers such as FDR [21] and the Concurrency Workbench [3]) do not allow constraints to be explored independently. Technically speaking, the term 'model checking' refers to determining whether a state machine is a model of a temporal logic formula. Exploration of constraints in their own right would require validity checking of temporal logic formulas, which is less tractable, and not usually supported by tools.

Static analysis. Traditional static analyses, being designed for compilers, check the code against a fixed repertoire of constraints. Recently, Sagiv, Reps and Wilhelm have developed a parametric shape analysis (PSA) [22] that can accommodate constraints in first-order logic. PSA is sound for 'yes' answers, and can thus prove that constraints hold, but not for 'no' answers, and it does not provide concrete counterexamples. The *PREfix* tool developed by Intrinsa (and now owned by Microsoft) finds anomalies in code by an interprocedural analysis that combines traditional dataflow with arithmetic constraint solving. It offers no soundness guarantees, but appears to be accurate, and has reportedly found several thousand bugs in the code of Windows 2000. The *Reflexion Model Tool* [18] checks gross structural properties of code by comparing the results of a static analysis, under a user-defined abstraction mapping, to the user's model.

Theorem proving. The *Extended Static Checker* (ESC) [4] finds errors in Java code by generating proof obligations using a weakest precondition semantics that are submitted to *Simplify*, a specialized theorem prover. ESC trades soundness for accuracy. Subtle violations of abstraction are possible which open loopholes in the conventional rules for modular reasoning. Since these rarely occur in practice, ESC ignores them, and although it may therefore miss errors, it will produce fewer spurious complaints. ESC can accommodate user-defined specifications that involve first-order formulas with uninterpreted functions, arithmetic and quantifiers.Nevertheless, ESC has been mostly used to catch array bounds violations and null pointer dereferences, and has yet to be applied to the kinds of design constraint we have described here.

7   Discussion

Our analysis plays two roles in the approach we have described: both in the exploration of the constraints themselves, and in checking the conformance of code to the constraints. For the latter, a key advantage of our analysis mechanism is that it treats elementary program statements as constraints, and can therefore take specifications of procedures as surrogates for their code. Libraries are easily handled by writing constraints for the procedures, which are then used by the analysis at each call site.

Nevertheless, it is not necessary that the same mechanism be used for both analyses. It seems likely that there are abstraction-based mechanisms more in the style of conventional static analyses that will be more suitable, at least some of the time, for analyzing code.

Existing static analyses cannot be easily adapted to this task for two reasons. First, most do not accommodate user-defined constraints. Second, the abstractions used tend to bound sets uniformly from above. To check a constraint that involves both existential and universal quantification, it will be necessary to compute both upper and lower bounds at once.

With Martin Rinard, we are looking into static analyses that can check conformance to design constraints, and which are compositional and can scale to large programs. It is not clear how these analyses will compare to our satisfaction-based analysis. Our guess is that they will scale more readily, but provide less accuracy. This suggests that it may be fruitful to apply a coarser static analysis on the program as a whole, and then, when the analysis fails and indicates that a design constraint may have been violated, to apply the satisfaction-based analysis locally in an attempt to find a counterexample.

Acknowledgments

The notion of design constraints was developed in collaboration with Martin Rinard. Mandana Vaziri worked with the author on the code analysis scheme, and did the shape analysis case study. Sarfraz Khurshid analyzed Intentional Naming. The analysis of COM was done with Kevin Sullivan, and extends his previous work. Albert Lee analyzed the CTAS code by hand as part of this masters thesis. Ilya Shlyakhter and Ian Schechter implemented parts of the Alloy analysis tool. The author would like to thank Michelle Eshow, CTAS's development manager, and her colleagues for help understanding CTAS, and Michael Jackson, for his insightful comments on an earlier draft of this paper. This research was funded in part by the MIT Center for Innovation in Product Development under NSF Cooperative Agreement Number EEC-9529140, by a grant from Nippon Telephone and Telegraph, by a grant from NASA, and by an endowment from Douglas and Pat Ross.

References

1. William Adjie-Winoto, Elliot Schwartz, Hari Balakrishnan, and Jeremy Lilley. The Design and Implementation of an Intentional Naming System. *Proc. 17th ACM Symposium on Operating Systems Principles (SOSP'99)*, Kiawah Island, SC. Dec. 1999.
2. The Bandera Project, Kansas State University. http://www.cis.ksu.edu/santos/bandera/.
3. R. Cleaveland and S. Sims. The NCSU Concurrency Workbench. In: *R. Alur and T. Henzinger, editors, Computer-Aided Verification (CAV'96)*, volume 1102 of Lecture Notes in Computer Science, pages 394–397, New Brunswick, NJ, July 1996. Springer-Verlag.
4. D. Detlefs, K. R. Leino, G. Nelson, and J. Saxe. *Extended static checking*. Technical Report 159, Compaq Systems Research Center, 1998.
5. Nurit Dor, Michael Rodeh & Mooly Sagiv. Detecting Memory Errors via Static Pointer Analysis. *Proceedings of the ACM SIGPLAN-SIGSOFT Workshop on Program Analysis for Software Tools and Engineering (PASTE'98)*, Montreal, June 1998.
6. William Harrison and Harold Ossher. Subject-Oriented Programming – A Critique of Pure Objects. *Conference on Object-Oriented Programming Systems, Languages, and Applications (OOPSLA'93)*, September 1993.

7. K. Havelund and T. Pressburger. Model Checking Java Programs Using Java PathFinder. To appear: *International Journal on Software Tools for Technology Transfer*, Springer-Verlag.
8. Gerard J. Holzmann. The Model Checker Spin. *IEEE Transactions on Software Engineering: Special issue on Formal Methods in Software Practice*, Volume 23, Number 5, May 1997, pp. 279–295.
9. Daniel Jackson and Jeannette Wing. Lightweight Formal Methods, *IEEE Computer*, April 1996.
10. Daniel Jackson. *Alloy: A Lightweight Object Modelling Notation*. Technical Report 797, MIT Laboratory for Computer Science, Cambridge, MA, February 2000.
11. Daniel Jackson and John Chapin. Simplifying Air-traffic Control: A Case Study in Software Design. *IEEE Software*, May 2000.
12. Daniel Jackson, Ian Schechter and Ilya Shlyakhter. Alcoa: the Alloy Constraint Analyzer. *Proc. International Conference on Software Engineering*, Limerick, Ireland, June 2000.
13. Daniel Jackson and Kevin Sullivan. *COM Revisited: Tool Assisted Modelling and Analysis of Software Structures*. Submitted for publication. Available at: http://sdg.lcs.mit.edu/~dnj/publications.
14. Daniel Jackson and Mandana Vaziri. *Using a SAT Solver to Find Bugs in Code*. Submitted for publication. Available at: http://sdg.lcs.mit.edu/~dnj/publications.
15. Daniel Jackson. *Automating First Order Logic*. Submitted for publication. Available at: http://sdg.lcs.mit.edu/~dnj/publications.
16. Sarfraz Khurshid and Daniel Jackson. *Exploring the Design of an Intentional Naming Scheme with an Automatic Constraint Analyzer*. Submitted for publication. Available at: http://sdg.lcs.mit.edu/~dnj/publications.
17. G. Kiczales, J. Lamping, A. Mendhekar, C. Maeda, C. V. Lopes, J. Loingtier and J. Irwin, Aspect-Oriented Programming. *Proceedings of European Conference on Object-Oriented Programming (ECOOP'97)*, pp. 220-242.
18. Gail C. Murphy, David Notkin and Kevin Sullivan. Software Reflexion Models: Bridging the Gap Between Source and High-Level Models. *Proc. Third ACM SIGSOFT Symposium on the Foundations of Software Engineering (FSE'95)*, October 1995.
19. P. Naur and B. Randell (eds). *Software Engineering: Report on a Conference sponsored by the NATO Science Committee*, Garmisch, Germany, October 1968, Brussels, Scientific Affairs Division, NATO, January 1969, 231 pp.
20. President's Information Technology Advisory Committee. *Report to the President. Information Technology Research: Investing in Our Future*. February 1999. Available at: http://www.ccic.gov/ac/report/
21. A.W. Roscoe. Model-checking CSP. In: *A Classical Mind: Essays in Honour of C.A.R. Hoare*. Prentice-Hall 1994, ISBN 0-13-294844-3.
22. Mooly Sagiv, Tom Reps and Reinhard Wilhelm. Parametric Shape Analysis via 3-Valued Logic. *Proc. ACM Symposium on Principles of Programming Languages (POPL'99)*, San Antonio, TX, Jan. 20–22, 1999, ACM, New York, NY, 1999.
23. J. Michael Spivey. *The Z Notation: A Reference Manual*. Second ed, Prentice Hall, 1992.
24. Kevin Sullivan, M. Marchukov and D. Socha. Analysis of a conflict between interface negotiation and aggregation in Microsoft's component object model. *IEEE Transactions on Software Engineering*, July/August, 1999.

Model Checking as Constraint Solving

Andreas Podelski

Max-Planck-Institut für Informatik
Im Stadtwald, 66123 Saarbrücken, Germany
podelski@mpi-sb.mpg.de

Abstract. We show how model checking procedures for different kinds of infinite-state systems can be formalized as a generic constraint-solving procedure, viz. the saturation under a parametric set of inference rules. The procedures can be classified by the solved form they are to compute. This solved form is a recursive (automaton-like) definition of the set of states satisfying the given temporal property in the case of systems over stacks or other symbolic data.

1 Introduction

In the large body of work on model checking for infinite-state systems (see e.g. [2,3,4,5,6,7,8,9,10,11,12,15,16,17,18,20,21,22,26,27,28]), we can distinguish two basic cases according to the infinite data domain for the program variables. In the first case, we have pushdown stacks or other 'symbolic' data implemented by pointer structures. These data are modeled by words or trees, and sets of states are represented by word automata or tree automata. In the second case, program variables range over reals or other numeric data, and sets of states are represented by arithmetic constraints. Accordingly, the respective model checking procedures operate on automata or on arithmetic constraints. Whereas they are essentially fixpoint procedures based on the predecessor or the successor operator in the second case, they seem to require ad-hoc reasoning techniques in the first case. In this paper, we show how all these procedures can be formalized as one generic constraint-solving procedure, viz. the saturation under a parametric set of inference rules; the procedures can be compared by the solved form they are to compute.

We will use constraints φ (such as $x = y + 1$ over the domain of reals or $x = a.y$ over the domain of words) in order to form Constraints Φ (such as $X = \{x \mid \exists y \in Y : x = y + 1\}$ or $X = \{x \mid \exists y \in Y : x = a.y\}$).[1] A specification of a transition system by a guarded-command program, together with a specification of a temporal property by a modal μ-calculus formula, translates effectively to a Constraint Φ such that the intended solution of Φ is the temporal property (i.e., the value of a variable X of Φ is the set of states satisfying the property). Model checking for the transition system and the temporal property amounts to solving that Constraint Φ. Solving Φ means transforming Φ into an equivalent Constraint Φ' in *solved form*.

---

[1] Notation: constraints φ are first-order, Constraints Φ are second-order.

J. Palsberg (Ed.): SAS 2000, LNCS 1824, pp. 22–37, 2000.

In each Constraint solving step, a direct consequence under a logical inference rule is added as a conjunct to the Constraint ("saturation"). When no more new conjuncts can be added, the Constraint is in solved form. This generic model checking procedure is parametrized by the set of inference rules.

The purpose of the solved form of a Constraint is to exhibit its set of solutions; technically, this means that known (and algorithmically more or less pleasing) tests for emptiness and for membership are applicable. (Strictly speaking, the test of the membership of the initial state of the system in this set is still part of the model checking procedure.)

We can compare the two cases of 'symbolic' vs. numeric data structures by the two basic cases of solved forms. The solved form is a recursive definition of sets of states in the first case, and a non-recursive definition (viz. a symbolic state enumeration) in the second case.

Our uniform definition of model checking and the classification according to solved forms allows us to contrast the two cases with each other. Model checking over the reals is 'harder' than over the words in the sense that solving a Constraint Φ over the reals means 'eliminating the recursion'. For example, the Constraint $X = \{x \mid \exists y \in X : x = y+1\} \cup \{0\}$ gets transformed into in its solved form $X = \{x \mid x \geq 0\}$; however, the Constraint $X = \{x \mid \exists y \in X : x = a.y\} \cup \{\varepsilon\}$ is already in solved form (representing the set a^* of all words $a.a \ldots a$ including the empty word ε). The first Constraint arises from the CTL formula $\mathrm{EF}(0)$ and the program consisting of the loop with the one instruction $\texttt{x:=x-1}$, the second from the CTL formula $\mathrm{EF}(\varepsilon)$ and the program with $\texttt{pop(a,x)}$.

Our technical setting uses concepts from logic programming. In order to address the reader who is not familiar with those concepts, we will first consider two concrete examples of infinite-state systems and use them to illustrate our approach (Sections 2 and 3). We then generally characterize the temporal property of a system in terms of a solution of a Constraint Φ (Section 4). In our formalization of the model checking procedure, the first step in the design of a concrete procedure is to define the solved form of a Constraint; we give a generic definition and its two instances corresponding to symbolic and numeric systems, respectively (Section 5). The second step is to instantiate the parameter of the generic Constraint-solving procedure, namely the set of inference rules, for concrete examples of infinite-state systems (Section 6).

2 Finite Automata as Infinite-State Systems

We will rephrase well-known facts about finite automata in order to illustrate our notions of constraints φ and Constraints Φ and the correspondence between a specific solution of Φ and a temporal property.

The notion of constraints φ. A finite automaton is given essentially by a *finite* edge-labeled directed graph $\mathcal{G}$. Some nodes of the graph $\mathcal{G}$ are marked as *initial* and some as *final*. We will write $Q = \{1, \ldots, n\}$ for its set of nodes and Σ for its set of edge labels. The graph defines a transition system. The states are pairs $\langle i, x \rangle$ consisting of a node i and a word x (i.e. x is an element of the free monoid Σ^* over the alphabet Σ). The edge $\langle i, a, j \rangle$ from node i to node j labeled by a defines the following state transitions:

state $\langle i, x \rangle$ can take a transition to state $\langle j, y \rangle$ if $\underline{x = a.y}$ holds.

The formula $x = a.y$ is an example of a constraint φ (over the variables x and y). The constraint is satisfied by words x and y if the first letter of x is a, and y is obtained from x by removing the first letter.

We note that a finite automaton defines a special case of an *infinite-state* transition system where each execution sequence is finite (infinite with self-loops on $\langle i, \varepsilon \rangle$). This view will be useful when we extend it to pushdown systems in Section 3.

The notion of Constraints Φ. It is well known that a finite automaton can be associated with a *regular system of equations*, which is a conjunction of equations of the form $p_i = [\varepsilon \cup] \bigcup_{\ldots} a.p_j$ where the union ranges over all edges $\langle i, a, j \rangle$ from node i to node j; the 'empty word' ε is a member of the union if the node i is marked final.

A regular system of equations is an example of a Constraint Φ (over the variables $p_1, \ldots, p_n$). Its variables range over sets of words. Being interested in the *least* solution, we can it equivalently as the conjunction of the following (superset) inclusions:

$$p_i \supseteq a.q_i \quad \text{(for each edge } \langle i, a, j \rangle),$$
$$p_i \supseteq \varepsilon \quad \text{(if the node } i \text{ is marked final).}$$

We next introduce a syntactic variant of the inclusion $p_i \supseteq a.q_i$ that makes explicit the role of constraints:

$$p_i \supseteq \{x \in \Sigma^* \mid \exists y \in \Sigma^* \, (\underline{x = a.y},\ y \in p_j)\}.$$

Identifying sets and unary predicates, we write the above inclusion in yet another syntactic variant, namely as a *clause* of a constraint data base or constraint logic program:[2]

$$p_i(x) \leftarrow x = a.y,\ p_j(y).$$

This notation leaves implicit the universal quantification of the variables x and y for each clause. Thus, the only free variables in the clause above are the *set variables* p_i and p_j. An inclusion of the form $p_i \supseteq \varepsilon$ translating the fact that the node i is marked final can be written as a special case of clause called *fact*:

$$p_i(x) \leftarrow x = \varepsilon.$$

---

[2] The close relationship between a clause $p(x) \leftarrow \ldots$ and an inclusion $p \supseteq \ldots$ underlines the fact that the "predicate symbols" p in clauses stand for second-order variables; they range over sets of (tuples of) data values.

Solutions of Constraints Φ and Temporal Properties. The correspondence between the least solution of a regular system of equations and the language recognized by a finite automaton is well known. If we note $[\![p_i]\!]$ the value of the set variable p_i in the least solution of the regular system (viz. the Constraint Φ), then the recognized language is the union of all sets of words $[\![p_i]\!]$ such that the node i is marked initial.

The set $[\![p_i]\!]$ consists of all words accepted by the finite automaton when starting from the node i. Now, we only need to realize that acceptance is a special case of a temporal property, namely the reachability of an *accepting state* which is of the form $\langle j, \varepsilon \rangle$ for a final node j:

$x \in \Sigma^\star$ is accepted from node $i \in Q$ iff $\langle i, x \rangle \longrightarrow^\star \langle j, \varepsilon \rangle$ for a final node j.

We introduce *accept* as the symbol for the *atomic proposition* that holds for all accepting states. Then, the temporal property is specified by the formula $EF(accept)$ in the syntax of CTL, or by the formula $\mu X.(accept \vee \Diamond X)$ in the syntax of the modal μ-calculus. We can now rephrase the above correspondence as the following identity between the value $[\![p_i]\!]$ of the variable p_i in the least solution of the Constraint Φ and the temporal property:

$$x \in [\![p_i]\!] \text{ iff } \langle i, x \rangle \in EF(accept). \tag{1}$$

In Section 4, we will generalize this correspondence (which holds also for other systems than just finite automata, other temporal properties than just reachability, and, accordingly, other solutions than just the least one).

3   Pushdown Systems

In the previous section, we have shown that a temporal property corresponds to a specific solution of a Constraint Φ for a special example. In that example, the Constraint Φ that is associated with the given transition system and the given temporal property is already in what we define to be the *solved form*. There is no reasonable way to simplify it any further; the tests for emptiness or membership are linear in the size of Φ (we carry over the standard algorithms for automata).

In contrast, in the case of *pushdown systems* to be introduced next, the associated Constraint Φ is not in solved form. The purpose of this section is to illustrate that model checking for pushdown systems (in the style of e.g. [6,18]) is done by solving Φ, i.e. by bringing Φ into an equivalent solved form. Our example temporal property is again reachability.

If we view the word x in the second component of a state $\langle i, x \rangle$ of the transition system induced by a finite automaton as the representation of a *stack*, then each edge $\langle i, a, j \rangle$ defines a *pop* operation (at node i, if the top symbol is a, pop it and go to node j). It is now natural to extend the notion of transition graphs by allowing edges that define *push* operations (at node i, push a on top of the stack and go to node j). Formally, the edge $\langle i, !a, j \rangle$ from node i to node j labeled by a together with "!" defines the following state transitions:

state $\langle i, x \rangle$ can take a transition to state $\langle j, y \rangle$ if $a.x = y$ holds.

In contrast with the previous case, infinite execution sequences are possible in the more general kind of transition system.

We extend the notion of regular systems of equations accordingly. Each edge $\langle i, !a, j \rangle$ corresponds to an inclusion of the form

$$p_i \supseteq \{x \mid \exists y \in \Sigma^* \, (a.x = y, \, y \in p_j)\}$$

which we will write equivalently as the clause

$$p_i(x) \leftarrow a.x = y, \, p_j(y).$$

The new kind of clause contains constraints of a new form (the letter a is appended to the left of the variable x appearing in the head atom).

As before, each edge $\langle i, a, j \rangle$ translates to a clause $p_i(x) \leftarrow x = a.y, \, p_j(y)$. If we are again interested in the reachability of accepting states defined as above (wrt. a given set of nodes marked final), we translate each marking of a node j as final to a clause $p_j(x) \leftarrow x = \varepsilon$ (we say that these clauses express the atomic proposition *accept*).

The Constraint Φ whose least solution characterizes the temporal property $\mathrm{EF}(accept)$ in the same sense as in (1) is formed of the conjunction of the two kinds of clauses translating pop resp. push edges of the transition graph, and of the third kind of clauses expressing the atomic proposition *accept*.

We do not know of any algorithms for the tests for emptiness or membership that apply directly to Constraints containing the three kinds of conjuncts. We now define the *solved form* of a Constraint Φ as the smallest conjunction containing all conjuncts of Φ and being closed under the two inference rules below.

$$\left.\begin{array}{l} p(x) \leftarrow a.x = y, \, q(y) \\ q(x) \leftarrow q'(x) \\ q'(x) \leftarrow x = a.y, \, r(y) \end{array}\right\} \vdash p(x) \leftarrow r(x)$$

$$\left.\begin{array}{l} p(x) \leftarrow q(x) \\ q(x) \leftarrow r(x) \end{array}\right\} \vdash p(x) \leftarrow r(x)$$

(2)

We note that the first of the two inference rules is obtained by applying logical operations to constraints φ over the logical structure of words. The conjunction of the two clauses $p(x) \leftarrow a.x = y, \, q(y)$ and $q(y) \leftarrow y = a.z, \, r(z)$ (the second clause is obtained by applying α-renaming to the clause $p(x) \leftarrow a.x = y, \, q(y)$ with the universally quantified variables x and y) yields the clause

$$p(x) \leftarrow a.x = y, \, y = a.z, r(z).$$

The logical operations that we now apply are: forming the conjunction of constraints (here, $a.x = y \wedge y = a.z$), testing its satisfiability and transforming it into the equivalent constraint $x = z$.

Given a Constraint Φ, we define the Constraint Φ' as the part of Φ without conjuncts of the form $p_i(x) \leftarrow a.x = y$, $p_j(y)$ (i.e. without the clauses that translate push edges). If Φ is in solved form, then the least solution of Φ is equal to the least solution of Φ' (as can be shown formally). Hence, the tests of emptiness or membership for the least solution of Φ can be restricted to the Constraint Φ'. The conjuncts of Φ' are of the form $p_i(x) \leftarrow x = a.y$, $p_j(y)$ (translating edges of a finite automaton) or $p_j(x) \leftarrow x = \varepsilon$ (translating the marking of final nodes) or $p(x) \leftarrow r(x)$ (translating "ε-transitions of a finite automaton); thus, Φ' corresponds to a finite automaton with ε-transitions (for which linear algorithms are again well known).

The model checking procedure for pushdown systems is simply the *Constraint solving procedure* that we define as the iterative addition of new conjuncts obtained by the inference step above (until no more new conjuncts can be added).

The *cubic* complexity bound for this procedure, which can be described by inference rules, can be inferred directly using the techniques of McAllester [23]; these techniques work by transferring known complexity bounds for deductive database queries.

Atomic Propositions specified by Regular Sets. It should be clear by now how we form the Constraint Φ corresponding to the temporal property $\mathrm{EF}(ap_{\mathcal{L}})$ where the atomic proposition $ap_{\mathcal{L}}$ is given by a family $\mathcal{L} = (L_i)_{i \in Q}$ of regular word languages $L_i \subseteq \Sigma^*$ for each node $i \in Q$; the atomic proposition holds for all states $\langle i, w \rangle$ where $w \in L_i$ (the atomic proposition *accept* is the special case where all languages L_i consist of the empty word ε). Each set L_i is recognized by a finite automaton with the set of nodes Q_i such that $Q \cap Q_i = \{i\}$ and L_i is the set of all words accepted from node i (all nodes different from i are new). We translate the finite automaton into a Constraint Φ_i such that value of the variable p_i in its least solution is L_i (all other variables are new). We now form the Constraint Φ as the conjunction of all clauses translating pop and push edges of the transition graph of the pushdown system and of all Constraints Φ_i.

Automata and Guarded Command Programs. The purpose of Sections 2 and 3 is to convey the intuition behind the general framework through two concrete examples. Since the general setting uses guarded command programs, we need to relate those with transition graphs of finite automata. An edge $\langle i, a, j \rangle$ from node i to node j labeled a specifies the same transition steps as the following guarded command:

$$z = i, \ head(x) = a \ [\![\ z := j, \ x := tail(x)$$

The guarded command program obtained by the translation of a transition graph has the program variables z (ranging over the finite set Q of program points) and x (ranging over words denoting the stack contents).

The guarded command above can be represented in another form, where primed variables stand for the value of the variable after the transition step.

Here, the guard constraint $\alpha(z, x)$ and the action constraint $\gamma(z, x, z', x')$ are logical formulas (we indicate their free variables in parenthesis; the variable y is quantified existentially at the outset of the guarded command).

$$\underbrace{z = i, \ x = a.y}_{\alpha(z,x)} \ \| \ \underbrace{z' = j, \ x' = y}_{\gamma(z,x,z',x')}$$

In the setting of Section 4, the guarded command will be translated to the conjunct $p(z, x) \leftarrow z = i, \ x = a.y, \ z' = j, \ x' = y, \ p(z', x')$ of the Constraint Φ; here p is a generic symbol for the (only one) variable of Φ. This translation is equivalent to the one given in Section 2, in the sense that $p_i(x)$ is equivalent to $p(i, x)$.

4   Temporal Properties and Constraints Φ

Given a specification of a transition system (possibly with an infinite state space) in form of a guarded command program $\mathcal{P}$ and of a temporal property in form of a modal μ-calculus formula Δ, we will construct a Constraint Φ whose solution (least, greatest or intermediate, according to the quantifier prefix of Δ) is the temporal property.

The program $\mathcal{P}$ is a set of guarded commands $\alpha \ \| \ \gamma$; the free variables of the guard constraint α are the program variables $x_1, \ldots, x_n$; its existentially quantified variables may be 'shared' with the action constraint γ which is a conjunction of equalities $x' = e(x_1, \ldots, x_n)$ with an expression e for each program variable x (we omit any further formalization). We use $\mathbf{x}$ for the tuple $x_1, \ldots, x_n$.

The formula Δ consists of a sequence of quantifiers μX or νX applied to a set of declarations of the form $X = \delta$, where the language of expressions δ is defined as follows. We assume the usual restrictions for the (closed, well-formed) formula Δ in positive normal form (negation is pushed to the atomic propositions; as usual, we close the set of atomic propositions under negation).

$$\delta \ \equiv \ ap \mid X_1 \vee X_2 \mid X_1 \wedge X_2 \mid \Diamond X \mid \Box X$$

The Constraint Φ is defined as the conjunction of the following clauses, where p_X is a new symbol for a variable of Φ (for each X occurring in Δ).

$$\Phi \ \equiv \ \left\{ \begin{array}{ll} p_X(\mathbf{x}) \leftarrow ap & \text{for } X = ap \quad\quad \text{ in } \Delta, \\ p_X(\mathbf{x}) \leftarrow p_{X_i}(\mathbf{x}) & \text{for } X = X_1 \vee X_2 \text{ in } \Delta, \ i = 1, 2 \\ p_X(\mathbf{x}) \leftarrow p_{X_1}(\mathbf{x}), \ p_{X_2}(\mathbf{x}) & \text{for } X = X_1 \wedge X_2 \text{ in } \Delta, \\ p_X(\mathbf{x}) \leftarrow \alpha, \ \gamma, \ p_{X'}(\mathbf{x}') & \text{for } X = \Diamond X' \quad\quad \text{ in } \Delta, \ \alpha \ \| \ \gamma \text{ in } \mathcal{P} \\ p_X(\mathbf{x}) \leftarrow \bigwedge_j \forall \ldots \alpha_j, \ \gamma_j, \ p_{X'}(\mathbf{x_j}) & \text{for } X = \Box X' \quad\quad \text{ in } \Delta \end{array} \right\}$$

In the last kind of clause, the conjunction $\bigwedge_j$ ranges over all guarded commands of the program $\mathcal{P}$; the primed variables in each guarded command are renamed apart (from $\mathbf{x}'$ to $\mathbf{x}'_j$; the renamed version of $\alpha \parallel \gamma$ is $\alpha_j \parallel \gamma_j$), and the universal quantifier ranges over all variables other than $\mathbf{x}$ and $\mathbf{x_j}$.[3]

We assume that the quantifier prefix of Δ is $\xi_1 X_1 \ldots \xi_m X_m$ where ξ_i is either μ or ν; i.e., the formula is of the form

$$\Delta \equiv \xi_1 X_1 \ldots \xi_m X_m \; \{X_i = \delta_i \mid i = 1, \ldots, m\}.$$

Then, the free variables of the Constraint Φ form the tuple $\langle p_{X_1}, \ldots, p_{X_m} \rangle$, and a solution of Φ can be represented as a tuple $\langle S_1, \ldots, S_m \rangle$ of sets of states (states are value tuples $\langle v_1, \ldots, v_n \rangle$ for the program variables $\langle x_1, \ldots, x_n \rangle$).

The intended solution $\langle [\![p_{X_1}]\!], \ldots, [\![p_{X_m}]\!] \rangle$ of Φ according to the quantifier prefix of Δ is defined as the fixpoint of the *logical consequence operator* T_Φ,

$$\langle [\![p_{X_1}]\!], \ldots, [\![p_{X_m}]\!] \rangle \;=\; \xi_1 p_{X_1} \ldots \xi_m p_{X_m} \; T_\Phi(\langle p_{X_1}, \ldots, p_{X_m} \rangle).$$

In order to define alternating fixpoints, we reformulate the usual logical consequence operator for constraint logic programs as a fixpoint operator T_Φ over tuples $\langle S_1, \ldots, S_m \rangle$ of sets of states (see also [13]); its application is defined by $T_\Phi(\langle S_1, \ldots, S_m \rangle) = (\langle S'_1, \ldots, S'_m \rangle)$ where

$$S'_j = \{\langle v_1, \ldots, v_n \rangle \mid \Phi \cup p_{X_1}(S_1) \cup \ldots \cup p_{X_m}(S_m) \vdash p_{X_j}(\langle v_1, \ldots, v_n \rangle)\}.$$

Here, $p_{X_k}(S_k)$ stands for the conjunction of formulas $p_{X_k}(\langle w_1, \ldots, w_n \rangle)$ where $\langle w_1, \ldots, w_n \rangle \in S_k$ (we always implicitly use the identification of sets and unary predicates p_X). The symbol $\vdash$ here refers to one single step of logical inference (the *modus ponens* rule, essentially). When using clauses with constraints φ (here, conjunctions $\alpha \wedge \gamma$ of guard and action constraints), the inference step is taken wrt. the logical structure for the specific constraints (the domain of reals, the monoid of words, etc.). The alternating fixpoints are well-defined due to our assumption that Δ is well-formed; we omit any further formal details.

Theorem 1. *Given a specification of a transition system in form of a guarded command program $\mathcal{P}$ and of a temporal property in form of a modal μ-calculus formula Δ, the set of all states satisfying the temporal property is the value $[\![p_{X_1}]\!]$ of the variable p_{X_1} under the solution of Φ specified by the quantifier prefix of Δ.*

Proof. The proof works by a logical formulation of the construction of an alternating tree automaton as in [1], expressing the next-state relation used there by the first-order constraints $\alpha \wedge \gamma$ that correspond to the guarded commands. These constraints are inserted into the tree-automaton clauses (see Figure 1) without changing their logical meaning; the clauses are then transformed into the form as they occur in Φ; again, one can show this transformation logically correct. ∎

---

[3] The universal quantification in the body of clauses goes beyond the usual notion of Horn clauses that is used in related approaches (see e.g. [14,15,16,25]). It is needed when successor values can be chosen nondeterministically. The direct-consequence operator T_Φ is still defined.

Reachability for Guarded Command Programs. As an example, we consider the most simple (and practically most important) temporal property, i.e. reachability, which is specified by the CTL formula $\mathrm{EF}(ap)$ or the modal μ-calculus formula

$$\Delta \equiv \mu X \mu X_1 \mu X_2 \left\{ \begin{array}{l} X =X_1 \vee X_2, \\ X_1=ap, \\ X_2=\Diamond X \end{array} \right\}.$$

Given Δ and a guarded command program $\mathcal{P}$ whose program variables form the tuple $\mathbf{x}$, we form the Constraint

$$\Phi \equiv \left\{ \begin{array}{l} p_X(\mathbf{x}) \leftarrow p_{X_1}(\mathbf{x}) \\ p_X(\mathbf{x}) \leftarrow p_{X_2}(\mathbf{x}) \\ p_{X_1}(\mathbf{x}) \leftarrow ap \end{array} \right\} \cup \{p_{X_2}(\mathbf{x}) \leftarrow \alpha,\ \gamma,\ p_X(\mathbf{x}') \mid \alpha \parallel \gamma \text{ in } \mathcal{P}\}$$

Following Theorem 1, we deduce that the set of states satisfying the temporal property Δ is the value $[\![p_X]\!]$ of the variable p_X under the least solution of Φ. The least solution is the fixpoint $\mu p_X \mu p_{X_1} \mu p_{X_2}\, T_\Phi(\langle p_X, p_{X_1}, p_{X_2}\rangle))$.

Equivalently, the value $[\![p_X]\!]$ is defined by the least solution of Φ' (defined as $\mu p_X\, T_{\Phi'}(p_X)$), where Φ' is a simplified version of Φ defined by

$$\Phi' \equiv \{p_X(\mathbf{x}) \leftarrow ap\} \cup \{p_X(\mathbf{x}) \leftarrow \alpha,\ \gamma,\ p_X \mid \alpha \parallel \gamma \text{ in } \mathcal{P}\}.$$

Inevitability. The greatest solution of the Constraint

$$\Phi'' \equiv \{p_X(\mathbf{x}) \leftarrow ap,\ \alpha,\ \gamma,\ p_X \mid \alpha \parallel \gamma \text{ in } \mathcal{P}\}$$

is the property defined by the CLT formula $\mathrm{EG}(ap)$ or the modal μ-calculus formula $\nu X\ \{ap \wedge \Diamond X\}$, which is the dual of the simplest case of a liveness property, namely inevitability.

Clark's completion. The conjunction of all clauses $p(\mathbf{x}) \leftarrow body_i$ defining the predicate p is, in fact, only a syntactic sugaring for the formula that expresses the logical meaning correctly, namely the equivalence (here, the existential quantification ranges over all variables but the ones in $\mathbf{x}$)

$$p(\mathbf{x}) \leftrightarrow \bigvee_i \exists \ldots\ body_i.$$

The two forms are equialent wrt. the least solution. The greatest solution, however, refers to the second form with equivalences (the so-called *Clark's completion*), or, equivalently, to the greatest fixpoint of T_Φ. All intermediate solutions are defined by intermediate fixpoints of T_Φ.

5   Solved Forms for Constraints Φ

We first give a general definition of solved forms (for all cases of data structures) that is only parametrized by a subclass of *solved-form clauses*. We will then instantiate the definition by specifying concrete subclasses for the two basic cases of data structures.

The idea behind solved-form clauses is that they form a fragment of monadic second-order logic (over the respective data structures) for which procedures implementing tests for emptiness and membership are available. Note that it makes sense here to admit also procedures that are possibly non-terminating (but hopefully practically useful); e.g., one may trade this possibility with a termination guarantee for the constraint solving procedure.

Definition 1 (General Solved Form). *Given a class of* solved-form clauses, *a Constraint Φ is said to be in* solved form *if it is equivalent to the Constraint Φ' that consists of all solved-form clauses of Φ.*

As always, the equivalence between Constraints Φ and Φ' refers to the solution specified by a given fixpoint (least, greatest, ..., possibly alternating).

Definition 2 (Solved Form (1) for Words). *The class of solved-form clauses defining the solved form of Constraints Φ for systems over words consists of all clauses of one of the three forms:*

$$p(x) \leftarrow x = a.y, \ q(y),$$
$$p(x) \leftarrow x = \varepsilon,$$
$$p(x) \leftarrow q(x).$$

In Section 2, we have seen that the class of clauses defined above corresponds to the notion of a finite automaton. (As noted in Section 4, we can write these clauses using a generic predicate symbol p, i.e. writing $p(i, x)$ instead of $p_i(x)$.)

Generally, we say that a class of clauses (then called *automaton clauses*) corresponds to a given class of automata if each Constraint Φ consisting of such clauses can be translated into an equivalent automaton in the class (i.e. such that the recognized languages and the values under the specific solution of the Constraint Φ coincide). This kind of correspondence holds between several notions of automata and their 'corresponding' form of *automaton clauses* (see Figure 1). In each case, one can define a new class of solved-form clauses.

We have usually in mind automata on finite words or finite trees, but one can consider also infinite objects (e.g. in order to model cyclic pointer structures), terms in algebras other than the tree algebra, certain forms of graphs etc..

The results in [13] imply the correspondence between fixpoints and acceptance conditions for Constraints Φ over words and trees; i.e., every alternating fixpoint specifying a solution of a conjunction of Horn clauses corresponds to a specific acceptance condition (on infinite runs, i.e. based on the *parity condition*) for the 'corresponding' automaton over words resp. trees. Thus, if Φ is in solved form, algorithms implementing emptiness and membership tests are known.

The correspondence between fixpoints and acceptance conditions for Constraints Φ generalizes from the domain of words or trees to any constraint domain. However, emptiness and membership are undecidable for (any interesting subclass of) *recursive* Constraints Φ over the reals (i.e. with conjuncts of the form $p(\mathbf{x}) \leftarrow \varphi, \ p(\mathbf{x}'))$, even if we consider the *least* solution only.

$p(x) \leftarrow x = a.y, \; p(y)$	finite automaton (on words)
$p(x) \leftarrow x = \varepsilon$	
$p(x) \leftarrow x = f(y, z), \; q(y), \; r(z)$	tree automaton
$p(x) \leftarrow x = a$	
$p(x) \leftarrow x = f(y, z), \; y = z, \; q(y), \; r(z)$	"equality on brother terms"
$p(x) \leftarrow q(x), \; r(x)$	alternation
$p(x) \leftarrow \neg q(x)$	negation
stratified	"weak alternating"
$\dots \nu p \mu q \dots$	automata with parity condition

Fig. 1. Automaton clauses and corresponding notions of automata

This leads to the following definition of *non-recursive* solved-form clauses. The definition means that the solution of a Constraint in solved form (2) is essentially presented as a finite union of infinite sets of states, these sets being denoted by constraints φ (whose free variables form the tuple $\mathbf{x} = \langle x_1, \dots, x_n \rangle$).

Definition 3 (Solved Form (2), for Reals). *The class of solved-form clauses defining the solved form of Constraints Φ for systems over reals consists of all clauses of the form (where φ is a constraint over reals)*

$$p(\mathbf{x}) \leftarrow \varphi.$$

Definition 3 is parametric wrt. a given notion of constraints φ; it can be reformulated for other domains such as the integers or the rationals. The free variables of the constraints φ correspond to the program variables; some program variables (the control variables) range over a finite domain of program locations; we can choose that domain as a finite subset of the constraint domain. We have in mind linear or non-linear arithmetic constraints over the reals or over the integers, as they are used in model checkers for network protocols with counters, timed, linear-hybrid or hybrid systems, etc.. The class of constraints is closed under conjunction and existential quantification; it may or may not be closed under disjunction. It comes with a test of satisfiability ("$\models \exists \mathbf{x} \, \varphi(\mathbf{x})$?"), entailment ("$\models \varphi(\mathbf{x}) \rightarrow \varphi'(\mathbf{x})$?") and satisfaction for a given tuple of values of the constraint domain ("$\models \varphi(v_1, \dots, v_n)$?").

6   Solving Constraints Φ

A *Constraint solving procedure* can be defined generically wrt. to a given set of inference rules: iteratively add direct consequences as conjuncts; start from the Constraint Φ constructed for the model checking problem (viz. for the program $\mathcal{P}$ and the temporal formula Δ); terminate when no more *new* consequences can be inferred. It is part of the inference system to specify whether 'new' refers to the semantics of all of Φ or the semantics or the syntax of one of the conjuncts of Φ.

Thus, a model checking procedure is specified by a set of inference rules. These define transformations of constraints into equivalent constraints (as always in this text, equivalence refers to the intended solutions).

The *soundness* of the model checking procedure holds by definition. The *completeness* (the solution of the subpart Φ' contains already the solution of the solved form of Φ) is trivial for the inference rule (3) given below for systems over reals. It requires more intricate reasoning in the case of the inference rule (2) for pushdown systems.

A possible alternative to ensure completeness is to check whether the solved-form clauses subsume all the other ones. To our knowledge, this alternative has not yet been explored in practical systems.

In the remainder of this section we show that one can express the main ideas of the model checking procedures for different examples of infinite-state systems by means of inference rules (the parameter of our generic procedure).

In Section 3, we have seen the set of inference rules (2) for *pushdown systems*. In the case of more general temporal properties (e.g. expressed with nested fixpoints), the inference rules must be extended to memorize the priority of the fixpoint operator for the 'eliminated' predicate q; this memorization technique is described in [13]. The solved form is here an alternating Rabin automaton with ε-transitions. Applying known results for those automata, we obtain the complexity result of [28] in a direct way.

In passing, we observe that the model checking problem for the subclass of *finite-state automata* viewed as infinite-state systems (with pop operations only) has the same complexity.

Real-Valued Systems. The set of inference rules that accounts for the symbolic model checking procedure for system over reals or integers (based on backward analysis) consists of the following rule. (Forward analysis is accounted for differently; see e.g. [19,16]).

$$\left.\begin{array}{l} p(\mathbf{x}) \leftarrow \alpha,\ \gamma,\ p(\mathbf{x}') \\ p(\mathbf{x}) \leftarrow \varphi \end{array}\right\} \vdash p(\mathbf{x}) \leftarrow \varphi[\mathbf{x}'/\mathbf{x}],\ \alpha,\ \gamma \qquad (3)$$

The application of the inference rule includes the test of satisfiability of the constraint $\varphi[\mathbf{x}'/\mathbf{x}] \wedge \alpha \wedge \gamma$. Note our conventions about notation: conjuncts in clauses are separated by commas; the constraint $\varphi[\mathbf{x}'/\mathbf{x}]$ is obtained by renaming the tuple $\mathbf{x}$ (of free variables of φ) to $\mathbf{x}'$ (recall that the free variables in the guard constraint α and the action constraint γ form the tuples $\mathbf{x}$ and $\langle x_1, \ldots, x_n, x_1', \ldots, x_n' \rangle$, respectively).

Meta-Transitions. The ultimate goal of a constraint solving procedure is to add enough 'interesting' conjuncts, i.e. conjuncts forming the part Φ' which is relevant according to the definition of a solved form (i.e., the part to which the emptiness or memberships tests refer). Other conjuncts may be inferred and added, however, in order to *accelerate* the inference of 'interesting' conjuncts. To give a simple example, the guarded command $z = \ell,\ x \geq 0 \parallel z' = \ell,\ x' = x + 1$ (an increment loop for the integer variable x at the program location ℓ) corresponds to the clause

$$p_X(z, x) \leftarrow z = \ell,\ x \geq 0,\ z' = \ell,\ x' = x + 1,\ p_X(z, x'). \tag{4}$$

This clause entails the clause (where the variable k is implicitely existentially quantified in $x' = x + k$)

$$p_X(z, x) \leftarrow z = \ell,\ x \geq 0,\ z' = \ell,\ x' = x + k,\ p_X(z, x'). \tag{5}$$

Boigelot [2] uses Presburger arithmetic in order to derive guarded commands called *meta-transitions* corresponding to clauses such as (5). One application of the inference rule (3) to the clause (5) yields a clause that subsumes all clauses obtained by its application to the clause in (4) in an infinite iteration.

Queue Systems. A system with one queue is similar to a pushdown system in that a dequeue operation corresponds to a pop operation and, hence, can be translated to a clause of the same form (for better legibility, we return to our notation of Section 3). A guarded command specifying an enqueue operation, however, is translated to a clause with the constraint $x.a = y$ expressing the concatenation to the right of the word x modeling the queue contents.

$$p(x) \leftarrow x = a.y,\ q(y) \qquad \text{(dequeue)}.$$
$$p(x) \leftarrow x.a = y,\ q(y) \qquad \text{(enqueue)}.$$

Model checking for systems with queues is a topic of ongoing research; see e.g. [2,3,7]. One possible (quite insufficient) inference rule is

$$\left. \begin{array}{l} p(x) \leftarrow x.a = y,\ q(y) \\ q(x) \leftarrow x = a.y,\ r(y) \\ r(x) \leftarrow x = \varepsilon \end{array} \right\} \vdash p(x) \leftarrow x = \varepsilon.$$

This rule can be generalized to any set of clauses specifying a finite automaton that accepts only words ending with the letter a (here, $q'_1, \ldots, q'_n$ are new).

$$\left. \begin{array}{l} p(x) \leftarrow \underline{x.a = y},\ q_1(y) \\ q_1(x) \leftarrow x = b_1.y,\ q_2(y) \\ \vdots \\ q_{n-1}(x) \leftarrow x = b_{n-1}.y,\ q_n(y) \\ q_n(x) \leftarrow \underline{x = a.y},\ r(y) \\ r(x) \leftarrow x = \varepsilon \end{array} \right\} \vdash \left\{ \begin{array}{l} p(x) \leftarrow \underline{x = y},\ q'_1(y) \\ q'_1(x) \leftarrow x = b_1.y,\ q'_2(y) \\ \vdots \\ q'_{n-1}(x) \leftarrow x = b_{n-1}.y,\ q'_n(y) \\ q'_n(x) \leftarrow \underline{x = \varepsilon} \end{array} \right.$$

This schematic inference rule is used by Boigelot and Godefroid (see [2,3]).

7   Related Work and Conclusion

Since a fixpoint equation is a constraint over sets of states, the existence of a characterization of a temporal property by a second-order Constraint is not surprising. Our characterization (in Theorem 1) using clausal syntax with first-order constraints seems to be the first one, however, that is useful for *symbolic* model checking (where 'symbolic' refers to first-order constraints) for a very general class of (nondeterministic) infinite-state systems. The characterization holds for the full modal μ-calculus and for arbitrary guarded command programs and is thus more general than in related approaches [1,15,14,16,19,18,25] (see also Footnote 3). In the case of finite-state systems, Φ is the alternating automaton constructed by Kupfermann, Vardi and Wolper [1] in a logical formulation; we generalize that construction and its extensions for pushdown systems [18] and for timed automata [19].

We have formalized model checking as a generic constraint-solving procedure that is parametrized by logical inference rules. This allows us to classify the two basic cases by the solved form, and to express the main ideas of model checking procedures concisely.

Our formalization provides a formal support for proving a model checking procedure correct (by checking soundness and completeness of the inference rules, possibly employing proof-theoretic (as opposed to graph-theoretic) techniques) and for analyzing its complexity (e.g. by writing the inference rules as bottom-up logic programs and applying syntactic criteria as suggested by McAllester [23]; see e.g. [17]).

Regarding future work, we note that the emptiness test or the test whether an initial state $\langle v_1, \ldots, v_n \rangle$ is a member of $[\![p_X]\!]$ (in the notation of Theorem 1) can be implemented by applying a *refutation* procedure to the conjunction of the formula $\neg \exists \mathbf{x} p_X(\mathbf{x})$ (or of the formula $\neg p_X(\langle v_1, \ldots, v_n \rangle)$, respectively) with the Constraint Φ. This is related to the procedures e.g. in [14,22,24,27,25]. Hybrid forms combining that procedure and the one given in Section 6 and the relation to ordered resolution have to be explored.

Acknowledgement

We thank Harald Ganzinger for discussions and for his suggestion of a general solved form, and Giorgio Delzanno and Jean-Marc Talbot for comments.

References

1. O. Bernholtz, M. Vardi, and P. Wolper. An automata-theoretic approach to branching-time model checking. In D. Dill, editor, *CAV 94: Computer-aided Verification*, LNCS, pages 142–155. Springer, 1994. 29, 35
2. B. Boigelot. *Symbolic Methods for Exploring Infinite State Spaces*. PhD thesis, University of Liège, May 1998. 22, 34

3. B. Boigelot and P. Godefroid. Symbolic verification of communications protocols with infinite state spaces using QDDs. In *Proceedings of CAV'96*, volume 1102 of *LNCS*, Berlin, 1996. Springer. 22, 34

4. B. Boigelot and P. Wolper. Symbolic Verification with Periodic Sets. In D. L. Dill, editor, *Proceedings of CAV'94: Computer-aided Verification*, volume 818 of *LNCS*, pages 55–67. Springer, 1994. 22

5. B. Boigelot and P. Wolper. Verifying Systems with Infinite but Regular State Space. In A. J. Hu and M. Y. Vardi, editors, *Proceedings of CAV'98: Computer-aided Verification*, volume 1427 of *LNCS*, pages 88–97. Springer, 1998. 22

6. A. Bouajjani, J. Esparza, and O. Maler. Reachability Analysis of Pushdown Automata: Application to Model Checking. In A. W. Mazurkiewicz and J. Winkowski, editors, *CONCUR '97: Concurrency Theory,*, volume 1243 of *LNCS*, pages 135–150. Springer, 1997. 22, 25

7. A. Bouajjani and P. Habermehl. Symbolic reachability analysis of FIFO-channel systems with nonregular sets of configuarations. *Theoretical Computer Science*, 221:211–250, 1999. 22, 34

8. T. Bultan, R. Gerber, and W. Pugh. Symbolic Model Checking of Infinite-state Systems using Presburger Arithmetics. In O. Grumberg, editor, *Proceedings of CAV'97: Computer-aided Verification*, volume 1254 of *LNCS*, pages 400–411. Springer, 1997. 22

9. O. Burkart, D. Caucal, F. Moller, and B. Steffen. Verification on infinite structures. In S. S. J. Bergstra, A. Ponse, editor, *Handbook of Process Algebra*. Elsevier Science Publisher B.V., 1999. to appear. 22

10. O. Burkart and B. Steffen. Composition, decomposition and model checking optimal of pushdown processes. *Nordic Journal of Computing*, 2(2):89–125, 1995. 22

11. O. Burkart and B. Steffen. Model–checking the full modal mu–calculus for infinite sequential processes. In P. Degano, R. Gorrieri, and A. Marchetti-Spaccamela, editors, *International Colloquium on Automata, Languages, and Programming (ICALP'97)*, volume 1256 of *LNCS*, pages 419–429. Springer, 1997. 22

12. W. Chan, R. Anderson, P. Beame, and D. Notkin. Combining Constraint Solving and Symbolic Model Checking for a Class of Systems with Non-linear Constraints. In O. Grumberg, editor, *Proceedings of the Ninth Conference on Computer Aided Verification (CAV'97)*, volume 1254 of *LNCS*, pages 316–327. Springer, 1997. 22

13. W. Charatonik, D. McAllester, D. Niwinski, A. Podelski, and I. Walukiewicz. The Horn mu-calculus. In V. Pratt, editor, *Proceedings of LICS'98: Logic in Computer Science*, pages 58–69. IEEE Computer Society Press, 1998. 29, 31, 33

14. W. Charatonik, S. Mukhopadhyay, and A. Podelski. The $S\mu$-calculus. Submitted to this conference. 29, 35

15. W. Charatonik and A. Podelski. Set-based analysis of reactive infinite-state systems. In B. Steffen, editor, *Proceedings of TACAS'98: Tools and Algorithms for the Construction and Analysis of Systems*, volume 1384 of *LNCS*, pages 358–375. Springer, 1998. 22, 29, 35

16. G. Delzanno and A. Podelski. Model checking in CLP. In R. Cleaveland, editor, *Proceedings of TACAS'99: Tools and Algorithms for the Construction and Analysis of Systems*, volume 1579 of *LNCS*, pages 223–239. Springer, 1999. 22, 29, 33, 35

17. J. Esparza and A. Podelski. Efficient algorithms for pre* and post* on interprocedural parallel flow graphs. In T. Reps, editor, *Proceedings of POPL'00: Principles of Programming Languages*, pages 1–11. IEEE, ACM Press, January 2000. 22, 35

18. A. Finkel, B. Willems, and P. Wolper. A direct symbolic approach to model checking pushdown systems. Electronic Notes in Theoretical Computer Science 9, www.elsevier.nl/locate/entcs, 13 pages, 1997. 22, 25, 35

19. L. Fribourg and J. Richardson. Symbolic Verification with Gap-order Constraints. Technical Report LIENS-93-3, Laboratoire d'Informatique, Ecole Normale Superieure, Paris, 1996. 33, 35

20. S. Graf and H. Saidi. Verifying invariants using theorem proving. In *Proceedings of CAV'96: Computer-aided Verification*, volume 1102 of *LNCS*, pages 196–207. Springer, 1996. 22

21. T. A. Henzinger, P.-H. Ho, and H. Wong-Toi. HyTECH: a Model Checker for Hybrid Systems. In O. Grumberg, editor, *Proceedings of CAV'97: Computer Aided Verification*, volume 1254 of *LNCS*, pages 460–463. Springer, 1997. 22

22. K. G. Larsen, P. Pettersson, and W. Yi. Compositional and symbolic model checking of real-time systems. In *Proceedings of the 16th Annual Real-time Systems Symposium*, pages 76–87. IEEE Computer Society Press, 1995. 22, 35

23. D. McAllester. On the complexity analysis of static analyses. In A. Cortesi and G. Filé, editors, *SAS'99: Static Analysis Symposium*, volume 1694 of *LNCS*, pages 312–329. Springer, 1999. 27, 35

24. S. Mukhopadhyay and A. Podelski. Model checking in Uppaal and query evaluation. In preparation. 35

25. Y. S. Ramakrishnan, C. R. Ramakrishnan, I. V. Ramakrishnan, S. A. Smolka, T. Swift, and D. S. Warren. Efficient Model Checking using Tabled Resolution. In O. Grumberg, editor, *Proceedings of CAV'97: Computer-aided Verification*, volume 1254 of *LNCS*, pages 143–154. Springer, 1997. 29, 35

26. T. R. Shiple, J. H. Kukula, and R. K. Ranjan. A Comparison of Presburger Engines for EFSM Reachability. In A. J. Hu and M. Y. Vardi, editors, *Proceedings of CAV'98: Computer-aided Verification*, volume 1427 of *LNCS*, pages 280–292. Springer, 1998. 22

27. H. B. Sipma, T. E. Uribe, and Z. Manna. Deductive Model Checking. In R. Alur and T. Henzinger, editors, *Proceedings of CAV'96: Computer-aided Verification*, volume 1102 of *LNCS*, pages 208–219. Springer, 1996. 22, 35

28. I. Walukiewicz. Pushdown processes: Games and model checking. In *Proceedings of CAV'96: Computer-aided Verification*, volume 1102 of *LNCS*, pages 62–74. Springer, 1996. 22, 33

Abstract Interpretation Based Semantics of Sequent Calculi

Gianluca Amato and Giorgio Levi

Università di Pisa, Dipartimento di Informatica
corso Italia 40, 56125 Pisa, Italy
{amato,levi}@di.unipi.it

Abstract. In the field of logic languages, we try to reconcile the proof theoretic tradition, characterized by the concept of uniform proof, with the classic approach based on fixpoint semantics. Hence, we propose a treatment of sequent calculi similar in spirit to the treatment of Horn clauses in logic programming. We have three different semantic styles (operational, declarative, fixpoint) that agree on the set of all the proofs for a given calculus. Following the guideline of abstract interpretation, it is possible to define abstractions of the concrete semantics, which model well known observables such as correct answers or groundness. This should simplify the process of extending important results obtained in the case of positive logic programs to the new logic languages developed by proof theoretic methods. As an example of application, we present a top-down static analyzer for properties of groundness which works for full intuitionistic first order logic.

1 Introduction

One of the greatest benefits of logic programming, as presented in [14], is that it is based upon the notion of *executable specifications*. The text of a logic program is endowed with both an operational (algorithmic) interpretation and an independent mathematical meaning which agree each other in several ways. The problem is that operational expressiveness (intended as the capability of directing the flow of execution of a program) tends to obscure the declarative meaning. Research in logic programming strives to find a good balance between these opposite needs.

Uniform proofs [17] have widely been accepted as one of the main tools for approaching the problem and to distinguish between logic without a clear computational flavor and logic programming languages. However, that of uniform proofs being a concept heavily based on proof theory, researches conducted along this line have always been quite far from the traditional approach based on fixpoint semantics. In turn, this latter tradition has brought up several important

---

[1] The proofs of the properties which appear in the text are available at the the following URL: http://www.di.unipi.it/~amato/papers.

J. Palsberg (Ed.): SAS 2000, LNCS 1824, pp. 38–57, 2000.

results concerning the effective utilization of Horn clauses as a real programming language. Among the others, problems such as compositionality of semantics [7], modularity [5,6], static analysis [13], debugging [8], have been tackled in this setting. Adapting these results to the new logic languages developed via the proof theoretic approach, such as λProlog [19] or LinLog [3], would probably require at least two things:

- provide a fixpoint semantics for these new languages;
- generalize a great number of concepts whose definition is too much tied to the case of Horn clauses.

This paper proposes a semantic framework which can be useful in such an effort. The main idea is to recognize proofs in the sequent calculi as the general counterpart of SLD resolutions for positive logic programs. Thus, the three well-known semantics (operational, declarative and fixpoint) for Horn clause logic can be reformulated within this general setting and directly applied to all the logic languages based on sequent calculi.

Moreover, these semantics are generalized to be parametric w.r.t. a *pre-interpretation*, which is essentially a choice of semantic domains and intended meanings for the inference rules. When a pre-interpretation is given, we have fixed a particular property of the proofs we want to focus our attention on (correct answers, resultants, groundness). Hence, classical abstractions such as correct answers or resultants, used in the semantic studies of logic programs, and abstractions for static analysis like groundness, can be retrieved in terms of properties of proofs. Expressed in such a way, rather than referring to a computational procedure like SLD resolution, they are more easily extendable to other logic languages.

It turns out that the most convenient way of defining pre-interpretations is through abstract interpretation theory [11]. In this way, we provide a semantic framework for the new proof-theoretic based logic languages to which most of the studies we have for positive logic programs can be easily adapted.

The paper is much inspired by [7]. After some preliminaries, we introduce the three semantic styles for sequent calculi, with respect to a particular concrete pre-interpretation. It is shown that the three semantics coincide on the set of proofs for a given calculus. Later, using techniques of abstract interpretation theory, the concept of observable is introduced, as an abstraction of a set of proofs. This gives corresponding notions of abstract semantics for sequent calculi. In general, the properties of the abstract semantics will depend on completeness properties of the abstract optimal semantic operators. For some observables, those that *separate sequents*, there is a strict correspondence between abstract semantics and semantics in a particular pre-interpretation induced by the observable.

Then, some examples of observables are provided: success sets, correct answers, groundness. All of them are presented in the case of full first-order intuitionistic logic or in a yet more general setting. This gives an idea of the process of importing well know observables for positive logic programs to broader fragments of logic. This should be the first step towards a more detailed semantic analysis of these extended languages. In particular, as an example of application of the proposed methodology, a top-down static interpreter for groundness analysis of intuitionistic logic has been implemented in PROLOG and it is presented in summary. Finally, possible future developments are discussed.

2   Proofs and Proof Schemas

2.1   Basic Definitions

Logics can be presented in several different ways: we will stick to a Gentzen-like proof-theoretic formulation. Let us fix two languages $\mathcal{D}$ and $\mathcal{G}$. We call *clauses* the elements of $\mathcal{D}$ and *goals* the elements of $\mathcal{G}$. If Γ and Δ are two sequences of clauses and goals respectively, $\Gamma \twoheadrightarrow \Delta$ is a *sequent*. If Δ is a sequence of length not greater than one, we have an *intuitionistic* sequent. In the following, we will use the letter S and its variants to denote sequents.

A *proof schema* is a rooted ordered tree with sequents as nodes. Given a proof schema p, we call hyp(p) (*hypotheses*) the sequence of leaves of p taken from a pre-order visit of p and we write th(p) (*theorem*) for the root of p. When we want to state that p is a proof schema with hyp(p) = $S_1, \ldots, S_n$ and th(p) = S, we write

$$p : S_1, \ldots, S_n \vdash S \ . \tag{1}$$

Note that a schema of height zero (when the root is also the only hypothesis) and a schema of height one with no hypotheses are different objects. If S is a sequent, a proof schema of S with height zero is the *empty proof schema* for S, and is denoted by ϵ_S. This is because we assume that leaves are different from nodes with out-degree zero. The former correspond to hypotheses, while the latter are sequents introduced by an axiom.

Example 1. If $\mathcal{D}$ and $\mathcal{G}$ are first order languages with unary predicate symbols p and r, the following is a proof schema

$$\frac{\dfrac{p(x) \twoheadrightarrow r(x) \qquad \cdot \twoheadrightarrow r(y)}{\cdot \twoheadrightarrow r(x) \wedge r(y)} \qquad \cdot \twoheadrightarrow \exists z.p(z)}{\forall z.p(z) \twoheadrightarrow \forall w.r(w)} \tag{2}$$

Note that it is not a proof in any of the standard logical systems. The following are respectively a proof schema $p : \cdot \vdash p(x) \twoheadrightarrow p(x)$ and the empty proof schema $p' : q(x) \twoheadrightarrow p(x) \vdash q(x) \twoheadrightarrow p(x) = \epsilon_{q(x) \twoheadrightarrow p(x)}$

$$p : \ \frac{}{p(x) \twoheadrightarrow p(x)} \qquad\qquad p' : \ \ q(x) \twoheadrightarrow p(x) \tag{3}$$

according to our convention on nodes with out-degree zero. □

Now, we fix a set $\mathcal{R}$ of proof schemas of height one. We call *inference rules* the elements of $\mathcal{R}$. A proof schema p, which is obtained by gluing together the empty proof schemas and the inference rules, is called *proof*. A proof with no hypothesis is said to be *final*. A sequent S is *provable* if there is a final proof rooted at S. Finally, we call *logic* a triple $\langle \mathcal{D}, \mathcal{G}, \mathcal{R} \rangle$.

Example 2. Assume $\mathcal{R}$ is the set of inference rules for first order logic. Then p and p' in the previous example are proofs. In particular, p is a final proof. Another proof, a bit more involved, is the following

$$\frac{\dfrac{\Gamma \twoheadrightarrow \forall x.p(x)}{\Gamma \twoheadrightarrow p(w)}}{\Gamma \twoheadrightarrow \exists w.p(w)} \tag{4}$$

where Γ is a list of sequents. □

In the following, we will often work with the logic $\mathcal{L}_{hc}$ of Horn clauses and with the first order intuitionistic logic $\mathcal{L}_i$. However, with the exception of Sect. 5, all the framework can be directly applied to a generic logic system. Just note that what we traditionally call inference rule, i.e. something like

$$\frac{\Gamma \twoheadrightarrow G_1 \quad \Gamma \twoheadrightarrow G_2}{\Gamma \twoheadrightarrow G_1 \wedge G_2} \ ,$$

should be viewed as a collection of different inference rules, one for each instance of G_1, G_2 and Γ.

2.2   Semantic Operators

Given a sequent S, we denote by Sch_S the set of all the proof schemas rooted at S. For each $p \in \mathsf{Sch}_S$ of the form

$$p : S_1, \ldots, S_n \vdash S \ , \tag{5}$$

we have a corresponding semantic operator $p : \mathsf{Sch}_{S_1} \times \cdots \times \mathsf{Sch}_{S_n} \twoheadrightarrow \mathsf{Sch}_S$ which works by gluing proof schemas of the input sequents together with p, to obtain a new proof schema of the output sequent S. If Sch is the set of all the proof schemas, $p : S_1, \ldots, S_n \vdash S \in \mathsf{Sch}$ and $X_i \subseteq \mathsf{Sch}$ for each i, we define a collecting variant of the semantic operator p, defined as

$$p(X_1, \ldots, X_n) = \{ p(p_1, \ldots, p_n) \mid \forall i. \ p_i \in X_i \cap \mathsf{Sch}_{S_i} \} \ . \tag{6}$$

We will write $p(X)$ as a short form for $p(X, \ldots, X)$ with n identical copies of X as input arguments.

Working with a semantic operator for each proof schema is quite uncomfortable, especially when reasoning in terms of abstractions. We can actually resort to a unique *gluing operator*. Given X_1 and X_2 subsets of Sch, we denote by $X_1 \vartriangleright X_2$ the set

$$X_1 \vartriangleright X_2 = \bigcup_{p \in X_1} p(X_2) \ . \tag{7}$$

In other words, $X_1 \vartriangleright X_2$ is the result of gluing together each proof schema in X_1 with all the "compatible" proof schemas in X_2. It turns out that $\vartriangleright$ is (roughly) the counterpart for sequent calculi of the $\bowtie$ operator for SLD derivations defined in [9].

Example 3. Consider the proof p in $\mathcal{L}_{hc}$ given by

$$\frac{\dfrac{\forall x.p(x) \twoheadrightarrow p(a) \qquad \forall x.r(x) \twoheadrightarrow r(b)}{\forall x.p(x), \forall x.r(x) \twoheadrightarrow p(a) \wedge r(b)}}{\forall x.p(x) \wedge \forall x.r(x) \twoheadrightarrow p(a) \wedge r(b)} \tag{8}$$

and the proofs p'

$$\frac{p(a) \twoheadrightarrow p(a)}{\forall x.p(x) \twoheadrightarrow p(a)} \tag{9}$$

and $p'' = \epsilon_{\forall x.r(x) \twoheadrightarrow r(b)}$. Then, the proof $p(p', p'')$ is

$$\frac{\dfrac{\dfrac{p(a) \twoheadrightarrow p(a)}{\forall x.p(x) \twoheadrightarrow p(a)} \qquad \forall x.r(x) \twoheadrightarrow r(b)}{\forall x.p(x), \forall x.r(x) \twoheadrightarrow p(a) \wedge r(b)}}{\forall x.p(x) \wedge \forall x.r(x) \twoheadrightarrow p(a) \wedge r(b)} \tag{10}$$

In particular, note that gluing with empty proofs has no effects.   □

3   The Concrete Semantics

Given a logic $\mathcal{L} = \langle \mathcal{D}, \mathcal{G}, \mathcal{R} \rangle$, we can introduce three different styles of semantics, similar in spirit to the operational, declarative and fixpoint semantics of classic logic programming. We follow the idea underlying [9] of having a common set of semantic operators for both the top-down (operational) and the bottom-up (fixpoint) styles.

3.1   Declarative Semantics

The fundamental idea is that a logic can be viewed as a signature for Σ-algebras, where sequents correspond to sorts and inference rules to term symbols. A Σ-algebra gives a choice of a semantic domain for each sequent and of a semantic function for each inference rule. Roughly, a model for a logic in a given Σ-algebra should assign, to each sequent, an element of its corresponding semantic domain, in such a way that this assignment is well-behaved w.r.t. the inference rules.

To be more precise, we call *pre-interpretation* the choice of a nonempty ordered set $\mathcal{I}(\Gamma \twoheadrightarrow \Delta)$ for each sequent and of a monotonic function $\mathcal{I}(r)$ for each inference rule r, where if $\mathrm{hyp}(r) = S_1, \ldots, S_n$ and $\mathrm{th}(r) = S$,

$$\mathcal{I}(r) = \mathcal{I}(S_1) \times \cdots \times \mathcal{I}(S_n) \to \mathcal{I}(S) \ . \tag{11}$$

Therefore, the concept of *pre-interpretation* is the same of ordered Σ-algebras as defined in [18].

Given a logic $\mathcal{L}$ with a pre-interpretation $\mathcal{I}$, an *interpretation* is a choice of an element $[\![S]\!] \in \mathcal{I}(S)$ for each sequent S. An interpretation is a *model* when, for each inference rule

$$r : S_1, \ldots, S_n \vdash S \ , \tag{12}$$

the following relation holds

$$\mathcal{I}(r)([\![S_1]\!], \ldots, [\![S_n]\!]) \sqsubseteq [\![S]\!] \ . \tag{13}$$

The notion of pre-interpretation gives us a great flexibility. In [1] it is shown how to obtain well known semantics such as correct answers or Heyting semantics for a generic sequent calculus.

When we talk of programming languages, the idea is that a program P corresponds to a sequence of clauses. Given a goal G and a model $[\![\_]\!]$, the corresponding semantics of G in the program P is given by $[\![P \twoheadrightarrow G]\!]$.

Example 4. In the logic $\mathcal{L}_{hc}$, consider the pre-interpretation $\mathcal{I}$ given by

- $\mathcal{I}(S) = \{\mathsf{true}, \mathsf{false}\}$ with $\mathsf{false} \sqsubseteq \mathsf{true}$;
- if $r \in \mathcal{R}$ is the inference rule $r : S_1, \ldots, S_n \vdash S$, then $\mathcal{I}(r)$ is the logical conjunction of the n input values. If r has no hypothesis, then $\mathcal{I}(r) = \mathsf{true}$.

If P is a definite logic program, i.e. a set of definite clauses, and $[\![\_]\!]$ is an interpretation, the set

$$I_P = \left\{ A \mid [\![\vec{\forall} P \twoheadrightarrow A]\!] = \mathsf{true} \text{ and } A \text{ is a ground atomic goal} \right\} \tag{14}$$

is a Herbrand interpretation, where $\vec{\forall} P$ is the universal closure of the clauses in P. Moreover, if $[\![\_]\!]$ is a model, I_P is a Herbrand model.

Note that, given a PROLOG clause G :- B, the corresponding clause in $\mathcal{L}_{hc}$ is the universally quantified formula $\vec{\forall}.(B \supset G)$. As a result, a query G for a definite program becomes $\exists.G$ in $\mathcal{L}_{hc}$. Actually, the sequent

$$\forall x.(p(x) \supset q(x)), \forall x.p(x) \twoheadrightarrow \exists y.q(y) \tag{15}$$

has an obvious final proof, but

$$p(x) \supset q(x), p(x) \twoheadrightarrow q(y) \tag{16}$$

is not provable since free variables are never instantiated in the sequent calculus for $\mathcal{L}_{hc}$. □

A major drawback of this approach is that the process of defining a pre-interpretation is quite arbitrary, especially for what concerns the inference rules. In the following, we try to overcome this problem by just sticking to a specific concrete pre-interpretation and deriving all the others by abstraction functions, according to the theory of abstract interpretation.

Given a logic $\mathcal{L}$, consider the *syntactic* pre-interpretation $\mathcal{I}_\mathcal{L}$ given by

- $\mathcal{I}_{\mathcal{L}}(S) = \langle \mathcal{P}(\mathsf{Sch}_S), \subseteq \rangle$ for each sequent S;
- $\mathcal{I}_{\mathcal{L}}(r)$ is the semantic function corresponding to $r \in \mathcal{R}$, as in (6).

Interpretations for $\mathcal{I}_{\mathcal{L}}$ are called *syntactical interpretations*. In the following, these will be denoted by subsets of Sch. The convention does not rise any ambiguities, since if $S_1 \neq S_2$, then $\mathsf{Sch}_{S_1} \cap \mathsf{Sch}_{S_2} = \emptyset$. A syntactical model, therefore, is a set of proof schemas closed under application of inference rules. We denote by Int the set of all the syntactical interpretations, which is a complete lattice under subset ordering. In the remaining of this section, when we talk of interpretations or models we always refer to the syntactical ones, unless otherwise stated.

It is possible to concisely express the condition of a syntactical interpretation I being a model using the glue operator. The property to be satisfied is

$$\mathcal{R} \diamond I \subseteq I \ . \tag{17}$$

Models form a complete lattice under the same ordering of the interpretations. However, it is not a sublattice, since the join operator and the bottom element differ. In particular, the bottom element of the lattice of models is what we call *declarative semantics* of $\mathcal{L}$ and we denote it by $\mathcal{D}(\mathcal{L})$.

$\mathcal{D}(\mathcal{L})$ turns out to be the set of final proofs of $\mathcal{L}$. Hence, the declarative semantics precisely captures all the terminating computations. For a valid treatment of compositionality, we also need information about partial computations [5]. If ϵ is the set of all the empty proof schemas, we call *complete declarative semantics* of $\mathcal{L}$, and we denote it by $\mathcal{D}_c(\mathcal{L})$, the least model greater then ϵ. It is possible to prove that $\mathcal{D}_c(\mathcal{L})$ is actually the set of all the proofs of $\mathcal{L}$.

3.2   Top-Down and Bottom-Up Semantics

The definition of the declarative semantics is non-constructive. We now present a bottom-up construction of the least model using an operator similar to the immediate consequence operator T_P of logic programming. The $T_{\mathcal{L}}$ operator, mapping interpretations to interpretations, is defined as follows

$$T_{\mathcal{L}}(I) = I \cup (\mathcal{R} \diamond I) \ . \tag{18}$$

We can prove that all the results which hold for the T_P operator apply to $T_{\mathcal{L}}$ as well. In particular an interpretation I is a model iff it is a fixpoint of $T_{\mathcal{L}}$. Moreover $T_{\mathcal{L}}$ is continuous, hence $T_{\mathcal{L}} \uparrow \omega$ is its least fixpoint. We call $T_{\mathcal{L}} \uparrow \omega$ the *fixpoint semantics* of $\mathcal{L}$. It trivially follows that the fixpoint and declarative semantics do coincide. Analogously to the complete declarative semantics, we can define a *complete fixpoint semantics* as $T_{\mathcal{L}}^{\omega}(\epsilon)$. As in the previous case, $T_{\mathcal{L}}^{\omega}(\epsilon) = \mathcal{D}_c(\mathcal{L})$.

Note that inference rules are essentially treated like Horn clauses for a predicate is_a_proof/1. For example, an inference rule like

$$\frac{\Gamma \twoheadrightarrow \varphi \quad \Gamma \twoheadrightarrow \psi}{\Gamma \twoheadrightarrow \varphi \wedge \psi} \tag{19}$$

corresponds to the Horn clause

$$\texttt{is\_a\_proof}(\texttt{der}(\Gamma \twoheadrightarrow \varphi \wedge \psi, [P_1, P_2])) : -$$
$$P_1 = \texttt{der}(\Gamma \twoheadrightarrow \varphi, \_), P_2 = \texttt{der}(\Gamma \twoheadrightarrow \psi, \_), \tag{20}$$
$$\texttt{is\_a\_proof}(P_1), \texttt{is\_a\_proof}(P_2)$$

where $\texttt{der}(Sequent, List\_of\_Proof\_Schemas)$ is a coding for proof schemas. In general, we have an infinite set of ground Horn clauses, since every instance of (19) counts as a different inference rule and variables in the logic $\mathcal{L}$ are coded as ground objects at the Horn clause level. These properties play a fundamental role when we try to modify the set of inference rules to obtain new derived logic systems, such as uniform logics [1].

The fixpoint construction is essentially a bottom-up process. Real interpreters, on the contrary, follow a top-down approach, since it is generally more efficient. We consider here a transition system $(\mathsf{Sch}, \longmapsto)$ that emulates such a behavior. Assume $p : S_1, \dots, S_n \vdash S$ is a proof schema and $r : S'_1, \dots, S'_m \vdash S_i$ is an inference rule. We can define a new proof schema $p' = p(\epsilon_{S_1}, \dots, r, \dots, \epsilon_{S_n})$ just replacing S_i in the hypotheses of p with the inference rule r. We write $p \longmapsto p'$ when the above conditions are satisfied. In general, it is possible to replace more than one hypothesis, hence we have the following transition rule

$$p \longmapsto p(r_1, \dots, r_n) \text{ when } \begin{cases} p : S_1, \dots, S_n \vdash S, \\ r_i \in \mathcal{R} \cup \epsilon \text{ and } \mathrm{th}(r_i) = S_i \text{ for each } 1 \le i \le n. \end{cases}$$
$$\tag{21}$$

We call *complete operational semantics* of $\mathcal{L}$ the interpretation

$$\mathcal{O}_c(\mathcal{L}) = \{p \in \mathsf{Sch} \mid \exists S. \ \epsilon_S \longmapsto^* p\} \ . \tag{22}$$

It is possible to give a collecting variant of the operational semantics construction, via a fixpoint operator $U_{\mathcal{L}}$ on interpretations which uses the gluing semantic operator:

$$U_{\mathcal{L}}(I) = I \rhd (\mathcal{R} \cup \epsilon) \ . \tag{23}$$

The idea is that $U_{\mathcal{L}}(I)$ contains all the proof schemas derived by I with a step of the transition system, i.e.

$$U_{\mathcal{L}}(I) = \{p' \mid \exists p \in I. \ p \longmapsto p'\} \ . \tag{24}$$

Actually, we can prove that $U_{\mathcal{L}}^{\omega}(\epsilon) = \mathcal{O}_c(\mathcal{L})$. Moreover, we have $U_{\mathcal{L}}^{\omega}(\epsilon) = \mathcal{D}_c(\mathcal{L})$. Hence, all the different styles of semantics do coincide.

From the implementation viewpoint, the great advantage of the top-down operational semantic w.r.t. the bottom-up fixpoint one is that we do not need to compute the entire semantics if we are only interested in part of it. An interpreter for a logic language typically works with a program P and a goal G, trying to obtain the proofs of the sequent $P \twoheadrightarrow G$. The semantics of every other sequent in the logic is computed only if it is needed for computing the semantics of $P \twoheadrightarrow G$.

We call *query* whatever sequent in the logic $\mathcal{L}$. According to this definition, a query is a pair made of a program and a goal. We define the *operational behavior* of $\mathcal{L}$ as a function $\mathcal{B}(\mathcal{L}) : \mathsf{Query} \to \mathsf{Int}$ such that

$$\mathcal{B}(\mathcal{L})_Q = \{p \in \mathsf{Sch} \mid \epsilon_Q \longmapsto^* p\} \ . \tag{25}$$

In other words, $\mathcal{B}(\mathcal{L})_Q$ is the set of proofs for the sequent Q in the logic $\mathcal{L}$. The fixpoint operator $U_{\mathcal{L}}$ can be used to compute $\mathcal{B}(\mathcal{L})$ since it is $\mathcal{B}(\mathcal{L})_Q = U_{\mathcal{L}}^{\omega}(\{\epsilon_Q\})$.

There is an immediate result of compositionality for $\mathcal{B}$. For each sequent S, consider the set $R = \{r_i\}_{i \in I}$ of all the inference rules rooted at S, such that $r_i : S_{i,1}, \dots, S_{i,m_i} \vdash S$. We have

$$\mathcal{B}(\mathcal{L})_S = \bigcup_{i \in I} r_i \left(\mathcal{B}(\mathcal{L})_{S_{i,1}}, \dots, \mathcal{B}(\mathcal{L})_{S_{i,m_i}} \right) \ . \tag{26}$$

Unfortunately, this result is not what we desire in most of the cases, as shown by the following example.

Example 5. When we work in $\mathcal{L}_{hc}$, the above compositionality result gives us the following property:

$$\mathcal{B}(\mathcal{L}_{hc})_{P \twoheadrightarrow G_1 \wedge G_2} = \mathcal{B}(\mathcal{L}_{hc})_{P \twoheadrightarrow G_1} \wedge \mathcal{B}(\mathcal{L}_{hc})_{P \twoheadrightarrow G_2} \ . \tag{27}$$

However, the classical result of and-compositionality for definite logic programs (w.r.t. correct answers or other observables) says that the semantics of $G_1 \wedge G_2$ can be derived from the semantics of G_1 and G_2. Since goals in definite programs become existentially quantified in our setting, we would like a relationship between $P \twoheadrightarrow \bar{\exists}.G_1 \wedge G_2$, $P \twoheadrightarrow \bar{\exists}.G_1$ and $P \twoheadrightarrow \bar{\exists}.G_2$. Unfortunately, this cannot be derived directly from (26). □

Note that $U_{\mathcal{L}}$ works with proofs with hypotheses. For this reason, it is not possible to retrieve only terminated computations using this fixpoint operator. This is not a flaw in the definition of the operator, but an intrinsic limit of all the kinds of top-down semantic refinements.

4 Abstraction Framework

The previous semantics are by far too detailed for most of the needs. However, it is now possible to use the techniques of abstract interpretation [11] to develop a range of abstract semantics for sequent calculi. We begin by defining the fundamental concept of *observable*.

Definition 1 (Observable). *An observable is a triple (D, α, γ) where D (the abstract domain) is an ordered set w.r.t. the relation $\sqsubseteq$ and $\alpha : \mathsf{Int} \to D$ (the abstraction function) is a monotonic function with γ as right adjoint.*

Since α and γ in (D, α, γ) uniquely determine each other [12], we will often refer to an observable just by the abstraction function.

An abstract interpretation for a logic $\mathcal{L}$ is an element of the abstract domain D. Given an interpretation I, it is possible to define an abstract counterpart $\alpha(I)$. Hence, it is possible to define abstract denotational, operational and fixpoint semantics as the abstractions of the corresponding concrete semantics. The question is whether it is possible to derive such abstract semantics working entirely in the abstract domain.

Example 6. Given a logic $\mathcal{L}$, take as abstract domain D_s the powerset of all the sequents with the standard ordering, and as abstraction function the following

$$\alpha_s(I) = \{S \mid \exists p \in I.\ \text{th}(p) = S \text{ and } \text{hyp}(S) = \emptyset\}\ . \tag{28}$$

The right adjoint of α is the function

$$\gamma_s(A) = \{p \mid \text{hyp}(S) \neq \emptyset \text{ or } \text{th}(p) \in A\}\ . \tag{29}$$

We call $(D_s, \alpha_s, \gamma_s)$ the observable of *success sets*, since it abstracts a set of proofs in the set of the theorems they prove. □

4.1   Abstract Semantic Operators

The only two operators we use in the specification of the concrete semantics are union and gluing. Once we define an abstraction, we have an abstract operator $\cup_\alpha$ correct w.r.t. $\cup$, defined as

$$\bigcup_\alpha \{A_j \mid j \in J\} = \alpha \left(\bigcup \{\gamma(A_j) \mid j \in J\} \right)\ . \tag{30}$$

In general, $\cup_\alpha$ is the least upper bound of those elements in D which are the image of some interpretation I. Moreover, it is a complete operator, i.e.

$$\bigcup_\alpha \{\alpha(I_j) \mid j \in J\} = \alpha \left(\bigcup \{I_j \mid j \in J\} \right)$$

for each collection $\{I_j\}_{j \in J}$ of interpretations.

We could define an abstract operator $\rhd_\alpha$ correct w.r.t. $\rhd$ as done for $\cup_\alpha$ in (30). However, $\rhd$ is never used in all its generality. Hence we prefer to consider the optimal abstract counterparts of the two unary operators $I \mapsto \mathcal{R} \rhd I$ and $I \mapsto I \rhd (\mathcal{R} \cup \epsilon)$. We define

$$\mathcal{R} \rhd_\alpha A = \alpha(\mathcal{R} \rhd \gamma(A))\ , \tag{31}$$
$$A \rhd_\alpha (\mathcal{R} \cup \epsilon) = \alpha(\gamma(A) \rhd (\mathcal{R} \cup \epsilon))\ . \tag{32}$$

When either $\mathcal{R} \rhd_\alpha A$ or $A \rhd_\alpha (\mathcal{R} \cup \epsilon)$ is complete, we say that the observable is respectively *denotational* or *operational*, following the terminology introduced in [2]. If, for each inference rule $r \in \mathcal{R}$, there is an abstract operator $\tilde{r}$ correct w.r.t. r as defined in (6), a correct abstract operator for $\mathcal{R} \rhd A$ can be defined as

$$\mathcal{R} \tilde{\rhd} A = \bigcup_\alpha \tilde{r}(A) \ . \tag{33}$$
$$\phantom{\mathcal{R} \tilde{\rhd} A = \bigcup_\alpha} {}_{r \in \mathcal{R}}$$

Moreover, if all the $\tilde{r}$'s are optimal or complete, the same holds for (33).

Example 7. With respect to the observable α_s, consider an inference rule r : $S_1, \dots, S_n \vdash S$. The corresponding optimal abstract operator r_{α_s} is given by

$$r_{\alpha_s}(X_1, \dots, X_n) = \begin{cases} \{S\} & \text{if } S_i \in X_i \text{ for each } i = 1 \dots n \\ \emptyset & \text{otherwise} \end{cases} \tag{34}$$

and it can be proved to be complete. Then, it turns out that the observable of success sets is denotational. An observable which is both operational and denotational is that of *plain resultants*, defined as

$$\alpha_r(I) = \{\langle S, (S_1, \dots, S_n) \rangle \mid \exists p \in I. \ p : S_1, \dots, S_n \vdash S\} \ . \tag{35}$$

with the obvious ordering by subsets. Note that what is generally called resultant is the reduced product [12] of α_r and the observable of computed answers.   □

4.2   Pre-interpretations and Observables

By means of the observables we want to recover the great generality given by the use of pre-interpretations, but in a more controlled way, in order to simplify the definition and comparison of different semantics.

Given a logic $\mathcal{L}$ and an observable (D, α, γ), we have a corresponding pre-interpretation $\mathcal{I}_\alpha$ given by

- $\mathcal{I}_\alpha(S) = \langle \{x \in D \mid x \sqsubseteq \alpha(\mathsf{Sch}_S)\}, \sqsubseteq \rangle$, where $\sqsubseteq$ is the ordering for D;
- $\mathcal{I}_\alpha(r) = \alpha \circ r \circ \gamma$.

The idea is that, with the use of pre-interpretations, we break an abstract interpretation in pieces, each one relative to a single sequent. If A is an abstract interpretation, a corresponding interpretation $[\![\_]\!]$ w.r.t. $\mathcal{I}_\alpha$ is

$$[\![S]\!]_\alpha = A \cap_\alpha \alpha(\mathsf{Sch}_S) \ , \tag{36}$$

for each sequent S, where $\cap_\alpha$ is the optimal abstract operator which is correct w.r.t. $\cap$. On the other side, given $[\![\_]\!]_\alpha$, we have the abstract interpretation

$$A = \bigcup_\alpha \{[\![S]\!]_\alpha \mid S \text{ is a sequent}\} \ . \tag{37}$$

However, in general, (36) and (37) do not form a bijection. Actually, an interpretation w.r.t. $\mathcal{I}_\alpha$ always keeps separate the semantics for different sequents, while the same does not happen for abstract interpretations.

Example 8. Consider the observable (D, α, γ) where $D = \{\text{true}, \text{false}\}$, with false $\sqsubseteq$ true and

$$\alpha(I) = \begin{cases} \text{true} & \text{if } \exists p \in I. \ \text{hyp}(p) = \emptyset \\ \text{false} & \text{otherwise} \end{cases} \tag{38}$$

The corresponding pre-interpretation $\mathcal{I}_\alpha$ is the same as the one defined in Example 4. Given the interpretation $[\![\_]\!]$ such that $[\![\bar{S}]\!] = \text{true}$ for a given sequent $\bar{S}$ and $[\![S]\!] = \text{false}$ for each $S \neq \bar{S}$, the composition of (36) and (37) is the interpretation $[\![\_]\!]'$ such that

$$[\![S]\!]' = \left(\bigcup_\alpha \{ [\![S']\!] \mid S' \text{ is a sequent} \} \right) \cap_\alpha \text{true} = \text{true} \tag{39}$$

for each sequent S. □

Given an observable α, we say that it *separates sequents* when

- $\gamma(\alpha(\text{Sch}_S)) = \text{Sch}_S$ for each sequent S;
- $\gamma(\alpha(\bigcup_S X_S)) = \bigcup_S \gamma(\alpha(X_S))$ if $X_S \subseteq \text{Sch}_S$ for each sequent S.

If α separates sequents, (36) and (37) form a bijection between the abstract interpretations which are in the image of α and the interpretations $[\![\_]\!]$ such that $[\![S]\!]$ is in the image of α for each sequent S. From this point of view, it seems that observables are even more general than pre-interpretations. On the other side, abstractions only cover a subset of all the pre-interpretations, those whose abstraction function has a right adjoint.

Example 9. It is easy to prove that α_s separates sequents. The corresponding pre-interpretation $\mathcal{I}_{\alpha_s}$ is isomorphic to the pre-interpretation $\mathcal{I}$ given in Example 4. Note that, thanks to abstract interpretation theory, we automatically obtain an optimal candidate for the abstract semantic functions from the choice of the abstract domain.

4.3 Abstract Semantics

We say that an abstract interpretation A is an *abstract model* when the corresponding interpretation $[\![\_]\!]_\alpha$ for $\mathcal{I}_\alpha$ given by (36) is a model. In formulas, this means that, for each inference rule $r : S_1, \dots, S_n \vdash S$,

$$\alpha \left(r \left(\gamma(A \cap_\alpha \alpha(\text{Sch}_{S_1})), \dots, \gamma(A \cap_\alpha \alpha(\text{Sch}_{S_n})) \right) \right) \sqsubseteq A \cap_\alpha \alpha(\text{Sch}_S) . \tag{40}$$

In turn, this is equivalent to say that $\gamma(A)$ is a syntactic model.

We would like to define the *abstract declarative semantics* $\mathcal{D}_\alpha(\mathcal{L})$ as the least abstract model for $\mathcal{L}$. However, since our abstract domain is a poset, we are not guaranteed that such an element exists. Nevertheless, when we work with a denotational observable, we have:

- $\mathcal{D}_\alpha(\mathcal{L}) = \alpha(\mathcal{D}(\mathcal{L}))$, where $\mathcal{D}_\alpha(\mathcal{L})$ is the least abstract model;

– $\mathcal{D}_{c,\alpha}(\mathcal{L}) = \alpha(\mathcal{D}_c(\mathcal{L}))$, where $\mathcal{D}_{c,\alpha}(\mathcal{L})$ is the least abstract model greater than $\alpha(\epsilon)$.

Other conditions, such as surjectivity of α, imply the existence of $\mathcal{D}_\alpha(\mathcal{L})$, whether or not α is denotational. However, in this case, we cannot be sure of the stated correspondence with $\alpha(\mathcal{D}(\mathcal{L}))$.

As in the concrete case, we want to recover $\mathcal{D}_\alpha(\mathcal{L})$ as the least fixpoint of a continuous operator. If the observable is denotational, we define by

$$T_{\mathcal{L},\alpha}(A) = A \cup_\alpha (\mathcal{R} \rhd_\alpha A) , \tag{41}$$

an abstract operator which is complete w.r.t. $T_\mathcal{L}$. Then, by well known results of abstract interpretation theory [12],

$$T_{\mathcal{L},\alpha} \uparrow \omega = \alpha(T_\mathcal{L} \uparrow \omega) = \mathcal{D}_\alpha(\mathcal{L}) , \tag{42}$$

$$T^\omega_{\mathcal{L},\alpha}(\alpha(\epsilon)) = \alpha(T^\omega_\mathcal{L}(\epsilon)) = \mathcal{D}_{c,\alpha}(\mathcal{L}) , \tag{43}$$

which are the required equalities.

Finally, let us come to the abstract operational semantics. In general, since we do not have an abstraction on the level of the single derivation, we can only abstract the collecting operational semantics given by $U_\mathcal{L}$. If $\rhd$ is operational, we define

$$U_{\mathcal{L},\alpha}(A) = A \rhd_\alpha (\mathcal{R} \cup \epsilon) , \tag{44}$$

which is a complete abstract operator w.r.t. $U_\mathcal{L}$. It is a well known result of abstract interpretation theory that

$$U^\omega_{\mathcal{L},\alpha}(\alpha(\epsilon)) = \alpha(U^\omega_\mathcal{L}(\epsilon)) = \alpha(D_c(\mathcal{L})) , \tag{45}$$

$$U^\omega_{\mathcal{L},\alpha}(\alpha(\{\epsilon_Q\})) = \alpha(U^\omega_\mathcal{L}(\{\epsilon_S\})) = \alpha(\mathcal{B}(\mathcal{L})_Q) . \tag{46}$$

Therefore, we have a top-down collecting construction of the abstract declarative semantics and of the operational behavior of $\mathcal{L}$.

Generally, if we replace the first equality with a "greater than" disequality in the equations (42), (43), (45) and (46), they become true for every observable α. In this case, the semantics computed in the abstract domain are correct w.r.t. the real abstract semantics.

5   Examples

Now that the theory is well established, we can focus our attention on its applications. We will recover two of the most common abstractions used in the field of logic programming, but working within the framework of the sequent calculus. The advantage is that our definitions do not depend on any computational procedure used to interpret the language. In turn, this makes it easier to extend the abstractions to different logic languages. Actually, the observables we are going to discuss are general enough to be applied to the full first-order intuitionistic logic. The drawback of this approach is that observables like computed answers, which rely on a specific computational mechanism, are not directly expressible.

In the following, we will assume to work in the domain of first-order intuitionistic logic. This means that $\langle \mathcal{D}, \mathcal{G} \rangle$ is a first-order language, while **Term** and **Var** are the corresponding sets of first-order terms and variables. To simplify the notation, in the forthcoming discussions we assume that, in each sequent, there is at most one quantification for each bound variable.

Here is a summary of the inference rule schemas we use for the sequent calculus of first-order intuitionistic logic.

$$\frac{\Gamma_1, B, \Gamma_2, C \twoheadrightarrow D}{\Gamma_1, C, \Gamma_2, B \twoheadrightarrow D} \; interchange \qquad \frac{\Gamma_1, B, B \twoheadrightarrow C}{\Gamma_1, B \twoheadrightarrow C} \; contraction$$

$$\frac{}{\Gamma, B \twoheadrightarrow B} \; id \qquad \frac{}{\Gamma, \bot \twoheadrightarrow \bot} \; trueR \qquad \frac{\Gamma \twoheadrightarrow \bot}{\Gamma \twoheadrightarrow B} \; \bot R$$

$$\frac{\Gamma \twoheadrightarrow B}{\Gamma \twoheadrightarrow B \vee C} \; \vee R_1 \qquad \frac{\Gamma \twoheadrightarrow B}{\Gamma \twoheadrightarrow C \vee B} \; \vee R_2 \qquad \frac{\Gamma, B \twoheadrightarrow D \quad \Gamma, C \twoheadrightarrow D}{\Gamma, B \vee C \twoheadrightarrow D} \; \vee L$$

$$\frac{\Gamma, B_1, B_2 \twoheadrightarrow C}{\Gamma, B_1 \wedge B_2 \twoheadrightarrow C} \; \wedge L \qquad \frac{\Gamma \twoheadrightarrow B \quad \Gamma \twoheadrightarrow C}{\Gamma \twoheadrightarrow B \wedge C} \; \wedge R$$

$$\frac{\Gamma \twoheadrightarrow B \quad \Gamma, C \twoheadrightarrow E}{\Gamma, B \supset C \twoheadrightarrow E} \; \supset L \qquad \frac{\Gamma, B \twoheadrightarrow C}{\Gamma \twoheadrightarrow B \supset C} \; \supset R$$

$$\frac{\Gamma, B[x/t] \twoheadrightarrow C}{\Gamma, \forall x.B \twoheadrightarrow C} \; \forall L \qquad \frac{\Gamma \twoheadrightarrow B[x/v]}{\Gamma \twoheadrightarrow \forall x.B} \; \forall R$$

$$\frac{\Gamma, B[x/v] \twoheadrightarrow C}{\Gamma, \exists x.B \twoheadrightarrow C} \; \exists L \qquad \frac{\Gamma \twoheadrightarrow B[x/t]}{\Gamma \twoheadrightarrow \exists x.B} \; \exists R$$

provided that the variable v does not occur in the lower sequents of the $\exists L$ and $\forall R$ schemas and B is an atomic formula in the id schema. When we want to denote a well defined inference rule, which is an instance of one of these schemas, we append appropriate indexes to the name of the schemas, like in $\exists R_{\Gamma, \exists z. \varphi, t(a)}$ for

$$\frac{\Gamma \twoheadrightarrow \varphi[z/t(a)]}{\Gamma \twoheadrightarrow \exists z. \varphi} \; .$$

5.1   Correct Answers

First of all, we want to extend the standard notion of correct answer for Horn clauses to the general case of first order intuitionistic logic. Given a goal **G** and a program P in pure logic programming, a correct answer θ is a function (substitution) from the variables in G to terms, with the interesting property that $\vec{\forall}P \twoheadrightarrow G\theta$ is provable. Since the real logical meaning of evaluating G in a program P is that of proving the closed sequent $\vec{\forall}P \twoheadrightarrow \vec{\exists}G$, we can think of an extension of the concept of correct answer to generic sequents $\Gamma \twoheadrightarrow \varphi$ as a mapping from existentially quantified variable in φ to terms. We require that $\Gamma \twoheadrightarrow \varphi\{\theta\}$ is provable for an appropriate notion of substitution $\{\theta\}$.

However, note the following facts:

- if we only work with Horn clauses and a sequent $\Gamma \twoheadrightarrow \exists x.\varphi$ is provable, we know that there exists a term t such that $\Gamma \twoheadrightarrow \varphi[x/t]$ is provable. This is not true in the general case. Therefore, we can think of using partial functions mapping variables to terms, so that we can choose not to give an instance for some of the variables;
- consider the two sequents $S = \Gamma \twoheadrightarrow \exists x.\varphi$ and $S' = \Gamma \twoheadrightarrow (\exists x.\varphi) \supset \psi$. The role of the two existential quantifiers is completely different. In the first case we are actually looking for a term t to substitute into the x. In the second case, we are producing a new object a, forcing the fact that $\varphi[x/a]$ holds. To be more precise, in a proof for S, we introduce the formula $\exists x.\varphi$ with the rule $\exists R$ or $\bot R$, while in a proof for S' we introduce it by $\exists L$. As a consequence, we want to restrict our attention to the first kind of existential quantifiers.

Given a formula φ, a variable x is said to be a *query variable* for φ if the subformula $\exists x.\varphi'$ positively occurs in φ for some φ'. A *(candidate) answer* θ for φ is a function from the query variables of φ to Term such that

- if $\exists x.\varphi'$ positively occurs in φ, $\theta(x)$ does not contain any variable which is quantified in φ';
- θ is idempotent, i.e. its domain (the set of variables for which θ is defined) and range (the set of variables which occur in its image) are disjoint.

Let us point out that, when φ has no positive existentially quantified variables, it has only a trivial candidate answer.

Given an answer θ for φ, we define the *instantiation* $\varphi\{\theta\}$ of φ via θ by induction on the structure of the goals, as follows:

$$
\begin{aligned}
\bot\{\theta\} &= \bot \\
A\{\theta\} &= A &&\text{if } A \text{ is an atomic goal} \\
(\varphi' \oplus \varphi'')\{\theta\} &= \varphi'\{\theta\} \oplus \varphi''\{\theta\} &&\text{for each binary logical symbol } \oplus \\
(\forall x.\varphi)\{\theta\} &= \forall x.(\varphi\{\theta\}) \\
(\exists x.\varphi)\{\theta\} &= \varphi[x/\theta(x)]\{\theta\} &&\text{if } \theta(x) \text{ is defined} \\
(\exists x.\varphi)\{\theta\} &= \exists x.\varphi\{\theta\} &&\text{if } \theta(x) \text{ is undefined.}
\end{aligned}
$$

In other words, $\varphi\{\theta\}$ is obtained by replacing every existentially quantified subformula $\exists x.\varphi'$ in φ such that $\theta(x) \neq \bot$ with $\varphi'[x/\theta(x)]$.

An answer for φ is said to be a *correct answer* for the sequent $\Gamma \rightarrowtail \varphi$ when $\Gamma \rightarrowtail \varphi\{\theta\}$ is provable. Given the standard functional ordering $\leq$ for candidate answers, it is easy to check that, if θ is a correct answer for the sequent S and $\theta' \leq \theta$, then θ' is a correct answer, too. A correct answer for φ is *total* when its domain coincides with the set of query variables for φ.

Example 10. Given the goal $G = \forall x.\exists y.p(x,y)$, the answers $\theta = \{y \rightsquigarrow f(x)\}$, $\theta' = \{y \rightsquigarrow a\}$ and $\theta'' = \{\}$ give origin to the instantiated goals $G\{\theta\} = \forall x.p(x, f(x))$, $G\{\theta'\} = \forall x.p(x,a)$ and $G\{\theta''\} = G$. It turns out that θ and θ'' are correct answers for the sequent $\forall x.p(x, f(x)) \rightarrowtail G$.

Note that $\theta = \{x \rightsquigarrow y\}$ is not a candidate answer for $G = \exists x.\forall y.p(x,y)$, since y is a bound variable in $\forall y.p(x,y)$.

Assume we want to restrict ourselves to the fragment of Horn clauses. Let P be a pure logic program and let G be a definite goal. A correct answer θ (in the classical framework) for G in P is said *total* when it is idempotent and $dom(\theta) = vars(G)$. Then, the two different definitions of total correct answers do coincide.

For example, let us consider the program p(X,X) and the goal p(X,Y). The substitution $\{X/Y\}$ is a (non total) correct answer in the classical setting, but $\{x/y\}$ is not a candidate answer for the sequent $\forall x.p(x,x) \rightarrowtail \exists x.\exists y.p(x,y)$. However, the equivalent correct answer $\{X/Z, Y/Z\}$ is total, and corresponds to a correct answer in our setting, too.

5.2   Groundness

A first order term t is *ground* when it contains no variables. If θ is a candidate answer for φ, a variable x is ground in θ if $\theta(x)$ is ground. We also say that θ is *grounding* for x. A typical problem of static analysis is to establish which variables are forced to be ground in all the correct answers for a sequent S. There are many studies on this subject for the case of Horn clauses (see, for example, [4]), and some works for hereditary Harrop formulas, too (see [15]).

Given the set $\mathsf{Gr} = \{g, ng\}$, a *groundness answer* for a formula φ is a partial function β from the query variables of φ to Gr. Note that we do not assume any ordering between g and ng. Given a candidate answer θ for φ, we define a corresponding groundness answer $\alpha_g(\theta)$, according to the following:

$$\alpha_g(\theta)(x) = \begin{cases} \bot & \text{if } \theta \text{ is undefined in } x, \\ g & \text{if } \theta \text{ is grounding for } x, \\ ng & \text{otherwise} \end{cases} \qquad (47)$$

If θ is a correct answer for S, then $\alpha_g(\theta)$ is called a *correct groundness answer* for S. Given the obvious functional ordering for groundness answers, it turns out that if β is correct for S and $\beta' \leq \beta$, then β' is correct.

Example 11. Let us give some examples of sequents and their corresponding correct groundness answers:

sequent	groundness answers
$\forall y.p(y) \twoheadrightarrow \exists x.p(x)$	$\{x/g\}\ \{x/ng\}$
$\forall y.p(a,y) \wedge p(y,b) \twoheadrightarrow \exists x.p(x,x)$	$\{x/g\}$
$p(a) \vee r(b) \twoheadrightarrow \exists x.p(x) \vee r(x)$	$\{x/g\}$
$\perp \twoheadrightarrow \exists x.p(x)$	$\{x/g\}\ \{x/ng\}$
$\forall y.p(y,y) \twoheadrightarrow \forall x_1.\exists x_2.p(x_1,x_2)$	$\{x_1/ng\}$
$\forall y.p(y,y) \twoheadrightarrow \exists x_1.\exists x_2.p(x_1,x_2)$	$\{x_1/g, x_2/g\}, \{x_1/ng, x_2/ng\}$
$\exists y.p(y) \twoheadrightarrow \exists x.p(x)$	$\{x/\perp\}$
$p(t(a)) \twoheadrightarrow \exists x.p(r(x))$	$\emptyset$

Note that we only give the maximal correct groundness answers, according with the functional ordering.

We are interested in effectively computing the set of correct groundness answers for a given input sequent. Using the theory presented in this paper, we have developed a top-down analyzer for groundness, which works for the full intuitionistic first-order logic. It is based on the idea that, given a proof of the sequent S, it is possible to derive a groundness answer for S by just examining the structure of the proof. In particular if $p = r(p1, \dots, p_n)$, it is:

$$
\text{ganswer}(p)(x) = \begin{cases} g & \text{if } r = \exists R_{\Gamma,\exists x.\varphi,t} \text{ and } t \text{ is ground,} \\ ng & \text{if } r = \exists R_{\Gamma,\exists x.\varphi,t} \text{ and } t \text{ is not ground,} \\ \{\text{ganswer}(p_i)(x)\} & \text{if } r \neq R_{\Gamma,\exists x.\varphi,t} \text{ and } x \text{ appears in } p_i, \\ \perp & \text{otherwise.} \end{cases}
$$

$$(48)$$

In general, if p is a final proof for S, we are not guaranteed that ganswer(p) is a correct groundness answer for S. For example, if $S = \exists x.t(x) \twoheadrightarrow \exists y.t(y)$ and p is the obvious corresponding final proof, it is ganswer(p) $= \{x/ng\}$, while the only correct answer is $\{x/\perp\}$. However, if β is a correct groundness answer for S, we can find a final proof p of S such that ganswer(p) $\geq \beta$. As a result, if I is the set of final proofs for S, then $\downarrow \{\text{ganswer}(p) \mid p \in I\}$ contains all the correct groundness answers for S. In the language of the theory of abstract interpretation, it means that $\downarrow \{\text{ganswer}(p) \mid p \in I\}$ is a correct approximation of the set of correct groundness answers.

Now, let us consider the function α_t which abstracts a formula φ with the same formula, where terms have been replaced by the set of variables occurring in them. We can trivially lift α_t to work with sequents.

If we name by $\langle \mathcal{D}', \mathcal{G}' \rangle$ the new language image of $\langle \mathcal{D}, \mathcal{G} \rangle$ via α_t, we can define a domain of *groundness with set resultants* D_{rg} such as

$$D_{rg} = \mathcal{P}_{\downarrow}\{\langle S, \beta, R \rangle \mid S \text{ is a sequent in } \langle \mathcal{D}', \mathcal{G}' \rangle,$$

$$R = \{S_1, \dots, S_n\} \text{ is a finite set of sequents in } \langle \mathcal{D}', \mathcal{G}' \rangle,$$

$$\beta \text{ is a groundness answer for } S\} \ .$$

$$(49)$$

where $\mathcal{P}_{\downarrow}(X)$ is the set of downward closed subsets of X, ordered by

$$\langle S, \beta, R \rangle \leq \langle S', \beta', R' \rangle \text{ iff } S = S' \wedge \beta \leq \beta' \wedge R \supseteq R' \tag{50}$$

We can define an abstraction from syntactical interpretations to the domain of groundness with resultants as

$$\alpha_{\mathrm{rg}}(I) = \{\langle \alpha_t(S), \beta, \{\alpha_t(S_1), \dots, \alpha_t(S_n)\}\rangle \mid \text{ there exists } p : S_1, \dots, S_n \vdash S \text{ in } I$$
$$\text{with ganswer}(p) = \beta\}$$
$$\tag{51}$$

We obtain an observable which can be effectively used for top-down analysis of groundness. The analyzer we have developed in PROLOG and which can be found at the URL http://www.di.unipi.it/~amato/papers/sas2000final.pl is an implementation of this observable, with some minor optimizations.

Example 12. By applying our analyzer to the sequents in the Example 11 we obtain precisely the same set of correct groundness answers, with the following exceptions:

sequent	groundness answers
$\exists y.p(y) \twoheadrightarrow \exists x.p(x)$	$\{x/g\}$
$p(t(a)) \twoheadrightarrow \exists x.p(r(x))$	$\{x/ng\}$

The previous example shows two different situations in which we lose precision. The first one is due to the fact that we abstract a term with the set of its variables, loosing the information about the functors. To solve this problem, the only solution is to improve our domain. The second situation arises from the interaction between positively and negatively occurring existential quantifiers, and can be addressed by improving the precision of the ganswer function. It should be possible to define a complete ganswer function, such that if p is a final proof for S, then ganswer(p) is a correct groundness answer for S. However, this involves examining the interaction between different quantifiers, and can possibly lead to a further generalization of the notion of correct answers, as a graph, linking quantifiers which produce "objects", introduced by $\forall R$ and $\exists L$, and quantifiers which consume "objects", introduced by $\forall L$ and $\exists R$.

If we restrict ourselves to Horn clauses logic, the abstraction function is quite precise, and we obtain a domain which, although expressed with a different formalism, has the same precision of $\mathcal{P}os$ [16,10].

6   Conclusions and Future Works

The usefulness of a general semantic framework strictly depends on its ability to be easily instantiated to well known cases while suggesting natural extensions to them. In the case of a framework which we want to use as a reference for the development of procedures for static analyses, we also require that theoretical descriptions can be implemented in a straightforward way.

In this paper we presented a semantic framework for sequent calculi modeled around the idea of the three semantics of Horn clauses and around abstract interpretation theory. With particular reference to groundness and correct answers, we have shown that well known concepts in the case of Horn clauses can be obtained as simple instances of more general definitions valid for much broader logics. This has two main advantages. First of all, we can instantiate the general concepts to computational logics other then Horn clauses, such as hereditary Harrop formulas. Moreover, the general definitions often make explicit the logical meaning of several constructions (such as correct answers), which are otherwise obscured by the use of small logical fragments. We think that, following this framework as a sort of guideline, it is possible to export most of the results for positive logic programs to the new logic languages developed following proof-theoretic methods.

Regarding the implementation of static analyzers from the theoretical description of the domains, not all the issues have been tackled. While a top-down analyzer can often be implemented straightforwardly, like our interpreter for groundness, the same definitely does not hold for bottom-up analyzers. Since for a bottom-up analysis we have to build the entire abstract semantics of a logic, we need a way to isolate a finite number of "representative sequents" from which the semantics of all the others can easily be inferred: it is essentially a problem of compositionality.

We are actually studying this problem and we think that extending the notion of a logic $\mathcal{L}$ with the introduction of some *rules for the decomposition of sequents* will add to the theoretical framework the power needed to easily derive compositional $T_{\mathcal{L}}$ operators, thus greatly simplifying the implementation of bottom-up analyzers.

Moreover, the problem of groundness analysis for intuitionistic logic could be further addressed. The precision we can reach with the proposed domain can be improved by refining the abstraction function, and the implementation of the analyzer could be reconsidered to make it faster. Finally, it should be possible to adapt the domain to work with intuitionistic linear logic.

We think that our approach to the problem of static analyses of logic programs is new. There are several papers focusing on logic languages other than Horn clauses [15] but, to the best of our knowledge, the problem has never been tackled before from the proof-theoretic point of view. An exception is [20], which, however, is limited to hereditary Harrop formulas and does not come out with any real implementation of the theoretical framework.

References

1. G. Amato. Uniform Proofs and Fixpoint Semantics of Sequent Calculi. DRAFT. Available at the following URL: http://www.di.unipi.it/~amato/papers/, 1999. 43, 45
2. Gianluca Amato and Giorgio Levi. Properties of the lattice of observables in logic programming. In M. Falaschi and M. Navarro, editors, *Proceedings of the APPIA-GULP-PRODE'97 Joint Conference on Declarative Programming*, 1997. 47

3. J. M. Andreoli. Logic programming with focusing proofs in linear logic. *Journal of Logic and Computation*, 2(3):297–347, 1992. 39
4. T. Armstrong, K. Marriott, P. Schachte, and H. Søndergaard. Boolean functions for dependency analysis: Algebraic properties and efficient representation. In B. Le Charlier, editor, *Proc. Static Analysis Symposium, SAS'94*, volume 864 of *Lecture Notes in Computer Science*, pages 266–280. Springer-Verlag, 1994. 53
5. A. Bossi, M. Gabbrielli, G. Levi, and M. C. Meo. A Compositional Semantics for Logic Programs. *Theoretical Computer Science*, 122(1–2):3–47, 1994. 39, 44
6. Antonio Brogi, Paolo Mancarella, Dino Pedreschi, and Franco Turini. Modular logic programming. *ACM Transactions on Programming Languages and Systems*, 16(4):1361–1398, July 1994. 39
7. M. Comini, G. Levi, and M. C. Meo. A theory of observables for logic programs. *Information and Computation*, 1999. To appear. 39
8. M. Comini, G. Levi, and G. Vitiello. Modular abstract diagnosis. In *International Workshop on Tools and Environments for (Constraint) Logic Programming, ILPS'97 Postconference Workshop*, 1997. 39
9. M. Comini and M. C. Meo. Compositionality properties of *SLD*-derivations. *Theoretical Computer Science*, 211(1 & 2):275–309, 1999. 41, 42
10. A. Cortesi, G. Filè, and W. Winsborough. *Prop* revisited: Propositional Formula as Abstract Domain for Groundness Analysis. In *Proc. Sixth IEEE Symp. on Logic In Computer Science*, pages 322–327. IEEE Computer Society Press, 1991. 55
11. P. Cousot and R. Cousot. Abstract Interpretation: A Unified Lattice Model for Static Analysis of Programs by Construction or Approximation of Fixpoints. In *Proc. Fourth ACM Symp. Principles of Programming Languages*, pages 238–252, 1977. 39, 46
12. P. Cousot and R. Cousot. Abstract Interpretation and Applications to Logic Programs. *Journal of Logic Programming*, 13(2 & 3):103–179, 1992. 47, 48, 50
13. S. K. Debray. Formal bases for dataflow analysis of logic programs. In G. Levi, editor, *Advances in logic programming theory*, pages 115–182. Clarendon Press, Oxford, 1994. 39
14. J. W. Lloyd. *Foundations of Logic Programming*. Springer-Verlag, 1987. Second edition. 38
15. F. Malésieux, O. Ridoux, and P. Boizumault. Abstract compilation of λProlog. In J. Jaffar, editor, *Joint International Conference and Symposium on Logic Programming*, pages 130–144, Manchester, United Kingdom, June 1998. MIT Press. 53, 56
16. K. Marriott and H. Sondergaard. Abstract Interpretation of Logic Programs: the Denotational Approach. In A. Bossi, editor, *Proc. Fifth Italian Conference on Logic Programming*, pages 399–425, 1990. 55
17. D. Miller, F. Pfenning, G. Nadathur, and A. Scedrov. Uniform proofs as a foundation for Logic Programming. *Annals of Pure and Applied Logic*, 51:125–157, 1991. 38
18. B. Möller. On the Algebraic Specification of Infinite Objects – Ordered and Cntinuous Models of Algebraic Types. *Acta Informatica*, 22:537–578, 1985. 42
19. G. Nadathur and D. Miller. An Overview of λProlog. In Kenneth A. Bowen and Robert A. Kowalski, editors, *Fifth International Logic Programmiong Conference*, pages 810–827. MIT Press, 1988. 39
20. P. Volpe. Abstractions of uniform proofs. In M. Hanus and M. Rodriguez-Artalejo, editors, *Algebraic and Logic Programming, Proc. 5th International Conference, ALP '96*, volume 1139 of *Lecture Notes in Computer Science*, pages 224–237. Springer-Verlag, 1996. 56

A Transformational Approach for Generating Non-linear Invariants[*]

S. Bensalem[1], M. Bozga[1], J.-C. Fernandez[2], L. Ghirvu[1], and Y. Lakhnech[1,**]

[1] VERIMAG
Centre Equation 2, avenue de Vignate F-38610 Gieres, France
Name@imag.fr
[2] LSR
681, rue de la Passerelle 38402 Saint Martin d'Hères Cedex, France
Fernandez@imag.fr

Abstract. Computing invariants is the key issue in the analysis of infinite-state systems whether analysis means testing, verification or parameter synthesis. In particular, methods that allow to treat combinations of loops are of interest. We present a set of algorithms and methods that can be applied to characterize over-approximations of the set of reachable states of combinations of self-loops. We present two families of complementary techniques. The first one identifies a number of basic cases of pair of self-loops for which we provide an exact characterization of the reachable states. The second family of techniques is a set of rules based on static analysis that allow to reduce n self-loops ($n \geq 2$) to $n-1$ independent pairs of self-loops. The results of the analysis of the pairs of self-loops can then be combined to provide an over-approximation of the reachable states of the n self-loops. We illustrate our methods by synthesizing conditions under which the Biphase Mark protocol works properly.

1 Introduction

This paper proposes techniques for computing over-approximations of the set of reachable states of a class of infinite state systems. The systems we consider are systems whose variables can be seen as *counters* that can be incremented by positive or negative constants or can be reset to some constant.

The problem of computing invariants of arithmetical programs in particular, and infinite state systems in general, has been investigated from the seventies. Abstract interpretation [CC77,CC92] is a precise and a formal framework which has been used to develop techniques to tackle this problem. As pioneering work in this field, one can mention M. Karr's work [Kar76] based on constant propagation for computing invariants that are systems of affine equations, P. & R. Cousot's work [CC76] which uses interval analysis to compute invariants of the form $x \in [a, b]$, $x \leq a$, etc., and the work by P. Cousot and N. Halbwachs [CH78]

---

[*] Work partially supported by Région Rhône-Alpes, France
[**] Contact author

J. Palsberg (Ed.): SAS 2000, LNCS 1824, pp. 58–72, 2000.
© Springer-Verlag Berlin Heidelberg 2000

which provides techniques that allow to compute linear constraints that relate the program variables.

In recent years, the subject has known a renewal of interest with the development of symbolic model-checking techniques for some classes of infinite state systems as timed and hybrid automata [HNSY92,HPR94], finite communicating automata [BG96,ABJ98], parameterized networks [KMM+97,ABJN99,BBLS], and automata with counters [BGP97,WB98].

In this paper, we consider transition systems with finite control and with counters as data variables. A transition consists of a guard and a set of assignments. A guard is given by a Presburger formula that may contain parameters, that is, variables that are neither initialized nor modified during execution. Assignments may increment the counters by positive or negative constants or set them to constant values. It should be noticed that this model is fairly general. Indeed, it is computationally equivalent to Turing machines and syntactically subsumes Timed Automa [AD94], Petri Nets with inhebitors, and Datalog Programs [FO97]. Indeed, each of these models can easily translated into our transition systems.

Given a transition syste we are interested in computing over-approximations of the set of reachable states from *parametric* initial states, that is, states of the form $\bar{x} = \bar{x}_0$, where $\bar{x}$ are the variables of the system and $\bar{x}_0$, are freeze variables (also called inactive auxiliary variables). In contrast to almost all the works mentioned above, the techniques we present allow to derive non-linear invariants. We concentrate on characterizing sets of states reachable by n-self-loops. This is not an essential restriction, since every system can be transformed into one with a single control location. Moreover, several spécification and programming languages such as UNITY [KJ89] or the synchronous language Lustre [CHPP87] consist of programs where all transitions are self-loops of a single control point. Notice also that it is clear that the combined effect of self-loops cannot in general be characterized by linear constraints. We present two families of complementary techniques. The first one is presented as set of results that identify a number of basic cases of pairs of self-loops for which we provide an exact characterization of the reachable states. The second family of techniques is a set of rules based on static analysis that allow to reduce n self-loops ($n \geq 2$) to $n - 1$ independent pairs of self-loops. The results of the analysis of the pairs of self-loops can then be combined to provide an over-approximation of the reachable states of the n self-loops.

The reduction techniques we present are in the same line as the decomposition rules presented by Fribourg and Olsèn in [FO97], where they consider Datalog programs, i.e., transition systems consisting of a single control location and counters and where only $x > 0$ is allowed as guard. Notable differences are, however, the fact that the systems they consider are syntactically more restricted and that their rules are exact.

To illustrate the techniques we present in this paper, we consider the Biphase mark protocol which is a parameterized protocol used as a convention for representing both a string of bits and clock edges in a square wave. Using our techniques we have been able to provide a full parametric analysis of this protocol.

2 Preliminaries

We assume an underlying assertion language $\mathcal{A}$ that includes first-order predicate logic and interpreted symbols for expressing the standard operations and relations over some concrete domains. We assume to have the set of integers among these domains. Assertions (we also say predicates) in $\mathcal{A}$ are interpreted in states that assign values to the variables of $\mathcal{A}$. Given a predicate P, we denote by $free(P)$ the set of free variables occurring in it. Similarly, if e is an expression in $\mathcal{A}$, we also write $free(e)$ to denote the set of all variables which occur in e. As expressiveness is not our issue in this paper, we will tacitly identify a predicate with the set of its models.

As computational model we use transition systems. We restrict ourselves to transition systems where the expressions occurring in an assignment to variables x are either constants or of the form $x + k$. Thus, a transition system is given by a tuple $(\mathcal{X}, \mathcal{Q}, \mathcal{T}, \mathcal{E}, \Pi)$ where $\mathcal{X}$ is a finite set of typed data variables, $\mathcal{Q}$ is a finite set of control locations, $\mathcal{T}$ is a finite set of transition names, $\mathcal{E}$ associates with each transition τ a pair $(\mathcal{E}_1(\tau), \mathcal{E}_2(\tau))$ consisting of a source and a target control location, and Π associates with each transition a guard $gua(\tau)$ which is an assertion in the Presburger fragment of $\mathcal{A}$ with free variables in $\mathcal{X}$ and a list $affe(\tau)$ of assignments of the form $x := x + k$ or $x := k$ with $x \in \mathcal{X}$ and $k \in \mathbb{Z}$ and such that for each $x \in \mathcal{X}$ there is at most one assignment $x := e$ in $affe(t)$. We denote by $\text{Base}(\tau)$ the set of variables occurring in τ. Notice that we allow *parameters* in the guards of the transitions; parameters can be seen as program variables that are not modified during execution. This allow us to model parameterized protocols as the Biphase protocol, which we consider later on, and to analyze these protocols using our techniques.

Clearly, $(\mathcal{Q}, \mathcal{T}, \mathcal{E})$ builds a labeled graph which we call the *control graph*. Henceforth, we denote the set of transitions τ with $\mathcal{E}_1(\tau) = \mathcal{E}_2(\tau) = q$ by $L(q)$, i.e., $L(q)$ is the set of self-loops in q. Moreover, we write $\tau(\bar{x})$, where $\bar{x}$ is a set of variables, for the projection of τ on $\bar{x}$, that is, the transition whose guard is obtained from the guard of τ by existentially quantifying all variables but $\bar{x}$ and whose assignments are obtained from τ by removing all assignments to other variables than $\bar{x}$.

A transition τ induces a relation $\xrightarrow{\tau}$ on configurations which are pairs of control locations and valuations of the variables in $\mathcal{X}$. Given a transition τ, and configurations (q, s) and (q', s'), (q', s') is called τ-*successor of* (q, s), denoted by $(q, s) \xrightarrow{\tau} (q', s')$, if $\mathcal{E}(\tau) = (q, q')$, s satisfies $gua(\tau)$ and s' satisfies $s'(x) = s(e)$, for each $x := e$ in $affe(\tau)$, $s'(x) = s(x)$, for each x that is not affected by τ. Given a regular language L over $\mathcal{T}$ and given configurations (q, s) and (q', s'), we say that (q', s') is L-*reachable from* (q, s), denoted by $(q, s) \xrightarrow{L} (q', s')$, if there exists a word $\tau_1 \cdots \tau_n \in L$ and configurations $(q_i, s_i)_{i \leq n}$ such that $(q_0, s_0) = (q, s)$, $(q_n, s_n) = (q', s')$, and $(q_i, s_i) \xrightarrow{\tau_i} (q_{i+1}, s_{i+1})$. If φ and φ' are predicates, we write $\varphi \xrightarrow{L} \varphi'$ to denote the fact that there exists a state s that satisfies φ and a state s' that satisfies φ' such that $s \xrightarrow{L} s'$. Identifying, a state with a predicate characterizing it, we also use the notations $\varphi \xrightarrow{L} s'$ and $s \xrightarrow{L} \varphi'$, respectively. Henceforth, given a control location q, in case all transitions in L have q as source and target locations, we omit mentioning q in configurations. Furthermore, given a predicate $\varphi(\bar{x}_0, \bar{x})$, where x_0 are freeze variables (also called inactive auxiliary variables), and given a set $L \subseteq L(q)$ of self-loops, we say that $\varphi(\bar{x}_0, \bar{x})$ is an L-invariant at q, if for every state s' that is L-reachable from a state s, $\varphi[s(\bar{x})/\bar{x}_0, s'(\bar{x})/\bar{x}]$ is valid. Thus, $\varphi(\bar{x}_0, \bar{x})$ is the set of states reachable from a parametric state $\bar{x} = \bar{x}_0$ by taking sequences of transitions in L. The predicate $\varphi(\bar{x}_0, \bar{x})$ corresponds to the strongest postcondition of so-called *most general formulas* used in [Gor75] and investigated in [AM80] in the context of axiomatic verification of recursive procedures.

3   Characterizing Reachable States of Self-Loops

Throughout this section, we fix a transition system $S = (\mathcal{X}, \mathcal{Q}, \mathcal{T}, \mathcal{E}, \Pi)$. Our goal is to transform S into a transition system $S^{\#}$ such that $S^{\#}$ does not contain self-loops and such that the set of states reachable from a state s in $S^{\#}$ is a super-set of the set of states reachable from s in S, that is, $S^{\#}$ is an abstraction of S [CC77]. Thus, we will entirely concentrate on self-loops. The motivation and justification behind this is many-fold. First, it is obvious that our model is as expressive as Turing machines, since a two counter-machine is trivially encoded in this model. Moreover, arithmetical programs, which can easily encoded in our model, represent an interesting class of programs that have been widely investigated starting with the pioneering work [CH78]. Moreover, even if we restrict the control graph to a single node, we obtain, as discussed in [FO97], an interesting class of Datalog programs. Our model allows to encode in a natural way Petri Nets with inhibitors.

The main idea behind the transformation of S into $S^{\#}$ is the following. Consider a control location q and let $\varphi(\bar{x}_0, \bar{x})$ be an $L(q)$-invariant at q. Then, we obtain $S^{\#}$ by applying the following transformations:

1. Add a new list of variables $\bar{x}_0$ with the same length as $\bar{x}$.
2. Remove all transitions in $L(q)$.
3. Let $\tau_1, \cdots, \tau_n$ be all transitions with $\mathcal{E}_2(\tau_i) = q$ and let $\bar{x} := \bar{e}_i$ be the assignment associated to τ_i. Add to $\bar{x} := \bar{e}_i$ the assignment $\bar{x}_0 := \bar{e}_i$.
4. Replace each assignment $\bar{x} := \bar{e}$ of a transition τ with $\mathcal{E}_1(\tau) = q$ and $\mathcal{E}_2(\tau) \neq q$, by the predicate $\exists \bar{y} \cdot \varphi(\bar{x}_0, \bar{y}) \wedge gua(\tau) \wedge \bar{x}' = \bar{e}[\bar{y}/\bar{x}]$, where $\bar{x}'$ stands for the state variables after taking the transition. Note that $S^{\#}$ does not satisfy the syntactic restrictions on assignments as introduced in Section2; it is, however, a transition system in the usual sense.

It is not difficult to check that $S^{\#}$ is indeed an abstraction of S. Notice also that in case all predicates $\varphi(\bar{x}_0, \bar{x})$ used in the transformation for characterizing reachable states by self-loops are exact, the obtained system $\mathcal{S}^{\#}$ is then an exact abstraction of $\mathcal{S}$.

Our approach in computing invariants characterizing the effect of a set of loops is based on the particular case of two self-loops that satisfy syntactic conditions that allow us to analyze each self-loop in isolation and on a set of static analysis techniques which allow us to reduce the analysis of n self-loops to the analysis of a number of particular cases.

Given two transitions τ_0 and τ_1 with $\mathrm{Base}(\tau_0) = \bar{x}$ and $\mathrm{Base}(\tau_1) = \bar{x}\bar{y}$, where $\bar{x}$ and $\bar{y}$ are two disjoint sets of variables, and such that $\bar{x}$ is assigned the list $\bar{c}$ of constants in τ_1. We say that τ_0 *enables* τ_1, if for every state s with $s(\bar{x}) = \bar{c}$, there exists a state s' such that $s \xrightarrow{\tau_0^*} s'$ and s' satisfies the projection on $\bar{x}$ of the guard of τ_1, i.e., s' satisfies $\exists \bar{y} \cdot gua(\tau_1)$. Notice that τ_0 does not enable τ_1 iff for every state s with $s(\bar{x}) = \bar{c}$, there is no state s' such that $s \xrightarrow{\tau_0^*} s'$ and s' satisfies $\exists \bar{y} \cdot gua(\tau_1)$.

Lemma 1. *Let τ_0 and τ_1 be two transitions such that $Base(\tau_0) = \bar{x}, Base(\tau_1) = \bar{x}\bar{y}$, where $\bar{x}$ and $\bar{y}$ are two disjoint sets of variables, and such that $\bar{x}$ is assigned the list $\bar{c}$ of constants in τ_1.*

Then, $s \xrightarrow{(\tau_0+\tau_1)^*} s'$ iff $s \xrightarrow{\tau_0^*} s'$ or there exists a state s'' such that 1) $s \xrightarrow{\tau_0^* \tau_1} s''$,

2) $\bar{x} = \bar{c} \xrightarrow{\tau_0^*} s'(\bar{x})$ and 3) one of the following conditions holds:

1. *τ_0 enables τ_1 and $s(\bar{y}) \xrightarrow{\tau_1(\bar{y})^*} s'(\bar{y})$ or*
2. *τ_0 does not enable τ_1 and $s(\bar{y}) \xrightarrow{\tau_1} s'(\bar{y})$.*

$\square$

Proof. We prove the implication from left to right by induction on the number of times transition τ_1 is taken from s to s'. Thus, suppose we have $s \xrightarrow{(\tau_0+\tau_1)^*} s'$. The induction basis follows immediately, since then we have $s \xrightarrow{\tau_0^*} s'$. Suppose now that τ_1 is taken n times with $n > 0$. Then, we have $s \xrightarrow{\tau_0^*} s_1 \xrightarrow{\tau_1} s'' \xrightarrow{(\tau_0+\tau_1)^*} s'$ and τ_1 is taken $n-1$ times in the computation from s'' to s'. In case, τ_0 does not enable τ_1, we have $s'' \xrightarrow{\tau_0^*} s'$. Hence, since $\bar{y} \cap \mathrm{Base}(\tau_0) = \emptyset$, $s'(\bar{y}) = s''(\bar{y})$ and $\bar{x} = \bar{c} \xrightarrow{\tau_0^*} s'(\bar{x})$. That is, $s(\bar{y}) \xrightarrow{\tau_1} s'(\bar{y})$ and $\bar{x} = \bar{c} \xrightarrow{\tau_0^*} s'(\bar{x})$.

Now, suppose that τ_0 enables τ_1, then, by induction hypothesis, $s''(\bar{y}) \xrightarrow{\tau_1(\bar{y})^*} s'(\bar{y})$. Since, $\bar{y} \cap \mathrm{Base}(\tau_0) = \emptyset$, $s(\bar{y}) = s_1(\bar{y})$. Consequently, $s(\bar{y}) \xrightarrow{\tau_1(\bar{y})^*} s'(\bar{y})$. Moreover, by induction hypothesis, $\bar{x} = \bar{c} \xrightarrow{\tau_0^*} s'(\bar{x})$.

$\square$

Lemma 1 states conditions under which the set of states reachable by repeated execution of the transitions τ_0 and τ_1 can be exactly characterized by *independently* considering the values of the variables $\bar{x}$ that can be reached by applying τ_0 and the values of $\bar{y}$ that can be reached by applying τ_1.

In the following, we present a lemma that allows us to apply a decomposition similar to Lemma 1 while allowing τ_0 to contain additional variables $\bar{z}$ disjoint from $\bar{x}$ and $\bar{y}$ that are not modified by τ_1.

Lemma 2. *Let τ_0 and τ_1 be two transitions such that $Base(\tau_0) = \bar{x}\bar{z}$, $Base(\tau_1) = \bar{x}\bar{y}$, where $\bar{x}$, $\bar{y}$ and $\bar{z}$ are mutually disjoint sets of variables, and such that the following conditions are satisfied:*

1. *For every state s', if true $\xrightarrow{\tau_1} s'$ then s' does not satisfy the guard of τ_1.*
2. *$\bar{x}$ is assigned the list $\bar{c}$ of constants in τ_1.*
3. *There is a list $\bar{c}'$ of constants such that, for every states s and s' with $s(\bar{x}) = \bar{c}$ and $s \xrightarrow{\tau_0^*} s'$, if s' satisfies the guard of τ_1 then $s'(\bar{z}) = s(\bar{z}) + \bar{c}'$.*
4. *For every state s with $s(\bar{x}) = \bar{c}$ there is a state s' such that $s \xrightarrow{\tau_0^*} s'$ and such that s' satisfies the projection on $\bar{x}$ of the guard of τ_1.*
5. *For all states s and s' with $s(\bar{x}) = s'(\bar{x}) = \bar{c}$ and for all $k \geq 0$, $s \xrightarrow{\tau_0^k}$ true iff $s' \xrightarrow{\tau_0^k}$ true.*

Then, $s \xrightarrow{(\tau_0+\tau_1)^*} s'$ iff $s \xrightarrow{\tau_0^*} s'$ or there exists a state s'' such that

1. *$s \xrightarrow{\tau_0^*\tau_1} s''$, $\bar{x} = \bar{c} \xrightarrow{\tau_0(x)^*} s'(\bar{x})$ and*
2. *there exists $k \in I\!\!N$ and a state s''' with $s'''(\bar{z}) = s''(\bar{z}) + k * \bar{c}$, $s(\bar{y}) \xrightarrow{\tau_1^{k+1}} s'(\bar{y})$, and $s'''(\bar{z}) \xrightarrow{\tau_0^*} s'(\bar{z})$.*

□

Proof. (sketch).

Using Condition 1., one can prove that $s \xrightarrow{(\tau_0+\tau_1)^*} s'$ iff $s \xrightarrow{\tau_0^*} s'$ or there are states s'' and s''' and $k \geq 0$ such that

$$s \xrightarrow{\tau_0^*\tau_1} s'' \xrightarrow{(\tau_0^+\tau_1)^k} s''' \xrightarrow{\tau_0^*} s'.$$

Let us consider the second case. Here, by Condition 2., we have $s''(\bar{x}) = \bar{c}$. Hence, by Condition 3., in any state reachable from s'' by applying $(\tau_0^+\tau_1)$ k'-times, the value of $\bar{z}$ is $s''(\bar{z}) + k' * \bar{c}'$. Therefore, $s'''(\bar{z}) = s''(\bar{z}) + k * \bar{c}$.

Notice that Condition 4., is used to prove the "only if" part of the statement. Condition 5. guarantees that s''' is reachable from s'' by $(\tau_0^+\tau_1)$ k-times. It also guarantees that the number of times τ_0 can be taking starting in a state satisfying $\bar{x} = \bar{c}$ does not depend on $\bar{z}$.

□

Remark 1. It is important to notice that Condition 2 is syntactic, so it can be easily checked. Moreover, the remaining conditions can be checked effectively, since the sets of reachable states involved are expressible in Presburger arithmetic. Indeed, if a language L is of the form $L_1 + \cdots + L_n$, where each L_i is either finite or of the form w^*, where w is a word, then the set of states reachable by L

from a (parametric) state $\bar{x} = \bar{x}_0$ is easily expressible in Presburger arithmetic. Nevertheless, it is easy to give sufficient syntactic conditions that can be easily checked. For instance, Condition 5. is satisfied, if $\bar{z}$ does not occur in the guard of transition τ_0.

Example 1.
Let us consider the following self-loops:

$$\begin{cases} \tau_0 : x < T & \to x := x + 1; z := z + 1 \\ \tau_1 : x = T \wedge y < C \to x := 0; y := y + 1 \end{cases}$$

It is easy to check that the premises of Lemma 2 are satisfied. Using the characterization stated by the lemma and after simplification, we obtain the following invariant:

$$(x - z = x_0 - z_0 \wedge x \geq x_0 \wedge z \geq z_0 \wedge y = y_0)$$
$$\vee \; \exists k \geq 1 \cdot$$
$$(y = y_0 + k \wedge y \leq C \wedge z = (z_0 - x_0) + k * T + x \wedge x \leq T)$$

□

Lemma 2 can be generalized as follows to the case where $\bar{z}$ is not augmented by the same list $\bar{c}$ of constants:

Lemma 3. *Assume the same premises as in Lemma 2 but condition 3. replaced by:*

There is a set I of values such that, for every states s and s' with $s(\bar{x}) = \bar{c}$ and $s \xrightarrow{\tau_0^*} s'$, if s' satisfies the guard of τ_1 then

3.a *there is $\bar{c}' \in I$ with $s'(\bar{z}) = s(\bar{z}) + \bar{c}'$ and*

3.b *for every $\bar{c}'' \in I$ there is a state s'' with $s''(\bar{z}) = s(\bar{z}) + \bar{c}''$, $s \xrightarrow{\tau_0^*} s''$, and such that s'' satisfies the guard of τ_1.*

Then, $s \xrightarrow{(\tau_0 + \tau_1)^*} s'$ iff $s \xrightarrow{\tau_0^*} s'$ or there exists a state s'' such that

1. $s \xrightarrow{\tau_0^* \tau_1} s''$, $\bar{x} = \bar{c} \xrightarrow{\tau_0(x)^*} s'(\bar{x})$ and

2. there exists $k \in \mathbb{N}$ and a state s''' with $s'''(\bar{z}) = s''(\bar{z}) + \sum_{i=1}^{i=k} \bar{c}_i$ with $\bar{c}_i \in I$, $s(\bar{y}) \xrightarrow{\tau_1^{k+1}} s'(\bar{y})$, and $s'''(\bar{z}) \xrightarrow{\tau_0^*} s'(\bar{z})$.

□

Example 2.
Let us consider the following self-loops:

$$\begin{cases} \tau_0 : x < T & \to x := x + 1; z := z + 1 \\ \tau_1 : t \leq x \leq T \wedge y < C \to x := 0; y := y + 1 \end{cases}$$

Now, applying Lemma 3 we obtain the following invariant:

$$(x - z = x_0 - z_0 \wedge x \geq x_0 \wedge z \geq z_0 \wedge y = y_0)$$
$$\vee \; \exists k \geq 1 \cdot$$
$$(y = y_0 + k \wedge y \leq C \wedge z \in (z_0 - x_0) + [k * t, k * T] + x \wedge x \leq T)$$

□

Remark 2. Notice that, if we remove Condition 3.b in Lemma 3, then only the "only if" part of the conclusion is true, that is, we have $s \xrightarrow{(\tau_0 + \tau_1)^*} s'$ implies $s \xrightarrow{\tau_0^*} s'$ or there exists a state s'' such that

1. $s \xrightarrow{\tau_0^* \tau_1} s''$, $\bar{x} = \bar{c} \xrightarrow{\tau_0^*} s'(\bar{x})$ and

2. there exists $k \in I\!N$ and a state s''' with $s'''(\bar{z}) = s''(\bar{z}) + \sum_{i=1}^{i=k} \bar{c}_i$ with $\bar{c}_i \in I$,

   $s(\bar{y}) \xrightarrow{\tau_1^{k+1}} s'(\bar{y})$, and $s'''(\bar{z}) \xrightarrow{\tau_0^*} s'(\bar{z})$.

This result can of course be used to derive an invariant that is not necessarily the strongest. □

4   Decomposition Techniques

We present hereafter heuristics which allow us to reduce the analysis of $n \geq 2$ self-loops to simpler cases such that, finally, we can apply the lemmata introduced in Section 3.

Basically, we consider the case of $n + 1$ loosely-coupled self-loops. We show that, their global analysis can be effectively reduced to n analysis of 2 self-loop problems, when some syntactic conditions on the sets of used variables occurs. The decomposition technique is stated by the following lemma and can be seen as a direct generalization of lemma 1.

Lemma 4. *Let $\tau_0, \tau_1, \cdots, \tau_n$ be transitions such that $Base(\tau_0) = \bar{x}_1 \cdots \bar{x}_n$, $Base(\tau_i) = \bar{x}_i \bar{y}_i$ and for each $i = 1, \cdots, n$, $\bar{x}_i$ is assigned by τ_i the list $\bar{c}_i$ of constants, and the sets of variables $\bar{x}_i$ and $\bar{y}_i$ are all pairwise disjoint.*

If each φ_i is a $(\tau_0(\bar{x}_i) + \tau_i)^*$-invariant, then $\bigwedge_{i=1}^n \varphi_i$ is a $(\tau_0 + \cdots + \tau_n)^*$-invariant. □

Example 3. Let us consider the following three self-loops borrowed from the description of the Biphase protocol, which we will consider in Section 5:

$$\begin{cases} \tau_0 : x < max \wedge y < max & \rightarrow x := x + 1 \quad y := y + 1 \\ \tau_1 : x \geq min \wedge n < cell & \rightarrow x := 0 \quad n := n + 1 \\ \tau_2 : y \geq min \wedge m < sample \rightarrow y := 0 \quad m := m + 1 \end{cases}$$

We can easily check that the premises of Lemma 4 are satisfied. Hence, we can split the analysis of the three self-loops into the independent analysis of the following sets each consisting of two self-loops, as shown below:

$$\begin{cases} \tau_0(x) : x < max & \rightarrow x := x + 1 \\ \tau_1 \quad : x \geq min \wedge n < cell \rightarrow x := 0 \quad n := n + 1 \end{cases}$$

$$\begin{cases} \tau_0(y) : y < max & \rightarrow y := y + 1 \\ \tau_2 \quad : y \geq min \wedge m < sample \rightarrow y := 0 \quad m := m + 1 \end{cases}$$

Each case can be analyzed independently using the results established in the previous section. We obtain that

$$\varphi_1 = (x \leq max \ \wedge \ n \leq cell)$$

is a $(\tau_0(x) + \tau_1)^*$-invariant and that

$$\varphi_2 = (y \leq max \ \wedge \ m \leq sample)$$

is a $(\tau_0(y) + \tau_2)^*$-invariant.

Thus, we can infer that

$$\varphi_1 \wedge \varphi_2 = (x \leq max \ \wedge \ n \leq cell \ \wedge \ y \leq max \ \wedge \ m \leq sample)$$

is a $(\tau_0 + \tau_1 + \tau_2)^*$-invariant. $\qquad\qquad\square$

However, the invariants obtained in this way are too weak. The reason is that by the decomposition of the set of loops we lost the overall constraint induced on $\bar{x}$ variables by the τ_0 loop. That is, all variables occurring in τ_0 are strongly related by this transition, and it is no more the case when taking the projections. The following lemma solves this problem by adding some *re-synchronization* variables in order to be able to reconstruct (at least partially) the existing relation among the $\bar{x}$ variables.

Lemma 5. *Let $\tau_0, \tau_1, \cdots, \tau_n$ be transitions s.t. the premises of Lemma 4 are satisfied. Let $(z_i)_{i=1,n}$ be fresh variables and let $\tau_0'(\bar{x}_i)$ be the transition obtained from $\tau_0(\bar{x}_i)$ augmented with the assignment $z_i := z_i + 1$.*

If each φ_i' is a $(\tau_0'(\bar{x}_i) + \tau_i)^*$-invariant, then $\exists z_1, \cdots z_n.(z_1 = \cdots = z_n \wedge \bigwedge_{i=1}^n \varphi_i')$ is a $(\tau_0 + \cdots + \tau_n)^*$-invariant. $\qquad\square$

Intuitively, variables z_i keep track of the number of times the transition τ_0 is executed in each case. In this way, the global invariant can be strengthened by adding the equality on z_i variables. That is, when considered together, the number of times τ_0 is executed must be the same in all $1 \leq i \leq n$ cases.

Example 4. Let us consider again the three-loops presented above. After splitting them and augmentation with fresh variables z_x and z_y, we obtain the following sets of self-loops to be analyzed:

$$\begin{cases} \tau_0(x) : x < max & \rightarrow x := x + 1 \quad z_x := z_x + 1 \\ \tau_1 \quad : x \geq min \wedge n < cell \rightarrow x := 0 \quad n := n + 1 \end{cases}$$

$$\begin{cases} \tau_0(y) : y < max & \rightarrow y := y + 1 \quad z_y := z_y + 1 \\ \tau_2 \quad : y \geq min \wedge m < sample \rightarrow y := 0 \quad m := m + 1 \end{cases}$$

Applying, Lemma 3, we obtain that

$$\varphi_1' = (x \leq max \ \wedge \ n \leq cell \ \wedge \ n \cdot min + x \leq z_x \leq n \cdot max + x)$$

is a $(\tau_0'(x) + \tau_1)^*$-invariant and that

$$\varphi_2' = (y \leq max \ \wedge \ m \leq sample \ \wedge \ m \cdot min + y \leq z_y \leq m \cdot max + y)$$

is a $(\tau_0'(y) + \tau_2)^*$-invariant.

The global invariant computed is then $\exists z_x, z_y.(z_x = z_y \wedge \varphi_1' \wedge \varphi_2')$, which can be simplified to

$$x \leq max \ \wedge \ n \leq cell \ \wedge \ y \leq max \ \wedge \ m \leq sample \ \wedge$$
$$n \cdot min + x \leq m \cdot max + y \ \wedge \ m \cdot min + y \leq n \cdot max + x.$$

This invariant is indeed stronger than the one computed in Example 3.   □

5   The Biphase Protocol

The biphase mark protocol is a convention for representing both a string of bits and clock edges in a square wave. It is widely used in applications where data written by one device is read by another. It is for instance used in commercially available micro-controllers as the Intel 82530 Serial Communication Controller and in the Ethernet.

We borrow the following informal description of the protocol from J. S. Moore:

> In the biphase mark protocol, each bit of messages is encoded in a *cell* which is logically divided into a *mark subcell* and a *code subcell*. During the mark subcell, the signal is held at the negation of its value at the end of the previous cell, providing an edge in the signal train which marks the beginning of the new cell. During the code subcell, the signal either returns to its previous value or does not, depending on whether the cell encodes a "1" or "0". The receiver is generally waiting for the edge that marks the arrival of a cell. When the edge is detected, the receiver counts off a fixed number of cycles, called *sampling distance*, and samples the signal there. The sampling distance is determined so as to make the receiver sample in the middle of the code subcell. If the sample is the same as the mark, a "0" was sent; otherwise a "1" was sent. The receiver takes up waiting for the next edge, thus *phase locking* onto the sender's clock.

The main interesting aspect (from the verification point of view) of this protocol is the analysis of the tolerable asynchrony between the sender and the receiver. Put more directly, the derivation of sufficient conditions on the jitter between the clock of the sender and the clock of the receiver such that the protocol works properly.

To our knowledge, there has been some work on the verification of instances of the protocol either using theorem-proving techniques [Moo93] or model-checking [IG99,Vaa] and one work presenting full parameter analysis using PVS and the Duration Calculus, however, without clock jitter.

Using the techniques presented earlier in this paper, we have been able to fully analyze the protocol and to derive parameterized sufficient conditions for its correctness.

5.1   Protocol Modeling

We use extended transition systems to model the protocol which consists of a sender and a receiver exchanging boolean value. Some of the transitions are marked with synchronization labels. Following, Vaandrager we model the clock drifts and jitter using two different clocks which will be reset independently and using two parameters min and max to bound the drift between these clocks. The models of the sender, the receiver and their product are given in Figure 1, Figure 2, and Figure 3.

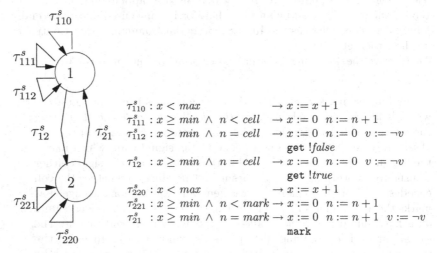

Fig. 1. The sender

5.2   Invariant Generation

Using the techniques presented before we are able to construct the following invariants for the product control locations:

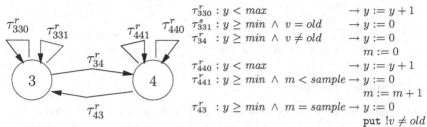

$$\tau^r_{330} : y < max \qquad\qquad\qquad \to y := y+1$$
$$\tau^s_{331} : y \geq min \ \wedge \ v = old \qquad \to y := 0$$
$$\tau^r_{34} \ : y \geq min \ \wedge \ v \neq old \qquad \to y := 0$$
$$m := 0$$
$$\tau^r_{440} : y < max \qquad\qquad\qquad \to y := y+1$$
$$\tau^r_{441} : y \geq min \ \wedge \ m < sample \to y := 0$$
$$m := m+1$$
$$\tau^r_{43} \ : y \geq min \ \wedge \ m = sample \to y := 0$$
$$\textbf{put} \ !v \neq old$$

Fig. 2. The receiver

$$\tau_{130}, \tau_{140}, \tau_{230}, \tau_{240} : x < max \ \wedge \ y < max \to x := x+1 \ \ y := y+1$$

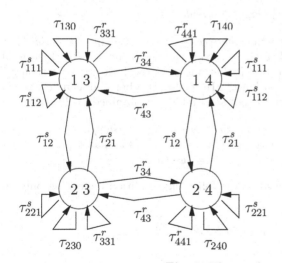

Fig. 3. The product

$$\varphi_{13} = x \leq max \ \wedge \ y \leq max \ \wedge \ n \leq cell$$
$$\varphi_{14} = x \leq max \ \wedge \ y \leq max \ \wedge \ n \leq cell \ \wedge \ m \leq sample$$
$$m \cdot min + y \leq n \cdot max + x \ \wedge \ n \cdot min + x \leq m \cdot max + y$$
$$\varphi_{23} = x \leq max \ \wedge \ y \leq max \ \wedge \ n \leq mark$$
$$\varphi_{24} = x \leq max \ \wedge \ y \leq max \ \wedge \ n \leq mark \ \wedge \ m \leq sample$$
$$m \cdot min + y \leq n \cdot max + x \ \wedge \ n \cdot min + x \leq m \cdot max + y$$

5.3   Parameter Synthesis

One of requirements for correctness of the protocol states that *the receiver does not sample too late*. That is, a bad behavior is obtained by allowing to take two consecutive **get** actions by the protocol, without no **put** action in between. For instance, such a scenario is possible when in state 14, the **get** transitions τ_{112}^s or τ_{12}^s are enabled before the **put** transition τ_{43}^r. To avoid such a situation, a sufficient condition will be if $\varphi_{14} \wedge (gua(\tau_{112}^s) \vee gua(\tau_{12}^s))$ is not satisfiable. This condition is the following:

$$x \leq max \ \wedge \ y \leq max \ \wedge \ n \leq cell \ \wedge \ m \leq sample$$
$$m \cdot min + y \leq n \cdot max + x \ \wedge \ n \cdot min + x \leq m \cdot max + y$$
$$x \geq min \ \wedge \ n = cell$$

and is equivalent after simplification to :

$$(cell + 1) \cdot min > (sample + 1) \cdot max$$

A second requirement states that *the receiver does not sample too early*. That is, wrong behavior occurs when the receiver samples before the mark sub-cell started. In this case, a bad scenario is that one in state 24 the **put** transition τ_{43}^r is enabled before the **mark** transition τ_{21}^s. Here also, this behavior can be avoided if the condition $\varphi_{24} \ \wedge \ gua(\tau_{43}^r)$ is not satisfiable. We obtained in this case:

$$x \leq max \ \wedge \ y \leq max \ \wedge \ n \leq mark \ \wedge \ m \leq sample$$
$$m \cdot min + y \leq n \cdot max + x \ \wedge \ n \cdot min + x \leq m \cdot max + y$$
$$y \geq min \ \wedge \ m = sample$$

and can be further simplified to the following condition depending only on parameters:

$$(sample + 1) \cdot min > (mark + 1) \cdot max$$

6   Conclusions

In this paper, we presented a set of techniques which allow to compute an over-approximation of the set of reachable states of a set of self-loops. The techniques we presented can be partitioned in two classes: 1.) exact techniques that under effectively checkable conditions allow to characterize the set of reachable states of pairs of self-loops without loss of information and 2.) techniques that allow to reduce more general cases of a set of self-loops to the analysis of a set of pairs of self-loops. Using, our techniques we have been able to synthesize a set of conditions on the parameters of the Biphase protocol that are sufficient to ensure its correctness.

We plan to implement our techniques using decision procedures for Presburger arithmetic to decide the conditions necessary for applying them. We also plan to apply these techniques for generating test cases for protocols and test objectives that involve data.

References

ABJ98.   P. Abdulla, A. Bouajjani, and B. Jonsson. On-the-fly analysis of systems with unbounded, lossy fifb channels. In *CAV'98*, volume 1427 of *LNCS*, pages 305-318, 1998. 59

ABJN99.   P.A. Abdulla, A. Bouajjani, B. Jonsson, and M. Nilsson. Handling Global Conditions in Parameterized System Verification. In N. Halbwachs and D. Peled, editors, *CAV '99*, volume 1633 of *LNCS*, pages 134-145. Springer-Verlag, 1999. 59

AD94.   R. Alur and D. Dill. A Theory of Timed Automata. *Theoretical Computer Science*, 126, 1994. 59

AM80.   K.R. Apt and L.G.L.T. Meertens. Completeness with finite systems of intermediate assertions for recursive program schemes. *SIAM J. Comp.*, 9:665-671, 1980. 61

BBLS.   K. Baukus, S. Bensalem, Y. Lakhnech, and K. Stahl. Abstracting wsis systems to verify parameterized networks'In *TACAS'OO*. 59

BG96.   B. Boigelot and P. Godefroid. Symbolic verification of communication protocols with infinite state spaces using QDDs. In *CAV'96*, volume 1102 of *LNCS*, pages 1-12, 1996. 59

BGP97.   Bultan, Gerber, and Pugh. Symbolic model checking of infinite state systems using presburger arithmetic. In *CAV: International Conference on Computer Aided Verification*, 1997. 59

CC76.   P. Cousot and R. Cousot. Static determination of dynamic properties of programs. In *Proc. 2nd Int. Symp. on Programming*, pages 106-130, 1976. 58

CC77.   P. Cousot and R. Cousot. Abstract interpretation: A unified lattice model for static analysis of programs by construction or approximation of fix-points. In *4th ACM symp. of Prog. Lang.*, pages 238-252. ACM Press, 1977. 58, 61

CC92.   P. Cousot and R. Cousot. Abstract interpretation frameworks. *J. Logic and Comp.*, 2(4):511-547, 1992. 58

CH78.   P. Cousot and N. Halbwachs. Automatic discovery of linear restraints among the variables of a program. In *5th ACM symp. of Prog. Lang.*, pages 84-97. ACM Press, 1978. 58, 61

CHPP87.   P. Caspi, N. Halbwachs, D. Pilaud, and J. Plaice. LUSTRE, adclarative language for programming synchronous systems. In *14th Symposium on Principles of Programming Langiages*, 1987. 59

FO97.   L. Fribourg and H. Olsen. A decompositional approach for computing least fized-points of datalog programs with z-counters. *Constraints,* 2(3/4) :305-335,1997. 59, 61

Gor75.   G. A. Gorelick. A complete axiomatic system for proving assertions about recursive and non-recursive programs. Technical report, Toronto, 1975. 61

HNSY92.   T.A. Henzinger, X. Nicollin, J. Sifakis, and S. Yovine. Symbolic model-checking for real-time systems. In *Seventh Annual IEEE Symposium on Logic in Computer Science,* pages 394-406. IEEE Computer Society Press, 1992. 59

HPR94.   N. Halbwachs, Y.-E. Proy, and P. Raymond. Verification of linear hybrid systems by means of convex approximations. In *Proceedings of the International Symposium on Static Analysis,* volume 818 of *LNCS,* pages 223-237. Springer-Verlag, 1994. 59

IG99.   S. Ivanov and W. 0. D. Griffioen. Verification of a biphase mark protocol. Report CSI-R9915, Computing Science Institute, University of Nijmegen, August 1999. 68

Kar76.   M. Karr. Affine relationships among variables of a program. *Acta Informatica,* 6:133-151, 1976. 58

KJ89.   K.M. Chandy and J. Misra. *Parallel Program Design.* Addison-Wesley, Austin, Texas, May 1989. 59

KMM+97.   Y. Kesten, 0. Maler, M. Marcus, A. Pnueli, and E. Shahar. Symbolic Model Checking with Rich Assertional Languages. In 0. Grumberg, editor, *Proceedings of CAV '97,* volume 1256 of *LNCS,* pages 424-435. Springer-Verlag, 1997. 59

Moo93.   J. S. Moore. A formal model of asynchronous communication and its use in mechanically verifying a biphase mark protocol. *Formal Aspects of Computing,* 3(1), 1993. 68

Vaa.   F. Vaandrager. Analysis of a biphase mark protocol with uppaal. Presentation at the meeting of the VHS-ESPRIT Project. 68

WB98.   P. Wolper and B. Boigelot. Verifying systems with infinite but regular state spaces. In *CAV'98,* volume 1427 of *LNCS,* pages 88-97, 1998. 59

Deriving Parallel Codes via Invariants

Wei-Ngan Chin[1], Siau-Cheng Khoo[1], Zhenjiang Hu[2], and Masato Takeichi[2]

[1] School of Computing, National University of Singapore, Singapore
{chinwn,khoosc}@comp.nus.edu.sg
[2] Department of Information Engineering, University of Tokyo, Japan
hu@ipl.t.u-tokyo.ac.jp, takeichi@u-tokyo.ac.jp

Abstract. Systematic parallelization of sequential programs remains a major challenge in parallel computing. Traditional approaches using program schemes tend to be narrower in scope, as the properties which enable parallelism are difficult to capture via ad-hoc schemes. In [CTH98], a systematic approach to parallelization based on the notion of preserving the *context* of recursive sub-terms has been proposed. This approach can be used to derive a class of divide-and-conquer algorithms. In this paper, we enhance the methodology by using *invariants* to guide the parallelization process. The enhancement enables the parallelization of a class of recursive functions with conditional and tupled constructs, which were not possible previously. We further show how such invariants can be discovered and verified systematically, and demonstrate the power of our methodology by deriving a parallel code for maximum segment product. To the best of our knowledge, this is the first systematic parallelization for the maximum segment product problem.

Keywords: Parallelization, Context Preservation, Invariants, Conditional Recurrences, Constraints.

1 Introduction

It is well-recognised that a key problem of parallel computing remains the development of efficient and correct parallel software. Many advanced language features and constructs have been proposed to alleviate the complexities of parallel programming, but perhaps the simplest approach is to stick with sequential programs and leave it to parallelization techniques to do a more decent transformation job. This approach could also simplify the program design and debugging processes, and allows better portability to be achieved.

A traditional approach to this problem is to identify a set of useful higher-order functions for which parallelization can be guaranteed. As an example, Blelloch's NESL language [BCH+93] supports two extremely important parallel primitives, scan and segmented scan, that together covers a wide range of parallel programs. Specifically, segmented scan can be used to express non-trivial problems (such as sparse matrix calculations and graph operations [Ble90]) that are difficult to parallelize due to their use of irregular data structures.

J. Palsberg (Ed.): SAS 2000, LNCS 1824, pp. 75–94, 2000.

However, before a programmer can use these higher-order parallel primitives, she must *manually match* her problem to the sequential form of scan and segmented scan (based on flattened list), shown below.[1]

$$
\begin{aligned}
&scan\ (\oplus)\ ([], w) &&= [] \\
&scan\ (\oplus)\ (x:xs, w) &&= [(w{\oplus}x)] +\!\!+ scan\ (\oplus)\ (xs, w{\oplus}x) \\[4pt]
&segscan\ (\oplus)\ ([], w) &&= [] \\
&segscan\ (\oplus)\ ((x,b):xs, w) &&= \textbf{if}\ b == 1\ \textbf{then}\ [(x,b)] +\!\!+ segscan\ (\oplus)\ (xs, x) \\
& && \quad\ \textbf{else}\ [(w{\oplus}x, b)] +\!\!+ segscan\ (\oplus)\ (xs, w{\oplus}x)
\end{aligned}
$$

(ASIDE : Our functions are defined using Haskell/ML style pattern-matching equations. Notationwise, [] denotes an empty sequence, $x : xs$ denotes an infix *Cons* data node with x as its head and xs as its tail. Also, $+\!\!+$ is the sequence concatenation operator.)

Note that operator $\oplus$ needs to be semi-associative[2]. This is required to help distribute/parallelize the above *scan* and *segscan* functions.

The process of *matching* a given program to a set of higher-order primitives is non-trivial, particularly for recursive functions with conditional and tupled constructs. As an example, consider a sequential program to find the minimum sum from all possible segments of elements.

$$
\begin{aligned}
&mss([x]) &&= x \\
&mss(x:xs) &&= min2(mis(x:xs), mss(xs)) \\[4pt]
&mis([x]) &&= x \\
&mis(x:xs) &&= \textbf{if}\ mis(xs) + x \le x\ \textbf{then}\ mis(xs) + x\ \textbf{else}\ x
\end{aligned}
$$

How may one match this function to an appropriate parallel primitive (*eg.* *scan*)? Alternatively, could we *directly derive* a parallel equivalent of this function?

While the sequential version of *mss* is straightforward to formulate, the same cannot be said for its parallel counterpart. Part of the complication stems from the presence of the conditional construct and the need to *invent* new auxiliary functions to circumvent its sequentiality.

In this paper, we propose a semi-automatic methodology for systematic derivation of parallel programs directly from their sequential equations. We focus on transforming recursive functions containing one or more conditional constructs, and make use of an *invariant*, where appropriate, to guide the transformation steps. In the case of *mis*, we first convert its sequential definition body

---

[1] The functions defined in this paper are written in Haskell syntax. Particularly, the parenthesis notation ($\cdot$) converts an infix operator (such as $\oplus$) into its equivalent prefix function.

[2] An operator $\oplus$ is said to be semi-associative if there exists a companion operator $\bar{\oplus}$ that is fully associative, such that $((a{\oplus}b){\oplus}c) = (a{\oplus}(b\bar{\oplus}c))$ holds. For example, $-$ and $\div$ are semi-associative operators with $+$ and $*$ as their respective companions. Note that *scan* and *segscan* are usually defined using the more restricted full-associative property whereby $\oplus = \bar{\oplus}$.

(the second equation) into a contextual form: $\textbf{if } \bullet \leq \alpha_1 \textbf{ then } \bullet + \alpha_2 \textbf{ else } \alpha_3$, where $\bullet = mis(xs)$, $\alpha_1 = 0$, $\alpha_2 = x$, and $\alpha_3 = x$. By using the invariant $\alpha_3 \geq \alpha_1 + \alpha_2$, we can derive a parallel version of mis (and mss) as follows:[3]

$$
\begin{aligned}
mss([x]) &= x \\
mss(xr \!+\!\!+\! xs) &= min2(mss(xr), min2(uT(xr) + mis(xs), mss(xs)))
\end{aligned}
$$

$$
\begin{aligned}
mis([x]) &= x \\
mis(xr \!+\!\!+\! xs) &= \textbf{if } mis(xs) \leq uH(xr) \textbf{ then } mis(xs) + uG(xr) \textbf{ else } mis(xr)
\end{aligned}
$$

$$
\begin{aligned}
uH([x]) &= 0 \\
uH(xr \!+\!\!+\! xs) &= min2(uH(xs), uH(xr) - uG(xs))
\end{aligned}
$$

$$
\begin{aligned}
uT([x]) &= x \\
uT(xr \!+\!\!+\! xs) &= min2(uT(xr) + uG(xs), uT(xs))
\end{aligned}
$$

$$
\begin{aligned}
uG([x]) &= x \\
uG(xr \!+\!\!+\! xs) &= uG(xs) + uG(xr)
\end{aligned}
$$

(ASIDE : The concatenation operator $\!+\!\!+\!$ also serves as a sequence splitting operation when used as a pattern in the LHS of equation. Operationally, a sequence may be implemented using a vector for easier data access and distribution. However, this paper shall focus on high-level parallelization issues, and omit detailed implementation concerns, such as data-type conversion & task distribution.)

The main contributions of this paper are:

- We *extend* the parallelization methodology proposed in [CTH98] to cover recursive functions with conditional and tupled constructs. These functions are hard to parallelize, but we circumvent this difficulty by using an appropriate normalization process. (Section 3)
- A novelty of our approach is the introduction of *invariants* to the parallelization process. To the best of our knowledge, this is the first use of invariants for the derivation of parallel programs. Such an effort significantly widens the class of parallelizable functions. (Section 4)
- Instead of relying on user-defined invariants to improve parallelization opportunity, we demonstrate *how invariants can be systematically generated and verified* through high-level constraint-solving techniques. (Section 4.3 with details in Appendix A)
- We demonstrate how the sequential code for maximum segment product problem can be systematically parallelized using our methodology. To the best of our knowledge, this is the first account of systematic parallelization for this particular problem.

---

[3] Here, we have used an inequality invariant during our parallelization. Alternatively, we can employ a stronger *equality* invariant $\alpha_3 = \alpha_1 + \alpha_2$. This will produce a very compact parallel code for mis.

The outline of the paper is as follows: Section 2 describes the syntax of the language processed by our method. Section 3 details our parallelization methodology. Section 4 discusses how invariants are discovered and verified through constraint solving. We then apply our methodology to the parallelization of maximum segment product problem in Section 5. Finally, we relate our work to existing works done in the research community, before concluding the paper.

2 Language

We are mainly interested in deriving a class of divide-and-conquer algorithms with simple split operators (e.g. ++). For simplicity, we shall focus on a strict first-order functional language. (Limited support for passing function names as parameters will also be provided through program schemes. For example, *ssc* in Figure 1 is essentially a function scheme with $\oplus$ as its function-type variable.)

Definition 1: *A First-Order Language*

$$F ::= \{f(p_{i,1}, \ldots, p_{i,n_i}) = t_i\}_{i=1}^m$$
$$t ::= v \mid c(t_1, \ldots, t_n) \mid \text{if } t_1 \text{ then } t_2 \text{ else } t_3$$
$$\mid f(t_1, \ldots, t_n) \mid \text{let } (v_1, \ldots, v_n) = t_1 \text{ in } t_2$$
$$p ::= v \mid c(p_1, \ldots, p_n)$$
$$v \in \text{Variables}; \quad c \in \text{Data constructors}; \quad f \in \text{Function names} \qquad \Box$$

This language contains the usual data constructor terms, function calls, **let** and **if** constructs. Also, each function f is defined by a set of pattern-matching equations.

We shall focus on sequential functions that are inductively defined over linear data types with an associative decomposition operator. For practical reasons, we restrict the linear data type to *List* with ++ as its decomposition operator. We shall only perform parallelization for a special sub-class of sequential functions, called *linear self-recursive* functions.

Definition 2: *Linear Self-Recursive Functions*
A function f is said to be *self-recursive* if it contains only self-recursive calls. In addition, it is said to be *linear self-recursive* (LSR) if its definition contains exactly one self-recursive call. $\qquad \Box$

Though our methodology can support LSR-functions with multiple recursion parameters and nested patterns, this paper shall restrict the sub-class of functions considered to the following form.

$$--- f([], \lfloor v_j \rfloor_{j=1}^n) = Ez$$
$$--- f(x : xs, \lfloor v_j \rfloor_{j=1}^n) = Er\langle f(xs, \lfloor Dr_j\langle v_j\rangle \rfloor_{j=1}^n)\rangle$$

$Er\langle\ \rangle$ denotes the *context* for the self-recursive call of f in the rhs of the definition, while $\lfloor Dr_j\langle\ \rangle \rfloor_{j=1}^n$ denote the *contexts* for the *accumulative* parameters $v_{j \in 1..n}$ appearing in the call to f. These expression contexts are referred to as *Recurring Contexts* (or *R-contexts* in short), as they capture the recurring subterms for

$$msp([x]) \quad =x$$
$$msp(x : xs) =max2(mip(x : xs),$$
$$msp(xs))$$
$$mip([x]) \quad =x$$
$$mip(x : xs) =$$
$$\quad \text{if } x > 0 \text{ then } max2(x, x*mip(xs))$$
$$\quad \text{else } max2(x, x*mipm(xs))$$
$$mipm([x]) \quad =x$$
$$mipm(x : xs) =$$
$$\quad \text{if } x > 0 \text{ then } min2(x, x*mipm(xs))$$
$$\quad \text{else } min2(x, x*mip(xs))$$

$$sbp([x]) \quad =conv(x)$$
$$sbp(x : xs) = \text{if } sbp(xs) \leq 0 \text{ then}$$
$$sbp(xs) + conv(x)$$
$$\text{else } 1$$
$$conv(x) = \text{if } x ==')' \text{ then } -1$$
$$\text{else (if } x ==' (' \text{ then } 1)$$
$$\text{else } 0$$
$$ssc\ (\oplus)\ ([], c) \quad =c$$
$$ssc\ (\oplus)\ (x : xs, c) = \text{if } p(x) \text{ then } c$$
$$\text{else } ssc\ (\oplus)\ (xs, c) \oplus x$$

Fig. 1. Sample Sequential Programs

each self-recursive function. Note that there exists exactly one self-recursive f call. $Er\langle\ \rangle$ and $\lfloor Dr_j\langle\ \rangle\rfloor_{j=1}^n$ do not contain other self or mutual-recursive calls. Also, x, xs are allowed to occur freely in E_r and $\lfloor Dr_j\rfloor_{j=1}^n$.

Several example functions are available in Fig. 1. Here, function msp computes the maximum segment product; function sbp checks a string for properly paired bracket; and ssc is a higher-order program scheme. Notice that both ssc and msp are LSR functions. However, mip, $mipm$, and sbp are not. Fortunately, these functions can be converted easily using the following two pre-processing techniques.

Firstly, *tupling* [Chi93,HITT97] may be used to eliminate multiple recursive calls. For simple cases such as duplication of calls in mis and sbp, tupling eliminates duplication via **let** abstraction. For more complicated cases, such as multiple mutual-recursive calls of mip and $mipm$, it generates an LSR-function $miptup$ such that for any list l, $miptup(l) = (mip(l), mipm(l))$. The generated $miptup$ function is:

$$miptup([x]) \quad = (x, x)$$
$$miptup(x : xs) = \text{let } (u, v) = miptup(xs)$$
$$\text{in if } x > 0 \text{ then } (max2(x, x*u), min2(x, x*v))$$
$$\text{else } (max2(x, x*v), min2(x, x*u))$$

Secondly, a *conditional normalization* procedure [CDG96] can be applied to combine recursive calls in different conditional branches together. Our conditionals are first expressed in a more general guarded form:

$$(\text{ if } b \text{ then } e_1 \text{ else } e_2) \quad \Leftrightarrow \quad \text{if } \begin{cases} b & \to e_1 \\ \neg b & \to e_2 \end{cases}$$

After that, the following duplicate elimination rule is applied to combine multiple self-recursive calls in different branches together.

$$\text{if } \{\ b_i \ \to\ E\langle e_i\rangle\ \}_{i \in N} \ \Rightarrow\ E\langle \text{if } \{\ b_i \ \to\ e_i\}_{i \in N}\rangle$$

For example, with *segscan*, we obtain:

$$segscan\ (\oplus)\ ([], w) \quad = []$$
$$segscan\ (\oplus)\ ((x, b) : xs, w) = (\ \textbf{if}\ b == 1\ \textbf{then}\ [(x, b)]\ \textbf{else}\ [(w \oplus x, b)]\ )\ \text{++}$$
$$segscan\ (\oplus)\ (xs,\ \textbf{if}\ b == 1\ \textbf{then}\ x\ \textbf{else}\ w \oplus x\ )$$

3 Parallelization Methodology

Our methodology for parallelization is based on the notion of generalizing from sequential examples. Given a LSR-function, f, we attempt to obtain a more *general* parallel equation directly from its sequential equation.

An earlier version of this methodology was presented in [CTH98]. However, this earlier work did not handle recursive functions, with conditional and tupled constructs, well. A major innovation of this paper is the use of *invariants* to facilitate parallelization. We shall first see why such invariants are *required*, and later show how they may be systematically *discovered and verified*.

The four steps of our parallelization methodology are now elaborated, using *mis* (the auxiliary function of *mss*) as our running example.

Step 1 : *R-Contexts Extraction & Normalization*
   The first step is to extract out R-contexts for both the recursive call and each of the accumulative arguments. In the case of *mis*, we have the following R-context.

$$(\hat{\lambda}\langle\bullet\rangle.\ \textbf{if}\ \alpha_0 + \underline{\bullet} \le \alpha_1\ \textbf{then}\ \underline{\bullet} + \alpha_2\ \textbf{else}\ \alpha_3\ )\textbf{where}\ \alpha_i = x\ \forall\ i \in 0 \ldots 3$$

We use the notation $\hat{\lambda}\langle\bullet\rangle.\cdots$ to represent an R-context parameterized by a special variable $\bullet$, is known as the *R-hole*. $\bullet$ captures the position of the recursive call/accumulative parameter. Also, *context variables* (e.g. $\{\alpha_i\}_{i \in 0..3}$) are used to capture each maximal subterm that does not contain $\bullet$.

To obtain a simpler R-context, we apply a normalization process to the original R-context. This process performs a series of semantic-preserving transformation to the R-context, aiming at reducing the *depths & occurrences* of the R-hole, and the *occurrences* of context variables. The heuristics used by the transformation is as follows.

Definition 3: *Heuristics for Context Normalization*
Consider a R-context with one or more R-holes. Our normalization attempts to:

- Minimise the *depth*[4] of the *R-holes* or their *proxies*. (A *proxy* is a local variable which denotes either a R-hole or its component – if the R-hole is a tuple.)
- Minimise the *number of occurrences* of the *context variables*, where possible.
- Minimise the *number of occurrences* of the *R-holes* or their *proxies*.   □

---

[4] Depth is defined to be the distance from the root of an expression tree. For example, the depths of variable occurrences c,x,xs,c in $(c+(x+sum(xs,c)))$ are 1,2,3,3 respectively.

A variety of laws, such as *associativity* and *distributivity*, will be employed in the normalization process. These laws are assumed to be supplied by the user beforehand. In the case of *mis*, we can normalize to obtain the following simpler R-context:

$$\hat{\lambda}\langle \bullet \rangle. \text{ if } \bullet \leq \alpha_1 \text{ then } \bullet + \alpha_2 \text{ else } \alpha_3 \quad \text{where } \alpha_1 = 0; \ \alpha_2 = x; \ \alpha_3 = x$$

Finally, we parameterise the R-context with respect to context variables, and obtain a *skeletal R-context*, $\mathcal{R}_{mis}$, defined by:

$$\mathcal{R}_{mis}(\alpha_1, \alpha_2, \alpha_3) \stackrel{def}{\equiv} \hat{\lambda}\langle \bullet \rangle. \text{ if } \bullet \leq \alpha_1 \text{ then } \bullet + \alpha_2 \text{ else } \alpha_3$$

Such a normalization is helpful in the following ways:

- It can faciliate *context preservation* in Step 2.
- It can minimise the occurrences of context variables. This can help reduce unnecessary auxiliary functions that are synthesized in Step 3.

Step 2 : *Context Preservation*

Our parallelization methodology is based on generalizing from sequential examples. This method relies on finding a second sequential equation with the same skeletal R-context as the first equation. The second equation can be obtained by unfolding the recursive call once, as follows.

$$f(x : (y : xs), \lfloor v_i \rfloor_{i=1}^{n})$$
$$= \sigma_1 Er \langle \sigma_2 Er \langle f(xs, \lfloor \sigma_2 \ Dr_i \langle \sigma_1 \ Dr_i \langle v_i \rangle \rangle \rfloor_{i=1}^{n}) \rangle \rangle$$
$$= (\sigma_1 Er \circ \sigma_2 Er) \langle f(xs, \lfloor (\sigma_2 \ Dr_i \circ \sigma_1 \ Dr_i) \langle v_i \rangle \rfloor_{i=1}^{n}) \rangle$$
$$\textbf{where } \sigma_1 = [xs \mapsto y : xs]; \ \sigma_2 = [x \mapsto y, \lfloor v_i \mapsto (\sigma_1 \ Dr_i) \langle v_i \rangle \rfloor_{i=1}^{n}]$$

In the above, $(\sigma \ Er)$ performs substitution of variables in the context Er by σ. Also, $(\sigma_1 Er \circ \sigma_2 Er)$ denotes context composition, in the obvious manner. In the case of *mis*, we obtain:

$$mis(x : (y : xs)) = ((\hat{\lambda}\langle \bullet \rangle. \text{ if } \bullet \leq 0 \text{ then } \bullet + x \text{ else } x \ )$$
$$\circ (\hat{\lambda}\langle \bullet \rangle. \text{ if } \bullet \leq 0 \text{ then } \bullet + y \text{ else } y \ )) \langle mis(xs) \rangle$$
$$= (\mathcal{R}_{mis}(0, x, x) \ \circ \ \mathcal{R}_{mis}(0, y, y)) \langle mis(xs) \rangle$$

Note that the respective R-contexts have been *replicated* by this unfold. In order to check if the second equation has the same skeletal R-context structure as the first equation, we must check if the following *context preservation* property holds for each of our R-contexts.

Definition 4: *Invariant-Based Context Preservation*

A R-context E is said to be *preserved modulo replication* under an *invariant P*, if there exists a skeletal R-context $\mathcal{R}$ such that the following holds:

$$(E \Rightarrow_{\eta}^{\star} \mathcal{R}(t_i)_{i \in N}) \ \wedge \ P(t_i)_{i \in N} \ \wedge$$
$$(((\ \mathcal{R}(\alpha_i)_{i \in N} \ \circ \ \mathcal{R}(\beta_i)_{i \in N}) \ \textbf{st } (P(\alpha_i)_{i \in N} \ \wedge \ P(\beta_i)_{i \in N}))$$
$$\Rightarrow_{\eta(\mathcal{R})}^{\star} (\ \mathcal{R}(\Omega_i)i \ \in \ N \ \textbf{st } P(\Omega_i)_{i \in N}))$$

where both $\Rightarrow_\eta{}^\star$ and $\Rightarrow_{\eta(\mathcal{R})}{}^\star$ denote respectively a series of normalization transformation. The former aims at normalizing the R-context E, as described in Step 1 above; the latter aims at transforming the replicated R-context to the desired skeletal R-context $\mathcal{R}$. α_i and β_i are context variables, and Ω_i denote subterms not containing R-hole, nor its proxies. The skeletal R-context $\mathcal{R}$ is said to be the *common context* despite replication/unfolding. Notationwise, $(e \ \mathbf{st} \ p)$ denotes an expression e that satisfies the invariant p.   □

The term $P(t_i)_{i\in N}$ specifies that the normalized R-context $\mathcal{R}\langle t_i\rangle_{i\,\in\,N}$ satisfies the invariant P; we call it the *pre-condition* for R-context. The other three terms on P ensure that all new R-context generated during context-preserving transformation also satisfy P; we call this the *invariance condition* for the invariant across R-context replication. This condition can be independently expressed as:
$$P(\alpha_i)_{i\,\in\,N} \wedge P(\beta_i)_{i\,\in\,N} \Rightarrow P(\Omega_i)_{i\,\in\,N}.$$

In the case of *mis*, we claim that $\mathcal{R}_{mis}(\alpha_1,\alpha_2,\alpha_3)$ is preserved modulo replication under the invariant $P_{mis}(\alpha_1,\alpha_2,\alpha_3) \overset{def}{\equiv} \alpha_3 \geq \alpha_1 + \alpha_2$. We will describe how such an invariant is discovered (and verified) in Section 4. Here, we illustrate how P_{mis} can be used to preserve R-context during transformation. We begin with the composition $\mathcal{R}_{mis}(\alpha_1,\ \alpha_2,\alpha_3) \circ \mathcal{R}_{mis}(\beta_1,\beta_2,\beta_3)$, assuming that the composition satisfies the invariance property $P'_{mis} \overset{def}{\equiv} P_{mis}(\alpha_1,\alpha_2,\alpha_3) \wedge P_{mis}(\beta_1,\beta_2,\beta_3)$. Note that at each transformation step, the expression under transformation satisfies P'_{mis}. Due to space constraint, we omit writing P'_{mis} in these steps, except for the first expression.

$((\hat{\lambda}\langle\bullet\rangle. \ \mathbf{if} \ \bullet \leq \alpha_1 \ \mathbf{then} \ \bullet + \alpha_2 \ \mathbf{else} \ \alpha_3 \ )\circ(\hat{\lambda}\langle\bullet\rangle. \ \mathbf{if} \ \bullet \leq \beta_1 \ \mathbf{then} \ \bullet + \beta_2 \ \mathbf{else} \ \beta_3) \ )$
$\quad \mathbf{st} \ (\alpha_3 \ \geq \ \alpha_1 \ + \ \alpha_2) \wedge (\beta_3 \ \geq \ \beta_1 \ + \ \beta_2)$

$\Rightarrow_{\eta(\mathcal{R}_{mis})}$ {definition of $\circ$}
$\hat{\lambda}\langle\bullet\rangle. \ \mathbf{if} \ (\mathbf{if} \ \bullet \leq \beta_1 \ \mathbf{then} \ \bullet + \beta_2 \ \mathbf{else} \ \beta_3) \leq \alpha_1 \ \mathbf{then} \ (\mathbf{if} \ \bullet \leq \beta_1 \ \mathbf{then} \ \bullet + \beta_2 \ \mathbf{else} \ \beta_3) + \alpha_2$
$\quad \mathbf{else} \ \alpha_3$

$\Rightarrow_{\eta(\mathcal{R}_{mis})}$ {float out $(\bullet \leq \beta_1)$ & simplify}
$\hat{\lambda}\langle\bullet\rangle. \ \mathbf{if} \ \bullet \leq \beta_1 \ \mathbf{then} \ \mathbf{if} \ \bullet + \beta_2 \leq \alpha_1 \ \mathbf{then} \ \bullet + \beta_2 + \alpha_2 \ \mathbf{else} \ \alpha_3$
$\quad \mathbf{else} \ \mathbf{if} \ \beta_3 \leq \alpha_1 \ \mathbf{then} \ \beta_3 + \alpha_2 \ \mathbf{else} \ \alpha_3$

$\Rightarrow_{\eta(\mathcal{R}_{mis})}$ {flatten nested if}
$\hat{\lambda}\langle\bullet\rangle.\mathbf{if} \begin{cases} (\bullet \leq \beta_1) \wedge (\bullet + \beta_2 \leq \alpha_1) & \rightarrow \bullet + \beta_2 + \alpha_2 \\ (\bullet \leq \beta_1) \wedge \neg(\bullet + \beta_2 \leq \alpha_1) & \rightarrow \alpha_3 \\ \neg(\bullet \leq \beta_1) \wedge (\beta_3 \leq \alpha_1) & \rightarrow \beta_3 + \alpha_2 \\ \neg(\bullet \leq \beta_1) \wedge \neg(\beta_3 \leq \alpha_1) & \rightarrow \alpha_3 \end{cases}$

$\Rightarrow_{\eta(\mathcal{R}_{mis})}$ {combine $\leq$ & regroup if}
$\hat{\lambda}\langle\bullet\rangle.\mathbf{if} \ \bullet \leq \ min2(\beta_1,\alpha_1 - \beta_2) \ \mathbf{then} \ \bullet + \beta_2 + \alpha_2 \ \mathbf{else}$
$\qquad \mathbf{if} \begin{cases} (\bullet \leq \beta_1) \wedge \neg(\bullet + \beta_2 \leq \alpha_1) & \rightarrow \alpha_3 \\ \neg(\bullet \leq \beta_1) \wedge (\beta_3 \leq \alpha_1) & \rightarrow \beta_3 + \alpha_2 \\ \neg(\bullet \leq \beta_1) \wedge \neg(\beta_3 \leq \alpha_1) & \rightarrow \alpha_3 \end{cases}$

$\Rightarrow_{\eta(\mathcal{R}_{mis})}$ {float nonrec $(\beta_3 \leq \alpha_1)$ & simplify}
$\hat{\lambda}\langle\bullet\rangle.\mathbf{if}\ \underline{\bullet} \leq\ min2(\beta_1, \alpha_1 - \beta_2)\ \mathbf{then}\ \underline{\bullet} + \beta_2 + \alpha_2\ \mathbf{else}$

$\quad \mathbf{if}\ \beta_3 \leq \alpha_1\ \mathbf{then}\ \boxed{\mathbf{if}\ \left\{ \begin{array}{ll} (\underline{\bullet} \leq \beta_1) \wedge \neg(\underline{\bullet} + \beta_2 \leq \alpha_1) & \rightarrow\ \alpha_3 \\ \neg(\underline{\bullet} \leq \beta_1) & \rightarrow\ \beta_3 + \alpha_2 \end{array} \right.}\ \mathbf{else}\ \alpha_3$

$\Rightarrow_{\eta(\mathcal{R}_{mis})}$ {simplify above box to $\beta_3 + \alpha_2$, using P'_{mis}}
$\hat{\lambda}\langle\bullet\rangle.\mathbf{if}\ \underline{\bullet} \leq\ min2(\beta_1, \alpha_1 - \beta_2)\ \mathbf{then}\ \underline{\bullet} + \beta_2 + \alpha_2\ \mathbf{else}$

$\quad \mathbf{if}\ \beta_3 \leq \alpha_1\ \mathbf{then}\ \boxed{\beta_3 + \alpha_2}\ \mathbf{else}\ \alpha_3$

$\Rightarrow_{\eta(\mathcal{R}_{mis})}$ {extract}
$\hat{\lambda}\langle\bullet\rangle.\ \mathbf{if}\ \underline{\bullet} \leq \Omega_1\ \mathbf{then}\ \underline{\bullet} + \Omega_2\ \mathbf{else}\ \Omega_3$
$\quad \mathbf{where}\quad \Omega_1 = min2(\beta_1,\ \alpha_1 - \beta_2)\ ;\ \Omega_2 = \beta_2 + \alpha_2\ ;$
$\qquad\qquad \Omega_3 = \mathbf{if}\ \beta_3 \leq \alpha_1\ \mathbf{then}\ \beta_3 + \alpha_2\ \mathbf{else}\ \alpha_3$

The second last transformation step above is valid because the test $(\underline{\bullet} \leq \beta_1)$ $\wedge\ \neg(\underline{\bullet} + \beta_2 \leq \alpha_1)$ is false under the condition that $\underline{\bullet} >\ min2(\beta_1, \alpha_1 - \beta_2)$, $\beta_3 \leq \alpha_1$, and P'_{mis} are true. In the last step, we obtain $\mathcal{R}_{mis}(\Omega_1, \Omega_2, \Omega_3)$. We state without proof the validity of the invariance property:
$$P_{mis}(\alpha_1, \alpha_2, \alpha_3) \wedge P_{mis}(\beta_1, \beta_2, \beta_3)\ \Rightarrow P_{mis}(\Omega_1, \Omega_2, \Omega_3).$$

The context-preserving transformation process described above is similar to the normalization process in that we aim to simplify the R-context. However, the former process is performed with a specific goal in mind: producing $\mathcal{R}_{mis}$. Goal-directed transformation can be effectively carried out by a technique called *rippling* [BvHSI93], that repeatedly minimises the difference between actual expression and the targeted skeletal R-context, $\mathcal{R}_{mis}$. The detail of this technique will be described in a forthcoming paper.

Step 3 : *Auxiliary Function Synthesis*

Successful context preservation ensures that a parallel equation can be derived from its sequential counterpart. This assurance was proven in [CTH98]. To synthesise the parallel equation for *mis*, we perform a second-order generalisation to obtain the following:

$$mis(xr \mathbin{+\!\!+} xs) = \mathbf{if}\ mis(xs) \leq uH(xr)\ \mathbf{then}\ mis(xs) + uG(xr)\ \mathbf{else}\ uJ(xr)$$

The RHS is essentially similar to R-contexts of *mis*, with the exception of new auxiliary functions (the second-order variables) uH, uG and uJ, to replace each of the earlier context variables, $\{\alpha_i\}_{i \in 1..3}$. Such functions are initially unknown. We apply an inductive derivation procedure to synthesize their definitions. For base case where $xr = [x]$, inductive derivation yields:

$$uH([x]) = 0\ ;\ uG([x]) = x\ ;\ uJ([x]) = x$$

For the inductive case we set $xr = xa \mathbin{+\!\!+} xb$, inductive derivation yields:

$$uH(xa\mathbin{+\!\!+}xb) \;=\; min2(uH(xb),\; uH(xa) \;-\; uG(xb))$$
$$uG(xa\mathbin{+\!\!+}xb) \;=\; uG(xb) \;+\; uG(xa)$$
$$uJ(xa\mathbin{+\!\!+}xb) \;=\; \textbf{if } uJ(xb) \;\le\; uH(xa) \textbf{ then } uJ(xb) + uG(xa) \textbf{ else } uJ(xa)$$

The above result is essentially equivalent to the following substitutions:

$$
\begin{array}{lll}
\alpha_1 = uH(xa) & \alpha_2 = uG(xa) & \alpha_3 = uJ(xa) \\
\beta_1 = uH(xb) & \beta_2 = uG(xb) & \beta_3 = uJ(xb) \\
\Omega_1 = uH(xa\mathbin{+\!\!+}xb) & \Omega_2 = uG(xa\mathbin{+\!\!+}xb) & \Omega_3 = uJ(xa\mathbin{+\!\!+}xb)
\end{array}
$$

The corresponding parallel definitions are:

$$mis([x]) \qquad = x$$
$$mis(xr\mathbin{+\!\!+}xs) \;=\; \textbf{if } mis(xs) \;\le\; uH(xr) \textbf{ then } mis(xs) + uG(xr) \textbf{ else } uJ(xr)$$

$$uH([x]) \qquad = 0$$
$$uH(xr\mathbin{+\!\!+}xs) \;=\; min2(uH(xs),\; uH(xr) - uG(xs))$$

$$uG([x]) \qquad = x$$
$$uG(xr\mathbin{+\!\!+}xs) \;=\; uG(xs) \;+\; uG(xr)$$

$$uJ([x]) \qquad = x$$
$$uJ(xr\mathbin{+\!\!+}xs) \;=\; \textbf{if } uJ(xs) \;\le\; uH(xr) \textbf{ then } uJ(xs) + uG(xr) \textbf{ else } uJ(xr)$$

Some of the functions synthesized may be identical to previously known functions. For example, uJ is identical to mis itself. Such duplicate functions can be detected syntactically and eliminated.

Step 4 : *Tupling*

While the equations derived may be parallel, they may be inefficient due to the presence of redundant function calls. To remove this inefficiency, we perform tupling transformation.

For mis, we remove its redundant calls by introducing the following tupled function which returns multiple results.

$$mistup(xs) \;=\; (mis(xs),\, uH(xs),\, uG(xs))$$

After tupling, we can obtain the following efficient parallel program, whereby duplicate calls are re-used, rather than re-computed. Note how m_b, h_a, g_a, g_b are used multiple times in the second recursive equation.

$$mistup([x]) \qquad = (0,\, x,\, x)$$
$$mistup(xa\mathbin{+\!\!+}xb) \;=$$
$$\quad \textbf{let } \{(m_a, h_a, g_a) = mistup(xa);\, (m_b, h_b, g_b) = mistup(xb)\}$$
$$\quad \textbf{in } (\,(\,\textbf{if } m_b \le h_a \textbf{ then } m_b + g_a \textbf{ else } m_a\,),\, min2(h_b, h_a - g_b),\, g_b + g_a\,)$$

4 Discovering Invariants

In general, it is non-trivial to preserve conditional R-context, particularly if it has multiple R-holes. This is because the number of R-holes may multiply after context replication. Our proposal to curbing such growth is to exploit *invariant* during normalization. This new technique generalises our earlier method for parallelization, and significantly widens its scope of application.

We have shown in Section 3 how an invariant can be used to achieve context presevation. It remains to be seen how an invariant can be discovered. Instead of relying on the user to provide an invariant, we achieve this eureka step by employing constraint-solving techniques to systematically generate and verify the invariant.

Invariant is originated from the need to facilitate normalization process during context preservation. Specifically, constraints may be added to achieve normalization; these constraints constitute the invariant. We have identified two scenarios under which constraints may be needed during normalization, namely: *conditional laws* and *conditional elimination*.

4.1 Conditional Laws

Some laws are conditional in nature. For example, the following four distributive laws for $*$ over $min2$ and $max2$ are conditional upon the sign of input c.

$$c*max2(a, b) = max2(c*a, c*b) \text{ if } c \geq 0$$
$$c*max2(a, b) = min2(c*a, c*b) \text{ if } c \leq 0$$
$$c*min2(a, b) = min2(c*a, c*b) \text{ if } c \geq 0$$
$$c*min2(a, b) = max2(c*a, c*b) \text{ if } c \leq 0$$

Before these laws can be used in normalization process, we require their corresponding conditions to be satisfied. These conditions may become the invariant for our R-context. Of course, we need to verify that they can be satisfied as a pre-condition, and they obey the invariance property. An example of how such conditional laws are applied is illustrated later in Section 5.

4.2 Conditional Elimination

During context preservation process, we may wish to eliminate some conditional branches so as to reduce the number of R-holes. A branch can be eliminatd by identifying constraint that is known *not* to be true at the branch. This constraint may become the invariant for the corresponding R-context.

We would have encountered this situation in Section 3, if we tried to preserve the contextual form of *mis* function, without any knowledge of invariant. We repeat the problematic intermediate step of the transformation here:

$$\hat{\lambda}\langle\bullet\rangle.\text{if } \bullet \leq min2(\beta_1, \alpha_1 - \beta_2) \text{ then } \bullet + \beta_2 + \alpha_2 \text{ else}$$

$$\text{if } \beta_3 \leq \alpha_1 \text{ then } \boxed{\text{if } \begin{cases} (\bullet \leq \beta_1) \wedge \neg(\bullet + \beta_2 \leq \alpha_1) & \to \alpha_3 \\ \neg(\bullet \leq \beta_1) & \to \beta_3 + \alpha_2 \end{cases}} \text{ else } \alpha_3$$

At this step, there are five occurrences of $\bullet$, instead of two in the original R-context. The three extraneous occurrences of $\bullet$ can be found in the *boxed* branch of the conditional shown in the last step of normalization.

A way to eliminate these redundant occurrences of the R-hole is to eliminate one of these two branches (and thus make the test in the remaining branch unnecessary). We therefore look for an invariant that enables such elimination. A technique we have devised is to gather the conditions associated with the two branches and attempt to find a constraint (exclusively in terms of either $\{\alpha_1, \alpha_2, \alpha_3\}$ or $\{\beta_1, \beta_2, \beta_3\}$) that holds for either branch. If found, the corresponding branch may be eliminated by using the *negated constraint as invariant*. This constraint-searching technique is formulated as $Ctx \vdash_B c$ where Ctx denotes the condition associated with a branch, and c represents the desired constraint expressed exclusively in terms of variables from B.

In the first branch, we obtain $\neg(\beta_3 < \beta_1 + \beta_2)$ as a candidate for invariant:

$$\neg(\bullet \leq min2(\beta_1, \alpha_1 - \beta_2)) \wedge \beta_3 \leq \alpha_1 \wedge (\bullet \leq \beta_1) \wedge \neg(\bullet + \beta_2 \leq \alpha_1) \atop \vdash_{\{\beta_1, \beta_2, \beta_3\}} \beta_3 < \beta_1 + \beta_2 \tag{1}$$

In the second branch, we find no candidate:

$$\neg(\bullet \leq min2(\beta_1, \alpha_1 - \beta_2)) \wedge \beta_3 \leq \alpha_1 \wedge \neg(\bullet \leq \beta_1) \atop \vdash_{\{\beta_1, \beta_2, \beta_3\}} \text{ no constraint found} \tag{2}$$

If $\neg(\beta_3 < \beta_1 + \beta_2)$ is the invariant (and indeed it is), then the context-preservation process can proceed, yielding the desired R-context form. Invariant validation, as well as the discovery of invariant, is the job of constraint solver.

4.3   Constraint Solving via CHR

A convenient tool for solving constraints is the *Constraint Handling Rules* (CHR) developed by Frühwirth [Frü98]. Using CHR, we can build tiny but specialised constraint-solvers for operators that handle variable arguments. Currently, we run CHR on top of a Prolog system (named ECL^iPS^e Prolog).

In this section, we demonstrate the use of CHR to help discover and verify the invariant found in Section 4.2. The CHR rules defined for this problem are given Appendix A. To discover the invariant for *mis* through conditional elimination, we supply the context of rule (1) (*ie.*, the premises) as a prolog program to ECL^iPS^e Prolog (Here, Ai and Bi represent α_i and β_i respectively; H denotes $\bullet$. The predicates used are self-explanatory):

```
br1(A1,A2,A3,B1,B2,B3,H) :- minus(A1,B2,T), min2(B1,T,U), gt(H,U),
        le(B3,A1), le(H,B1), add(H,B2,S), gt(S,A1).
```

We then ask Prolog to show us those constraints that are consistent with the context. Following is the session (shortened for presentation sake) we have with Prolog. Note that constraints (19), (21), and (41) jointly infer that $\beta_3 < \beta_1 + \beta_2$:

```
[eclipse 6]: br1(A1,A2,A3,B1,B2,B3,H).
Constraints:
(19) le(H_892, B1_754)
(21) add(H_892, B2_296, _1397)
(41) lt(B3_986, _1397)
yes.
[eclipse 7]:
```

To verify that $\neg(\beta_3 < \beta_1 + \beta_2)$ is an invariant, we first verify its pre-condition. Referring to the initial R-context of *mis*, we use CHR to verify the following proposition:

$$(\alpha_1 = 0) \wedge (\alpha_2 = x) \wedge (\alpha_3 = x) \vdash (\alpha_3 \geq \alpha_1 + \alpha_2). \tag{3}$$

To verify the invariance condition, we feed CHR with the following formula:

$$(\alpha_3 \geq \alpha_1 + \alpha_2) \wedge (\beta_3 \geq \beta_1 + \beta_2) \vdash (\Omega_3 \geq \Omega_1 + \Omega_2) \tag{4}$$

Algorithmically, we prove the validity of both formulae (3) and (4) by a standard technique called *refutation*. That is, we attempt to find a condition under which the negation of a formula is true. Failing to do so, we conclude that the formula is true. Following is the Prolog program for verifying formula (4):

```
premise(V1,V2,V3) :- add(V1,V2,R), le(R,V3).    % generic premise
omega1(A1,B1,B2,R) :- minus(A1,B2,T), min2(B1,T,R).
omega2(A2,B2,R) :- add(A2,B2,R).
omega3(A1,A2,A3,B3,R) :- le(B3,A1), add(A2,B3,R).
omega3(A1,A2,A3,B3,R) :- gt(B3,A1), R=A3.
neg_inv(A1,A2,A3,B1,B2,B3,R1,R2,R3) :-           % Negated formula
  premise(A1,A2,A3),premise(B1,B2,B3),omega1(A1,B1,B2,R1),
  omega2(A2,B2,R2),omega3(A1,A2,A3,B3,R3),add(R1,R2,RR),gt(RR,R3).
```

Following is extracted from a session with ECL^{i}PS^e Prolog:

```
[eclipse 7]: neg_inv(A1,A2,A3,B1,B2,B3,R1,R2,R3).
no (more) solution.
[eclipse 8]:
```

5 MSP : A Bigger Example

Our parallelization method is not just a nice theoretical result. It is also practically useful for parallelizing more complex programs. In particular, we could systematically handle recursive functions with conditional and tupled constructs that are often much harder to parallelize. Let us examine a little known problem, called *maximum segment product* [Ben86], whose parallelization requires deep human insights otherwise.

Given an input list $[x_1, \ldots, x_n]$, we are interested to find the maximum product of all non-empty (contiguous) segments, of the form $[x_i, x_{i+1}, \ldots, x_j]$ where $1 \leq i \leq j \leq n$. A high-level specification of msp is the following generate-and-test algorithm.

$$msp(xs) \;=\; max(map(prod, segs(xs)))$$

Here, $segs(xs)$ returns all segments for an input list xs, while $map(prod, segs(xs))$ applies $prod$ to each sublist from $segs(xs)$, before max chooses the largest value. While clear, this specification is grossly inefficient. However, it can be transformed by fusion [Chi92a,TM95,HIT96] to a sequential algorithm. The transformed msp, together with two auxiliary functions, mip, and $mipm$, were given in Figure 1.

Functions mip and $mipm$ are mutually recursive and not in LSR-form. Nevertheless, we could use the automated tupling method of [Chi93,HITT97] to obtain a tupled definition of $miptup$, as elaborated earlier in Section 2.

We focus on the parallelization of $miptup$ as it must be parallelized before its parent msp function. We could proceed to extract its initial R-context[5] (shown below) to check if it could be parallelized.

$$\hat{\lambda}\,\langle \bullet \rangle.\, \mathbf{let}\ (u, v)\ =\ \underline{\bullet}\ \mathbf{in}\ \mathbf{if}\ \alpha_1 > 0\ \mathbf{then}\ (max2(\alpha_2, \alpha_3 * u),\ min2(\alpha_4, \alpha_5 * v))$$
$$\mathbf{else}\ (max2(\alpha_6, \alpha_7 * v),\ min2(\alpha_8, \alpha_9 * u))$$
$$\mathbf{where}\ \alpha_1 = x\ ;\ \alpha_2 = x\ ;\ \alpha_3 = x\ ;\ \alpha_4 = x\ ;\ \alpha_5 = x\ ;$$
$$\alpha_6 = x\ ;\ \alpha_7 = x\ ;\ \alpha_8 = x\ ;\ \alpha_9 = x$$

Note the use of local variables u, v as proxies for the R-hole. The depth and occurrences of these proxies should thus be minimised, where possible, during normalization. Application of context preservation can proceed as follows.

$$(\ \hat{\lambda}\,\langle \bullet \rangle.\, \mathbf{let}\ (u, v)\ =\ \underline{\bullet}\ \mathbf{in}\ \mathbf{if}\ \alpha_1 > 0\ \mathbf{then}\ (max2(\alpha_2, \alpha_3 * u), min2(\alpha_4, \alpha_5 * v))$$
$$\mathbf{else}\ (max2(\alpha_6, \alpha_7 * v), min2(\alpha_8, \alpha_9 * u)))$$
$$\circ\ (\ \hat{\lambda}\,\langle \bullet \rangle.\, \mathbf{let}\ (u, v)\ =\ \underline{\bullet}\ \mathbf{in}\ \mathbf{if}\ \beta_1 > 0\ \mathbf{then}\ (max2(\beta_2, \beta_3 * u), min2(\beta_4, \beta_5 * v))$$
$$\mathbf{else}\ (max2(\beta_6, \beta_7 * v), min2(\beta_8, \beta_9 * u)))$$

$\Rightarrow_\eta$ {tupled & conditional normalization}

$$\hat{\lambda}\,\langle \bullet \rangle.\mathbf{let}\ (u, v) = \underline{\bullet}\ \mathbf{in}$$

$$\mathbf{if}\ \begin{cases} (\beta_1 > 0) \wedge (\alpha_1 > 0) \\ \quad \rightarrow (\ max2(\alpha_2, \alpha_3 * max2(\beta_2, \beta_3 * u))\ ,\ min2(\alpha_4, \alpha_5 * min2(\beta_4, \beta_5 * v))\ ) \\ (\beta_1 > 0) \wedge \neg(\alpha_1 > 0) \\ \quad \rightarrow (max2(\alpha_6, \alpha_7 * min2(\beta_4, \beta_5 * v))\ ,\ min2(\alpha_8, \alpha_9 * max2(\beta_2, \beta_3 * u))\ ) \\ \neg(\beta_1 > 0) \wedge (\alpha_1 > 0) \\ \quad \rightarrow (max2(\alpha_2, \alpha_3 * max2(\beta_6, \beta_7 * v))\ ,\ min2(\alpha_4, \alpha_5 * min2(\beta_8, \beta_9 * u))\ ) \\ \neg(\beta_1 > 0) \wedge \neg(\alpha_1 > 0) \\ \quad \rightarrow (max2(\alpha_6, \alpha_7 * min2(\beta_8, \beta_9 * u))\ ,\ min2(\alpha_8, \alpha_9 * max2(\beta_6, \beta_7 * v))\ ) \end{cases}$$

---

[5] Note that the skeletal R-context always have its variables uniquely re-named to help support reusability and the context preservation property.

To normalize further, we need to distribute $*$ into $max2$ and $min2$. This could only be done with the set of distributive laws provided in Section 4.1.

Each of these laws has a *condition* attached to it. If this condition is not present in the R-context, we must add them as required constraint before the corresponding distributive law can be applied (Sec 4.1). Doing so results in the following successful context preservation.

$\Rightarrow_\eta$ {add selected constraints & normalize further}

$\hat{\lambda}\langle\bullet\rangle.\textbf{let } (u, v) = \bullet \textbf{ in}$

$\textbf{if} \begin{cases} (\beta_1 > 0) \wedge (\alpha_1 > 0) \\ \quad \rightarrow \begin{pmatrix} max2(max2(\alpha_2, \alpha_3*\beta_2), (\alpha_3*\beta_3)*u)), \\ min2(min2(\alpha_4, \alpha_5*\beta_4), (\alpha_5*\beta_5)*v) \end{pmatrix} \\ (\beta_1 > 0) \wedge \neg(\alpha_1 > 0) \\ \quad \rightarrow \begin{pmatrix} max2(max2(\alpha_6, \alpha_7*\beta_4), (\alpha_7*\beta_5)*v)), \\ min2(min2(\alpha_8, \alpha_9*\beta_2), (\alpha_9*\beta_3)*u) \end{pmatrix} \\ \neg(\beta_1 > 0) \wedge (\alpha_1 > 0) \\ \quad \rightarrow \begin{pmatrix} max2(max2(\alpha_2, \alpha_3*\beta_6), (\alpha_3*\beta_7)*v)), \\ min2(min2(\alpha_4, \alpha_5*\beta_8), (\alpha_5*\beta_9)*u) \end{pmatrix} \\ \neg(\beta_1 > 0) \wedge \neg(\alpha_1 > 0) \\ \quad \rightarrow \begin{pmatrix} max2(max2(\alpha_6, \alpha_7*\beta_8), (\alpha_7*\beta_9)*u)), \\ min2(min2(\alpha_8, \alpha_9*\beta_6), (\alpha_9*\beta_7)*v) \end{pmatrix} \end{cases}$

$\textbf{st } \{\alpha_3 \geq 0; \ \alpha_5 \geq 0; \ \alpha_7 \leq 0; \ \alpha_9 \leq 0 \}$

$\Rightarrow_\eta$ {re−group branches & form skeletal R−ctx }

$\hat{\lambda}\langle\bullet\rangle.\textbf{let } (u, v) = \bullet \textbf{ in if } \Omega_1 > 0 \textbf{ then } (max2(\Omega_2, \Omega_3*u), \ min2(\Omega_4, \Omega_5*v))$
$\qquad\qquad\qquad \textbf{else } (max2(\Omega_6, \Omega_7*v), \ min2(\Omega_8, \Omega_9*u))$

$\textbf{where } \Omega_1 = \alpha_1*\beta_1$
$\qquad\quad \Omega_2 = \textbf{if } \alpha_1 > 0 \textbf{ then } max2(\alpha_2, \alpha_3*\beta_2) \textbf{ else } max2(\alpha_6, \alpha_7*\beta_8)$
$\qquad\quad \Omega_3 = \textbf{if } \alpha_1 > 0 \textbf{ then } \alpha_3*\beta_3 \textbf{ else } \alpha_7*\beta_9$
$\qquad\quad \Omega_4 = \textbf{if } \alpha_1 > 0 \textbf{ then } min2(\alpha_4, \alpha_5*\beta_4) \textbf{ else } min2(\alpha_8, \alpha_9*\beta_6)$
$\qquad\quad \Omega_5 = \textbf{if } \alpha_1 > 0 \textbf{ then } \alpha_5*\beta_5 \textbf{ else } \alpha_9*\beta_7$
$\qquad\quad \Omega_6 = \textbf{if } \alpha_1 > 0 \textbf{ then } max2(\alpha_2, \alpha_3*\beta_6) \textbf{ else } max2(\alpha_6, \alpha_7*\beta_4)$

$\qquad\quad \Omega_7 = \textbf{if } \alpha_1 > 0 \textbf{ then } \alpha_3*\beta_7 \textbf{ else } \alpha_7*\beta_5$
$\qquad\quad \Omega_8 = \textbf{if } \alpha_1 > 0 \textbf{ then } min2(\alpha_4, \alpha_5*\beta_8) \textbf{ else } min2(\alpha_8, \alpha_9*\beta_2)$
$\qquad\quad \Omega_9 = \textbf{if } \alpha_1 > 0 \textbf{ then } \alpha_5*\beta_9 \textbf{ else } \alpha_9*\beta_3$

We can now form an invariant from the constraints collected during transformation. To do so, we take into consideration the conditional context in which these constraints are used. We thus derive at the formula $(\alpha_1 > 0 \Rightarrow \alpha_3 \geq 0 \wedge \alpha_5 \geq 0) \wedge (\alpha_1 \leq 0 \Rightarrow \alpha_7 \leq 0 \wedge \alpha_9 \leq 0)$. We verify that this is indeed an invariant by proving its pre-condition and invariance condition. We omit the detail constraint solving in this paper.

Next, we synthesize the auxiliary functions needed for defining the parallel version of *miptup*. After eliminating duplicated functions, we obtain:

$$miptup([x]) \quad = (x, x)$$
$$miptup(xr \mathbin{+\!\!+} xs) =$$
$$\quad \textbf{let } (u, v) = miptup(xs)$$
$$\quad \textbf{in if } uH1(xr) > 0 \textbf{ then}$$
$$\qquad (max2(uH2(xr), uH1(xr)*u), min2(uH4(xr), uH1(xr)*v))$$
$$\qquad \textbf{else } (max2(uH2(xr), uH1(xr)*v), min2(uH4(xr), uH1(xr)*u))$$

$$uH1([x]) \quad = x$$
$$uH1(xr \mathbin{+\!\!+} xs) = uH1(xr)*uH1(xs)$$

$$uH2([x]) \quad = x$$
$$uH2(xr \mathbin{+\!\!+} xs) = \textbf{if } uH1(xr) > 0 \textbf{ then } max2(uH2(xr), uH1(xr)*uH2(xs))$$
$$\qquad\qquad\qquad \textbf{else } max2(uH2(xr), uH1(xr)*uH4(xs))$$

$$uH4([x]) \quad = x$$
$$uH4(xr \mathbin{+\!\!+} xs) = \textbf{if } uH1(xr) > 0 \textbf{ then } min2(uH4(xr), uH1(xr)*uH4(xs))$$
$$\qquad\qquad\qquad \textbf{else } min2(uH4(xr), uH1(xr)*uH2(xs))$$

Finally, by tupling the definitions of $uH2$ and $uH4$ together, we obtain a tupled function that is identical to the components of $miptup$. Consequently, we can derive a very compact parallel algorithm shown below.

$$miptup([x]) \quad = (x, x)$$
$$miptup(xr \mathbin{+\!\!+} xs) =$$
$$\quad \textbf{let } (a, b) = miptup(xr); (u, v) = miptup(xs)$$
$$\quad \textbf{in if } uH1(xr) > 0 \textbf{ then } (max2(a, uH1(xr)*u), min2(b, uH1(xr)*v))$$
$$\qquad \textbf{else } (max2(a, uH1(xr)*v), min2(b, uH1(xr)*u))$$

$$uH1([x]) \quad = x$$
$$uH1(xr \mathbin{+\!\!+} xs) = uH1(xr)*uH1(xs)$$

With these equations, we can proceed to parallelize the parent function $msptup$ using context preservation and normalization. Its parallel equations are:

$$msp(xr \mathbin{+\!\!+} xs) = \textbf{let } (a, b) = miptup(xr); (u, v) = miptup(xs)$$
$$\qquad\qquad \textbf{in } max2(max2(max2(msp(xr), msp(xs)),$$
$$\qquad\qquad\qquad\qquad max2(mfp(xr) + a, mfp(xr) + b)),$$
$$\qquad\qquad\qquad max2(mfpm(xr) + a, mfpm(xr) + b))$$

$$mfp([x]) \quad = x$$
$$mfp(xr \mathbin{+\!\!+} xs) = \textbf{if } uH1(xs) > 0 \textbf{ then } max2(mfp(xr)*uH1(xs), mfp(xs))$$
$$\qquad\qquad\qquad \textbf{else } max2(mfpm(xr)*uH1(xs), mfp(xs))$$

$$mfpm([x]) \quad = x$$
$$mfpm(xr \mathbin{+\!\!+} xs) = \textbf{if } uH1(xr) > 0 \textbf{ then } min2(mfpm(xr)*uH1(xs), mfpm(xs))$$
$$\qquad\qquad\qquad \textbf{else } min2(mfp(xr)*uH1(xs), mfpm(xs))$$

Tupling can again be applied to obtain a work-efficient parallel program.

6   Related Works

Generic program schemes have been advocated for use in structured parallel programming, both for imperative programs expressed as first-order recurrences through a classic result of [Sto75] and for functional programs via Bird's homomorphism [Ski90]. Unfortunately, most sequential specifications fail to match up *directly* with these schemes. To overcome this shortcoming, there have been calls to constructively transform programs to match these schemes, but these proposals [Roe91,GDH96] often require deep intuition and the support of ad-hoc lemmas – making automation difficult. Another approach is to provide more specialised schemes, either statically [PP91] or via a procedure [HTC98], that can be directly matched to sequential specification. Though cheap to operate, the generality of this approach is often called into question.

On the imperative language (e.g. Fortran) front, there have been interests in parallelization of reduction-style loops. A work similar to ours was independently conceived by Fischer & Ghoulum [FG94,GF95]. By modelling loops via functions, they noted that function-type values could be reduced (in parallel) via associative function composition. However, the propagated function-type values could only be efficiently combined if they have a template closed under composition. This requirement is similar to the need to find a common R-context under recursive call unfolding, which we discovered earlier in [Chi92b]. Being based on loops, their framework is less general and less formal. No specific techniques, other than simplification, have been offered for checking if closed template is possible. Also, without invariant handling, their approach is presently limited.

The power of constraints have not escaped the attention of traditional work on finding parallelism in array-based programs. Through the use of constraints, Pugh showed how *exact dependence analysis* can be formulated to support better vectorisation[Pug92]. Our work is complimentary to Pugh's in two respects. Firstly, we may take advantage of practical advances in his constraint technology. Secondly, we tackle a different class of reduction-style sequential algorithms, with inherent dependences across recursion. Thus, instead of checking for the absence of dependence, we transform the sequential dependences into divide-and-conquer counterparts with the help of properties, such as associativity and distributivity. We originally planned to use the Omega calculator for our constraint solving. However, some of our problems (e.g. *msp*) require constraints that fall outside the linear arithmetic class accepted by Pugh's system. This forces us to turn to CHR to build our own specialised constraint solvers.

7   Conclusion

We have presented a systematic methodology for parallelizing sequential programs. The method relies on the successful preservation of replicated R-contexts for the recursive call and each accumulative argument. The notion of context preservation is central to our parallelization method. A key innovation in this paper is the introduction of *invariants* to obtain context preservation. To support this, some constraint-solving techniques have been proposed. Finally, we demonstrated the power of our methodology by applying it to parallelize a non-trivial problem: maximum segment product.

We are currently working on an implementation system to apply context preservation and invariant verification semi-automatically. Apart from the heuristic of minimising both the depths and number of occurrences of R-holes, we have also employed the *rippling* technique [BvHSI93], which has been very popular in automated theorem-proving. It may also be possible for our method to recover from failures when a given R-context could not be preserved. In particular, the resulting context may suggest either a *new* or a *generalized* R-context that could be attempted. This much enhanced potential for parallelization is made possible by our adoption of appropriate strategies and techniques (including constraint handling) for guiding their applications.

Acknowledgment

The authors would like to thank the anonymous referees for their comments. This work was supported by the research grant RP3982693.

References

BCH+93. G.E. Blelloch, S Chatterjee, J.C. Hardwick, J. Sipelstein, and M. Zagha. Implementation of a portable nested data-parallel language. In *4th Principles and Practice of Parallel Programming*, pages 102–111, San Diego, California (ACM Press), May 1993. 75

Ben86.   Jon Bentley. *Programming Pearls*. Addison-Wesley, 1986. 87

Ble90.   Guy E. Blelloch. *Vector Models for Data Parallel Computing*. MIT Press, Cambridge, MA, 1990. 75

BvHSI93. A. Bundy, F. van Harmelen, A. Smaill, and A. Ireland. Rippling: A heuristic for guiding inductive proofs. *Artificial Intelligence*, 62:185–253, 1993. 83, 92

CDG96.   W.N. Chin, J Darlington, and Y. Guo. Parallelizing conditional recurrences. In *2nd Annual EuroPar Conference*, Lyon, France, (LNCS 1123) Berlin Heidelberg New York: Springer, August 1996. 79

Chi92a.   Wei-Ngan Chin. Safe fusion of functional expressions. In *7th ACM LISP and Functional Programming Conference*, pages 11–20, San Francisco, California, June 1992. ACM Press. 88

Chi92b.   Wei-Ngan Chin. Synthesizing parallel lemma. In *Proc of a JSPS Seminar on Parallel Programming Systems, World Scientific Publishing*, pages 201–217, Tokyo, Japan, May 1992. 91

Chi93.   Wei-Ngan Chin. Towards an automated tupling strategy. In *ACM SIGPLAN Symposium on Partial Evaluation and Semantics-Based Program Manipulation*, pages 119–132, Copenhagen, Denmark, June 1993. ACM Press. 79, 88

CTH98.   W.N. Chin, A. Takano, and Z. Hu. Parallelization via context preservation. In *IEEE Intl Conference on Computer Languages*, Chicago, U.S.A., May 1998. IEEE CS Press. 75, 77, 80, 83

FG94.   A.L. Fischer and A.M. Ghuloum. Parallelizing complex scans and reductions. In *ACM SIGPLAN Conference on Programming Language Design and Implementation*, pages 135–136, Orlando, Florida, ACM Press, 1994. 91

Frü98.   Thom Frühwirth. Theory and practice of constraint handling rules. *Journal of Logic Programming*, 37((1–3)):95–138, Oct 1998. 86

GDH96.   Z.N. Grant-Duff and P. Harrison. Parallelism via homomorphism. *Parallel Processing Letters*, 6(2):279–295, 1996. 91

GF95.   A.M. Ghuloum and A.L. Fischer. Flattening and parallelizing irregular applications, recurrent loop nests. In *3rd ACM Principles and Practice of Parallel Programming*, pages 58–67, Santa Barbara, California, ACM Press, 1995. 91

HIT96.   Z. Hu, H. Iwasaki, and M. Takeichi. Deriving structural hylomorphisms from recursive definitions. In *ACM SIGPLAN International Conference on Functional Programming*, pages 73–82, Philadelphia, Pennsylvannia, May 1996. ACM Press. 88

HITT97.   Z. Hu, H. Iwasaki, M. Takeichi, and A. Takano. Tupling calculation eliminates multiple traversals. In *2nd ACM SIGPLAN International Conference on Functional Programming*, pages 164–175, Amsterdam, Netherlands, June 1997. ACM Press. 79, 88

HTC98.   Z. Hu, M. Takeichi, and W.N. Chin. Parallelization in calculational forms. In *25th Annual ACM Symposium on Principles of Programming Languages*, pages 316–328, San Diego, California, January 1998. ACM Press. 91

PP91.   SS. Pinter and RY. Pinter. Program optimization and parallelization using idioms. In *ACM Principles of Programming Languages*, pages 79–92, Orlando, Florida, ACM Press, 1991. 91

Pug92.   William Pugh. The omega test: A fast practical integer programming algorithm for dependence analysis. *Communications of ACM*, 8:102–114, 1992. 91

Roe91.   Paul Roe. *Parallel Programming using Functional Languages (Report CSC 91/R3)*. PhD thesis, University of Glasgow, 1991. 91

Ski90.   D. Skillicorn. Architecture-independent parallel computation. *IEEE Computer*, 23(12):38–50, December 1990. 91

Sto75.   Harold S. Stone. Parallel tridiagonal equation solvers. *ACM Transactions on Mathematical Software*, 1(4):287–307, 1975. 91

TM95.   A. Takano and E. Meijer. Shortcut deforestation in calculational form. In *ACM Conference on Functional Programming and Computer Architecture*, pages 306–313, San Diego, California, June 1995. ACM Press. 88

A   A Tiny Constraint Solver in CHR

In CHR, we define both *simplification* and *propagation* rules for constraints over variables. Simplification rules are used by CHR to replace existing constraints with simpler, logically equivalent, constraints, whereas propagation rules add new constraints which are logically redundant but may cause further simplification. The CHR rules used in the case of *mis* is defined below:

```
%% Rules for Negation.
ne(A,B) <=> A=B | fail.          % "<=>" is a simplification rule
```

```
ne(A,B) ==> ne(B,A).              % "==>" is a propagation rule
%% Rules for inequalities.
le(A,B) <=> A=B | true.           % reflexive
le(A,B),le(B,A) <=> A = B.        % antisymmetry
le(A,B),le(B,C) ==> le(A,C).      % transitive

lt(A,B) <=> A=B | fail.           % non-reflexive
lt(A,B),le(B,A) <=> fail.         % asymmetry
le(A,B),lt(B,A) <=> fail.         % asymmetry
lt(A,B),lt(B,A) <=> fail.         % asymmetry
lt(A,B),le(B,C) ==> lt(A,C).      % transitive
le(A,B),lt(B,C) ==> lt(A,C).      % transitive
lt(A,B),lt(B,C) ==> lt(A,C).      % transitive
le(A,B), ne(A,B) <=> lt(A,B).
ge(A,B) <=> le(B,A).
gt(A,B) <=> lt(B,A).
%% Rules for addition.
add(X,Y,Z) <=> Y=0 | X=Z.         % zero
add(X,Y,Z) <=> X=Z | Y=0.         % zero
add(X,Y,Z) ==> add(Y,X,Z).            % commutative
add(X,Y,Z), add(Z,U,W) ==> add(Y,U,R),add(X,R,W).   % associative
add(X1,Y,Z1), add(X2,Y,Z2) ==> le(Z1,Z2) | le(X1,X2). %
add(X1,Y,Z1), add(X2,Y,Z2) ==> lt(X1,X2) | lt(Z1,Z2). %
add(X1,Y,Z1), add(X2,Y,Z2) ==> lt(Z1,Z2) | lt(X1,X2). %
add(X1,Y,Z1), add(X2,Y,Z2) ==> gt(X1,X2) | gt(Z1,Z2). %
add(X1,Y,Z1), add(X2,Y,Z2) ==> gt(Z1,Z2) | gt(X1,X2). %
%% Rules for subtraction
minus(X,Y,Z) <=> add(Y,Z,X).      % normalise
%% Rules for minimum operation.
min2(A,B,C) <=> gt(A,B) | C = B.
min2(A,B,C) <=> le(A,B) | A = C.
min2(A,B,C) ==> min2(B,A,C).          % commutative
min2(A,B,C),min2(C,D,E) ==> min2(B,D,F),min2(A,F,E). % associative
%% Rules for maximum operation.
max2(A,B,B) <=> min2(A,B,A).
```

Safety of Strictness Analysis via Term Graph Rewriting

David Clark[1], Chris Hankin[1], and Sebastian Hunt[2]

[1] Department of Computing, Imperial College, London SW7 2BZ
{djc,clh}@doc.ic.ac.uk
[2] Department of Computing, City University, London EC1V 0HB
seb@soi.city.ac.uk

Abstract. A safe abstraction is presented for a restricted form of term graph rewriting. This abstraction can be seen as a formalisation of the rewrite system employed by the strictness analyser in the Concurrent Clean compiler. Programs written in a core functional language are interpreted as graph rewriting systems using a form of equational term graph rewriting due to Ariola and Arvind. Abstract graphs are defined by extending the signature of ordinary graphs and it is shown how to extend a rewriting system on ordinary graphs to one on abstract graphs. An abstraction relation between abstract graphs is used to define a notion of safety with respect to a variant of Ariola and Arvind's direct approximation semantics, and this notion of safety is shown to be adequate for strictness analysis. Abstract reduction is defined as the union of the extended rewrite system with additional 'heuristic' reductions and shown to be safe.

1 Introduction

In this paper we present a safe abstraction for a restricted form of term graph rewriting system and show how it can form the basis of a strictness analyser for an untyped core functional language. This work grows out of work by Eric Nöcker on the strictness analyser used in the Clean compiler [16, 17] and subsequent attempts to provide a satisfactory formal account of the method.

1.1 Background

Nöcker's 1988 paper on the strictness analyser used in the Clean compiler [16, 17] did not give a formal account of the algorithm. Claims made for the algorithm included the ability to find higher order strictness information, a high speed of execution of the algorithm and a high speed of execution of the resulting code. (Apart from some material in Nöcker's thesis [18] little has been published to back up these claims.) As a method of strictness analysis it seems formidable in practice but the lack of a formalisation meant that it was not possible to prove that the algorithm was correct. Surprisingly, this has remained the situation until the time of writing.

J. Palsberg (Ed.): SAS 2000, LNCS 1824, pp. 95–114, 2000.
© Springer-Verlag Berlin Heidelberg 2000

The algorithm can be seen as having two parts: a method of rewriting so-called abstract graphs together with a collection of heuristics which are used to safely force termination of rewrite sequences. In this paper we provide the first complete account of the first part of the algorithm and account for some, but not all, of the heuristics.

The Clean strictness analyser works by manipulating abstract graphs, which are just graphs over an extended signature. The additional symbols in the extended signature are used to allow a single abstract graph to represent a set of ordinary graphs. In this, Nöcker's work is clearly inspired by abstract interpretation [10, 1, 15]. The intuitions behind the symbols used to construct abstract graphs are as follows: $\perp$ represents Ω, the undefined graph; $\top$ represents all graphs; union symbols (rendered as $\oplus$ below) are used to represent a point of non-deterministic choice within an abstract graph. (In the formalisation of the current paper, $\perp$ is indistinguishable from Ω and so the only additional symbols used are $\top$ and $\oplus$.)

1.2   Related Work

There are a number of earlier papers which attempt to formalise the algorithm. We briefly review these.

The first and (hitherto) most complete formal account of the strictness analyser, is found in a pair of papers by Goubault et al [12, 22], which show how to place the algorithm into an abstract interpretation framework. The first of these papers [12] uses the syntax of abstract graphs to define a class of the lattices required by abstract interpretation: each abstract graph is unravelled to a set of regular trees and a standard ordering on trees is used to induce an ordering on abstract graphs. There are two drawbacks with this approach. Firstly, sharing information is lost. Secondly, to have a lattice based on regular trees, graphs containing cycles via $\oplus$ have to be disallowed and precisely such graphs are used in a key way in the Clean strictness analyser to represent lists. The second paper [22] shows the rewriting of abstract graphs and the heuristics to be safe for this restricted class of abstract graphs.

Nöcker, a co-author of [22], made another attempt to formalise the algorithm in a paper [18] which gives a formal framework for abstract reduction for term rewriting. The paper speculates on extending the formalisation to term graphs via infinitary term rewriting but falls short of completing the extension. Hankin and Clark [8] attempted to improve upon the the ordering in [12] but their ordering also excludes cycles via $\oplus$.

The approach taken by Schütz et al [20] is, in effect, to do away with union symbols altogether and develop a theory based on non-deterministic rewriting. (The paper does contain a brief informal description of how unions are used to obtain an efficient implementation. No attempt is made to formalise this use of unions or prove it correct.) The result is interesting but it uses term rewriting rather than graph rewriting and so does not apply directly to the Clean strictness analyser. However this work inspired a related approach to term graph rewriting by Clark [9] which sketched a proof for the correctness of abstract reduction.

Although our formalisation is *not* presented as an abstract interpretation, there are striking similarities (see Sect. 7). Despite these similarities, it is not yet clear whether our approach can be alternatively formalised as an abstract interpretation.

One distinctive feature of our work (and Nöcker's original work) is that while ⊕ seems to play the role taken by ⊔ in abstract interpretation, it is treated in a purely syntactic manner, not as the join operation in a lattice. In this, our work is reminiscent of Chuang and Goldberg's syntactic approach to fixed point computation [7]. More generally, the use of direct syntactic/operational approaches in reasoning about program behaviour has proved very successful in recent years (see [11] for some good examples). An example which is close in spirit to the style of reasoning employed in the current paper is the use of the notion of subject-reduction in the work of Wright and Felleisen [25].

1.3   Our Contribution

In the current paper we avoid the limitations of earlier approaches by working directly with graphs, defining an abstraction relation between abstract graphs, and defining a weak notion of homomorphism which allows us to compare abstract graphs directly without unravelling. Our definitions do not give us a lattice of abstract graphs. Nonetheless, as we show, using these definitions it is possible to state and prove safety in a direct operational manner.

We believe that our formalisation is complete with respect to the clean strictness analyser, in the following sense: all those abstract graphs which are used in the analyser are allowed by our framework and we conjecture that no alternative to our notion of safety will allow more strictness properties to be inferred from the results of abstract reduction. However, our work does not constitute a complete proof of correctness for the analyser since it does not address the 'loop detection' heuristics which are used to force termination (see Sect. 6 and Sect. 7).

1.4   Outline

In Sect. 2 we define a functional language and interpret its programs as term graph rewriting systems of a restricted form (which we call simple functional GRSs). In Sect. 3 we define abstract graphs and an abstraction relation between ordinary and abstract graphs, and show how a simple functional GRS on ordinary graphs can be extended to one on abstract graphs. In Sect. 4 we define a variant of a direct approximation style semantics for our restricted class of rewriting systems. In Sect. 5 we state our notion of safety using this semantics and show it to be adequate for strictness analysis. In Sect. 6 we define abstract reduction and show how to prove it safe by establishing that it commutes with the extended simple functional GRS introduced in Sect. 3. Finally, in Sect. 7 we summarise and suggest directions for future work. Proofs of key results are sketched in an appendix.

2 Graph Rewriting Systems

Following Barendsen and Smetsers [6], we describe a core functional language and show how its programs can be interpreted as term graph rewriting systems.

Let x, y, z range over a set Var of variables. A set $\mathcal{F}$ of function symbols and a set $\mathcal{C}$ of constructor symbols, determines a signature $\mathcal{S} = \mathcal{F} \cup \mathcal{C}$. All symbols in $\mathcal{S}$ are assumed to have a fixed arity: let $\mathcal{S}^k$ ($\mathcal{F}^k$, $\mathcal{C}^k$) denote the subset of symbols in $\mathcal{S}$ ($\mathcal{F}$, $\mathcal{C}$) having arity $k \geq 0$ and let S^k (F^k, C^k) range over $\mathcal{S}^k$ ($\mathcal{F}^k$, $\mathcal{C}^k$).

The syntax of a core functional language of supercombinators is as follows.

$$T ::= x \mid S^k(T_1, \dots, T_k) \mid \mathsf{let}\ x_1 = T_1, \dots, x_n = T_n\ \mathsf{in}\ T \mid$$
$$\mathsf{case}\ T\ \mathsf{of}\ P_1 \to E_1; \dots; P_k \to E_k$$
$$P ::= C^k(x_1, \dots, x_k)$$

In $\mathsf{let}\ x_1 = T_1, \dots, x_n = T_n\ \mathsf{in}\ T$, each x_i is bound in all T_i as well as in T (so this let is really a letrec). Function definitions are equations (one per function symbol F) of the form $F(\boldsymbol{x}) = T$.

Higher order functions are modelled in a standard way [13] by allowing partial applications of functions to less than their complete complement of arguments. This is done by requiring $\mathcal{F}$ to contain a binary application symbol @ and, for each $k \geq 1$, $F \in \mathcal{F}^k$, $0 \leq j < k$, requiring $\mathcal{C}^j$ to contain a constructor symbol C_F^j. Then $C_F^j(E_1, \dots, E_j)$ represents the partial curried application $F E_1 \dots E_j$ and the meaning of @ is given by equations of the form:

$$@(C_F^j(\boldsymbol{x}), y) = C_F^{j+1}(\boldsymbol{x}, y) \qquad @(C_F^{k-1}(\boldsymbol{x}), y) = F(\boldsymbol{x}, y).$$

To interpret programs in this language as graph rewriting systems, we use a restricted version of a form of equational term graph rewriting due to Ariola and Arvind [3]. This form of graph rewriting corrects a defect in the earlier work of Barendregt et al [5] concerning collapsing rules and cycles (see Ariola and Klop [2] for a discussion). The solution depends on the use of a special 'unboxed' constant $\circlearrowleft$, where the key feature of unboxed constants is that they can be freely substituted for variables in the terms used to represent graphs. We use the formalism of Ariola and Arvind [3], rather than that of Ariola and Klop [2], because we exploit the distinction between boxed and unboxed constants ($\top$ is unboxed) and because a variant of the graph model in the former allows us to define safety of our abstraction in a natural way.

Definition 2.1 (GRS Term). *Let* UC *denote some subset of* $\mathcal{C}^0 \cup \{\circlearrowleft\}$ *nominated as the unboxed constants[1]. We require that* $\circlearrowleft \in$ UC. *Let* v, w *range over* Var $\cup$ UC. *The GRS terms over signature* $\mathcal{S}$, *denoted* Ter($\mathcal{S}$), *are defined as follows:*

$$L, M, N ::= \mathsf{let}\ \{x_1 = E_1, \dots, x_n = E_n\}\ \mathsf{in}\ v$$
$$E ::= M \mid v \mid S^k(v_1, \dots, v_k) \mid \Omega$$

---

[1] In [3] all nullary symbols are unboxed.

Here and in the remainder of the paper, writing $S^k(v)$ should be taken to imply $S^k \notin \mathrm{UC}$ in the case that $k = 0$.

In a term $M =$ let $\{x = E\}$ in v, the order of bindings is irrelevant, all x_i are required to be distinct and are bound in all E_i as well as v (so let is a letrec). The sets $\mathrm{FV}(M)$ and $\mathrm{BV}(M)$ of the free and bound variables, respectively, of M are defined in the usual way. $\mathrm{Ter}^\circ(\mathcal{S})$ denotes the closed terms.

The root of M, denoted $\mathrm{root}(M)$, is v.

In [3], a unique canonical form is defined for each term by flattening nested lets, removing 'trivial' bindings of the form $x = v$ and substituting v everywhere for x, and removing garbage. This is formalised in [3] as a strongly normalising reduction system on terms. For example, the reduction rule for flattening has the form:

$$\text{let } \{x = E, y = \text{let } \{x' = E'\} \text{ in } w, x'' = E''\} \text{ in } v$$
$$\rightarrow \text{let } \{x = E, y = w, x' = E', x'' = E''\} \text{ in } v$$

(assuming all bound variables distinct and the bound and free variables disjoint). Removal of trivial bindings is straightforward apart from those of the form $x = x$ (the substitution has no effect, so removal of the binding would result in x becoming free): these are dealt with by substituting $\circlearrowright$ for x.

Definition 2.2 (Canonical Form). *A term* let $\{x = E\}$ in v *is in canonical form if:*

1. *each E_i is either Ω or of the form $S^k(v_1, \ldots, v_k)$;*
2. *each x_i is reachable from v (the term is garbage free).*

Let $\overline{M}$ denote the result of flattening and removal of trivial bindings, and let $\mathrm{GC}(N)$ denote N with garbage removed. Then $\mathrm{GC}(\overline{M})$ is said to be the canonical form for M.

Terms M and N are said to be graph equivalent, *written $M \equiv N$, if the canonical forms for M and N are the same up to renaming of bound variables.*

Canonical forms correspond in an obvious way to rooted labelled digraphs which are finite and connected. As an example, consider the term

let $\{x' = \text{let } \{x = A(y, z), z = \Omega\} \text{ in } x, y = F(x', y'), y' = C\}$ in x'.

Assuming $C \in \mathrm{UC}$, this has canonical form let $\{x = A(y, z), y = F(x, C), z = \Omega\}$ in x, which directly corresponds to the following graph:

Predicates and relations defined on terms in canonical form are to be understood as being implicitly extended to arbitrary terms via their canonical forms. For example, the rooted homomorphism preorder $\leqslant$ (see Def. 2.4) is extended to arbitrary terms thus: $M \leqslant N$ iff $GC(\overline{M}) \leqslant GC(\overline{N})$.

The correspondence between canonical forms and graphs makes it possible to transpose many familiar graph definitions to terms in canonical form.

Definition 2.3 (Label, Vertex, Edge, Path). *Let $M = $ let $\{x = E\}$ in v be in canonical form.*

1. *For $x \in \mathrm{BV}(M)$ such that x is not bound to Ω, the label for x is the unique $S \in \mathcal{S}$ such that x is bound to $S(y)$.*
2. *The set of vertices of M, denoted $\mathrm{vert}(M)$, is $\mathrm{FV}(M) \cup \mathrm{BV}(M) \cup \mathrm{UC}$.*
3. *An edge[2] in M is a pair (x, v) of vertices of M such that $x = S^k(v_1, \ldots, v_k)$ is a binding in M with $v = v_j$ for some $1 \leq j \leq k$.*
4. *For $n \geq 0$, a path of length n in M is a sequence $v_0 \cdots v_n$ of $n + 1$ vertices of M, such that, for every $0 \leq i < n$, (v_i, v_{i+1}) is an edge in M.*

Definition 2.4 (Homomorphism). *Given terms M and N in canonical form, a homomorphism from M to N is a map $\sigma : \mathrm{vert}(M) \rightarrow \mathrm{vert}(N)$ such that:*

1. $\sigma(v) = v$, *if $v \notin \mathrm{BV}(M)$;*
2. *if x is bound to $S^k(v)$ in M, then $\sigma(x)$ is bound to $S^k(\sigma(v))$ in N.*

(We write $\sigma(v)$ to mean $\sigma(v_1), \ldots, \sigma(v_k)$.) If, furthermore, $\sigma(\mathrm{root}(M)) = \mathrm{root}(N)$, then σ is called a rooted homomorphism *and we write $\sigma : M \leqslant N$. We write $M \leqslant N$ to mean that there exists such a σ.*

Note that if x is bound to Ω in M, it is not necessary to have $\sigma(x)$ bound to Ω in N (or, indeed, even to have $\sigma(x) \in \mathrm{BV}(N)$).

It is easily verified that (rooted) homomorphisms compose and that the identity is a rooted homomorphism, hence $\leqslant$ is a preorder (which, in fact, induces $\equiv$).

We now introduce Ariola and Arvind's formalisation of the general notion of term graph rewrite rule.

Definition 2.5 (GRS Rewrite Rule). *A GRS rewrite rule (henceforth, just rewrite rule) ρ has the form:*

$$\frac{z = E_l, x_1 = E_1, \ldots, x_n = E_n}{z \rightarrow E_r}$$

($n \geq 0$) where, letting $\mathrm{lhs}(\rho)$ denote the term let $\{z = E_l, x_1 = E_1, \ldots, x_n = E_n\}$ in z *and letting $\mathrm{rhs}(\rho)$ denote E_r:*

1. $\mathrm{lhs}(\rho)$ *is in canonical form and does not contain Ω (thus E_l and each E_i must be of the form $S^k(v)$);*

---

[2] The notions of edge and path defined here contain less information than the standard ones but are sufficient for our purposes. The standard ones can be defined in similar fashion.

2. $FV(rhs(\rho)) \subseteq FV(lhs(\rho)) \cup BV(lhs(\rho))$.

The closure of $lhs(\rho)$ *is* let $\{y = \Omega, x = E, z = E_l\}$ in z *where* $y = FV(lhs(\rho))$.

Note that the function/constructor distinction plays no role in the above definition. This notion of rewrite rule is actually far too general for our purposes and so below (Def. 2.8) we define a restricted form which is adequate for the core functional language described above.

Definition 2.6 (Redex). *Let P be a set of rewrite rules. Given term M in canonical form, a P-redex in M is a pair (ρ, σ), where ρ is in P and σ is a homomorphism from the closure of $lhs(\rho)$ to M.*

Let L be the closure of $lhs(\rho)$. Then $\sigma(root(L))$ (which is necessarily in $BV(M)$) is known as the root *of the redex. Note that the domain of σ contains $FV(rhs(\rho))$.*

Definition 2.7 (Rewrite). *Let P be a set of rewrite rules, let $M = $ let $\{x_1 = E_1, \ldots, x_n = E_n\}$ in v and let $\Delta = (\rho, \sigma)$ be a P-redex in M. Let x_i be the root of Δ. M is said to* rewrite *to $GC(\overline{N})$ by Δ if $N = M[x_i \leftarrow (rhs(\rho))^\sigma]$, where E^σ denotes the application of σ as a substitution on the free variables of E, and $M[x_i \leftarrow E]$ denotes the term* let $\{x_1 = E_1, \ldots, x_i = E, \ldots, x_n = E_n\}$ in v.

If M rewrites to M' by some P-redex Δ, we write $M \xrightarrow{P} M'$. We write $\xrightarrow{P}{}_{\!\twoheadrightarrow}$ for the transitive reflexive closure of $\xrightarrow{P}$ and we write $\xrightarrow{P}{}_{=}$ for the reflexive closure.

Definition 2.8 (Simple Functional GRS). *A rewrite rule ρ is said to be* left-linear *if the graph represented by $lhs(\rho)$ is a tree. A* simple functional GRS *over S is a set P of left-linear rewrite rules of a limited form, namely, for each function symbol $F \in \mathcal{F}$:*

1. *either a single rewrite rule of the form*

$$\frac{z = F(y)}{z \to E}$$

   (note that y is a vector of variables, not arbitrary vertices);
2. *or a family of n rewrite rules, each of either of the following two forms:*

$$\frac{z = F(y_0, y), \; y_0 = C_i(x_i)}{z \to E_i} \qquad \frac{z = F(C_i, y)}{z \to E_i},$$

   with each C_i a distinct constructor symbol, $1 \leq i \leq n$.

When function symbol F is defined by a family of rules as in (2) we say that F is pattern-matching.

Any program written in the core functional language described at the beginning of this section can be translated in a straightforward manner into a simple functional GRS. In essence, each use of case is translated to a pattern-matching function definition (in general, this will involve lifting the locally bound variables of a case to the top level, as in lambda-lifting). See Barendsen and Smetsers [6] for examples.

Say that $\xrightarrow{\alpha}$ *subcommutes* with $\xrightarrow{\beta}$ if $\xleftarrow{\alpha};\xrightarrow{\beta} \subseteq \xrightarrow{\beta}_=;_=\xleftarrow{\alpha}$. A rewrite relation is said to be *subcommutative* if it subcommutes with itself. It is a standard result that subcommutativity implies confluence (see eg [14]).

Proposition 2.9. *The rewrite relation generated by a simple functional GRS is subcommutative, hence confluent, up to $\equiv$.*

Proof. The restrictions placed on the form of rules allowed in a simple functional GRS ensure that the rules are non-overlapping (non-interfering in the terminology of [3]). Subcommutativity is immediate by Theorem 4.8 in [3]. □

3   Abstracting a Simple Functional GRS

In this section we define abstract GRS terms as a superset of the ordinary GRS terms and go on to define an abstraction relation on abstract terms. We then define a way of extending a simple functional GRS on ordinary terms to one on abstract terms.

Definition 3.1 (Abstract GRS Term). *An abstract GRS term over S is a GRS term over the signature $S^{\#} = \mathcal{F} \cup \mathcal{C}^{\#}$, where $\mathcal{C}^{\#}$ is $\mathcal{C}$ plus the following (assumed new) constructor symbols:*

1. $\top$, *of arity* 0, $\top \in \mathrm{UC}$;
2. *for each* $k \geq 1$, *the union symbol* $\oplus^k$ *of arity* k *(we will often omit the superscript* k*).*

Let H, J, K range over abstract terms.

Note that the abstract terms over S include the terms over S as a special case: $\mathrm{Ter}(S) \subset \mathrm{Ter}(S^{\#})$.

Our formalisation of the meaning of $\oplus$ is provided below by the notions of choice set and weak homomorphism. The first of these goes to heart of our graph-based approach, showing how each vertex labelled $\oplus$ is used to represent a set of non-$\oplus$ vertices.

Definition 3.2 (Choice Set). *Let H be an abstract term in canonical form. Given $v \in \mathrm{vert}(H)$, a choice path for v is a path $v = v_0, \ldots, v_n$ in M such that, for all $0 \leq i < n$, v_i is labelled $\oplus$. Let the set of definite vertices of H, denoted $\mathrm{dvert}(H)$, be the set $\{v \in \mathrm{vert}(H) \mid v$ is not labelled $\oplus\}$.*

The choice set for $v \in \mathrm{vert}(H)$, denoted $\chi(v)$, is the smallest set $X \subseteq \mathrm{dvert}(H)$ such that:

1. $\circlearrowright \in X$ *if there is a choice path* $v = v_0 \cdots v_i \cdots v_n = v_i$ *with* $0 \leq i < n$;
2. $v' \in X$ *if there is a choice path* $v = v_0 \cdots v_n = v'$ *and* v' *is not labelled* $\oplus$.

Lemma 3.3. *If $v \in \mathrm{dvert}(H)$ then $\chi(v) = \{v\}$. If x is bound to $\oplus^k(v)$ in H, then $\chi(x) = \chi(v_1) \cup \cdots \cup \chi(v_k)$.*

The definition of homomorphism (Def. 2.4) requires that all labels are preserved. Given the role played by $\oplus$ labels, it is inappropriate to require them to be strictly preserved when comparing abstract graphs. The following provides a weakening of the notion of homomorphism which reflects the special status of $\oplus$:

Definition 3.4 (Weak Homomorphism). *Given abstract terms H and J in canonical form, a weak homomorphism from H to J is a map $\sigma : \mathrm{dvert}(H) \to \mathrm{dvert}(J)$ such that:*

1. *$\sigma(v) = v$, if $v \notin \mathrm{BV}(H)$;*
2. *if x is bound to $S^k(v)$ in H, $S^k \neq \oplus^k$, then $\sigma(x)$ is bound to $S^k(w)$ in J and $\forall i, 1 \leq i \leq k. \forall v \in \chi(v_i). \sigma(v) \in \chi(w_i)$.*

If, furthermore, $\forall v \in \chi(\mathrm{root}(H)). \sigma(v) \in \chi(\mathrm{root}(J))$, then σ is called a rooted weak homomorphism and we write $\sigma : H \lesssim J$. We write $H \lesssim J$ to mean that there exists such a σ.

It is easily verified that (rooted) weak homomorphisms compose and that the identity is a rooted weak homomorphism, hence $\lesssim$ is a preorder.

Example 3.5 (Weak Homomorphism).

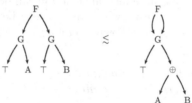

There is a unique rooted weak homomorphism σ which maps the nodes labelled F, G, A, B on the left to their counterparts on the right (we assume neither A or B is unboxed). Since $\top$ is unboxed, the definition of weak homomorphism forces $\sigma(\top) = \top$. Note that, like a homomorphism, a weak homomorphism cannot decrease sharing. Hence there is no weak homomorphism from right to left.

The notions of choice set and weak homomorphism capture the meaning of $\oplus$ but they do not say anything about the meaning of $\top$. To do this we define a relation between abstract terms as follows:

Definition 3.6 (Abstraction Morphism). *Given abstract terms H and J, both in canonical form, let $\tau : \mathrm{dvert}(H) \to \mathrm{dvert}(J)$. The relation $\leq_\tau \subseteq \mathrm{dvert}(H) \times \mathrm{dvert}(J)$ is defined as follows: $v \leq_\tau w$ iff $w = \tau(v) \vee w = \top$. Then τ is an abstraction morphism from H to J if:*

1. *$\tau(v) = v$, if $v \notin \mathrm{BV}(H)$;*
2. *if x is bound to $S^k(v)$ in H, $S^k \neq \oplus^k$, then either $\tau(x) = \top$, or $\tau(x)$ is bound to $S^k(w)$ in J and $\forall i, 1 \leq i \leq k. \forall v \in \chi(v_i). \exists w \in \chi(w_i). v \leq_\tau w$.*

If, furthermore, $\forall v \in \chi(\text{root}(H)). \exists w \in \chi(\text{root}(J)). v \leq_\tau w$, then τ is called a rooted abstraction morphism *and we write $\tau : H \underset{\sim}{\trianglelefteq} J$. We say that H is* abstracted *by J, written $H \underset{\sim}{\trianglelefteq} J$, if there exists such a τ.*

It is easily verified that (rooted) abstraction morphisms compose and that the identity is a rooted abstraction morphisms, hence $\underset{\sim}{\trianglelefteq}$ is a preorder. Clearly, all terms are abstracted by $\top$.

Example 3.7 (Abstraction).

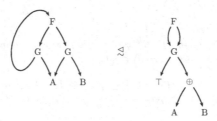

There is a unique rooted abstraction morphism τ from left to right. Note that τ must map the two vertices labelled G on the left to a single vertex on the right.

Note the similarity between the definition of abstraction morphism and the definition of weak homomorphism. In fact, abstraction can be seen as a conservative extension of weak homomorphism, which in turn can be seen as a conservative extension of $\leqslant$, as shown by the following lemma:

Lemma 3.8. *1. $\leqslant \,\subseteq\, \underset{\sim}{\leq} \,\subseteq\, \underset{\sim}{\trianglelefteq}$.*

2. $\underset{\sim}{\trianglelefteq}$ restricts to $\underset{\sim}{\leq}$ on terms not containing $\top$.

3. $\underset{\sim}{\leq}$ restricts to $\leqslant$ on terms not containing $\oplus$.

We now define a simple functional GRS P# for rewriting abstract graphs. The main burden of our remaining technical development is to define an appropriate notion of safety and to show that rewriting abstract graphs using P# safely approximates the rewriting of ordinary graphs using P. Unlike previous approaches (eg [17, 22]), we do not define an abstract evaluator based on an abstract notion of pattern matching. Instead, we provide rewrite rules which apply whenever $\oplus$ or $\top$ occur in the pattern position for a pattern-matching function.

Definition 3.9 (Extension of a Simple Functional GRS). *Let P be a simple functional GRS. Then the extension of P to abstract terms, denoted P#, is P extended with additional rules for each pattern-matching F as follows: let the rule set for F in P comprise n rules, each of either of the two forms:*

$$\frac{z = F(y_0, \boldsymbol{y}),\ y_0 = C_i(\boldsymbol{x}_i)}{z \to E_i} \qquad \frac{z = F(C_i, \boldsymbol{y})}{z \to E_i},$$

We add to P# the following rules:

1.

$$z = F(y_0, \boldsymbol{y}), \ y_0 = \oplus^k(z_1, \ldots, z_k)$$
$$\overline{\qquad z \to H \qquad}$$

for each $\oplus^k$, where H is the term

let $\{z' = \oplus^k(z_1', \ldots, z_k'), \ z_1' = F(z_1, \boldsymbol{y}), \ \ldots, \ z_k' = F(z_k, \boldsymbol{y})\}$ in z'

(z' and each z_i, z_i' fresh). We call these the $\oplus$-lifting rules.

2.

$$z = F(\top, \boldsymbol{y})$$
$$\overline{\qquad z \to J \qquad}$$

where J is the term[3]

let $\{z' = \oplus^n(z_1, \ldots, z_n), \ z_1 = E_1^\sigma, \ \ldots, \ z_n = E_n^\sigma\}$ in z',

(each z_i fresh) and $\sigma(x) = \begin{cases} x & \text{if } x \in \boldsymbol{y} \\ \top & \text{otherwise.} \end{cases}$ We call these the $\top$ rules.

Note that $\mathrm{P}\#$ is itself a simple functional GRS. The rewrite relation $\xrightarrow{\mathrm{P}\#}$ on $\mathrm{Ter}(\mathcal{S}^\#)$ is easily seen to be a conservative extension of $\xrightarrow{\mathrm{P}}$ on $\mathrm{Ter}(\mathcal{S})$.

Example 3.10 (Rewriting by $\mathrm{P}\#$). Suppose F is defined in P by the pair of rules:

$$\frac{z = F(\mathrm{Nil})}{z \to \mathrm{Nil}} \qquad \frac{z = F(y), \ y = \mathrm{Cons}(x_1, x_2)}{z \to F(x_2)}$$

Then we have the $\mathrm{P}\#$ rewrite sequence:

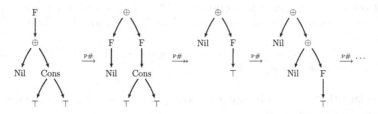

It is clear from this example that not all abstract graphs have a normal form with respect to $\xrightarrow{\mathrm{P}\#}$.

---

[3] J will be different for different choices of ordering $i = 1 \ldots n$ on the rules for F. However, since $\oplus^n$ is a commutative operator with respect to the semantic precongruence induced by $\lesssim$ (see Sect. 5), the differences are not semantically significant.

4 The Graph Model

We require a safety result which states that rewriting an abstract term H by the rules in P# gives information which is valid for all terms M such that $M \trianglelefteq H$. We state our safety property in terms of a variant of the direct approximation style semantics defined in [3]. We begin by defining what we regard as the directly observable part of a closed term.

Definition 4.1 (Directly Observable Approximation). *Let $S = \mathcal{F} \cup \mathcal{C}$ be a signature. Given $M \in \mathrm{Ter}^\circ(S)$, let $U_M = \{z \in \mathrm{BV}(M) \mid z$ does not have a label in $\mathcal{C}\}$. The map $\omega : \mathrm{Ter}^\circ(S) \to \mathrm{Ter}^\circ(C)$ is defined by $\omega(M) = M[U_M \leftarrow \Omega]$. $\omega(M)$ is known as* the directly observable approximation of M.

The following lemma collects together some basic facts about ω:

Lemma 4.2. *Let H, J be closed abstract terms over S. Let $\longrightarrow$ be the rewrite relation generated by any simple functional GRS over $S^\#$.*

1. $\omega(H) \leqslant H$.
2. $\omega(H) \leqslant J \Rightarrow \omega(H) \leqslant \omega(J)$.
3. $\omega(H) \lesssim J \Rightarrow \omega(H) \lesssim \omega(J)$.
4. $\omega(H) \trianglelefteq J \Rightarrow \omega(H) \trianglelefteq \omega(J)$.
5. $H \longrightarrow\!\!\!\!\rightarrow J \Rightarrow \omega(H) \leqslant \omega(J)$.

Definition 4.3 (Context). A context over signature S *is a GRS term* let $\{x_1 = E_1, \ldots, x_n = E_n\}$ in v *except that (at most) one E_i is allowed to be $\square$. Let $\mathrm{Ctx}(S)$ denote the contexts over signature S.*

Let $\mathfrak{C}, \mathfrak{D}$ range over contexts. If $\mathfrak{C}$ is a context containing the binding $x_i = \square$, the result of placing a term M in $\mathfrak{C}$, written $\mathfrak{C}[M]$, is the term $\mathfrak{C}[x_i \leftarrow M]$. If $\square$ *does not occur in $\mathfrak{C}$ then $\mathfrak{C}[M] = \mathfrak{C}$.*

Definition 4.4 (Compatible Relation). *We say that a binary relation R on terms is* compatible *if, for all contexts $\mathfrak{C}$, for all terms M, N, if $M \, R \, N$ then $\mathfrak{C}[M] \, R \, \mathfrak{C}[N]$.*

A compatible preorder is said to be a precongruence. *A compatible equivalence relation is said to be a* congruence.

It is standard that if R is a preorder (precongruence) then $R \cap R^{-1}$ is an equivalence relation (congruence).

Lemma 4.5. *The following are compatible:*

1. *The transitive reflexive closure of any rewrite relation generated by a set of GRS rewrite rules;*
2. $\leqslant$, $\lesssim$ and $\trianglelefteq$.

Definition 4.6 (Observational Preorder and Observational Equivalence). *Let* P *be a simple functional GRS over signature S and let $M, N \in$ Ter(S) be in canonical form. We say that M is observably less than N with respect to* P*, written $M \precsim_P N$, if, for all contexts $\mathfrak{C} \in$ Ctx(S) such that $\mathfrak{C}[M]$ and $\mathfrak{C}[N]$ are closed, $\forall M' \twoheadleftarrow^P \mathfrak{C}[M]. \exists N' \twoheadleftarrow^P \mathfrak{C}[N]. \omega(M') \leqslant \omega(N')$. We say that M and N are observationally equivalent with respect to* P*, written $M \cong_P N$, if $M \precsim_P N$ and $N \precsim_P M$.*

We will omit the P *subscripts when it is not confusing to do so.*

It is easily verified that $\precsim$ is a preorder (hence $\cong$ is an equivalence relation). Furthermore, because the definition of $\precsim$ quantifies over all contexts, it follows directly that $\precsim$ is in fact a precongruence (hence $\cong$ is a congruence). The following result is an easy consequence of Lemma 4.2(5) plus confluence:

Proposition 4.7. *If $M \xrightarrow{P}\!\!\!\!\twoheadrightarrow N$ then $M \cong_P N$.*

5 Safety

The previous section defines a semantic precongruence, $\precsim$, based on the rooted graph homomorphism preorder $\leqslant$ and rewriting by a simple functional GRS P. In this section we define a natural analogue of $\precsim$ for abstract terms, based on the abstraction preorder $\trianglelefteq$ and rewriting by P#. As we show below, this 'abstract' precongruence is sound with respect to $\precsim$, in the sense that it restricts to a subrelation of $\precsim$ on ordinary terms.

Definition 5.1 (Semantic Extension). *Let $S = \mathcal{F} \cup \mathcal{C}$, let R be a binary relation on Ter$^\circ(\mathcal{C})$ and let* P *be a simple functional GRS over S. The semantic extension of R with respect to* P*, denoted $[R]_P \subseteq$ Ter$(S) \times$ Ter(S) is defined thus: $M [R]_P N$ iff for all contexts $\mathfrak{C} \in$ Ctx(S) such that $\mathfrak{C}[M]$ and $\mathfrak{C}[N]$ are closed, $\forall M' \twoheadleftarrow^P \mathfrak{C}[M]. \exists N' \twoheadleftarrow^P \mathfrak{C}[N]. \omega(M') R \omega(N')$.*

It is easily seen that, if R is a preorder then so is $[R]_P$, for any P. Note that $\precsim_P$ is $[\leqslant]_P$ (where $\leqslant$ is implicitly restricted to Ter$^\circ(\mathcal{C}) \times$ Ter$^\circ(\mathcal{C})$).

Proposition 5.2. *Let* P *be a simple functional GRS over S. Then*

$$[\trianglelefteq]_{P\#} \restriction \text{Ter}(S) \times \text{Ter}(S) \subseteq \precsim_P$$

(where $R \restriction X$ denotes the restriction of R to X).

Proof. See Appendix.

Remark 5.3. We conjecture that $[\trianglelefteq]_{P\#}$ is in fact a conservative *extension* of $[\leqslant]_P$ (ie, that $\subseteq$ can be strengthened to $=$ in the statement of the proposition). In the current setting it is not clear that this is a useful property.

This result shows that, in principle, P# can be used to predict the semantics of terms with respect to P. This is not obviously useful, since $\xrightarrow{\text{P\#}}$ is no easier to compute than $\xrightarrow{\text{P}}$. In particular, it is easy to see that, in general, $[\lesssim]_{\text{P\#}}$ will be undecidable. Clearly we must settle for a sound method - one which allows us to decide a subrelation of $[\lesssim]_{\text{P\#}}$, which, by the proposition, in turn decides a subrelation of $\sqsubseteq_{\text{P}}$. The key to developing such a method is to show that $\lesssim$ is itself a safe approximation to $[\lesssim]_{\text{P\#}}$. Proving this directly is not straightforward and we postpone it to Sect. 6 (Corollary 6.6).

Definition 5.4 (Safety). *Let* P *be a simple functional GRS over* S *and let* R *be a binary relation on* $\text{Ter}(S^{\#})$. *We say that* R *is safe if* $R \subseteq [\lesssim]_{\text{P\#}}$.

Note that, because $[\lesssim]_{\text{P\#}}$ is a preorder, R is safe iff R^* is safe. The following results shows this notion of safety to be adequate for strictness analysis:

Proposition 5.5. *Let* P *be a simple functional GRS over* S. *Let* $\xrightarrow{\text{AR}}$ *be some notion of abstract reduction for* P *(that is,* $\xrightarrow{\text{AR}}$ *is a binary relation on* $\text{Ter}(S^{\#})$*). If* $\lesssim$ *is safe and* $\xrightarrow{\text{AR}}$ *is safe then* $H \xrightarrow{\text{AR}} \Omega \Rightarrow M \cong_{\text{P}} \Omega$ *for all* $M \lesssim H$.

Note that M need not be closed. This result entails, for example, that if $\lesssim$ and $\xrightarrow{\text{AR}}$ are safe, then $F(\Omega, \top) \xrightarrow{\text{AR}} \Omega$ implies $F(\Omega, x) \cong_{\text{P}} \Omega$, with x free. (This is clearly an analogue of the usual denotational definition of strictness in the first argument of a binary function: $\forall d.\, f(\bot, d) = \bot$. Formalising this would involve the elaboration of a denotational model for P but it is easy to see that trivially non-terminating programs, such as let $\{z = L(0)\}$ in z where $L(x) \to L(x)$, are $\cong_{\text{P}} \Omega$.)

6   Abstract Reduction

We assume given some simple functional GRS P over a signature $S = \mathcal{F} \cup \mathcal{C}$.

We define a relation $\xrightarrow{\text{AR}}$, and show that it is safe. $\xrightarrow{\text{AR}}$ is defined as the union of a number of subrelations, R_i, each of which has the following property:

$$H\, R_i\, J \Rightarrow \omega(H) \lesssim \omega(J) \tag{1}$$

This allows us to establish safety of $\xrightarrow{\text{AR}}$ via a commutativity property:

Lemma 6.1. *Let* $\xrightarrow{\text{AR}} = \bigcup_{i \in I} R_i$ *with each* $R_i \subseteq \text{Ter}(S^{\#}) \times \text{Ter}(S^{\#})$. *If each* R_i *satisfies (1) and each* R_i^* *is compatible, then* $\xrightarrow{\text{AR}}$ *is safe if it commutes with* $\xrightarrow{\text{P\#}}$.

Proof. See Appendix.

It follows easily from Prop. 4.7 that $\xrightarrow{\text{P\#}}$ is safe, so it is reasonable to include $\xrightarrow{\text{P\#}}$ in $\xrightarrow{\text{AR}}$. Now consider Example 3.10. The function F is clearly strict but we do not have $F(\Omega) \xrightarrow{\text{P\#}} \Omega$. We would like to add an 'Ω-lifting rewrite rule' $F(\Omega, y) \to \Omega$ for every pattern-matching F. Unfortunately this is not well-defined, since Ω is disallowed in the left hand sides of rewrite rules, but the idea motivates the following definition:

Definition 6.2. *Let H, J be abstract terms in canonical form. Then $H \xrightarrow{\Omega_L} GC(\overline{J})$ iff there exist pattern-matching F^k, bound variables $z, y_0 \in BV(H)$, and vertices $v_1, \ldots, v_{k-1} \in \text{vert}(H)$, such that y_0 is bound to Ω in H and z is bound to $F^k(y_0, v_1, \ldots, v_{k-1})$ in H and $J = H[z \leftarrow \Omega]$.*

Lemma 6.3.   *1. $\xrightarrow{\Omega_L}$ is compatible and $\xrightarrow{\Omega_L}$ satisfies (1).*

2. $\xrightarrow{\Omega_L}$ subcommutes with itself and with $\xrightarrow{P}$ for any simple functional GRS P.

Nöcker's analysis method amounts to defining $\xrightarrow{AR}$ as $\xrightarrow{P\#} \cup \xrightarrow{\Omega_L}$ plus some 'heuristic' reductions which are used to force termination. There are two forms of heuristic described in [17]. The first of these dynamically coarsens the abstract graph by replacing some parts of it by $\top$ (this may be done when some bound on the number of rewrite steps is reached). The second form performs checks to detect looping behaviour in the abstract evaluator and responds by either replacing parts of the graph by Ω or introducing a cycle into the graph. In addition, Nöcker's analyser applies a number of reduction rules to simplify subgraphs involving $\oplus$ (for example: $\oplus(x, y, y) \rightarrow \oplus(x, y)$).

We do not account for the heuristics based on loop-detection in the current paper. Replacement by $\top$ and the simplification of $\oplus$ subgraphs are subsumed by including $\lesssim$ in $\xrightarrow{AR}$. Thus we arrive at the following notion of abstract reduction:

Definition 6.4. $\xrightarrow{AR} = \xrightarrow{P\#} \cup \xrightarrow{\Omega_L} \cup \lesssim$.

Theorem 6.5. $\xrightarrow{AR}$ *commutes with* $\xrightarrow{P\#}$.

Proof. See Appendix.

Corollary 6.6. $\lesssim$ *and* $\xrightarrow{AR}$ *are safe.*

Proof. The subrelations $\lesssim$, $\xrightarrow{P\#}$, $\xrightarrow{\Omega_L}$ are each compatible (Lemma 4.5, Lemma 6.3(1)) and satisfy (1) (Lemma 4.2, Lemma 6.3(1)) thus safety of $\xrightarrow{AR}$ follows by Lemma 6.1. Safety of $\lesssim$ is implied by safety of $\xrightarrow{AR}$, since $\lesssim \subseteq \xrightarrow{AR}$. □

7   Conclusions and Further Work

Nöcker's method of abstract reduction is an intuitively appealing approach to program analysis which is quite unlike any of the other approaches to strictness analysis which have been proposed in the literature. In this paper we have succeeded for the first time in formalising abstract reduction and proving its correctness without any restrictions on the class of abstract graphs. Future work will address the correctness of the heuristics based on loop-detection, which are used in the Clean strictness analyser to force termination. We do not believe that this will require a change to our formalisation. The main technical requirement is to establish a standardisation result, allowing semantic properties to be inferred from cyclic behaviour along particular (rather than all) reduction paths.

Being tailored to strictness analysis, the approach that we have taken is rather *ad hoc*. Ideally, we would like to establish a general framework and explore the application of abstract reduction to other program analyses. To start with, it may be relatively easy to adapt the results of this paper to binding time analysis. Beyond that, a striking aspect of the notion of abstraction developed in this paper is that it is sensitive to differences in sharing. Information about sharing properties can be very useful to language implementors [21, 6, 24] and it will be interesting to see if a form of sharing analysis can be developed by adapting our technique.

Another future direction would be to develop similar techniques for other forms of operational semantics. It would be an advantage to have a framework which applied directly to lambda calculi, rather than having to work with supercombinators. One possibility would be to use the rewriting theory of cyclic lambda calculi developed by Ariola and Blom [4]. An alternative would be to use an abstract machine approach, such as that used by Moran and Sands [19].

Finally, it remains open whether abstract reduction can be formalised within the framework of abstract interpretation. We can draw the following analogies: Collecting interpretation $\sim$ graphs built using $\oplus$, ordered by $\lesssim$, plus the $\oplus$-lifting rules; Abstraction of the collecting semantics $\sim$ graphs built using $\top$, ordered by $\lhd$, plus the $\top$ rules; Widening $\sim$ heuristics modelled by $\unlhd$. But many unanswered questions remain.

We would like to thank Richard Kennaway, Matthias Felleisen, Thomas Jensen and the anonymous referees for their suggestions and comments.

References

[1] S. Abramsky and C.L. Hankin, editors. *Abstract Interpretation of Declarative Languages*. Computers and Their Applications. Ellis Horwood, 1987. 96

[2] Z. Ariola and J. W. Klop. Equational term graph rewriting. *Fundamentae Informatica*, 26(3,4):207–240, June 1996. 98

[3] Zena Ariola and Arvind. Properties of a first-order functional language with sharing. *Theoretical Computer Science*, 146(1–2):69–108, July 1995. 98, 99, 102, 106

[4] Zena Ariola and Stefan Blom. Cyclic lambda calculi. In *Proc. TACS'97*. Springer-Verlag, February 1997. LNCS 1281. 110

[5] H.P. Barendregt, M.C.J.D. van Eekelen, J.R.W. Glauert, J.R. Kennaway, M.J. Plasmeijer, and M.R. Sleep. Term graph rewriting. In *Proc. PARLE 87*, volume 2, pages 141–158. Springer-Verlag LNCS 259, Eindhoven, The Netherlands, June 1987. 98

[6] Erik Barendsen and Sjaak Smetsers. Uniqueness typing for functional languages with graph rewriting semantics. *Mathematical Structures in Computer Science*, 6:579–612, 1996. 98, 102, 110

[7] Tyng-Ruey Chuang and Benjamin Goldberg. A syntactic approach to fixed point computation on finite domains. In *Proc. 1992 ACM Conference on LISP and Functional Programming*. ACM, June 1992. 97

[8] D. J. Clark and C. Hankin. A lattice of abstract graphs. In M. Bruynooghe and J Penjam, editors, *Proc. Programming Language Implementation and Logic Programming*, pages 318–331, Tallinn, Estonia, August 1993. Springer-Verlag LNCS 714. 96

[9] David J. Clark. *Term Graph Rewriting and Event Structures*. PhD thesis, Imperial College, University of London, 1996. 96

[10] P. Cousot and R. Cousot. Abstract interpretation: A unified lattice model for static analysis of programs by construction or approximation of fixed points. In *Proc. Fourth ACM Symposium on Principles of Programming Languages*, pages 238–252, Los Angeles, 1977. 96

[11] Andrew D. Gordon and Andrew M. Pitts, editors. *Higher Order Operational Techniques in Semantics*. Publications of the Newton Institute. Cambridge University Press, 1998. 97

[12] E. Goubault and C. L. Hankin. A lattice for the abstract interpretation of term graph rewriting systems. In *Term Graph Rewriting, theory and practice*, pages 131–140. John Wiley and Sons Ltd., 1993. 96

[13] J. R. Kennaway, J. W. Klop, M. R. Sleep, and F. J. de Vries. Comparing curried and uncurried rewriting. *J. Symbolic Computation*, 21:15–39, 1996. 98

[14] Jan Willem Klop. Term rewriting systems. In Samson Abramsky, Dov M. Gabbay, and Tom Maibaum, editors, *Handbook of Logic in Computer Science*, volume 2, pages 1–116. Oxford University Press, New York, 1992. 102

[15] F. Nielson, H. R. Nielson, and C. L. Hankin. *Principles of Program Analysis*. Springer, 1999. 96

[16] E. Nöcker. Strictness analysis based on abstract reduction of term graph rewrite systems. In *Proc. Workshop on Implementation of Lazy Functional Languages*, 1988. 95

[17] E. Nöcker. Strictness analysis using abstract reduction. In *Proc. Conference on Functional Programming Languages and Computer Architectures (FPCA '93)*, Copenhagen, 1993. ACM Press. 95, 104, 109

[18] E. Nöcker. *Efficient Functional Programming*. PhD thesis, Department of Computer Science, University of Nijmegen, Toernooiveld 1, 6525 ED Nijmegen, The Netherlands, 1994. 95, 96

[19] David Sands and Andrew Moran. Improvement in a lazy context: an operational theory for call-by-need. In *Proc. Twenty-sixth ACM Symposium on Principles of Programming Languages*, San Antonio, Texas, January 1999. 110

[20] M. Schütz, M. Schmidt-Schauß and S. E. Panitz. Strictness analysis by abstract reduction using a tableau calculus. In A. Mycroft, editor, *Proc. Static Analysis, Second International Symposium, SAS '95*, number 983 in Lecture Notes in Computer Science, pages 348–365, Glasgow, UK, September 1995. Springer Verlag. 96

[21] David N. Turner, Philip Wadler, and Christian Mossin. Once upon a type. In *Proc. 7'th International Conference on Functional Programming and Computer Architecture*, San Diego, California, June 1995. 110

[22] M. C. J. van Eekelen, E. Goubault, C. L. Hankin, and E. Nöcker. Abstract reduction: Towards a theory via abstract interpretation. In *Term Graph Rewriting, theory and practice*, pages 117–130. John Wiley and Sons Ltd., 1993. 96, 104

[23] Vincent van Oostrom. *Confluence for Abstract and Higher-Order Rewriting*. PhD thesis, Vrije Universiteit, Amsterdam, 1994. 112, 113

[24] Keith Wansbrough and Simon Peyton Jones. Once upon a polymorphic type. In *Proc. Twenty-sixth ACM Symposium on Principles of Programming Languages*, San Antonio, Texas, January 1999. 110

[25] Andrew K. Wright and Matthias Felleisen. A syntactic approach to type sound-ness. *Information and Computation*, 115(1):38–94, 15 November 1994. 97

A   Appendix: proof outlines for key results

Proof: Proposition 5.2

Suppose $M \ [\overset{\triangleleft}{\sim}]_{\text{P\#}} N$ with $M, N \in \text{Ter}(\mathcal{S})$ and suppose $M' \overset{\text{P}}{\twoheadleftarrow} \mathfrak{C}[M]$, with $\mathfrak{C} \in \text{Ctx}(\mathcal{S})$ a closing context for M and N. We must show that there exists $N' \overset{\text{P}}{\twoheadleftarrow} \mathfrak{C}[N]$ such that $\omega(M') \leqslant \omega(N')$. Since $\overset{\text{P}}{\longrightarrow} \subseteq \overset{\text{P\#}}{\longrightarrow}$, by definition of $[\overset{\triangleleft}{\sim}]_{\text{P\#}}$ there exists $J \overset{\text{P\#}}{\twoheadleftarrow} \mathfrak{C}[N]$ with $\omega(M') \overset{\triangleleft}{\sim} \omega(J)$. Then we may take $N' = J$, since $\overset{\text{P\#}}{\twoheadrightarrow}$ and $\overset{\triangleleft}{\sim}$ conservatively extend $\overset{\text{P}}{\twoheadrightarrow}$ and $\leqslant$, respectively.

Proof: Lemma 6.1

Assume $H \overset{\text{AR}}{\twoheadrightarrow} J$. Let $\mathfrak{C} \in \text{Ctx}(\mathcal{S}^{\#})$ be a closing context for H and J. Suppose that $H' \overset{\text{P\#}}{\twoheadleftarrow} \mathfrak{C}[H]$. We must show that there exists $J' \overset{\text{P\#}}{\twoheadleftarrow} \mathfrak{C}[J]$ such that $\omega(H') \overset{\triangleleft}{\sim} \omega(J')$. Compatibility of $\overset{\text{AR}}{\twoheadrightarrow}$ follows from compatibility of the R_i^* (by induction on the length of the $\overset{\text{AR}}{\twoheadrightarrow}$ sequence), thus, by our initial assumption we have $\mathfrak{C}[H] \overset{\text{AR}}{\twoheadrightarrow} \mathfrak{C}[J]$. Then, by commutativity, we have $H' \overset{\text{AR}}{\twoheadrightarrow} J' \overset{\text{P\#}}{\twoheadleftarrow} \mathfrak{C}[J]$ for some J'. Since each R_i satisfies (1), so does $\overset{\text{AR}}{\twoheadrightarrow}$ (by induction on the length of the $\overset{\text{AR}}{\twoheadrightarrow}$ sequence) and hence $\omega(H') \overset{\triangleleft}{\sim} \omega(J')$.

Proof: Theorem 6.5

We begin by factoring $\overset{\triangleleft}{\sim}$ into the composition of a more primitive form of ab-straction with $\lesssim$. We then prove commutativity using Vincent van Oostrom's method of decreasing diagrams [23].

Definition A.1 (Simple Abstraction). *Let H, J be abstract terms in canon-ical form such that $\text{FV}(J) \subseteq \text{FV}(H)$ and $\text{BV}(J) \subseteq \text{BV}(H)$. Define the relation $\leq \subseteq \text{vert}(H) \times \text{vert}(J)$ thus: $v \leq w$ iff $w = v \vee w = \top$. Then H is simply abstracted by J, written $H \lhd J$, if:*

1. $\text{root}(H) \leq \text{root}(J)$;
2. *if x is bound to $S^k(v)$ in H and $x \in \text{BV}(J)$, then x is bound to $S^k(w)$ in J and $\forall i, 1 \leq i \leq k. v_i \leq w_i$.*

$\lhd$ is easily seen to be a partial order.

Lemma A.2. *1. $\lhd \subseteq \overset{\triangleleft}{\sim}$.*
2. $H \overset{\triangleleft}{\sim} K$ iff there exists J such that $H \lhd J \lesssim K$.

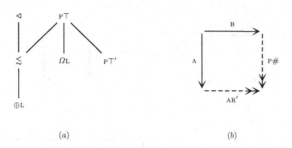

(a) (b)

Fig. 1. applying van Oostrom's method

To use van Oostrom's method, we must present $\xrightarrow{\text{P\#}}$ and $\xrightarrow{\text{AR}}$ as unions of labelled subrelations (we actually present slightly different relations which have the same transitive reflexive closure as these). Let $\xrightarrow{\oplus\text{L}}$ be the reflexive closure of the rewrite relation generated by just the $\oplus$-lifting rules in P# and let $\xrightarrow{\text{PT}}$ be the reflexive closure of the rewrite relation generated by P plus the T rules in P#. It is immediate from the definitions that

$$\xrightarrow{\text{P\#}}_{=} \;=\; \xrightarrow{\text{PT}} \cup \xrightarrow{\oplus\text{L}}$$

Now let $\xrightarrow{\text{PT}'} = \xrightarrow{\text{PT}}$, let $\xrightarrow{\vartriangleleft} = \vartriangleleft$, let $\xrightarrow{\lesssim} = \lesssim$, and define:

$$\xrightarrow{\text{AR}'} \;=\; \xrightarrow{\text{PT}'} \cup \xrightarrow{\oplus\text{L}} \cup \xrightarrow{\Omega\text{L}}_{=} \cup \xrightarrow{\vartriangleleft} \cup \xrightarrow{\lesssim}$$

It is an easy consequence of Lemma A.2 plus transitivity of $\lesssim$ that $\xrightarrow{\text{AR}'}\!\!\!\twoheadrightarrow \;=\; \xrightarrow{\text{AR}}\!\!\!\twoheadrightarrow$; thus it suffices to prove that $\xrightarrow{\text{AR}'}$ commutes with $\xrightarrow{\text{P\#}}$. Next we define a strict order $\prec$ on the labels of the subrelations; the Hasse diagram is shown in Fig. 1(a). Now we consider each $(\text{A},\text{B}) \in \{\text{PT},\oplus\text{L}\} \times \{\text{PT}',\oplus\text{L},\Omega\text{L},\vartriangleleft,\lesssim\}$, and show that, in each case, the diagram of Fig. 1(b) can be completed in a way which respects $\prec$ in the manner required by Theorem 2.3.5 of [23].

All the cases in $\{\text{PT},\oplus\text{L}\} \times \{\text{PT}',\oplus\text{L},\Omega\text{L}\}$ are very simple using subcommutativity (Prop. 2.9, Lemma 6.3(2)). The remaining four cases are summarised by the commuting squares in Fig. 2.

Cases (1), (2) and (3) are straightforward. Case (4) is more involved. In general, the PT redex rewritten down the left hand side will be just one member of a family comprising the set $\sigma^{-1}(\sigma(z))$, where z is the root of the PT redex and σ is the weak homomorphism witnessing $\lesssim$ along the upper edge. Intuitively, this family identifies a set of PT and ΩL redexes whose residuals we need to rewrite along the lower horizontal edge. However, not every member of this family need be the root of a redex, since the definition of weak homomorphism allows the presence of vertices labelled $\oplus$ to 'break' potential redexes. It can be shown that all these potential redexes can be exposed by use of $\lesssim$ and $\oplus$L. Similarly, $\sigma(z)$ may be the root of a 'broken' redex on the right, hence the use of $\oplus$L rewrites

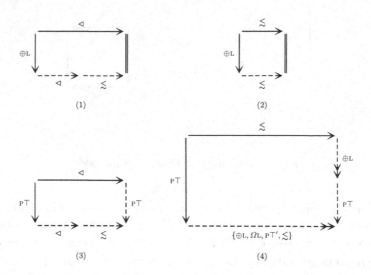

Fig. 2. proof cases for Theorem 6.5

down the right hand side. Formalising the argument involves the following key definition and lemmas:

Definition A.3 (Trace and Fragment). *Let H be in canonical form. Let Δ be a redex in H by a $\oplus$-lifting rule, let z be the root of Δ, and let $H \longrightarrow H'$ by Δ. By the definition of the $\oplus$-lifting rules (Def. 3.9), z is bound to $F(y_0, \boldsymbol{v})$ in H, for some pattern matching F, and y_0 is bound to $\oplus^k(\boldsymbol{w})$. As a result of the rewrite, all references to z in H are replaced by references to a fresh variable z' bound to $\oplus^k(z'_1, \ldots, z'_k)$ in H' with each z'_i bound to $F(w_i, \boldsymbol{v})[z'/z]$. We call z' the trace of z by Δ and we call the z'_i the fragments of z by Δ.*

Lemma A.4. *Say that $\sigma : H \lesssim K$ is strong on z if, for all $x \in \sigma^{-1}(z)$, if x is bound to $F(\boldsymbol{v})$ and F is pattern-matching, then v_1 is not labelled $\oplus$.*

Let K contain a redex Δ by one of the $\oplus$-lifting rules, let the root of Δ be z, and let $K \longrightarrow K'$ by Δ. If $\sigma : H \lesssim K$ is strong on z then there exists $\sigma' : H \lesssim K'$ such that σ' is strong on each of the fragments of z by Δ.

Lemma A.5. *Let $\Delta = (\rho, \sigma_\Delta)$ be a PT-redex in K and let z be the root of Δ. Let $\sigma : H \lesssim K$ be strong on z and let $\{x_1, \ldots, x_n\} = \{x \in \sigma^{-1}(z) \mid x \text{ is not bound to } \Omega\}$. Then:*

1. *There are only two possibilities for each x_i: (a) x_i is the root of a redex $\Delta_i = (\rho, \sigma_i)$ in H; (b) x_i is bound to $F(y_i, \boldsymbol{v})$ in H with F pattern-matching and y_i bound to Ω (thus x_i is the root of a ΩL redex).*
2. *For $1 \leq i \leq n$ define J_i according to the cases in part (1): (a) $J_i = (\mathrm{rhs}(\rho))^{\sigma_i}$; (b) $J_i = \Omega$. If $K \longrightarrow K'$ by Δ, then $\mathrm{GC}(\overline{H[\boldsymbol{x} \leftarrow \boldsymbol{J}]}) \lesssim K'$.*

Checking Cleanness in Linked Lists

Nurit Dor[1,*], Michael Rodeh[2], and Mooly Sagiv[1]

[1] Department of Computer Science, Tel-Aviv University, Israel
{nurr,sagiv}@math.tau.ac.il
[2] IBM Research Laboratory in Haifa

Abstract. A new algorithm is presented that automatically uncovers memory errors such as NULL pointers dereference and memory leaks in C programs. The algorithm is *conservative*, i.e., it can never miss an error but may report "false alarms". When applied to several intricate C programs manipulating singly linked lists, the new algorithm yields more accurate results, does not report **any** false alarm and usually runs even faster and consumes less space than a less precise algorithm.

1 Introduction

Many nasty bugs result from misusing memory by NULL pointer dereference, access to freed storage, or memory leaks. We refer to these errors as **memory cleanness errors** since they should never occur in bug-free programs. No wonder that many academic and commercial projects are aimed at producing tools that detect classes of memory cleanness problems (see Section 4.1).

This paper does not intend to introduce another shape analysis or pointer analysis algorithms. Instead, we focus on detecting cleanness violations by using such algorithms. The main result of this research is a cleanness checking algorithm that detects non-trivial bugs but does not yield too many false alarms. We focus on C programs. However cleanness violations including the one addressed by this paper also occur in Java programs. Some of them are detected by the Java virtual machine at run-time[1].

1.1 Main Results

In this paper we describe algorithms that automatically discover memory cleanness errors in C programs. The algorithms are *conservative*, i.e., they never miss an error but they may generate "false alarms". We applied the algorithms to C programs which manipulate singly linked lists. Two major results have been obtained:

---

* This research was supported by a grant from the Ministry of Science,Israel.

[1] The third top ranked bug by Java users in Sun's bug parade site as for August 1999 http://developer.java.sun.com/developer/bugParade/bugs/4014323.html deals with Java's image memory leaks. Users report system crashes due to such memory leaks.

J. Palsberg (Ed.): SAS 2000, LNCS 1824, pp. 115–135, 2000.

- A new, efficient and quite precise algorithm for detecting memory cleanness errors (see Section 2). It does not yield **any** false alarm on quite intricate C programs (see Table 1). On programs manipulating more complicated data structures such as cyclic lists and tree, it produces false alarms. It represents memory states as Shape Graphs with Reachability from stack variables (see [5]) and thus we call it $SG+R$. To assess the usability of our new algorithm we implemented it using PAG – a program analyzer generator developed at Saarland University [15]. On bad examples $SG+R$ can be rather slow. However, it is reasonably efficient on non-trivial programs that we tried. It runs significantly faster than the algorithm described in [5] since it avoids the cost of transitive closure. It also compares favorably with verification systems aimed at showing memory cleanness since it does not require loop invariants. Interestingly, $SG+R$ runs significantly faster than the verification system described in [13] on the programs we tried. For example, on the procedure swap shown in Fig. 1(c) the $SG+R$ algorithm runs in less than 0.01 seconds as opposed to 21.

program	description
search.c	searches for an element in a linked list
null_deref.c	searches a linked list but with a typical error of not checking for the end of the list
delete.c	deletes a given element from a linked list
del_all.c	deletes an entire linked list
insert.c	inserts an element into a sorted linked list
merge.c	merges two sorted linked lists into one sorted list
reverse.c	reverses a linked list via destructive updates
fumble.c	an erroneous version of reverse.c which loses the list
rotate.c	performs a cyclic rotation when given pointers to the first and last elements
swap.c	swaps the first and second elements of a list, fails when the list is 1 element long (see Fig. 1)

Table 1. Description of the analyzed programs. Some of these interesting programs are from *LCLint* [7], [13] and from first-year students. They are all in the format shown in Fig. 1 and available at http://www.math.tau.ac.il/~nurr.

- We use two of the well known pointer analysis techniques to check cleanness and compare their cost and effectiveness to our new algorithm. The first technique is **flow-sensitive points-to** analysis [1,24] (referred to as PT). The second algorithm, SG, uses Shape Graphs and is a slight variant of the shape analysis technique described in [21]. The SG algorithm is similar to $SG+R$ except that it does not (explicitly) track reachability from stack variables. Our results are reported in Table 2 and Table 3. We compare time, space and the number of false alarms. We believe that space is more important than time since it is less implementation dependent and since it is normally the bottleneck in scaling program analysis algorithms to handle large programs (see also Section 3). We conclude that:

- As expected, the PT algorithm is the cheapest of the three but it is quite imprecise. In fact, it cannot be used at all to check for memory leakage errors which are quite problematic even in Java.
- The SG algorithm is less effective than the $SG+R$ algorithm and is sometimes slower. This is an evidence to a general phenomenon in program analysis were a less precise algorithm can be sometimes less efficient in practice since the less precise algorithm may fail to detect the important program invariants, thereby, abstracting situations that can never occur in the program and thus consuming more time and space.

program	$SG+R$		SG		PT	
	time	space	time	space	time	space
search.c	0.02	860	0.04	934	0.01	357
null_deref.c	0.03	968	0.02	1042	0.02	403
delete.c	0.05	1632	0.1	2147	0.01	560
del_all.c	0.02	400	0.01	446	0.01	317
insert.c	0.02	1834	0.05	2272	0.03	1035
merge.c	2.08	4931	1718	138466	0	810
reverse.c	0.03	922	0.03	946	0.01	380
fumble.c	0.04	868	0.04	803	0.02	343
rotate.c	0.01	886	0.01	969	0	552
swap.c	0	478	0.01	573	0	295

Table 2. The CPU time (in seconds) and space (counted as the total number of edges, see Section 3) used to analyze the tested programs using the three implementations.

1.2   Limitations

The $SG+R$ algorithm does not handle pointer arithmetic, casting, and function pointers. There are also a few simplifying assumptions for ease of implementation. These features, which we can handle but preferred to ignore in this implementation, are: (i) address-of; (ii) arrays; and (iii) recursive functions. The current implementation analyzes programs and handle procedures by call-string [25] which is provided by PAG.

1.3   Outline of the Rest of this Paper

The rest of this paper in organized as follows. Section 2 describes the $SG+R$ algorithm. Section 3 describes the implementations and compares the algorithms.

program	real errors	false alarms					
		$SG+R$		SG		PT	
		leak	ref	leak	ref	leak	ref
search.c	0	0	0	2	0	5	0
null_deref.c	3	0	0	2	0	5	0
delete.c	0	0	0	2	0	7	0
del_all.c	0	0	0	0	0	6	4
insert.c	0	0	0	2	0	7	1
merge.c	0	0	0	6	0	8	5
reverse.c	0	0	0	0	0	7	0
fumble.c	1	0	0	0	0	6	0
rotate.c	0	0	0	2	0	5	1
swap.c	3	0	0	0	0	5	0

Table 3. The precision of the three algorithms in terms of false alarms reported on the tested programs (see Section 3).

We conclude by discussing related work and assessing the potential and limitations of our approach (Section 4).

2   The $SG+R$ Algorithm

This section describes the $SG+R$ algorithm for cleanness checking. The algorithm is a standard iterative dataflow analysis algorithm (e.g., see [16]). It iteratively computes a finite set of "abstract descriptions" of all the stores that occur at a given program point. It starts with the abstract description of the initial store at the beginning of the program and then it repeatedly applies *transfer functions* for every program statement and condition until a fixed point is reached. Upon termination, it checks the cleanness conditions against the abstract description.

The algorithm is *conservative*, i.e., upon termination, every store that can possibly occur when the execution of a program reaches a given program point, *pt*, is described by some abstract description computed at *pt*. However, it may happen that an abstract description at *pt* describes a store that cannot occur at *pt*, either because the class of inputs that is being considered is too broad or since the algorithm over approximates the storage configurations. This means that the algorithm can never miss a potential error but may report "false alarms."

The rest of this section is organized as follows: In Section 2.1, our memory abstraction is described. Then, in Section 2.2, we demonstrate the transfer functions. Finally, in Section 2.3 we explain how cleanness is checked.

2.1 Shape Graphs with Reachability

A *shape graph* is an abstraction of the memory states in which the actual values of both data and pointer cells are ignored. Instead, the shape graph captures the "shape" of the data structures and the relationships between different stack (and static) pointer variables. Heap cells are represented by *shape-nodes* and sets of "indistinguishable" heap cells are represented by a single shape-node, called a *summary-node*. The number of these shape graphs depends on the program but not on its input.

Fig. 1(a) shows a declaration of a linked list data type in C and the main function that creates the list and then invokes the **swap** function shown in Fig. 1(c) that swaps the first two elements via destructive updating. This program is used as a running example in this section. Fig. 2 shows the three shape graphs that occur when the $SG+R$ algorithm analyzes the **create_list** function: the shape graph g_1 represents the situation in which c is NULL; g_2 represents a one element linked list, g_3 represents linked list of two or more elements pointed-to by c. In g_3, the shape node n_2 represents the tail of the list pointed-to by c.

```
                          List* create_list() {
   typedef struct           List *e,*c;
   node {                   int i,size;                    List* swap(List *c) {
     struct node *n;                                         List *p;
     int data;              c = NULL;                        s₁: if ( c!=NULL) {
   } List;                  scanf("%d",&size);               s₂:   p = c;
                            for(i=0; i<size; i++) {          s₃:   c = c→n;
                              e = malloc(sizeof(List));      s₄:   p→n = c→n;
   main() {                   e→data = i;                    s₅:   c→n = p;
     List *c;                 e→next = c;                    }
     c = create_list();       c = e;                         s₆: return c;
     c = swap(c);           }                              }
   }                        return c;
                          }
         (a)                        (b)                            (c)
```

Fig. 1. A C program with (a) a declaration of a linked list data type and a main function, (b) a function that creates a NULL terminated list and (c) a function that uses destructive updating to swap the first two elements of a list.

Formally, a shape graph is a directed graph with a set of shape-nodes, *variable-edges* connecting pointer variables to shape nodes, and *selector-edges* connecting shape nodes.

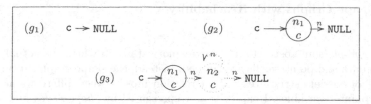

Fig. 2. The shape graphs that arise from the analysis of the `create_list` function shown in Fig. 1(b). Shape nodes are circles, named by n_i. Appearance of name p below the name n_i means, "the cell(s) represented by n_i are reachable from p", i.e., $p \in reach(n)$.

Shape Node A shape node n has the following properties:

- The set $ptb(n)$ consists of the stack variables that are directly pointing to all the concrete heap cells represented by n. In g_3, $ptb(n_1) = \{c\}$ and $ptb(n_2) = \emptyset$. In the shape graph there is a variable-edge from every variable in $ptb(n)$ to the node n. For vividness reasons, the ptb property is not displayed in the figures inside the shape node. Note, that exactly one heap cell is represented by n if $ptb(n)$ is nonempty.
- The set $reach(n)$ consist of the stack variables that via (chains of) selectors reach all the concrete heap cells represented by n. In graph, g_3, $reach(n_1) = \{c\}$ and $reach(n_2) = \{c\}$ since all heap cells represented by n_2 are reachable-from c. Pictorially we display the variables in $reach$ of a node below the name of the node.

  The shape graph shown in Fig. 3 corresponds to a memory state in which c points to a linked list of length four or more, and x points in between the second and the last element of the list. Node n_1 represents the first list element, n_3 represents the element pointed-to by x. Node n_2 represents all the elements between the element pointed-to by c and the element pointed-to by x. It has the properties $ptb(n_2) = \emptyset$ and $reach(n_2) = \{c\}$. Node n_4 represents all the list elements that are the tail of the list, it has the properties $ptb(n_4) = \emptyset$ and $reach(n_4) = \{c, x\}$. Nodes n_2 and n_4 are distinguishable as they represent disjoint sets of heap cells.

- The Boolean flag $unshared(n)$ holds the value $true$ for nodes representing heap cells that cannot be pointed-to by more than one selector. In g_3, $unshared(n_1) = true$ and $unshared(n_2) = true$, since no heap cell represented by n_2 can be pointed-to by two or more selectors. This implies that two incoming selector-edges into n_2 cannot simultaneously occur in any concrete state of data store.

  As a matter of notation we use the term $is(n)$ to describe nodes n with $unshared(n) = false$. For example, n_3 in shape graph g_{12} of Fig. 4 is shared.

- The Boolean flag $alloc(n)$ indicates nodes which represent allocated heap cells. This flag is false for nodes representing freed memory cells. We need this information to detect usage of dead storage.
- The Boolean flag $unique(n)$ indicates that n is a *unique node*, i.e., it represents exactly one heap cell. Nodes n with $unique(n) = false$ may represent more than one heap cell and are therefore called *summary nodes*. The node n_2 in g_3 is a summary node. Summary nodes are drawn as dotted circles.

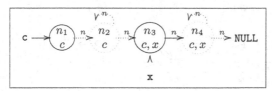

Fig. 3. A shape graph that arises in the $SG+R$ algorithm when x traverses a linked list pointed-to by c.

There is a special shape node NULL representing NULL pointers. It is important to understand that properties of a node are conservative approximations of the actual properties of all the heap cells represented by that node. For instance, every pointer variable in $reach(n)$ must reach all heap cells represented by n but the converse need not hold, it may be that a variable x does not belong to $reach(n)$ and yet for every heap cell, l, represented by n there is a selector path from x to l. In particular, a node n with $reach(n) = \emptyset$ may represent nongarbage storage. Similar situation holds for the Boolean flags. If some Boolean property, B, holds for a node n then for all heap cells represented by n B holds. The opposite need not hold. For example node n with $unique(n) = false$ may represent a single heap cell.

Selector Edges There are two types of selector-edges: *definite* and *indefinite*. Definite edges are drawn as solid lines and indefinite edges are drawn as dotted lines (the reader may notice the analogy with [22] which is not explained here for reasons of space). Selector edges are labeled with the name of the selector.

An indefinite selector-edge from a node m into n indicates that the heap cells represented by m may have a selector into a heap cell represented by n. In g_3, the indefinite edge from n_2 to itself represents selectors into next list elements. This is an indefinite edge since it might not hold for all the heap cells represented by n_2, e.g., between the second and the fourth element. In some situations, the analysis can be more precise by taking into account the fact that a selector-edge is definite, i.e., it always exists.

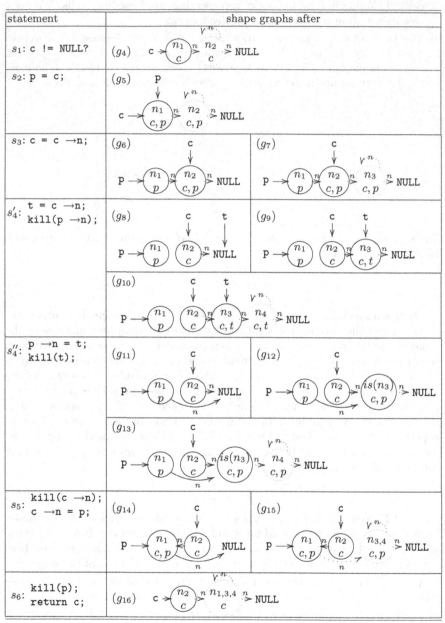

Fig. 4. The shape graphs that arise when the $SG+R$ algorithm is applied to the function in Fig. 1(c) with the input shape graph g_3 of Fig. 2.

2.2   Handling Statements and Conditions

In this section we sketch the application of the iterative algorithm to the running example. The algorithm iteratively computes a set of shape graphs at every program point. To guarantee that the number of shape graphs is finite, we merge shape nodes with the same properties to summary nodes. This causes a lose in precision but ensures that the algorithm terminates. Note that the number of shape nodes can be exponential in the number of stack variables. However, measurements reported in the next section seem to indicate that this is not a problem, at least for the tested programs.

The iterative algorithm analyzes the running example by applying the sequence of transfer functions belonging to the statements of the swap function to each of the shape graphs in Fig. 2. Conditions are partly analyzed and shape graphs are not propagated if the condition is not met. In the analysis of g_1 the condition at statement s_1 is not met and the shape graph is immediately propagated to the **return** statement s_6. The analysis of g_2 is not explained here. Instead, Fig. 4 follows the evolution of g_3, which is the interesting one. The condition at statement s_1 is met and g_3 is propagated to statement s_2.

Statement s_2 generates a shape graph representing concrete stores where c and p point to the heap cell represented by n_1. Therefore, in g_5, node n_1 represents a heap cell pointed-to by c and p and thus $ptb(n_1) = \{c, p\}$. Also, since n_2 represents heap cells reachable-from c before the statement, after the statement it represents heap cells reachable-from c and p and thus $reach(n_2) = \{c, p\}$. We see that for this statement, the update of reachability information is fairly simple. We defer the explanation of updating reachability of general assignments to the end of this subsection.

One of the interesting and complicated aspects of shape analysis is the way linked lists are traversed. Statement s_3 demonstrates this: in the shape graph before this statement (g_5) we know that n_2 is unshared ($unshared(n_2) = true$). Therefore (only) two types of concrete memory states can be represented by this shape graph: (i) memory states in which c and p both point to lists with exactly two elements, and (ii) memory states in which c and p both point to lists of length three or more. The shape analysis algorithm conservatively assumes that both situations can happen. Hence, the statement c=c→n leads to two shape graphs g_6 and g_7. The difference between these graphs is the presence of a summary node n_3 in g_7 indicating that the list contains more than two elements. In both of these shape graphs, n_1 represents heap cells pointed-to by (and reached-by) p while n_2 represents heap cells pointed-to by c and reachable-from p and c. Node n_3 in g_7 represents heap cells not pointed-to by any variables but reachable-from p and c. This operation of advancing a pointer down the list is called *materialization* in [3,21] since a new shape node (in this example the node pointed-to by c was materialized).

Now, statement s_4 is analyzed on the two shape graphs resulting from statement s_3. Our implementation uses a front-end to break complicated statements into simpler ones in a usual way. Every assignment of the form $l = r$ is performed by: (i) generating a new temporary, say t, to store r; (ii) uninitializing l, denoted by kill(l); (iii) assigning t to l; and (iv) uninitializing t (of course the first and the last stages can be sometimes avoided). So far, we have ignored this issue for ease of understanding. Since s_4 is rather complex, we chose to break this statement into four stages (as in the implementation). For reasons of space, we show two stages at each row in Fig. 4.

The effect of statement t = c→n on g_6 is simply to assign NULL to t, and then kill(p→n) removes the selector edge from the heap cell pointed-to by p. As a result, in g_8, n_1 does not have selector edges. Also, the only heap cell reachable-from p is the one directly pointed-to by p, represented by n_1.

The effect of statement t = c→n on g_7 is to materialize a new node representing the heap cell pointed-to by t, thus generating two graphs and then kill(p→n) removes the selector edge from the heap cell pointed-to by p. As a result, node n_1 in the resulting shape graphs g_9 and g_{10} does not have selector edges. Also, the only heap cell reachable-from p is the one directly pointed-to by p, represented by n_1.

Next, the assignment p→n = t is performed on g_8 which connects the selector edge of n_1 to NULL and then kill(t) results in g_{11}. Performing this assignment on g_9 and g_{10} is more interesting since before this statement the heap cell represented by n_3 may have an incoming selector edge. Therefore, this statement results in $unshared(n_3)$ set to $false$. After kill(t), we get the graph g_{12} (from g_9) and g_{13} (from g_{10}). Note that n_3 and n_4 in g_{13} are not merged since n_3 has $unshared = false$ and n_4 has $unshared = true$. As we shall see, this is what allows us to eventually conclude that c points to a linked list at s_6. The update of reachability for this statement is explained in Section 2.2.

The statement kill(c→n) at s_5 also performs destructive update on the selector from c which removes the selector edge from the heap cell pointed-to by c into the heap cell pointed-to by c→n. Therefore, the analysis removes the selector edge from n_2. Moreover, the heap cell represented by n_3 is unshared, causing $unshared(n_3)$ to be set to $true$, but now n_3 and n_4 have the same properties (excluding $unique$ which is not used as a node distinction). Thus, these nodes are merged, and therefore after c→n = p we get g_{15} where node $n_{3,4}$ corresponds to n_3 and n_4 in g_{13} and to n_3 in g_{12}.

Before statement s_6, we join the abstract representation from the true path and the false path of the if statement at s_1. Since at each program point, we maintain a set of shape graphs, the join is a set-union operation generating the set containing graphs g_1,g_{14},g_{15} and more (those evolved from g_2). This operation is not shown in Fig. 4 since it only follows the evolution of g_3.

At statement s_6, the local variables are uninitialized and thus kill(p) causes $ptb(n_1)$ from g_{14} to be set to empty, and thus nodes n_1 and $n_{3,4}$ are now merged, resulting in g_{16}.

The reader is referred to [21,22,17] for more elaborations on shape analysis algorithms. Our way of conservatively and efficiently updating reachability in linear time is new and thus explained in the next subsection.

Updating Reachability A statement such as s_4 which assigns a new value to a selector of a variable p can affect the reachability from other stack variables "upstream" from p→n. Fig. 5(a) contains an interesting concrete store which demonstrates the most complicated case arising in cyclic graphs. If the statement kill(y→n) is performed on this store, l_4 will no longer be reachable-from x but l_2 (and l_1 and l_3) will. Our current analysis therefore conservatively handles reachability in this case: we remove the reachability from all the variables x that can reach the heap cell pointed-to by y. Thus, when the statement is performed on Fig. 5(b), we conservatively lose the fact that x is in $reach(n_2)$. In our running example as well as in all the other programs this does not lead to false alarms since no cyclic lists are created. The advantage of our simplified approach is that it can be implemented in time linear in the size of the shape graph. A more precise and more expensive solution is described in [20].

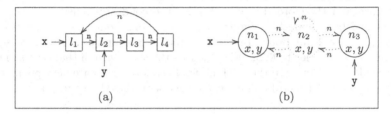

Fig. 5. A cyclic concrete store (a) and the corresponding shape graph (b).

2.3   Cleanness Checking

Every statement has a cleanness precondition, i.e., a requirement that every store occurring at this statement must satisfy. For example a statement, st, of the form y = x requires that x points to either NULL or to an allocated heap cell before this statement. For example, st is not clean when x is uninitialized or refers to a freed heap cell. Our tool conservatively checks cleanness preconditions by investigating the resulting shape graphs. For each shape graph g that occurs before a statement st, we impose conditions that guarantee that the preconditions of st are met by every store represented by g. These conditions are explained below. They can be justified using the theory of abstract interpretation, see [4]. This is beyond the scope of this paper. Since the iterative algorithm is itself conservative, we conclude that our tool can never miss a cleanness violation.

For each program point, our tool displays the shape graphs that violate the cleanness conditions with an appropriate error message. The programmer can see results of the analysis graphically and determine whether it is an error or a false alarm. Of course, false alarms can be generated when the shape graph at a given point describes memory states that can never occur at that point. However, since the analysis is conservative, it will never miss a cleanness violation. We try to avoid reporting cleanness errors from the same cause at different program points.

We conclude this subsection by specifying the cleanness conditions on shape graphs.

Pointer Reference Condition When referring to a pointer x we check that there is a definite variable-edge from x to a node n with $alloc(n) = true$. (For simplicity, the NULL node has $alloc = true$). Here, we use the fact that the analysis guarantees that if x can be uninitialized it must yield a shape graph where there is no variable-edge from x. Similarly, if x may point to a freed storage, there must be a shape graph where there is a selector edge from x to a node n with $alloc(n) = false$. All references in our running example are safe.

Pointer Dereference Condition Every pointer dereference should produce a reference and therefore the pointer reference condition must hold and also there should be no variable edge from x to the NULL node. For example, when analyzing the swap function in Fig. 1(c) on the shape graph g_2 in Fig. 2 we report a potential dereference to NULL. Fig. 6 shows the shape graph that arises. There is a variable edge from c to the NULL node. Therefore, the statement p→n=c→n is not safe. The tool reports an error message with this shape graph.

Memory Leakage Condition The memory leakage precondition is more complicated and we will explain it on each of the two operations kill(x) and kill(x→n), where memory leakage can occur. We only check memory leakage if the statement does not raise other cleanness errors explained before.

When the statement kill(x) is applied, we need to assure that either: (i) x is uninitialized; (ii) x is pointing to NULL; or (iii) x is pointing to a heap cell which is also reachable from a different stack variable y. On the shape graph we check that either: (i) There is no variable edge from x; (ii) There is a variable edge from x to NULL; or (iii) There is a variable edge from x to a node n and either: (a) there is a different variable y, $y \in ptb(n)$ or $y \in reach(n)$; or (b) there is a definite incoming selector edge into n.

The condition (iii)(b) may seem surprising since a definite incoming selector-edge may only emanate from a node n' representing garbage heap cells. In this case we choose not to report memory leakage since this error was issued when n' became inaccessible.

When the statement kill(x→n) is applied, we need to assure that either: (i) x→n is uninitialized; (ii) x→n is pointing to NULL; or (iii) the heap cell pointed-to by x→n can be reached from a different stack variable y.

On the shape graph, let n_x be target of the variable-edge from x (which must exist since this statement does not raise a dereference violation). We check that either: (i) There is no selector-edge from n_x. (ii) There is a unique selector-edge from n_x and it is to NULL. (iii) For each successor node, n', of n_x (a node that has an incoming selector-edge from n_x) either: (a) there is a different variable y, $y \in ptb(n')$ or $y \in reach(n')$, or (b) there is a definite incoming selector edge into n'.

Note that this case is slightly more complicated than the kill(x) case mainly because there can be more than one outgoing selector-edge from n_x. As before we try to avoid reporting the same error twice.

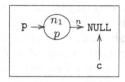

Fig. 6. A shape graph that arises after statement s_3, c=c→n, when the shape analysis algorithm is applied to the function in Figure 1(c) with input shape graph g_2 in Fig. 2.

3   Comparison

In this section we describe the implementation of the algorithms and analyze the results of applying the algorithms to the programs listed in Table 1.

3.1   Implementation Issues

All algorithms were implemented using PAG. The time is measured by PAG running on a Linux system on a PC Pentium 166 Mhz with 128MB.

All analyses conservatively take into account conditions of the form of pointer (in)equalities. For ease of implementation, the treatment of NULL pointers is improved by source-to-source transformation that uses a special variable to indicate NULL. The cleanness checking is for: (i) NULL dereference; (ii) usage of uninitialized pointers; (iii) usage of dead storage; and (iv) memory leakage.

The *PT* analysis computes the well-known points-to information. It represents the possibly many objects allocated at calls to malloc by creating a named object based on the number of the node in the control flow graph (CFG). The analysis is flow-sensitive, i.e., it considers the control flow of the program. For detecting usages of uninitialized storage we keep a special location called **garbage** which all pointers are initialized to. An additional analysis that enables the removal of over-conservative selector edges to garbage is done. The analysis indicates storage that may have been freed.

Cleanness checking in the *PT* algorithm is rather straightforward. The cleanness preconditions are: (i) In a reference to pointer x, x should not point to **garbage** or to a possibly freed storage; (ii) In a dereference to pointer x, x must not point to NULL; (iii) In assignments to x, the precondition is that another pointer or selector points to the same location as x. Note that in our example the pointers points-to the heap. Therefore, in every assignment to a previously assigned pointer we report a potential memory leakage. This is since we can not guarantee that another pointer points to the same location as x.

The SG algorithm is similar to the $SG+R$ algorithm but it does not track down the reachability information. A node in the shape graph is not characterized by the set of reached-by variables. In practice, the SG and the $SG+R$ algorithms are the same implementation with a flag indicating whether to update or not the reachability. Cleanness checking in the SG algorithm is exactly the same as in the $SG+R$ algorithm but in the SG algorithm $reach(n)$ is always empty.

The SG algorithm is a slight improvement, in terms of precision of the [21] algorithm in that the SG algorithm computes a set of shape graphs for each point in the program while the [21] algorithm combines the different shape graphs at a program point to one shape graph. This implies that the [21] algorithm will have at least as many false alarms as the SG algorithm but we do not know if it will run faster.

Precision Table 3 lists the number of real errors in the program (three of the tested programs are incorrect) and the number of false alarms reported by the algorithms. All algorithms are conservative, they do not miss any errors. Therefore, the interesting number is the number of false alarms. Measuring false alarms provides a true indication as to the precision of the pointer analysis as opposed to say, the number of shape graphs or points-to pairs. We classify the false alarms into two types. The first type, *leak*, are false alarms on memory leakage. The *ref* false alarms column counts pointer reference and pointer dereference false alarms (see Sections 2.3 for the $SG+R$ algorithm). The reason for this separation is that one does expects the PT algorithm to effectively detect pointer reference errors but not memory leakage errors.

From the table we can establish the following observations:

- The $SG+R$ algorithm yields no false alarms on the tested programs. This indicates that the abstraction used by the $SG+R$ algorithm has the exact precision needed for analyzing the linked list programs. It does generate false alarms on tree manipulation programs or when infeasible control flow paths are conservatively taken into account.
- The SG algorithm does not yield false alarms of type *ref*. This indicates that the relation between program variables which is kept by the abstraction of the SG algorithm in the nodes' *ptb* property is enough to avoid *ref* false alarms.
- Explicit reachability information is needed to avoid false alarms on memory leakage. The SG algorithm reports false alarms on memory leakage on almost all programs. A common false alarm, repeated in many programs, is upon correctly traversing a list. Fig. 7 is an example of a shape graph that arises when traversing a list inside a loop. This graph represents a data structure where c points to the head and x points to an element (third and on) inside the structure[2]. Processing the statement x=x→n generates a false alarm on

---

[2] From this shape graph we do not know that it represents a list.

memory leakage. This is because node n_3 is not pointed-to by any other variable, it does not have a definite incoming edge and we do not know that it is reachable-from c. In the $SG+R$ algorithm these false alarms are avoided since we know that the node is reachable-from c.

- The PT algorithm is useless for checking memory leakage. Every assignment to a previously allocated heap pointer is a potential leakage. This is unfortunate since there are true bugs in programs that are only detected when checking for memory leaks. For example, the program `fumble.c` that erroneously loses part of the list.

- The PT algorithm is not precise enough to avoid false alarms of type *ref*. In four out of the ten programs it reports false alarms, most of them on NULL dereference. The PT algorithm does not track information about relations between the variables in the program needed in order to correctly analyze conditions and to avoid false alarms.

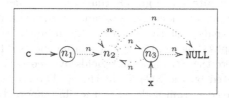

Fig. 7. A shape graph that arise by the SG algorithm when correctly traversing a linked list. Processing the statement x=x→n on this shape graph yields a false alarm.

Cost Table 2 lists the time and space requirements of the implementations on the analyzed programs. The PT algorithm is the fastest, running a few milliseconds on all programs. The $SG+R$ and SG algorithms are similar in the time requirement with one exception, the program `merge.c`. This is the most complicated program to analyze and the $SG+R$ algorithm runs significantly faster than the SG algorithm.

The time measurement is not a precise comparison since it is dependent on both the PAG and our not-very-efficient implementation. Although the space and time measurements fit one another very well, we regard the space measurement as a more precise comparison. We count the space as the number of total edges (variables and selectors) arising in all points in the program. For the PT algorithm an edge corresponds to a points-to pair. In all programs the space requirement was the smallest in the PT algorithm.

The space comparison between the SG and the $SG+R$ is surprising. The worst case space-complexity of the SG algorithm is smaller than that of the $SG+R$ algorithm. But, the space requirement of the SG algorithm is larger than that of the $SG+R$ algorithm. In all programs but one the number of edges in the SG algorithm is greater than that of the $SG+R$ algorithm.

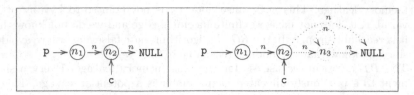

Fig. 8. The shape graphs that arise after statement c=c→n when the SG algorithm is applied to the function shown in Figure 1(c) on a shape graph representing a linked list of length two or more elements (g_3 shown in Fig. 2 without reachability).

The reason for this extra edges is that in the SG algorithm there is less information, it does not contain any explicit information on the reachability from stack variables. This lack of information causes the analysis to be over-conservative and generate shape graphs that are not generated by the $SG+R$ algorithm. For example, consider the program swap.c shown in Fig. 1 and the result of the $SG+R$ analysis on this program shown in Fig. 4. The SG algorithm yields the shape graphs shown in Fig. 8 after statement s_3. This is the first point of the program where the SG algorithm yields over-conservative shape graphs that are not generated by the $SG+R$ algorithm. The second shape graph has an over-conservative edge from node n_2 to the NULL node. This edge will cause the analysis to generate more redundant shape graphs as it progress through the program.

Additional information used to compare the SG and the $SG+R$ algorithms is the total number of shape graphs that arise during the analysis and the maximal number of shape graphs generated at a single point in the program. Table 4 lists this information[3]. Again, in all programs but one the SG generates more shape graphs than the $SG+R$ algorithm.

4   Conclusion

4.1   Related Work

Dynamic Cleanness Checking The vast majority of cleanness checking tools detect violations at run-time (e.g., see [2,29,18]). They can be effective in localizing the source of a violation — where a NULL pointer is dereferenced or where leaking memory is created. The Java run-time environment also checks for memory violations. However, it is clear that the effectiveness of run-time checking depends on the proper choice of test cases to uncover violations. Since run-time tools are intrusive, they are rarely used when the code is run in production. For example, the experimental results of Safe-C [2] show that execution

---

[3] This information is unavailable for the PT algorithm since in this algorithm there is only one set of points-to relations for each point in the program.

program	$SG+R$		SG	
	total	max	total	max
search.c	202	14	217	17
null_deref.c	226	20	241	23
delete.c	296	21	374	26
del_all.c	118	8	144	6
insert.c	301	17	362	19
merge.c	444	46	11416	1393
reverse.c	194	14	202	14
fumble.c	191	14	186	12
rotate.c	148	5	157	6
swap.c	134	5	144	6

Table 4. A comparison between the $SG+R$ and the SG algorithms of the total number of shape graphs (column 1) and the maximal number of shape graphs that arises at a single point in the program (column 2).

overhead of cleanness checking ranges from 130% to 540%. These tools demand manual runs and therefore they do not assure us against bugs.

Of course, any conservative tool including ours can also be used in conjunction with a dynamic tool to reduce the cost of run-time checks. The static tool can indicate which run-time checks are redundant. For example, the absence of memory leakage implies that garbage collection need not be invoked.

Static Cleanness Checking The *LCLint* tool can discover certain cleanness violations by statically analyzing programs. The tool, which both industry and academia use, has already been successfully applied to uncover some bugs in real life C programs. It is quite efficient but is less ambitious than the SG and the $SG+R$ algorithms on heap allocated data structures. It requires the user to supply annotations. It simplifies the analysis of loops by making it non conservative. For example, it does not detect the error in program null_deref.c. Similar comments go to the Prefix tool [19].

Compaq's Systems Research Center also aims at developing tools for static cleanness checking [6]. They have developed a tool called *Extended Static Checking* that uses verification technology, but feels to the programmer more like a type-checker. It requires simple annotations of pre- and post-conditions from the programmer. The tool uses program verification to find violations of certain cleanness conditions, such as NULL dereference and array bound violations. The tool was originally designed for Modula3 and was ported for Java. The $SG+R$ algorithm compares favorably with the ESC tool for programs manipulating linked list since we automatically infer strong invariants. However, we currently cannot precisely handle arrays.

The algorithm of [13] is able to verify not only that a program is clean but also to show that it is correct with respect to a given partial specification. However, it depends on user-provided loop invariants, it is applicable only to a subset of Pascal, and its complexity is non elementary, i.e. $2^{2^{2^{\cdot}}}$. Our comparisons indicate that the $SG+R$ algorithm is faster by a factor of 10 to 100 than their algorithm.

Fradet, Gaugne, and Le Métayer suggest a Hoare-like logic that defines programs that obey the no-NULL dereference cleanness condition in a subset of C [9]. Although they propose a conservative algorithm that automatically checks a subset of the logic, this method cannot be extended to automatically check many programs since it cannot always phrase the loop invariants.

It is possible to use slicing techniques [11,12,8] to locate cleanness violations. However, current-slicing techniques yield very conservative results in languages that support pointers and references (especially in the presence of recursive data structures). In other words, it seems that current slicing tools will yield an excessive number of false alarms.

Related Work on Pointer Analysis Many conservative algorithm were proposed to analyze the content of the heap (e.g., [14,3,26,10,22]). Each of these algorithms can be used to provide conservative cleanness with different levels of cost and effectiveness. However, it should be noted that the practical benefits of these algorithms are not proved yet (despite the interesting results in [28] which shows that shape analysis can be used for parallelizations). Therefore, we believe that our work contributes to the understanding of the benefits, costs, and limitations of pointer analysis in general and shape analysis in particular.

4.2   Usability and Scalability

The usability of cleanness checking tools depend on many factors including: (i) The ability to detect nontrivial bugs; (ii) The ease of use; and (iii) The ability to scale for large realistic programs. An easy to use tool should: (i) Report minimal false alarms; (ii) Demand minimal interaction with the user in general, in particular annotations; and (iii) Provide useful error messages.

In this paper, we focused on the aspect of detection of nontrivial bugs and on ease-of-use. We are encouraged by the fact that $SG+R$ can detect bugs in C programs manipulating singly linked lists without any false alarms. Our tool is automatic, it analyzes the program without any interaction with the user and it runs reasonably fast. We use PAG and the XVCG tool [23] for pictorial representation of the shape graphs and the CFG. Last, the algorithm have already generalized to handle many data structures including trees and doubly linked lists [22].

The worst case complexity of our algorithm is quite high. It is linear in the size of the shape graphs. The number of shape nodes is exponential in the number of pointer stack variables and the number of shape graphs is exponential in the number of shape nodes. But the average time and space requirements of our algorithm depend on the number of different aliasing configuration between program variables. Our initial experience indicates that this number does not necessarily correspond to the program size. For example, it takes 360 CPU seconds to analyze a C program of size 1106 lines, and we generated 20 cleanness messages.

Scaling our techniques for real large programs without generating too many false alarms is a task that will take a significant effort. Examples of techniques that may be useful are:

- User annotations can help, e.g., by requiring that the programmer specifies pre- and post-conditions. One possibility is to use C assert statements or Java extensions such as [27].
- Better interprocedural analysis can improve the precision and the cost of the analysis. Currently we use the automatic call-string approach of PAG to handle procedures. This approach is inadequate since it is both imprecise and expensive.
- Programming languages such as Java simplify cleanness checking by restricting pointer manipulations and by supporting object oriented programming. This can help in improving the efficiency and the effectiveness of static cleanness checking (as opposed to the Java virtual machine which enforces some cleanness at run-time).
- Finally in some cases, practical tools can be developed by ignoring several kinds of errors at the cost of not being conservative. For example, the Prefix tool assumes that procedure parameters are not aliased. This can lead to undetection of certain errors.

Acknowledgements

We are grateful to T. Ball for the merge.c program which has a high contribution to the understanding of the capabilities and limitations of our algorithms. We are also grateful for the helpful comments of T. Reps, N. Rinetskey and R. Wilhelm which led to substantial improvements to this paper.

References

1. L. O. Andersen. *Program Analysis and Specialization for the C Programming Language*. PhD thesis, DIKU, Univ. of Copenhagen, May 1994. 116
2. T.M. Austin, S.E. Breach, and G.S. Sohi. Efficient detection of all pointer and array access errors. In *SIGPLAN Conf. on Prog. Lang. Design and Impl.* ACM Press, 1994. 130
3. D.R. Chase, M. Wegman, and F. Zadeck. Analysis of pointers and structures. In *SIGPLAN Conf. on Prog. Lang. Design and Impl.*, pages 296–310, New York, NY, 1990. ACM Press. 123, 132
4. P. Cousot and R. Cousot. Systematic design of program analysis frameworks. In *Symp. on Princ. of Prog. Lang.*, pages 269–282, New York, NY, 1979. ACM Press. 125

5. N. Dor, M. Rodeh, and M. Sagiv. Detecting memory errors via static pointer analysis. In *Proceedings of the ACM SIGPLAN-SIGSOFT Workshop on Program Analysis for Software Tools and Engineering (PASTE'98)*, pages 27–34, June 1998. Available at "http://www.math.tau.ac.il/~ nurr/paste98.ps.gz". 116

6. Cop. Digital Equipment. Extended static checking. Available at "http://www.research.digital.com/SRC/esc/Esc.html", 1998. 131

7. D. Evans. Static detection of dynamic memory errors. In *SIGPLAN Conf. on Prog. Lang. Design and Impl.*, 1996. Available at "http://www.cs.virginia.edu/ evans/pldi96-abstract.html". 116

8. J. Field, G. Ramalingam, and F. Tip. Parametric program slicing. In *ACM Symp. on Princ. of Prog. Lang.*, pages 379–392, January 1995. 132

9. P. Fradet, R. Gaugne, and D. Métayer. Static detection of pointer errors: an axiomatisation and a checking algorithm. In *Proc. European Symposium on Programming, ESOP'96 , LNCS*, 1996. 132

10. R. Ghiya and L. Hendren. Putting pointer analysis to work. In *Symp. on Princ. of Prog. Lang.*, New York, NY, 1998. ACM Press. 132

11. S. Horwitz and T. Reps. The use of program dependence graphs in software engineering. In *Proceedings of the Fourteenth International Conference on Software Engineering*, pages 392–411. ACM, New York, May 1992. 132

12. D. Jackson. Aspect, an economical bug detector. In *Proceedings of the 13th International Conference on Software Engineering*, pages 13–22, May 1994. 132

13. J.L. Jensen, M.E. Joergensen, N.Klarlund, and M.I. Schwartzbach. Automatic verification of pointer programs using monadic second-order logic. In *SIGPLAN Conf. on Prog. Lang. Design and Impl.*, 1997. 116, 131

14. N.D. Jones and S.S. Muchnick. Flow analysis and optimization of Lisp-like structures. In S.S. Muchnick and N.D. Jones, editors, *Program Flow Analysis: Theory and Applications*, chapter 4, pages 102–131. Prentice-Hall, Englewood Cliffs, NJ, 1981. 132

15. Florian Martin. PAG – an efficient program analyzer generator. *International Journal on Software Tools for Technology Transfer*, 2(1):46–67, 1998. 116

16. Steven Muchnick. *Advanced Compiler Design and Implementation*. Morgan Kaufmann, 1997. 118

17. F. Nielson, H. R. Nielson, and C. L. Hankin. *Principles of Program Analysis*. Springer, 1999. 124

18. Cop. Parasoft. Insure++. Available at "http://www.parasoft.com/", 1999. 130

19. Cop. Prefixco. Prefix automated code reviewer. Available at "http://www.prefixco.com/", 1999. 131

20. M. Sagiv, T. Reps, and R. Wilhelm. Parametric shape analysis via 3-valued logic. Tech. Rep. TR-1383, Comp. Sci. Dept., Univ. of Wisconsin, Madison, WI, July 1998. Available at "http://www.cs.wisc.edu/wpis/papers/parametric.ps". 125

21. M. Sagiv, T. Reps, and R. Wilhelm. Solving shape-analysis problems in languages with destructive updating. *Trans. on Prog. Lang. and Syst.*, 20(1):1–50, January 1998. 116, 123, 124, 128

22. M. Sagiv, T. Reps, and R. Wilhelm. Parametric shape analysis via 3-valued logic. In *Symp. on Princ. of Prog. Lang.*, 1999. Available at "http://www.cs.wisc.edu/wpis/papers/popl99.ps". 121, 124, 132

23. G. Sander. Graph layout through the vcg tool. *Graph Drawing, DIMACS International Workshop GD'94*, pages 194–205, 1995. 132

24. M. Shapiro and S. Horwitz. Fast and accurate flow-insensitive points-to analysis. In *Symp. on Princ. of Prog. Lang.*, pages 1–14, 1997. 116

25. M. Sharir and A. Pnueli. Two approaches to interprocedural data flow analysis. In S.S. Muchnick and N.D. Jones, editors, *Program Flow Analysis: Theory and Applications*, chapter 7, pages 189–234. Prentice-Hall, Englewood Cliffs, NJ, 1981. 117

26. J. Stransky. A lattice for abstract interpretation of dynamic (Lisp-like) structures. *Inf. and Comp.*, 101(1):70–102, Nov. 1992. 132

27. Reliable Systems.   Icontract – desgin by contract.   Available at "http://www.reliable-systems.com/", 1999. 133

28. Emilio Zapata. Automatic parallelization of irregular applications. In *SPA99*, 1999. 132

29. B. Zorn and P. Hilfinger. A memory allocation profilers for c and lisp programs. Available at "ftp://gatekeeper.dec.com/pub/misc/mprof-3.0.tar.z", 1991. 130

Confidentiality Analysis of Mobile Systems

Jérôme Feret

Laboratoire d'Informatique de l'École Normale Supérieure
ENS-LIENS, 45, rue d'Ulm, 75230 PARIS cédex 5, FRANCE
`jerome.feret@ens.fr`
`http://www.di.ens.fr/~feret`

Abstract. We propose an abstract interpretation-based analysis for automatically detecting all potential interactions between the agents of a part of a mobile system, without much knowledge about the rest of it. We restrict our study to mobile systems written in the π-calculus, and introduce a non-standard semantics which restores the link between channels and the processes that have created them. This semantics also allows to describe the interaction between a system and an unknown context. It is, to the best of our knowledge, the first analysis for this problem. We then abstract this non-standard semantics into an approximated one so as to automatically obtain a non-uniform description of the communication topology of mobile systems which compute in hostile contexts.

1 Introduction

Growing requirements of society impose the use of widely spread mobile systems of processes. In such systems the communication topology dynamically changes during processes computations, so that their analysis is a very difficult task. Furthermore, the size of systems, such as the Internet for instance, is large enough to prevent a single person from knowing the whole system. That is why we are interested in validating properties on a mobile system, which is a part of bigger one, called its context, without having precise knowledge of this context.

We address the problem of proving the confidentiality of such a mobile system: we propose to automatically infer a sound and accurate description of the topology of the interactions between the agents of this mobile system, in order to prove that private information can only be communicated to authorized agents. This description should be non-uniform, in order to distinguish between recursive instances of processes. This allows for instance to prove that in an *ftp* protocol the response to a query is returned to the correct customer.

We propose an automatic abstract interpretation-based analysis for the full π-calculus [18,19] which is a suitable formalism to describe mobile systems of processes. We present a new non-standard semantics, in the style of Venet's work [22], which mainly consists of labeling each recursive instance of processes with markers, in a deterministic way inferred during process creation. This labeling allows to trace precisely the origin of channels and to distinguish between recursive instances of processes, which cannot be done with the standard semantics. Besides, we require no further restrictions on the π-calculus. Moreover, our

J. Palsberg (Ed.): SAS 2000, LNCS 1824, pp. 135–154, 2000.

semantics is general enough to approximate the potential behaviour of a small known system in any unknown context.

Several abstractions of our non-standard semantics can be deduced, using Abstract Interpretation, we propose a generic abstract semantics to describe the interactions between processes and between the system's context, in order to automatically prove confidentiality properties. The implementation of the product between this semantics and another one focusing on counting occurrences of processes during computations [13] has lead to original results.

The standard semantics is given in Sect. 3. We define the non-standard semantics in Sect. 4. We design a generic abstract analysis to validate confidentiality of systems in Sect. 5 and instantiate it in Sect. 6.

Acknowledgments. We deeply thank anonymous referees for their significant comments on an early version. We wish also to thank Patrick and Radhia Cousot, Arnaud Venet, Ian Mackie, François Maurel, David Monniaux and François Pottier, for their comments and discussions.

2   Related Work

The problem of proving the confidentiality of a mobile system has been studied extensively. Several type-based methods have been proposed to capture non-interference properties between processes in [1,16] or to study information flow properties in [15]. All these works rely on the use of a partial order of security levels, and consist in statically checking that, owing analyzed properties, low security level agents cannot violate higher security level information.

Control flow analysis only focus on the flow information. Several uniform (or monovariant) analyses have been proposed [3,4]. Non-uniform (or polyvariant) analysis allows to describe the interaction between iterations of the same recursive process. This is not achievable by type-based methods, since the same security level is inferred for all recursive instances of the same process. For instance, in [20] to prove the confidentiality of a customer-server protocol, the set of customers has to be known before the beginning of the analysis. Only very few non-uniform analyses are available. Some alias analyses to infer pointer equality relationships are non-uniform, e.g. [12] which refines a uniform analysis (trivially based on type declaration). This has been applied by Colby to design a non-uniform control flow analysis for CML in [6]. This requires a good uniform approximation of the control flow of a system before starting the non-uniform analysis.

Our study follows Venet's work on the π-calculus [22], which allows to infer a sound non-uniform description of the topology of communication between the agents of *friendly systems* [18], in where resources cannot be nested. We consider the full π-calculus with nested replications. Moreover, we consider any open system and approximate the interaction between this system and its context which, to the best of our knowledge has never been achieved in a control flow analysis of the π-calculus. In particular, contrary to [1] we can propagate interactions without immediately reporting an error. Our framework can be easily adapted to other formalisms such as *the mobile ambients* [5], for instance.

3 π-calculus

π-calculus [18,19] is a formalism used to describe mobile systems, which is based on the use of processes and channels. We consider a lazy synchronous version of the polyadic π-calculus, inspired by the asynchronous version introduced by Turner [21] and the chemical abstract machine [2] in which communication primitives are very simple while ensuring the same expressive power. Let *Channel* be a countable set of channel names. The standard semantics of the π-calculus, given in Fig. 1, relies on the use of both a reduction relation to define results of processes computations, and a congruence relation to reveal redexes by making the processes meet.

Example 1. We model a system S which describes an *ftp* protocol. A resource creates repeatedly a new customer which sends a query to the server, composed with data and his email address. Data processing is abstracted away to make everything simpler. The server receives the query and returns the data back to the customer's email.

Syntax of S is given as follows:

$$S := (\nu \text{ port})(\nu \text{ gen}) \ (\textbf{Server} - \textbf{Customer} - \text{gen!}[])$$

where

$$\textbf{Server} := *\text{port}?[info,add] \ (add![info])$$
$$\textbf{Customer} := *\text{gen}?[] \ ((\nu \ data) \ (\nu \ email) \ \text{port}![data,email] - \text{gen}![])$$

For example, a short computation of S is given as follows:

$$
\begin{aligned}
S \rightarrow &(\nu \text{ port})(\nu \text{ gen})(\nu \ data_1)(\nu \ email_1) \\
&(\textbf{Server} - \textbf{Customer} - \text{port}![data_1,email_1] - \text{gen}![] \ ) \\
\rightarrow &(\nu \text{ port})(\nu \text{ gen})(\nu \ data_1)(\nu \ email_1) \\
&(\textbf{Server} - \textbf{Customer} - email_1![data_1] - \text{gen}![] \ ) \\
\rightarrow &(\nu \text{ port})(\nu \text{ gen})(\nu \ data_1)(\nu \ email_1) \ (\nu \ data_2)(\nu \ email_2) \\
&(\textbf{Server} - \textbf{Customer} - \text{gen}![] - email_1![data_1] - \text{port}![data_2,email_2]) \\
\rightarrow &(\nu \text{ port})(\nu \text{ gen})(\nu \ data_1)(\nu \ email_1) \ (\nu \ data_2)(\nu \ email_2) \\
&(\textbf{Server} - \textbf{Customer} - \text{gen}![] - email_1![data_1] - email_2![data_2]) \quad \square
\end{aligned}
$$

As illustrated in the above example, the configuration of a mobile system S at any stage is always congruent to one of the particular form, $(\nu \ c)(P_1 \mid ... \mid P_n)$ where c is a sequence of names, and P_1, ..., P_n are sub-processes beginning with a matching, a message, an input guard or a replication guard. Those are syntactic copies of sub-processes of S, which have been substituted during the communications. Standard semantics does not allow to trace neither the origin of those processes, nor the origin of the channels they have declared, because of the use of α-conversion: in example 1, it is impossible to express that in the sub-process $email_n![data_n]$, channels $email_n$ and $data_n$ have been created by the same recursive instance of the resource **Customer**.

$$P ::= action.P \qquad \text{(Action)}$$
$$\quad -\ (P \mid P) \qquad \text{(Parallel composition)}$$
$$\quad -\ \emptyset \qquad\qquad \text{(End of a process)}$$

$$action ::= c![x_1, ..., x_n] \quad \text{(Message)}$$
$$\quad -\ c?[x_1, ..., x_n] \quad \text{(Input guard)}$$
$$\quad -\ *c?[x_1, ..., x_n] \quad \text{(Replication guard)}$$
$$\quad -\ (\nu\ x) \qquad\qquad \text{(Channel creation)}$$

where $c, x_1, ..., x_n, x, y \in Channel$, $n \geqslant 0$. Input guard, replication guard and channel creation are the only name binders, i.e in $c?[x_1, ..., x_n]P$ (resp. $(\nu\ x)P$), occurrences of x_1, x_2, ..., x_n (resp. x) in P are considered bound. Usual rules about scopes, substitution and α-conversion apply. We denote by $\mathcal{FN}(P)$ the set of free names of P, i.e names which are not under a scope binder and by $\mathcal{BN}(P)$ the set of bound names of P.

(a) Syntax

$$(\nu\ x)P \equiv (\nu\ y)P[x \leftarrow y] \text{ if } y \notin \mathcal{FN}(P) \qquad \text{(α-conversion)}$$
$$P \mid Q \equiv Q \mid P \qquad\qquad\qquad\qquad \text{(Commutativity)}$$
$$P \mid (Q \mid R) \equiv (P \mid Q) \mid R \qquad\qquad\qquad \text{(Associativity)}$$
$$(\nu\ x)(\nu\ y)P \equiv (\nu\ y)(\nu\ x)P \qquad\qquad\quad \text{(Swapping)}$$
$$((\nu\ x)P) \mid Q \equiv (\nu\ x)(P \mid Q) \quad \text{ if } x \notin \mathcal{FN}(Q) \qquad \text{(Extrusion)}$$

where $c, x, y \in Channel$

(b) Congruence relation

$$c![x_1, ..., x_n]P \mid c?[y_1, ..., y_n]Q \rightarrow P \mid Q[y_1 \leftarrow x_1, ..., y_n \leftarrow x_n]$$
$$c![x_1, ..., x_n]P \mid *c?[y_1, ..., y_n]Q \rightarrow P \mid Q[y_1 \leftarrow x_1, ..., y_n \leftarrow x_n] \mid *c?[y_1, ..., y_n]Q$$

$$\frac{P \rightarrow Q}{(\nu\ x)P \rightarrow (\nu\ x)Q} \qquad \frac{P' \equiv P \quad P \rightarrow Q \quad Q \equiv Q'}{P' \rightarrow Q'} \qquad \frac{P \rightarrow P'}{P \mid Q \rightarrow P' \mid Q}$$

where $c, x_1, ..., x_n, y_1, ..., y_n \in Channel$

(c) Reduction relation

Fig. 1. The chemical semantics

4   Non-standard Semantics

The non-standard semantics is a refined semantics, which aims at explicitly specifying the links between channels and the instances of processes which have declared them. Any instance of a process is identified unambiguously by a marker in order to distinguish that instance from all others. Tracing the origin of channel names is then easily done by identifying each new channel name with the marker of the process which has created it. Venet, in [22], has designed such a non-standard semantics, but its applies only to a small part of the π-calculus, called *the friendly systems* [18]. It especially requires resources not to be nested, and the system to be closed. We propose a new non-standard semantics in order to remove those restrictions.

4.1   Closed Systems

Let Lbl be an infinite set of labels. We denote by Id the set of all binary trees the leaves of which are all labeled with ε and the nodes of which are labeled with a pair (i, j) where both i and j are in Lbl. The tree having a node labeled a, a left sibling t_1 and a right one t_2 is denoted by $N(a, t_1, t_2)$.

Let us first consider the case of a closed mobile system S in the π-calculus (the general case will be considered in Sect 4.2) and assume without any loss of generality that two channel binders of S are never used on the same channel name. We locate syntactic components of S by marking each sign ? and ! occurring in S with distinct labels in Lbl, the subset of Lbl used in labeling S is denoted by Lbl_{used}. A non-standard configuration is a set of thread instances, where a thread instance is a triplet composed with a syntactic component, a marker and an environment. The syntactic component is a copy of a sub-process of S, the marker is calculated at the creation of the thread and the environment specifies the semantic value of each free name of the syntactic component. Thread instances are created at the beginning of the system computation and while processes are running. In both cases, several threads are spawned, corresponding to a set of syntactic components, calculated by applying the function *Agent*, defined as follows, either on S for initial threads, or on the continuation of running processes.

$$Agent(\emptyset) = \{\}$$
$$Agent(x!^i[x_1, ..., x_n]P) = \{x!^i[x_1, ..., x_n]P\}$$
$$Agent(y?^i[y_1, ..., y_n]P) = \{y?^i[y_1, ..., y_n]P\}$$
$$Agent(*y?^i[y_1, ..., y_n]P) = \{*y?^i[y_1, ..., y_n]P\}$$
$$Agent(P \mid Q) = Agent(P) \cup Agent(Q)$$
$$Agent((\nu\ x)P) = Agent(P)$$

Markers are binary trees in Id. Initial thread markers are ε, while new threads markers are calculated recursively from the marker of the threads whose computation has lead to their creation:

- when an execution does not involve fetching a resource, the marker of the computed thread is just passed to the threads in its continuation;
- when a resource is fetched, markers of new threads in its continuation are $N((i, j), id_*, id_!)$, where $(*y?^i[\overline{y}]P, id_*, E_*)$ is the resource thread and $(x!^j[\overline{x}]Q, id_!, E_!)$ the message thread.

Environments map each free name of syntactic components to a pair (a, b) where a is a bound name of $\mathcal{S}$ and b is a marker. Intuitively, a refers to the binder $(\nu\, a)$ which has been used in declaring the channel, and b is the marker of the thread which has declared it. While threads are running, environments are calculated in order to mimic the standard semantics.

The translation of a labeled system $\mathcal{S}$ into a set of initial threads and non-standard computation rules are given in Fig. 3. Standard and non-standard semantics are in *bisimulation*. The proof relies on that non-standard computations cannot yield conflicts between threads markers.

Example 2. We give the non-standard configuration describing the *ftp* server, just after that two connections with customers have been completed.

Labelling of $\mathcal{S}$ is given as follows:

$$\mathcal{S} := (\nu\, \mathrm{port})(\nu\, \mathrm{gen})\ (\textbf{Server} - \textbf{Customer} - \mathrm{gen}!^6[])$$

where

$$\textbf{Server} := *\mathrm{port}?^1[\mathit{info}, \mathit{add}]\ (\mathit{add}!^2[\mathit{info}])$$
$$\textbf{Customer} := *\mathrm{gen}?^3[]\ ((\nu\, \mathit{data})\ (\nu\, \mathit{email})\ \mathrm{port}!^4[\mathit{data}, \mathit{email}] - \mathrm{gen}!^5[])$$

The non-standard configuration is given as follows, each sub-process is denoted by the first label occurring in its syntax.

$$
\left\{
\begin{array}{l}
\left(1, \varepsilon, \left\{ \mathrm{port}\ \mapsto (\mathrm{port}, \varepsilon) \right\} \right)\\[4pt]
\left(3, \varepsilon, \left\{ \begin{array}{ll} \mathrm{gen} & \mapsto (\mathrm{gen}, \varepsilon)\\ \mathrm{port} & \mapsto (\mathrm{port}, \varepsilon) \end{array} \right\} \right)\\[8pt]
\left(2, \mathit{id}_1', \left\{ \begin{array}{ll} \mathit{add} & \mapsto (\mathit{email}, \mathit{id}_1)\\ \mathit{info} & \mapsto (\mathit{data}, \mathit{id}_1) \end{array} \right\} \right)\\[8pt]
\left(2, \mathit{id}_2', \left\{ \begin{array}{ll} \mathit{add} & \mapsto (\mathit{email}, \mathit{id}_2)\\ \mathit{info} & \mapsto (\mathit{data}, \mathit{id}_2) \end{array} \right\} \right)\\[8pt]
\left(5, \mathit{id}_2, \left\{ \mathrm{gen}\ \mapsto (\mathrm{gen}, \varepsilon) \right\} \right)
\end{array}
\right\}
\quad \text{where} \quad
\left\{
\begin{array}{l}
\mathit{id}_1 = N((3,6), \varepsilon, \varepsilon)\\
\mathit{id}_1' = N((1,4), \varepsilon, \mathit{id}_1)\\
\mathit{id}_2 = N((3,5), \varepsilon, \mathit{id}_1)\\
\mathit{id}_2' = N((1,4), \varepsilon, \mathit{id}_2)
\end{array}
\right.
$$

We shall remark that, since $\mathcal{S}$ has no embedded resources, markers are all sequences, instead of trees. It explicitly appears that each time a copy of sub-process 2 is created, both channels *add* and *info* are bound to two channel names created by the same replication of the resource 3.   □

4.2   Interactions with a Context

We now extend our non-standard semantics to open systems. An open system $\mathcal{S}$ is a part of a bigger closed system, the rest of which is called its context. The context is a set of processes, concurrently running with the processes of $\mathcal{S}$. We represent this context by the set of names it shares with $\mathcal{S}$, called unsafe names, and approximate it as an intruder which is able to form any possible process working on these channel names. An interaction between $\mathcal{S}$ and its context, may only consist in a communication between a process $p_{\mathcal{S}}$ of the first one and a

$$C_0(\mathcal{S}) = \{(p, \varepsilon, E_p) \mid p \in Agent(\mathcal{S})\}, \text{ where } E_p = \begin{cases} \mathcal{FN}(p) & \to \mathcal{BN}(\mathcal{S}) \times Id \\ x & \mapsto (x, \varepsilon) \end{cases}.$$

(a) C_0 calculates the set of initial threads

Let C be a non-standard configuration,
if there are $\lambda, \mu \in C$,
with $\lambda = (y?^i[y_1, ..., y_n]P, id_?, E_?)$ and $\mu = (x!^j[x_1, ..., x_n]Q, id_!, E_!)$,
such that $E_?(y) = E_!(x)$,
then $C \to_2 C'$,
where $C' = (C \setminus \{\lambda, \mu\}) \cup (f_?(Agent(P))) \cup (f_!(Agent(Q)))$,

$$f_? : Ag \mapsto \left(Ag, id_?, \begin{cases} z \mapsto E_?(z) & \text{if } z \in \mathcal{FN}(Ag) \cap \mathcal{FN}(y?^i[y_1, ..., y_n]P) \\ y_k \mapsto E_!(x_k) & \text{if } y_k \in \mathcal{FN}(Ag) \\ z \mapsto (z, id_?) & \text{if } \begin{cases} z \in \mathcal{FN}(Ag) \cap \mathcal{BN}(y?^i[y_1, ..., y_n]P) \\ z \notin \{y_k \mid k \in [[1; n]]\} \end{cases} \end{cases} \right)$$

and $f_! : Ag \mapsto \left(Ag, id_!, \begin{cases} z \mapsto E_!(z) & \text{if } z \in \mathcal{FN}(Ag) \cap \mathcal{FN}(x!^j[x_1, ..., x_n]Q) \\ z \mapsto (z, id_!) & \text{if } z \in \mathcal{FN}(Ag) \cap \mathcal{BN}(x!^j[x_1, ..., x_n]Q) \end{cases} \right).$

(b) Non-standard communication

Let C be a non-standard configuration,
if there are $\lambda, \mu \in C$,
with $\lambda = (*y?^i[y_1, ..., y_n]P, id_?, E_?)$ and $\mu = (x!^j[x_1, ..., x_n]Q, id_!, E_!)$,
such that $E_?(y) = E_!(x)$,
then $C \to_2 C'$,
where $C' = (C \setminus \{\mu\}) \cup (f_?(Agent(P))) \cup (f_!(Agent(Q)))$,
$id_* = N((i, j), id_?, id_!)$

$$f_? : Ag \mapsto \left(Ag, id_*, \begin{cases} z \mapsto E_?(z) & \text{if } z \in \mathcal{FN}(Ag) \cap \mathcal{FN}(y?^i[y_1, ..., y_n]P) \\ y_k \mapsto E_!(x_k) & \text{if } y_k \in \mathcal{FN}(Ag) \\ z \mapsto (z, id_*) & \text{if } \begin{cases} z \in \mathcal{FN}(Ag) \cap \mathcal{BN}(y?^i[y_1, ..., y_n]P) \\ z \notin \{y_k \mid k \in [[1; n]]\} \end{cases} \end{cases} \right)$$

and $f_! : Ag \mapsto \left(Ag, id, \begin{cases} z \mapsto E_!(z) & \text{if } z \in \mathcal{FN}(Ag) \cap \mathcal{FN}(x!^j[x_1, ..., x_n]Q) \\ z \mapsto (z, id_!) & \text{if } z \in \mathcal{FN}(Ag) \cap \mathcal{BN}(x!^j[x_1, ..., x_n]Q) \end{cases} \right).$

(c) Non-standard resource fetching

Fig. 3. Non-standard semantics for close systems

process p_{cont} of the second one, via an unsafe name. This communication is called spying when p_{cont} is the receiver, and spoiling when p_{cont} is the message sender. While spying, the context listens to new channel names which get unsafe. While spoiling, the context may pass any name to $\mathcal{S}$, either an unsafe name created by a binder of $\mathcal{S}$ or a name created by the context itself, thus we have to introduce an infinite set of unsafe names that the context may have created. At last, spoiling may lead to a resource fetching, which would require to create an unambiguous marker, otherwise the consistency of the semantics would not be preserved.

Since α-conversion allows us to choose the names of new channels created by the context, we may assume those channels have been declared by recursive instances of a single process. Choosing $cont_?$, $cont_!$ $\in Lbl \setminus Lbl_{used}$ and $ext \in Channel \setminus \mathcal{BN}(\mathcal{S})$, such channels will be seen as if they were created by the binder $(\nu\ ext)$ of a recursive instance of a process whose marker is t_n, where t_n is recursively defined as follows:

$$\begin{cases} t_0 = N((cont_?,\ cont_!), \varepsilon, \varepsilon) \\ t_{n+1} = N((cont_?,\ cont_!), \varepsilon, t_n) \end{cases}.$$

We then denote by $\mathcal{EN}$ the set $\{(ext, t_n) \mid n \in \mathbb{N}\}$ and assume that every spoiling message are syntactic copies of a single process, whose first sign is labeled with $cont_!$. The coherence of our semantics mainly relies on the fact that during a computation, there cannot have been two different instances of a single process with the same marker. We guarantee this property by associating to each spoiling message an hypothetical fresh marker t_n.

A non-standard configuration is now a triplet $(C, Unsafe, Unused)$, where C is a set of threads, $Unsafe$ is a set of pairs (a, id), such that channel names created by the binder $(\nu\ a)$ of the recursive instance of a process whose marker was id is unsafe, and $Unused$ is a set of fresh markers which have not been used as markers for spoiling message. $\mathcal{S}$ may start with several initial configurations, since free names have to be chosen among the set of initial unsafe names. The transition relation $\looparrowright$ holds both with computations inside the mobile system $\mathcal{S}$ and computations involving the system $\mathcal{S}$ and its context. Initial non-standard configurations and computation rules are given in Figs. 4 and 6.

5   Abstract Semantics

We denote by $\mathcal{C}$ the set of all possible non-standard configurations. The set of all possible non-standard configurations a system may take during a finite computation is given by its collecting semantics [7], and can be expressed as the least fix point of the $\sqcup$-complete endomorphism $\mathbb{F}$ on the complete lattice $(\wp(\mathcal{C}), \subseteq, \cup, \emptyset, \cap, \mathcal{C})$ defined as follows:

$$\mathbb{F}(X) = C_0(\mathcal{S}) \cup \{C \mid \exists C' \in X\ :\ C' \looparrowright C\}.$$

$$(\{(p, \varepsilon, E_p) \mid p \in Agent(\mathcal{S})\}, \mathcal{EN}, \{t_n \mid n \in \mathbb{N}\}) \in C_0(\mathcal{S})$$
$$\iff \begin{cases} \forall p \in Agent(\mathcal{S}),\ \forall x \in \mathcal{FN}(p), \\ \quad E_p(x) = (x, \varepsilon)\ if\ x \in \mathcal{BN}(\mathcal{S}), \\ \quad \exists n\ such\ that\ E_p(x) = (ext, t_n)\ otherwise \end{cases}$$

Fig. 4. Non-standard initial configurations for open systems

$$\frac{C \to_2 C'}{(C, \textit{Unsafe}, \textit{Unused}) \leadsto (C', \textit{Unsafe}, \textit{Unused})}$$

(a) Non-standard safe transitions

Let $(C, \textit{Unsafe}, \textit{Unused})$ be a non-standard configuration,
if there is $\lambda \in C$, with $\lambda = (x!^j[x_1, ..., x_n]P, id_!, E_!)$,
such that $E_!(x) \in \textit{Unsafe}$,
then $(C, \textit{Unsafe}, \textit{Unused}) \leadsto (C', \textit{Unsafe}', \textit{Unused})$,
where $C' = (C \setminus \{\lambda\}) \cup (f_!(\textit{Agent}(P)))$,

$$f_! : Ag \mapsto \left(Ag, id_!, \begin{cases} z \mapsto E(z) & \text{if } z \in \mathcal{FN}(Ag) \cap \mathcal{FN}(x!^j[x_1, ..., x_n]P) \\ z \mapsto (z, id_!) & \text{if } z \in \mathcal{FN}(Ag) \cap \mathcal{BN}(x!^j[x_1, ..., x_n]P) \end{cases} \right)$$

and $\textit{Unsafe}' = \textit{Unsafe} \cup \{E(x_k) \mid k \in [|1; n|]\}$.

(b) Non-standard spied communication

Let $(C, \textit{Unsafe}, \textit{Unused})$ be a non-standard configuration,
if there are $\lambda \in C$, with $\lambda = (y?^i[y_1, ..., y_n]P, id_?, E_?)$ and $u_1, ..., u_n \in \textit{Unsafe}$,
such that $E_?(y) \in \textit{Unsafe}$,
then $(C, \textit{Unsafe}, \textit{Unused}) \leadsto (C', \textit{Unsafe}, \textit{Unused})$,
where $C' = (C \setminus \{\lambda\}) \cup (f_?(\textit{Agent}(P)))$,

$$f_? : Ag \mapsto \left(Ag, id_?, \begin{cases} z \mapsto E_?(z) & \text{if } z \in \mathcal{FN}(Ag) \cap \mathcal{FN}(y?^i[y_1, ..., y_n]P) \\ y_k \mapsto u_k & \text{if } y_k \in \mathcal{FN}(Ag) \\ z \mapsto (z, id_?) & \text{if } \begin{cases} z \in \mathcal{FN}(Ag) \cap \mathcal{BN}(y?^i[y_1, ..., y_n]P) \\ z \notin \{y_k \mid k \in [|1; n|]\} \end{cases} \end{cases} \right).$$

(c) Non-standard spoilt communication

Let $(C, \textit{Unsafe}, \textit{Unused})$ be a non-standard configuration,
if there are $\lambda \in C$, with $\lambda = (*y?^i[y_1, ..., y_n]P, id_?, E_?)$, $u_1, ..., u_n \in \textit{Unsafe}$, $id \in \textit{Unused}$,
such that $E_?(y) \in \textit{Unsafe}$,
then $(C, \textit{Unsafe}, \textit{Unused}) \leadsto (C', \textit{Unsafe}, \textit{Unused}')$
where $C' = C \cup (f_?(\textit{Agent}(P)))$,
$id_* = N((i, cont_!), id_?, id)$,

$$f_? : Ag \mapsto \left(Ag, id_*, \begin{cases} z \mapsto E_?(z) & \text{if } z \in \mathcal{FN}(Ag) \cap \mathcal{FN}(y?^i[y_1, ..., y_n]P) \\ y_k \mapsto u_k & \text{if } y_k \in \mathcal{FN}(Ag) \\ z \mapsto (z, id_*) & \text{if } \begin{cases} z \in \mathcal{FN}(Ag) \cap \mathcal{BN}(y?^i[y_1, ..., y_n]P) \\ z \notin \{y_k \mid k \in [|1; n|]\} \end{cases} \end{cases} \right),$$

and $\textit{Unused}' = \textit{Unused} \setminus \{id\}$.

(d) Non-standard spoilt resource fetching

Fig. 6. Non-standard transitions for open systems

Usually, this semantics is not decidable, we use abstract interpretation [8] to design an abstract domain in which a description of the collecting semantics will be finitely designed. We introduce two lattices, left as parameter of our abstraction, $(Id_1^\sharp, \sqsubseteq_1, \cup_1, \perp_1, \cap_1, \top_1)$ and $(Id_2^\sharp, \sqsubseteq_2, \cup_2, \perp_2, \cap_2, \top_2)$, to respectively represent sets of markers and sets of pairs of markers, related to their concrete domains via two monotone maps, γ_1 and γ_2:

$$\gamma_1 \; : \; (Id_1^\sharp, \sqsubseteq_1) \to (\wp(Id), \subseteq), \text{ with } \gamma_1(\perp_1) = \emptyset \,,$$

$$\gamma_2 \; : \; (Id_2^\sharp, \sqsubseteq_2) \to (\wp(Id \times Id), \subseteq) \text{ with } \gamma_2(\perp_2) = \emptyset \,.$$

Let Pro be the set of all sub-processes of $\mathcal{S}$, and Can be the set $\{(p, x, y) \mid p \in Pro, \; x \in \mathcal{FN}(p), \; y \in \{ext\} \cup \mathcal{BN}(\mathcal{S})\}$. Can is the set of all possible interactions between agents of $\mathcal{S}$. The interaction (p, x, y) denotes the fact that the channel name $x \in \mathcal{FN}(p)$ has been declared by the $(\nu\, y)$ binder, if $y \neq ext$, or has been declared by the context otherwise. Our abstract domain is then the product of three functional domains:

$$\mathcal{C}^\sharp = (C_{Pro}^\sharp \times C_{Com}^\sharp \times C_{Esc}^\sharp) \text{ where } \begin{cases} C_{Pro}^\sharp : & Pro & \to Id_1^\sharp \\ C_{Com}^\sharp : & Can & \to Id_2^\sharp \\ C_{Esc}^\sharp : \mathcal{BN}(\mathcal{S}) \cup \{ext\} & \to Id_1^\sharp \end{cases} .$$

$C_{Pro}^\sharp$ maps each sub-process to the set of markers it may be marked with. $C_{Com}^\sharp$ maps each interaction (P, x, y) to the set of pairs of markers (id_1, id_2), such that x is the free name of a thread whose marker was id_1; this thread may have been declared by the $(\nu\, y)$ binder of a thread whose marker was id_2. Finally $C_{Esc}^\sharp$ maps each names x to the set of markers id such that a channel name declared by the binder $(\nu\, x)$ of a thread whose marker was id may be unsafe.

An abstract configuration $C^\sharp = (f_{pro}^\sharp, f_{can}^\sharp, f_{esc}^\sharp)$ is then related to a set of concrete configurations by the monotone map γ, where $\gamma(C^\sharp)$ is:

$$\left\{ A \in \wp(\mathcal{C}) \;\middle|\; \begin{array}{l} \forall (C, esc, unused) \in A, \\ \begin{cases} \exists (x, id) \in esc & \Longrightarrow & id \in \gamma_1(f_{esc}^\sharp(x)) \\ \exists (P, id, E) \in C, & \Longrightarrow & id \in \gamma_1(f_{pro}^\sharp(P)) \\ \begin{pmatrix} \exists (P, id, E) \in C, \\ \exists x \in \mathcal{FN}(P) \end{pmatrix} & \Longrightarrow & \begin{pmatrix} (id, id') \in \gamma_2(f_{can}^\sharp(P, x, y)) \\ \text{where } E(x) = (y, id') \end{pmatrix} \end{cases} \end{array} \right\} .$$

The abstract semantics is given by an initial abstract configuration $C_0^\sharp$ and a transition relation $\rightharpoonup$, in Figs. 7 to 12. In the relation $C_1^\sharp \rightharpoonup C_2^\sharp$, $C_2^\sharp$ represents new interactions between agents induced by an abstract computation. The transition relation $\rightharpoonup$ uses several abstract primitives, which must satisfy some soundness conditions:

- two abstract projections: $\Pi_1 : Id_2^\sharp \to Id_1^\sharp$ and $\Pi_2 : Id_2^\sharp \to Id_1^\sharp$, such that $\{u \in Id \mid \exists v \in Id \text{ such that } (u, v) \in \gamma_2(c)\} \subseteq \gamma_1(\Pi_1(c))$ and $\{v \in Id \mid \exists u \in Id \text{ such that } (u, v) \in \gamma_2(c)\} \subseteq \gamma_1(\Pi_2(c))$;

$$\text{where } \begin{cases} i_{pro}^{\sharp} = \begin{cases} Pro \rightarrow Id_1^{\sharp} \\ P \mapsto \varepsilon_1^{\sharp} & \text{if } P \in (Agent(S)) \\ P \mapsto \bot_1^{\sharp} & \text{otherwise} \end{cases} \\ i_{can}^{\sharp} = \begin{cases} Can \rightarrow Id_2^{\sharp} \\ (P, x, x) \mapsto \varepsilon_2^{\sharp} & \text{if } \begin{cases} P \in (Agent(S)) \\ x \in BN(S) \cap FN(P) \end{cases} \\ (P, x, ext) \mapsto (Inj_1(\varepsilon_1^{\sharp})) \cap_2 (Inj_2(t^{\sharp})) & \text{if } \begin{cases} P \in (Agent(S)) \\ x \in FN(S) \cap FN(P) \end{cases} \\ (P, x, y) \mapsto \bot_2^{\sharp} & \text{otherwise} \end{cases} \\ i_{esc}^{\sharp} = \begin{cases} BN(S) \cup \{ext\} \rightarrow Id_1^{\sharp} \\ ext \mapsto t^{\sharp} \\ x \mapsto \bot_1^{\sharp} \text{ if } x \in BN(S) \end{cases} \end{cases}$$

Fig. 7. Initial abstract configuration

- two abstract injections: $Inj_1 : Id_1^{\sharp} \rightarrow Id_2^{\sharp}$ and $Inj_2 : Id_1^{\sharp} \rightarrow Id_2^{\sharp}$,
  such that $\{(u,v) \in Id \times Id \mid u \in \gamma_1(c)\} \subseteq \gamma_2(Inj_1(c))$
  and $\qquad \{(u,v) \in Id \times Id \mid v \in \gamma_1(c)\} \subseteq \gamma_2(Inj_2(c))$;
- two abstract joins: $\underset{= \rightarrow}{\bowtie} : Id_2^{\sharp} \times Id_2^{\sharp} \rightarrow Id_2^{\sharp}$ and $\underset{\leftarrow =}{\bowtie} : Id_2^{\sharp} \times Id_2^{\sharp} \rightarrow Id_2^{\sharp}$,
  such that $\left\{ (u,v) \in Id \times Id \mid \exists w \in \Sigma^* \begin{array}{l} (w,u) \in \gamma_2(c) \\ (w,v) \in \gamma_2(c') \end{array} \right\} \subseteq \gamma_2(\underset{= \rightarrow}{\bowtie}(c,c'))$
  and $\left\{ (u,v) \in Id \times Id \mid \exists w \in Id \begin{array}{l} (v,w) \in \gamma_2(c) \\ (u,w) \in \gamma_2(c') \end{array} \right\} \subseteq \gamma_2(\underset{\leftarrow =}{\bowtie}(c,c'))$;
- two abstract marker creators: $push_1^{(i,j)} : Id_1^{\sharp} \times Id_1^{\sharp} \rightarrow Id_1^{\sharp}$
  and $push_2^{(i,j)} : Id_1^{\sharp} \times Id_2^{\sharp} \rightarrow Id_2^{\sharp}$,
  such that $\left\{ N((i,j),u,v) \mid \begin{array}{l} u \in \gamma_1(c_g) \\ v \in \gamma_1(c_d) \end{array} \right\} \subseteq \gamma_1(push_1^{(i,j)}(c_g, c_d))$
  and $\left\{ (N((i,j),u,v),w) \mid \begin{array}{l} u \in \gamma_1(c_g) \\ (v,w) \in \gamma_2(c_d) \end{array} \right\} \subseteq \gamma_2(push_2^{(i,j)}(c_g, c_d))$;
- an abstract marker duplicator: $dpush : Id_1^{\sharp} \rightarrow Id_2^{\sharp}$,
  such that $\{(u,u) \mid u \in \gamma_1(c)\} \subseteq \gamma_2(dpush(c))$;
- initial abstract markers: $\varepsilon_1^{\sharp} \in Id_1^{\sharp}$, $\varepsilon_2^{\sharp} \in Id_2^{\sharp}$, $t^{\sharp} \in Id_1^{\sharp}$ such that
  $\{\varepsilon\} \subseteq \gamma_1(\varepsilon_1^{\sharp})$, $\{(\varepsilon,\varepsilon)\} \subseteq \gamma_2(\varepsilon_2^{\sharp})$ and $\{t_n \mid n \in \mathbb{N}\} \subseteq \gamma_1(t^{\sharp})$.

Roughly speaking, Π_1 (resp. Π_2) projects every pair of markers onto its first (resp. second) component. Inj_1 (resp. Inj_2) constructs for every marker the set of pair whose first (resp. second) component is that marker. $\underset{\leftarrow =}{\bowtie}$ and $\underset{= \rightarrow}{\bowtie}$ allow to calculate and propagate relational information between the components of a pair of markers throughout communication and resource fetching computations. $push_1^{(i,j)}$ constructs every marker of the processes created during a replication, using the set of markers of the resource given in its first argument and the set of markers of the message sender given in its second argument. $push_2^{(i,j)}$

acts similarly to $push_1^{(i,j)}$, but it takes into account relational information about markers of the free channels names of the message sender. *dpush* duplicates every marker into a pair of markers, this is used while creating new channel names.

All these conditions imply the following proposition:

Proposition 1. *If $C \in \gamma(C^\sharp)$ and $C \hookrightarrow D$, then there exists $D^\sharp$ such that $C^\sharp \rightharpoonup D^\sharp$ and $D \in \gamma(C^\sharp \sqcup D^\sharp)$.*

As a consequence, the abstract counterpart $\mathbb{F}^\sharp$ of $\mathbb{F}$, defined by

$$\mathbb{F}^\sharp(C^\sharp) = C_0^\sharp \sqcup C^\sharp \sqcup \{\overline{C}^\sharp \mid C^\sharp \rightharpoonup \overline{C}^\sharp\},$$

satisfies the soundness condition $\mathbb{F} \circ \gamma \subseteq \gamma \circ \mathbb{F}^\sharp$. Using Kleene's theorem, we prove the soundness of our analysis:

Theorem 1. $lfp_0 \mathbb{F} \subseteq \bigcup_{n \in \mathbb{N}} \gamma(\mathbb{F}^{\sharp n}(\bot_\sharp))$

We compute a sound approximation of our abstract semantics by using a widening operator [7,9] $\nabla : C^\sharp \times C^\sharp \to C^\sharp$ satisfying the following properties:

- $\forall C_1^\sharp, C_2^\sharp \in C^\sharp, C_1^\sharp \sqcup C_2^\sharp \sqsubseteq C_1^\sharp \nabla C_2^\sharp$
- for all increasing sequence $(C_n^\sharp) \in (C^\sharp)^{\mathbb{N}}$, the sequence (C_n^∇) defined as

$$\begin{cases} C_0^\nabla = C_0^\sharp \\ C_{n+1}^\nabla = C_n^\nabla \nabla C_{n+1}^\sharp \end{cases}$$

is ultimately stationary.

We can easily construct a widening operator ∇ on our abstract domain from existing widening operators ∇_1 on Id_1 and ∇_2 on Id_2.

Theorem 2. *Abstract iteration[9,10] The abstract iteration (C_n^∇) of $\mathbb{F}^\sharp$ defined as follows*

$$\begin{cases} C_0^\nabla = \bot \\ C_{n+1}^\nabla = \begin{cases} C_n^\nabla & \text{if } \mathbb{F}^\sharp(C_n^\nabla) \sqsubseteq C_n^\nabla \\ C_n^\nabla \nabla \mathbb{F}^\sharp(C_n^\nabla) & \text{otherwise} \end{cases} \end{cases}$$

is ultimately stationary and its limit C^∇ satisfies $lfp_0 \mathbb{F} \subseteq \gamma(C^\nabla)$.

Let $(f_{pro}^\sharp, f_{can}^\sharp, f_{esc}^\sharp)$ be an abstract configuration,
we consider $u \in Channel$ and $y?^i[y_1, ..., y_n]P$, $x!^j[x_1, ..., x_n]Q$ two sub-processes,
such that

$$f_{can}^\sharp(y?^i[y_1, ..., y_n]P, y, u) = id_\sharp^?,$$
$$f_{can}^\sharp(x!^j[x_1, ..., x_n]Q, x, u) = id_\sharp^!,$$
$$\perp_1 \neq (\Pi_2(id_\sharp^?)) \cap_1 (\Pi_2(id_\sharp^!)),$$

and we introduce

$$id_{can} \triangleq (\Pi_2(id_\sharp^?)) \cap_1 (\Pi_2(id_\sharp^!)),$$
$$idpro^? \triangleq \Pi_1(id_\sharp^? \cap_2 Inj_2(id_{can})),$$
$$idpro^! \triangleq \Pi_1(id_\sharp^! \cap_2 Inj_2(id_{can})),$$
$$id_k^t \triangleq \underset{=\rightarrow}{\bowtie} (\underset{\leftarrow =}{\bowtie} (id_\sharp^?, id_\sharp^!), f_{can}^\sharp(x!^j[x_1, ..., x_n]Q, x_k, t)) \cap_2 Inj_1(idpro^?).$$

Then we have

$$(f_{pro}^\sharp, f_{can}^\sharp, f_{esc}^\sharp) \rightharpoonup (g_{pro}^\sharp, g_{can}^\sharp, \emptyset)$$

where $g_{pro}^\sharp = \begin{cases} p \mapsto idpro^? & \text{if } p \in (Agent(P)) \\ q \mapsto idpro^! & \text{if } q \in (Agent(Q)) \} \end{cases}$

and $g_{can}^\sharp =$

$$
\begin{cases}
(p, z, z) \mapsto dpush(idpro^?) & \text{if} \begin{cases} p \in (Agent(P)) \\ z \in \mathcal{BN}(P) \cap \mathcal{FN}(p) \\ z \notin \{y_i \mid i \in [|1; n|]\} \end{cases} \\[2em]
(p, y_k, t) \mapsto id_k^t & \text{if} \begin{cases} p \in (Agent(P)) \\ y_k \in \mathcal{BN}(P) \cap \mathcal{FN}(p) \end{cases} \\[2em]
(p, z, t) \mapsto f_{can}^\sharp(y?^i[y_1, ..., y_n]P, z, t) \cap_2 Inj_1(idpro^?) & \text{if} \begin{cases} p \in (Agent(P)) \\ z \in \mathcal{FN}(P) \cap \mathcal{FN}(p) \\ z \neq y \end{cases} \\[2em]
(p, y, u) \mapsto f_{can}^\sharp(y?^i[y_1, ..., y_n]P, y, u) \cap_2 Inj_2(id_{can}) & \text{if} \begin{cases} p \in (Agent(P)) \\ y \in \mathcal{FN}(P) \cap \mathcal{FN}(p) \end{cases} \\[2em]
(q, z, z) \mapsto dpush(idpro^!) & \text{if} \begin{cases} p \in (Agent(Q)) \\ z \in \mathcal{BN}(Q) \cap \mathcal{FN}(q) \end{cases} \\[2em]
(q, z, t) \mapsto f_{can}^\sharp(x!^j[x_1, ..., x_n]Q, z, t) \cap_2 Inj_1(idpro^!) & \text{if} \begin{cases} q \in (Agent(Q)) \\ z \in \mathcal{FN}(Q) \cap \mathcal{FN}(q) \\ z \neq x \end{cases} \\[2em]
(q, x, u) \mapsto f_{can}^\sharp(x!^j[x_1, ..., x_n]Q, x, u) \cap_2 Inj_2(id_{can}) & \text{if} \begin{cases} p \in (Agent(Q)) \\ x \in \mathcal{FN}(Q) \cap \mathcal{FN}(q). \end{cases}
\end{cases}
$$

Fig. 8. Abstract communication

Let $(f_{pro}^\sharp, f_{can}^\sharp, f_{esc}^\sharp)$ be an abstract configuration,
we consider $u \in Channel$ and $*y?^i[y_1, ..., y_n]P$, $x!^j[x_1, ..., x_n]Q$ two sub-processes,
such that

$$f_{can}^\sharp(*y?^i[y_1, ..., y_n]P, y, u) = id_\sharp^?,$$
$$f_{can}^\sharp(x!^j[x_1, ..., x_n]Q, x, u) = id_\sharp^!,$$
$$\perp_1 \neq (\Pi_2(id_\sharp^?)) \cap_1 (\Pi_2(id_\sharp^!)),$$

and we introduce

$$id_{can} \triangleq (\Pi_2(id_\sharp^?)) \cap_1 (\Pi_2(id_\sharp^!)),$$
$$idpro^? \triangleq \Pi_1(id_\sharp^? \cap_2 Inj_2(id_{can})),$$
$$idpro^! \triangleq \Pi_1(id_\sharp^! \cap_2 Inj_2(id_{can})),$$
$$id_{s,t} \triangleq Inj_1(idpro^!) \cap_2 \underset{=\longrightarrow}{\bowtie} (\underset{\longleftarrow=}{\bowtie} (id_\sharp^!, id_\sharp^?), f_{can}^\sharp(y?^i[y_1, ..., y_n]P, s, t)),$$
$$id_k^t \triangleq f_{can}^\sharp(x!^j[x_1, ..., x_n]Q, x_k, t).$$

Then we have

$$(f_{pro}^\sharp, f_{can}^\sharp, f_{esc}^\sharp) \longrightarrow (g_{pro}^\sharp, g_{can}^\sharp, \emptyset)$$

where $g_{pro}^\sharp = \begin{cases} p \mapsto idpro^? \mid p \in (Agent(P)) \\ q \mapsto idpro^! \mid q \in (Agent(Q)) \end{cases}$

and $g_{can}^\sharp =$

$$
\begin{cases}
(p, z, z) \mapsto dpush(push_1^{(i,j)}(idpro^?, idpro^!)) & \text{if } \begin{cases} p \in (Agent(P)) \\ z \in \mathcal{BN}(P) \cap \mathcal{FN}(p) \\ z \notin \{y_i \mid i \in [|1; n|]\} \end{cases} \\[6pt]
(p, y_k, t) \mapsto push_2^{(i,j)}(idpro^?, id_k^t) & \text{if } \begin{cases} p \in (Agent(P)) \\ y_k \in \mathcal{BN}(P) \cap \mathcal{FN}(p) \end{cases} \\[6pt]
(p, z, t) \mapsto push_2^{(i,j)}(idpro^?, id_{z,t}) & \text{if } \begin{cases} p \in (Agent(P)) \\ z \in \mathcal{FN}(P) \cap \mathcal{FN}(p) \\ z \neq y \end{cases} \\[6pt]
(p, y, u) \mapsto push_2^{(i,j)}(idpro^?, id_{y,u}) \cap_2 Inj_2(id_{can}) & \text{if } \begin{cases} p \in (Agent(P)) \\ y \in \mathcal{FN}(P) \cap \mathcal{FN}(p) \end{cases} \\[6pt]
(q, z, z) \mapsto dpush(idpro^!) & \text{if } \begin{cases} q \in (Agent(Q)) \\ z \in \mathcal{BN}(Q) \cap \mathcal{FN}(q) \end{cases} \\[6pt]
(q, z, t) \mapsto f_{can}^\sharp(x!^j[x_1, ..., x_n]Q, z, t) \cap_2 Inj_1(idpro^!) & \text{if } \begin{cases} q \in (Agent(Q)) \\ z \in \mathcal{FN}(Q) \cap \mathcal{FN}(q) \\ z \neq x \end{cases} \\[6pt]
(q, x, u) \mapsto f_{can}^\sharp(x!^j[x_1, ..., x_n]Q, x, u) \cap_2 Inj_2(id_{can}) & \text{if } \begin{cases} q \in (Agent(Q)) \\ x \in \mathcal{FN}(Q) \cap \mathcal{FN}(q). \end{cases}
\end{cases}
$$

Fig. 9. Abstract resource fetching

Let $(f_{pro}^\sharp, f_{can}^\sharp, f_{esc}^\sharp)$ be an abstract configuration,
we consider $u \in Channel$ and $x!^j[x_1, ..., x_n]Q$ a sub-process, such that
$$f_{can}^\sharp(x!^j[x_1, ..., x_n]Q, x, u) = id_\sharp^!,$$
$$\perp_1 \neq (f_{esc}^\sharp(u)) \sqcap_1 (\Pi_2(id_\sharp^!)),$$
and we introduce
$$id_{can} \triangleq (f_{esc}^\sharp(u)) \sqcap_1 (\Pi_2(id_\sharp^!)),$$
$$idpro^! \triangleq \Pi_1(id_\sharp^! \sqcap_2 Inj_2(id_{can})).$$
Then we have $(f_{pro}^\sharp, f_{can}^\sharp, f_{esc}^\sharp) \rightarrow (g_{pro}^\sharp, g_{can}^\sharp, g_{esc}^\sharp)$
where
$$g_{pro}^\sharp = \{q \mapsto idpro^! \text{ if } q \in (Agent(Q)),$$
$g_{can}^\sharp =$

$$\begin{cases}
(q, z, z) \mapsto dpush(idpro^!) & \text{if } \begin{cases} q \in (Agent(Q)) \\ z \in \mathcal{BN}(Q) \cap \mathcal{FN}(q) \end{cases} \\
(q, z, t) \mapsto f_{can}^\sharp(x!^i[x_1, ..., x_n]Q, z, t) \sqcap_2 Inj_1(idpro^!) & \text{if } \begin{cases} q \in (Agent(Q)) \\ z \in \mathcal{FN}(Q) \cap \mathcal{FN}(q) \\ z \neq x \end{cases} \\
(q, x, u) \mapsto f_{can}^\sharp(x!^i[x_1, ..., x_n]Q, x, u) \sqcap_2 Inj_2(id_{can}) & \text{if } \begin{cases} q \in (Agent(Q)) \\ x \in \mathcal{FN}(Q) \cap \mathcal{FN}(q), \end{cases}
\end{cases}$$

$$g_{esc}^\sharp = \{t \mapsto \Pi_2(f_{can}^\sharp(Q, x_k, t) \sqcap_2 Inj_1(idpro^!)), \forall k \in [|1; n|].$$

Fig. 10. Abstract spied communication

Let $(f_{pro}^\sharp, f_{can}^\sharp, f_{esc}^\sharp)$ be an abstract configuration,
we consider $u \in Channel$ and $y?^i[y_1, ..., y_n]P$ a sub-process, such that
$$f_{can}^\sharp(y?^i[y_1, ..., y_n]P, y, u) = id_\sharp^?,$$
$$\perp_1 \neq (f_{esc}^\sharp(u)) \sqcap_1 (\Pi_2(id_\sharp^?)),$$
and we introduce
$$id_{can} \triangleq (f_{esc}^\sharp(u)) \sqcap_1 (\Pi_2(id_\sharp^?)),$$
$$idpro^? \triangleq \Pi_1(id_\sharp^? \sqcap_2 Inj_2(id_{can})).$$
Then we have $(f_{pro}^\sharp, f_{can}^\sharp, f_{esc}^\sharp) \rightarrow (g_{pro}^\sharp, g_{can}^\sharp, \emptyset)$
where
$$g_{pro}^\sharp = \{p \mapsto idpro^? \text{ if } p \in (Agent(P)),$$
$g_{can}^\sharp =$

$$\begin{cases}
(p, z, z) \mapsto dpush(idpro^?) & \text{if } \begin{cases} p \in (Agent(P)) \\ z \in \mathcal{BN}(P) \cap \mathcal{FN}(p) \\ z \notin \{y_i \mid i \in [|1; n|]\} \end{cases} \\
(p, z, t) \mapsto f_{can}^\sharp(y?^i[y_1, ..., y_n]Q, z, t) \sqcap_2 Inj_1(idpro^?) & \text{if } \begin{cases} p \in (Agent(P)) \\ z \in \mathcal{FN}(P) \cap \mathcal{FN}(p) \\ z \neq y \end{cases} \\
(p, y, u) \mapsto f_{can}^\sharp(y?^i[y_1, ..., y_n]P, y, u) \sqcap_2 Inj_2(id_{can}) & \text{if } \begin{cases} p \in (Agent(P)) \\ y \in \mathcal{FN}(P) \cap \mathcal{FN}(p) \end{cases} \\
(p, y_k, t) \mapsto (Inj_1(idpro^?) \sqcap_2 Inj_2(f_{esc}^\sharp(t))) & \text{if } \begin{cases} p \in (Agent(P)) \\ y_k \in \mathcal{BN}(P) \cap \mathcal{FN}(p). \end{cases}
\end{cases}$$

Fig. 11. Abstract spoilt communication

Let $(f_{pro}^{\sharp}, f_{can}^{\sharp}, f_{esc}^{\sharp})$ be an abstract configuration,
we consider $u \in Channel$ and $*y?^i[y_1, ..., y_n]P$ a sub-process, such that
$$f_{can}^{\sharp}(*y?^i[y_1, ..., y_n]P, y, u) = id_{\sharp}^?$$
$$\perp_1 \neq (\Pi_2(id_{\sharp}^?)) \cap_1 (f_{esc}^{\sharp}(u)),$$
and we introduce
$$id_{can} \triangleq (\Pi_2(id_{\sharp}^?)) \cap_1 (f_{esc}^{\sharp}(u)),$$
$$idpro^? \triangleq \Pi_1(id_{\sharp}^? \cap_2 Inj_2(id_{can})),$$
$$idpro^* \triangleq push_1^{(i,cont_!)}(idpro^?, t^{\sharp}),$$
$$id_{s,t} \triangleq Inj_1(t^{\sharp}) \cap_2 Inj_2(\Pi_2(f_{can}^{\sharp}(y?^i[y_1, ..., y_n]P, s, t) \cap_2 Inj_1(idpro_?))).$$
Then we have $(f_{pro}^{\sharp}, f_{can}^{\sharp}, f_{esc}^{\sharp}) \rightharpoonup (g_{pro}^{\sharp}, g_{can}^{\sharp}, \emptyset)$
where $g_{pro}^{\sharp} = \left\{ p \mapsto idpro^* \mid p \in (Agent(P)) \right\}$
and
$g_{can}^{\sharp} =$

$$
\begin{cases}
(p, z, z) \mapsto dpush(idpro^*) & \text{if } \begin{cases} p \in (Agent(P)) \\ z \in \mathcal{BN}(P) \cap \mathcal{FN}(p) \\ z \notin \{y_i \mid i \in [\![1; n]\!]\} \end{cases} \\
(p, y_k, t) \mapsto Inj_1(idpro^*) \cap_2 Inj_2(f_{esc}^{\sharp}(t)) & \text{if } \begin{cases} p \in (Agent(P)) \\ y_k \in \mathcal{BN}(P) \cap \mathcal{FN}(p) \end{cases} \\
(p, z, t) \mapsto push_2^{(i,cont_!)}(idpro^?, id_{z,t}) & \text{if } \begin{cases} p \in (Agent(P)) \\ z \in \mathcal{FN}(P) \cap \mathcal{FN}(p) \\ z \neq y \end{cases} \\
(p, y, u) \mapsto push_2^{(i,cont_!)}(idpro^?, id_{y,u}) \cap_2 Inj_2(id_{can}) & \text{if } \begin{cases} p \in (Agent(P)) \\ y \in \mathcal{FN}(P) \cap \mathcal{FN}(p). \end{cases}
\end{cases}
$$

Fig. 12. Abstract spoilt resource fetching

6   Abstract Domains

Many domains can be used to instantiate the parametric domains $Id_1^{\sharp}$ and $Id_2^{\sharp}$ and their associated primitives, depending on which complexity and which level of accuracy we expect. We have explained in [13, Sect. 6.1] that an inexpensive uniform analysis can be obtained by instantiating both $Id_1^{\sharp}$ and $Id_2^{\sharp}$ with the lattice $\{\perp, \top\}$ with the following concretization functions:

$$\gamma_1 : \begin{cases} \perp \mapsto \emptyset \\ \top \mapsto Id \end{cases} \quad \text{and} \quad \gamma_2 : \begin{cases} \perp \mapsto \emptyset \\ \top \mapsto Id \times Id \end{cases} .$$

For the sake of comparison, this analysis is at least as accurate as the one of Nielson et al. [3] and takes into account unreachable code.

Non-uniform analyses [6,22] are much more expensive. We obtain an accurate analysis by using the reduced product of both a non relational domain Id_1^{un} (resp. Id_2^{un}) and a relational domain Id_1^{rel} (resp. Id_2^{rel}) to represent sets of markers (resp. sets of pairs of markers). Non relational domains provide an intelligible description of markers, whereas relational domains are used in comparing processes and channels markers.

We denote by $\Sigma = (Lbl_{used} \cup \{cont_?, cont_!\})^2$ the set of useful pairs of labels. For the sake of simplicity, we first approximate every tree marker by the words of Σ^* written on the right combs of its elements, where the right comb of a tree is defined as follows:

$$\begin{cases} right\_comb(\varepsilon) = \varepsilon \\ right\_comb(N(a, b, c)) = a.right\_comb(c) \end{cases}$$

This abstraction is motivated by the following theorem:

Theorem 3. *Let* $(C_0, unsafe_0, unused_0) \rightsquigarrow \ldots \rightsquigarrow (C_n, unsafe_n, unused_n)$, *be a non-standard computation sequence, where* $(C_0, unsafe_0, unused_0) \in C_0(\mathcal{S})$.

If there exist $i, j \in [[0, n]]$, $(p, id, E) \in C_i$ *and* $(p', id', E') \in C_j$, *such that* $right\_comb(id) = right\_comb(id')$ *then* $id = id'$.

Our non relational domain is based on the use of *regular languages* on Σ. Id_1^{un} is the set of regular languages on Σ, while Id_2^{un} is the set of pairs of languages on Σ, defined pair wise. Associated abstract primitives are not detailed due to lack of space, a full description of these primitives is given in [13, Sect. 6.3]. Since there exist infinite chains in Id_1^{un}, a computable analysis needs a widening operator ∇. A convenient choice for $L_1 \nabla L_2$ consists in the quotient of the minimal automaton $(G, \rightarrow)$ of $L_1 \cup L_2$ by the relation $\sim_n$, defined as follows, where n is a fixed integer:

- $a \sim_0 b \Longleftrightarrow true$;

- $a \sim_{n+1} b \Longleftrightarrow \begin{cases} \forall c \text{ such that } a \xrightarrow{\lambda} c, \exists c' \text{ such that } c \sim_n c' \text{ and } b \xrightarrow{\lambda} c' \\ \forall c \text{ such that } b \xrightarrow{\lambda} c, \exists c' \text{ such that } c \sim_n c' \text{ and } a \xrightarrow{\lambda} c' \end{cases}$.

Our relational approximation abstracts numerical relations between the number of occurrences of each label in sets of words and in sets of pairs of words. We assign to each $\lambda \in \Sigma$ two distinct variables x_λ and y_λ. We denote by $\mathcal{V}_1$ the set $\{x_\lambda \mid \lambda \in \Sigma\}$, and by $\mathcal{V}_2$ the set $\{x_\lambda \mid \lambda \in \Sigma\} \cup \{y_\lambda \mid \lambda \in \Sigma\}$. The abstract domains $\wp(\mathbb{N}^{\mathcal{V}_1})$ and $\wp(\mathbb{N}^{\mathcal{V}_2})$ are respectively related to $\wp(Id)$ and $\wp(Id \times Id)$ by two monotone maps $\gamma_{\mathcal{V}_1}$ and $\gamma_{\mathcal{V}_2}$ defined as follows:

$$\gamma_{\mathcal{V}_1}(A) = \{u \in \Sigma^* \mid \exists (n_t)_{t \in \mathcal{V}_1} \in A, \forall \lambda \in \Sigma, n_{x_\lambda} = |u|_\lambda\},$$

$$\gamma_{\mathcal{V}_2}(A) = \left\{ (u, v) \in \Sigma^* \times \Sigma^* \;\middle|\; \exists (n_t)_{t \in \mathcal{V}_2} \in A, \forall \lambda \in \Sigma, \begin{cases} n_{x_\lambda} = |u|_\lambda \\ n_{y_\lambda} = |v|_\lambda \end{cases} \right\}.$$

Many relational numerical domains have been introduced in the literature [17,11,14]. We propose to use Karr's affine relationship equality relations domain. We define Id_1^{rel} by the set of affine equality relations systems on the set of variables $\mathcal{V}_1$, while Id_2^{rel} is the set of affine equality relations systems on the set of variables $\mathcal{V}_\in$. Those domains are fully described in [17].

$$\begin{cases} (1, \text{port}, \text{port}) & \mapsto \left((\varepsilon, \varepsilon), \left\{ x_\lambda = y_\lambda = 0, \ \forall \lambda \in \Sigma \right) \right. \\ (2, \text{add}, \text{email}) & \mapsto \left(\begin{matrix} ((1,4)(3,5)^*(3,6), (3,5)^*(3,6)), \\ \begin{cases} y_\lambda = x_\lambda, \ \forall \lambda \in \Sigma \setminus \{(1,4)\} \\ x_\lambda = 0, \ \forall \lambda \in \Sigma \setminus \{(1,4); (3,5); (3,6)\} \\ x_{(3,6)} = x_{(1,4)} = 1 \\ y_{(1,4)} = 0 \end{cases} \end{matrix} \right) \\ (2, \text{info}, \text{data}) & \mapsto \left(\begin{matrix} ((1,4)(3,5)^*(3,6), (3,5)^*(3,6)), \\ \begin{cases} y_\lambda = x_\lambda, \ \forall \lambda \in \Sigma \setminus \{(1,4)\} \\ x_\lambda = 0, \ \forall \lambda \in \Sigma \setminus \{(1,4); (3,5); (3,6)\} \\ x_{(3,6)} = x_{(1,4)} = 1 \\ y_{(1,4)} = 0 \end{cases} \end{matrix} \right) \\ (3, \text{port}, \text{port}) & \mapsto \left((\varepsilon, \varepsilon), \left\{ x_\lambda = y_\lambda = 0, \ \forall \lambda \in \Sigma \right) \right. \\ (3, \text{gen}, \text{gen}) & \mapsto \left((\varepsilon, \varepsilon), \left\{ x_\lambda = y_\lambda = 0, \ \forall \lambda \in \Sigma \right) \right. \\ (4, \text{port}, \text{port}) & \mapsto \left(\begin{matrix} ((3,5)^*(3,6), \varepsilon), \\ \begin{cases} y_\lambda = 0, \ \forall \lambda \in \Sigma \\ x_\lambda = 0, \ \forall \lambda \in \Sigma \setminus \{(3,5); (3,6)\} \\ x_{(3,6)} = 1 \end{cases} \end{matrix} \right) \\ (4, \text{email}, \text{email}) & \mapsto \left(\begin{matrix} ((3,5)^*(3,6), (3,5)^*(3,6)), \\ \begin{cases} y_\lambda = x_\lambda, \ \forall \lambda \in \Sigma \\ x_\lambda = 0, \ \forall \lambda \in \Sigma \setminus \{(3,5); (3,6)\} \\ x_{(3,6)} = 1 \end{cases} \end{matrix} \right) \\ (4, \text{data}, \text{data}) & \mapsto \left(\begin{matrix} ((3,5)^*(3,6), (3,5)^*(3,6)), \\ \begin{cases} y_\lambda = x_\lambda, \ \forall \lambda \in \Sigma \\ x_\lambda = 0, \ \forall \lambda \in \Sigma \setminus \{(3,5); (3,6)\} \\ x_{(3,6)} = 1 \end{cases} \end{matrix} \right) \\ (5, \text{gen}, \text{gen}) & \mapsto \left(\begin{matrix} (3,5)^*(3,6), \varepsilon), \\ \begin{cases} y_\lambda = 0, \ \forall \lambda \in \Sigma) \\ x_\lambda = 0, \ \forall \lambda \in \Sigma \setminus \{(3,5); (3,6)\} \\ x_{(3,6)} = 1 \end{cases} \end{matrix} \right) \\ (6, \text{gen}, \text{gen}) & \mapsto \left((\varepsilon, \varepsilon), \left\{ x_\lambda = y_\lambda = 0, \ \forall \lambda \in \Sigma \right) \right. \end{cases}$$

Fig. 13. $f^\sharp_{can}$: the *ftp* server analysis

Example 3. Our analysis may be used in proving the confidentiality of our *ftp* server. We denote by $C^\sharp = (f^\sharp_{pro}, f^\sharp_{can}, f^\sharp_{esc})$ the result of our analysis. $f^\sharp_{can}$ is given in Fig. 13 while $f^\sharp_{esc}$ maps each channel to $\perp_1$. These results are precise enough to prove that channels *data* (resp. *email*) can be passed only to channels *info* (resp. *add*), and cannot be listened to by any processes of an unknown context. Furthermore, using theorem 3, we can conclude that anytime a process 4 is spawned, its free channels are bound to channels created by the same recursive instance of resource 3. □

7   Conclusion

We have designed a powerful non-standard semantics, which is able to describe the behaviour of any mobile system expressed in the π-calculus, while tracing precisely the origin of channels. Moreover, our abstraction allows to analyze the behaviour of a part of a system whatever its context may be, which has many applications, such as analyzing a system part by part or analyzing the security of a known system inside a hostile context.

We have approximated this non-standard semantics into an abstract one, which focuses on confidentiality properties. We have obtained results which have at least the same level of accuracy than those obtained on *the friendly systems* [22], while our semantics works on the full π-calculus and can be applied to open mobile system. Analyzing a system part by part may lead to more accurate results than analyzing a complete system, especially while detecting mutual exclusion [13].

References

1. Martin Abadi. Secrecy by typing in security protocol. In *Proc. 5th FPCA*, volume 523 of *Lecture Notes in Computer Science*, pages 427–447. Springer-Verlag, 1991. 136

2. G. Berry and G. Boudol. The chemical abstract machine. *Theoretical Computer Science*, 96:217–248, 1992. 137

3. C. Bodei, P. Degano, F. Nielson, and H. R. Nielson. Control flow analysis for the π-calculus. In *Proc. CONCUR'98*, number 1466 in Lecture Notes in Computer Science, pages 84–98. Springer-Verlag, 1998. 136, 150

4. C. Bodei, P. Degano, F. Nielson, and H. R. Nielson. Static analysis of processes for no read-up and no write-down. In *Proc. FOSSACS'99*, number 1578 in Lecture Notes in Computer Science, pages 120–134. Springer-Verlag, 1999. 136

5. L. Cardelli and A. D. Gordon. Mobile ambients. In *Foundations of Software Science and Computational Structures*, volume 1378 of *Lecture Notes in Computer Science*, pages 140–155. Springer, 1998. 137

6. C. Colby. Analyzing the communication topology of concurrent programs. In *Symposium on Partial Evaluation and Program Manipulation*, 1995. 136, 150

7. P. Cousot. Semantic foundations of program analysis. In S.S. Muchnick and N.D. Jones, editors, *Program Flow Analysis: Theory and Applications*, chapter 10, pages 303–342. Prentice-Hall, Inc., Englewood Cliffs, 1981. 142, 146

8. P. Cousot and R. Cousot. Abstract interpretation: a unified lattice model for static analysis of programs by construction or approximation of fixpoints. In *Conference Record of the Fourth ACM Symposium on Principles of Programming Languages*, pages 238–252, Los Angeles, California, U.S.A., 1977. 144

9. P. Cousot and R. Cousot. Abstract interpretation frameworks. *Journal of logic and computation*, 2(4):511–547, August 1992. 146

10. P. Cousot and R. Cousot. Comparing the Galois connection and widening-narrowing approaches to abstract interpretation. In *Programming Language Implementation and Logic Programming, Proceedings of the Fourth International Symposium, PLILP'92*, volume 631 of *Lecture Notes in Computer Science*, pages 269–295. Springer-Verlag, 1992. 146

11. P. Cousot and N. Halbwachs. Automatic discovery of linear restraints among variables of a program. In *Proceedings of the Fifth Conference on Principles of Programming Languages*. ACM Press, 1978. 151

12. A. Deutsch. A storeless model of aliasing and its abstraction using finite representations of right-regular equivalence relations. In *Proceedings of the 1992 International Conference on Computer Languages*, pages 2–13. IEEE Computer Society Press, Los Alamitos, California, U.S.A., 1992. 136

13. J. Feret. Conception de π-*sa* : un analyseur statique générique pour le π-calcul. Mémoire de dea, SPP, september 1999. Electronically available at http://www.di.ens.fr/~feret/dea.html. 136, 150, 151, 153

14. P. Granger. Static analysis of linear congruence equalities among variables of a program. In *TAPSOFT'91*, volume 493. Lecture Notes in Computer Science, 1991. 151

15. Matthew Hennessy and James Riely. Resource access control in systems of mobile agents. In U. Nestmann and B. Pierce, editors, *3rd International Workshop on High-Level Concurrent Languages (HLCL'98)*, volume 16(3) of *Electronic Notes in Theoretical Computer Science*, Nice, September 1998. Elsevier. Available from http://www.elsevier.nl/locate/entcs. Full version available as Sussex CSTR 98/02, 1998. Available from http://www.cogs.susx.ac.uk/. 136

16. K. Honda, V. Vasconcelos, and N. Yoshida. Secure information flow as types process behaviour. In *Proc. ESOP'00*, number 1782 in Lecture Notes in Computer Science. Springer-Verlag, 2000. 136

17. M. Karr. Affine relationships among variables of a program. *Acta Informatica*, pages 133–151, 1976. 151

18. R. Milner. The polyadic π-calculus: a tutorial. In *Proceedings of the International Summer School on Logic and Algebra of Specification*. Springer Verlag, 1991. 135, 136, 137, 139

19. R. Milner, J. Parrow, and D. Walker. A calculus of mobile processes. *Information and Computation*, 100:1–77, 1992. 135, 137

20. James Riely and Matthew Hennessy. Secure resource access for mobile agents. Draft. Available from http://www.depaul.edu/~jriely, June 1999. 136

21. D. N. Turner. *The Polymorphic Pi-Calculus: Theory and Implementation*. PhD thesis, Edinburgh University, 1995. 137

22. A. Venet. Automatic determination of communication topologies in mobile systems. In *Proceedings of the Fifth International Static Analysis Symposium SAS'98*, volume 1503 of *Lecture Notes in Computer Science*, pages 152–167. Springer-Verlag, 1998. 135, 136, 139, 150, 153

Unified Analysis of Array and Object References in Strongly Typed Languages

Stephen Fink[1], Kathleen Knobe[2], and Vivek Sarkar[1]

[1] IBM Thomas J. Watson Research Center
P. O. Box 704, Yorktown Heights, NY 10598, USA
[2] Compaq Cambridge Research Laboratory
One Cambridge Center, Cambridge, MA 02139, USA

Abstract. We present a simple, unified approach for the analysis and optimization of object field and array element accesses in strongly typed languages, that works in the presence of object references/pointers. This approach builds on Array SSA form [14], a uniform representation for capturing control and data flow properties at the level of array elements. The techniques presented here extend previous analyses at the array element level [15] to handle both array element and object field accesses uniformly.

In the first part of this paper, we show how SSA-based program analyses developed for scalars and arrays can be extended to operate on object references in a strongly typed language like Java. The extension uses Array SSA form as its foundation by modeling object references as indices into hypothetical *heap arrays*. In the second part of this paper, we present two new sparse analysis algorithms using the heap array representation; one identifies redundant loads, and the other identifies dead stores. Using strong typing to help disambiguation, these algorithms are more efficient than equivalent analyses for weakly typed languages. Using the results of these algorithms, we can perform scalar replacement transformations to change operations on object fields and array elements into operations on scalar variables.

We present preliminary experimental results using the Jalapeño optimizing compiler infrastructure. These results illustrate the benefits obtained by performing redundant load and dead store elimination on Java programs. Our results show that the (dynamic) number of memory operations arising from array-element and object-field accesses can be reduced by up to 28%, resulting in execution time speedups of up to 1.1×.

Keywords: static single assignment (SSA) form, Array SSA form, load elimination, store elimination, scalar replacement, Java object references.

1 Introduction

Classical compiler analyses and optimizations have focused primarily on properties of scalar variables. While these analyses have been used successfully in practice for several years, it has long been recognized that more ambitious analyses must also consider non-scalar variables such as objects and arrays.

J. Palsberg (Ed.): SAS 2000, LNCS 1824, pp. 155–174, 2000.
© Springer-Verlag Berlin Heidelberg 2000

Past work on analysis and optimization of array and object references can be classified into three categories — 1) analysis of array references in scientific programs written in languages with named arrays such as Fortran, 2) analysis of pointer references in weakly typed languages such as C, and 3) analysis of object references in strongly typed languages such as Modula-3 and Java. This research focuses on the third category.

Analysis and optimization algorithms in the first category were driven by characteristics of the programming language (Fortran) used to write scientific programs. These algorithms typically use dependence analysis [22] to disambiguate array references, and limit their attention to loops with restricted control flow. The algorithms in this category did not consider the possibility of pointer-induced aliasing of arrays, and hence do not apply to programming languages (such as C and Java) where arrays might themselves be aliased.

Analysis and optimization algorithms in the second category face the daunting challenge of dealing with pointer-induced aliases in a weakly typed language. A large body of work has considered pointer analysis techniques (e.g., [17,6,13,16,7,12]) that include powerful methods to track pointer references both intra- and inter-procedurally. However, many of these techniques have limited effectiveness for large "real-world" programs because the underlying language semantics force highly conservative default assumptions. In addition, these algorithms are known to be complex and time-consuming in practice.

The research problem addressed by our work falls in the third category viz., efficient and effective analysis and optimization of array and object references in strongly typed object-oriented languages such as Java. Recent work on type-based alias analysis [11] has demonstrated the value of using type information in such languages in analysis and optimization.

In this paper, we present a new unified approach for analysis and optimization of object field and array element accesses in strongly typed languages, that works in the presence of object references/pointers. We introduce a new abstraction called *heap arrays*, which serves as a uniform representation for array and object references. Our approach is flow-sensitive, and therefore more general than past techniques for type-based alias analysis. In addition, our approach leverages past techniques for sparse analyses, namely Array SSA form (SSA) [14,15] and scalar global value numbering [1], to obtain analysis and optimization algorithms that are more efficient than the algorithms used for weakly type languages such as C.

To illustrate this approach, we present two new analysis algorithms for strongly typed languages: one identifies redundant loads, and one identifies dead stores. We have implemented our new algorithms in the Jalapeño optimizing compiler [3], and we present empirical results from our implementation. Our results show that the (dynamic) number of memory operations arising from array-element and object-field accesses can be reduced by up to 28%, resulting in execution time speedups of up to 1.1×.

Our interest in efficient analysis arises from our goal of optimizing large Java programs. For this context, we need optimization algorithms that are efficient enough to apply at runtime in a dynamic optimizing compiler [3]. However, we believe that the approach developed in this paper will also apply to other applications that require efficient analysis, such as program understanding tools that need to scale to large programs.

The rest of the paper is organized as follows. Section 2 outlines the foundations of our approach: Section 2.1 introduces heap arrays, and Section 2.2 summarizes an extension of global value numbering to efficiently precompute *definitely-same* and *definitely-different* information for heap array indices. Section 3 describes our algorithms to identify redundant loads and dead stores. Section 4 contains our preliminary experimental results. Section 5 discusses related work, and Section 6 contains our conclusions.

2   Analysis Framework

In this Section, we describe a unified representation called *extended Array SSA* form, which can be used to perform sparse dataflow analysis of values through scalars, array elements, and object references. First, we introduce a formalism called *heap arrays* which allows us to analyze object references with the same representation used for named arrays [14]. Then, we show how to use the extended Array SSA representation and global value numbering to disambiguate pointers with the same framework used to analyze array indices.

2.1   Heap Arrays

In this section, we describe our approach to analyzing accesses to object fields and array elements as accesses to elements of hypothetical *heap arrays*. The partitioning of memory locations into heap arrays is analogous to the partitioning of memory locations using type-based alias analysis [11]. The main difference is that our approach also performs a flow-sensitive analysis of element-level accesses to the heap arrays.

We model accesses to object fields as follows. For each field x, we introduce a hypothetical one-dimensional heap array, $\mathcal{H}^x$. Heap array $\mathcal{H}^x$ consolidates all instances of field x present in the heap. Heap arrays are indexed by object references. Thus, a GETFIELD[1] of $p.x$ is modeled as a read of element $\mathcal{H}^x[p]$, and a PUTFIELD of $q.x$ is modeled as a write of element $\mathcal{H}^x[q]$. The use of distinct heap arrays for distinct fields leverages the fact that accesses to distinct fields must be directed to distinct memory locations in a strongly typed language. Note that field x is considered to be the same field for objects of types C_1 and C_2, if x is declared in class C_1 and class C_2 extends class C_1 *i.e.*, if C_2 is a subclass of C_1.

Recall that arrays in an OO language like Java are also allocated in the heap — the program uses both an object reference and an integer subscript to access an array element. Therefore, we model such arrays as *two-dimensional*

---

[1] We use GETFIELD and PUTFIELD to denote general field access operators that may appear in three-address statements, not necessarily in Java bytecode.

heap arrays, with one dimension indexed by the object reference, and the second dimension indexed by the integer subscript. To avoid confusion, we refer to the array declared in the program as a "program array", and its representation in our model as its corresponding heap array.

The notation $\mathcal{H}^{\mathcal{T}[\,]\mathcal{R}}$ denotes a heap array, where $\mathcal{R}$ is the rank (dimensionality) of the underlying program array, and $\mathcal{T}$ is the element type. We introduce a distinct heap array for each distinct array type in the source language. Java contains seven possible array element types — bytes, chars, integers, longs, floats, doubles and objects. We denote the heap arrays for one-dimensional program arrays of these element types by $\mathcal{H}^{b[\,]}$, $\mathcal{H}^{c[\,]}$, $\mathcal{H}^{i[\,]}$, $\mathcal{H}^{l[\,]}$, $\mathcal{H}^{f[\,]}$, $\mathcal{H}^{d[\,]}$, and $\mathcal{H}^{O[\,]}$ respectively[2]. Thus, a read/write of a one-dimensional integer program array element a[i] corresponds to a read/write of heap array element $\mathcal{H}^{i[\,]}[a,i]$. In general, heap arrays for $\mathcal{R}$-dimensional arrays of these types are denoted by $\mathcal{H}^{b[\,]\mathcal{R}}$, $\mathcal{H}^{i[\,]\mathcal{R}}$, $\mathcal{H}^{l[\,]\mathcal{R}}$, $\mathcal{H}^{f[\,]\mathcal{R}}$, $\mathcal{H}^{d[\,]\mathcal{R}}$, and $\mathcal{H}^{O[\,]\mathcal{R}}$.

Note that we have only one heap array, $\mathcal{H}^{O[\,]\mathcal{R}}$, that represents all $\mathcal{R}$-dimensional arrays of objects. We could refine this approach by examining all the object array types used in the method being compiled, and replacing $\mathcal{H}^{O[\,]\mathcal{R}}$ by a set of heap arrays, one for each LCA (Least Common Ancestor) in the class hierarchy of the object array types.

Having modeled object and array references as accesses to named arrays, we can rename heap arrays and scalar variables to build an extended version of Array SSA form [14]. First, we rename heap arrays so that each renamed heap array has a unique static definition. This includes renaming of the dummy definition inserted at the start block to capture the unknown initial value of the heap array.

We insert three kinds of ϕ functions to obtain an *extended* Array SSA form that we use for data flow analyses[3]. Figure 1 illustrates the three types of ϕ function.

1. A *control* ϕ (denoted simply as ϕ) corresponds to the standard ϕ function from scalar SSA form [10], which represents a control flow merge of a set of reaching definitions.
2. A *definition* ϕ ($d\phi$) is used to deal with "non-killing" definitions. In scalar SSA, form a definition of a scalar kills the value of that scalar previously in effect. An assignment to an array element, however, must incorporate previous values. $d\phi$ functions were introduced in our past work on Array SSA form [14,15].
3. A *use* ϕ ($u\phi$) function creates a new name whenever a statement reads a heap array element. $u\phi$ functions were not used in prior work, and represent the extension in "extended" Array SSA form.
   The main purpose of the $u\phi$ function is to link together load instructions for the same heap array in control flow order. Intuitively, the $u\phi$ function

---

[2] By default, $\mathcal{R} = 1$ in our notation *i.e.,* we assume that the array is one-dimensional if $\mathcal{R}$ is not specified.

[3] The extended Array SSA form can also be viewed as a sparse data flow evaluation graph [8] for a heap array.

creates a new SSA variable name, with which a sparse dataflow analysis can associate a lattice variable.

We present one dataflow algorithm that uses the $u\phi$ for redundant load identification and one algorithm (dead store elimination) that does not require a new name at each use. In this latter case the $u\phi$ function is omitted.

We will sometimes need to distinguish between references (definitions and uses) that correspond directly to references in source and references added by construction of our extended Array SSA form. We refer to the first as *source* references and the second as *augmenting* references. In figure 1.c the references to $x_1[j]$, $x_2[k]$ and $x_3[i]$ are source references. The other references in that code fragment are all augmenting references.

Original program:

```
{x in
effect here. }
x[j] := ...
```

Original program:

```
{x in
effect here. }
if ... then
    x[j] := ...
endif
```

Original program:

```
{x in
effect here. }
x[j] := ...
... := x[k]
... := x[i]
```

Insertion of $d\phi$:

```
{x₀ in
effect here. }
x₁[j] := ...
x₂ := dφ(x₁,x₀)
```

Insertion of ϕ:

```
{x₀ in
effect here. }
if ... then
    x₁[j] := ...
    x₂ := dφ ...
endif
x₃ := φ(x₂, x₀)
```

Insertion of $u\phi$:

```
{x₀ in
effect here. }
x₁[j] := ...
x₂ := dφ(x₁,x₀)
... := x₂[k]
x₃ := uφ(x₂)
... := x₃[i]
x₄ := uφ(x₃)
```

(a)   (b)   (c)

Fig. 1. Three examples of ϕ nodes in extended Array SSA form.

The $d\phi$ and $u\phi$ functions in extended Array SSA form do not lead to excessive compile-time overhead because we introduce at most one $d\phi$ function for each heap array def and at most one $u\phi$ function for each heap array use. Instructions that operate on scalar variables do not introduce any heap array operations[4]. So, the worst-case size of the extended Array SSA form is proportional to the

---

[4] Note that local variables (stack elements) cannot be subject to pointer-induced aliasing in a strongly typed language such as Java.

size of the scalar SSA form that would be obtained if each heap array access is modeled as a def. Past empirical results have shown the size of scalar SSA form to be linearly proportional to the size of the input program [10], and the same should hold for extended Array SSA form.

2.2 Definitely-Same and Definitely-Different Analyses for Heap Array Indices

In this section, we show how the heap arrays of extended Array SSA form reduce questions of pointer analysis to questions regarding array indices. In particular, we show how global value numbering and allocation site information can be used to efficiently compute *definitely-same* (DS) and *definitely-different* (DD) information for heap array indices. For simplicity, the DS and DD analyses described in this section are limited in scope to scalar references.

As an example, consider the following Java source code fragment annotated with heap array accesses:

```
r = p ;
q = new Type1 ;
p.y = ... ;      // Hʸ[p] := ...
q.y = ... ;      // Hʸ[q] := ...
... = r.y ;      // ... := Hʸ[r]
```

Our analysis goal is to identify the redundant load of r.y, enabling the compiler to replace it with a use of scalar temporary that captures the value stored into p.y. We need to establish two facts to perform this transformation: 1) object references p and r are identical (definitely same) in all program executions, and 2) object references q and r are distinct (definitely different) in all program executions.

For a program in SSA form, we say that $DS(a, b) = true$ if and only if variables a and b are known to have exactly the same value at all points that are dominated by the definition of a and dominated by the definition of b. Analogous to DS, DD denotes a "definitely-different" binary relation *i.e.*, $DD(a, b) = true$ if and only if a and b are known to have distinct (non-equal) values at all points that are dominated by the definition of a and dominated by the definition of b.

The problem of determining if two symbolic index values are the same is equivalent to the classical problem of *global value numbering* [1,18,21]. We use the notation $\mathcal{V}(i)$ to denote the value number of SSA variable i. Therefore, if $\mathcal{V}(i) = \mathcal{V}(j)$, then $DS(i, j) = true$. For the code fragment above, the statement, p = r, ensures that p and r are given the same value number (*i.e.*, $\mathcal{V}(p) = \mathcal{V}(r)$), so that $DS(p, r) = true$.

In general, the problem of computing DD is more complex than value numbering. Note that DD, unlike DS, is not an equivalence relation because DD is not transitive. $DD(a, b) = true$ and $DD(b, c) = true$, does not imply that $DD(a, c) = true$.

For object references, we use allocation-site information to compute the $\mathcal{DD}$ relation. In particular, we rely on two observations:

1. Object references that contain the results of distinct allocation-sites must be different.
2. An object reference containing the result of an allocation-site must differ from any object reference that occurs at a program point that dominates the allocation site. (As a special case, this implies that the result of an allocation site must be distinct from all object references that are method parameters.)

For example, in the above code fragement, the presence of the allocation site in q = new Type1 ensures that $\mathcal{DD}(p, q) = true$.

For array references, we currently rely on classical dependence analysis to compute the $\mathcal{DD}$ relationship within shared loops. Global $\mathcal{DD}$ is the subject of future work.

Although the computations of $\mathcal{DD}$ for object references and array indices differ, the algorithms presented here use both types of $\mathcal{DD}$ relation in the same way, resulting in a unified analysis for arrays and objects. This unified approach applies, for example, to analysis of Java arrays, which are themselves accessed by reference. In this case we need to determine 1) if two arrays references are definitely not aliased and 2) if the array indices referenced are definitely not the same.

In the remainder of the paper, we assume that the index of a heap array is, in general, a vector whose size matches the rank of the heap array *e.g.*, an index into a one-dimensional heap array $\mathcal{H}^x$ will be a vector of size 1 (*i.e.*, a scalar), and an index into a two-dimensional heap array $\mathcal{H}^{b[\,]}$ will be a vector of size 2. (For Java programs, heap arrays will have rank ≤ 2 since all program arrays are one-dimensional.) Given a vector index $k = (k_1, \ldots)$, we will use the notation $\mathcal{V}(k)$ to represent a vector of value numbers, $(\mathcal{V}(k_1), \ldots)$. Thus, $\mathcal{DS}(j, k)$ is *true* if and only if vectors j and k have the same size, and their corresponding elements are definitely-same *i.e.*, $\mathcal{DS}(j_i, k_i) = true$ for all i. Analogously, $\mathcal{DD}(j, k)$ is *true* if and only if vectors j and k have the same size, and at least one pair of elements is definitely-different *i.e.*, $\mathcal{DD}(j_i, k_i) = true$ for some i.

3   Scalar Replacement Algorithms

In this Section, we introduce two new analyses based on extended Array SSA form. These two analyses form the backbone of *scalar replacement* transformations, which replace accesses to memory by uses of scalar temporaries. First, we present an analysis to identify fully redundant loads. Then, we present an analysis to identify dead stores.

Figure 2 illustrates three different cases of scalar replacement for object fields. All three cases can be identified by the algorithms presented in this paper. For the original program in figure 2(a), introducing a scalar temporary T1 for the store (def) of p.x can enable the load (use) of p.x to be eliminated *i.e.*, to

Original program:

```
p   := new Type1
q   := new Type1
 .   .
p.x :=  ...
q.x :=  ...
... := p.x
```

Original program:

```
p   := new Type1
q   := new Type1
 .   .   .
...   := p.x
q.x :=  ...
... := p.x
```

Original program:

```
p   := new Type1
q   := new Type1
r   := p
 .   .
p.x :=  ...
q.x :=  ...
r.x :=  ...
```

After redundant load
elimination:

```
p   := new Type1
q   := new Type1
 .   .
T1  :=  ...
p.x := T1
q.x :=  ...
... := T1
```

After redundant load
elimination:

```
p   := new Type1
q   := new Type1
 .   .
T2  := p.x
...   := T2
q.x :=  ...
... := T2
```

After dead store
elimination:

```
p   := new Type1
q   := new Type1
r   := p
 .   .
q.x :=  ...
r.x :=  ...
```

(a)   (b)   (c)

Fig. 2. Object examples of scalar replacement

Original program:

```
x[p]    :=  ...
x[p+1]  :=  ...
...  := x[p]
```

Original program:

```
...   := x[p]
x[p+1]  :=  ...
...   := x[p]
```

Original program:

```
x[p]    :=  ...
x[p+1]  :=  ...
x[p]    :=  ...
```

(a)   (b)   (c)

Fig. 3. Array examples of scalar replacement

be replaced by a use of T1. Figure 2(b) contains an example in which a scalar temporary (T2) is introduced for the first load of p.x, thus enabling the second load of p.x to be eliminated *i.e.*, replaced by T2. Finally, figure 2(c) contains an example in which the first store of p.x can be eliminated because it is known to be dead (redundant); no scalar temporary needs to be introduced in this case.

Figure 3 shows array-based examples. To highlight the uniform approach for both arrays and objects, these examples are totally analagous to the object based examples in figure 2.

Past algorithms for scalar replacement (*e.g.*, [4,2]) have been based on data dependence analysis or on exhaustive (dense) data flow analysis (*e.g.*, [5]). In this section, we show how extended Array SSA form, augmented with the definitely-same and definitely-different analysis information described in section 2.2, can be used to obtain a simple sparse scalar replacement algorithm. In addition, the use of SSA form enables our algorithm to find opportunities for scalar replacement that are not discovered by past algorithms that focus exclusively on innermost loops.

The rest of this section is organized as follows. Section 3.1 describes our analysis to identify redundant loads with respect to previous defs and previous uses, and Section 3.2 outlines our algorithm for dead store elimination.

3.1   Redundant Load Elimination

Input: Intermediate code for method being optimized, augmented with the $\mathcal{DS}$ and $\mathcal{DD}$ relations defined in Section 2.2.

Output: Transformed intermediate code after performing scalar replacement.

Algorithm:

1. **Build extended Array SSA form for each heap array.**
   Build Array SSA form, inserting control ϕ, $d\phi$ and $u\phi$ functions as outlined in Section 2.1, and renaming of all heap array definitions and uses.
   As part of this step, we annotate each call instruction with dummy defs and uses of each heap array for which a def or a use can reach the call instruction. If interprocedural analysis is possible, the call instruction's heap array defs and uses can be derived from a simple flow-insensitive summary of the called method.
2. **Perform index propagation.**
   (a) Walk through the extended Array SSA intermediate representation, and for each ϕ, $d\phi$, or $u\phi$ statement, create a dataflow equation with the appropriate operator as listed in Figures 5, 6 or 7.
   (b) Solve the system of dataflow equations by iterating to a fixed point.
   After index propagation, the lattice value of each heap array, A_i, is $\mathcal{L}(A_i) = \{ \mathcal{V}(\boldsymbol{k}) \mid$ location $A[\boldsymbol{k}]$ is "available" at def A_i (and all uses of A_i) $\}$.
3. **Scalar replacement analysis.**
   (a) Compute $UseRepSet = \{$ use $A_j[\boldsymbol{x}] \mid \exists\ \mathcal{V}(\boldsymbol{x}) \in \mathcal{L}(A_j) \}$ *i.e.*, use $A_j[\boldsymbol{x}]$ is placed in $UseRepSet$ if and only if location $A[\boldsymbol{x}]$ is available at the def of A_j and hence at the use of $A_j[\boldsymbol{x}]$. (Note that A_j uniquely identifies a use, since all uses are renamed in extended Array SSA form.)
   (b) Compute $DefRepSet = \{$ def $A_i[\boldsymbol{k}] \mid \exists$ use $A_j[\boldsymbol{x}] \in UseRepSet$ with $\mathcal{V}(\boldsymbol{x}) = \mathcal{V}(\boldsymbol{k}) \}$ *i.e.*, def $A_i[\boldsymbol{k}]$ is placed in $DefRepSet$ if and only if a use $A_j[\boldsymbol{x}]$ was placed in $UseRepSet$ with $\mathcal{V}(\boldsymbol{x}) = \mathcal{V}(\boldsymbol{k})$.
4. **Scalar replacement transformation.**
   Apply scalar replacement actions selected in step 3 above to the *original* program and obtain the transformed program.

Fig. 4. Overview of Redundant Load Elimination algorithm.

Figure 4 outlines our algorithm for identifying uses (loads) of heap array elements that are redundant with respect to prior defs and uses of the same heap array. The algorithm's main analysis is *index propagation*, which identifies the set of indices that are *available* at a specific def/use A_i of heap array A.

$\mathcal{L}(A_2)$	$\mathcal{L}(A_0) = \top$	$\mathcal{L}(A_0) = \langle (i_1), \ldots \rangle$	$\mathcal{L}(A_0) = \bot$
$\mathcal{L}(A_1) = \top$	$\top$	$\top$	$\top$
$\mathcal{L}(A_1) = \langle (i') \rangle$	$\top$	UPDATE($(i'), \langle (i_1), \ldots \rangle$)	$\langle (i') \rangle$
$\mathcal{L}(A_1) = \bot$	$\bot$	$\bot$	$\bot$

Fig. 5. Lattice computation for $\mathcal{L}(A_2) = \mathcal{L}_{d\phi}(\mathcal{L}(A_1), \mathcal{L}(A_0))$ where $A_2 := d\phi(A_1, A_0)$ is a definition ϕ operation

$\mathcal{L}(A_2)$	$\mathcal{L}(A_0) = \top$	$\mathcal{L}(A_0) = \langle (i_1), \ldots \rangle$	$\mathcal{L}(A_0) = \bot$
$\mathcal{L}(A_1) = \top$	$\top$	$\top$	$\top$
$\mathcal{L}(A_1) = \langle (i') \rangle$	$\top$	$\mathcal{L}(A_1) \cup \mathcal{L}(A_0)$	$\mathcal{L}(A_1)$
$\mathcal{L}(A_1) = \bot$	$\bot$	$\bot$	$\bot$

Fig. 6. Lattice computation for $\mathcal{L}(A_2) = \mathcal{L}_{u\phi}(\mathcal{L}(A_1), \mathcal{L}(A_0))$ where $A_2 := u\phi(A_1, A_0)$ is a use ϕ operation

$\mathcal{L}(A_2) = \mathcal{L}(A_1) \sqcap \mathcal{L}(A_0)$	$\mathcal{L}(A_0) = \top$	$\mathcal{L}(A_0) = \langle (i_1), \ldots \rangle$	$\mathcal{L}(A_0) = \bot$
$\mathcal{L}(A_1) = \top$	$\top$	$\mathcal{L}(A_0)$	$\bot$
$\mathcal{L}(A_1) = \langle (i_1), \ldots \rangle$	$\mathcal{L}(A_1)$	$\mathcal{L}(A_1) \sqcap \mathcal{L}(A_0)$	$\bot$
$\mathcal{L}(A_1) = \bot$	$\bot$	$\bot$	$\bot$

Fig. 7. Lattice computation for $\mathcal{L}(A_2) = \mathcal{L}_\phi(\mathcal{L}(A_1), \mathcal{L}(A_0)) = \mathcal{L}(A_1) \sqcap \mathcal{L}(A_0)$, where $A_2 := \phi(A_1, A_0)$ is a control ϕ operation

(a) Extended Partial Array SSA form:	(b) After index propagation:	(c) Scalar replacement actions selected:	(d) After transforming original program:

`p := new Type1`
`q := new Type1`
`. . .`
$\mathcal{H}_1^x[p] := \ldots$
$\mathcal{H}_2^x := d\phi(\mathcal{H}_1^x, \mathcal{H}_0^x)$
$\mathcal{H}_3^x[q] := \ldots$
$\mathcal{H}_4^x := d\phi(\mathcal{H}_3^x, \mathcal{H}_2^x)$
$\ldots := \mathcal{H}_4^x[p]$
$\mathcal{H}_5^x := u\phi(\mathcal{H}_4^x)$
	$\mathcal{L}(\mathcal{H}_0^x) = \{ \}$
	$\mathcal{L}(\mathcal{H}_1^x) = \{\mathcal{V}(p)\}$
	$\mathcal{L}(\mathcal{H}_2^x) = \{\mathcal{V}(p)\}$
	$\mathcal{L}(\mathcal{H}_3^x) = \{\mathcal{V}(q)\}$
	$\mathcal{L}(\mathcal{H}_4^x) = \{\mathcal{V}(p), \mathcal{V}(q)\}$
	$\mathcal{L}(\mathcal{H}_5^x) = \{\mathcal{V}(p), \mathcal{V}(q)\}$
		$UseRepSet = \{\mathcal{H}_4^x[p]\}$
		$DefRepSet = \{\mathcal{H}_1^x[p]\}$
			`p := new Type1`
			`q := new Type1`
			`. . .`
			$A\_temp_{\mathcal{V}(p)} := \ldots$
			`p.x :=` $A\_temp_{\mathcal{V}(p)}$
			`q.x := ...`
			$\ldots := A\_temp_{\mathcal{V}(p)}$

Fig. 8. Trace of load elimination algorithm from figure 4 for program in figure 2(a)

Index propagation is a dataflow problem, which computes a lattice value $\mathcal{L}(\mathcal{H})$ for each heap variable $\mathcal{H}$ in the Array SSA form. This lattice value $\mathcal{L}(\mathcal{H})$ is a set of value number vectors $\{i_1, \ldots\}$, such that a load of $\mathcal{H}[i]$ is available (previously stored in a register) if $\mathcal{V}(i) \in \mathcal{L}(\mathcal{H})$. Figures 5, 6 and 7 give the lattice computations which define the index propagation solution. The notation UPDATE$(i', \langle i_1, \ldots \rangle)$ used in the middle cell in figure 5 denotes a special update of the list $\mathcal{L}(A_0) = \langle i_1, \ldots \rangle$ with respect to index i'. UPDATE involves four steps:

1. Compute the list $T = \{\ i_j \mid i_j \in \mathcal{L}(A_0)$ and $\mathcal{DD}(i', i_j) = true\ \}$. List T contains only those indices from $\mathcal{L}(A_0)$ that are *definitely different* from i'.
2. Insert i' into T to obtain a new list, I.
3. If the size of list I exceeds the threshold size Z, then one of the indices in I is dropped from the output list so as to satisfy the size constraint. (Since the size of $\mathcal{L}(A_0)$ must have been $\leq Z$, it is sufficient to drop only one index to satisfy the size constraint.)
4. Return I as the value of UPDATE$(i', \langle i_1, \ldots \rangle)$.

After index propagation, the algorithm selects an array use (load), $A_j[x]$, for scalar replacement if and only if index propagation determines that an index with value number $\mathcal{V}(x)$ is available at the def of A_j. If so, the use is included in *UseRepSet*, the set of uses selected for scalar replacement. Finally, an array def, $A_i[k]$, is selected for scalar replacement if and only if some use $A_j[x]$ was placed in *UseRepSet* such that $\mathcal{V}(x) = \mathcal{V}(k)$. All such defs are included in *DefRepSet*, the set of defs selected for scalar replacement.

Figure 8 illustrates a trace of this load elimination algorithm for the example program in figure 2(a). Figure 8(a) shows the partial Array SSA form computed for this example program. The results of index propagation are shown in figure 8(b). These results depend on definitely-different analysis establishing that $\mathcal{V}(p) \neq \mathcal{V}(q)$ by using allocation site information as described in Section 2.2. Figure 8(c) shows the scalar replacement actions derived from the results of index propagation, and Figure 8(d) shows the transformed code after performing these scalar replacement actions. The load of p.x has thus been eliminated in the transformed code, and replaced by a use of the scalar temporary, $A\_temp_{\mathcal{V}(p)}$.

We now present a brief complexity analysis of the redundant load elimination algorithm in Figure 4. Note that index propagation can be performed separately for each heap array. Let k be the maximum number of defs and uses for a single heap array. Therefore, the number of $d\phi$ and $u\phi$ functions created for a single heap array will be $O(k)$. Based on past empirical measurements for scalar SSA form [10], we can expect that the number of control ϕ functions for a single heap array will also be $O(k)$ in practice (since there are $O(k)$ names created for a heap array). Recall that the maximum size of a lattice value list, as well as the maximum height of the lattice, is a compiler-defined constant, Z. Therefore, the worst case execution-time complexity for index propagation of a *single heap array* is $O(k \times Z^2)$.

To complete the complexity analysis, we define a size metric for each method, $S = \max(\#\text{ instrs in method}, k \times (\#\text{ call instrs in method}))$. The first term (#

instrs in method) usually dominates the max function in practice. Therefore, the worst-case complexity for index propagation for all heap arrays is

$$\sum_{\text{heap array } A} O(k_A \times Z^2) = O(S \times Z^2),$$

since $\sum_A k_A$ must be $O(S)$. Hence the execution time is a linear with a Z^2 factor. As mentioned earlier, the value of Z can be adjusted to trade off precision and overhead. For the greatest precision, we can set $Z = O(k)$, which yields a worst-case $O(S \times k^2)$ algorithm. In practice, k is usually small resulting in linear execution time. This is the setting used to obtain the experimental results reported in Section 4.

We conclude this section with a brief discussion of the impact of the Java Memory Model (JMM). It has been observed that redundant load elimination can be an illegal transformation for multithreaded programs written for a memory model, such as the JMM, that includes the memory coherence assumption [20]. (This observation does not apply to single-threaded programs.) However, it is possible that the Java memory model will be revised in the future, and that the new version will not require memory coherence [19]. However, if necessary, our algorithms can be modified to obey memory coherence by simply treating each $u\phi$ function as a $d\phi$ function $i.e.$, by treating each array use as an array def. Our implementation supports these semantics with a command-line option. As in interesting side note, we observed that changing the data-flow equations to support the strict memory model involved changing fewer than ten lines of code.

3.2   Dead Store Elimination

In this section, we show how our Array SSA framework can be used to identify redundant (dead) stores of array elements. Dead store elimination is related to load elimination, because scalar replacement can convert non-redundant stores into redundant stores. For example, consider the program in Figure 2(a). If it contained an additional store of p.x at the bottom, the first store of p.x will become redundant after scalar replacement. The program after scalar replacement will then be similar to the program shown in Figure 2(c) as an example of dead store elimination.

Our algorithm for dead store elimination is based on a backward propagation of $DEAD$ sets. As in load elimination, the propagation is $sparse$ $i.e.$, it goes through ϕ nodes in the Array SSA form rather than basic blocks in a control flow graph. However, $u\phi$ functions are not used in dead store elimination, since the ordering of uses is not relevant to identifying a dead store. Without $u\phi$ functions, it is possible for multiple uses to access the same heap array name. Hence, we use the notation $\langle A, s \rangle$ to refer to a specific use of heap array A in statement s.

Consider an augmenting def A_i, a source or augmenting use $\langle A_j, s \rangle$, and a source def A_k in Array SSA form. We define the following four sets:

$$DEAD_{def}(A_i) = \{ \mathcal{V}(x) | \text{element } x \text{ of array } A \text{ is dead at augmenting def } A_i \}$$
$$DEAD_{use}(\langle A_j, s \rangle) = \{ \mathcal{V}(x) \mid \text{element } x \text{ of array } A \text{ is dead at source use of } A_j$$
$$\text{in statement } s \}$$
$$KILL(A_k) = \{ \mathcal{V}(x) \mid \text{element } x \text{ of array } A \text{ is killed by source def of } A_k \}$$
$$LIVE(A_i) = \{ \mathcal{V}(x) \mid \exists \text{ a source use } A_i[x] \text{ of augmenting def } A_i \}$$

The *KILL* and *LIVE* sets are local sets; *i.e.*, they can be computed immediately without propagation of data flow information. If A_i "escapes" from the procedure (*i.e.*, definition A_i is exposed on procedure exit), then we must conservatively set $LIVE(A_i) = \mathcal{U}_{ind}^A$, the universal set of index value numbers for array A. Note that in Java, every instruction that can potentially throw an exception must be treated as a procedure exit, although this property can be relaxed with some interprocedural analysis.

1. **Propagation from the LHS to the RHS of a control ϕ:**
   Consider an augmenting statement s of the form, $A_2 := \phi(A_1, A_0)$ involving a control ϕ.
   In this case, the uses, $\langle A_1, s \rangle$ and $\langle A_0, s \rangle$, must both come from augmenting defs, and the propagation of $DEAD_{def}(A_2)$ to the RHS is a simple copy *i.e.*, $DEAD_{use}(\langle A_1, s \rangle) = DEAD_{def}(A_2)$ and $DEAD_{use}(\langle A_0, s \rangle) = DEAD_{def}(A_2)$.
2. **Propagation from the LHS to the RHS of a definition ϕ:**
   Consider a $d\phi$ statement s of the form $A_2 := d\phi(A_1, A_0)$. In this case use $\langle A_1, s \rangle$ must come from a source definition, and use $\langle A_0, s \rangle$ must come from an augmenting definition. The propagation of $DEAD_{def}(A_2)$ and $KILL(A_1)$ to $DEAD_{use}(\langle A_0, s \rangle)$ is given by the equation, $DEAD_{use}(\langle A_0, s \rangle) = KILL(A_1) \cup DEAD_{def}(A_2)$.
3. **Propagation to the LHS of a ϕ statement from uses in other statements:**
   Consider a definition or control ϕ statement of the form $A_i := \phi(\dots)$. The value of $DEAD_{def}(A_i)$ is obtained by intersecting the $DEAD_{use}$ sets of all uses of A_i, and subtracting out all value numbers that are not definitely different from every element of $LIVE(A_i)$. This set is specified by the following equation:

$$DEAD_{def}(A_i) = \left(\bigcap_{s \text{ is a } \phi \text{ use of } A_i} DEAD_{use}(\langle A_i, s \rangle) \right) - \{ v | \exists w \in$$

$$LIVE(A_i) s.t. \neg DD(v, w) \}$$

Fig. 9. Data flow equations for $DEAD_{def}$ and $DEAD_{use}$ sets

The data flow equations used to compute the $DEAD_{def}$ and $DEAD_{use}$ sets are given in Figure 9. The goal of our analysis is to find the maximal

$DEAD_{def}$ and $DEAD_{use}$ sets that satisfy these equations. Hence our algorithm will initialize each $DEAD_{def}$ and $DEAD_{use}$ set to $= \mathcal{U}_{ind}^{A}$ (for renamed arrays derived from original array A), and then iterate on the equations till a fixpoint is obtained. After $DEAD$ sets have been computed, we can determine if a source definition is redundant quite simply as follows. Consider a source definition, $A_1[j] := \ldots$, followed by a definition ϕ statement, $A_2 := d\phi(A_1, A_0)$. Then, if $\mathcal{V}(j) \in DEAD(A_2)$, then def (store) A_1 is redundant and can be eliminated.

As in the index propagation analysis in Section 3.1, the worst-case execution-time complexity for dead store elimination is $O(S \times k^2)$, where S is the size of the input method and k is an upper bound on the number of defs and uses for a single heap array. In practice, k is usually small resulting in linear execution time.

4   Experimental Results

We present an experimental evaluation of the scalar replacement algorithms using the Jalapeño optimizing compiler [3]. The performance results in this section were obtained on an IBM F50 Model 7025 system with four 166MHz PPC604e processors running AIX v4.3. The system has 1GB of main memory. Each processor has split 32KB first-level instruction and data caches and a 256KB second-level cache.

The Jalapeño system is continually under development; the results in this section use the Jalapeño system as of April 5, 2000. For these experiments, the Jalapeño optimizing compiler performed a basic set of standard optimizations including copy propagation, type propagation, null check elimination, constant folding, devirtualization, local common subexpression elimination, load/store elimination, dead code elimination, and linear scan register allocation. Previous work [3] has demonstrated that Jalapeño performance with these optimizations is roughly equivalent to that of the industry-leading IBM product JVM and JIT. The runs use Jalapeño's non-generational copying garbage collector with 300MB of heap (which is shared by the application and by all components of the Jalapeño JVM).

Our preliminary implementation has several limitations. Our current implementation does not eliminate the null-pointer and array-bounds checks for redundant loads. We do not use any interprocedural summary information, as the Jalapeño optimizing compiler assumes on "open-world" due to dynamic class loading. We do not perform any loop-invariant code motion or partial redundancy elimination to help eliminate redundant loads in loops. Most importantly, the Jalapeño optimizing compiler still lacks many classical scalar optimizations, which are especially important to eliminate the register copies and reduce register pressure introduced by scalar replacement. For these reasons, these experimental results should be considered a lower bound on the potential gains due to scalar replacement, and we expect the results to improve as Jalapeño matures.

Note that since the entire Jalapeño JVM is implemented in Java, the optimizing compiler compiles not only application code and library code, but also VM code. The results in this section thus reflect the performance of the entire body of Java code which runs an application, which includes VM code and libraries. Furthermore, the compiler inlines code across these boundaries.

For our experiments, we use the seven codes from the SPECjvm98 suite [9], and the Symantec suite of compiler microbenchmarks. For the SPEC codes, we use the medium-size (-s10) inputs. Note that this methodology does *not* follow the official SPEC run rules, and these results are not comparable with any official SPEC results. The focus of our measurements was on obtaining dynamic counts of memory operations. When we report timing information, we report the best wall-clock time from three runs.

Program	getfield	putfield	getstatic	put-static	aload	astore	Total
compress	171158111	33762291	4090184	377	39946890	19386949	268344802
jess	17477337	372777	109024	27079	7910971	60241	25957429
db	2952234	166079	88134	35360	2135244	428809	5805860
mpegaudio	81362707	13571793	18414632	3511	155893220	25893308	295139171
jack	9117580	2847032	226457	171130	1005661	860617	14228477
javac	5363477	1797152	188401	3421	449841	223629	8025921
mtrt	26474627	4788579	53134	1927	8237230	800812	40356309
symantec	28553709	15211818	41	0	303340062	123075060	470180690

Table 1. Dynamic counts of memory operations, without scalar replacement.

We instrumented the compiled code to count each of the six types of Java memory operations eligible for optimization by our scalar replacement algorithms: getfield, putfield, getstatic, putstatic, aload and astore. Table 1 shows the dynamic count of each operation during a sample run of each program.

Program	getfield	putfield	getstatic	putstatic	aload	astore	Total
compress	25.9%	0.0%	0.0%	0.0%	0.0%	0.0%	16.5%
jess	1.0%	0.0%	0.0%	0.0%	0.0%	0.0%	0.7%
db	21.8%	0.0%	0.0%	0.0%	0.0%	0.0%	11.1%
mpegaudio	57.1%	9.0%	0.0%	0.0%	20.3%	10.6%	27.8%
jack	15.2%	0.9%	0.1%	0.0%	0.0%	0.0%	9.9%
javac	3.2%	0.0%	0.0%	0.0%	0.1%	0.0%	2.2%
mtrt	1.0%	0.0%	0.1%	0.0%	0.0%	0.0%	0.7%
symantec	7.9%	3.8%	0.0%	0.0%	33.2%	0.4%	22.1%

Table 2. Percentage of (dynamic) memory operations eliminated.

Table 2 shows the percentage of each type of memory operation eliminated by our scalar replacement algorithms. The table shows that overall, the algorithms eliminate between 0.7% and 27.8% of the loads and stores. The table shows that redundant load elimination eliminates many more operations than dead store elimination. On two codes, (mpegaudio and symantec), elimination of loads from arrays play a significant role. On the others, the algorithm eliminates mostly getfields. Interestingly, the algorithms are mostly ineffective at eliminating references to static variables; however, table 1 shows that these references are relatively infrequent.

Program	Time (no scalar replacement)	Time (scalar replacement)	Speedup
compress	5.75	5.32	1.08
jess	1.80	1.80	1.00
db	1.98	1.97	1.00
mpegaudio	7.25	6.59	1.10
jack	8.13	8.12	1.00
javac	2.61	2.60	1.00
mtrt	3.07	3.05	1.00
symantec	16.22	15.46	1.05

Table 3. Speedup due to scalar replacement.

Table 3 shows the improvement in running time due to the scalar replacement algorithm. The results show that the scalar replacement transformations give speedups of at least 1.05× on each of the three codes where the optimizations were most effective. Mpegaudio shows the greatest improvement with a speedup of 1.1×.

We conclude this section with a brief discussion of the impact of scalar replacement on register allocation. It has been observed in the past that scalar replacement can increase register pressure [5]. For example, the scalar replacement transformations shown in Figure 2(a) and Figure 2(b) eliminate load instructions at the expense of introducing temporaries with long live ranges. In our initial experiments, this extra register pressure resulted in performance degradations for some cases. We addressed the problem by introducing heuristics for live range splitting into our register allocator, which solved the problem.

5   Related Work

Past work on analysis and optimization of array and object references can be classified into three categories — analysis of array references in scientific programs written in languages with named arrays such as Fortran, analysis of pointer references in weakly typed languages such as C, and analysis of object references in strongly typed languages such as Modula-3 and Java. Our research builds on past work in the third category.

The analysis framework based on heap arrays reported in this paper can be viewed as a flow-sensitive extension of *type-based alias analysis* as in [11]. Three different versions of type-based alias analysis were reported in [11] — *TypeDecl* (based on declared types of object references), *FieldTypeDecl* (based on type declarations of fields) and *SMTypeRefs* (based on an inspection of assignment statements in the entire program). All three versions are flow-insensitive. The disambiguation provided by heap arrays in our approach is comparable to the disambiguation provided by *FieldTypeDecl* analysis. However, the use of value numbering and Array SSA form in our approach results in flow-sensitive analyses of array and object references that are more general than the three versions of type-based alias analysis in [11]. For example, none of the three versions would disambiguate references p.x and q.x in the example discussed earlier in Figure 2(a).

In the remainder of this section, we briefly compare our approach with relevant past work in the first two categories of analysis and optimization of array and object references.

The first category is analysis and optimization of array references in scientific programs. The early algorithms for scalar replacement (*e.g.,* [4]) were based on data dependence analysis and limited their attention to loops with restricted control flow. More recent algorithms for scalar replacement (*e.g.,* [5,2]) use analyses based on PRE (partial redundancy elimination) as an extension to data dependence analysis. However, all these past algorithms focused on accesses to elements of named arrays, as in Fortran, and did not consider the possibility of pointer-induced aliasing of arrays. Hence, these algorithms are not applicable to programming languages (such as C and Java) where arrays might themselves be aliased.

The second category is analysis and optimization of pointer references in weakly typed languages such as C. Analysis of such programs is a major challenge because the underlying language semantics forces the default assumptions to be highly conservative. It is usually necessary to perform a complex points-to analysis before pointer references can be classified as *stack*-directed or *heap-directed* and any effective optimization can be performed [12]. To address this challenge, there has been a large body of research on flow-sensitive pointer-induced alias analysis in weakly typed languages *e.g.,* [17,6,13,16,7]. However, these algorithms are too complex for use in efficient analysis of strongly typed languages, compared to the algorithms presented in this paper. Specifically, our algorithms analyze object references in the same SSA framework that has been used in the past for efficient scalar analysis. The fact that our approach uses global value numbering in SSA form (rather than pointer tracking) to determine if two pointers are the same or different leads to significant improvements in time and space efficiency. The efficiency arises because SSA generates a single value partition whereas pointer tracking leads to a different connection graph at different program points.

6   Conclusions and Future Work

In this paper, we presented a unified framework to analyze object-field and array-element references for programs written in strongly-typed languages such as Java and Modula-3. Our solution incorporates a novel approach for modeling object references as heap arrays, and on the use of global value numbering and allocation site information to determine if two object references are known to be same or different. We presented new algorithms to identify fully redundant loads and dead stores, based on sparse propagation in an extended Array SSA form. Our preliminary experimental results show that the (dynamic) number of memory operations arising from array-element and object-field accesses can be reduced by up to 28%, resulting in execution time speedups of up to 1.1×.

In the near future, we plan to use our extended Array SSA compiler infrastructure to extend other classical scalar analyses to deal with memory accesses. An interesting direction for longer-term research is to extend SSA-based value numbering (and the accompanying $\mathcal{DS}$ and $\mathcal{DD}$ analyses) to include the effect of array/object memory operations by using the Array SSA analysis framework. This extension will enable more precise analysis of nested object references of the form a.b.c, or equivalently, indirect array references of the form a[b[i]]. Eventually, our goal is to combine conditional constant and type propagation, value numbering, PRE, and scalar replacement analyses with a single framework that can analyze memory operations as effectively as scalar operations.

Acknowledgments

We thank David Grove, Michael Hind, Harini Srinivasan, Mark Wegman and Bill Thies for their comments and suggestions. Thanks also to the entire Jalapeño team for their contribution to the infrastructure used for the experimental results reported in this paper.

References

1. Bowen Alpern, Mark N. Wegman, and F. Kenneth Zadeck. Detecting Equality of Variables in Programs. *Fifteenth ACM Principles of Programming Languages Symposium*, pages 1–11, January 1988. San Diego, CA. 156, 160
2. R. Bodik and R. Gupta. Array Data-Flow Analysis for Load-Store Optimizations in Superscalar Architectures. *Lecture Notes in Computer Science*, (1033):1–15, 1995. Proceedings of Eighth Annual Workshop on Languages and Compilers for Parallel Computing, Columbus, Ohio, August 1995. 162, 171
3. Michael G. Burke, Jong-Deok Choi, Stephen Fink, David Grove, Michael Hind, Vivek Sarkar, Mauricio J. Serrano, V. C. Sreedhar, Harini Srinivasan, and John Whaley. The Jalapeño Dynamic Optimizing Compiler for Java. In *ACM Java Grande Conference*, June 1999. 156, 168

4. David Callahan, Steve Carr, and Ken Kennedy. Improving Register Allocation for Subscripted Variables. *Proceedings of the ACM SIGPLAN '90 Conference on Programming Language Design and Implementation, White Plains, New York*, pages 53–65, June 1990. 162, 171

5. Steve Carr and Ken Kennedy. Scalar Replacement in the Presence of Conditional Control Flow. *Software—Practice and Experience*, (1):51–77, January 1994. 162, 170, 171

6. David R. Chase, Mark Wegman, and F. Kenneth Zadeck. Analysis of Pointers and Structures. *Proceedings of the ACM SIGPLAN '90 Conference on Programming Language Design and Implementation, White Plains, New York*, 25(6):296–310, June 1990. 156, 171

7. Jong-Deok Choi, Michael Burke, and Paul Carini. Efficient flow-sensitive interprocedural computation of pointer-induced aliases and side effects. In *20th Annual ACM SIGACT-SIGPLAN Symposium on the Principles of Programming Languages*, pages 232–245, January 1993. 156, 171

8. Jong-Deok Choi, Ron Cytron, and Jeanne Ferrante. Automatic Construction of Sparse Data Flow Evaluation Graphs. *Conference Record of the Eighteenth Annual ACM Symposium on Principles of Programming Languages*, January 1991. 158

9. The Standard Performance Evaluation Corporation. SPEC JVM98 Benchmarks. http://www.spec.org/osg/jvm98/, 1998. 169

10. Ron Cytron, Jeanne Ferrante, Barry K. Rosen, Mark N. Wegman, and F. Kenneth Zadeck. Efficiently Computing Static Single Assignment Form and the Control Dependence Graph. *ACM Transactions on Programming Languages and Systems*, 13(4):451–490, October 1991. 158, 160, 165

11. Amer Diwan, Kathryn S. McKinley, and J. Eliot B. Moss. Type-based alias analysis. In *SIGPLAN '98 Conference on Programming Language Design and Implementation*, pages 106–117, May 1998. 156, 157, 171

12. Rakesh Ghiya and Laurie J. Hendren. Putting pointer analysis to work. In *25th Annual ACM SIGACT-SIGPLAN Symposium on the Principles of Programming Languages*, pages 121–133, January 1998. 156, 171

13. Laurie J. Hendren, Joseph Hummel, and Alexandru Nicolau. Abstractions for recursive pointer data structures: Improving the analysis of imperative programs. *Proceedings of the ACM SIGPLAN '92 Conference on Programming Language Design and Implementation*, pages 249–260, June 1992. 156, 171

14. Kathleen Knobe and Vivek Sarkar. Array SSA form and its use in Parallelization. In *25th Annual ACM SIGACT-SIGPLAN Symposium on the Principles of Programming Languages*, January 1998. 155, 156, 157, 158

15. Kathleen Knobe and Vivek Sarkar. Conditional constant propagation of scalar and array references using array SSA form. In Giorgio Levi, editor, *Lecture Notes in Computer Science, 1503*, pages 33–56. Springer-Verlag, 1998. Proceedings from the *5th International Static Analysis Symposium*. 155, 156, 158

16. William Landi, Barbara G. Ryder, and Sean Zhang. Interprocedural side effect analysis with pointer aliasing. *Proceedings of the ACM SIGPLAN '93 Conference on Programming Language Design and Implementation*, pages 56–67, May 1993. 156, 171

17. J. R. Larus and P. N. Hilfinger. Detecting conflicts between structure accesses. *Proceedings of the ACM SIGPLAN '88 Conference on Programming Language Design and Implementation*, 23(7):21–34, July 1988. 156, 171

18. Steven S. Muchnick. *Advanced Compiler Design & Implementation*. Morgan Kaufmann Publishers, Inc., San Francisco, California, 1997. 160

19. William Pugh. A new memory model for Java. Note sent to the JavaMemoryModel mailing list, http://www.cs.umd.edu/ pugh/java/memoryModel, October 22, 1999. 166

20. William Pugh. Fixing the Java Memory Model. In *ACM Java Grande Conference*, June 1999. 166

21. Barry K. Rosen, Mark N. Wegman, and F. Kenneth Zadeck. Global Value Numbers and Redundant Computations. *Fifteenth ACM Principles of Programming Languages Symposium*, pages 12–27, January 1988. San Diego, CA. 160

22. Michael J. Wolfe. *Optimizing Supercompilers for Supercomputers*. Pitman, London and The MIT Press, Cambridge, Massachusetts, 1989. In the series, Research Monographs in Parallel and Distributed Computing. 156

Polymorphic versus Monomorphic Flow-Insensitive Points-To Analysis for C[*]

Jeffrey S. Foster[1], Manuel Fähndrich[2], and Alexander Aiken[1]

[1] University of California
Berkeley, 387 Soda Hall #1776, Berkeley, CA 94720
{jfoster,aiken}@cs.berkeley.edu
[2] Microsoft Research, One Microsoft Way, Redmond, WA 98052
maf@microsoft.com

Abstract We carry out an experimental analysis for two of the design dimensions of flow-insensitive points-to analysis for C: polymorphic versus monomorphic and equality-based versus inclusion-based. Holding other analysis parameters fixed, we measure the precision of the four design points on a suite of benchmarks of up to 90,000 abstract syntax tree nodes. Our experiments show that the benefit of polymorphism varies significantly with the underlying monomorphic analysis. For our equality-based analysis, adding polymorphism greatly increases precision, while for our inclusion-based analysis, adding polymorphism hardly makes any difference. We also gain some insight into the nature of polymorphism in points-to analysis of C. In particular, we find considerable polymorphism available in function parameters, but little or no polymorphism in function results, and we show how this observation explains our results.

1 Introduction

When constructing a constraint-based program analysis, the analysis designer must weigh the costs and benefits of many possible design points. Two important tradeoffs are:

- Is the analysis *polymorphic* or *monomorphic*? A polymorphic analysis separates analysis information by call site, while monomorphic analysis conflates all call sites. A polymorphic analysis is more precise but also more expensive than a corresponding monomorphic analysis.
- What is the underlying constraint relation? Possibilities include equalities (solved with unification) or more precise and expensive inclusions (solved with dynamic transitive closure), among many others.

Intuitively, if we want the greatest possible precision, we should use a polymorphic inclusion-based analysis, while if we are mostly concerned with efficiency, we should use a monomorphic equality-based analysis. But how much

---

[*] This research was supported in part by the National Science Foundation Young Investigator Award No. CCR-9457812, NASA Contract No. NAG2-1210, an NDSEG fellowship, and an equipment donation from Intel.

J. Palsberg (Ed.): SAS 2000, LNCS 1824, pp. 175–199, 2000.

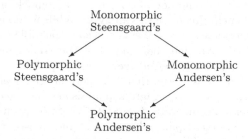

Figure1. Relation between the four analyses. There is an edge from analysis x to analysis y if y is *at least as precise* as x.

more precision does polymorphism add, and what do we lose by using equality constraints? In this paper, we try to answer these questions for a particular constraint-based program analysis, *flow-insensitive points-to analysis for C*. Our goal is to compare the tradeoffs between the four possible combinations of polymorphism/monomorphism and equality constraints/inclusion constraints.

Points-to analysis computes, for each expression in a C program, a set of abstract memory locations (variables and heap) to which the expression could point. Our monomorphic inclusion-based analysis (Sect. 4.1) implements a version of Andersen's points-to analysis [4], and our monomorphic equality-based analysis (Sect. 4.2) implements a version of Steensgaard's points-to analysis [29]. To add polymorphism to Andersen's and Steensgaard's analyses (Sect. 4.3), we use Hindley-Milner style parametric polymorphism [21].

Our analyses are designed such that monomorphic Andersen's analysis is at least as precise as monomorphic Steensgaard's analysis [16,28], and similarly for the polymorphic versions. Given the construction of our analyses, it is a theorem that the hierarchy of precision shown in Fig. 1 always holds. The main contribution of this work is the quantification of the exact relationship among these analyses. A secondary contribution of this paper is the development of polymorphic versions of Andersen's and Steensgaard's points-to analyses.

Running the analyses on our suite of benchmarks, we find the following results (see Sect. 5), where $\ll$ is read "is significantly less precise than." In general,

Monomorphic Steensgaard's $\ll$
Polymorphic Steensgaard's $\ll$
Polymorphic Andersen's

Monomorphic Steensgaard's $\ll$
Monomorphic Andersen's $\approx$
Polymorphic Andersen's

The exact relationships vary from benchmark to benchmark. These results are rather surprising—why should polymorphism not add much precision to Andersen's analysis but benefit Steensgaard's analysis? While we do not have definitive answers to these questions, Sect. 5.3 suggests some possible explanations.

Notice from this table that monomorphic Andersen's analysis is approximately as precise as polymorphic Andersen's analysis, while polymorphic Steensgaard's analysis is much less precise than polymorphic Andersen's analysis. Note, however, that polymorphic Steensgaard's analysis and monomorphic Andersen's analysis are in general incomparable (see Sect. 5.1). Still, given that polymorphic analyses are much more complicated to understand, reason about, and implement than their monomorphic counterparts, these results suggest that monomorphic Andersen's analysis may represent the best design choice among the four analyses. This may be a general principle: in order to improve a program analysis, developing a more powerful monomorphic analysis may be preferable to adding context-sensitivity, one example of which is Hindley-Milner style polymorphism.

Carrying out an experimental exploration of even a portion of the design space for non-trivial program analyses is a painstaking task. In interpreting our results there are two important things to keep in mind. First, our exploration of even the limited design space of flow-insensitive points-to analysis for C is still partial—there are dimensions other than the two that we explore that may not be orthogonal and may lead to different tradeoffs. For example, it may matter how precisely heap memory is modeled, how strings are modeled, whether C **structs** are analyzed by field or all fields are summarized together, and so on. Section 5 details our choices for these parameters. Also, Hindley-Milner style polymorphism is only one way to add context-sensitivity to a points-to analysis, and other approaches (e.g., polymorphic recursion [15]) may yield different tradeoffs.

Second, our experiments measure the relative precision of each analysis. They do not measure the relative impact of each analysis in a compiler. For example, it may be that some points-to sets are more important than others to an optimizer, and thus increases in precision may not always lead to better optimizations. However, a more precise analysis should not lead to worse optimizations than a less precise analysis. We should also point out that it is difficult to separate the benefit of a pointer analysis in a compiler from the design of the rest of the optimizer. Measures of relative precision have the advantage of being independent of the specific choices made in using the analysis information by a particular tool.

2   Related Work

Andersen's [4] and Steensgaard's [29] points-to analyses are only two choices in a vast array of possible alias analyses, among them [5,6,7,8,9,10,11,15,19,20,27,28,31,33,34]. As our results suggest, the benefit of polymorphism (more generally, *context-sensitivity*) may vary greatly with the particular analysis.

Hindley-Milner style polymorphism [21] has been studied extensively. The only direct applications of Hindley-Milner polymorphism to C of which we are aware are the analyses in this paper, the polymorphic recursive analysis proposed in [15] (see below), and the Lackwit system [23]. Lackwit, a software engineering tool, computes ML-style types for C and appears to scale very well to large programs.

Mossin [22] develops a polymorphic flow analysis based on polymorphic recursion and atomic subtyping constraints. Mossin's system starts with a type-annotated program and infers atomic flow constraints, whereas we infer the type and flow annotations simultaneously and do not have an atomic subtyping system. [15] develops an efficient algorithm for both subtyping and equality-based polymorphic recursive flow analyses, and shows how to construct a polymorphic recursive version of Steensgaard's analysis. (In contrast, in this paper we use Hindley-Milner style polymorphism, which can be less precise.) We believe that the techniques of [15] can also be adapted to Andersen's analysis.

Other research has explored making monomorphic inclusion-based analyses scalable. [14] describes an online cycle-elimination algorithm for simplifying inclusion constraints. [30] describes a related optimization technique, *projection merging*, which merges multiple projections of the same set variable. Our current implementation uses both of these techniques, which makes it possible to run the polymorphic inclusion-based analysis on our larger benchmarks.

Finally, we discuss a selection of related analyses. Wilson and Lam [31] propose a flow-sensitive alias analysis that distinguishes calls to the same function in different aliasing contexts. Their system analyzes a function once for each aliasing pattern of its actual parameters. In contrast, we analyze each function only once, independently of its context, by constructing types that summarize functions' points-to effects in any context.

Ruf [26] studies the tradeoff between context-sensitivity and context-insensitivity for a particular dataflow-style alias analysis, discovering that context-sensitivity makes little appreciable difference in the accuracy of the results. Our results partially agree with his. For Andersen's inclusion-based analysis we find the same trend. However, for Steensgaard's equality-based analysis, which is substantially less precise than Ruf's analysis, adding polymorphism makes a significant difference

Emami, Ghiya, and Hendren [11] propose a flow-sensitive, context-sensitive analysis. The scalability of this analysis is unknown.

Landi and Ryder [20] study a very precise flow-sensitive, context-sensitive analysis. Their flow-sensitive system has difficulty scaling to large programs; recent work has focused on combined analyses that apply different alias analyses to different parts of a program [35].

Chatterjee, Ryder, and Landi [6] propose an analysis for Java and C++ that uses a flow-sensitive analysis with conditional points-to relations whose validity depends on the aliasing and type information provided by the context. While the style of polymorphism used in [6] appears related to Hindley-Milner style polymorphism, the exact relationship is unclear.

Das [7] proposes a monomorphic alias analysis with precision close to Andersen's analysis but cost close to Steensgaard's analysis. The effect of adding polymorphism to Das's analysis is currently unknown but cannot yield more precision than polymorphic Andersen's analysis.

3   Constraints

Our analyses are formulated as non-standard type systems for C. We follow the usual approach for constraint-based program analysis: As the analyses infer types for a program's expressions, a system of typing constraints is generated on the side. The solution to the constraints defines the points-to graph of the program.

Our analyses are implemented with the Berkeley Analysis Engine (BANE) [1], which is a framework for constructing constraint-based analyses. BANE supports analyses involving multiple *sorts* of constraints, two of which are used by our points-to analyses. Our implementation of Andersen's analysis uses inclusion (or *set*) constraints [2,18]. Our implementation of Steensgaard's analysis uses a mixture of equality (or *term*) and inclusion constraints. The rest of this section provides background on the constraint formalisms.

Each sort of constraint comes equipped with a constraint relation. The relation between set expressions is $\subseteq$, and the relation between term expressions is $=$. For our purposes, *set expressions se* consist of set variables $\mathcal{X}, \mathcal{Y}, \ldots$ from a family of variables *Vars* (caligraphic text denotes variables), terms constructed from n-ary constructors $c \in Con$, a special form $proj(c, i, se)$, an empty set 0, and a universal set 1.

$$se ::= \mathcal{X} \mid c(se_1, \ldots, se_n) \mid proj(c, i, se) \mid 0 \mid 1$$

Similarly, *term expressions* are of the form

$$te ::= \mathcal{X} \mid c(te_1, \ldots, te_n) \mid 0$$

Here 0 represents a special, distinguished nullary constructor.

Each constructor c is given a *signature* S_c specifying the arity, variance, and sort of c. If S is the set of sorts (in this case, $S = \{\textbf{Term}, \textbf{Set}\}$), then constructor signatures are of the form

$$c : \iota_1 \times \cdots \times \iota_{\text{arity}(c)} \to S$$

where ι_i is s (covariant) or $\bar{s}$ (contravariant) for some $s \in S$. Intuitively, a constructor c is *covariant* in an argument $\mathcal{X}$ if the set denoted by a term $c(\ldots, \mathcal{X}, \ldots)$ becomes larger as $\mathcal{X}$ increases. Similarly, a constructor c is *contravariant* in an argument $\mathcal{X}$ if the set denoted by a term $c(\ldots, \mathcal{X}, \ldots)$ becomes smaller as $\mathcal{X}$ increases. To improve readability, we mark contravariant arguments with overbars.

One example constructor from Andersen's analysis is

$$lam : \textbf{Set} \times \overline{\textbf{Set}} \times \textbf{Set} \to \textbf{Set}$$

The *lam* constructor models function types. The first (covariant) argument names the function, the second (contravariant) argument represents the domain, and the third (covariant) argument represents the range.

Steensgaard's analysis uses a constructor

$$ref : \textbf{Set} \times \textbf{Term} \times \textbf{Term} \rightarrow \textbf{Term}$$

to model locations. The first field models the set of aliases of this location, and the second and third fields model the contents of this location. See Sect. 4.2 for a discussion of why a set is needed for the first field. More discussion of mixed constraints can be found in [12,13].

Our system also includes *conditional equality constraints* $L \leq R$ (defined on terms) to support Steensgaard's analysis (see Sect. 4.2). The constraint $L \leq R$ holds if either $L = R$ or $L = 0$ holds. Intuitively, if L is ever unified with a constructed term, then the constraint $L \leq R$ becomes $L = R$. Otherwise $L \leq R$ makes no constraint on R.

Our language of set constraints has no explicit operation to select components of a constructor. Instead we use constraints of the form

$$L \subseteq c(\ldots, \mathcal{Y}_i, \ldots) \tag{$*$}$$

to make $\mathcal{Y}_i$ contain $c^{-i}(L)$ if c is covariant in i, and to make $c^{-i}(L)$ contain $\mathcal{Y}_i$ if c is contravariant in i. However, such a constraint is inconsistent if L contains terms whose head constructor is not c. To overcome this limitation, we define constraints of the form

$$L \subseteq proj(c, i, \mathcal{Y}_i)$$

This constraint has the same effect as $(*)$ on the elements of L constructed with c, and no effect on the other elements of L.

Solving a system of constraints involves computing an explicit *solved form* of all solutions or of a particular solution. See [3,12,13] for a thorough discussion of the constraint solver used in BANE.

4   The Analyses

This section develops monomorphic and polymorphic versions of Andersen's and Steensgaard's analyses. The presentation of the monomorphic version of Andersen's analysis mostly follows [14,30] and is given primarily to make the paper self contained.

For a C program, points-to analysis computes a set of abstract memory locations (variables and heap) to which each expression could point. Andersen's and Steensgaard's analyses compute a *points-to graph* [11]. Graph nodes represent abstract memory locations, and there is an edge from a node x to a node y if x may contain a pointer to y. Informally, the analyses begin with some initial points-to relationships and close the graph under the rule

For an assignment $e_1 = e_2$, anything in the points-to set for e_2 must also be in the points-to set for e_1.

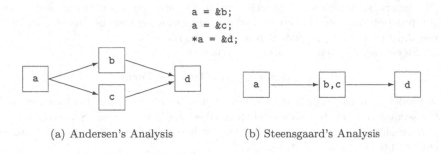

(a) Andersen's Analysis   (b) Steensgaard's Analysis

Figure2. Example points-to graph

For Andersen's analysis, each node in the points-to graph may have directed edges to any number of other nodes. For Steensgaard's analysis, each node may have at most one out-edge, and graph nodes are coalesced if necessary to enforce this requirement. Figure 2 shows the points-to graph for a simple C program computed by Andersen's analysis (a) and Steensgaard's analysis (b).

4.1   Andersen's Analysis

In Andersen's analysis, types τ represent sets of abstract memory locations and are described by the following grammar:

$$\rho ::= \mathcal{P}_{\mathbf{x}} \mid l_{\mathbf{x}}$$
$$\tau ::= \mathcal{X} \mid \mathit{ref}(\rho, \tau, \overline{\tau}) \mid \mathit{lam}(\rho, \overline{\tau}, \tau)$$

Here the constructor signatures are

$$\mathit{ref} : \mathbf{Set} \times \mathbf{Set} \times \overline{\mathbf{Set}} \to \mathbf{Set}$$
$$\mathit{lam} : \mathbf{Set} \times \overline{\mathbf{Set}} \times \mathbf{Set} \to \mathbf{Set}$$

$\mathcal{X}$ and $\mathcal{P}_{\mathbf{x}}$ are set variables, and $l_{\mathbf{x}}$ is a constant (a constructor of arity 0). Contravariant arguments are marked with overbars. Note that function types $\mathit{lam}(\cdots)$ are contravariant in the domain (second argument) and covariant in the range (third argument).

Memory locations can be thought of as abstract data types with two operations, one to *get* the value stored in the location and one to *set* it. Intuitively, the *get* and *set* operations have types

- $\mathit{get} : \mathtt{void} \to \mathcal{X}$
- $\mathit{set} : \mathcal{X} \to \mathtt{void}$

where $\mathcal{X}$ is the type of data held in the memory location. Dereferencing a location corresponds to applying the *get* operation, and updating a location corresponds to applying the *set* operation. Note that the type variable $\mathcal{X}$ appears covariantly in the type of the *get* operation and contravariantly in the type of the *set* operation.

Translating this intuition into a set constraint formulation, the location of a variable x is modeled with the type $ref(l_{\mathbf{x}}, \mathcal{X}, \overline{\mathcal{X}})$, where $l_{\mathbf{x}}$ is a constant representing the name of the location, the covariant occurrence of $\mathcal{X}$ represents the *get* method, and the contravariant occurrence of $\mathcal{X}$ (marked with an overbar) represents the *set* method. For convenience, we choose not to represent the void components of the *get* and *set* methods' types.

We also associate with each location x a set variable $\mathcal{P}_{\mathbf{x}}$ and add the constraints $\mathcal{X} \subseteq proj(ref, 1, \mathcal{P}_{\mathbf{x}})$ and $\mathcal{X} \subseteq proj(lam, 1, \mathcal{P}_{\mathbf{x}})$. This constrains $\mathcal{P}_{\mathbf{x}}$ to contain the set of abstract locations, including functions, in the points-to set $\mathcal{X}$. The points-to graph is then defined by the least solution of $\mathcal{P}_{\mathbf{x}}$ for every location x. In the set formulation, the least solution for the points-to graph shown in Fig. 2a is

$$\mathcal{P}_{\mathbf{a}} = \{l_{\mathbf{b}}, l_{\mathbf{c}}\} \qquad \mathcal{P}_{\mathbf{b}} = \{l_{\mathbf{d}}\} \qquad \mathcal{P}_{\mathbf{c}} = \{l_{\mathbf{d}}\}$$

In addition to reference types we also must model function types, since C allows pointers to functions to be stored in memory. The type $lam(l_{\mathbf{f}}, \overline{\tau_1}, \tau_2)$ represents the function named f (every C function has a name) with argument τ_1 and return value τ_2. For simplicity the grammar allows only one argument. In our implementation, arguments are modeled with an ordered record $\{\tau_1, \ldots, \tau_n\}$ [25].[1]

Figure 3 shows a fragment of the type rules for the monomorphic version of Andersen's analysis. Judgments are of the form $A \vdash e : \tau; C$, meaning that in typing environment A, expression e has type τ under the constraints C. For simplicity we present only the interesting type rules. The full rules for all of C can be found in [16].

We briefly discuss the rules. To avoid having separate rules for *l*- and *r*-values, we model all variables as *l*-types. Thus the type of a variable x is our representation of its location, i.e., a *ref* type.

- Rule (Var_A) states that typings in the environment trivially hold.
- The address-of operator (Addr_A) adds a level of indirection to its operand by adding a *ref* constructor. The location (first) and *set* (third) fields of the resulting type are 0 and 1, respectively, because &e is not itself an *l*-value and cannot be updated.
- The dereferencing operator (Deref_A) removes a *ref* and makes the fresh variable $\mathcal{T}$ a superset of the points-to set of τ. Note the use of *proj* in case τ also contains a function type.
- The assignment rule (Asst_A) uses the same technique as (Deref_A) to *get* the contents of the right-hand side, and then uses the contravariant *set* field of the *ref* constructor to store the contents in the left-hand side location. See [16] for detailed explanations and examples.

---

[1] Note that we do not handle variable-length argument lists (varargs) correctly even with records. Handling varargs requires compiler- and architecture-specific knowledge of the layout of parameters in memory. See Sect. 5.

$$\overline{A \vdash \mathbf{x} : A(\mathbf{x}); \emptyset} \qquad\qquad\qquad (\mathrm{Var}_A)$$

$$\frac{A \vdash e : \tau; C}{A \vdash \&e : ref(0, \tau, \overline{1}); C} \qquad\qquad (\mathrm{Addr}_A)$$

$$\frac{\begin{array}{c} A \vdash e : \tau; C \\ C' = C \ \wedge \ \tau \subseteq proj\,(ref, 2, \mathcal{T}) \end{array}}{A \vdash *e : \mathcal{T}; C'} \qquad (\mathrm{Deref}_A)$$

$$\frac{\begin{array}{c} A \vdash e_1 : \tau_1; C_1 \ A \vdash e_2 : \tau_2; C_2 \\ C = C_1 \ \wedge \ C_2 \ \wedge \\ \tau_1 \subseteq proj\,(ref, 3, \mathcal{T}) \ \wedge \\ \tau_2 \subseteq proj\,(ref, 2, \mathcal{T}) \end{array}}{A \vdash e_1 {=} e_2 : \tau_2; C} \qquad (\mathrm{Asst}_A)$$

$$\frac{A[\mathbf{x} \mapsto ref(l_{\mathbf{x}}, \mathcal{X}, \overline{\mathcal{X}})] \vdash e : \tau; C}{A \vdash \mathtt{let}\ x\ \mathtt{in}\ e\ \mathbf{ni} : \tau; C} \qquad (\mathrm{LetRef}_A)$$

$$\frac{\begin{array}{c} \tau_f = ref(0, lam(l_{\mathbf{f}}, \overline{\mathcal{X}}, \mathcal{R}_{\mathbf{f}}), \overline{1}) \\ \tau_x = ref(l_{\mathbf{x}}, \mathcal{X}, \overline{\mathcal{X}}) \\ A[\mathbf{f} \mapsto \tau_f, \mathbf{x} \mapsto \tau_x] \vdash e : \tau; C \\ C' = C \ \wedge \ \tau \subseteq proj\,(ref, 2, \mathcal{R}_{\mathbf{f}}) \end{array}}{A \vdash \mathtt{fun}\ \mathbf{f}\ \mathbf{x} \ = \ e : \tau_f; C'} \qquad (\mathrm{Lam}_A)$$

$$\frac{\begin{array}{c} A \vdash *e_1 : \tau_1; C_1 \ A \vdash e_2 : \tau_2; C_2 \\ C = C_1 \ \wedge \ C_2 \ \wedge \\ \tau_2 \subseteq proj\,(ref, 2, \mathcal{T}) \ \wedge \\ \tau_1 \subseteq proj\,(lam, 2, \mathcal{T}) \ \wedge \\ \tau_1 \subseteq proj\,(lam, 3, \mathcal{R}) \end{array}}{A \vdash e_1\ e_2 : ref(0, \mathcal{R}, \overline{1}); C} \qquad (\mathrm{App}_A)$$

Figure3. Constraint generation rules for Andersen's analysis. $\mathcal{T}$ and $\mathcal{R}$ stand for fresh variables

- The rule (LetRef$_A$) introduces new variables. Since this is C, all variables are in fact updateable references, and we allow them to be uninitialized.
- The rule (Lam$_A$) defines a possibly-recursive function $\mathbf{f}$ whose result is e. We lift each function type to an l-type by adding a ref as in (Asst$_A$). For simplicity the C issues of promotions from function types to pointer types, and the corresponding issues with * and & applied to functions, are ignored. These issues are handled correctly by our implementation. Notice a function type contains the value of its parameter, $\mathcal{X}$, not a reference $ref(l_{\mathbf{x}}, \mathcal{X}, \overline{\mathcal{X}})$. Analogously the range of the function type is also a value.
- Function application (App$_A$) constrains the formal parameter of a function type to contain the actual parameter, and makes the return type of the function a lower bound on fresh variable $\mathcal{R}$. Notice the use of $*e_1$ in the hypothesis of this rule, which we need because the function, an r-type, has

been lifted to an l-type in (Lam$_S$). The result $\mathcal{R}$, which is an r-type, is lifted to an l-type by adding a ref constructor, as in (Addr$_A$).

4.2 Steensgaard's Analysis

Intuitively, Steensgaard's analysis replaces the inclusion constraints of Andersen's analysis with equality constraints. The type language is a small modification of the previous system:

$$\rho ::= \mathcal{P}_\mathbf{x} \mid \mathcal{L}_\mathbf{x} \mid l_\mathbf{x}$$
$$\tau ::= \mathcal{X} \mid ref(\rho, \tau, \eta)$$
$$\eta ::= \mathcal{X} \mid lam(\tau, \tau)$$

with constructor signatures

$$ref : \mathbf{Set} \times \mathbf{Term} \times \mathbf{Term} \to \mathbf{Term}$$
$$lam : \mathbf{Term} \times \mathbf{Term} \to \mathbf{Term}$$

As before, ρ denotes locations and τ denotes updateable references. Following [29], in this system function types η are always structurally within $ref(\cdots)$ types because in a system of equality constraints we cannot express a union $ref(\ldots) \cup lam(\ldots)$. For a similar reason location sets ρ consist solely of variables $\mathcal{P}_\mathbf{x}$ or $\mathcal{L}_\mathbf{x}$ and are modeled as sets (see below).

Each program variable $\mathbf{x}$ is modeled with the type $ref(\mathcal{L}_\mathbf{x}, \mathcal{X}, \mathcal{F}_\mathbf{x})$, where $\mathcal{L}_\mathbf{x}$ is a **Set** variable. For each location $\mathbf{x}$ we add a constraint $l_\mathbf{x} \subseteq \mathcal{L}_\mathbf{x}$, where $l_\mathbf{x}$ is a nullary constructor (as in Andersen's analysis). We also associate with location $\mathbf{x}$ another set variable $\mathcal{P}_\mathbf{x}$ and add the constraint $\mathcal{X} \leq ref(\mathcal{P}_\mathbf{x}, *, *)$, where $*$ stands for a fresh unnamed variable.

We compute the points-to graph by finding the least solution of the $\mathcal{P}_\mathbf{x}$ variables. For the points-to graph in Fig. 2b, the result is

$$\mathcal{P}_\mathsf{a} = \{l_\mathsf{b}, l_\mathsf{c}\} \qquad \mathcal{P}_\mathsf{b} = \{l_\mathsf{d}\} \qquad \mathcal{P}_\mathsf{c} = \{l_\mathsf{d}\}$$

Notice that b and c are inferred to be aliased, i.e., $\mathcal{L}_\mathsf{b} = \mathcal{L}_\mathsf{c}$. If we had instead used nullary constructors directly in the ρ field of ref, or had the ρ field been a **Term** sort, then the constraints would have been inconsistent, since $l_\mathsf{b} \neq l_\mathsf{c}$.

In Steensgaard's formulation [29], the relation between locations $\mathbf{x}$ and their corresponding term variables $\mathcal{P}_\mathbf{x}$ is implicit. While this suffices for a monomorphic analysis, in a polymorphic analysis maintaining this map is problematic, as generalization, simplification, and instantiation (see Sect. 4.3) all cause variables to be renamed.

Mixed constraints provide an elegant solution to this problem. By explicitly representing the mapping from locations to location names in a constraint formulation, we guarantee that any sound constraint manipulations preserve this mapping.

Figure 4 shows the constraint generation rules for Steensgaard's analysis. The rules are similar to the rules for Andersen's analysis. Again, we briefly discuss the rules. As before, all variables are modeled as l-types.

$$\overline{A \vdash \mathbf{x} : A(\mathbf{x}); \emptyset} \qquad (\text{Var}_S)$$

$$\frac{A \vdash e : \tau; C}{A \vdash \&e : ref(*, \tau, *); C} \qquad (\text{Addr}_S)$$

$$\frac{\begin{array}{c} A \vdash e : \tau; C \\ C' = C \ \wedge \ \tau \leq ref(*, \mathcal{T}, *) \end{array}}{A \vdash *e : \mathcal{T}; C'} \qquad (\text{Deref}_S)$$

$$\frac{\begin{array}{c} A \vdash e_1 : \tau_1; C_1 \qquad A \vdash e_2 : \tau_2; C_2 \\ C = C_1 \ \wedge \ C_2 \ \wedge \\ \tau_1 \leq ref(*, \mathcal{T}_1, *) \ \wedge \ \tau_2 \leq ref(*, \mathcal{T}_2, *) \ \wedge \\ \mathcal{T}_2 \leq \mathcal{T}_1 \end{array}}{A \vdash e_1 = e_2 : \tau_2; C} \qquad (\text{Asst}_S)$$

$$\frac{A[\mathbf{x} \mapsto ref(\mathcal{L}_{\mathbf{x}}, \mathcal{X}, \mathcal{F}_{\mathbf{x}})] \vdash e : \tau; C}{A \vdash \mathtt{let}\ x\ \mathtt{in}\ e\ \mathtt{ni} : \tau; C} \qquad (\text{LetRef}_S)$$

$$\frac{\begin{array}{c} \tau_f = ref(*, ref(\mathcal{L}_{\mathbf{f}}, \mathcal{T}_{\mathbf{f}}, lam(\mathcal{X}, \mathcal{R}_{\mathbf{f}})), *) \\ \tau_x = ref(\mathcal{L}_{\mathbf{x}}, \mathcal{X}, \mathcal{F}_{\mathbf{x}}) \\ A[\mathbf{f} \mapsto \tau_f, \mathbf{x} \mapsto \tau_x] \vdash e : \tau; C \\ C' = C \ \wedge \ \tau \leq ref(*, \mathcal{T}, *) \ \wedge \ \mathcal{T} \leq \mathcal{R}_{\mathbf{f}} \end{array}}{A \vdash \mathtt{fun}\ \mathbf{f}\ \mathbf{x}\ =\ e : \tau_f; C'} \qquad (\text{Lam}_S)$$

$$\frac{\begin{array}{c} A \vdash *e_1 : \tau_1; C_1 \qquad A \vdash e_2 : \tau_2; C_2 \\ C = C_1 \ \wedge \ C_2 \ \wedge \\ \tau_1 \leq ref(*, *, \mathcal{F}) \ \wedge \ \mathcal{F} \leq lam(\mathcal{Y}, \mathcal{R}) \ \wedge \\ \tau_2 \leq ref(*, \mathcal{T}, *) \ \wedge \ \mathcal{T} \leq \mathcal{Y} \end{array}}{A \vdash e_1\ e_2 : ref(*, \mathcal{R}, *); C} \qquad (\text{App}_S)$$

Figure 4. Constraint generation rules for Steensgaard's analysis. $\mathcal{T}, \mathcal{T}_1, \mathcal{T}_2, \mathcal{Y}$, and $\mathcal{R}$ are fresh variables. Each occurrence of $*$ is a fresh, unnamed variable

- Rules (Var_S) and (LetRef_S) are unchanged from Andersen's analysis.
- Rule (Addr_S) adds a level of indirection to its operand.
- Rule (Deref_S) removes a ref and makes fresh variable $\mathcal{T}$ contain the points-to set of τ.
- The assignment rule (Asst_S) makes fresh variables $\mathcal{T}_i$ contain the points-to sets of each e_i. (Asst_S) conditionally equates $\mathcal{T}_1$ with $\mathcal{T}_2$, i.e., if e_2 is a pointer, its points-to set is unified with the points-to set of e_1. Using conditional unification increases the accuracy of the analysis [29].
- Function definition (Lam_S) behaves as in Andersen's analysis. Here, $ref(\mathcal{L}_{\mathbf{f}},\ \mathcal{T}_{\mathbf{f}}, lam(\mathcal{X}, \mathcal{R}_{\mathbf{f}}))$ represents the function type and the outermost ref lifts the function type to an l-type. Again a function type contains the r-types of its parameter and return value rather than their l-types. Notice that the type of the function $\mathbf{f}$ points to is stored in the second (τ) field of $\mathbf{f}$'s type $\tau_{\mathbf{f}}$, not in the third (η) field. Thus in the assignment rule (Asst_S),

$$\frac{A \vdash e : \tau ; C \quad \vec{\mathcal{X}} \notin \mathrm{fv}(A)}{A \vdash e : \forall \vec{\mathcal{X}}.\tau \backslash C ; C} \qquad \text{(Quant)}$$

$$\frac{A \vdash e : \forall \vec{\mathcal{X}}.\tau \backslash C' ; C \quad \vec{y} \text{ fresh}}{A \vdash e : \tau[\vec{\mathcal{X}} \mapsto \vec{y}] ; C \wedge C'[\vec{\mathcal{X}} \mapsto \vec{y}]} \qquad \text{(Inst)}$$

Figure5. Rules for quantification

the $\mathcal{T}_i$ variables contain both the functions and memory locations that the e_i point to.

- Function application (App$_S$) conditionally equates the formal and actual parameters of a function type and evaluates to the return type. Note the use of $*e_1$ in the hypothesis of this rule, which is needed since the function type has been lifted to an l-type. Intuitively, this rule expands the application $(\mathtt{fun\ f\ x} = e)\ e_2$ into the sequence $\mathtt{x} = e_2; e$.

4.3   Adding Polymorphism

This section describes how the monomorphic analyses are extended to polymorphic analyses. While ultimately we find polymorphism unprofitable for our points-to analyses, this section documents a number of practical insights for the implementation of polymorphism in analysis systems considerably more elaborate than the Hindley/Milner system.

The rules in Figs. 3 and 4 track the constraints generated in the analysis of each expression. The monomorphic analyses have one global constraint system. In the polymorphic analyses, each function body has a distinct constraint system.

We introduce polymorphic constrained types of the form $\forall \vec{\mathcal{X}}.\tau \backslash C$. The type $\forall \vec{\mathcal{X}}.\tau \backslash C$ represents any type of the form $\tau[\vec{\mathcal{X}} \mapsto \vec{se}]$ under constraints $C[\vec{\mathcal{X}} \mapsto \vec{se}]$, for any choice of $\vec{se}$. Figure 5 shows the additional rules for quantification. The notation $\mathrm{fv}(A)$ stands for the free variables of environment A. Rule (Quant) states that we may quantify a type over any variables not free in the type environment. (Inst) allows us to instantiate a quantified type with fresh variables, adding the constraints from the quantified type to the system. These rules are standard [24].

We restrict quantification to non-*ref* types to avoid well-known problems with mixing updateable references and polymorphism [32]. In practical terms, this means that after analyzing a function definition, we can quantify over its parameters and its return value. The rule (Inst) says that we may instantiate a quantified type with fresh variables, adding the constraints from the quantified type to the environment.

If used naïvely, rule (Quant) amounts to analyzing a program in which all function calls have been inlined. In order to make the polymorphic analyses tractable, we perform a number of simplifications to reduce the sizes of quantified types. See [17] for a discussion of the simplifications we use.

As an example of the potential benefit of polymorphic points-to analysis, consider the following atypical C program:

```
int *id(int *x) { return x; }

int main() {
    int a, b, *c, *d;
    c = id(&a); d = id(&b);
}
```

In the notation in this paper `id` is defined as **fun** id x $=$ x. In monomorphic Andersen's analysis all inputs to `id` flow to all outputs. Thus we discover that c and d both point to a and b. Polymorphic Andersen's analysis assigns `id` type

$$\forall \mathcal{X}, \mathcal{R}_{\text{id}}. \, lam(l_{\text{id}}, \overline{\mathcal{X}}, \mathcal{R}_{\text{id}}) \backslash$$
$$ref(l_{\text{x}}, \mathcal{X}, \overline{\mathcal{X}}) \subseteq proj(ref, 2, \mathcal{R}_{\text{id}})$$

Solving these constraints and simplifying (see [17]) yields

$$\forall \mathcal{X}. \, lam(l_{\text{id}}, \overline{\mathcal{X}}, \mathcal{X}) \backslash \emptyset$$

In other words, `id` is the identity function. Because this type is instantiated for each call of `id`, the points-to sets are computed exactly: c points to a and d points to b.

There are several important observations about the type system. First, function pointers do not have polymorphic types. Consider the following example:

```
int *f(...) { ... }
int foo(int *(*g)()) { x = g(...); y = g(...); z = f(...); }
int main() { foo(f); }
```

Within the body of `foo`, the type of g appears in the environment (with a monomorphic type), so variables in the type of g cannot be quantified. Hence both calls to g use the same instance of f's type. The call directly through f can use a polymorphic type for f, and hence is to a fresh instance.

Second, we do not allow the types of mutually recursive functions to be polymorphic within the recursive definition. Thus we analyze sets of mutually recursive functions monomorphically and then generalize the types afterwards.

Finally, we require that function definitions be analyzed before function uses. We formally state this requirement using the following definition:

Definition 1. The *function dependence graph (FDG)* of a program is a graph $G = (V, E)$ with vertices V and edges E. V is the set of all functions in the program, and there is an edge in E from f to g iff function f contains an occurrence of the name of g.

A function's successors in the FDG for a program must be analyzed before the function itself. Note that the FDG is trivial to compute from the program text.

1.	Make a fresh global constraint system *Glob*
2.	Construct the function dependence graph *G*
3.	For each non-root strongly-connected component *S* of *G* in final depth-first order
3a.	Make a fresh constraint system *C*
3b.	Analyze each f ∈ *S* monomorphically in *C*
3c.	Quantify each f ∈ *S* in *C*, applying simplifications
3d.	Compute *C′* = *C* simplified and merge *C′* into *Glob*
4.	Analyze the root SCC in *Glob*

Figure6. Algorithm 1: Bottom-up pass

Figure 6 shows the algorithm for analyzing a program polymorphically. Each strongly-connected component of the FDG is visited in final depth-first order. We analyze each mutually-recursive component monomorphically and then apply quantification. We merge the simplified system C' into the top-level constraint system *Glob*, replacing *Glob* by *Glob* ∧ C'. Notice that we do not require a call graph for the analysis, but only the FDG, which is statically computable.

4.4   Reconstructing Local Information

After applying the bottom-up pass of Fig. 6, the analysis has correctly computed the points-to graph for the global variables and the local variables of the outermost function, usually called main. (There is no need to quantify the type of main, since its type can only be used monomorphically.) At this point we have lost alias information for local variables, for two reasons. First, applying simplifications during the analysis may eliminate the points-to variables corresponding to local variables completely. Second, whenever we apply (Inst) to instantiate the type of a function f, we deliberately lose information about the types of f's local variables by replacing their points-to type variables with fresh type variables.

The points-to set of a local variable depends on the context(s) in which f is used. To reconstruct points-to information for locals, we keep track of the instantiated types of functions and use these to flow context information back into the original, unsimplified constraint system.

Figure 7 gives the algorithm for reconstructing the points-to information for the local variables of function f on a particular path or set of paths *P* in the FDG. Note that Algorithm 2 requires f ∈ *P*. The constraints given are for Andersen's analysis. For Steensgaard's analysis we replace ⊆ constraints by the appropriate ≤ constraints. (Note that for Steensgaard's analysis there may be more precise ways of computing summary information. See [15].) In Algorithm 2, the constraint systems along the FDG path are merged into a fresh constraint system, and then the types of the actual parameters from each instance are linked to the types of the formal parameters of the original type. We also link the return values of the original type to the return values of the instances.

1.   Let $C = Glob \wedge \bigwedge_{\mathbf{g} \in P} C_{\mathbf{g}}$ be a fresh system
2.   For each function $\mathbf{g} \in P$
2a.   Let $lam(l_{\mathbf{g}}, \overline{\mathcal{G}_1}, \mathcal{R}_1), \ldots, lam(l_{\mathbf{g}}, \overline{\mathcal{G}_n}, \mathcal{R}_n)$ be the instances of $\mathbf{g}$'s function type.
2b.   Let $lam(l_{\mathbf{g}}, \overline{\mathcal{G}}, \mathcal{R})$ be $\mathbf{g}$'s original function type
2c.   Add constraints $\mathcal{G}_i \subseteq \mathcal{G}$ and $\mathcal{R} \subseteq \mathcal{R}_i$ for $i \in [1..n]$.
3.   Compute the points-to sets for $\mathbf{f}$'s locals in C.

Figure7. Algorithm 2: Top-down pass for function $\mathbf{f}$ on FDG path or set of FDG paths P

This algorithm computes the points-to sets for the local variables of $\mathbf{f}$ along FDG path P. Because this algorithm is parameterized by the FDG path, it lets the analysis client choose the precision of the desired information. An interactive software engineering tool may be interested in a particular use of a function (corresponding to a single path from $\mathbf{f}$ to the root), while a compiler, which must produce code that works for all instances, would most likely be interested in all paths from $\mathbf{f}$ to the root of the FDG.

In our experiments (Sect. 5), to compute information for function $\mathbf{f}$ we choose P to be all of $\mathbf{f}$'s ancestors in the FDG. This corresponds exactly to a points-to analysis in which $\mathbf{f}$ and its ancestors are monomorphic and all other functions are polymorphic. Clearly there are cases in which this choice will lead to a loss of precision. However, the other natural alternative, to compute alias information for each of $\mathbf{f}$'s instances separately, would yield an exponential algorithm. By treating $\mathbf{f}$ monomorphically, in an FDG of size n Algorithm 2 requires copying $O(n^2)$ (unsimplified) constraint systems.

5   Experiments

We have implemented our analyses using BANE [1]. BANE manages the details of constraint representation and solving, quantification, instantiation, and simplification. Our analysis tool generates constraints and decides when and what to quantify, instantiate, and simplify.

Our analysis handles almost all features of C, following [29]. The only exceptions are that we do not correctly model expressions that rely on compiler-specific choices about the layout of data in memory, e.g., variable-length argument lists or absolute addressing.

Our experiments cover the four possible combinations of polymorphism (polymorphic or monomorphic) and analysis precision (inclusion-based or equality-based). Table 1 lists the suite of C programs on which we performed the analyses.[2] The size of each program is listed in terms of preprocessed source lines

---

[2] We modified the `tar-1.11.2` benchmark to use the built-in malloc rather than a user-defined malloc in order to model heap usage more accurately.

Table1. Benchmark programs

Name	AST Nodes	Preproc Lines	Name	AST Nodes	Preproc Lines
allroots	700	426	less-177	15179	11988
diff.diffh	935	293	li	16828	5761
anagram	1078	344	flex-2.4.7	29960	9345
genetic	1412	323	pmake	31148	18138
ks	2284	574	make-3.72.1	36892	15213
ul	2395	441	tar-1.11.2	38795	17592
ft	3027	1180	inform-5.5	38874	12957
compress	3333	651	sgmls-1.1	44533	30941
ratfor	5269	1532	screen-3.5.2	49292	23919
compiler	5326	1888	cvs-1.3	51223	31130
assembler	6516	2980	espresso	56938	21537
ML-typecheck	6752	2410	gawk-3.0.3	71140	28326
eqntott	8117	2266	povray-2.2	87391	59689
simulator	10946	4216			

and number of AST nodes. The AST node count is restricted to those nodes the analysis traverses, e.g., this count ignores declarations.

As with most C programs, our benchmark suite makes extensive use of standard libraries. After analyzing each program we also analyze a special file of hand-coded stubs modeling the points-to effects of all library functions used by our benchmark suite. These stubs are not included in the measurements of points-to set sizes, and we only process the stubs corresponding to library functions that are actually used by the program. The stubs are modeled in the same way that regular functions are modeled. Thus they are treated monomorphically in the monomorphic analyses, and polymorphically in the polymorphic analyses.

To model heap locations, we generate a fresh global variable for each syntactic occurrence of a `malloc`-like function in a program. In certain cases it may be beneficial to distinguish heap locations by call path, though we did not perform this experiment. We model structures as atomic, i.e., every field of a structure shares the same location. Recent results [33] suggest some efficient alternative approaches.

For the polymorphic analyses, when we apply Algorithm 2 (Fig. 7) to compute the analysis results for function f, we choose P to be the set of all paths from f to the root of the FDG.

5.1 Precision

Figures 8 and 9 graph for each benchmark the average size of the points-to sets at the dereference sites in the program. A higher average size indicates lower precision. Missing data points indicate that the analysis exceeded the memory capacity of the machine (2GB).

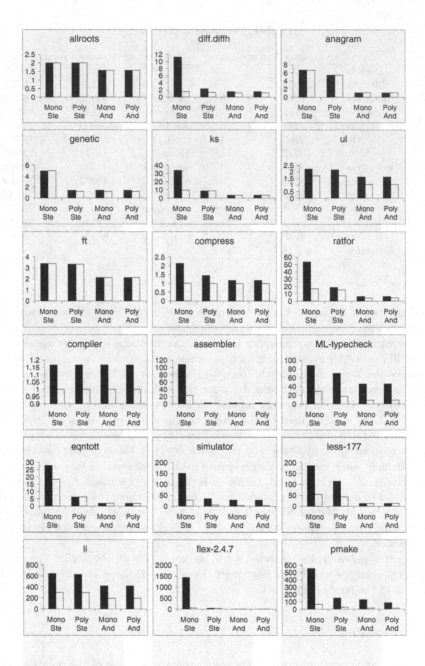

Figure8. Average points-to sizes at dereference sites. The black bars give the results when strings are modeled; the white bars give the results when strings are not modeled

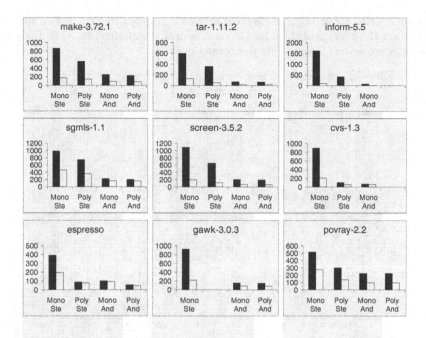

Figure9. Continuation of Fig. 8. Average points-to sizes at dereference sites. The black bars give the results when strings are modeled; the white bars give the results when strings are not modeled

We also measure the precision of the analyses both when each string is modeled as a distinct location and when strings are completely ignored (modeled as 0). Note the different scales on different graphs. For the purposes of this experiment, functions are not counted in points-to sets, and multi-level dereferences are counted separately (e.g., in ****x** there are two dereferences). Array indexing on known arrays (expressions of type array) is not counted as dereferencing.

Table 2 gives the numeric values graphed in Figs. 8 and 9 and more detailed information about the distribution of points-to sets. Due to lack of space, we only give the data for the experiments that model strings as distinct locations. See [17] for the data when strings are modeled as 0. For each analysis style, we list the running time, the average points-to set sizes at dereference sites, and the number of dereference sites with points-to sets of size 1, 2, and 3 or more, plus the total number of non-empty dereference sites. (Most programs have some empty dereference sites because of dead code.) We also list the size of the largest points-to set.

Recall from the introduction that for a given dereference site, it is a theorem that the points-to sets computed by the four analyses are in the inclusion relations shown in Fig. 1. More precisely, there is an edge from analysis x in Fig. 1

Table2. Data for string modeling experiments graphed in Fig. 8. The running times are the average of three for the monomorphic experiments, while the polymorphic experiments were only performed once.

Name	Monomorphic Steensgaard's		Num. deref sites					Polymorphic Steensgaard's			Num. deref sites				
	Time (s)	Av.	1	2	3+	tot	max	Up Tm (s)	Dn Tm (s)	Av.	1	2	3+	tot	max
allroots	0.17	2.00	0	42	0	42	2	0.27	0.29	2.00	0	42	0	42	2
diff.diffh	0.23	11.25	12	1	23	36	17	0.29	0.55	2.36	14	13	9	36	5
anagram	0.25	6.74	11	1	30	42	9	0.37	1.00	5.45	12	0	30	42	8
genetic	0.36	4.95	22	8	46	76	15	0.45	1.18	1.43	62	10	4	76	10
ks	0.43	33.83	3	13	99	115	39	0.53	1.38	8.86	3	13	99	115	10
ul	0.49	2.22	55	129	54	238	4	0.59	2.97	2.16	55	137	46	238	4
ft	0.65	3.39	29	8	133	170	4	1.05	4.58	3.35	37	0	133	170	4
compress	0.73	2.13	181	44	36	261	8	0.94	5.32	1.44	181	44	36	261	3
ratfor	1.65	53.41	36	4	125	165	80	2.71	30.90	18.65	36	7	122	165	62
compiler	1.15	1.17	65	13	0	78	2	2.47	5.76	1.17	65	13	0	78	2
assembler	2.54	108.03	79	31	273	383	213	5.22	58.96	2.98	223	36	124	383	120
ML-typecheck	2.92	88.41	28	0	285	313	97	3.92	60.87	70.33	28	27	258	313	85
eqntott	2.70	27.82	68	110	436	614	42	3.45	54.17	6.17	76	133	405	614	11
simulator	3.78	150.11	24	13	259	296	223	5.70	118.20	33.71	105	5	186	296	89
less-177	5.66	185.55	69	13	490	572	219	18.28	321.89	114.13	80	14	478	572	173
li	18.67	643.88	8	0	933	941	657	33.33	695.71	629.01	8	0	933	941	644
flex-2.4.7	64.33	1431.68	13	0	1613	1626	1445	22.09	818.25	43.83	15	2	1609	1626	1226
pmake	20.98	556.19	40	2	2501	2543	570	373.97	4416.16	151.69	100	9	2434	2543	218
make-3.72.1	40.05	863.25	90	222	3170	3482	975	265.43	1045.70	556.94	311	158	3013	3482	666
tar-1.11.2	26.10	597.13	87	70	2031	2188	656	23.16	776.65	356.20	183	114	1888	2185	434
inform-5.5	47.81	1618.62	21	0	1268	1289	1648	2601.61	67608.52	408.47	28	0	1261	1289	601
sgmls-1.1	69.70	987.71	96	11	2382	2489	1046	126.08	3961.22	749.20	123	15	2351	2489	867
screen-3.5.2	64.79	1093.00	27	9	4915	4951	1110	65.37	1991.28	656.86	112	36	4803	4951	768
cvs-1.3	47.42	894.44	97	680	2276	3053	1242	124.80	2949.33	100.18	1159	141	1753	3053	367
espresso	34.40	391.59	101	530	5479	6110	456	104.65	3368.75	86.78	1238	595	4277	6110	171
gawk-3.0.3	78.30	927.57	139	50	4930	5119	966	—	—	—	—	—	—	—	—
povray-2.2	64.72	515.85	761	407	8044	9212	618	111.38	6606.45	299.41	1027	659	7526	9212	434

Name	Monomorphic Andersen's		Num. deref sites					Polymorphic Andersen's			Num. deref sites				
	Time (s)	Av.	1	2	3+	tot	max	Up Tm (s)	Dn Tm (s)	Av.	1	2	3+	tot	max
allroots	0.18	1.57	18	24	0	42	2	0.14	0.22	1.57	18	24	0	42	2
diff.diffh	0.18	1.56	25	2	9	36	3	0.21	0.49	1.56	25	2	9	36	3
anagram	0.24	1.10	38	4	0	42	2	0.16	0.72	1.10	38	4	0	42	2
genetic	0.22	1.43	62	10	4	76	10	0.21	0.76	1.43	62	10	4	76	10
ks	0.37	3.58	9	22	84	115	5	0.33	0.98	3.58	9	22	84	115	5
ul	0.24	1.61	184	8	46	238	4	0.23	1.61	1.61	184	8	46	238	4
ft	0.42	2.12	75	0	95	170	3	0.56	2.25	2.12	75	0	95	170	3
compress	0.34	1.18	215	46	0	261	2	0.41	1.42	1.18	215	46	0	261	2
ratfor	0.63	6.27	56	9	100	165	47	1.22	5.99	6.27	56	9	100	165	47
compiler	0.57	1.17	65	13	0	78	2	0.96	5.07	1.17	65	13	0	78	2
assembler	1.07	2.87	225	36	122	383	120	3.02	80.46	2.87	225	36	122	383	120
ML-typecheck	0.99	45.87	101	30	182	313	78	1.79	14.81	45.87	101	30	182	313	78
eqntott	1.03	1.92	239	199	176	614	5	1.50	11.20	1.92	239	199	176	614	5
simulator	1.35	28.53	107	10	179	296	72	2.32	51.70	27.78	107	10	179	296	71
less-177	2.55	12.98	221	92	259	572	110	4.35	184.03	12.72	238	101	233	572	110
li	4.44	421.23	28	0	913	941	465	189.49	9929.88	421.23	28	0	913	941	465
flex-2.4.7	4.81	6.22	734	204	688	1626	1226	8.61	173.97	6.21	735	204	687	1626	1226
pmake	5.11	129.16	401	98	2044	2543	175	21.38	682.71	88.64	452	98	1993	2543	144
make-3.72.1	9.02	250.85	619	268	2595	3482	494	13.18	390.35	230.12	652	264	2566	3482	487
tar-1.11.2	6.89	69.07	330	741	1117	2188	200	7.74	327.48	66.11	336	742	1107	2185	194
inform-5.5	6.95	80.51	657	20	612	1289	227	—	—	—	—	—	—	—	—
sgmls-1.1	8.14	224.11	687	321	1481	2489	506	40.52	1121.89	205.63	703	323	1463	2489	492
screen-3.5.2	7.45	206.48	339	39	4573	4951	241	1277.15	2028.85	195.83	342	44	4565	4951	232
cvs-1.3	10.82	71.27	1281	192	1580	3053	203	—	—	—	—	—	—	—	—
espresso	12.89	101.21	1824	300	3986	6110	175	28.81	967.64	56.34	1973	304	3833	6110	152
gawk-3.0.3	12.40	157.28	1177	226	3716	5119	237	22.14	763.62	148.77	1184	228	3707	5119	225
povray-2.2	22.40	223.61	2474	588	6150	9212	402	169.51	5574.82	223.61	2474	588	6150	9212	402

to analysis y if for each expression e, the points-to set computed for e by analysis x contains the points-to set computed for e by analysis y. Two issues arise when interpreting the average points-to set size metric. First, when two analyses are related by inclusion the average size of points-to sets is a valid measure of precision. Thus we can use our metric to compare any two analyses *except* polymorphic Steensgaard's analysis and monomorphic Andersen's analysis.

For these two analyses there is no direct inclusion relationship. For a given expression e, if e_S is the points-to set computed by polymorphic Steensgaard's analysis and e_A is the points-to set computed by monomorphic Andersen's analysis, it may be that $e_S \not\subseteq e_A$ and $e_S \not\supseteq e_A$. Detailed examination of the points-to sets computed by polymorphic Steensgaard's analysis and monomorphic Andersen's analysis reveals that this does occur in practice, and thus the two analyses are incomparable in our metric. The best we can do is observe that monomorphic Andersen's analysis is almost as precise as polymorphic Andersen's analysis, and polymorphic Steensgaard's analysis is less precise than polymorphic Andersen's analysis.

Second, it is possible for a polymorphic analysis to determine that a monomorphically non-empty points-to set is in fact empty, and thus have a larger average points-to set size than its monomorphic counterpart (since only non-empty points-to sets are included in this average). However, we can eliminate this possibility by counting the total number of nonempty dereference sites. (A polymorphic analysis cannot have more nonempty dereference sites than its monomorphic counterpart.) The data in Table 2 shows that for all benchmarks except `tar-1.11.2`, the total number of non-empty dereference sites is the same across all analyses, and the difference between the polymorphic and monomorphic analyses for `tar-1.11.2` is miniscule. Therefore we know that averaging the sizes of non-empty dereference sites is a valid measure of precision.

5.2   Speed

Table 2 also lists the running times for the analyses. The running times include the time to compute the least model of the $\mathcal{P}_X$ variables, i.e., to find the points-to sets. For the polymorphic analyses, we separate the running times into the time for the bottom-up pass and the time for the top-down pass.

For purposes of this experiment, whose goal is to compare the precision of monomorphic and polymorphic points-to analysis, the running times are largely irrelevant. Thus we have made little effort to make the analyses efficient, and the running times should all be taken with a grain of salt.

5.3   Discussion

The data presented in Figs. 8 and 9 and Table 2 shows two striking and consistent results:

1. Polymorphic Andersen's analysis is hardly more precise than monomorphic Andersen's analysis.
2. Polymorphic Steensgaard's analysis is much more precise than monomorphic Steensgaard's analysis.

The only exceptions to these trends are some of the smaller programs (`all-roots`, `ul`, `ft`, `compiler`, `li`), for which polymorphic Steensgaard's analysis is not much more precise than monomorphic Steensgaard's analysis, and one larger program, espresso, for which Polymorphic Andersen's analysis is noticeably more precise than Monomorphic Andersen's analysis. Additionally, notice that for all programs except espresso, polymorphic Steensgaard's analysis has a higher average points-to set size than monomorphic Andersen's analysis. (Recall that this does not necessarily imply strictly increased precision.)

To understand these results, consider the following code skeleton:

```
void f() { ... h(a); ... }
void g() { ... h(b); ... }
void h(int *c) { ... }
```

In Steensgaard's equality-based monomorphic analysis, the types of all arguments for all calls sites of a function are equated. In the example, this results in $a = b = c$, where a is a's points-to type, b is b's points-to type, and c is c's points-to type. In the polymorphic version of Steensgaard's analysis, a and b can be distinct. Our measurements show that separating function parameters is important for points-to analysis.

In contrast, in Andersen's monomorphic inclusion-based system, the points-to types of arguments at call sites are potentially separated. In the example, we have $a \subseteq c$ and $b \subseteq c$. However, function results are all conflated (i.e., every call site has the same result, the union of points-to results over all call sites). The fact that polymorphic Andersen's analysis is hardly more precise than monomorphic Andersen's analysis suggests that separating function parameters is by far the most important form of polymorphism present in points-to analysis for C.

Thus, we conclude that polymorphism for points-to analysis is useful primarily for separating inputs, which can be achieved very nearly as well by a monomorphic inclusion-based analysis. This conclusion begs the question: Why is there so little polymorphism in points-to results available in C? Directly measuring the polymorphism available in output side effects of C functions is difficult, although we hypothesize that C functions tend to side-effect global variables and heap data (which our analyses model as global) rather than stack-allocated data.

We can measure the polymorphism of result types fairly directly. Table 3 lists for each benchmark the number of call sites and percentage of calls that occur in void contexts. These results emphasize that most C functions are called for their side effects: for 25 out of 27 benchmarks, at least half of all calls are in void contexts. Thus, there is a greatly reduced chance that polymorphism can be beneficial for Andersen's analysis.

It is worth pointing out that the client for a points-to analysis can also have a significant, and often negative, impact on the polymorphism that actually can be exploited. In the example above, when computing points-to sets for h's local variables we conflate information for all of c's contexts. This summarization effectively removes much of the fine detail about the behavior of h in different calling contexts. However, many applications require points-to information that is valid in every calling context. In addition, if we attempt to distinguish all call paths, the analysis can quickly become intractable.

Table3. Potential polymorphism. The measurements include library functions.

Name	Call Sites	% Void	Name	Call Sites	% Void
allroots	55	69	less-177	1091	56
diff.diffh	67	58	li	1243	37
anagram	59	75	flex-2.4.7	1205	79
genetic	79	75	pmake	1943	56
ks	101	84	make-3.72.1	1955	50
ul	103	74	tar-1.11.2	1586	54
ft	152	70	inform-5.5	2593	72
compress	138	73	sgmls-1.1	1614	62
ratfor	306	75	screen-3.5.2	2632	75
compiler	448	89	cvs-1.3	3036	55
assembler	519	66	espresso	2729	51
ML-typecheck	430	31	gawk-3.0.3	2358	51
eqntott	364	61	povray-2.2	3123	59
simulator	677	75			

6   Conclusion

We have explored two dimensions of the design space for flow-insensitive points-to analysis for C: polymorphic versus monomorphic and inclusion-based versus equality-based. Our experiments show that while polymorphism is potentially beneficial for equality-based points-to analysis, it does not have much benefit for inclusion-based points-to analysis. Even though we feel that added engineering effort can make the running times of the polymorphic analyses much faster, the precision would still be the same.

Monomorphic Andersen's analysis can be made fast [30] and often provides far more precise results than monomorphic Steensgaard's analysis. Polymorphic Steensgaard's analysis is in general much less precise than polymorphic Andersen's analysis, which is in turn little more precise than monomorphic Andersen's analysis. Additionally, as discussed in Sect. 4.3, implementing polymorphism is a complicated and difficult task. Thus, we feel that monomorphic Andersen's analysis may be the best choice among the four analyses.

Acknowledgements

We thank the anonymous referees for their helpful comments. We would also like to thank Manuvir Das for suggestions for the implementation.

References

1. A. Aiken, M. Fähndrich, J. S. Foster, and Z. Su. A Toolkit for Constructing Type- and Constraint-Based Program Analyses. In X. Leroy and A. Ohori, editors, *Proceedings of the second International Workshop on Types in Compilation*, volume 1473 of *Lecture Notes in Computer Science*, pages 78–96, Kyoto, Japan, Mar. 1998. Springer-Verlag. 179, 189

2. A. Aiken and E. L. Wimmers. Solving Systems of Set Constraints. In *Proceedings, Seventh Annual IEEE Symposium on Logic in Computer Science*, pages 329–340, Santa Cruz, California, June 1992. 179

3. A. Aiken and E. L. Wimmers. Type Inclusion Constraints and Type Inference. In *FPCA '93 Conference on Functional Programming Languages and Computer Architecture*, pages 31–41, Copenhagen, Denmark, June 1993. 180

4. L. O. Andersen. *Program Analysis and Specialization for the C Programming Language*. PhD thesis, DIKU, Department of Computer Science, University of Copenhagen, May 1994. 176, 177

5. M. Burke, P. Carini, J.-D. Choi, and M. Hind. Flow-Insensitive Interprocedural Alias Analysis in the Presence of Pointers. In K. Pingali, U. Banerjee, D. Gelernter, A. Nicolau, and D. Padua, editors, *Proceedings of the Seventh Workshop on Languages and Compilers for Parallel Computing*, volume 892 of *Lecture Notes in Computer Science*, pages 234–250. Springer-Verlag, 1994. 177

6. R. Chatterjee, B. G. Ryder, and W. A. Landi. Relevant Context Inference. In *Proceedings of the 26th Annual ACM SIGPLAN-SIGACT Symposium on Principles of Programming Languages*, pages 133–146, San Antonio, Texas, Jan. 1999. 177, 178

7. M. Das. Unification-based Pointer Analysis with Directional Assignments. In *Proceedings of the 2000 ACM SIGPLAN Conference on Programming Language Design and Implementation*, Vancouver B.C., Canada, June 2000. To appear. 177, 179

8. S. Debray, R. Muth, and M. Weippert. Alias Analysis of Executable Code. In *Proceedings of the 25th Annual ACM SIGPLAN-SIGACT Symposium on Principles of Programming Languages*, pages 12–24, San Diego, California, Jan. 1998. 177

9. A. Deutsch. Interprocedural May-Alias Analysis for Pointers: Beyond k-limiting. In *Proceedings of the 1994 ACM SIGPLAN Conference on Programming Language Design and Implementation*, pages 230–241, Orlando, Florida, June 1994. 177

10. N. Dor, M. Rodeh, and M. Sagiv. Detecting Memory Errors via Static Pointer Analysis. In *Proceedings of the ACM SIGPLAN/SIGSOFT Workshop on Program Analysis for Software Tools and Engineering*, pages 27–34, Montreal, Canada, June 1998. 177

11. M. Emami, R. Ghiya, and L. J. Hendren. Context-Sensitive Interprocedural Points-to Analysis in the Presence of Function Pointers. In *Proceedings of the 1994 ACM SIGPLAN Conference on Programming Language Design and Implementation*, pages 242–256, Orlando, Florida, June 1994. 177, 178, 180

12. M. Fähndrich. *BANE: A Library for Scalable Constraint-Based Program Analysis*. PhD thesis, University of California, Berkeley, 1999. 180

13. M. Fähndrich and A. Aiken. Program Analysis using Mixed Term and Set Constraints. In P. V. Hentenryck, editor, *Static Analysis, Fourth International Symposium*, volume 1302 of *Lecture Notes in Computer Science*, pages 114–126, Paris, France, Sept. 1997. Springer-Verlag. 180

14. M. Fähndrich, J. S. Foster, Z. Su, and A. Aiken. Partial Online Cycle Elimination in Inclusion Constraint Graphs. In *Proceedings of the 1998 ACM SIGPLAN Conference on Programming Language Design and Implementation*, pages 85–96, Montreal, Canada, June 1998. 178, 180

15. M. Fähndrich, J. Rehof, and M. Das. Scalable Context-Sensitive Flow Analysis using Instantiation Constraints. In *Proceedings of the 2000 ACM SIGPLAN Conference on Programming Language Design and Implementation*, Vancouver B.C., Canada, June 2000. To appear. 177, 178, 188

16. J. S. Foster, M. Fähndrich, and A. Aiken. Flow-Insensitive Points-to Analysis with Term and Set Constraints. Technical Report UCB//CSD-97-964, University of California, Berkeley, Aug. 1997. 176, 182

17. J. S. Foster, M. Fähndrich, and A. Aiken. Polymorphic versus Monomorphic Flow-insensitive Points-to Analysis for C. Technical report, University of California, Berkeley, Apr. 2000. 186, 187, 192

18. N. Heintze and J. Jaffar. A Decision Procedure for a Class of Set Constraints. In *Proceedings, Fifth Annual IEEE Symposium on Logic in Computer Science*, pages 42–51, Philadelphia, Pennsylvania, June 1990. 179

19. M. Hind and A. Pioli. Assessing the Effects of Flow-Sensitivity on Pointer Alias Analyses. In G. Levi, editor, *Static Analysis, Fifth International Symposium*, volume 1503 of *Lecture Notes in Computer Science*, pages 57–81, Pisa, Italy, Sept. 1998. Springer-Verlag. 177

20. W. Landi and B. G. Ryder. A Safe Approximate Algorithm for Interprocedural Pointer Aliasing. In *Proceedings of the 1992 ACM SIGPLAN Conference on Programming Language Design and Implementation*, pages 235–248, San Francisco, California, June 1992. 177, 178

21. R. Milner. A Theory of Type Polymorphism in Programming. *Journal of Computer and System Sciences*, 17:348–375, 1978. 176, 178

22. C. Mossin. *Flow Analysis of Typed Higher-Order Programs*. PhD thesis, DIKU, Department of Computer Science, University of Copenhagen, 1996. 178

23. R. O'Callahan and D. Jackson. Lackwit: A Program Understanding Tool Based on Type Inference. In *Proceedings of the 19th International Conference on Software Engineering*, pages 338–348, Boston, Massachusetts, May 1997. 178

24. M. Odersky, M. Sulzmann, and M. Wehr. Type Inference with Constrained Types. In B. Pierce, editor, *Proceedings of the 4th International Workshop on Foundations of Object-Oriented Languages*, Jan. 1997. 186

25. D. Rémy. Typechecking records and variants in a natural extension of ML. In *Proceedings of the 16th Annual ACM SIGPLAN-SIGACT Symposium on Principles of Programming Languages*, pages 77–88, Austin, Texas, Jan. 1989. 182

26. E. Ruf. Context-Insensitive Alias Analysis Reconsidered. In *Proceedings of the 1995 ACM SIGPLAN Conference on Programming Language Design and Implementation*, pages 13–22, La Jolla, California, June 1995. 178

27. M. Sagiv, T. Reps, and R. Wilhelm. Parametric Shape Analysis via 3-Valued Logic. In *Proceedings of the 26th Annual ACM SIGPLAN-SIGACT Symposium on Principles of Programming Languages*, pages 105–118, San Antonio, Texas, Jan. 1999. 177

28. M. Shapiro and S. Horwitz. Fast and Accurate Flow-Insensitive Points-To Analysis. In *Proceedings of the 24th Annual ACM SIGPLAN-SIGACT Symposium on Principles of Programming Languages*, pages 1–14, Paris, France, Jan. 1997. 176, 177

29. B. Steensgaard. Points-to Analysis in Almost Linear Time. In *Proceedings of the 23rd Annual ACM SIGPLAN-SIGACT Symposium on Principles of Programming Languages*, pages 32–41, St. Petersburg Beach, Florida, Jan. 1996. 176, 177, 184, 185, 189

30. Z. Su, M. Fähndrich, and A. Aiken. Projection Merging: Reducing Redundancies in Inclusion Constraint Graphs. In *Proceedings of the 27th Annual ACM SIGPLAN-SIGACT Symposium on Principles of Programming Languages*, Boston, Massachusetts, Jan. 2000. To appear. 178, 180, 196

31. R. P. Wilson and M. S. Lam. Efficient Context-Sensitive Pointer Analysis for C Programs. In *Proceedings of the 1995 ACM SIGPLAN Conference on Programming Language Design and Implementation*, pages 1–12, La Jolla, California, June 1995. 177, 178

32. A. K. Wright. Simple Imperative Polymorphism. In *Lisp and Symbolic Computation 8*, volume 4, pages 343–356, 1995. 186

33. S. H. Yong, S. Horwitz, and T. Reps. Pointer Analysis for Programs with Structures and Casting. In *Proceedings of the 1999 ACM SIGPLAN Conference on Programming Language Design and Implementation*, pages 91–103, Atlanta, Georgia, May 1999. 177, 190

34. S. Zhang, B. G. Ryder, and W. A. Landi. Program Decomposition for Pointer Aliasing: A Step toward Practical Analyses. In *Fourth Symposium on the Foundations of Software Engineering*, Oct. 1996. 177

35. S. Zhang, B. G. Ryder, and W. A. Landi. Experiments with Combined Analysis for Pointer Aliasing. In *Proceedings of the ACM SIGPLAN/SIGSOFT Workshop on Program Analysis for Software Tools and Engineering*, pages 11–18, Montreal, Canada, June 1998. 178

Efficient Inference of Static Types for Java Bytecode*

Etienne M. Gagnon, Laurie J. Hendren, and Guillaume Marceau

Sable Research Group, School of Computer Science
McGill University, Montreal, Canada
[gagnon,hendren,gmarceau]@sable.mcgill.ca

Abstract. In this paper, we present an efficient and practical algorithm for inferring static types for local variables in a 3-address, stackless, representation of Java bytecode.

By decoupling the type inference problem from the low level bytecode representation, and abstracting it into a *constraint system*, we show that there exists verifiable bytecode that cannot be statically typed. Further, we show that, without transforming the program, the static typing problem is NP-hard. In order to get a practical approach we have developed an algorithm that works efficiently for the usual cases and then applies efficient program transformations to simplify the hard cases.

We have implemented this algorithm in the Soot framework. Our experimental results show that all of the 17,000 methods used in our tests were successfully typed, 99.8% of those required only the first stage, 0.2% required the second stage, and no methods required the third stage.

1 Introduction

Java bytecode is rapidly becoming an important intermediate representation. This is predominately because Java bytecode interpreters and JIT-compilers are becoming more common, and such interpreters / compilers are now a standard part of popular web browsers. Thus, Java bytecode (henceforth referred to as simply bytecode) has become a target representation for a wide variety of compilers, including compilers for Ada [23], ML [14], Scheme [5], and Eiffel [20].

Bytecode has many interesting properties, including some guarantees about verifiable bytecode that ensure that verified bytecode programs are *well-behaved*. For example, verifiable bytecode guarantees that each method invocation has the correct number and type of arguments on the Java expression stack. Verification is done partly statically via a flow analysis of the bytecode, and partly via checks that are executed at runtime. As part of the static verification, a flow analysis is used to estimate the type of each local variable and each location on the expression stack, for each program point. However, as we will show in section 3 this is **not** the same typing problem as the one addressed in this paper.

Although bytecode has many good features, it is not an ideal representation for program analysis / optimization or program understanding. For analysis /

---

* This work has been supported in part by FCAR and NSERC.

J. Palsberg (Ed.): SAS 2000, LNCS 1824, pp. 199–220, 2000.

optimization, the expression stack complicates both the analyses and subsequent transformations. In addition, the stack-based representation does not map nicely to real register-based architectures. For these sorts of optimizing compiler applications a more traditional three-address code is preferable, and is used in many optimizing Java compilers. For program understanding, the bytecode is too low-level, and one would like to present a higher-level view to the programmer. One example of a high-level representation is decompiling bytecode back to Java. Note that to be generally useful such decompilers should work for any verifiable bytecode, not just bytecode produced by Java compilers.[1]

When bytecode is translated to a three-address representation or high-level representation it is important that all variables should be given a static type that is correct for all uses of that variable. For a decompiler, each variable needs to have a declared type that is type correct for all uses of that variable. For three-address representations, the type of a variable can be used to improve analysis and optimization. We have found having types for local variables to be indispensable in our compiler, and one example use, improving the quality of the call graph, is presented in section 7.2.

In this paper, we address the problem of inferring a *static type* for each variable in a three-address representation of bytecode called Jimple[26,25]. Jimple is part of the Soot compiler framework that is used for both compiler optimizations and decompilation. It is a fairly standard representation, so our results should apply to other similar representations.

In order to give a feel for the problem, consider the simple example in Figure 1. Figure 1(a) gives an untyped method in a Jimple-like intermediate representation. Note that there is some type information which comes directly from the bytecode. For example, the signature of method f is specified in the bytecode, so we know a fixed type for the return value, and we know some type information from **new** instructions. However, local variables, such as a, b, c and s do not have an explicit type in the bytecode. We can determine correct types for these variables by collecting type constraints. Figure 1(b) shows the class hierarchy, and figure 1(c) shows the constraints imposed by each statement. We formulate the typing problem as a graph problem. Figure 1(d) shows a graph that represents both the class hierarchy and the type constraints on the variables. Types in the hierarchy are shown as double circles which we call *hard nodes*, while type variables are shown as single circles which we call *soft nodes*. A solution to the typing problem is found by coalescing nodes together. If nodes can be coalesced so that each coalesced node contains exactly one hard node, then we have found a solution to the typing problem. Figure 1(e) shows one possible coalescing of the graph, and this corresponds to the typed method in Figure 1(e). Note that there may be more than one correct solution. For this example another correct solution would be to assign a, b and c the type Object. In general, we prefer

---

[1] Also note that by combining a compiler that translates from a high-level language X to bytecode with a decompiler from bytecode to Java, one has a tool for translating from X to Java.

a typing that gives more specific types since this will help more in subsequent analyses.

```
public java.lang.String f()
{    <unknown> a;
     <unknown> b;
     <unknown> c;
     <unknown> s;

s1:  c = new C();
s2:  b = new B();
     if ( ... )
s3:    a = c;
     else
s4:    a = b;
s5:  s = a.toString();
s6:  return(s);
}
```

(a) untyped method

```
class A extends Object
{ ... }

class B extends A
{ public String toString() ...;
  ...
}

class C extends A
{ public String toString() ...;
  ...
}
```

(b) class hierarchy

$$
\begin{aligned}
\text{s1:} & \ T(c) \leftarrow C \\
\text{s2:} & \ T(b) \leftarrow B \\
\text{s3:} & \ T(a) \leftarrow T(c) \\
\text{s4:} & \ T(a) \leftarrow T(b) \\
\text{s5:} & \ Object \leftarrow T(a) \\
       & \ T(s) \leftarrow String \\
\text{s6:} & \ String \leftarrow T(s)
\end{aligned}
$$

(c) constraints

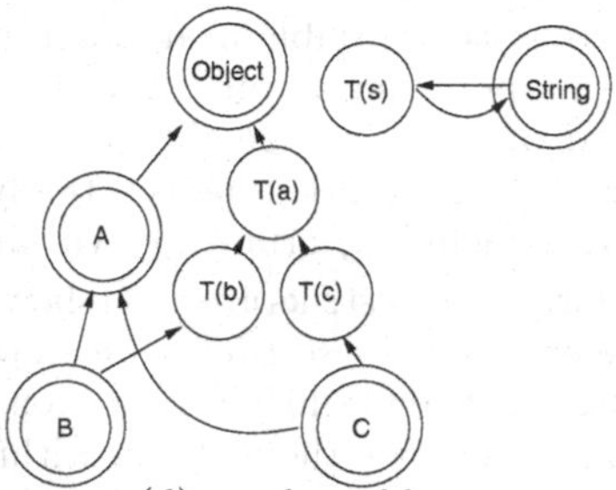

(d) graph problem

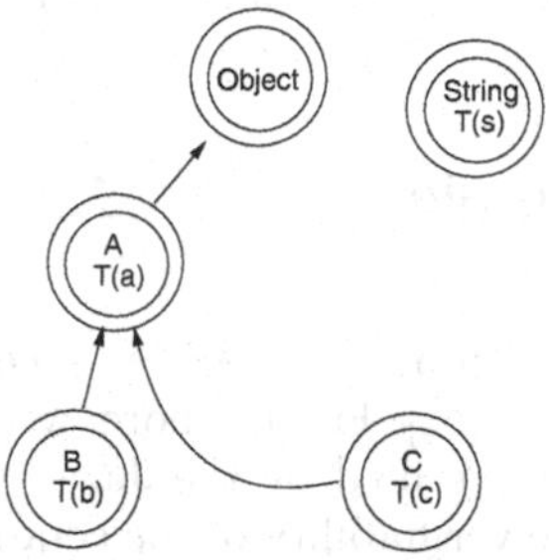

(e) solution

```
public java.lang.String f()
{    A a;
     B b;
     C c;
     java.lang.String s;

s1:  c = new C();
s2:  b = new B();
     if ( ... )
s3:    a = c;
     else
s4:    a = b;
s5:  s = a.toString();
s6:  return(s);
}
```

(f) typed method

Fig. 1. Simple example of static typing

The type inference problem would seem easy at first glance, and for our simple example it would be quite easy to deduce types during the bytecode to Jimple translation. However, there are three points that make the general typing problem difficult: (1) the program point specific nature of the bytecode verification, (2) multiple inheritance due to interfaces, and (3) the correct typing of arrays. In fact, we will show that the type inference problem is NP-hard. However, we propose an efficient, polynomial time, multi-stage algorithm that bypasses this complexity by performing program transformations that simplify the type inference problem, without affecting program semantics, when a difficult case is encountered. Our algorithm performs two kinds of transformations: (1) variable splitting at object creation sites, and (2) insertion of type casts that are guaranteed to succeed at run-time. Our experimental results show that all of the 16,492 methods extracted from 2,787 JDK 1.1 and SPEC jvm98 classes were typed by our algorithm, without inserting any type casts. Variable splitting was only applied in 29 methods.

It is important to contrast this work, where we find a *static* type consistent with *all* uses of a variable, with other type inference analyses where the main focus is to statically infer the set of dynamic (or concrete) types that a variable could hold, at a particular program point at run-time [17,18,1,2]. We will call such algorithms *run-time type analysis* to distinguish them from our *static-type analysis*. For our example program in Figure 1(a), run-time type analysis would infer that the variable a at program point s1 could have type B, whereas at program point s5 a could have types {B, C}. In our typing problem we need to find **one** static type that is consistent with **all** uses of a. As we show in section 7.2, our static type is actually a reasonably good starting point for other analyses, including a run-time type analysis we have built on top of typed Jimple.

Our paper is structured as follows. In section 2 we present our three-address representation. In section 3 we show some examples to demonstrate why this typing problem is difficult. In section 4, we define the general static type inference problem, and give the main algorithm for programs without arrays. In section 5 we present extensions to our algorithm to handle arrays. In section 6 we show how to infer integer types. Section 7 contains our experimental results. Finally, we review related work in section 8 and present our conclusions in section 9.

2   A 3-Address Representation: Jimple

We assume that the reader is already familiar with Java bytecode. A complete description of the *class file format* can be found in [13]. Furthermore, we assume that all analyzed bytecode would be successfully verified by the Java bytecode verifier[13]. It is important to remember that the verifiability of the code implies that it is *well behaved*, but it does not imply that it is *well typed*.

While the bytecode format seems of great interest for implementing an interpreter, it is not well suited for reasoning about bytecode, since many operands are on the stack and thus do not have explicit names. In order to alleviate this difficulty, many Java optimizing compilers convert bytecode to a more traditional 3-address-code, where all stack-based operations are transformed into local variable based operations. This is made possible by the conditions met by verified bytecode, most notably: the constant stack depth at each program point, and the explicit maximum depth of stack and number of local variables used in the body of a method.

The bytecode to 3-address-code transformation is done by computing the stack depth at each program point, introducing a new local variable for each stack depth, and then rewriting the instruction using the new local variables[2]. For example:

```
iload_1    (stack depth before 0 after 1)
iload_2    (stack depth before 1 after 2)
iadd       (stack depth before 2 after 1)
istore_1   (stack depth before 1 after 0)
```

is transformed into:

```
stack_1 = local_1
stack_2 = local_2
stack_1 = stack_1 iadd stack_2
local_1 = stack_1
```

In producing the 3-address-code it is simple to retain all type information contained in bytecode instructions. So, for instance, every virtual method contains the complete signature of the called method, as well as the name of the class declaring the method. However, as there are no explicit types for locals or stack locations, it is more difficult to find types for these variables. In our compiler we produce a 3-address representation called Jimple, that is first created in an untyped version, where the types of local variables are unknown. Every verifiable bytecode program has an equivalent *untyped* Jimple representation.

In final preparation, prior to applying the typing algorithms outlined in this paper, a data flow analysis is applied on the Jimple representation, computing definition-use and use-definition (*du-ud*) chains. Then, all local variables are split into multiple variables, one for each web of du-ud chains. Our example would be transformed to:

```
stack_1_0 = local_1_0
stack_2_0 = local_2_0
stack_1_1 = stack_1_0 iadd stack_2_0
local_1_1 = stack_1_1
```

Note that stack_1 has been split into stack_1_0 and stack_1_1, and similarly local_1 has been split into local_1_0 and local_1_1. This splitting is quite important, because a single local or stack location in the bytecode can refer to different types at different program points. This form of Jimple looks overly long, with many spurious copy statements. In our framework the code is cleaned up using standard techniques for copy propagation and elimination.

3 Challenges of Typing

The static typing problem looks quite simple at first, but there are subtle points that make the problem difficult. In this section we illustrate some difficulties by

---

[2] In reality, the stack analysis, the introduction of new local variables, and the transformation are not as straight-forward as it looks here. This is due to the presence of subroutines (the *jsr* bytecode instruction) and double-word values (*long, double*). A complete description of the bytecode to Jimple transformation can be found in [26,25].

showing differences between the typing problem for a 3-address representation with local variables, and the typing approximation done by the Java verifier. Another subtle point is how to deal with arrays, and this is dealt with in Section 5.

3.1   Declared Variable Types versus Types at Program Points

Part of the Java verifier is a flow analysis that estimates, at each program point, the type of values stored in each local variable and each stack location. This type information is used to ensure that each bytecode instruction is operating on data of the correct type. In our typing problem we wish to give a type to each variable that is correct for **all** uses and definitions of that variable (i.e. the same type must be correct at multiple program points).

Consider Figure 2 where two methods hard and harder illustrate the point. In method hard, the Java verifier would infer that x has type CA at program point s1 and type CB at program point s2. For program point s3 the verifier merges the types from each branch by taking their closest common superclass, which is Object. Thus, for three different program points, the verifier has three different types. However, for our problem, we want to assign one type to local variable x. In this case, it is possible to satisfy all constraints and assign type Object to variable x. However, to find consistent types the whole method must be analyzed, the types cannot be computed "on-the-fly" as is done in the verifier.

Now consider method harder in Figure 2. This is similar to the previous case, but now it is not possible to give a single static type to variable y. At program point s1 y **must** have type CA and at program point s2 y **must** have type CB. In order to statically type this program, it must be transformed to include extra copy statements (as one would get by translating from an SSA form) or by introducing type casts. Note that one would not see the harder case in bytecode produced from an ordinary Java compiler, however we have seen cases like this in bytecode produced by compilers for other languages.

```
class CA extends Object { f(){...} ... }
class CB extends Object { g(){...} ... }
class MultiDef extends Object          void harder()
{ void hard()                          { <untyped> y;
  { <untyped> x;                          if( ... )
     if( ... )                      s1:    { y = new CA(); y.f(); }
s1:   x =  new CA();                     else
     else                           s2:    { y = new CB(); y.g(); }
s2:   x =  new CB();                s3:  y.toString();
s3: x.toString();                        }
  }                                  }
```

Fig. 2. Multiple definition and use points

3.2   Problems Due to Interfaces

Interfaces in Java give a restricted form of multiple inheritance, and this leads to problems in finding a static typing in some cases. Consider the example in

Figure 3(a), where the class hierarchy is defined as in Figure 3(b). At program point s1 aa has interface type IC, and at program point s2 aa has interface type ID. The difficulty comes at the merge point because there is no single superinterface for IC and ID, rather there are two unrelated choices, IA and IB. The Java verifier will choose the type Object, and then check the invokeinterface calls at **runtime**. These runtime checks will pass, and so from the verification point of view, this program is well-behaved.

```
class InterfaceDemo                      class CC implements IC
{ IC getC() { return new CC(); }         { void f() {}
  ID getD() { return new CD(); }           void g() {}
                                         }
  void hardest()
  { <untyped> aa;                        class CD implements ID
                                         { void f() {}
    if( ... )                              void g() {}
s1:   aa = getC();                       }
    else
s2:   aa = getD();

s3: aa.f(); // invokeinterface IA.f      Interface IA { void f(); }
s4: aa.g(); // invokeinterface IB.g      Interface IB { void g(); }
  }                                      Interface IC extends IA, IB {}
}                                        Interface ID extends IA, IB {}
         (a) untyped program                      (b) hierarchy
```

Fig. 3. Typing interfaces

Now consider our problem of finding one static type for aa. In this case there is no solution, even though the bytecode is verifiable. If we chose type IA, then the type at statement s4 is wrong, if we chose type IB, the type at statement s3 is wrong, if we chose type IC, the type at statement s2 is wrong, and if we chose type ID, the type at statement s1 is wrong. In fact, one can not write a Java program like this Jimple program and give a correct static type to aa. However, remember that our Jimple code comes from bytecode produced from any compiler or bytecode optimizer, and so this situation may occur in verifiable bytecode.

One might be tempted to think that adding extra copies of the variable, like in SSA form would solve this problem as well. However, if we rewrite 3(a) in SSA form, we get:

```
    if( ... )
s1:   aa1 = getC();
    else
s2:   aa2 = getD();

s3a: aa3 = phi(aa1, aa2);
s3: aa3.f(); // invokeinterface IA.f
s4: aa3.g(); // invokeinterface IB.g
```

Clearly this does not solve the problem, there is still no type solution for aa3.

4   Three-Stage Algorithm

4.1   Algorithm Overview

The goal of the typing algorithm is to find a static type assignment for all local variables such that all type restrictions imposed by Jimple instructions on their arguments are met. In order to solve this problem, we abstract it into a *constraint system*. For convenience of implementation (and description), we represent this constraint system as a directed-graph.

We initially restrict our type inference problem to programs that do not include arrays, nor array operations. This allows us to illustrate the constraint system.

Finding whether there exists or not a static-type assignment that solves this constraint system is similar to solving the UNIFORM-FLAT-SSI problem, which Tiuryn and Pratt have shown to be NP-Complete[24]. Thus, the overall typing problem is NP-Hard.

Given this complexity result, we have chosen to design an efficient algorithm that may perform program transformations to make the typing problem simpler. We first give an overview of our algorithm, and then describe each stage in more detail.

An Efficient 3-Stage Algorithm The algorithm consists of three stages. The first stage constructs a directed-graph of program constraints. Then, it merges the connected components of the graph, and removes transitive constraints. Finally, it merges single constraints. At this point, it succeeds if all variables have valid types, or it fails if a variable has no type, or if a type error was detected in the process.

If the first stage fails to deliver a solution, the second stage applies a variable splitting transformation, and then reruns stage 1 on the transformed program. We have only found one situation where variable splitting is required, and that is for variables which are assigned new objects (i.e. for statements of the form x = new A()).

If stage 2 fails, then stage 3 proceeds as follows. A new constraints graph is built, where this graph only encodes *variable definition* constraints. In this graph, *variable use* constraints are not recorded, and interface inheritance is ignored. In other words, each interface has a single parent java.lang.Object. Then, the constraints system is solved using the *least common ancestor* LCA of classes and interfaces (which is now always unique). Once all variables are assigned a type, *use constraints* are checked on every original Jimple statement, and type casts are added as needed to satisfy the constraints. The verifiability of the original program guarantees that these inserted casts will always succeed at run-time.

Handling Arrays This section describes the basic constraint system for programs without arrays. We extend the constraint system, with extra notation for array constraints, in Section 5. We then show how to transform an array problem into a *restricted problem* (with no array constraints), and how to propagate the solution of the restricted problem back to the original array problem.

Implementing the Algorithm We have implemented the algorithm, but in this paper we do not discuss implementation details. It is quite straightforward to achieve a simple implementation using efficient algorithms for strongly-connected components and fast union on disjoint sets [6].

4.2   Stage 1

Constraint System   In this section, we show how to transform the type inference problem into a constraint system represented as a directed graph. Intuitively, the graph represents the constraints imposed on local variables by Jimple instructions in the body of a method. In this initial version, we assume that the analyzed Jimple code contains no arrays and no array operations. Further, we infer primitive types as defined for Java bytecode [13]. In particular, *boolean*, *byte*, *short*, and *char* are all treated as *int*. Section 6 presents an algorithm that can be used to infer these different integer types.

The *constraint graph* is a directed graph containing the following components:

1. *hard node*: represents an explicit type;
2. *soft node*: represents a type variable; and
3. *directed edge*: represents a constraint between two nodes.

A directed edge from node b to node a, represented in the text as $a \leftarrow b$, means that b should be *assignable* to a, using the standard *assignment compatibility* rules of Java [13,10]. Simply stated, b should be of the same type as a, or a should be a *superclass* (or *superinterface*) of b.

The graph is constructed via a single pass over the Jimple code, adding nodes and edges to the graph, as implied by each Jimple instruction. The collection of constraints is best explained by looking at a few representative Jimple statements. We will look at the simple assignment statement, the assignment of a *binary* expression to a local variable, and a virtual method invocation. All other constructions are similar.

A *simple assignment* is an assignment between two local variables $[a = b]$. If variable b is assigned to variable a, the constraints of *assignment compatibility* imply that $T(a) \leftarrow T(b)$, where $T(a)$ and $T(b)$ represent the yet unknown respective types of a and b. So, in this case, we need to add an edge from $T(b)$ to $T(a)$ (if not already present). This is shown in figure 4.

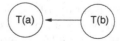

Fig. 4. b assigned to a

An assignment with a more complex right-hand-side results in more constraints. For example, the statement $[a = b + 3]$, generates the following constraints: $T(a) \leftarrow T(b)$, $T(a) \leftarrow int$, and $int \leftarrow T(b)$.

Our last and most complicated case is a method invocation, where constraints are generated for the receiver, the actuals, and the variable on the left-hand-side. For example, consider $[a = b.equals(c)]$, or with the full type signature: $a =$

virtualinvoke b.[boolean java.lang.Object.equals(java.lang.Object)] (c). We get the following constraints, each involving a hard node: (1) *java.lang.Object ← T(b)*, from the declaring class of *equals*; and (2) *java.lang.Object ← T(c)*, from the argument type in the method signature; and (3) *T(a) ← int*, because the return type of *equals* is *boolean* (we have a single integer type).

As shown in figure 1, our type inference problem now consists of merging soft nodes with hard nodes, such that all *assignment compatibility* constraints, represented by edges, are satisfied. Merging a soft node with a hard node is equivalent to inferring a type for a local variable. If no such solution exists (or it is too costly to find), or if a node needs more than one associated type (e.g. a soft node is merged with two or more hard nodes), then the first stage of the inference algorithm fails.

Connected Components   Our first transformation on the constraint graph consists of finding its connected components (or cycles). Every time a connected component is found, we merge together all nodes of connected component, as illustrated in figure 5.

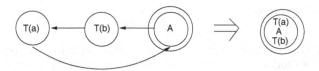

Fig. 5. Merging connected components

This is justified because every node in a connected component is indirectly *assignable* to and from any other node in the same connected component. It follows that all these nodes must represent the same type, in any solution to the type inference problem.

We can divide connected components into three kinds. First, there are connected components without hard nodes. In this case, nodes are simply merged, and all constraints of all nodes are propagated to the representative node[3]. Second, some connected components have a single hard node. In this case, all soft nodes are merged with the hard node, then all constraints are verified. If any constraint can't be satisfied, the first stage of the algorithm fails. Third, it may be that a connected component has two or more hard nodes. When this occurs, the first stage fails.

In this step, we also take advantage of the verifier restrictions on primitive types to merge respectively all values in a *transitive relation* with any of the primitive types: *int, long, float,* and *double*. Figure 6 shows an example of primitive type merge. It is enough that a node be indirectly assignable to *or* from a primitive type hard node to be merged with it. This is because there is no automatic conversion between primitive types.

Transitive Constraints   Once the connected components are removed from the constraint graph, we are left with a directed-acyclic-graph (DAG). Our next

---

[3] Constraints from the representative node to itself are eliminated.

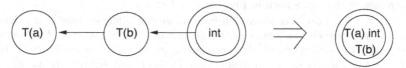

Fig. 6. Merging primitive types

transformation consists of removing redundant constraints (edges) from this DAG by eliminating any transitive constraints in the graph. A transitive constraint from a node y to a node x, is a constraint $x \leftarrow y$ such that there exists another constraint $p \leftarrow y$ where p is not x and there is a path from p to x in the directed graph.

Transitive constraints are removed regardless of the kind of nodes involved (soft, hard), with the exception of hard-node to hard-node constraints[4]. This is shown in figure 7.

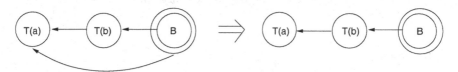

Fig. 7. Removing transitive constraints

Single Constraints Nodes that have only one parent or one child constraint can be simplified. A node x is said to have a *single parent constraint* to a node y, if $y \leftarrow x$ and for any $p \neq y$ there is no constraint $p \leftarrow x$. A node x is said to have a *single child constraint* to a node y, if $x \leftarrow y$ and for any $p \neq y$ there is no constraint $x \leftarrow p$.

Our next transformation consists of merging soft nodes that have single constraints to other nodes. To improve the accuracy of our results, we do this using the following priority scheme:

1. Merge single child constraints: Merge x with y when x is a soft node with a single child constraint to any other node y. (Merging with children results in lower (thus more precise) types in the type hierarchy).
2. Merge with least common ancestor: This is a special case. When x is a soft node that only has child constraints to hard nodes representing *class types*, we can safely replace these constraints by a single child constraint to the hard node representing the least common ancestor of the class types involved. Then we can merge the resulting single child constraint.
3. Merge single soft parent constraints: Merge x with y when x is a soft node with a single parent constraint to another *soft node y*.
4. Merge remaining single parent constraints: Merge x with y when x is a soft node with a single parent constraint to another node y.

---

[4] Hard-node to hard-node constraints represent the type hierarchy.

Examples of this are shown in Figures 1 and 8.

When a soft node has no explicit parent, we can safely assume that it has the hard node representing *java.lang.Object* as parent. We also introduce (as does the verifier) a *null* type, which is a descendant of all reference types. When a soft node has no child, which means that it was never *defined*, we assume that it has *null* as a child.

Stage 1 succeeds if all soft nodes are merged with hard nodes at the end of this step. It fails when merging a soft node with a hard node exposes an invalid constraint, or when there remains a soft node at the end of the step.

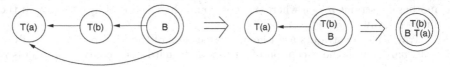

Fig. 8. Merging single constraints

4.3   Stage 2

In some cases, stage 1 fails to deliver a solution. In our experiments, this only happened in cases similar to the problem exposed in method **harder** of Figure 2. More precisely, the source of the problem is that Java and other languages use a simple **new** expression to both create and initialize a new object, whereas in bytecode, the same operation is done in two separate steps: the object is created using the **new** bytecode, but it is then initialized by invoking the <init> method on the newly created object. This is shown in Figure 9, where the method called **java** shows the method as it would appear in Java, and the method called **three_address** shows the extra <init> instructions that are exposed at the bytecode level.

```
class CA
  extends Object
  { ... }                      void three_address()    void fixed_three_address()
class CB                       { <untyped> y;          { <untyped> y, y1, y2;
  extends Object                 if( ... )               if( ... )
  { ... }                        { y =  new CA();        { y1 =  new CA();
class MultiDef                     y.[CA.<init>()]();      y = y1;
  extends Object               }                           y1.[CA.<init>]();
{ void java()                                            }
  { Object y;                  else                     else
    if( ... )                    { y =  new CB();         { y2 =  new CB();
      y = new CA();                y.[CB.<init>()]();       y = y2;
    else                       }                           y2.[CB.<init>]();
      y = new CB();            y.toString();             }
    y.toString();           }                           y.toString();
  }                                                    }
}
```

Fig. 9. Object creation in Java versus 3-address code

In stage 2, we solve this problem by introducing copy statements at every object creation site. This is shown in Figure 9 in the method `fixed_three_address`. After inserting the extra copy statements, we simply reapply stage 1.

Experimental results show us that this very simple transformation is very effective at solving all type inference difficulties found in code generated from normal compilers.

4.4   Stage 3

It is possible that the previous stages fail and this would happen with the method `hardest` in Figure 3. However, current compilers and programs seem not to expose such difficult cases. In the future, optimizing compilers could get more aggressive, and programmers might start designing more elaborate interface hierarchies. In order to provide a complete, yet efficient type inference algorithm, we designed this third stage.

First, we note that, due to the *good behavior* guarantees provided by the bytecode verifier, a very crude solution to all type inference problems would be to separate local variables into sets of: reference, double, float, long and int variables. Then, assign the type *java.lang.Object* to all reference variables. Finally, introduce type casts at every location where *use constraints* would be violated. All the introduced casts are guaranteed to succeed at runtime.

But this solution would be somewhat useless in the context of an three-address code optimizer, as type information would be too general, and it would not offer much information in decompiled Java programs.

Our solution also depends on the *good behavior* of verifiable bytecode, but offers a much improved type accuracy without sacrificing simplicity. We simply rebuild the constraint graph without *use constraints*[5], and we ignore the interface hierarchy by assuming that all interfaces have a single parent *java.lang.Object*. In this hierarchy, every two types have an LCA.

As in stage 1, we merge strongly connected components. But, in this *definition constraints* graph, all hard-node to soft-node constraints are parent constraints. So, no strongly connected component contains a hard node. Thus, this step will not detect any type error.

Then, as in stage 1, we eliminate transitive constraints and merge single constraints. When merging single constraints, we replace multiple child constraints from a soft node to hard nodes by a single child constraint from the soft node to the node representing the LCA type of classes and interfaces involved. Unlike stage 1, this is guaranteed to deliver a solution.

The type assignment of this solution may violate some use constraints. So, in a last step, we check every three-address statement for constraint violations, and introduce type casts as needed.

Figure 10 shows this solution applied to the examples in Figure 2 (`harder`), and Figure 3 (`hardest`).

---

[5] A *definition constraint* is a constraint imposed by a definition e.g. $x = new\ A$ is a definition of x, and so it introduces a constraint that would be included in this graph. A *use constraint* in imposed by a use of a variable e.g. *return(x)* uses x and so any constraints imposed by this use would not be included in the graph.

```
    void harder()
    { Object y;
      if( ... )
s1:    { y =  new CA();
           ((CA) y).f(); }
      else
s2:    { y =  new CB();
           ((CB) y).g(); }
s3: y.toString();
    }
```

(a) Figure 2 (harder) solution

```
    void hardest()
    { Object aa;

      if( ... )
s1:    aa = getC();
      else
s2:    aa = getD();

s3: ((IA) aa).f(); // invokeinterface IA.f
s4: ((IB) aa).g(); // invokeinterface IB.g
    }
```

(b) Figure 3 (hardest) solution

Fig. 10. Adding casts

5 Array Constraints

To infer types in programs using arrays, we introduce array constraints in the constraints graph. An *array constraint* represents the relation between the type of an array and the type of its elements. We write $A \mapsto B$, to indicate that B is the element type of array type A (or more simply, A is an array of B). In graphs, we represent these constraints using dashed directed edges from the array type to the element type.

This simple addition allows us to collect constraints for all three-address statements. For example, the program fragment a[d] = b; c = a; generates the following constraints: $a \mapsto b, d \leftarrow int$, and $c \leftarrow a$.

In Java bytecode, $(A[] \leftarrow B[])$ *iff* $(A \leftarrow B)$ and $(A \leftarrow B[])$ *iff* $(A \in \{Object,$ *Serializable, Cloneable*$\}$). We take advantage of this to build an equivalent constraints graph without any array constraints. Then we solve the new problem using the algorithm presented in Section 4. Finally, we use this solution to infer the type of arrays, reversing our first transformation. This transformation is applied in both stage 1 and stage 3, if needed.

We now give a more detailed description of this process. First, we compute the array depth of soft nodes in the constraints graph using a work list algorithm and the following rules:

- Every hard node has an array depth equal to the number of dimensions of the array type it represents, or 0 if it is not an array type.
- *null* has array depth ∞. (*null* is descendant of all types, including array types of all depth[6]).
- A soft node with one or more child constraint has an array depth equal to the smallest *array depth* of its children.
- A soft node with an array constraint has a depth equal to one + the depth of its element node.
- When we verify our solution, a soft node with one or more parent constraints must have an array depth greater or equal to the greatest *array depth* of its parents[7]. (This rule is not used in stage 3).

---

[6] We could also use 256, as Java arrays are limited to 255 dimensions.

[7] If this rule fails, stage 1 fails.

We merge with *null* all soft nodes with array depth equal to ∞. Then, we complete the constraints graph by adding all missing array constraints (and soft nodes) so that every node of array depth n greater than 0 (called *array node*) has an array constraint to a node of array depth $n - 1$.

The final step in the transformation is to change all constraints between *array soft nodes* and other nodes into constraints between *non-array nodes* using the following rules:

- Change a constraint between two nodes of equal depth into a constraint between their respective element nodes.
- Change a constraint between two nodes of different depth into a constraint between the element type of lowest depth node and *java.lang.Cloneable* and *java.io.Serializable*.

This is illustrated in figure 11.

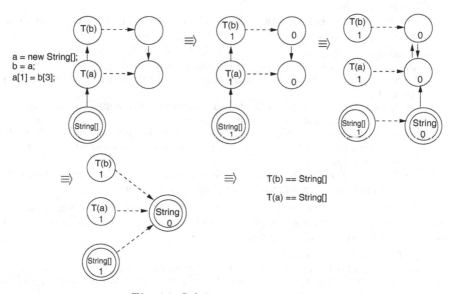

Fig. 11. Solving array constraints

Then we use the algorithm of section 4 to solve the typing problem on the graph of non-array nodes. Then we use this solution to infer the type of array nodes. For example, if $x \mapsto y$, and $y = A$, then $x = A[]$

In order to correctly handle the case of primitive array types (*boolean[]...[]*, *short[]...[]*, *char[]...[]*, *byte[]...[]*), we merge these hard nodes with all their same-depth neighbors before constraints propagation[8].

---

[8] This is necessary because the depth 0 for all these types is *int*.

6   Integer Types

While the algorithm presented in previous sections infers the necessary types for optimizing three-address code, these types are not sufficient for Java decompilers. All `boolean`, `byte`, `short`, `char` values are automatically operated upon as `int` values by the bytecode interpreter. Furthermore, the Java verifier does not check for consistent use of these types.

It is thus possible to construct bytecode programs with dubious semantics as:

```
boolean erroneous(int a)   // boolean return value
{ return a;   // valid bytecode!
}
void dubious()
{ <unknown> b = erroneous(5);
  System.out.[void println(int)](b);   // prints 1 or 5?
}
```

We developed an algorithm that infers the basic types `boolean`, `byte`, `short`, `char`, `int` for all variables that are assigned an `int` type by the initial 3-stage algorithm.

This algorithm operates in two stages. The first stage uses the type hierarchy in Figure 12(a), and consists of:

- Constraints collection.
- Merging connected components. (This may fail).
- Merging single relations by aplying the following rules until a fixed point is reached:
    - Replacing all multiple child dependencies between a single soft node and multiple hard nodes by a dependency on the *least common ancestor* type.
    - Replacing all multiple parent dependencies between a single soft node and multiple hard nodes by a dependency on the *greatest common descendent* type.
    - Merging a soft node with a single parent or single child hard node representing either `boolean`, `byte`, `short`, `char` or, `int`.

If this stage fails to deliver a solution (remaining soft node, conflicting parent or child constraints), then a second stage is performed using the type hierarchy in Figure 12(b) and the following steps:

- *Definition constraints* collection.
- Merging connected components. (This always succeeds).
- Merging single relation by aplying the following rules until a fixed point is reached:
    - Replacing all multiple child dependencies between a single soft node and multiple hard nodes by a dependency on the *least common ancestor* type.
    - Merging a soft node with a single child hard node.

This will always deliver a solution. In the final type assignment, [0..127] is replaced by `byte`, and [0..32767] is replaced by `char`. Finally, *use constraints* are verified and type casts are added as required.

The second stage might introduce *narrowing* type casts, and thus possibly change the semantics of the program. However, this would only happen when programs have dubious semantics to begin with. In our experiments, we have not discovered a case where stage 2 was needed.

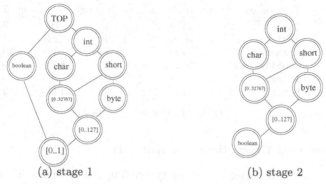

(a) stage 1   (b) stage 2

Fig. 12. Integer type hierarchy

7   Experimental Results

The typing algorithm presented in this paper has been implemented in the Soot framework[21]. The typing algorithm accepts untyped Jimple as input, and outputs typed Jimple. Typed Jimple is used by subsequent analyses including class hierarchy analysis, pointer analysis and a Jimple to Java decompiler.

In this section we present the results of two set of experiments done using our implementation. The first set of experiments was performed to test the robustness of the typing algorithm as well as to gather empirical data about the complexity of type constraints in programs compiled from various languages. In the second experiment, the inferred types of Jimple were used to improve Class Hierarchy Analysis.

7.1   Typing Java Bytecode

We have applied our typing algorithm on class files produced by compilers of five different languages: Java[10], Eiffel[20], Ada[23], Scheme[5] and ML[14]. Table 1 shows a selection of our results to show the general trends. The benchmarks are as follows: **javac** is the Sun's javac compiler, **jdk1.1** is everything in Sun's java class library for jdk1.1, **kalman** is a numeric Ada benchmark, **compile_to_c** is the SmallEiffel compiler (version 0.79), **lexgen** is a lexer generator used in the Standard ML of New Jersey benchmark suite, and **boyer** is one of the Gabriel Scheme benchmarks.

The *# methods* column gives the total number of methods in the benchmark. The next two columns give the number of methods that could be typed using various steps of stage 1. The *conn. comp.* column counts the number of methods that could be completely typed by finding connected components, while the *single cons.* column counts the number of methods that needed both connected components and the removal of single constraints. The *stage 2* column counts the number of methods that required the stage 2. The *stage 3* column counts the number of methods that needed stage 3. It is interesting to note that a significant number of methods were typed using only connected components, and none of the 16959 methods required insertion of type casts (stage 3).

Language	Benchmark	# methods	conn. comp.	single cons.	stage 2	stage 3
java:	`javac`	1179	383	796	3	0
java:	`jdk1.1`	5060	2818	2228	14	0
ada:	`kalman`	735	463	262	10	0
eiffel:	`compile_to_c`	7521	1562	5959	0	0
ml:	`lexgen`	209	140	69	0	0
scheme:	`boyer`	2255	820	1433	2	0

Table 1. Required steps

7.2   Improving Class Hierarchy Analysis

One of the motivations for producing typed Jimple was for use in compiler analyzes and optimizations, and our second experiment illustrates one such use. In this experiment we measured the gains in the precision of the conservative call graph built using *class hierarchy analysis* (CHA)[4,7,8]. The basic idea is that for each virtual call of the form $o.f(a_1, a_2, \ldots, a_n)$, one needs to determine all possible methods f that could be called given the receiver o and a given class hierarchy. If the call graph is built using untyped Jimple, then type information provided by a method signature must be used to estimate the type of the receiver o. This type is correct, but may be too general and thus CHA may be too conservative about the destination of a virtual (or interface) call. If the call graph is built using typed Jimple, then each receiver has an inferred type provided by our algorithm, and this is often a tighter type than the type in the signature. This improved type information reduces the number of possible destinations for the call, and provides a better call graph on which further analysis can be made.

source program language name		call-graph edges untyped Jimple (#)	call-graph edges typed Jimple (#)	Reduction (%)
java:	`jack`	10583	10228	3
java:	`javac`	26320	23625	10
java:	`jimple`	51350	33464	35
ada:	`rudstone`	8151	7806	4
eiffel:	`illness`	3966	3778	5
ml:	`nucleic`	5009	4820	4

Table 2. Call graph reduction

Table 2 shows the number of call-graph edges for both untyped and typed Jimple, and the percent reduction due to using typed Jimple. Again we present a selection of benchmarks from a variety of compilers. Note that the very object-oriented benchmarks like `javac` (10%) and `jimple` (35%) show significant reductions if the static type of the receiver is known. This means that subsequent analyses, including run-time type analysis, will start with a significantly better approximation of the call graph. The other benchmarks show a reduction in the 3% to 5% range, which is not as significant. This is mostly due to the fact that these benchmarks have a much simpler call graph to begin with, and so there is not much room for improvement.

These results serve to illustrate one benefit of typed Jimple. In fact the types are useful for a wide variety of other analyses including: (1) finding when an invokeinterface can be replaced by an invokevirtual call (i.e. when the inferred type of the receiver is a class, but the instruction is an invokeinterface), (2) deciding when a method can be safely inlined without violating access rules, (3) giving types to variables in decompiled code, and (4) as a basis for grouping variables by type (i.e. a coarse grain run-time type analysis or side-effect analysis can group variables by declared type).

8   Related Work

Related work has been done in the fields of type inference, typed assembly languages, and decompilation.

This work is a refinement of a preliminary report by Gagnon and Hendren[9]. In our preliminary work we proposed an exponential algorithm to solve difficult cases, whereas in this work we avoid the exponential case by applying program transformations, and we introduce the 3-stage approach. Further, this paper addresses the problem of assigning different integer types.

In [12], Knoblock and Rehof present a superficially similar algorithm to type Java bytecode. Their approach is different on many aspects. Their algorithm only works with programs in SSA form. It consists of adding new types and changing the interface hierarchy so that every two interfaces have a LUB and a SUP in the resulting type lattice. Changing the type hierarchy has unfortunate consequences: decompiled programs expose a type hierarchy that differs from the original program, the globality of such a change makes this algorithm useless in a dynamic code optimizers like HotSpot[22]. Our algorithm, on the other hand, works with any 3-address code representation and has no global side effects. It is thus suitable for use in a dynamic enviroment.

Type inference is a well known problem. There has been considerable work on type inference for modern object-oriented languages. Palsberg and Schwartzbach introduced the *basic type inference algorithm* for Object-Oriented languages [17]. Subsequent papers on the subject extend and improve this initial algorithm [18,1,2]. These algorithms infer dynamic types, i.e. they describe the set of possible types that can occur at runtime. Further, most techniques need to consider the whole program.

As we emphasized in the introduction, our type problem is different in that we infer static types. Further, we have a very particular property of having some type information from the bytecode, including the types of methods. This means that our type inference can be intra-procedural, and just consider one method body at a time.

Work has been done by Morrisett et al.[16] on stack-based typed assembly language. This work differs in that their typed assembly language is directly produced from a higher level language. Their work emphasizes the importance of having type information to perform aggressive optimizations. We agree that types are important for optimization, and this is one good reason we need our type inference.

Our technique is related to the type inference performed by Java decompilers[15,11,27,3] and other Java compilers that convert from bytecode to C, or other intermediate representations. Proebsting and Watterson have written a paper[19] on decompilation in Java. Their paper is mainly focused on reconstruction high-level control statements from primitive goto branches. In their text, they wrongfully dismiss the type inference problem as being solvable by well known techniques similar to the Java verifier's algorithm. As we have shown in this paper, the problem is NP-Hard in general, and some bytecode programs require program transformations in order to be typeable statically.

9   Conclusion

In this paper we presented a static type inference algorithm for typing Java bytecode. We based our methods on a 3-address representation of Java bytecode called Jimple. In effect, we perform the translation of untyped 3-address code to typed 3-address code, where all local variables have been assigned a static type.

We have presented a constraint system that can be used to represent the type inference problem. Using this representation, we developed a simple, fast and effective multi-stage algorithm that was shown to handle all methods in a set of programs (and libraries) produced from five different source languages. We emphasized the difference between *well behaved* bytecode as defined by the Java verifier, and *well typed* bytecode, as required by a static typing algorithm. Our experimental results show that this efficient analysis can significantly improve the results of further analyzes like Class Hierarchy Analysis.

Acknowledgments

We thank Raja Vallée-Rai and other Sable research group members for their work on developing Jimple and the Soot framework.

References

1. Ole Agesen. Constraint-based type inference and parametric polymorphism. In Baudouin Le Charlier, editor, *SAS'94—Proceedings of the First International Static Analysis Symposium*, volume 864 of *Lecture Notes in Computer Science*, pages 78–100. Springer, September 1994. 202, 217
2. Ole Agesen. The Cartesian product algorithm: Simple and precise type inference of parametric polymorphism. In Walter G. Olthoff, editor, *ECOOP'95—Object-Oriented Programming, 9th European Conference*, volume 952 of *Lecture Notes in Computer Science*, pages 2–26, Åarhus, Denmark, August 1995. Springer. 202, 217
3. Ahpah Software Inc. http://zeus.he.net/~pah/products.html. 218
4. David F. Bacon and Peter F. Sweeney. Fast static analysis of C++ virtual function calls. In *Proceedings of the Conference on Object-Oriented Programming Systems, Languages, and Applications*, volume 31 of *ACM SIGPLAN Notices*, pages 324–341, New York, October 1996. ACM Press. 216

5. Per Bothner. Kawa - compiling dynamic languages to the Java VM, 1998. 199, 215

6. Thomas H. Cormen, Charles E. Leiserson, and Ronald L. Rivest. *Introduction to Algorithms.* MIT Press; McGraw-Hill Book, Cambridge New York, 1990. 207

7. Jeffrey Dean, David Grove, and Craig Chambers. Optimization of object-oriented programs using static class hierarchy analysis. In Walter G. Olthoff, editor, *ECOOP'95—Object-Oriented Programming, 9th European Conference*, volume 952 of *Lecture Notes in Computer Science*, pages 77–101, Åarhus, Denmark, August 1995. Springer. 216

8. Mary F. Fernandez. Simple and effective link-time optimization of Modula-3 programs. In *Proceedings of the ACM SIGPLAN'95 Conference on Programming Language Design and Implementation (PLDI)*, pages 103–115, La Jolla, California, June 1995. 216

9. Etienne M. Gagnon and Laurie J. Hendren. Intra-procedural inference of static types for java bytecode. Technical Report Sable 1998-5, McGill University, Montreal, Canada, October 1998. http://www.sable.mcgill.ca/publications/. 217

10. James Gosling, Bill Joy, and Guy Steele. *The Java Language Specification.* The Java Series. Addison-Wesley, 1997. 207, 215

11. Innovative Software. http://world.isg.de. 218

12. T. Knoblock and J. Rehof. Type elaboration and subtype completion for Java bytecode. In *Proceedings 27th ACM SIGPLAN-SIGACT Symposium on Principles of Programming Languages.*, pages 228–242, January 2000. 217

13. Tim Lindholm and Frank Yellin. *The Java Virtual Machine Specification.* The Java Series. Addison-Wesley, Reading, MA, USA, Jannuary 1997. 202, 207

14. MLJ. http://research.persimmon.co.uk/mlj/. 199, 215

15. Mocha. http://www.brouhaha.com/~eric/computers/mocha.html. 218

16. G. Morrisett, K. Crary, N. Glew, and D. Walker. Stack-based typed assembly language. *Lecture Notes in Computer Science*, 1473:28–52, 1998. 217

17. Jens Palsberg and Michael I. Schwartzbach. Object-Oriented Type Inference. In *Proceedings of the OOPSLA '91 Conference on Object-oriented Programming Systems, Languages and Applications*, pages 146–161, November 1991. Published as ACM SIGPLAN Notices, volume 26, number 11. 202, 217

18. J. Plevyak and A. A. Chien. Precise concrete type inference for object-oriented languages. *ACM SIGPLAN Notices*, 29(10):324–324, October 1994. 202, 217

19. Todd A. Proebsting and Scott A. Watterson. Krakatoa: Decompilation in Java (does bytecode reveal source?). In USENIX, editor, *The Third USENIX Conference on Object-Oriented Technologies and Systems (COOTS), June 16–19, 1997. Portland, Oregon*, pages 185–197, Berkeley, CA, USA, June 1997. USENIX. 218

20. Small Eiffel. http://SmallEiffel.loria.fr/. 199, 215

21. Soot. http://www.sable.mcgill.ca/soot/. 215

22. Sun Microsystems Inc. http://java.sun.com/products/hotspot/. 217

23. Tucker Taft. Programming the Internet in Ada 95. In Alfred Strohmeier, editor, *Reliable software technologies, Ada-Europe '96: 1996 Ada-Europe International Conference on Reliable Software Technologies, Montreux, Switzerland, June 10–14, 1996: proceedings*, volume 1088, pages 1–16, 1996. 199, 215

24. Jerzy Tiuryn. Subtype inequalities. In *Proceedings, Seventh Annual IEEE Symposium on Logic in Computer Science*, pages 308–315, Santa Cruz, California, June 1992. IEEE Computer Society Press. 206

25. Raja Vallée-Rai, Phong Co, Etienne Gagnon, Laurie Hendren, Patrick Lam, and Vijay Sundaresan. Soot - a Java bytecode optimization framework. In *Proceedings of CASCON '99*, 1999. 200, 203

26. Raja Vallée-Rai, Etienne Gagnon, Laurie Hendren, Patrick Lam, Patrice Pominville, and Vijay Sundaresan. Optimizing Java Bytecode using the Soot framework: It is feasible? In David Watt, editor, *CC2000—International Conference on Compiler Construction*, pages 18–34, Berlin, Germany, March 2000. 200, 203
27. WingSoft Corporation. http://www.wingsoft.com/wingdis.shtml. 218

Abstract Interpretation of Game Properties[*]

Thomas A. Henzinger[1], Rupak Majumdar[1], Freddy Mang[1], and
Jean-François Raskin[1,2]

[1] Department of Electrical Engineering and Computer Sciences
University of California at Berkeley, CA 94720-1770, USA
[2] Département d'Informatique, Faculté des Sciences
Université Libre de Bruxelles, Belgium
{tah,rupak,fmang,jfr}@eecs.berkeley.edu

Abstract. We apply the theory of abstract interpretation to the verification of game properties for reactive systems. Unlike properties expressed in standard temporal logics, game properties can distinguish adversarial from collaborative relationships between the processes of a concurrent program, or the components of a parallel system. We consider two-player concurrent games —say, component vs. environment— and specify properties of such games —say, the component has a winning strategy to obtain a resource, no matter how the environment behaves— in the alternating-time μ-calculus ($A\mu$). A sound abstraction of such a game must at the same time restrict the behaviors of the component and increase the behaviors of the environment: if a less powerful component can win against a more powerful environment, then surely the original component can win against the original environment.

We formalize the concrete semantics of a concurrent game in terms of controllable and uncontrollable predecessor predicates, which suffice for model checking all $A\mu$ properties by applying boolean operations and iteration. We then define the abstract semantics of a concurrent game in terms of abstractions for the controllable and uncontrollable predecessor predicates. This allows us to give general characterizations for the soundness and completeness of abstract games with respect to $A\mu$ properties. We also present a simple programming language for multi-process programs, and show how approximations of the maximal abstraction (w.r.t. $A\mu$ properties) can be obtained from the program text. We apply the theory to two practical verification examples, a communication protocol developed at the Berkeley Wireless Research Center, and a protocol converter. In the wireless protocol, both the use of a game property for specification and the use of abstraction for automatic verification were instrumental to uncover a subtle bug.

[*] This research was supported in part by the DARPA (NASA) grant NAG2-1214, the DARPA (Wright-Patterson AFB) grant F33615-C-98-3614, the MARCO grant 98-DT-660, the ARO MURI grant DAAH-04-96-1-0341, and the NSF CAREER award CCR-9501708.

J. Palsberg (Ed.): SAS 2000, LNCS 1824, pp. 220–240, 2000.

1   Introduction

In compositional verification, one attempts to decompose the task of proving that a system behaves correctly into subtasks which prove that the individual components of the system behave correctly. Often such a proof decomposition cannot proceed blindly, because an individual component may behave correctly only if put into a certain context. Then, some assumptions about the environment of the component are necessary for the subproof to go through. The interaction between a component and its environment is naturally modeled as a two-player infinite game on a state space. If the interaction is synchronous, then the game is *concurrent*: in each round, both players choose their moves simultaneously and independently, and the combination of the two moves determines the next state. (*Turn-based* games for modeling asynchronous or interleaved interaction, where in each round only one of the two players has a choice, can be considered a special case of concurrent games.) If player 1 represents a component, and player 2 represents the environment assumptions, then a typical property of interest is "Does player 1 have a strategy to reach a goal, say, obtain a resource, no matter how player 2 behaves." A rich logic for specifying such game properties formally is the *alternating-time μ-calculus*, denoted $A\mu$ [1], which subsumes several temporal logics for expressing game properties. In [29] the abstract interpretation of the more special case of turn-based games is considered, but the model checking problem of a general class of game properties is not considered.

While there exist algorithms for model checking game properties [1,16], as usual in model checking, the involved state spaces may be prohibitively large. The common remedy is *abstraction*: the verification engineer attempts to simplify the component model and the environment assumptions as much as possible while still preserving soundness. If the simplifications are sound, and satisfy the desired property, then we can be sure that the actual system also satisfies the property. (By contrast, completeness must often be sacrificed: it may be that the actual system is correct, while the simplified system is not. If an error is found which has no counterpart in the actual system, then some of the simplifying assumptions must be reversed.) For linear-time and branching-time properties, it is well-known how to choose sound simplifications, and how to characterize complete ones. For example, if the objective is to establish a temporal requirement for all traces of a system, then a sound simplification must allow more traces; if the objective is to establish a temporal requirement for some trace, then a sound simplification must allow fewer traces. For game properties, the situation is more complicated. For example, with respect to the property "Does player 1 have a strategy to reach a goal," a simplification is sound if it restricts the power of player 1 and at the same time increases the power of player 2. In this paper, we give a general characterization of soundness and completeness for simplifying games with respect to $A\mu$ properties. This theory is then applied to two practical verification examples, a wireless communication protocol and a protocol converter.

We work in the *abstract-interpretation* framework of [7,9], which makes precise the notion of "simplification" used informally in the previous paragraph. We first give a set of predicates which are sufficient for model checking all $A\mu$ properties by applying boolean operations and iteration. Following [9], this is called the *collecting semantics* of a game. The essential ingredients of the collecting semantics are the *player-i controllable predecessor* predicate, which relates a state q with a set σ of states if player i can force the game from q into σ in a single round, and its dual, the *player-i uncontrollable predecessor* predicate, which relates q with σ if player i cannot prevent the game from moving from q into σ in a single round. We then define what it means for an abstraction of the collecting semantics and the corresponding abstract model checking algorithm to be *sound* (if an abstract state q^α satisfies an $A\mu$ formula, then so do all states in the concretization of q^α), and *complete* (q^α satisfies an $A\mu$ formula if some state in the concretization of q^α does). The completeness of abstractions will be characterized in terms of the *alternating bisimilarity* relation of [2]. This contrasts with the cases in linear-time and branching-time domains: for linear-time properties, completeness requires trace equivalence; for branching-time properties, bisimilarity. Our results can thus be seen to be systematic generalizations of the abstract-interpretation theory for temporal requirements from (single-player) transition systems [6,26,12,14,11] to (mutli-player) game structures.

While our development applies to concurrent game structures in general, in practice it is preferable to derive the abstraction of the collecting semantics directly from the text of a program [7,14]. Such a direct computation (defined by structural induction on the programming language) may lose precision, and we typically obtain only an approximation of the *maximal* abstraction (an abstract state q^α satisfies an $A\mu$ formula if all states in the concretization of q^α do). We introduce a simple programming language for multi-process programs based on guarded commands [18]. We interpret processes as players in a concurrent game, and show how to compute approximations of the maximal abstraction directly from the program text. We present both *domain abstraction*, a nonrelational form of abstraction where each variable is interpreted over an abstract domain, and *predicate abstraction*, a relational abstraction which permits more accuracy by relating the values of different variables via abstract predicates [24].

Abstract interpretation has been used successfully in the automated verification of reactive systems [13,14,23,5,27]. We illustrate the application of the theory to the automated verification of game properties with two practical examples. The first example originates from the *Two-Chip Intercom* (TCI) project of the Berkeley Wireless Research Center [4]. The TCI network is a wireless local network which allows approximately 40 remotes, one for each user, to transmit voice with point-to-point and broadcast communication. The operation of the network is coordinated by a base station, which assigns channels to the users through a TDMA scheme. Properties specifying the correct operation of each remote can be given in the game logic $A\mu$: each remote must behave correctly in an environment containing the base station and arbitrarily many other remotes. We verified the protocol for a base station and an arbitrary number of remotes. Since the system is infinite state, in order to use our model checkerMOCHA [3], we needed to abstract it to a finite instance. A bug was found on an abstract version of the protocol. The violated property involves an adversarial behavior of the base station with respect to a remote, and cannot be specified directly in a nongame logic like CTL. Thus, both game properties and abstract interpretation were necessary in the verification process.

The second example concerns the automatic synthesis of a protocol converter between a message sender which speaks the alternating-bit protocol and a receiver which speaks a simple two-phase protocol. We view the problem as a special case of *controller synthesis*, which is in turn a special case of $A\mu$ model checking. We view the composition of the sender and the receiver as the system to be controlled, and the protocol converter as the controller to be synthesized. The requirements of the converter is written in the game logic $A\mu$. Using predicate and domain abstractions, we are able to check for the existence and construct a converter which satisfies the requirements.

2   Structures and Logics for Games

Alternating Transition Systems. An *alternating transition system* [1] is a tuple $S = \langle \Sigma, Q, \Delta, \Pi, \pi \rangle$ with the following components: (i) Σ is the (finite) set of *players*. (ii) Q is a (possibly infinite) set of *states*. (iii) $\Delta = \{\delta_i : Q \to 2^{2^Q} \mid i \in \Sigma\}$ is a set of *transition functions*, one for each player in Σ, which maps each state to a nonempty set of *choices*, where each choice is a set of possible next states. Whenever the system is in state q, each player $a \in \Sigma$ independently and simultaneously chooses a set $Q_a \in \delta_a(q)$. In this way, a player a ensures that the next state of the system will be in its choice Q_a. However, which state in Q_a will be next depends on the choices made by the other players, because the successor of q must lie in the intersection $\bigcap_{a \in \Sigma} Q_a$ of the choices made by all players. We assume that the transition function is nonblocking and the players together choose a unique next state: if $\Sigma = \{a_1, \ldots, a_n\}$, then for every state $q \in Q$ and every set $Q_1, \ldots, Q_n$ of choices $Q_i \in \delta_{a_i}(q)$, the intersection $Q_1 \cap \ldots \cap Q_n$ is a singleton. Note that we do not lose expressive power by considering only deterministic games, because nondeterminism can be modeled by an additional player. (iv) Π is a set of *propositions*. (v) $\pi : \Pi \to 2^Q$ maps each proposition to a set of states.

From the definition it can be seen that alternating transition systems can model general *concurrent games*, and includes as a special case turn-based games. For two states q and q' and a player $a \in \Sigma$, we say q' is an *a-successor* of q if there exists a set $Q' \in \delta_a(q)$ such that $q' \in Q'$. For two states q and q', we say q' is a *successor* of q if for all players $a \in \Sigma$, the state q' is an *a-successor* of q. A *computation* $\eta = q_0 q_1 \ldots$ is a finite or infinite sequence of states such that q_{i+1} is a successor of q_i for all $i \geq 0$. A computation produces a *trace* $\tau = \pi(q_0)\pi(q_1)\ldots$ of sets of propositions. A *strategy* for a player $a \in \Sigma$ is a mapping $f_a : Q^+ \to 2^Q$ such that for $w \in Q^*$ and $q \in Q$, we have $f_a(w \cdot q) \in \delta_a(q)$. Thus, the strategy f_a maps a finite nonempty prefix $w \cdot q$ of a computation to a set in $\delta_a(q)$: this set contains possible extensions of the computation as suggested to player a by the strategy. For fixed strategies $F = \{f_a \mid a \in \Sigma\}$, the computation $\eta = q_0 q_1 \ldots$

is consistent with F if for all $i \geq 0$, $q_{i+1} \in f_a(q_0 q_1 \ldots q_i)$ for all $a \in \Sigma$. For a state $q \in Q$, we define the *outcome* $\mathcal{L}_F(q)$ of F with source q as the set of possible traces produced by the computations which start from state q, and are consistent with the strategies F.

For ease of presentation, we consider in the following only two players, whom we call player 1 and player 2 respectively, i.e., $\Sigma = \{1, 2\}$. The results generalize immediately to multiple players.

Alternating-Time μ-Calculus. A *game logic* L is a logic whose formulas are interpreted over the states of alternating transition systems; that is, for every L-formula φ and every alternating transition system S, there is a set $\llbracket \varphi \rrbracket_S$ of states of S which satisfy φ. The L *model checking problem* for a game logic L and an alternating transition system S asks, given an L-formula φ and a state q of S, whether $q \in \llbracket \varphi \rrbracket_S$.

The formulas of the *alternating time μ-calculus* [1] are generated by the grammar

$$\varphi ::= p \mid \overline{p} \mid x \mid \varphi \vee \varphi \mid \varphi \wedge \varphi \mid \langle\!\langle I \rangle\!\rangle \bigcirc \varphi \mid [\![I]\!] \bigcirc \varphi \mid (\mu x \colon \varphi) \mid (\nu x \colon \varphi),$$

for propositions p in some set Π^L of propositions, variables x in some set X of variables, and teams of players $I = 1, 2, \{1, 2\}$. Let $S = \langle \Sigma, Q, \Delta, \Pi, \pi \rangle$ be an alternating transition system whose propositions include all propositions on which formulas are constructed; that is, $\Pi^L \subseteq \Pi$. Let $\mathcal{E} \colon X \to 2^Q$ be a mapping from the variables to sets of states. We write $\mathcal{E}[x \mapsto \rho]$ for the mapping that agrees with $\mathcal{E}$ on all variables, except that $x \in X$ is mapped to $\rho \subseteq Q$. Given S and $\mathcal{E}$, every formula φ defines a set $\llbracket \varphi \rrbracket_{S, \mathcal{E}} \subseteq Q$ of states:

$$
\begin{aligned}
\llbracket p \rrbracket_{S, \mathcal{E}} &= \pi(p); \\
\llbracket \overline{p} \rrbracket_{S, \mathcal{E}} &= Q \backslash \pi(p); \\
\llbracket x \rrbracket_{S, \mathcal{E}} &= \mathcal{E}(x); \\
\llbracket \varphi_1 \{{\vee \atop \wedge}\} \varphi_2 \rrbracket_{S, \mathcal{E}} &= \llbracket \varphi_1 \rrbracket_{S, \mathcal{E}} \{{\cup \atop \cap}\} \llbracket \varphi_2 \rrbracket_{S, \mathcal{E}}; \\
\llbracket \{{\langle\!\langle 1 \rangle\!\rangle \atop [\![1]\!]}\} \bigcirc \varphi \rrbracket_{S, \mathcal{E}} &= \{q \in Q \mid (\{{\exists \sigma \in \delta_1(q). \forall \tau \in \delta_2(q) \atop \forall \sigma \in \delta_1(q). \exists \tau \in \delta_2(q)}\}) r \in \sigma \cap \tau \colon r \in \llbracket \varphi \rrbracket_{S, \mathcal{E}})\}; \\
\llbracket \{{\langle\!\langle 1, 2 \rangle\!\rangle \atop [\![1, 2]\!]}\} \bigcirc \varphi \rrbracket_{S, \mathcal{E}} &= \{q \in Q \mid (\{{\exists \sigma \in \delta_1(q). \exists \tau \in \delta_2(q) \atop \forall \sigma \in \delta_1(q). \forall \tau \in \delta_2(q)}\}) r \in \sigma \cap \tau \colon r \in \llbracket \varphi \rrbracket_{S, \mathcal{E}})\}; \\
\llbracket \{{\mu \atop \nu}\} x \colon \varphi \rrbracket_{S, \mathcal{E}} &= \{{\cap \atop \cup}\} \{\rho \subseteq Q \mid \rho = \llbracket \varphi \rrbracket_{S, \mathcal{E}[x \mapsto \rho]}\}.
\end{aligned}
$$

If we restrict ourselves to the closed formulas, then we obtain a game logic, denoted $A\mu$: the state $q \in Q$ *satisfies* the $A\mu$-formula φ if $q \in \llbracket \varphi \rrbracket_{S, \mathcal{E}}$ for any variable mapping $\mathcal{E}$; that is, $\llbracket \varphi \rrbracket_S = \llbracket \varphi \rrbracket_{S, \mathcal{E}}$ for any $\mathcal{E}$.

The logic $A\mu$ is very expressive and embeds the game logics ATL and ATL* [1]. For example, the ATL-formula $\langle\!\langle 1 \rangle\!\rangle \varphi_1 \mathcal{U} \varphi_2$ can be expressed in $A\mu$ as $(\mu x \colon \varphi_2 \vee (\varphi_1 \wedge \langle\!\langle 1 \rangle\!\rangle \bigcirc x))$. Note that the fragment which restricts all game quantifiers $\langle\!\langle I \rangle\!\rangle$ and $[\![I]\!]$ to the team $I = \{1, 2\}$ is the standard μ-calculus. Thus, our results include as a special case the results of [14].

Collecting Semantics of Alternating Transition Systems. Alternating transition systems provide an *operational semantics* to our model of systems with interacting components. In addition, we isolate the operators we need to evaluate on an alternating transition system in order to compute the set of states where a formula of the logic $A\mu$ holds. We call these operators, following [7,8], the *collecting semantics* of the alternating transition system. The collecting semantics of an alternating transition system may be thought of as an instrumented version of the operational semantics in order to gather useful information about temporal properties of a system. Given an alternating transition system $S = \langle \Sigma, Q, \Delta, \Pi, \pi \rangle$, the collecting semantics consists of the following operators.

States satisfying a proposition or the negation of a proposition. For every proposition $p \in \Pi$, and its negation $\bar{p}$, we define $\langle\!| p |\!\rangle = \pi(p)$ and $\langle\!| \bar{p} |\!\rangle = Q \setminus \pi(p)$.

Controllable and uncontrollable predecessors. We define the *player-1 controllable predecessor* relation $CPre_1 : 2^Q \to 2^Q$ as $q \in CPre_1(\sigma)$ iff $\exists \tau \in \delta_1(q). \forall \tau' \in \delta_2(q). \tau \cap \tau' \subseteq \sigma$ The state q is in the set of controllable predecessors of the set of states σ if player 1 can make a choice such that for all choices of player-2, the successor state of q lies in the set σ. Thus in q, player 1 has the ability to force the next state of the game into σ. We define the *player-1 uncontrollable predecessor* relation $UPre_1 : 2^Q \to 2^Q$ as $q \in UPre_1(\sigma)$ iff $\forall \tau \in \delta_1(q). \exists \tau' \in \delta_2(q). \tau \cap \tau' \subseteq \sigma$. So the state q is in the set of uncontrollable predecessors of the set of states σ if for each choice of player 1 in q, there exists a choice of player 2 such that the successor state of q is in σ. Thus in q, player 1 cannot force the game outside σ without the cooperation of player 2, or equivalently, player 1 cannot avoid σ. We can similarly define the player 2 controllable and uncontrollable predecessor relations $CPre_2$ and $UPre_2$. The team-$\{1, 2\}$ predecessor relations $CPre_{\{1,2\}}$ and $UPre_{\{1,2\}}$ are defined as:

$$q \in CPre_{\{1,2\}}(\sigma) \text{ iff } \exists \tau \in \delta_1(q). \exists \tau' \in \delta_2(q). \tau \cap \tau' \subseteq \sigma$$
$$q \in UPre_{\{1,2\}}(\sigma) \text{ iff } \forall \tau \in \delta_1(q). \forall \tau' \in \delta_2(q). \tau \cap \tau' \subseteq \sigma$$

From the definitions above, we can establish the following propositions.

Proposition 1. *The operators $CPre_I$ and $UPre_I$ (for $I = 1, 2, \{1, 2\}$) are duals of each other, that is, if $\sigma \subseteq Q$ is a set of states and $\neg \sigma = Q \setminus \sigma$, then $CPre_I(\sigma) = \neg UPre_I(\neg \sigma)$.*

Proposition 2. *The operators $CPre_I$ and $UPre_I$ are monotonic, that is, for all sets of states σ_1, σ_2 such that $\sigma_1 \subseteq \sigma_2 \subseteq Q$, we have $CPre_I(\sigma_1) \subseteq CPre_I(\sigma_2)$ and $UPre_I(\sigma_1) \subseteq UPre_I(\sigma_2)$.*

Model Checking with Game Operators The definition of $A\mu$ naturally suggests a model checking method for finite state systems, where fixpoints are computed by successive approximations; note that the operators $CPre_I$ and $UPre_I$ for $I = 1, 2, \{1, 2\}$ correspond naturally to the semantics of the logical formulas $\langle\!\langle I \rangle\!\rangle \bigcirc$ and $[\![I]\!] \bigcirc$. For alternating transition systems with a collecting semantics defined by the above operators, one can similarly define a model checking

Semi-algorithm ModelCheck
Input: the collecting semantics of an alternating transition system with
operators $\langle\!\langle \cdot \rangle\!\rangle$, $CPre_I$, $UPre_I$, a formula $\varphi \in A\mu$, and a mapping E
with domain X.

Output: $[\varphi]_{S,E} :=$
        if $\varphi = p$ **then return** $\langle\!\langle p \rangle\!\rangle$;
        if $\varphi = \bar{p}$ **then return** $\langle\!\langle \bar{p} \rangle\!\rangle$;
        if $\varphi = (\varphi_1 \vee \varphi_2)$ **then return** $[\varphi_1]_{S,E} \cup [\varphi_2]_{S,E}$;
        if $\varphi = (\varphi_1 \wedge \varphi_2)$ **then return** $[\varphi_1]_{S,E} \cap [\varphi_2]_{S,E}$;
        if $\varphi = \langle\!\langle I \rangle\!\rangle \bigcirc \varphi'$ **then return** $CPre_I([\varphi']_{S,E})$;
        if $\varphi = [\![I]\!] \bigcirc \varphi'$ **then return** $UPre_I([\varphi']_{S,E})$;
        if $\varphi = (\mu x : \varphi')$ **then**
                $T_0 := \emptyset$;
            for $i = 0, 1, 2, \ldots$ **do**
                $T_{i+1} := [\varphi']_{S,E[x \mapsto T_i]}$
            until $\quad T_{i+1} \subseteq T_i$;
            return T_i;
        if $\varphi = (\nu x : \varphi')$ **then**
                $T_0 := Q$;
            for $i = 0, 1, 2, \ldots$ **do**
                $T_{i+1} := [\varphi']_{S,E[x \mapsto T_i]}$
            until $\quad T_{i+1} \supseteq T_i$;
            return T_i.

Fig. 1. $A\mu$ model checking

procedure that uses boolean operations, as well as the predecessor operations
$CPre_I$ and $UPre_I$ [1]. The procedure ModelCheck of Figure 1 takes as input an
alternating transition system S described by its collecting semantics, a formula
$\varphi \in A\mu$, and an environment E mapping variables to sets of states, and produces
a set $[\varphi]_{S,E}$ of states.

Theorem 1. *If the semi-algorithm* ModelCheck *terminates, then* $[\varphi]_{S,E} = [\![\varphi]\!]_S$
for any closed formula φ *of* $A\mu$ *and any environment* E.

In general, the fixpoints may not converge in a finite number of steps, and
transfinite iteration may be required.

3   Abstractions of Alternating Transition Systems

Let Q^α be a set of *abstract states* and $\gamma : Q^\alpha \to 2^Q$ be a *concretization function*
that maps each abstract state q^α to a set of concrete states $\gamma(q^\alpha)$ which q^α
represents. We define a *precision order* $\preceq \subseteq Q^\alpha \times Q^\alpha$ on the abstract domain, as
$q_1^\alpha \preceq q_2^\alpha$ iff $\gamma(q_1^\alpha) \subseteq \gamma(q_2^\alpha)$. Thus q_1^α is *more precise than* q_2^α if the set of concrete
states represented by q_1^α is a subset of the set of concrete states represented
by q_2^α. So by definition, γ is monotonic w.r.t. $\preceq$. Let $\hat{\gamma}(\sigma^\alpha) = \bigcup \{\gamma(q^\alpha) \mid q^\alpha \in \sigma^\alpha\}$

denote the set extension of γ. We extend the order $\preceq$ over sets of abstract states, giving $\hat{\preceq} \subseteq 2^{Q^\alpha} \times 2^{Q^\alpha}$, as $\sigma_1^\alpha \hat{\preceq} \sigma_2^\alpha$ iff $\hat{\gamma}(\sigma_1^\alpha) \subseteq \hat{\gamma}(\sigma_2^\alpha)$. A set σ_1^α of abstract states is an *approximation* of a set σ_2^α of abstract states if $\sigma_1^\alpha \hat{\preceq} \sigma_2^\alpha$.

Given an alternating transition system S with state space Q and set of abstract states Q^α with concretization function γ, we want to compute the abstraction of the concrete semantics of any $A\mu$-formula φ, denoted $[\![\varphi]\!]_S^\alpha$. An abstract interpretation is *sound* if properties that we establish with the abstract algorithm are true in the concrete semantics; i.e., $\hat{\gamma}([\![\varphi]\!]_S^\alpha) \subseteq [\![\varphi]\!]_S$ In the sequel, we only consider sound abstract interpretations. Conversely, an abstract interpretation is *complete* if properties that are true on the concrete domain can be established by the abstract interpretation; i.e., $[\![\varphi]\!]_S \subseteq \hat{\gamma}([\![\varphi]\!]_S^\alpha)$. In general, an abstract interpretation is not complete unless strong conditions are fulfilled by the abstract domain and the concretization function. We will give a necessary and sufficient condition on the abstract domain and the concretization function for complete model checking of $A\mu$-properties. In addition to soundness and completeness, one is also interested in the *maximality* of abstract interpretations. The abstract interpretation is maximal if we have for all abstract state $q^\alpha \in Q^\alpha$, if $\gamma(q^\alpha) \subseteq [\![\varphi]\!]_S$ then $q^\alpha \in [\![\varphi]\!]_S^\alpha$. This means that if a property is true in all concrete states represented by an abstract state q^α, then the abstract model checking algorithm is able to establish it. As for completeness, maximality is also lost unless we impose strong conditions on the abstract domain and operations necessary to compute the abstract semantics. We refer the interested reader to [21,22] for a general treatment of maximality in abstract interpretation.

Abstraction of the Collecting Semantics. We have shown in the previous section that $[\![\varphi]\!]_S$ can be computed using the collecting semantics of S. We now explain how the collecting semantics can be abstracted. For each component $\langle \cdot \rangle$, $CPre_I$, and $UPre_I$ of the collecting semantics. We define the abstract counterpart $\langle \cdot \rangle^\alpha$, $CPre_I^\alpha$, and $UPre_I^\alpha$.

Abstract semantics of propositions. For each proposition $p \in \Pi^L$ we define $\langle p \rangle^\alpha = \{q^\alpha \in Q^\alpha \mid \gamma(q^\alpha) \subseteq \langle p \rangle\}$ and $\langle \bar{p} \rangle^\alpha = \{q^\alpha \in Q^\alpha \mid \gamma(q^\alpha) \subseteq \langle \bar{p} \rangle\}$. From this it follows that the abstract semantics for propositions is sound. Moreover, for abstract states q^α, r^α with $q^\alpha \preceq r^\alpha$, if $r^\alpha \in \langle p \rangle^\alpha$ then $q^\alpha \in \langle p \rangle^\alpha$. Note that given a proposition $p \in \Pi^L$ and an abstract state q^α, we can have $q^\alpha \notin \langle p \rangle^\alpha$ and $q^\alpha \notin \langle \bar{p} \rangle^\alpha$. This occurs when the abstract state q^α represents at the same time concrete states where the proposition p evaluates to true and other states where the proposition p evaluates to false.

Abstract controllable and uncontrollable predecessors. Let q^α be an abstract state and σ^α be a set of abstract states, we define the abstract controllable predecessor relation as: $q^\alpha \in CPre_I^\alpha(\sigma^\alpha)$ iff $\forall q \in \gamma(q^\alpha)$. $q \in CPre_I(\hat{\gamma}(\sigma^\alpha))$. So an abstract state q^α is included in the abstract controllable predecessors of an abstract region σ^α if all the concrete states represented by q^α are in the controllable predecessors of the set of concrete states represented by the set of abstract states σ^α.

Similarly, the abstraction of the uncontrollable predecessor relation is defined as $q^\alpha \in UPre_I^\alpha(\sigma^\alpha)$ iff $\forall q \in \gamma(q^\alpha)$. $q \in UPre_I(\hat{\gamma}(\sigma^\alpha))$. The soundness and the maximality of the abstract controllable and uncontrollable predecessors follow from the definitions.

Lemma 1. Soundness and maximality. *For every set σ^α of abstract states, $\hat{\gamma}(CPre_I^\alpha(\sigma^\alpha)) \subseteq CPre_I(\hat{\gamma}(\sigma^\alpha))$ and $\hat{\gamma}(UPre_I^\alpha(\sigma^\alpha)) \subseteq UPre_I(\hat{\gamma}(\sigma^\alpha))$, expressing soundness. Also, if $q^\alpha \notin CPre_I^\alpha(\sigma^\alpha)$ then $\gamma(q^\alpha) \not\subseteq CPre_I(\hat{\gamma}(\sigma^\alpha))$ and if $q^\alpha \notin UPre_I^\alpha(\sigma^\alpha)$ then $\gamma(q^\alpha) \not\subseteq UPre_I(\hat{\gamma}(\sigma^\alpha))$, expressing maximality.*

Abstract Model Checking of the Alternating-Time μ-Calculus. An *abstract model checking algorithm* takes as input an abstraction of the collecting semantics of the alternating transition system and an $A\mu$ formula φ, and computes a set of abstract states. This defines the *abstract semantics* of φ. Let AbsModelCheck be the abstract model checking algorithm obtained from ModelCheck by replacing the concrete collecting semantics $\langle \cdot \rangle$, $CPre_I$, and $UPre_I$ by their respective abstract collecting semantics $\langle \cdot \rangle^\alpha$, $CPre_I^\alpha$, and $UPre_I^\alpha$ for $I = 1, 2, \{1, 2\}$. The soundness of AbsModelCheck is proved by induction on the structure of formulas, using the soundness of the abstraction of the collecting semantics.

Theorem 2. Soundness of AbsModelCheck. *The abstract model checking algorithm AbsModelCheck is sound, i.e., if the algorithm AbsModelCheck produces the abstract region $[\varphi]_S^\alpha$ on input formula φ and the abstract collecting semantics of S, then for all abstract states $q^\alpha \in [\varphi]_S^\alpha$, and for all concrete states $q \in \gamma(q^\alpha)$, we have $q \in [\![\varphi]\!]_S$.*

In the proof of soundness, we can replace each of the predicates $\langle \cdot \rangle^\alpha$, $CPre_I^\alpha$, and $UPre_I^\alpha$ by approximations without losing the soundness of the abstract model checking algorithm. This is because any approximation of the sound abstraction of the collecting semantics remains sound. This statement is made precise in the following lemma.

Lemma 2. Approximation. *The soundness of the abstract model checking algorithm AbsModelCheck is preserved if the predicates $\langle \cdot \rangle^\alpha$, $CPre_I^\alpha$, and $UPre_I^\alpha$ are replaced by approximations $\langle \cdot \rangle^A$, $CPre_I^A$, and $UPre_I^A$ such that:*

1. *for all $p \in \Pi^L$, we have $\langle p \rangle^A \tilde{\preceq} \langle p \rangle^\alpha$, and $\langle \bar{p} \rangle^A \tilde{\preceq} \langle \bar{p} \rangle^\alpha$;*
2. *for all $\sigma^\alpha \subseteq Q^\alpha$, we have $CPre_I^A(\sigma^\alpha) \tilde{\preceq} CPre_I^\alpha(\sigma^\alpha)$;*
3. *for all $\sigma^\alpha \subseteq Q^\alpha$, we have $UPre_I^A(\sigma^\alpha) \tilde{\preceq} UPre_I^\alpha(\sigma^\alpha)$.*

Although the abstract interpretations for the propositions and the controllable and uncontrollable predecessors are maximal, unfortunately the maximality is not preserved by the abstract model checking algorithm AbsModelCheck. This is because the abstract model checking algorithm is defined compositionally. This is a well-known fact [7], and the loss of precision occurs already with boolean connectives. For example, let S be an alternating transition system with four states $Q = \{q_1, q_2, q_3, q_4\}$, and let $Q^\alpha = \{a_1, a_2, a_3\}$ be an abstract domain with three abstract states. Let the concretization function γ be given by $\gamma(a_1) = \{q_1, q_2\}$, $\gamma(a_2) = \{q_2, q_3\}$, and $\gamma(a_3) = \{q_3, q_4\}$. Let p be a proposition, with $[\![p]\!]_S = \{q_1, q_2\}$, and $[\![\bar{p}]\!]_S = \{q_3, q_4\}$. Note that $[p \vee \bar{p}]^{\alpha}_{S,E}$ is not maximal. In fact, even if $\gamma(a_2) \subseteq [\![p \vee \bar{p}]\!]_S$, we have $a_2 \notin [p \vee \bar{p}]^{\alpha}_{S,E}$

Abstract LTL Control. The formulas of *linear-time temporal logic* LTL are defined inductively by the grammar

$$\varphi ::= p \mid \neg\varphi \mid \varphi_1 \vee \varphi_2 \mid \bigcirc\varphi \mid \varphi_1 \mathcal{U} \varphi_2,$$

for propositions p in some set Π^L of propositions. Formulas are evaluated over *traces* in the standard way [20]. From these formulas, we define the formulas $\Diamond p = \mathit{true} \mathcal{U} p$ and $\Box p = \neg\Diamond\neg p$ as usual. Player 1 can *control the state q of an alternating transition system S for the* LTL *formula φ* if player 1 has a strategy f_1 such that for all strategies f_2 of player 2, every trace $\rho \in \mathcal{L}_{f_1,f_2}(q)$ satisfies the formula φ. The LTL *control problem* asks, given an alternating transition system S and an LTL formula φ, which states of S can be controlled by player 1 for φ. The LTL *controller-synthesis problem* asks, in addition, for the construction of witnessing strategies. The alternating-time μ-calculus can express controllability of LTL formulas [1], that is, for each LTL formula φ, there is an equivalent $A\mu$ formula ψ such that for all alternating transition systems S, player 1 can control a state q of S for φ iff $q \in [\![\psi]\!]_S$. For example, the $A\mu$ formula $\nu X \mu Y.(p \wedge \langle\!\langle 1 \rangle\!\rangle \bigcirc X) \vee \langle\!\langle 1 \rangle\!\rangle \bigcirc Y$ holds at a state if player 1 has a strategy to enforce computations in which the observable p occurs infinitely often, and this is equivalent to the LTL control requirement $\Box\Diamond p$. Thus, an algorithm for model checking $A\mu$ can be used to solve the LTL control problem. In particular, we can use algorithm ModelCheck of Figure 1 to solve the LTL control problem.

Given an LTL requirement φ and the abstraction of the collecting semantics of an alternating transition system S, we can solve the LTL control problem on the abstract system in the following way. We construct an $A\mu$ formula ψ equivalent to φ, and use the abstract model checking algorithm AbsModelCheck to compute the set of abstract states $[\![\psi]\!]^{\alpha}_S$. From the soundness of the abstract model checking algorithm, we can conclude that player 1 can control φ from all concrete states in $\hat{\gamma}([\![\psi]\!]^{\alpha}_S)$. Moreover, from the result of the abstract model checking algorithm, one can derive a controller for player 1 in the concrete system [28,17].

Completeness of Abstract Model Checking of Games. A necessary and sufficient characterization of completeness is provided by considering the *alternating bisimilarity relation* [2] on the state space of an alternating transition system. A binary relation $\cong \subseteq Q \times Q$ on the states of an alternating transition system is an *alternating bisimulation* if $q \cong r$ implies the following three conditions:

(1) $\pi(q) = \pi(r)$.

(2) For every set $T \in \delta_1(q)$ there exists a set $T' \in \delta_1(r)$ such that for every set $R' \in \delta_2(r)$ there exists a set $R \in \delta_1(q)$ such that if $(T \cap R) = \{q'\}$ and $(T' \cap R') = \{r'\}$ then $q' \cong r'$.

(3) For every set $T' \in \delta_1(r)$ there exists a set $T \in \delta_1(q)$ such that for every set $R \in \delta_2(q)$ there exists a set $R' \in \delta_1(r)$ such that if $(T \cap R) = \{q'\}$ and $(T' \cap R') = \{r'\}$ then $q' \cong r'$.

Two states q and r are *alternating bisimilar*, denoted $q \cong^B r$, if there is an alternating bisimulation $\cong$ such that $q \cong r$. Let $Q^{\cong^B}$ denote the set of alternating bisimilarity classes of states, and let $q_1^{\cong^B}, q_2^{\cong^B}, \ldots$ refer to classes in $Q^{\cong^B}$. In [2], it is shown that two states on an alternating transition system satisfy the same alternating-time μ-calculus formulas iff they are alternating bisimilar. Using this characterization, we can show that if the abstract model checking algorithm is complete, then for each alternating bisimilarity class $q^{\cong^B} \in Q^{\cong^B}$ there is a set of abstract states whose concretization is exactly the class $q^{\cong^B}$. The proof is by contradiction; if not, we can either find an $A\mu$ formula that can distinguish two concrete states that are in the concretization of the same abstract state, or show that the concretization of all the abstract states is strictly included in the set of concrete states implying that the abstract interpretation cannot be complete. This shows that the abstract domain and the concretization function must refine the alternating bisimilarity relation for the abstract model checking algorithm to be complete. Moreover, by induction on the structure of formulas we can prove the converse: if the set of abstract states refine the alternating bisimilarity classes then the abstract model checking algorithm is complete.

Theorem 3. Completeness of AbsModelCheck. *The abstract model checking algorithm* AbsModelCheck *is (sound and) complete on an alternating transition system S with state space Q if and only if the abstract domain Q^α and the concretization function γ satisfy that for every alternating bisimilar class $q^{\cong^B} \in Q^{\cong^B}$, there exists $\sigma^\alpha \subseteq Q^\alpha$ such that $\hat{\gamma}(\sigma^\alpha) = q^{\cong^B}$.*

Thus, to achieve completeness, each alternating bisimilarity class should be the image of a set of abstract states under the concretization function. In general, the abstract model checking algorithm is sound, but not necessarily complete. This means that if an $A\mu$ property fails to hold on the abstract system, we cannot conclude that it does not hold in the concrete system. In order to disprove a property, we have to check if the negation of the property holds on the abstract system. Of course, neither the property nor its negation may hold at a state, in which case we have to refine our abstraction. Moreover, the abstract interpretation can be used to produce both under and overapproximations of a region satisfying a formula (to construct an overapproximation of a formula, we compute an underapproximation of the negation of the formula by concretizing the abstract region returned by the abstract model checking algorithm, and take the complement of the resulting set). Using techniques in [19,10], this can give more precise approximations of a region where the formula holds.

4   Multi-process Programs: Concrete and Collecting Semantics

While the theory in the previous sections provides ways to model check an abstract system via its abstract collecting semantics, the abstract collecting semantics is derived from the (concrete) collecting semantics. In practice it is often preferable to be able to compute the abstract collecting semantics directly from the syntax of a program [7,14,25]. We introduce a simple programming language that is able to model concurrent games and show how to construct an abstraction of the collecting semantics directly from the program text.

Multi-process Programs. We consider a simple programming formalisms based on Dijkstra's guarded command language [18]. Let X be a set of variables interpreted over some possibly infinite domains. We denote by $X' = \{x' \mid x \in X\}$ the set of variables obtained by priming each variable in X. A valuation v of the variables X is a function which maps each of the variables in X into a value in its domain. Denote by $\mathcal{V}_X$ the set of all possible valuations of the variables X. For any valuation v, we write v' the valuation obtained by priming each domain variable of v. For any predicate φ over the variables X and a valuation $v \in \mathcal{V}_X$, denote by $\varphi[v]$ the truth value of the predicate with all the free variables interpreted according to the valuation v.

Given a set of program variables X, a Y-*action* ξ (guarded command) has the form $\| \; guard \rightarrow update$, where $Y \subseteq X$, the guard $guard$ is a boolean predicate over X, and the update relation $update$ is a boolean predicate over $X \cup Y'$. We also write $guard_\xi$ and $update_\xi$ to represent the guard and update relation of ξ respectively. Given a valuation $v \in \mathcal{V}_X$, the action ξ is said to be *enabled* if the guard $guard_\xi[v]$ evaluates to true. We assume that for every Y-action, the update relation is functional, that is, for all valuation functions $v \in \mathcal{V}_X$, there is exactly one valuation function $u \in \mathcal{V}_Y$ such that $update_\xi[v \cup u']$ holds. A Y-*process* Φ is a finite set of Y-actions. We say that the set of variables Y is *the controlled variables* of Φ. We require that for any valuation of the program variables, at least one action in the process is enabled.

To model two-player games, we partition the program variables X into two disjoint sets X_1, X_2 , i.e., $X = X_1 \uplus X_2$. Intuitively, X_i contains the variables updated by player i. A *program* $P = (\Phi_1, \Phi_2)$ over X is a pair of processes such that Φ_i is an X_i-process. Each process of the program can be defined by composing smaller processes, each of which controls a subset of the variables. For two processes Φ_1 and Φ_2 with disjoint controlled variables, their *composition* $\Phi_1 \| \Phi_2$ is the process $\Phi = \{\| \; guard_\xi \wedge guard_\eta \rightarrow update_\xi \wedge update_\eta \mid \xi \in \Phi_1 \wedge \eta \in \Phi_2\}$.

Example 1. Consider the program in Figure 3, depicting a protocol converter that operates between a lossy sender implementing an alternating-bit protocol, and a lossless receiver. The lossy sender *Sender* communicates with the converter through a pair of two-phase handshake lines, namely *sendreq* and *recvreq*. It signals the sending of a new message by inverting the variable *sendreq*, and

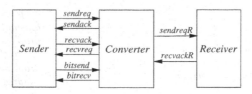

Fig. 2. An lossy sender speaking the alternating bit protocol communicating with a two-phase receiver through a protocol converter. The converter is to be synthesized.

expects an acknowledgement from the converter at a later time. It also sends a bit *bitsend* to the converter together with the message it sent. (The actual message is not modeled.) The sender is lossy in the sense that it may not signal the converter that a new message has been sent (by not inverting the variable *sendreq*), and it may just drop the acknowledgement sent by the converter (by inverting the variable *recvack*). If there is a loss, the variable *drop* will be set to *true*. The *Receiver* simply checks if there is a new message sent by the converter, and returns an acknowledgement after it has consumed the message. The *Monitor* process counts the number of messages received and sent by the converter. In this program Φ_2 is the composition *Sender∥Receiver∥Monitor*. The process Φ_1 is the *most* nondeterministic process which set the variables *sendack*, *sendreqR*, *recvreq*, and *bitrecv* to arbitrary values.

Concrete Semantics of Programs. The *concrete interpretation* of a program $P = \{\Phi_1, \Phi_2\}$ over the program variables X is the alternating transition system $S_P = \langle \Sigma, Q, \Delta, \Pi, \pi \rangle$, where (i) $\Sigma = \{1, 2\}$ (the two players of the program P). (ii) $Q = \mathcal{V}_X$, i.e., a state of S_P is a valuation of the program variables. (iii) $\Delta = (\delta_1, \delta_2)$ with $\delta_i : \mathcal{V}_X \rightarrow 2^{2^{\mathcal{V}_X}}$ is the transition function of player i and is defined as $\delta_i(v) = \{u \mid \xi \in \Phi_i \wedge guard_\xi[\![v]\!] \wedge update_\xi[\![v \cup u']\!]\}$. (iv) Π is a set of boolean predicates over the program variables X. (v) π maps an element p of Π to the set of states that satisfy p. Intuitively, for $i \in \{1, 2\}$, player i controls the actions in Φ_i. A program is run in steps. At each step, player 1 chooses an enabled action $\xi \in \Phi_1$, and updates the values of the variables in X_1 according to the predicate $update_\xi$. Independently and simultaneously, player 2 chooses an enabled action $\eta \in \Phi_2$ and updates the values of the variables in X_2 according to $update_\eta$.

Collecting Semantics of Programs. Given a program P over the set of variables X, let $(\!| \cdot |\!)$, $CPre_I$, $UPre_I$ (for $I = 1, 2, \{1, 2\}$) be the collecting semantics of S_P. We construct predicate formulas that represent the collecting semantics of the program P. Let R be a predicate over the variables X. We say R *represents* a state v of S_P if $R[\![v]\!]$ is true. We use predicates on X to denote the set of states they represent, and naturally extend operations defined on sets of states

$$\| \ pc = s_0 \qquad\qquad\qquad\qquad\qquad\qquad \rightarrow \quad \begin{array}{l} drop' := false; pc' := s_1; \\ bitsend' := \neg bitsend; \end{array}$$

$$\| \ pc = s_1 \wedge (recvack = recvreq) \qquad\qquad \rightarrow \quad \begin{array}{l} drop' := false; pc' := s_1; \\ sendreq' := \neg sendreq; \end{array}$$

$$\| \ pc = s_1 \wedge (recvack = recvreq) \qquad\qquad \rightarrow \quad \begin{array}{l} drop' := true; pc' := s_1; \\ sendreq' := sendreq; \end{array}$$

$$\| \ pc = s_1 \wedge (recvack \neq recvreq) \wedge (bitsend = bitrecv) \rightarrow \quad \begin{array}{l} drop' := false; pc' := s_0; \\ recvack' := \neg recvack; \end{array}$$

$$\| \ pc = s_1 \wedge (recvack \neq recvreq) \wedge (bitsend \neq bitrecv) \rightarrow \quad \begin{array}{l} drop' := false; pc' := s_1; \\ recvack' := \neg recvack; \end{array}$$

$$\| \ pc = s_1 \wedge (recvack \neq recvreq) \qquad\qquad \rightarrow \quad \begin{array}{l} drop' := true; pc' := s_1; \\ recvack' := \neg recvack; \end{array}$$

Sender

$$\| \ (sendack R \neq sendreq R) \ \rightarrow \ sendack R' := \neg sendack R;$$
$$\| \ (sendack R = sendreq R) \ \rightarrow \ sendack R' := sendack R;$$

Receiver

$$\| \ sendreq \neq sendack \qquad\qquad\qquad \rightarrow \ count' := count + 1;$$
$$\| \ sendreq R \neq sendack R \qquad\qquad\qquad \rightarrow \ count' := count - 1;$$
$$\| \ (sendreq R = sendack R) \wedge (sendreq = sendack) \ \rightarrow \ count' := count;$$

Monitor

Fig. 3. An alternating-bit sender, a simple receiver and a monitor

to predicates. Given a predicate R representing a set of states of S_P, we define the player-1 controllable predecessor predicate $\Psi_P^{CPre_1}(R)$ as:

$$\Psi_P^{CPre_1}(R) \equiv \bigvee_{\xi \in \Phi_1} \left(guard_\xi \wedge \bigwedge_{\eta \in \Phi_2} \left(guard_\eta \rightarrow \forall X' . (update_\xi \wedge update_\eta \rightarrow R') \right) \right)$$

where R' is the predicate obtained by substituting each free variable in the predicate R by its primed counterpart. Similarly, we define the player-1 uncontrollable predecessor predicate $\Psi_P^{UPre_1}(R)$ as:

$$\Psi_P^{UPre_1}(R) \equiv \bigwedge_{\xi \in \Phi_1} \left(guard_\xi \rightarrow \bigvee_{\eta \in \Phi_2} \left(guard_\eta \wedge \exists X' . (update_\xi \wedge update_\eta \wedge R') \right) \right)$$

The other predicates, $\Psi_P^{CPre_I}(R)$ and $\Psi_P^{UPre_I}(R)$ for $I = 2, \{1, 2\}$, can be defined similarly. The following proposition states that the predicates constructed above exactly coincide with the collecting semantics of the program P.

Proposition 3. *The computed formulas* $\langle \Psi_P^{CPre_I}(R), \Psi_P^{UPre_I}(R) \rangle$ *from the program* P *are equivalent to the collecting semantics of the alternating transition* *system S_P of the program P, that is, for every state v of S_P, and every predicate R representing the set of states σ, we have $v \in CPre_I(\sigma)$ iff $\Psi_P^{CPre_I}(R)[v]$, and $v \in UPre_I(\sigma)$ iff $\Psi_P^{UPre_I}(R)[v]$.*

5 Abstract Interpretation of Multi-process Programs with Respect to Game Properties

In this section we show two methods of computing an approximation of the abstraction of the collecting semantics directly from the program text.

Abstract Interpretation via Domain Abstraction. In abstract interpretation via domain abstraction, we are given for each program variable $x \in X$ a fixed abstract domain over which the variable is interpreted. Let $\mathcal{V}_X^\alpha$ be the set of abstract valuations of X, i.e., valuations of the variables over their abstract domains. Let $\gamma : \mathcal{V}_X^\alpha \to 2^{\mathcal{V}_X}$ be a concretization function mapping an abstract valuation (an abstract state) to the set of concrete valuations (the set of concrete states). To derive sound abstractions of the collecting semantics from the program text, we introduce, for $\xi \in \Phi_i$ and $i \in \{1, 2\}$, predicates $guard_\xi^C$, $guard_\xi^F$ over the variables X, and predicates $update_\xi^C$, $update_\xi^F$ over the variables $X \cup X'$. These predicates represent over (or *free*) and under (or *constrained*) approximations for the guards and update relations of the program. We define formally the free and constrained versions of the guard and update relations as follows.

- The predicate $guard_\xi^F$ is a *free abstract interpretation of guard$_\xi$* iff for all $u \in \mathcal{V}_X^\alpha$, $guard_\xi^F[u]$ is true if there exists a concrete valuation v in the concretization of u on which $guard_\xi[v]$ evaluates to true; i.e., $\forall u \in \mathcal{V}_X^\alpha. \exists v \in \gamma(u). (guard_\xi[v] \to guard_\xi^F[u])$
- The predicate $update_\xi^F$ is a *free abstract interpretation of update$_\xi$* iff for all $u_1, u_2 \in \mathcal{V}_X^\alpha$, $update_\xi^F[u_1, u_2']$ evaluates to true if there exists a pair of concrete valuations (v_1, v_2) represented by (u_1, u_2) on which $update_\xi$ evaluates to true; i.e., $\forall u_1, u_2 \in \mathcal{V}_X^\alpha. \exists v_1 \in \gamma(u_1), v_2 \in \gamma(u_2). (update_\xi[v_1 \cup v_2'] \to update_\xi^F[u_1 \cup u_2'])$.
- The predicate $guard_\xi^C$ is a *constrained abstract interpretation of guard$_\xi$* iff $guard_\xi^C$ evaluates to true on u if all concrete valuations v in the concretization of u make $guard_\xi$ evaluates to true; i.e., $\forall u \in \mathcal{V}_X^\alpha. \forall v \in \gamma(u). (guard_\xi^C[u] \to guard_\xi[v])$
- The predicate $update_\xi^C$ is a *constrained abstract interpretation of update$_\xi$* iff for all $u_1, u_2 \in \mathcal{V}_X^\alpha$, $update_\xi^C[u_1, u_2']$ evaluates to true if all pairs of concrete valuations (v_1, v_2) represented by (u_1, u_2) make $update_\xi$ true; i.e., $\forall u_1, u_2 \in \mathcal{V}_X^\alpha. \forall v_1 \in \gamma(u_1), v_2 \in \gamma(u_2). (update_\xi^C[u_1 \cup u_2'] \to update_\xi[v_1 \cup v_2'])$.

We now show how to approximate the abstraction of the collecting semantics directly from the program text by nonstandard interpretations of the guard and update predicates of the program P. For $I = 1, 2, \{1, 2\}$ and a set of abstract states represented by the predicate R^α, we construct the parameterized formulas $\Psi_P^{CPre_I^\alpha}(R^\alpha)$ and $\Psi_P^{UPre_I^\alpha}(R^\alpha)$ from $\Psi_P^{CPre_I}(R)$ and $\Psi_P^{UPre_I}(R)$ as follows: we replace every predicate that appears positively by its constrained version and every predicate that appears negatively by its free version. For example, the formula $\Psi_P^{CPre_1^\alpha}(R^\alpha)$ is as follows:

$$\bigvee_{\xi \in \Phi_1} \left(guard_\xi^C \wedge \bigwedge_{\eta \in \Phi_2} \left(guard_\eta^F \to \forall X'. \, (update_\xi^F \wedge update_\eta^F \to R^{\alpha\prime}) \right) \right)$$

We similarly obtain abstractions of the other formulas. Since we are always approximating conservatively, the following proposition holds.

Proposition 4. *Domain-based abstract interpretation produces approximations; i.e., for every predicate R^α representing the set of abstract states σ^α, we have $\Psi_P^{CPre_1^\alpha}(R^\alpha) \stackrel{\hat{}}{\preceq} CPre_1^\alpha(\sigma^\alpha)$, and $\Psi_P^{UPre_1^\alpha}(R^\alpha) \stackrel{\hat{}}{\preceq} UPre_1^\alpha(\sigma^\alpha)$.*

Abstract Interpretation via Predicate Abstraction. Domain-based abstraction computes abstractions from the program text compositionally, and may often produce crude approximations. An alternative method of constructing abstractions of the collecting semantics from the program text is *predicate abstraction*. In predicate abstraction, the abstract state is represented by a set of propositional predicates (called *abstraction predicates*) [24,15] over the variables X of a program. An abstract state assigns truth values to each abstraction predicate. The concretization function γ maps an abstract state to the set of concrete states that satisfy the predicates.

The abstraction of the collecting semantics under predicate abstraction may be approximated directly from the program text. Whereas we can still construct the abstract predicates compositionally by substituting for each concrete predicate (*guard* or *update*) a conjunction of the abstraction predicates that implies (or is implied by) the concrete predicate, very often this leads to an overly crude abstraction. Therefore we sacrifice compositionality in order to obtain a more precise approximation of the abstraction of the collecting semantics. The approximation of the abstraction of the collecting semantics is derived as follows (we show the computation explicitly for $\Psi_P^{CPre_1^\alpha}$, the other operators can be constructed similarly). For each pair $\xi \in \Phi_1$, $\eta \in \Phi_2$ of moves of player 1 and player 2, we compute the formula

$$\chi_{\xi\eta}(R^\alpha) = guard_\xi \wedge \left(guard_\eta \to \forall X'. \, (update_\xi \wedge update_\eta \to \hat{\gamma}(R^\alpha)') \right)$$

Thus, the predicate $\chi_{\xi\eta}(R^\alpha)$ holds at a concrete state v if we reach $\hat{\gamma}(R^\alpha)$ from v when player 1 plays move (action) ξ and player 2 plays move η. We replace each predicate $\chi_{\xi\eta}(R^\alpha)$ by a boolean combination of abstraction predicates $\chi_{\xi\eta}^\alpha(R^\alpha)$ which is implied by $\chi_{\xi\eta}(R^\alpha)$ to obtain a sound approximation of the abstraction of $\chi_{\xi\eta}(R^\alpha)$. Finally, $\Psi_P^{CPre_1^\alpha}(R^\alpha)$ is obtained by existentially quantifying over the

$$
\begin{aligned}
&\| \ \neg reset\_rt \wedge pc = RESET \wedge conn &\rightarrow\ & pc' := WAITC;\, req'_{ID} := ConnReq; \\
&\| \ \neg reset\_rt \wedge pc = WAITC \wedge ack = (ID, 1) &\rightarrow\ & pc' := CONN;\, req'_{ID} := NoReq; \\
&\| \ \neg reset\_rt \wedge pc = WAITC \wedge ack = (ID, 0) &\rightarrow\ & pc' := RESET;\, req'_{ID} := NoReq; \\
&\| \ \neg reset\_rt \wedge pc = CONN \wedge disc &\rightarrow\ & pc' := WAITD;\, req'_{ID} := DiscReq; \\
&\| \ \neg reset\_rt \wedge pc = WAITD \wedge ack = (ID, 1) &\rightarrow\ & pc' := RESET;\, req'_{ID} := NoReq; \\
&\| \ \neg reset\_rt \wedge pc = WAITD \wedge ack = (ID, 0) &\rightarrow\ & pc' := RESET;\, req'_{ID} := DiscReq; \\
&\| \ reset\_rt &\rightarrow\ & pc' := RESET;\, req'_{ID} := NoReq;
\end{aligned}
$$

Fig. 4. A remote whose id is ID.

$$
\begin{aligned}
&\| \ \neg reset\_bs \wedge req_{id} = ConnReq \wedge \neg register[id] &\rightarrow\ & register'[id] := true;\, ack'_{id} := 1; \\
&\| \ \neg reset\_bs \wedge req_{id} = ConnReq \wedge register[id] &\rightarrow\ & ack'_{id} := 0; \\
&\| \ \neg reset\_bs \wedge req_{id} = DiscReq \wedge \neg register[id] &\rightarrow\ & ack'_{id} := 0; \\
&\| \ \neg reset\_bs \wedge req_{id} = DiscReq \wedge register[id] &\rightarrow\ & register'[id] := false;\, ack'_{id} := 1; \\
&\| \ reset\_bs \wedge register[id] &\rightarrow\ & register'[i] := false;\, ack'_{id} := 0
\end{aligned}
$$

Fig. 5. A process of the base station. The complete base station is the composition of the above processes for each remote id.

moves of player 1 and universally quantifying over the moves of player 2 from the predicates $\chi^{\alpha}_{\xi\eta}$; formally, $\Psi_P^{CPre_1^{\alpha}}(R^{\alpha}) = \bigvee_{\xi \in \Phi_1} \bigwedge_{\eta \in \Phi_2} \chi^{\alpha}_{\xi\eta}$. Thus $\Psi_P^{CPre_1^{\alpha}}(R^{\alpha})$ is true at an abstract state if there is a move that player 1 can make, such that for all moves that player 2 makes, the game ends up in R^{α}. The other formulas are obtained similarly. We call this computation the *predicate-based abstract interpretation* of programs. The following proposition holds because in the construction of the operators we have always taken sound approximations.

Proposition 5. *Predicate-based abstract interpretation produces approximations; i.e., for every predicate R^{α} representing the set of abstract states σ^{α}, we have $\Psi_P^{CPre_1^{\alpha}}(R^{\alpha}) \hat{\preceq} CPre_1^{\alpha}(\sigma^{\alpha})$, and $\Psi_P^{UPre_1^{\alpha}}(R^{\alpha}) \hat{\preceq} UPre_1^{\alpha}(\sigma^{\alpha})$.*

6 Two Examples

We illustrate the methods introduced in the previous sections through two practical verification examples.

A Wireless Communication Protocol. This example is taken from the Two-Chip Intercom (TCI) project at the Berkeley Wireless Research Center [4]. The TCI network is a wireless local network which allows approximately 40 *remotes*, one for each user, to transmit voice with point-to-point and broadcast communication. The operation of the network is coordinated by a central unit called the base station which assigns channels to the users through the Time Division Multiplexing Access scheme.

We briefly describe a simplified model of the actual protocol used in TCI. The protocol operates as follows. Before any remote is operational, it has to register at the base station. A remote (Figure 4) has a state variable pc, which can be $RESET$ or $CONN$. If the remote is in the $RESET$ state, it can accept a connection request $conn$ from the user. The remote in turn sends a connection request to the base station and waits for an acknowledgement. It moves to the $CONN$ state if it receives a positive acknowledgement, or to the $RESET$ state otherwise. Once the remote is in the $CONN$ state, it can be disconnected by accepting a $disc$ request from the user.

A base station (Figure 5) keeps track of the states of the remotes in the database $register$. If it receives a connection request $ConnReq$ from a remote, it checks if the remote is already registered. If not, it registers the remote, and sends back a positive acknowledgement. If the remote is already registered, a negative acknowledgement is sent back. A similar process occurs if the remote wishes to disconnect. Both the remote and the base station has an external reset signal ($reset\_rt$ and $reset\_bs$) that can reset the units to the reset state.

We consider this protocol for a system with a base station and an arbitrary number of remotes. A natural property that such a system should have is the following: for any remote, say $remote_1$, no matter what the base station and the other remotes do, there should be a way to connect to the base station. However, the original protocol contained a bug, which we found in the course of the verification. We found the bug by proving the opposite, i.e., no matter what this remote does, the base station and the other remotes are able to keep this remote out of the network. This can be written as (assuming the two players in our system are the remote $remote_1$, and the base station together with all other remotes, denoted by Env): $\varphi = \langle\langle Env, remote_1 \rangle\rangle \Diamond [\![remote_1]\!] \Box (pc_1 \neq CONN)$, where pc_1 is the state variable in $remote_1$.

We automatically detected the bug using automated model checking. Since the system was infinite state, we could not apply model checking directly, and we needed to use abstraction to reduce the problem to a finite instance. By symmetry, it suffices to show the bug for the first remote, $remote_1$. We prove the property as follows: for every $i \neq 1$ we abstract the variable pc_i of $remote_i$ into one value, say $\bot$. To check the property, we need to constrain the behavior of the remotes. We choose the simplest form of constrained predicates, namely $false$. In other words, these remotes simply deadlock and therefore they can be removed from our consideration. For variables of $remote_1$ and the base station, we use the trivial (identity) abstraction. The property is proved by model checking on this abstract system in our model checker MOCHA [3].

To understand why this bug occurs, consider the following scenario. Suppose the remote has already been connected to the base station. The user $resets$ the remote and it returns to the reset state immediately. Now suppose the user instructs the remote to send a connection request to the base station. The base station, however, still has the remote being registered and therefore it simply refuses to grant any further connection permission. Note also that the property violated is a true game property: it cannot be expressed directly in a nongame logic like CTL. Thus, both abstraction and game properties were necessary in the automatic detection of this bug.

238   Thomas A. Henzinger et al.

Protocol Converter Synthesis. As an example of predicate abstraction, we consider the automatic synthesis of a protocol converter operates between the lossy sender *Sender* and a the lossless receiver *Receiver* in Example 1. We require our protocol converter *cv* to satisfy the following property (note that the converter is synthesized from the the the process Φ_1):

$$\langle\!\langle cv \rangle\!\rangle \Box ((\mathit{count} = 0 \lor \mathit{count} = 1) \land (\Box\Diamond\neg\mathit{drop} \Rightarrow \Box\Diamond(\mathit{sendreqR} \neq \mathit{sendackR})))$$

This formula specifies that the converter has a strategy that ensures the following two properties. First, the difference between the number of messages received and sent by the converter has to be either 0 or 1. Second, if the lossy sender is fair, there should be an infinite number of messages received by the receiver.

The abstract predicates used are $pc = s_0$, $pc = s_1$, $(\mathit{sendreq} = \mathit{sendack})$, $(\mathit{recvreq} = \mathit{recvack})$, $(\mathit{bitsend} = \mathit{bitrecv})$, $(\mathit{sendreqR} = \mathit{sendackR})$ and $\mathit{drop} = \mathit{true}$. Moreover, we abstract the domain of the variable *count* to $\{0, 1, \bot\}$ where the abstract values 0 and 1 represent the values 0 and 1 respectively, and the abstract value $\bot$ represents all other values. Using these predicate and domain abstractions we are able to check that a converter that meets the requirement exists. Using methods in [28,17], the actual converter can be synthesized.

References

1. R. Alur, T.A. Henzinger, and O. Kupferman. Alternating-time temporal logic. In *Proceedings of the 38th Annual Symposium on Foundations of Computer Science*, pages 100–109. IEEE Computer Society Press, 1997. 221, 223, 224, 226, 229
2. R. Alur, T.A. Henzinger, O. Kupferman, and M.Y. Vardi. Alternating refinement relations. In D. Sangiorgi and R. de Simone, editors, *CONCUR 97: Concurrency Theory*, Lecture Notes in Computer Science 1466, pages 163–178. Springer-Verlag, 1998. 222, 229, 230
3. R. Alur, T.A. Henzinger, F.Y.C. Mang, S. Qadeer, S.K. Rajamani, and S. Tasiran. MOCHA: modularity in model checking. In *CAV 98: Computer-aided Verification*, Lecture Notes in Computer Science 1427, pages 521–525. Springer-Verlag, 1998. 222, 237
4. Berkeley Wireless Research Center. http://bwrc.eecs.berkeley.edu. 222, 236
5. E.M. Clarke, O. Grumberg, and S. Jha. Verifying parameterized networks using abstraction and regular languages. In *CONCUR 95: Concurrency Theory*, Lecture Notes in Computer Science 962, pages 395–407. Springer-Verlag, 1995. 222
6. E.M. Clarke, O. Grumberg, and D.E. Long. Model checking and abstraction. In *Proceedings of the 19th Annual Symposium on Principles of Programming Languages*, pages 343–354. ACM Press, 1992. 222
7. P. Cousot and R. Cousot. Abstract interpretation: a unified lattice model for the static analysis of programs by construction or approximation of fixpoints. In *Proceedings of the Fourth Annual Symposium on Principles of Programming Languages*. ACM Press, 1977. 221, 222, 225, 228, 231
8. P. Cousot and R. Cousot. Abstract interpretation and application to logic programs. *Journal of Logic Programming*, 13(2/3):103–179, 1992. 225
9. P. Cousot and R. Cousot. Abstract interpretation frameworks. *Journal of Logic and Computation*, 2(4):511–547, 1992. 221, 222

10. P. Cousot and R. Cousot. Refining model checking by abstract interpretation. *Automated Software Engineering*, 6(1):69–95, 1999. 230
11. P. Cousot and R. Cousot. Temporal abstract interpretation. In *Proceedings of the 27th Annual Symposium on Principles of Programming Languages*, pages 12–25. ACM Press, 2000. 222
12. D.R. Dams. *Abstract Interpretation and Partition Refinement for Model Checking*. PhD thesis, Eindhoven University of Technology, The Netherlands, 1996. 222
13. D.R. Dams, R. Gerth, G. Döhmen, R. Herrmann, P. Kelb, and H. Pargmann. Model checking using adaptive state and data abstraction. In *CAV 94: Computer-Aided Verification*, Lecture Notes in Computer Science 818, pages 455–467. Springer-Verlag, 1994. 222
14. D.R. Dams, R. Gerth, and O. Grumberg. Abstract interpretation of reactive systems. *ACM Transactions on Programming Languages and Systems*, 19(2):253–291, 1997. 222, 224, 231
15. S. Das, D. Dill, and S. Park. Experience with predicate abstraction. In *CAV 99: Computer-aided Verification*, Lecture Notes in Computer Science 1633, pages 160–171. Springer-Verlag, 1999. 235
16. L. de Alfaro, T.A. Henzinger, and O. Kupferman. Concurrent reachability games. In *Proceedings of the 39th Annual Symposium on Foundations of Computer Science*, pages 564–575. IEEE Computer Society Press, 1998. 221
17. L. de Alfaro, T.A. Henzinger, and R. Majumdar. Symbolic algorithms for infinite-state games. Technical report, University of California, Berkeley, 2000. 229, 238
18. E.W. Dijkstra. *A Discipline of Programming*. Prentice-Hall, 1976. 222, 231
19. D.L. Dill and H. Wong-Toi. Verification of real-time systems by successive over- and underapproximation. In *CAV 95: Computer-aided Verification*, Lecture Notes in Computer Science 939, pages 409–422. Springer-Verlag, 1995. 230
20. E.A. Emerson. Temporal and modal logic. In J. van Leeuwen, editor, *Handbook of Theoretical Computer Science*, volume B, pages 995–1072. Elsevier Science Publishers, 1990. 229
21. R. Giacobazzi, F. Ranzato, and F. Scozzari. Complete abstract interpretations made constructive. In *MFCS 98: Mathematical Foundations of Computer Science*, Lecture Notes in Computer Science 1450, pages 366–377. Springer-Verlag, 1998. 227
22. R. Giacobazzi, F. Ranzato, and F. Scozzari. Making abstract interpretation complete. *Journal of the ACM*, 2000. To appear. 227
23. S. Graf. Verification of a distributed cache memory by using abstractions. In *CAV 94: Computer-aided Verification*, Lecture Notes in Computer Science 818, pages 207–219. Springer-Verlag, 1994. 222
24. S. Graf and H. Saïdi. Construction of abstract state graphs with pvs. In *CAV 97: Computer-aided Verification*, Lecture Notes in Computer Science 1254, pages 72–83. Springer-Verlag, 1997. 222, 235
25. C. Loiseaux, S. Graf, J. Sifakis, A. Bouajjani, and S. Bensalem. Property preserving abstractions for the verification of concurrent systems. *Formal Methods in System Design*, 6:11–44, 1995. 231
26. D.E. Long. *Model checking, abstraction, and compositional verification*. PhD thesis, Carnegie Mellon University, Pittsburgh, PA, 1993. 222
27. K.L. McMillan. Verification of infinite state systems by compositional model checking. In *CHARME 99: Correct Hardware Design and Verification Methods*, Lecture Notes in Computer Science 1703, pages 219–233. Springer-Verlag, 1999. 222

28. P.J. Ramadge and W.M. Wonham. Supervisory control of a class of discrete-event processes. *SIAM Journal of Control and Optimization*, 25(1):206–230, 1987. 229, 238

29. P. Stevens. Abstract interpretation of games. In *Proceedings of the 2nd International Workshop on Verification, Model Checking and Abstract Interpretation*, 1998. 221

FULLDOC: A Full Reporting Debugger for Optimized Code*

Clara Jaramillo[1], Rajiv Gupta[2], and Mary Lou Soffa[1]

[1] Department of Computer Science, University of Pittsburgh
Pittsburgh, PA 15260, USA
{cij,soffa}@cs.pitt.edu
[2] Department of Computer Science, University of Arizona
Tucson, AZ 85721, USA
gupta@cs.arizona.edu

Abstract. As compilers increasingly rely on optimizations to achieve high performance, the effectiveness of source level debuggers for optimized code continues to falter. Even if values of source variables are computed in the execution of the optimized code, source level debuggers of optimized code are unable to always report the expected values of source variables at breakpoints.

In this paper, we present FULLDOC, a debugger that can report all of the expected values of source variables that are computed in the optimized code. FULLDOC uses statically computed information to guide the gathering of dynamic information that enables full reporting. FULLDOC can report expected values at breakpoints when reportability is affected because values have been overwritten early, due to code hoisting or register reuse, or written late, due to code sinking. Our debugger can also report values that are path sensitive in that a value may be computed only along one path or the location of the value may be different along different paths. We implemented FULLDOC for C programs, and experimentally evaluated the effectiveness of reporting expected values. Our experimental results indicate that FULLDOC can report 31% more values than are reportable using only statically computed information. We also show improvements of at least 26% over existing schemes that use limited dynamic information.

1 Introduction

Ever since optimizations were introduced into compilers more than 30 years ago, the difficulty of debugging optimized code has been recognized. This difficulty has grown with the development of increasingly more complex code optimizations, such as path sensitive optimizations, code speculation, and aggressive register allocation. The importance of debugging optimized code has also increased over the years as almost all production compilers apply optimizations.

* Supported in part by NSF grants CCR-940226, CCR-9808590 and EIA-9806525, and a grant from Hewlett Packard Labs to the University of Pittsburgh and NSF grants CCR-9996362 and CCR-0096122 to the University of Arizona.

J. Palsberg (Ed.): SAS 2000, LNCS 1824, pp. 240–260, 2000.
© Springer-Verlag Berlin Heidelberg 2000

Two problems surface when trying to debug optimized code from the viewpoint of the source code. The *code location* problem relates to determining the position of a breakpoint in the optimized code that corresponds to the breakpoint in the source code. The *data value* problem is the problem of reporting the values of the source variables that a user *expects* to see at a breakpoint in the source code, even though the optimizer may have reordered or deleted the statements computing the values, or overwritten the values by register allocation.

Techniques have been developed that tackle both the code location and data value problems with the goal of reporting expected values when they can be determined from the optimized code but also reporting when an expected value cannot be determined. Progress has been made in the development of debuggers that report more and more expected values. The early techniques focused on determining expected values using information computed statically [8,4,3,15,1]. Recent techniques have proposed using information collected during execution, along with the static information, to improve the reportability of values [5,16]. Dhamdhere et al. [5] time stamp basic blocks to obtain part of the execution path of the optimized code, which is used to dynamically determine currency (whether the actual values of source variables during the optimized code execution are the expected values) at breakpoints. Wu et al. [16] selectively take control of the optimized program execution and then emulate instructions in the optimized code in the order that mimics the execution of the unoptimized program. This execution reordering enables the reporting of some of the expected values of source variables where they occur in the source. Despite all the progress, none of the techniques are able to report all possible expected values of variables at all breakpoints in the source program.

In this paper, we present FULLDOC, a **FULL** reporting **D**ebugger of **O**ptimized **C**ode that reports all expected values that are computed in the optimized program. We call this level of reporting "full reporting." That is, the only values we cannot report are those that are deleted; however in these cases, we report the value has been deleted. It should be noted that techniques exist for recovering some of these values in certain circumstances [8]. For example, if a statement is deleted due to copy propagation, it is sometimes possible to report the value if the copy is available. Since these recovery techniques can be incorporated into all debuggers, regardless of what else they do, we choose not to include these techniques, knowing that they can improve the results of all debuggers of optimized code, including FULLDOC. As illustrated in Figure 1, FULLDOC can report more expected values that are computed in the optimized code than Wu et al. [16] and Dhamdhere et al. [5]. Our technique is non-invasive in that the code that executes is the code that the optimizer generated. Also, unlike the emulation technique [16], we do not execute instructions in a different order and thus avoid the problem of masking user and optimizer errors. FULLDOC works on programs written in C, syntactically mapping breakpoints in the source code to the corresponding positions in the optimized code.

FULLDOC extends the class of reportable expected values by judiciously using both static and dynamic information. The overall strategy of our technique

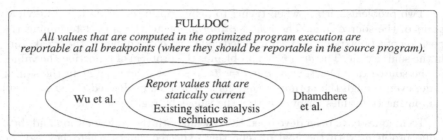

Fig. 1. Reportability of debugger strategies

is to determine by static program analysis those values that the optimizer has placed in a precarious position in that their values may not be reportable. The reportability of these values may depend on run time and debugging information, including the placement of the breakpoints and the paths taken in a program's execution. Thus, during execution, our strategy employs *invisible breakpoints* [17] to gather dynamic information that aids in the reporting of precariously placed values. We employ three schemes, all transparent to the user during a debugging session, to enable full reporting. To report values that are overwritten early with respect to a breakpoint either because of code motion or register reuse, FULLDOC saves the values before they are overwritten and deletes them as soon as they are no longer needed for reporting. FULLDOC only saves the values if they are indeed the expected values at the breakpoint. To report values that are written late with respect to a breakpoint because of code sinking, FULLDOC prematurely executes the optimized program until it can report the value, saving the values overwritten by the roll ahead execution so that they can be reported at subsequent breakpoints. When reportability of a variable at a breakpoint is dependent on the execution path of the optimized code, FULLDOC dynamically records information to indicate the impact of the path on the reportability of a value, and thus is able to report values that are path sensitive either because the computation of the value or the location is dependent on the path.

We implemented our technique and demonstrate its effectiveness and practicality through experimentation. We also show that the technique is practical in terms of the run time overhead.

The capabilities of FULLDOC are as follows.

- Every value of a source level variable that is computed in the optimized program execution is reportable at all breakpoints in the source code where the value of the variable should be reportable. Therefore, we can report more expected values that are computed in the optimized program execution than any existing technique. Values that are not computed in the optimized program execution are the only values that we do not report. However, FULL-DOC can incorporate existing techniques that recover some of these values.
- Run time overhead is minimized by performing all analysis during compilation. FULLDOC utilizes debugging information generated during compila-

tion to determine the impact of reportability of values at user breakpoints and to determine the invisible breakpoints that must be inserted to report affected values.

– Our techniques are transparent to the user. If a user inserts a breakpoint where the reportability of values is affected at the breakpoint or a potential future breakpoint, FULLDOC automatically inserts invisible breakpoints to gather dynamic information to report the expected values.
– Errors in the optimized code are not masked.
– User breakpoints can be placed between any two source level statements, regardless of the optimizations applied.
– The optimized program is not modified except for setting breakpoints.
– Statement level optimizations that hoist and sink code are supported, including speculative code motion, path sensitive optimizations (e.g., partial redundancy elimination), and register allocation.

This paper is organized by Section 2 describing the challenges of reporting expected values using examples. Section 3 describes our approach and implementation. Section 4 presents experimental results. Related work is discussed in Section 5, and concluding remarks are given in Section 6.

2   Challenges of Reporting Expected Values

The reportability of a variable's value involved in an optimization is affected by 1) register reuse, code reordering, and code deletion, 2) the execution path, including loop iterations, and 3) the placement of breakpoints. In this section, we consider the effect of optimizations that can cause a value of a variable to be overwritten early, written late, or deleted. Within each of these cases, we consider the impact of the path and the placement of breakpoints. We demonstrate how our approach handles these cases. In the figures, the paths highlighted are the regions in which reportability is affected; reportability is not affected in the other regions.

2.1   Overwritten Early in the Optimized Program

A value val of a variable v is *overwritten early* in the optimized program if val' prematurely overwrites v's value. The application of a code hoisting optimization and register reuse can cause values to be overwritten early. For example, consider the unoptimized program and its optimized version in Figure 2(a), where X^n refers to the nth definition of X. X^2 has been speculatively hoisted, and as a result, the reportability of X is affected. Regardless of the execution path of the optimized code, a debugger cannot report the expected value of X at a breakpoint b along region ① by simply displaying the *actual* contents of X. The *expected* value of X at b is the value of X^1, but since X^2 is computed early, causing the previous value (i.e., X^1) to be overwritten early, the actual value of X at b is X^2.

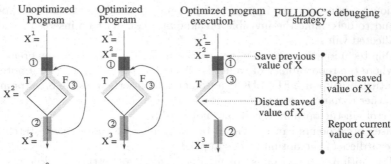

(a) X^2 is speculatively hoisted   b) true path taken during execution

Fig. 2. Overwritten early example

The path can also affect reportability. Assume now that a breakpoint b is placed in region ②. The expected value of X at b is either X^2, if the true path is taken, or X^1, if only the false path is taken within each loop iteration. However, since X^2 is computed before the branch, the actual value of X at b in the optimized code is X^2. Thus, when execution follows the true path, the expected value of X at b can be reported, but when only the false path is taken, its value cannot be reported.

The number of loop iterations can also affect reportability. The expected value of X at a breakpoint b along region ③ depends not only on whether the true path was taken but also on the current loop iteration. During the first loop iteration, the expected value is X^1. On subsequent loop iterations, the expected value is either X^2 (if the true path is taken) or X^1 (if only the false path is taken on prior loop iterations). However, since X^2 is computed before the loop, the actual value of X at b in the optimized code is X^2. When execution follows the true path, the debugger can report the expected value of X at b on subsequent loop iterations; otherwise, the debugger cannot report the expected value of X.

Using only dynamic currency determination [5], the expected value of X at breakpoints along region ① cannot be reported because the value has been overwritten. The emulation technique [16] can report the expected value of X along region ① and along the true path of region ③, but since the technique is not path sensitive, the expected value cannot be reported along region ② and along the false path of region ③ due to iterations.

FULLDOC can report all of these expected values. During the execution of the optimized code, if a value is overwritten early **with respect to a breakpoint**, FULLDOC saves the value in a *value pool*. FULLDOC only saves what is necessary and discards values when they are no longer needed for reporting. Figure 2(b) illustrates FULLDOC's strategy when the optimized program in Figure 2(a) executes along the true path, assuming the loop executes one time. FULLDOC saves X^1 before the assignment to X^2 and reports the saved value X^1 at breakpoints along regions ① and ③. FULLDOC discards the saved value when execution reaches the original position of X^2. At breakpoints along the non-highlighted path and region ②, FULLDOC reports the current value of X. Notice that values are saved only as long as they could be reportable in the source program, and thus, our save/discard mechanism automatically disambiguates which value to report at breakpoints along region ②. If X^1 is currently saved at the breakpoint, then only the false path was executed and the saved value is reported. Otherwise if X^1 is not currently saved, then the true path was executed and the current value of X is reported. Notice that this saving strategy, as well as the other strategies, are performed with respect to user breakpoints. In other words, if a user does not insert breakpoints along the regions where the reportability of X is affected, then FULLDOC does not save the value of X.

2.2 Written Late in the Optimized Program

A value *val* of a variable v is *written late* in the optimized program if the computation of *val* is delayed due to, for example, code sinking and partial dead code elimination. In Figure 3(a), suppose X^2 is partially dead along the false path and moved to the true branch. As a result, the expected value of X at a breakpoint b along regions ① and ② is not reportable in the optimized code.

Consider a breakpoint b placed in region ③. The expected value of X at b is X^2. However, the actual value of X at b in the optimized code is either X^2 (if the true path is taken) or X^1 (if the false path is taken). Thus, only when execution follows the true path, can the expected value of X at b be reported. Reportability can also be affected by loop iterations, which has the same effect as for the overwritten early case.

Using only dynamic currency determination [5], the expected value of X at breakpoints along region ③ can be reported provided the true path is taken but not along regions ① and ②. Since the emulation technique [16] is not path sensitive, the expected value of X along region ③ cannot be reported. We can report values in ① and ③ provided the true path is taken. Note that values in

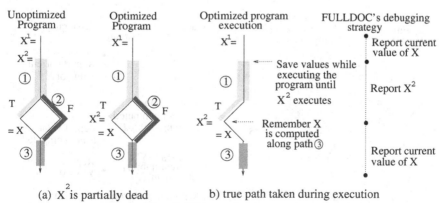

(a) X^2 is partially dead   b) true path taken during execution

Fig. 3. Written late example

regions ①, ②, and ③ could possibly be reported by all schemes if recovery techniques are employed.

If a requested value is written late **with respect to a breakpoint**, FULL-DOC prematurely executes the optimized code, saving previously computed values before they are overwritten (so that they can be reported at subsequent breakpoints). Figure 3(b) illustrates FULLDOC's strategy when the optimized program in Figure 3(a) executes along the true path. At breakpoints along region ①, FULLDOC reports the expected value of X by further executing the optimized code, saving previously computed values before they are overwritten. The roll ahead execution stops once X^2 executes. At breakpoints along the non-highlighted path and region ③, FULLDOC reports X^2.

2.3 Computed in the Unoptimized Program but not in the Optimized Program

Finally, we consider the case where a statement is deleted and thus its value is not computed in the optimized code. For example, in Figure 4(a), suppose Y^2 is dead in the unoptimized program and deleted. The expected value of Y at a breakpoint b along region ① is Y^2, which cannot be reported in the optimized code.

Now consider placing a breakpoint at region ②. The expected value of Y at b along region ② is either Y^1 (if the true path is taken) or Y^2 (if the false path is taken). However, since Y^2 was deleted, the actual value of Y at b in the optimized code is Y^1. Thus, along the true path, the actual value is the expected value and can be reported, but along the false path, the expected value cannot be reported.

The emulation technique [16] cannot report the expected value of Y along region ② because it is not path sensitive. Dynamic currency determination [5] as well as our technique can report the expected value of Y at breakpoints along region ② if the true path is taken.

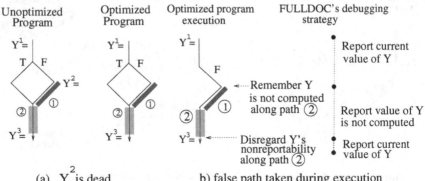

(a) Y^2 is dead   b) false path taken during execution
Fig. 4. Not computed in the optimized program example

Figure 4(b) illustrates FULLDOC's strategy when the optimized program in Figure 4(a) executes along the false path. At a breakpoint along the non-highlighted paths, FULLDOC reports the current value of Y. When execution reaches the original position of Y^2, FULLDOC knows Y is not reportable along regions ① and ②, and reports the expected value of Y is not computed. When execution reaches Y^3, FULLDOC disregards the non-reportability information of Y.

3   FULLDOC's Approach and Implementation

FULLDOC uses three sources of *debug information* for its debugging capabilities. First, as optimizations are applied, a *code location mapping* is generated between the source and optimized code. Second, after code is optimized and generated by the compiler, static analysis is applied to gather information about the reportability of expected values. This *reportability debug information* is used when user breakpoints are inserted, special program points are reached in the program execution, and when a user breakpoint is reached. Third, during execution, *dynamic debug information* indicating that these special points have been reached is used as well as the position of the user breakpoints to enable full reporting.

Figure 5 illustrates FULLDOC's strategy with respect to a user inserting breakpoints. When the user inserts breakpoints either before the program executes or during program execution, FULLDOC uses the code location mapping to determine the corresponding breakpoints in the optimized code. FULLDOC uses the reportability debug information to determine the impact on reportability at the breakpoints and potential future breakpoints:

- If a value is *overwritten early* with respect to a breakpoint, FULLDOC inserts *invisible breakpoints* [17] to *save* the value during execution as long as the value should be reportable and *discard* the value when it is no longer needed.
- If the reportability of a variable with respect to a breakpoint is path sensitive, FULLDOC inserts invisible breakpoints to update the dynamic debug information regarding the reportability of the value.

Figure 6 illustrates FULLDOC's strategy when a breakpoint is reached. If a user breakpoint is reached, FULLDOC informs the user. FULLDOC responds to user queries by using both static and dynamic information. For invisible breakpoints, FULLDOC performs the following actions. For a value that is *overwritten*

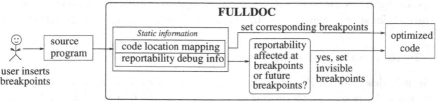

Fig. 5. FULLDOC's strategy with respect to user inserting breakpoints

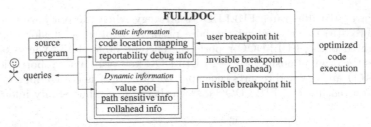

Fig. 6. FULLDOC's strategy with respect to breakpoints hit

early, FULLDOC *saves* the value in a *value pool* and *discards* the value when it is no longer needed for reporting. For a value that is path sensitive, FULLDOC updates the *path sensitive info* regarding the reportability of the value depending on the execution path taken.

When execution reaches a user breakpoint and the user requests the value of a variable, FULLDOC uses the reportability debug information and dynamic debug information to determine the reportability of the value. If the value is available at the location (in memory or register) of the variable or in the value pool, FULLDOC reports the value. If the requested value is *written late* with respect to the breakpoint, FULLDOC uses the reportability debug information to *roll ahead* with the execution of the optimized code, saving previously computed values before they are overwritten. It *stops* execution once the value is computed and reports the value to the user if it is computed. If the value is not computed in the execution, FULLDOC informs the user that the value is not reportable.

3.1   Code Location Mapping

The code location mapping captures the correspondence between the optimized code and the source code. This code location mapping is used by FULLDOC to map between user breakpoints in the source code and corresponding breakpoints in the optimized code. This mapping is also used to compute the reportability debug information, described in the next section. For each statement in the source code, the code location mapping associates the statement with (1) its original position in the optimized code, that is, the position in the control flow graph G_{opt} prior to the application of optimizations and (2) its corresponding statement(s) in the optimized code. Initially the optimized code starts as an identical copy of the source program with mappings between original positions and corresponding statements in the two programs. As optimizations are applied, the code location mapping is maintained between the source and optimized code.

3.2   Reportability Debug Information

We now describe the reportability debug information computed through static analysis of the optimized code that is provided to FULLDOC as well as how FULLDOC employs this information at run time and collects dynamic debug information in response to the user setting breakpoints and requesting values of variables at these breakpoints.

Simply Reportable

```
AvailAtBkpts[b,v] = {l} or {(d1,l1), (d2,l2), ...}
```

If the value of variable v is always reportable at breakpoint b, then AvailAt-Bkpts[b,v] provides the location (memory location or register name) where the value of v can be found. In case the value can always be found at the same location, no matter what execution path is taken, l provides the location.

However, it is possible that the location of v depends on the path taken during execution because b is reachable by multiple definitions of v, each of which stores the value of v in a different location (e.g., a different register). In this case, the execution path taken determines the latest definition of v that is encountered and hence the location where the value of v can be found. Each of the potential definition-location pairs ((di,li)) are provided by AvailAtBkpts[b,v] in this case. When a breakpoint is set at b, the debugger *activates* the recording of the definition of v that is encountered from among (d1, d2, ...) by inserting invisible breakpoints at each of these points. When an invisible breakpoint is hit during execution, the debugger records the latest definition encountered by overwriting the previously recorded definition.

Overwritten Early

```
EarlyAtBkpts[b] = {es: es overwrites early w.r.t. breakpoint b}
SaveDiscardPoints[es] = (save, {discard1, discard2, ...})
```

If the user sets a breakpoint at b, then for each statement es that over-writes early in EarlyAtBkpts[b], we activate the save and discard points in SaveDiscardPoints[es] by inserting invisible breakpoints. This ensures that the values of variables overwritten early with respect to breakpoint b will be saved and available for reporting at b from the value pool in case they are re-quested by the user. Note that the save and discard points must be activated immediately when a breakpoint is set by the user so that all values that may be requested by the user, when the breakpoint is hit, are saved. If a discard point is reached along a path and nothing is currently saved because a save point was not reached along the same path, the debugger simply ignores the discard point. The example in Figure 2, where X is overwritten early, is handled by this case.

Written Late

```
LateAtBkpts[b] = {ls: ls writes late w.r.t. breakpoint b}
StopPoints[ls] = {stop1, stop2, ...}
```

Assume the user sets a breakpoint at b. Then for each statement ls ∈ LateAtBkpts[b], we must first determine if ls is written late with respect to the next instance of the breakpoint b. If the original position of ls is reached during execution but the current position of ls is not reached (before the break-point b is hit), then ls is written late. We determine this information as follows. For each statement ls that is written late, we insert invisible breakpoints at the original and current positions of ls and record if the original position of ls is encountered during execution. When the current position of ls is reached during execution, the recorded information is discarded. Now, suppose execution reaches b, and the user requests the value of a variable v such that v is written late by a statement ls in LateAtBkpts[b]. If the original position of ls is currently recorded, then v is late at the current instance of the breakpoint b and the execution of the program rolls ahead until one of the stop points in StopPoints[ls] is encountered. At a stop point, either the value of v has just been computed or it is known that it will definitely not be computed (recall that sinking of partially dead code can cause such situations to arise). Unlike the overwritten early case where the save and discard points were activated when a breakpoint was set, here the stop points are activated when the breakpoint is hit and a request for a value that is written late is made. The example in Figure 3, where the reportability of X along region ① is affected, is handled by this case.

Never Reportable because Deleted Along a Path

```
NotRepDelAtBkpts[b] = {v: v is never reportable at b (deleted)}
NotRepLateAtBkpts[b] = {v: v is never reportable at b (late)}
```

When (partial) dead code removal is performed, the value of a variable de-fined by the deleted statement becomes unreportable. For each breakpoint b, the variables whose values are never reportable at b, no matter what execution path is taken, are recorded in NotRepDelAtBkpts[b] and NotRepLateAtBkpts[b], for statements removed from paths by dead code elimination and partial dead code elimination, respectively. When the user requests the value of a variable v at breakpoint b, if v is in NotRepDelAtBkpts[b] or NotRepLateAtBkpts[b], we report to the user that the value is not reportable because the statement that computes it has been deleted along the execution path. The example in Figure 4, where the reportability of Y is affected along region ①, is handled by this case. Also, the example in Figure 3, where the reportability of X is affected along region ② is handled by this case.

Path Sensitive Nonreportability/Reportability when Deleted

```
MaybeDelAtBkpts[b] = {ds: ds may be deleted w.r.t. breakpoint b}
EndDelPoints[ds] = {EndDel1, EndDel2, ...}
PotFutBkptsDel[b] = {ds: ds may be deleted at later breakpoints}
```

A value may be deleted on one path (in which case it is not reportable) and not deleted on another path (in which case it is reportable). In this path sensitive case, the reportability information must be updated during execution, based on the paths that are actually executed (i.e., program points reached).

If a user sets a breakpoint at b, invisible breakpoints are set at each of the original positions of any deleted statement ds in MaybeDelAtBkpts[b] to record if one of these positions is encountered during execution. Invisible breakpoints are also set at the end of the definition range of ds, stored in EndDelPoints[ds]. When EndDeli in EndDelPoints[ds] is reached during execution, the recorded information is discarded. Now consider the case when breakpoint b is reached, and the user requests the value of variable v defined by some statement ds in MaybeDelAtBkpts[b]. If the dynamically recorded information shows that the original position of ds was encountered, the debugger reports that the value of v was not computed as ds was deleted. Otherwise the debugger reports the current value of v. The example in Figure 4, where the reportability of Y along region ② is path sensitive, is handled by this case.

We use the same strategy for each deleted statement in PotFutBkptsDel[b], which prevents FULLDOC from setting invisible breakpoints too late. PotFut-BkptsDel[b] holds the deleted statements where reportability could be affected at potential future breakpoints even though reportability is not necessarily affected at b, and invisible breakpoints must now be set so that during the execution to breakpoint b, FULLDOC gathers the appropriate dynamic information for the potential future breakpoints.

Path Sensitive Nonreportability/Reportability when Written Late

```
MaybeLateAtBkpts[b] = {ls: ls may be late w.r.t. breakpoint b}
EndLatePoints[ls] = {EndLate1, EndLate2, ...}
PotFutBkptsLate[b] = {ls: ls may be late at later breakpoints}
```

Sinking code can also involve path sensitive reporting, because a statement may be sunk on one path and not another. This case is opposite to the previous one in that if a late statement is encountered, it is reportable. If the user sets a breakpoint at b, the debugger initiates the recording of the late statements in MaybeLateAtBkpts[b] by setting invisible breakpoints at the new positions of the late statements. The debugger will discard the recorded information of a late statement ls when a EndLatei in EndLatePoints[ls] is encountered (EndLatePoints[ls] holds the end of the definition range of ls). Now consider the case when breakpoint b is reached, and the user requests the value of variable v defined by some statement ls in MaybeLateAtBkpts[b]. If the dynamically recorded information shows that the late statement ls was encountered, the debugger reports the current value of v. Otherwise the debugger reports that the value of v is not reportable. The example in Figure 3, where the reportability of X along region ③ is path sensitive, is handled by this case.

The same strategy applies for each late statement ds in PotFutBkpts-Late[b], which prevents FULLDOC from setting invisible breakpoints too late.

3.3   Computing the Reportability Debug Information

The code location mapping is used to compute the reportability debug information. The algorithm in Figure 7 gives an overview of how this debug information

1 For each source definition D_v
2   If D_v overwrites x early then
3   Let `discard1`, `discard2`, ... = the corresponding positions of original
            definitions of x that are reachable from $ARHead(D_v)$ in the optimized code
4   `SaveDiscardPoints` $[D_v]$ = $(ARHead(D_v)$, {`discard1`, `discard2`,...})
5   For each breakpoint B along a path from D_v to `discard1`, `discard2`,...,
6   `EarlyAtBkpts[B]` = `EarlyAtBkpts[B]` $\cup$ { D_v }
7   Else If D_v writes late in the optimized code then
8   `StopPoints` $[D_v]$ = {$ARHead(D_v)$} $\cup$ {$p : p$ is an earliest possible program
                point along paths from $ORHead(D_v)$ where D_v will not execute}
9   For each breakpoint B along paths $ORHead(D_v)$ to $p \in$ `StopPoints` $[D_v]$,
10   `LateAtBkpts[B]` = `LateAtBkpts[B]` $\cup$ { D_v }
11 Compute `AvailAtBkpts[,]`, `NotRepDelAtBkpts[]`, and `NotRepLateAtBkpts[]`
        by comparing ranges using $ORHead(D_v)$ and $ARHead(D_v)$
12 Compute `MaybeDelAtBkpts[]` and `MaybeLateAtBkpts[]` by determining when
        deleted and late statements occur on one path and not another
13 Compute `EndDelPoints[]`, `EndLatePoints[]`, `PotFutBkptsDel[]`, and
        `PotFutBkptsLate[]` by using reachability

Fig. 7. Algorithm to compute the reportability debug information

is computed. Lines $2 - 6$ determine what values are overwritten early and compute the `SaveDiscardPoints[]` and `EarlyAtBkpts[]` information. Lines $7 - 10$ determine what values are written late and compute the `StopPoints[]` and `LateAtBkpts[]`. Lines 11-13 determine the rest of the debug information by using data flow analysis. More details about the particular steps follow.

Determining Statements that Overwrite Early or Write Late. We determine where values are overwritten early due to register reuse. Suppose D_x is a definition of a variable x and the location of x is in register r in the optimized code. If D_x reaches an assignment to r in which r is reassigned to another variable or temporary, then x is overwritten early at the reassignment.

To determine where values of variables are overwritten early due to code hoisting optimizations, we compare, using G_{opt}, the original positions of the definitions and their actual positions in the optimized program. Let $ARHead(D_v)$ denote the actual position of a definition D_v and let $ORHead(D_v)$ denote the corresponding original position of D_v. We determine the existence of a path P from $ARHead(D_v)$ to $ORHead(D_v)$ such that P does not include backedges of loops enclosing both $ARHead(D_v)$ and $ORHead(D_v)$. The backedge restriction on P ensures that we only consider the positions of the same instance of D_v before and after optimization. This restricted notion of a path is captured by the *SimplePath* predicate.

Definition. The predicate $SimplePath(x, y)$ is true if $\exists$ path P from program point x to program point y in G_{opt} and P does not include backedges of loops enclosing both x and y.

If $SimplePath(ARHead(D_v), ORHead(D_v))$ is true and the location of v at the program point before $ARHead(D_v)$ is the same location that is used to hold the value of D_v, then v is overwritten early at D_v in the optimized code. For example, in Figure 2, $SimplePath(ARHead(X^2), ORHead(X^2))$ is true, and thus, X is overwritten early at X^2.

To determine where values of variables are written late in the optimized program, we similarly compare, using G_{opt}, the original positions of the definitions and their actual positions in the optimized program. That is, for a definition D_v, we determine the existence of a path P from $ORHead(D_v)$ to $ARHead(D_v)$ such that P does not include backedges enclosing both points. Thus, if $Simple\text{-}Path(ORHead(D_v), ARHead(D_v))$ is true, then definition D_v is written late in the optimized code. For example, in Figure 3, X is written late at X^2 because $SimplePath(ORHead(X^2), ARHead(X^2))$ is true.

Computing `SaveDiscardPoints[]` and `EarlyAtBkpts[]`. If a value of x is overwritten early at D_v in the optimized code, then a save point is associated at the position of D_v in the optimized code, and discard points are associated at the corresponding positions of original definitions of x that are reachable from D_v in the optimized code. Data flow analysis is used to determine reachable original definitions, which is similar to the reachable definitions problem. After the save and discard points of D_v are computed, we determine the breakpoints where reportability is affected by D_v. $D_v \in$ `EarlyAtBkpts[b]` if b lies along paths from save to corresponding discard points of D_v. `EarlyAtBkpts[]` is easily computed by solving the following data flow equation on G_{opt}:

$$EarlyAt(B) = \bigcup_{N \in pred(B)} Gen_{ea}(N) \cup (EarlyAt(N) - Kill_{ea}(N))$$

where

$Gen_{ea}(B) = \{D_v : D_v \text{ overwrites early and a save point of } D_v \text{ is at } B\}$ and
$Kill_{ea}(B) = \{D_v : D_v \text{ overwrites early and a discard point of } D_v \text{ is at } B\}$.

Then $D_v \in$ `EarlyAtBkpts[B]` if $D_v \in EarlyAt(B)$. For example, in Figure 2, `SaveDiscardPoints[`X^2`]` $= (ARHead(X^2), \{ORHead(X^2), ORHead(X^3)\})$. For a breakpoint b along regions ①, ②, and ③, `EarlyAtBkpts[b]` $= \{X^2\}$.

Computing `StopPoints[]` and `LateAtBkpts[]`. For a definition D_v that is written late, `StopPoints` $[D_v]$ are the earliest points at which execution can stop because either (1) the late value is computed or (2) a point is reached such that it is known the value will not be computed in the execution. A stop point of D_v is associated at the $ARHead(D_v)$. Stop points are also associated with the earliest points along paths from $ORHead(D_v)$ where the appropriate instance of D_v does not execute. That is, $p \in StopPoint(D_v)$ if

$$p = ARHead(D_v) \vee \qquad (1)$$
$$(D_v \notin ReachableLate(p) \wedge \qquad (2)$$
$$\not\exists\, p'(SimplePath(p', p) \wedge p' \in StopPoint(D_v))). \qquad (3)$$

Condition 1 ensures a stop point is placed at D_v. Condition 2 ensures the rest of the stop points are not placed at program points where the appropriate instance of the late statement would execute. Condition 3 ensures stop points are placed at the earliest points. $ReachableLate(p)$ is the set of statements written late that are reachable at p. $ReachableLate()$ is easily computed by solving the following data flow equation on G_{opt}:

$$ReachableLate(B) = \bigcap_{N \in succ(B)} Gen_{rl}(N) \cup (ReachableLate(N) - Kill_{rl}(N))$$

where
  $Gen_{rl}(B) = \{D_v : ARHead(D_v) = B\}$ and
  $Kill_{rl}(B) = \{D_v : ORHead(D_v) = B\}.$

Consider the example in Figure 3. $StopPoints\ [X^2] = \{ARHead(X^2),$ program point at the beginning of the false path$\}$. After the stop points of D_v are computed, we determine the breakpoints where reportability is affected by D_v. $D_v \in$ `LateAtBkpts[b]` if b lies along paths from $ORHead(D_v)$ to the stop points of D_v. `LateAtBkpts[b]` is easily computed using data flow analysis.

Computing `AvailAtBkpts[,]`. The code location mapping is used to construct program ranges of a variable's value which correspond to the unoptimized code (*real* range) and the optimized code (*actual* range). By comparing the two ranges, we can identify program ranges in the optimized code corresponding to regions where the value of the variable is always available for reporting. If breakpoint B is in this program range for a variable v then `AvailAtBkpts[B,v]` is computed by performing data flow analysis to propagate the locations (memory and registers) of variables within these program ranges.

Computing `NotRepDelAtBkpts[]` and `NotRepLateAtBkpts[]`. To determine the values of variables that are not reportable along a breakpoint because of the application of dead code elimination, we propagate the deleted statements where reportability is affected (regardless of the execution path taken) through the optimized control flow graph G_{opt} by solving the data flow equation:

$$NonRepDel(B) = \bigcap_{N \in pred(B)} Gen_{nrd}(N) \cup (NonRepDel(N) - Kill_{nrd}(N))$$

where
  $Gen_{nrd}(B) = \{D_v : ORHead(D_v) = \{B\} \wedge D_v$ is deleted$\}$ and
  $Kill_{nrd}(B) = \{D_v : ORHead(D_v') = \{B\} \wedge D_v'$ is a definition of $v\}.$

Then for each breakpoint B, $v \in$ `NotRepDelAtBkpts[B]` if $\exists D_v$ such that $D_v \in NonRepDel(B)$. For example, in Figure 4(a), for a breakpoint B along region ①, $Y \in$ `NotRepDelAtBkpts`$[B]$. `NotRepLateAtBkpts[]` is computed similarly.

Computing `MaybeDelAtBkpts[]` and `MaybeLateAtBkpts[]`. To determine the values of variables that may not be reportable along a path when deleted, we first compute the data flow equation on G_{opt}:

$$MaybeDel(B) = \bigcup_{N \in pred(B)} Gen_{md}(N) \cup (MaybeDel(N) - Kill_{md}(N))$$

where

$Gen_{md}(B) = \{D_v : ORHead(D_v) = \{B\} \wedge D_v \text{ is deleted}\}$ and
$Kill_{md}(B) = \{D_v : ORHead(D'_v) = \{B\} \wedge D'_v \text{ is a definition of } v\}$.

Then $v \in$ `MaybeDelAtBkpts[B]` if $\exists D_v$ such that $D_v \in MaybeDel(B) \wedge D_v \notin NonRepDel(B)$. For example, in Figure 4(a), for a breakpoint B along region②, $Y \in$ `MaybeDelAtBkpts`$[B]$ because $Y^2 \in MaybeDel(B) \wedge Y^2 \notin NonRepDel(B)$. `MaybeLateAtBkpts[]` is computed similarly.

Computing `EndDelPoints[]` and `EndLatePoints[]`. For a variable v of a deleted statement `ds` $\in$ `MaybeDelAtBkpts[]`, `EndDelPoints[ds]` are the corresponding positions of original definitions of v that are reachable from $ORHead(\text{ds})$ in G_{opt}. For example, in Figure 4(a), `EndDelPoints[Y]` = the original position of Y^3, which is $ORHead(Y^3)$. Similarly, for a variable v of a late statement `ls` $\in$ `MaybeLateAtBkpts[]`, `EndLatePoints[ls]` are the corresponding positions of original definitions of v that are reachable from $ORHead(\text{ls})$.

Computing `PotFutBkptsDel[]` and `PotFutBkptsLate[]`. For each deleted statement D_v in `MaybeDelAtBkpts[]`, $D_v \in$ `PotFutBkptsDel[b]` if b lies along paths from the $ORHead(D_v)$ to the corresponding positions of original definitions of v that are reachable from $ORHead(D_v)$ in the optimized code. `PotFutBkptsLate[]` is computed similarly.

4 Experiments

We implemented FULLDOC by first extending LCC [6], a compiler for C programs, with a set of optimizations, including (coloring) register allocation, loop invariant code motion, dead code elimination, partial dead code elimination, partial redundancy elimination, copy propagation, and constant propagation and folding. We also extended LCC to perform the analyses needed to provide the debug information to FULLDOC, given in the previous section. We then implemented FULLDOC, using the debug information generated by LCC, and fast breakpoints [11] for the implementation of invisible breakpoints.

We performed experiments to measure the improvement in the reportability of expected values for a suite of programs, namely YACC and some SPEC95 benchmarks. Rather than randomly generate user breakpoints, we placed a user breakpoint at every source statement and determined the improvement in reportability of FULLDOC over a technique that uses only static information. We also report for each breakpoint, the reasons why reportability is affected, and thus we can compare the improvement of our technique over techniques that cannot report overwritten values or path sensitive values.

Table 1 shows for each benchmark, the percentage of values that could not be reported by (1) using only statically computed information and (2) FULLDOC. The first row gives the percentages of values that were deleted along all paths, and are thus not reportable in FULLDOC (as noted, FULLDOC could recover some of these values, as other debuggers can [8]). The next two rows give the percentages of values whose reportability is affected because they are overwritten early, either because of code hoisting (row 2) or a register being overwritten early (row 3). If a debugger does not include some mechanism for "saving" values overwritten early, it would not be able to report these values. The next three rows give the percentages of values whose reportability is affected because the statements that computed the values were affected by partial dead code elimination. Row 4 indicates the percentages of values that are not reportable along paths before the sunk values. Row 5 indicates the percentages of values that are not reportable along paths where the sunk values are never computed. Row 6 indicates the percentages of values that are not reportable along paths because the reportability of the values sunk is path sensitive. If a debugger does not include some mechanism to "roll ahead" the execution of the optimized program, it would not be able to report these values. The next two rows give the results when reportability is affected by path sensitive information. The seventh row gives the percentages that were not reportable for path sensitive deletes. In this case, the values may have been deleted on paths that were executed. The eighth row gives the results when the location of a value is path sensitive. A technique that does not include path sensitive information would fail to report these values. The last row gives the total percentages that could not be reported. On average, FULLDOC cannot report 8% of the local variables at a source breakpoint while a debugger using only static information cannot report 30%, which means FULLDOC can report 31% more values than techniques using only statically computed information. From these numbers, FULLDOC can report at least 28% more values than the emulation technique [16] since neither path sensitivity nor register overwrites were handled. FULLDOC can report at least

Table 1. Percentage of local variables per breakpoint that are not reportable

Problems	yacc		compress		go		m88ksim		ijpeg	
	static info	FULL DOC	static info	FULL DOC	static info	FULL DOC	static info	FULL DOC	static info	FULL DOC
deleted-all paths	0.96	0.96	15.03	15.03	0.75	0.75	1.87	1.87	10.42	10.42
code hoisting	0.19	0.00	0.34	0.00	0.30	0.00	0.14	0.00	4.15	0.00
reg overwrite	42.65	0.00	17.24	0.00	9.44	0.00	1.83	0.00	15.87	0.00
code sinking (rf)	0.19	0.00	0.64	0.09	1.40	0.39	0.57	0.07	1.79	0.09
del on path	0.00	0.00	0.02	0.02	0.10	0.10	0.06	0.06	0.28	0.28
path sens late	0.00	0.00	0.18	0.09	0.51	0.18	0.41	0.37	0.58	0.39
path sens delete	8.27	6.07	0.18	0.00	2.25	0.74	0.00	0.00	2.36	1.20
path sens location	3.95	0.00	0.07	0.00	1.14	0.00	0.32	0.00	1.43	0.00
total	56.21	7.03	33.70	15.23	15.89	2.16	5.20	2.37	36.88	12.38

Table 2. Static statistics

		yacc	compress	go	m88ksim	ijpeg
no. source statements		168	354	10876	5778	8214
% statements affected		85	57	59	52	56
number of table entries	code hoisting	10	77	1502	987	2374
	reg overwrite	517	234	11819	3961	9655
	code sinking (rf)	13	177	5355	1839	3745
	path sens late	0	117	2912	1203	1833
	path sens delete	66	37	1785	397	1452
	path sens location	48	59	1937	301	1447
% increase compile time		12.1	8.8	11.0	9.6	13.1

26% more values than dynamic currency determination technique [5] since early overwrites were not preserved and no roll ahead mechanism is employed.

In Table 2, we present statistics from the static analysis for FULLDOC. The first two rows show the number of source statements and the percentage of source statements whose reportability is affected by optimizations. The next 6 rows give the number of entries in each of the tables generated for use at run time. It should be noted that the largest table is for register overwrites. The last row shows that the increase in compilation for computing all the debug information averaged only 10.9%.

In Table 3, we show the average number of invisible breakpoints per source code statement that was encountered during execution. These numbers are shown for each of the various types of invisible breakpoints. These numbers indicate that not much overhead is incurred at run time for invisible breakpoints. The last three rows display the overhead imposed by the roll ahead execution of the optimized program. On average, 9.7% of the source assignment statements were executed during the roll aheads. The maximum number of statements executed during a roll forward ranges from 5 to 4102 values, which means at most 5 to 4102 number of values are saved from the roll ahead at any given moment. The average roll ahead of source assignment statements ranges from 2 to 7 statements. The size of the value pool holding values that are overwritten early was small with the maximum size ranging from 8 entries to 77 entries, indicating that optimizations are not moving code very far.

Thus, our experiments show that the table sizes required to hold the debug information and the increase in compile time to compute debug information are both quite modest. The run time cost of our technique, which is a maximum of less than one fast breakpoint per source level statement if all possible values are requested by the user at all possible breakpoints, is also reasonable. The payoff of our technique is substantial since it reports at least 26% more values than the best previously known techniques.

The presence of pointer assignments in a source program can increase our overheads because our strategies rely on determining the ranges in which the reportability of variables are affected. For control equivalent code motion (as-

Table 3. Runtime statistics

		yacc	compress	go	m88ksim	ijpeg
% breakpoints where reportability affected		94	95	67	21	92
avg. no. invisible breakpoints per source statement	code hoisting	0.12	0.03	0.04	0.05	0.35
	reg overwrite	1.03	0.13	0.26	0.02	0.35
	code sinking (rf)	0.03	0.03	0.07	0.03	0.12
	path sens late	0.10	0.05	0.13	0.04	0.23
	path sens delete	0.09	0.00	0.03	0.01	0.23
	path sens location	0.07	0.02	0.02	0.00	0.05
	overall	1.44	0.26	0.56	0.18	1.37
	(duplicates removed) overall	0.56	0.14	0.37	0.17	0.43
% source assignments executed for roll forwards		1.33	4.11	17.39	6.01	19.8
maximum roll forward length		5	60	314	4102	1482
average roll forward length		2	4	7	5	4

signments are not introduced into new paths nor removed from paths), we can statically determine the ranges in which reportability of values are affected even in the presence of pointer assignments. For the case when the reportability of a value of a variable is affected and the end of its reportable range is possibly at a pointer assignment (because of code deletion and non-control equivalent code motion), our strategy has to dynamically track the range in which the reportability of the value of the variable is affected.

5   Related Work

The difficulty of debugging optimized code has long been recognized [8], with most work focusing on the development of source level debuggers of optimized code [8,17,13,4,7,9,2,12,3,15,1] that use static analysis techniques to determine whether expected values of source level variables are reportable at breakpoints. Recent work on source level debuggers of optimized code utilizes some dynamic information to provide more expected values. By emulating (at certain program points) the optimized code in an order that mimics the execution of the unoptimized program, some values of variables that are otherwise not reportable by other debuggers can be reported in [16]. However, as pointed out in [16], altering the execution of the optimized program masks certain user and optimizer errors. Also, the emulation technique does not track paths and cannot report values whose reportability is path sensitive. The dynamic currency determination technique proposed in [5] can also report some values of variables that are not reportable by other debuggers by time stamping basic blocks to obtain a partial history of the execution path, which is used to precisely determine what variables are reportable at breakpoints; but values that are overwritten early by either code hoisting or register reuses are not always reportable. Recovery techniques [8], which can be incorporated into all debuggers including FULLDOC, are employed in [16] and [5] to recompute some of the nonreportable values in certain circumstances.

Instead of reporting expected values with respect to a source program, the Optdbx debugger [14] reports values with respect to an optimized source program version. Also, Optdbx uses invisible breakpoints to recover evicted variables.

Another approach to debugging optimized code is COP [10], a comparison checker for optimized code, which verifies that given an input, the semantic behaviors of both the unoptimized and optimized code versions are the same. This can be incorporated into a debugger to report all values, including deleted values. However, this technique requires the execution of both the unoptimized and optimized programs.

6 Conclusions

This paper presents FULLDOC, a **FULL** reporting **D**ebugger of **O**ptimized **C**ode that reports all expected values that are computed in the optimized program. That is, every value of a source level variable that is computed in the optimized program execution is reportable at all breakpoints in the source code where the value of the variable should be reportable. Experimental results show that FULLDOC can report 31% more values than techniques relying on static information and at least 26% more over existing techniques that limit the dynamic information used. FULLDOC's improvement over existing techniques is achieved by statically computing information to guide the gathering of dynamic information that enables full reporting. The only values that FULLDOC cannot reported are those that are not computed in the optimized program execution.

References

1. Adl-Tabatabai, A. and Gross, T. Source-Level Debugging of Scalar Optimized Code. In *Proceedings ACM SIGPLAN'96 Conf. on Programming Languages Design and Implementation*, pages 33–43, May 1996. 241, 258
2. Brooks, G., Hansen, G. J., and Simmons, S. A New Approach to Debugging Optimized Code. In *Proceedings ACM SIGPLAN'92 Conf. on Programming Languages Design and Implementation*, pages 1–11, June 1992. 258
3. Copperman, M. Debugging Optimized Code Without Being Misled. *ACM Transactions on Programming Languages and Systems*, 16(3):387–427, 1994. 241, 258
4. Coutant, D. S., Meloy, S., and Ruscetta, M. DOC: A Practical Approach to Source-Level Debugging of Globally Optimized Code. In *Proceedings ACM SIGPLAN'88 Conf. on Programming Languages Design and Implementation*, pages 125–134, June 1988. 241, 258
5. Dhamdhere, D. M. and Sankaranarayanan, K. V. Dynamic Currency Determination in Optimized Programs. *ACM Transactions on Programming Languages and Systems*, 20(6):1111–1130, November 1998. 241, 244, 245, 246, 256, 258
6. Fraser, C. and Hanson, D. *A Retargetable C Compiler: Design and Implementation*. Benjamin/Cummings, 1995. 255
7. Gupta, R. Debugging Code Reorganized by a Trace Scheduling Compiler. *Structured Programming*, 11(3):141–150, 1990. 258

8. Hennessy, J. Symbolic Debugging of Optimized Code. *ACM Transactions on Programming Languages and Systems*, 4(3):323–344, July 1982. 241, 256, 258

9. Holzle, U., Chambers, C., and Ungar, D. Debugging Optimized Code with Dynamic Deoptimization. In *Proceedings ACM SIGPLAN'92 Conf. on Programming Languages Design and Implementation*, pages 32–43, June 1992. 258

10. Jaramillo, C., Gupta, R., and Soffa, M. L. Comparison Checking: An Approach to Avoid Debugging of Optimized Code. In *ACM SIGSOFT Symposium on Foundations of Software Engineering and European Software Engineering Conference*, pages 268–284, September 1999. 259

11. Kessler, P. Fast Breakpoints: Design and Implementation. In *Proceedings ACM SIGPLAN'90 Conf. on Programming Languages Design and Implementation*, pages 78–84, June 1990. 255

12. Pineo, P. P. and Soffa, M. L. Debugging Parallelized Code using Code Liberation Techniques. *Proceedings of ACM/ONR SIGPLAN Workshop on Parallel and Distributed Debugging*, 26(4):103–114, May 1991. 258

13. Pollock, L. L. and Soffa, M. L. High-Level Debugging with the Aid of an Incremental Optimizer. In *21st Annual Hawaii International Conference on System Sciences*, volume 2, pages 524–531, January 1988. 258

14. Tice, C. *Non-Transparent Debugging of Optimized Code*. PhD dissertation, University of California, Berkeley, 1999. Technical Report UCB-CSD-99-1077. 258

15. Wismueller, R. Debugging of Globally Optimized Programs Using Data Flow Analysis. In *Proceedings ACM SIGPLAN'94 Conf. on Programming Languages Design and Implementation*, pages 278–289, June 1994. 241, 258

16. Wu, L., Mirani, R., Patil H., Olsen, B., and Hwu, W. W. A New Framework for Debugging Globally Optimized Code. In *Proceedings ACM SIGPLAN'99 Conf. on Programming Languages Design and Implementation*, pages 181–191, May 1999. 241, 244, 245, 246, 256, 258

17. Zellweger, P. T. An Interactive High-Level Debugger for Control-Flow Optimized Programs. In *Proceedings ACM SIGSOFT/SIGPLAN Software Engineering Symposium on High-Level Debugging*, pages 159–171, 1983. 242, 247, 258

Partial Redundancy Elimination on Predicated Code*

Jens Knoop[1], Jean-François Collard[2], and Roy Dz-ching Ju[3]

[1] Universität Dortmund
D-44221 Dortmund, Germany
knoop@ls5.cs.uni-dortmund.de
[2] Intel Corp. – Microcomputer Software Lab
[3] Intel Corp. – Microprocessor Research Lab
Santa Clara, CA 95052
{jean-francois.j.collard,roy.ju}@intel.com

Abstract. *Partial redundancy elimination* (*PRE*) is one of the most important and widespread optimizations in compilers. However, current PRE-techniques are inadequate to handle *predicated code*, i.e., programs where instructions are guarded by a 1-bit register that dynamically controls whether the effect of an instruction should be committed or nullified. In fact, to exclude corrupting the semantics they must be overly conservative making them close to useless. Since predicated code will be more and more common with the advent of the IA-64 architecture, we present here a family of PRE-algorithms tailored for predicated code. Conceptually, the core element of this family can be considered the counterpart of *busy code motion* of [17]. It can easily be tuned by two orthogonal means. First, by adjusting the power of a preprocess feeding it by information on predication. Second, by relaxing or strengthening the constraints on synthesizing predicates controlling the movability of computations. Together with extensions towards *lazy code motion*, this results in a family of PRE-algorithms spanning a range from tamed to quite aggressive algorithms, which is illustrated by various meaningful examples.

Keywords: Partial redundancy elimination, predicated code, IA-64, busy code motion, lazy code motion, data-flow analysis, optimization.

1 Motivation

Partial redundancy elimination (*PRE*) is one of the most important and widespread optimizations in compilers. Intuitively, it aims at avoiding unnecessary recomputations of values at run-time. Technically, this is achieved by storing the value of computations for later reuse in temporaries. Classical PRE-techniques, however, are inadequate when instructions are predicated. In order to exclude corrupting the program semantics, they have to be overly conservative. This is

---

* Part of this work was done while the second author was working at CNRS/PR*i*SM Laboratory, University of Versailles, 78035 Versailles, France.

J. Palsberg (Ed.): SAS 2000, LNCS 1824, pp. 260–280, 2000.

illustrated in the example of Figure 1(a), where statements are written using the syntax of the IA-64 [4,6] for predication. In this example, the predicates p and q guarding the execution of the statements will always have different truth values according to the semantics of the IA-64 machine model (cf. Section 2). Classical PRE-techniques, however, are by no means prepared to incorparate such information. Hence, they have to conservatively assume that variable a is modified between the two computation sites of $a + b$. Consequently, they fail to achieve the desired optimization of Figure 1(b).

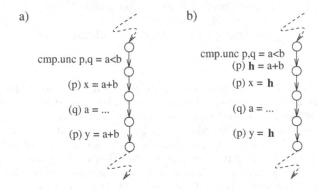

a)

cmp.unc p,q = a<b

(p) x = a+b

(q) a = ...

(p) y = a+b

b)

cmp.unc p,q = a<b
(p) **h** = a+b

(p) x = **h**

(q) a = ...

(p) y = **h**

Fig. 1. Illustrating the essence of PRE on predicated code.

Intuitively, the reason for this is that, in standard PRE, branching is interpreted nondeterministically. It is the key to (efficient) decidability and hence to an algorithmic solution of the problem. In predicated code, nondeterminism is no longer adequate. Though one could easily represent each predicated statement by an if-then-else-like graph structure, which would allow us to directly apply the standard PRE-techniques, this would be close to useless because it introduces many non-existent paths.[1] As a consequence, lots of redundancies, as the one in the example of Figure 1 could not be eliminated. Moreover, a transformation performed on such an extended graph would introduce the problem of how to retranslate it into predicated code.

On the other hand, simply neglecting the effects of predication is usually incorrect and corrupts the program semantics. In fact, the transformation displayed in Figure 1(b) is correct if and only if the conjunction of p and q is provably always false.

In this article, we therefore develop a new approach for PRE, which is tailored for predicated code. Conceptually, the basic algorithm we present can be considered the counterpart of *busy code motion* of [16,17]. Like busy code mo-

---

[1] Approaches like *qualified data flow analysis* of [12] aim at figuring out "spurious" paths on ordinary code. Generally, however, this works to some extent only, and it is not clear how to generalize these approaches to predicated code.

tion the new approach relies on two unidirectional data-flow analyses. First, a *hoistability* analysis moving computations to their *earliest down-safe* computation points. I.e., to the earliest points satisfying that the computation will be used on every program path starting there and reaching the end node without an intervening modification of any of its operands. Second, a *redundancy* analysis identifying all computations which are totally redundant after the hoisting step of the algorithm. Both analyses are fed by predicate information yielded by an independent preprocessing step. In addition, the predicate information allows us to identify and suppress *off-predicated* insertions, i.e., insertions whose guarding predicate is equivalent to *false* at the program point under consideration.[2]

Together, this results in the following overall structure of our algorithm:

1. *Analysis Phase* (Section 3.1):
   (a) *Preprocessing*: Computing predicate information (Section 3.1.1)
   (b) *Hoistability* analysis: Computing down-safety (Section 3.1.2)
   (c) *Redundancy* analysis: Computing redundant and off-predicated insertions (Section 8.3)
2. *Transformation Phase* (Section 3.2):
   Insertions and replacements: Insert computations, which are not redundant or off-predicated, and replace all original computations by references to temporaries. (Section 3.2.1)

This algorithm (as well as its extensions) works for arbitrary control flow, and constitutes the kernel of a family of PRE-algorithms for predicated code of different power. In fact, we will demonstrate how the basic algorithm can easily be tuned by simply modifying certain parameters in order to comply with given demands on the transformational power. This ranges from conservative tamed to quite aggressive versions differing in the constraints imposed on "synthesizing" new predicates providing control on the movability of computations. Moreover, extensions in the fashion of *lazy code motion* (cf. [16,17]) towards taking the lifetimes of temporaries into account are possible, too.

The power of the complete approach is demonstrated by the example of Figure 2, which is complex enough to illustrate its central features. By convention, p0 denotes the always true and false the always false predicate. The rationale for this notation is that several predicated architectures, including the IA-64, feature a p0 predicate which cannot be written and whose value is always equal to true. In the example of Figure 2, our approach is unique to achieve the optimizations displayed in Figure 3. The basic version of our algorithm

1. ... eliminates the redundancy of the evaluation of x+y in the assignments to a and b at the edges **4** and **6**, and
2. ... the redundancy of the evaluation of x+y in the assignments to c, d and e at the edges **10**, **18**, and **22** (Note that a and b do not reach the destination node of edge **12**, and that due to the instruction x=0 at edge **9**, expression x+y cannot be hoisted across this edge.)

---

[2] Off-predicated insertions, and, more generally, off-predicated statements, can be eliminated without changing the semantics but enhancing the performance.

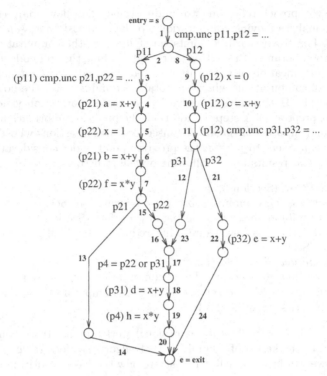

Fig. 2. Running example: Illustrating the power of the new PRE-approach.

The full version of our algorithm, which makes a step towards "semantic PRE" on predicates (cf. [20]) additionally

3. ... eliminates the redundancy of the evaluation of **x∗y** at edge **19** by inserting an assignment at edge **5** and edge **12**.[3]

The processing of this example is presented in full detail in [14], where we also discuss the necessity of a PRE framework on predicated code, including the issues, such as why PRE before if-conversion (cf. [8]) or reverse if-conversion (cf. [27]) does not suffice. Right now, it is worth noting that our PRE framework can handle any type of predicated code so long as the preprocessing stage, which is largely an independent phase to our core PRE algorithm and will be discussed in Section 3.1, can analyze the predicates in a program correctly.

Related Work. PRE has been pioneered by the algorithm of Morel and Renvoise [22], and thoroughly been studied in the literature.

---

[3] Note that also the basic version hoists the computation of **x∗y** at edge **19**. However, this gets stuck at edge **17** thereby failing to eliminate this partial redundancy.

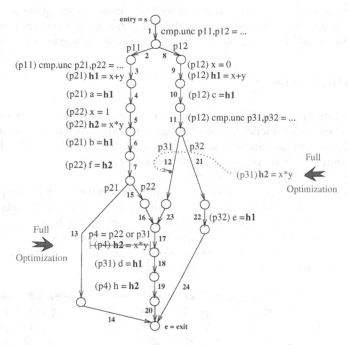

Fig. 3. The motivating example: Basic and full optimization.

The (intraprocedural) state-of-the-art algorithms fall into two major groups. First, algorithms aiming at eliminating redundancies among lexically identical terms, also known as *syntactic PRE* (cf. [3,5,16,17,22,25]). Second, algorithms aiming at eliminating redundancies also among lexically different, yet semantically equivalent computations, also known as *semantic PRE* (cf. [2,20,24,26]). The enhanced transformational power of the algorithms of the second group comes at the price of usually significantly higher computational costs.

Common to all of these approaches is that they are not prepared for dealing with predicated code. This also holds for the approaches of [8], which is restricted to single-entry/single-exit acyclic regions, and of [10]. They are capable of introducing predicated statements in order to enhance code sinking for enlarging the power of partial dead-code elimination, but are not capable of systematically working on predicated code.

In fact, to the best of our knowledge, the approach we are going to present here is the first one systematically extending PRE to predicated code. Basically, it falls into the group of syntactic PRE-approaches. However, in [14] we show how to extend it towards semantic PRE at almost no costs on both the conceptual and computational side. This is actually required in order to succeed in eliminating the partial redundancy of x*y at edge **19** in the example of Figure 2 (cf. [14]).

On purpose, the presentation in this article focuses on the phenomena showing up for PRE on predicated code, on their illustration by meaningful examples, and on the impact they have on the design decisions underlying our approach.

2   Preliminaries

Predication. In this article, we assume the architectural support of general predicated execution model in the IA-64 architecture [4,6], in which the execution of an instruction can be guarded by a qualifying predicate. The following form of compare instructions is provided to set predicates:

(qp) cmp.crel.ctype p1,p2=r2,r3

Predicates p1 and p2 are two target predicates. Predicate qp is the qualifying predicate. The two source operands, r2 and r3, are compared based on the relation specified by crel. There are a number of comparsion types, and we list three most relevant ones in the following table to describe their behaviors, where nc indicates "no change." The outcome of the crel comparison is in variable result. Note that unc is short for unconditional.

ctype	qp==0		qp==1 && result==0		qp==1 && result==1	
unc	p1=0	p2=0	p1=0	p2=1	p1=1	p2=0
or	p1=nc	p2=nc	p1=nc	p2=nc	p1=1	p2=1
and	p1=nc	p2=nc	p1=0	p2=0	p1=nc	p2=nc

To explore predication, a compiler generally incorporates a technique called *if-conversion* (cf. [1]), which eliminates branch instructions and converts affected instructions to appropriate predicated form.

An execution trace includes all of the instructions being executed. A trace belongs to the *domain* of predicate p if all the instructions on this trace are executed when p is true. The domain of p includes all such traces. Note that the notion of domain is purely for the discussion purpose, and we never have the need to enumerate traces. We call a predicate which explicitly appears in the instruction stream a *materialized predicate*.

Flow Graphs. As usual we represent programs by *directed flow graphs* $G = (N, E, \mathbf{s}, \mathbf{e})$ with node set N, edge set E, a unique start node $\mathbf{s}$, and a unique end node $\mathbf{e}$, which are assumed to have no predecessors and successors, respectively. Edges represent the branching structure and the (possibly predicated) statements of a program, while nodes represent program points. Edges leaving a node with more than one successor are labeled by a (*qualifying*) *predicate*, edges leaving a node with only one successor are labeled by a (possibly predicated) statement (including the empty statement *skip*). We denote the set of all qualifying predicates occurring in G by $\mathcal{Q}$, and the set of all statements by $\mathcal{S}$. With these notations, E is the disjoint union of the sets E_S and $E_{\mathcal{Q}}$, denoting the sets of edges labeled by a statement and a predicate, respectively. In particular, we define a function $qualPred : E_{\mathcal{Q}} \rightarrow \mathcal{Q}$, which maps an edge of $E_{\mathcal{Q}}$ to the qualifying predicate it is labeled with. Nodes with more than one successor are called *branch nodes*, nodes with more than one predecessor *join nodes*. We denote the corresponding subsets of N by N_B and N_J, respectively.

Without loss of generality we assume that edges leading to a join node have been split by inserting a synthetic node. The edges emerging thereby are labeled by *skip*. This allows us to insert computations uniformly at the "arrowheads" of edges, and avoids blocking of the code motion process by so-called *critical edges*, i.e. edges going from branch nodes to join nodes (cf. [16]).

We denote the set of predecessors and successors of a node n by $pred(n)=_{df}$ $\{\,m\mid (m,n)\in E\,\}$ and $succ(n)=_{df}\{\,m\mid (n,m)\in E\,\}$. Additionally, $src(e)$ and $dst(e)$, $e\in E$, denote the *source node* and the *destination node* of edge e. We assume that every node of a flow graph G lies on a path from **s** to **e**. Finally, let $\mathcal{P}$ denote the powerset operator, and $\mathcal{B}=_{df}\{true, false\}$ the set of Boolean truth values. Note that $\mathcal{B}$ can be considered a subset of $\mathcal{Q}$ by identifying *true* and p0.

3   PRE on Predicated Code

This section defines the base concepts in the PRE. First, a candidate pattern for code motion is as usual an expression or *term* that actually appears in the program and which we may want to place somewhere else in the program. "Placing somewhere else" is done in two steps: *Insertion* of evaluations of the term, the result of the evaluation being stored in a fresh temporary, and *replacement* of occurrences that are proved to be redundant with respect to evaluations that already existed or were introduced.

To do so, the analysis relies, as usual for PRE, on two fundamental local predicates *Comp* and *Transp* (local in the sense that they are attached to a single edge and depend on this edge's properties only), which are here tailored for taking qualifying predicates into account. $Comp_\pi$ gives the predicate that qualifies a *computation* of the term, π, in the considered edge, if any, while $Transp_\pi$ tells us whether the current edge is *transp*arent for hoisting π, when guarded by the predicate passed as argument to it.

- *CM-candidate patterns*: terms t
- *Local predicates*: ... defined for every edge $e\in E$ with respect to an arbitrary, but fixed CM-candidate pattern $\pi\equiv t$. We assume that $e\equiv(p)\ v:=t'$ for $e\in E_S$, and $e\equiv p$ for $e\in E_Q$.

  1. $Comp_\pi : E\to\mathcal{Q}$ defined by
  $$Comp_\pi(e)=_{df}\begin{cases}p & \text{if } e\in E_S\wedge\pi\in SubTerms(t')\\ false & \text{otherwise}\end{cases}$$

  2. $Transp_\pi : E\to(\mathcal{Q}\to\mathcal{B})$ defined by
  $$Transp_\pi(e)(q)=_{df}\begin{cases}(v\neq q\wedge v\notin SubTerms(\pi))\vee q\Rightarrow\bar{p} & \text{if } e\in E_S\\ true & \text{otherwise}\end{cases}$$

- *Pattern of insertions*: (qp) $\mathbf{h}_\pi := \pi$, where $\mathbf{h}_\pi$ is a fresh variable for the program under consideration, and qp is a qualifying predicate which for every insertion point is computed in the course of the code motion process.
- *Replacement candidates*: occurrences of the CM-candidate pattern π.

The definition of the predicate $Comp_\pi(e)$ directly reflects the semantics of predicated statements in the IA-64 architecture. Considering for illustration the statement (p) $x = a + b$, and a program run, where p equals *false* when reaching this statement, predication does not prevent the evaluation of the right-hand-side term $a + b$, rather it excludes that the value is eventually assigned to the left-hand-side variable x. However, the evaluation of the right-hand-side can be interrupted at any intermediate stage when it turns out that the guarding predicate is false. Hence, placing $a + b$ immediately before (p) $x = a + b$ is generally unsafe as one cannot be sure that it will be computed (and committed) by this statement. On the other hand, when guarded by p, it will be safe in this sense.

In distinction to the definition of $Comp_\pi$, which only relies on the parameter e, the predicate $Transp_\pi$ relies on a second argument, a qualifying predicate q. Intuitively, the truth value of $Transp_\pi$ with respect to an edge e and predicate q indicates, whether an occurrence of the computation pattern π guarded by q can safely be hoisted across the statement attached to e. This is true, if the left-hand-side variable v of the statement at e does neither modify an operand of π (i.e., $v \notin SubTerms(\pi)$) nor modify q itself (i.e., $v \neq q$), or if the statement of e would be off-predicated, whenever the evaluation of π guarded by q would be committed (i.e., $q \Rightarrow \bar{p}$, where $\Rightarrow$ stands for logical implication).

Based on these local predicates, we will present the hoistability and redundancy analyses for computation patterns, which constitute the algorithmic kernel of our approach, in the following section. The semantic domain they are operating on is the powerset of (materialized) qualifying predicates $\mathcal{P}(\mathcal{Q})$.[4]

3.1 Analysis Phase

3.1.1 Preprocessing: Analysing Predicates
The analyses involved in the transformation rely on information on the relationships between predicates (see e.g. the definitions of the local predicates *Comp* and *Transp* above). In our approach we assume that this information is provided by an independent preprocess. The requirement for this preprocessing is to analyze the predicates in a program and be able to answer the queries from our PRE algorithm on union ($\sqcup$) and intersection ($\sqcap$) for given predicates correctly (though maybe conservatively). A union query can also be used to derive a subset or superset relation between predicates. An intersection query can be used to derive a disjoint relation.

Though the PRE transformation will always be correct, it will be the more powerful the more precise the information on the relationships between predicates is. Exchanging the preprocess by a different one is an easy means for trading

---

[4] Aggressive versions of the algorithm may synthesize qualifying predicates in the course of the PRE process enlarging the semantic domain (cf. Section 4).

power against efficiency of the transformation. Note, the PRE-transformation itself has not to be modified. It is invariant under modifications of the preprocess.

There are several published predicate analysis techniques which meet the requirement of being the preprocessing phase to our PRE framework.

- The *predicate partition graph (PPG)* of [9,13]. The techniques in these work analyze predicates and control flow in a program and construct a graph to represent the relations among predicates. A *partition* of the predicate is a division of the domain of the predicate into multiple disjoint subsets, where the union of these subsets is equal to the domain. The constructed graph in this approach is called *Predicate Partition Graph* $G = (Q, E)$, where each node in Q represents a predicate p and each edge (p, p_1) represents that there exists a partition in p such that p_1 is a subset of this partition. An edge in G is directed and the edges created from the same partition are marked. Techniques are discussed in [13] to perform the union and intersection operations for the given predicates and approximate the results if necessary. A valid PPG is acyclic. Thanks to the property that edges represent partitions, the PPG is a lattice with a natural (strict) partial order denoted by $\sqsubseteq$ (resp. $\sqsubset$).
- The *predicate hierarchy graph (PHG)* of [21]. In this approach, a *Predicate Hierarchy Graph (PHG)* is a graphical representation of boolean equations for all of the predicates in a hyperblock. The PHG is composed of predicate and condition nodes. Conditions are added as children to their respective parent predicate nodes. Subsequent predicates are added to their parent condition nodes. A boolean expression is built for a predicate to determine the condition under which the predicate is true. The corresponding expressions of given predicates are ANDed or Ored together to answer an intersection or union query, respectively.
- The *P-facts* approach of [7]. The predicate extraction mechanism in this work allows the compiler to find how predicates are defined and used. This knowledge is expressed as logically invariant expressions, or P-facts, that are guaranteed to hold, regardless of the execution trace, the results of comparisons and the values of other predicates. These P-facts will be used later to determine feasible execution paths, i.e. execution paths which do not violate any of the P-facts gathered. The P-facts associated with given predicates are ANDed or ORed by a symbolic package which simplifies logic equations to answer an intersection or union query, respectively.

3.1.2 Hoistability Analysis Intuitively, the first step of our PRE-algorithm moves computations to the earliest points satisfying that their values will be used on every program continuation reaching the end node without an intervening modification of any of their operands. This property is usually known as *very busyness* or *anticipability* of a computation (cf. [11,22]). In [16,18,25] it is called *down-safety*. In order to emphasize the operational character we speak here of hoistability. It requires a backward analysis of the argument program, and relies on the local semantic functional

$$[\![\ ]\!]^{\pi}_{hst} : E \to (\mathcal{P}(\mathcal{Q}) \to \mathcal{P}(\mathcal{Q}))$$

where the index "hst" reminds to "hoistable." It is defined as follows:

$$\forall Q \in \mathcal{P}(\mathcal{Q}). \ [\![\ e\ ]\!]^{\pi}_{hst}(Q) =_{df} \mathcal{C}_{\mathcal{U}}(\{\ Comp_{\pi}(e)\} \cup \{\ q \in Q \mid Transp^{\pi}(e)(q)\})$$

The induced analysis is indeed a counterpart of the ordinary very busyness analysis, however, it is tailored for the predicated scenario. Intuitively, if for every predicate q of Q there is on every path from the destination node of e to the end node $\mathbf{e}$ of G a computation of π which is guarded by a predicate implying q such that an evaluation of π at both sites yields the same value, then this property holds analogously for every predicate of $[\![\ e\ ]\!]^{\pi}_{hst}(Q)$ for the source node of e.

Most important in the definition of $[\![\ ]\!]^{\pi}_{hst}$ is the operator $\mathcal{C}_{\mathcal{U}} : \mathcal{P}(\mathcal{Q}) \to \mathcal{P}(\mathcal{Q})$. It introduces a semantic flavour into the otherwise syntactic treatment of predicates during the hoistability analysis. $\mathcal{C}_{\mathcal{U}}$ denotes an *(upper) closure operator* on $\mathcal{P}(\mathcal{Q})$ with respect to the logical $\vee$ on materialized predicates.[5] I.e., for all $Q \in \mathcal{P}(\mathcal{Q})$, $\mathcal{C}_{\mathcal{U}}(Q)$ is the smallest set $Q' \in \mathcal{P}(\mathcal{Q})$ such that

- $Q \subseteq Q'$
- If $q, q' \in Q'$ and $q \sqcup q' = q'' \in Q$, then $q'' \in Q'$

Intuitively, enlarging the set of "hoistable" predicates by $\mathcal{C}_{\mathcal{U}}$ enhances the power of the hoistability analysis to move predicated computations across branch nodes as hoistability information must be "met" there for preserving safety of the transformation. This is discussed in the next paragraph. Here, just note that for all edges $e \in E_{\mathcal{Q}}$, the function $[\![\ e\ ]\!]^{\pi}_{hst}$ equals the identity on $\mathcal{P}(\mathcal{Q})$.

Fundamental for the fixed-point characterization of the set of hoistable program points is a "meet"-operator defined on the powerset lattice of $\mathcal{Q}$. In essence, it is given by the set-theoretic meet on $\mathcal{P}(\mathcal{Q})$, however, adapted to taking qualifying predicates at branch nodes into account. To this end, we introduce for every node $n \in N \backslash \{\mathbf{e}\}$ a k-ary, $k =_{df} |\ succ(n)\ |$, function $\mathcal{M}_n : \mathcal{P}(\mathcal{Q})^k \to \mathcal{P}(\mathcal{Q})$. It is defined by $\mathcal{C}_{\mathcal{U}} \circ \mathcal{M}'_n$, if $n \in N_B$, and by $\mathcal{M}'_n$, otherwise, where the i-th component of the domain of $\mathcal{M}_n$ is assumed to correspond with the i-th successor m_i of n. The functions $\mathcal{M}'_n$, $n \in N \backslash \{\mathbf{e}\}$, are defined as follows:[6]

---

[5] Restricting $\mathcal{C}_{\mathcal{U}}$ to materialized predicates avoids the introduction of computations, which are off-predicated with non-materialized predicates as in the example of Figure 4(d). Their computation costs may easily exceed those of a saved computation. On the other hand, it may prevent moving a computation out of a loop. Dropping this requirement is an easy means for getting a more aggressive hoisting algorithm.

[6] Defining $\mathcal{M}'_n(Q_1, \dots, Q_k) =_{df} \bigcap_{i \in \{1, \dots, k\}} Q_i$, we get a "tamed" version of hoisting.

$$\forall\,(Q_1,\dots,Q_k) \in \mathcal{P}(\mathcal{Q})^k.\ \mathcal{M}'_n(Q_1,\dots,Q_k)=_{df}$$

$$(i) \qquad \bigcap_{i\in\{1,\dots,k\}} Q_i$$

$$(ii)\ \cup\ \begin{cases} \displaystyle\bigcup_{i\in\{1,\dots,k\}} \{q \in Q_i \mid q \Rightarrow qualPred(\,(n,m_i)\,)\} & \text{if } n \in N_B \\ \emptyset & \text{otherwise} \end{cases}$$

In this definition, line (i) handles the standard case: it collects the set of predicates controlling a computation on every path starting at the branch node. Line (ii), intuitively, collects argumentwise the predicates implying the guarding predicate of the corresponding program branch. Note, line (i) is "conservative." Hoisting is in any sense safe. Line (ii), however, may introduce off-predicated computations along some paths. If this is undesirable, it can simply be avoided by dropping it from the definition. This shows the flexibility of our approach, and the ease and elegance of tuning the algorithm.

Finally, note that for $n \in N\backslash(N_B\cup\{e\})$, the function $\mathcal{M}_n$ is 1-ary. Hence, for these nodes $\mathcal{M}_n$ equals the identity on $\mathcal{P}(\mathcal{Q})$. Based on the functions $\mathcal{M}_n$, $n \in N\backslash(N_B \cup \{e\})$, the fixed-point characterization of the set of hoistable program points is as follows.

Equation System 1 (Hoistability).

$$\mathsf{hst}(n) = \begin{cases} \emptyset & \text{if } n = \mathbf{e} \\ \mathcal{M}_n\{[\![\,(n,m)\,]\!]_{hst}^{\pi}(\mathsf{hst}(m)) \mid m \in succ(n)\} & \text{otherwise} \end{cases}$$

Denoting by hst^* the greatest solution of Equation System 6, we can now determine the earliest safe computation points. To this end we introduce the function $E\text{-}HST_\pi : N \to \mathcal{P}(\mathcal{Q})$. In essence, this function maps every node to the set of predicates under whose control computation π can safely be hoisted to n, but not to all of n's predecessors. Intuitively, for every q in the image of $E\text{-}HST_\pi$ for some n, it is safe to insert an occurrence of $(q)\,\mathbf{h}_\pi = \pi$, while it is not for some of n's predecessors. Safety of the insertion here means that whenever the computation of the right-hand side of the insertion guarded by q is committed, then there is on every *feasible* program path starting at the insertion site and reaching the end node an original computation of π guarded by a predicate, which is implied by q. In other words, the value computed at the insertion site will be used on every program path starting there. The term "feasible" is here related to the definition of the operators $\mathcal{M}'_n$ introduced above. This means, if they are defined with respect to line (i) only, feasible means *every* path according to the usual nondeterministic interpretation of branching conditions. If it is defined with respect to lines (i) and (ii), feasible means the subset of paths respecting the implications taken care of by line (ii). If the computation of an insertion is not committed, this feasibility constraint does not apply. In this case, there may be paths on which this insertion has been added as an off-predicated one.

It is worth noting that certain insertions can be suppressed. This is because insertions predicated by q, for which there is a $q' \in E\text{-}HST_\pi(n)$ with $q \Rightarrow q'$ are obviously redundant. This is taken into account by means of a non-deterministic *cut* operator defined on $\mathcal{P}(\mathcal{Q})$, which we denote by *Cut*. It maps an argument $Q \in \mathcal{P}(\mathcal{Q})$ to a *maximal* subset Q' of Q satisfying

$$\forall q, q' \in Q'. \text{ If } q \Rightarrow q' \text{ then } q = q'$$

Note that Q' is usually not uniquely determined by this constraint. If there are elements q and q' in Q with $q \Longleftrightarrow q'$, then *Cut* has a non-trivial choice. The function $E\text{-}HST_\pi : N \rightarrow \mathcal{P}(\mathcal{Q})$ is now defined as follows:

$$\forall n \in N. \ E\text{-}HST_\pi(n) =_{df} Cut(\mathbf{hst}^*(n) \backslash \bigcup \{\mathbf{hst}^*(m) \mid m \in pred(n)\})$$

As assignments are attached to edges rather than nodes, we introduce next the "predicate" $Insert_{cpt_\pi} : E_X \rightarrow \mathcal{P}(\mathcal{Q})$ induced by $E\text{-}HST_\pi$.[7] It is defined by:[8]

$$\forall e \in E_X. \ Insert_{cpt_\pi}(e) =_{df} E\text{-}HST_\pi(dst(e))$$

The index "cpt" (short for "conceptually") reminds to the fact that insertions need not immediately be done by an implementation. In fact, usually some of them are globally redundant with respect to other insertions or off-predicated, and will only be detected by the following redundancy analysis. For clarity, however, we make this insertion step here explicit. It is given by:

– For all edges $e \in E$ with $Insert_{cpt_\pi}(e) \neq \emptyset$ do: Insert at the very end of e an occurrence of the instantiated computation pattern (p) $\mathbf{h}_\pi := \pi$, which is preceded by the statement initializing the qualifying predicate p:[9]

$$p = \bigvee \{q \mid q \in Insert_{cpt_\pi}(e)\}$$

Before proceeding with the redundancy analysis, it should be noted that in the definition of $E\text{-}HST_\pi$ simply subtracting the union $\bigcup \{\mathbf{hst}^*(m) \mid m \in pred(n)\}$ is sound because of the edge splitting we assumed for G. The edge splitting guarantees that every edge ending in a join node is labeled by skip. This guarantees the validity of the first part of Lemma 1, which directly implies the required statements of its second and third part.

Lemma 1. *1.* $\forall n \in N_J \ \forall m \in pred(n). \ \mathbf{hst}^*(n) = \mathbf{hst}^*(m)$
2. $\forall n \in N \ \forall m \in pred(n). \ \mathbf{hst}^*(m) = \bigcup \mathbf{hst}^*(n') \mid n' \in pred(n)\}$
3. $\forall e \in E. \ dst(e) \in N_J \Rightarrow Insert_{cpt_\pi}(e) = \emptyset$

---

[7] Note that $Insert_{cpt}$ is not really a predicate as its domain is the powerset of $\mathcal{Q}$. We call it a predicate here in order to emphasize its role as counterpart of the insertion predicate known from PRE-algorithms for conventional settings.

[8] We assume that $\mathbf{s}$ is reached by a "virtual" edge $e_{virtual}$, where in case of need, i.e., if $E\text{-}HST_\pi(\mathbf{s}) \neq \emptyset$, the required insertions are made. The extension of E by $e_{virtual}$ is indicated by the index X.

[9] Usually, this statement must be split into a sequence of 3-address statements.

3.1.3 Redundancy Analysis In this step, redundant insertions and computations are identified, which are globally redundant with respect to the hoisted computations specified by $Insert_{cpt_\pi}$. This property is usually known as *availability* [22] or *up-safety* [17], and defined with respect to the original occurrences of the computation pattern under consideration. Here, however, it is defined and computed with respect to their hoisted counterparts. The redundancy analysis requires a forward analysis of the program, and relies on the local semantic functional

$$[\![\ ]\!]^\pi_{rd} : E \to (\mathcal{P}(\mathcal{Q}) \to \mathcal{P}(\mathcal{Q}))$$

where the index "rd" reminds to *redundancy*. It is defined as follows:

$$\forall e \in E \ \forall Q \in \mathcal{P}(\mathcal{Q}). \ [\![\ e\ ]\!]^\pi_{rd}(Q) =_{df} \mathcal{C}_\mathcal{L}(Insert_{cpt_\pi}(e) \cup \{q \in Q \mid Transp_\pi(e)(q)\})$$

The intuition given for the hoistability analysis by referring to very busyness applies here analogously by referring to availability. In particular, like the hoistability analysis, also the redundancy analysis, i.e., the functions $[\![\ e\ ]\!]_{rd}$, $e \in E$, rely on a closure operator. This time, however, it is a *(lower) closure operator* on $\mathcal{P}(\mathcal{Q})$, essentially with respect to $\sqcap$, in symbols $\mathcal{C}_\mathcal{L} : \mathcal{P}(\mathcal{Q}) \to \mathcal{P}(\mathcal{Q})$. For all $Q \in \mathcal{P}(\mathcal{Q})$, $\mathcal{C}_\mathcal{L}(Q)$ is the smallest set $Q' \in \mathcal{P}(\mathcal{Q})$ such that

- $Q \subseteq Q'$
- If $q' \in Q'$ and $q \in Q$ such that $q \Rightarrow q'$, then $q \in Q'$

Like the upper closure operator $\mathcal{C}_\mathcal{U}$, the lower closure operator $\mathcal{C}_\mathcal{L}$ introduces a semantic flavour in the redundancy analysis. It allows us to syntactically detect occurrences of predicated computations, which are redundant with respect to insertions guarded by syntactically different predicates.

The fixed point characterization of the redundancy analysis is now as follows.

Equation System 2 (Redundancy).

$$\mathbf{rd}(n) = \begin{cases} Insert_{cpt_\pi}(e_{virtual}) & \text{if } n = \mathbf{s} \\ \bigcap\{[\![\ (m,n)\ ]\!]^\pi_{rd}(\mathbf{rd}(m)) \mid m \in pred(n)\} & \text{otherwise} \end{cases}$$

Let $\mathbf{rd}^*$ denote the greatest solution of Equation System 8. We are now ready to present the transformation step of our PRE-algorithm.

3.2 Transformation Phase

3.2.1 Insertions and Replacements In this step all original computations are replaced by the temporary $\mathbf{h}_\pi$ associated with the computation pattern π. Moreover, all insertions made after the hoistability analysis,[10] which are either redundant or off-predicated are eliminated. While the first step, i.e., replacing the original computations, is trivial, the second step, i.e., removing redundant and

---

[10] For explanatory reasons we assumed that these insertions have been made. In an actual implementation this can be avoided as sketched at the end of this section.

off-predicated insertions, relies on the predicate $Remove_\pi$ defined next. Here, At_e, $e \in E_X$, relies on information delivered by the preprocessing step discussed in Section 3.1. Intuitively, $At_e(p \Rightarrow false)$ is *true*, if and only if at edge e the qualifying predicate p is equivalent to *false*. In this case, the computation inserted under the control of p is off-predicated and can be suppressed.

- $Remove_\pi : E \to \mathcal{P}(\mathcal{Q})$ defined for all $e \in E$ by $Remove_\pi(e) =_{df}$

$$\{p \in Insert_{cpt_\pi}(e) \mid At_e(p \Rightarrow false) \vee (\exists q \in \mathbf{rd}^*(src(e)). \ p \Rightarrow q)\}$$

The final transformation step, which for the running example of Figure 2 yields the basic optimization displayed in Figure 3, is as follows. Its result is the counterpart of the busy-code-motion transformation of [17] for predicated code.

1. Remove all insertions at edges predicated by an element of $Remove_\pi(e)$.
2. Replace all original occurrences of the computation pattern π by the temporary $\mathbf{h}_\pi$, the one which is uniquely associated with π.

Actually, the first step above reduces to replace the initialization statement

$$p = \bigvee_{q \in Insert_{cpt_\pi}(e)} q \quad \text{by} \quad p = \bigvee_{q \in Insert_{cpt_\pi}(e) \setminus Remove_\pi(e)} q$$

Pragmatics. As mentioned in Section 3.1, an implementation need not to make insertions already after the hoistability analysis and to clean-up here. To achieve this it suffices to replace the insertion predicate $Insert_{cpt_\pi}$ by the predicate $Insert_\pi : E_X \to \mathcal{P}(\mathcal{Q})$ defined as follows:[11]

$$\forall e \in E_X. \ Insert_\pi(e) =_{df} Insert_{cpt_\pi}(e) \setminus Remove_\pi(e)$$

4   Tuning the Algorithm

Central for the transformational power of the algorithm is the hoistability analysis. Essentially, it is controlled by the (1) *closure* operator $\mathcal{C}_\mathcal{U}$, and the (2) *meet* operator $\mathcal{M}$. They are in fact the knobs for tuning the algorithm. We sketched this already in Section 3.1, but demonstrate it here in more detail using the example of Figure 4 for illustration.

Simply by adapting the definitions of $\mathcal{C}_\mathcal{U}$ and $\mathcal{M}$, we obtain variants of the algorithm ending up with either of the programs of Figure 4(b), (c), or (d). While (b) is the most conservative one, which is safe in the strong sense known from conventional PRE of not to introduce any kind of a new computation on a path (this includes off-predicated computations, too.), (c) and (d) take the specialities of predication into account. The transformation underlying (c) may introduce off-predicated computations along some paths, however, off-predicated

---

[11] Presenting the algorithm this way, the predicate *Remove* should be renamed to "UnnecessaryInserts." Unnecessary because they are totally redundant or off-predicated.

by materialized predicates only (see the insertion guarded by $r1$). In contrast, the transformation underlying (d) may introduce off-predicated computations along some paths, which are off-predicated by both materialized and non-materialized predicates (see the insertion guarded by $r4$. The disjunctive constituents $r2$ and $r3$ of $r4$ do not correspond to a materialized predicate).

5   Main Results

In this section we summarize the main results on our PRE-transformation, which we call P-PRE, where the first "P" reminds to "Predicated." First, P-PRE is sound, i.e., insertions are *safe*, and replacements are *correct*. As usual, this means that insertions do not introduce on any path a new (committed) computation of the computation pattern under consideration. For replacements it means that at every use site of a temporary, the temporary stores the same value that would result from a re-evaluation of the computation it replaces. We have:

Theorem 1 (Soundness). *P-PRE is sound, i.e., insertions are safe and replacements are correct.*

Moreover, P-PRE reduces the computational cost of the argument program. On every path the number of computations performed in the transformed program is at most as large as in the original program.

Theorem 2 (Improvement). *P-PRE is improving, i.e., the number of computations of the pattern under consideration performed in the transformed program is on every path smaller or equal to that in the original one.*

Without taking execution frequency profiles into account, improvement is actually the best we can hope for. This is in contrast to the conventional setting, where PRE can be organized to produce *computationally optimal* results, i.e., programs, where no path can be improved any further by means of semantics preserving PRE.[12] On predicated code, however, we are faced with the problem of incomparable minima. This is illustrated in the example of Figure 5. The redundancy between the computations of $a + b$ at edge **2** and **8** in Figure 5(a) can only be removed by introducing a redundancy between the computations of $a+b$ at edge **4** and **11** (cf. Figure 5(b)). In fact, trying to remove this redundancy without re-introducing the former one as shown in Figure 5(c) introduces on the "left-most" path through this program fragment a committed computation of $a + b$ — the one guarded by q —, whenever p is false when passing edge **1**. In this case, however, the corresponding paths of the programs in Figure 5 (a) and (b) would have been free of committed computations of $a + b$. Hence, the two programs of Figure 5 (a) and (b) are of incomparable quality, since the "left-most" path is improved by impairing the "right-most" one. Note that there is no program which improves on both the programs of Figure 5(a) and (b).

---

[12] Note that the impact of instruction level parallelism as provided e.g. by architectures like the IA-64 is an orthogonal issue of later compilation phases, which applies similarly to predicated and unpredicated code.

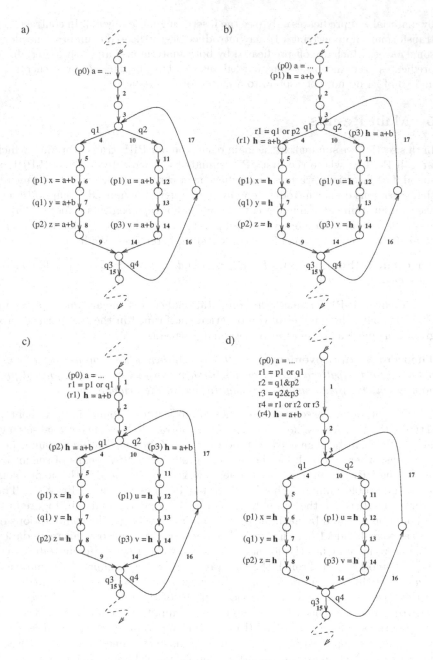

Fig. 4. Tuning the algorithm is easy.

Theorem 3 (Computational Optimality). *On predicated code, computationally optimal PRE-results are in general impossible.*

The impossibility of computational optimality for PRE in general is actually quite typical for advanced settings. Examples, for which this has been shown, too, include semantic PRE, interprocedurally syntactic PRE, and syntactic PRE for parallel programs (cf. [15] for an overview). In fact, predication introduces phenomena which are quite similar to those one encounters for semantic PRE.

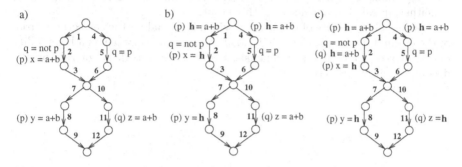

Fig. 5. Computational optimality in general impossible.

Complexity. In comparison to traditional PRE, where a term pattern can be placed in time linear in the program size, the data domain $\mathcal{P}(\mathcal{Q})$ the hoistability and redundancy analyses operate on adds here the number of qualifying predicates as a multiplicative factor to the worst-case time complexity. In practice, however, we expect that the refined analyses working on $\mathcal{P}(\mathcal{Q})$ are almost as efficient as their traditional counterparts working on the lattice of Boolean truth values as the impact of qualifying predicates is usually limited to small program fragments reducing the "effectively observable" chain length of $\mathcal{P}(\mathcal{Q})$.

6   Discussing Design Decisions

Up-safety/down-safety vs. hoistability/redundancy: Correctness. In contrast to *busy code motion* of [17], where the computation of insertion points is based on a pair of a down-safety and up-safety analysis,[13] our approach here is based on a pair of a hoistability and redundancy analysis. While this design decision is irrelevant for the conventional setting, it is important for the setting with predicated code here. In the conventional setting of [17], placing a computation at a certain program point is safe, if it is up-safe or down-safe. Intuitively, this

---

[13] Down-safety and up-safety are also known as very busyness (anticipability) and availability, respectively (cf. [23]).

means, placing a computation at a certain program point n is safe, i.e., it does not introduce the computation of a new value on any path from the program's entry to its exit, if it is computed on all paths originating in **s**, before reaching n without a subsequent modification of any of its operands, or if it is computed on all paths after passing n without such a modification.

The correctness of the transformation as specified in [17] relies on this decomposability of safety into up-safety and down-safety (cf. Safety Lemma [17]).

In the setting here, safety is not decomposable this way. This is demonstrated in the example of Figure 6. Though $a + b$ will be computed (and committed!) on every (maximal) path passing the join node, hence it is safe at this point, it is neither up-safe nor down-safe at this point.

Because of the failure of this lemma, which is crucial for the correctness proof of the original transformation, we decided to base our approach on a hoistability and a subsequent redundancy analysis. Correctness thus does not rely on the decomposability of safety.

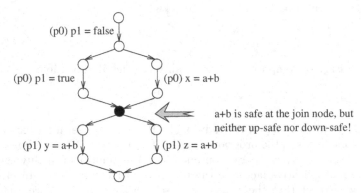

Fig. 6. Failure of the decomposability of safety into up-safety and down-safety.

Data domain $\mathcal{Q}$ vs. $\mathcal{P}(\mathcal{Q})$: Transformational power. A second important design decision concerns the data domain the analyses involved in the transformation rely on. An obvious alternative to working on the power set of $\mathcal{Q}$, would be to work on $\mathcal{Q}$ exploiting e.g. the lattice structure of the PPG (if this is used by the preprocess for providing predicate information), and to directly operate on $\mathcal{Q}$ instead of $\mathcal{P}(\mathcal{Q})$. While the design decision above, was motivated by the issue of *correctness*, the one here is motivated by the one of *transformational power*. In fact, a hoistability analysis working on $\mathcal{Q}$ instead of $\mathcal{P}(\mathcal{Q})$ is inherently weaker because of the domain's greater coarseness in comparison to $\mathcal{P}(\mathcal{Q})$.

In essence, the reason for the loss of transformational power lies in the observation that "the more liberal a predicate is guarding the execution of a computation, the less mobile it is." This is illustrated in the example of Figure 7(a). While the hoisting of $a + b$ guarded by p0 is blocked by the assignment to a at edge **4**, the one guarded by p is not because the conjunction of p and q is always false. While, however, a hoistability analysis working on $\mathcal{Q}$ (correctly) detects that $a + b$ guarded by p0 can safely be hoisted to $dst(4)$, it fails by merging the informations on p and p0 that only p0, however, not p is blocked by the assignment to a. In effect, this prevents hoisting the computation of $a + b$ at **11** out of the loop (cf. Figure 7(b)). In contrast, the finer granularity of $\mathcal{P}(\mathcal{Q})$ allows our analysis to keep track on both informations. As illustrated in Figure 7(c), this enables our analysis to remove the partially redundant computation of $a + b$ at edge **11** from the loop.

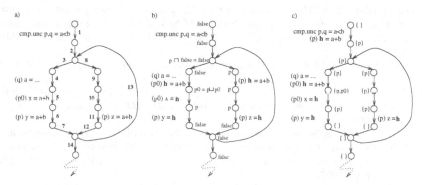

Fig. 7. $\mathcal{Q}$ vs. $\mathcal{P}(\mathcal{Q})$.

7   Conclusions

The advent of new architectures like the IA-64 supporting predicated code imposes new challenges on optimizing compilers. As demonstrated here for PRE, classical techniques are usually inadequate when transferred straightforwardly. In this article, we thus proposed a new approach for PRE, which is tailored for predicated code, while simultaneously retaining as much as possible of the structure and philosophy underlying its traditional counterparts. The basic algorithm of this approach can be considered the counterpart of *busy code motion*. It constitutes the kernel of a family of PRE-algorithms for predicated code of varying power. The members of these family can be derived simply by adapting certain input parameters acting like tuning-knobs for the overall approach. In fact, the pattern of the algorithms remains the same. Similarly, this holds for exchanging the preprocessing step providing information on predicates. Both steps are conceptually clearly separated in our approach making it extremely flexible and highly adaptable to one's specific needs. We believe that the methodology used here to adapt a classical optimization to predicated code may be of important impact for the transfer of other techniques, too. Currently, we are investigating an adaptation of the techniques for *partial dead-code elimination* [18] and *assignment motion* [19].

References

1. J. R. Allen, K. Kennedy, C. Porterfield, and J. Warren. Conversion of control dependence to data dependence. In *Conf. Rec. 10th Symp. on Principles of Prog. Lang.* (*POPL'83*), pages 177 – 189. ACM, NY, 1983. 265

2. R. Bodík and S. Anik. Path-sensitive value-flow analysis. In *Conf. Rec. 25th Symp. on Principles of Prog. Lang.* (*POPL'98*), pages 237 – 251. ACM, NY, 1998. 264

3. P. Briggs and K. D. Cooper. Effective partial redundancy elimination. In *Proc. ACM SIGPLAN Conf. Prog. Lang. Design and Impl.* (*PLDI'94*), volume *29*,6 of *ACM SIGPLAN Not.*, pages 159 – 170, 1994. 264

4. Intel Corp. IA-64 Application Developer's Architecture Guide, May 1999. 261, 265

5. D. M. Dhamdhere, B. K. Rosen, and F. K. Zadeck. How to analyze large programs efficiently and informatively. In *Proc. ACM SIGPLAN Conf. Prog. Lang. Design and Impl.* (*PLDI'92*), volume *27*,7 of *ACM SIGPLAN Not.*, pages 212 – 223, 1992. 264

6. C. Dulong. The IA-64 architecture at work. *IEEE Computer*, 31(7):24 – 32, 1998. 261, 265

7. A. E. Eichenberger and E. S. Davidson. Register allocation for predicated code. In *Proc. 28th Int. Symp. on Microarchitecture* (*MICRO-28*), volume 26, pages 180 – 191, 1995. 268

8. J. Z. Fang. Compiler algorithms on If-conversion, speculative predicate assignment and predicated code optimizations. In *Proc. 9th Int. Workshop on Languages and Compilers for Parallel Computing* (*LCPC'96*), LNCS 1239, pages 135 – 153. Springer-V., 1997. 263, 264

9. D. M. Gillies, D. C. R. Ju, R. Johnson, and M. Schlansker. Global predicate analysis and its application to register allocation. In *Proc. 29th Int. Symp. on Microarchitecture* (*MICRO-29*), volume 27, 1996. 268

10. R. Gupta, D. Berson, and J. Z. Fang. Path profile guided partial dead code elimination using predication. In *Proc. 5th IEEE Int. Conf. on Parallel Arch. and Comp. Techniques* (*PACT'97*), pages 102 – 115. IEEE Comp. Soc., CA, 1997. 264

11. M. S. Hecht. *Flow Analysis of Computer Programs.* Elsevier, North-Holland, 1977. 268

12. L. H. Holley and B. K. Rosen. Qualified data flow problems. *IEEE Trans. Softw. Eng.*, 1(SE-7):60 – 78, 1981. 261

13. R. Johnson and M. Schlansker. Analysis techniques for predicated code. In *Proc. 29th Int. Symp. on Microarchitecture* (*MICRO-29*), volume 27, pages 100 – 113, 1996. 268

14. J. Knoop, J.-F. Collard, and R. D. Ju. Partial redundancy elimination on predicated code: Motivation and algorithm. Technical Report 731/2000, Fachbereich Informatik, Universität Dortmund, Germany, 2000. 263, 264

15. J. Knoop and O. Rüthing. Optimization under the perspective of soundness, completeness, and reusability. In E.-R. Olderog and B. Steffen, editors, *Correct System Design – Recent Insights and Advances*, LNCS State-of-the-Art Survey, vol. 1710, pages 288 – 315. Springer-V., 1999. (Invited contribution). 276

16. J. Knoop, O. Rüthing, and B. Steffen. Lazy code motion. In *Proc. ACM SIGPLAN Conf. Prog. Lang. Design and Impl.* (*PLDI'92*), volume *27*,7 of *ACM SIGPLAN Not.*, pages 224 – 234, 1992. 261, 262, 264, 266, 268

17. J. Knoop, O. Rüthing, and B. Steffen. Optimal code motion: Theory and practice. *ACM Trans. Prog. Lang. Syst.*, 16:1117–1155, 1994. 260, 261, 262, 264, 272, 273, 276, 277

280   Jens Knoop et al.

18. J. Knoop, O. Rüthing, and B. Steffen. Partial dead code elimination. In *Proc. ACM SIGPLAN Conf. Prog. Lang. Design and Impl. (PLDI'94)*, volume *29*,6 of *ACM SIGPLAN Not.*, pages 147 – 158, 1994. 268, 279

19. J. Knoop, O. Rüthing, and B. Steffen. The power of assignment motion. In *Proc. ACM SIGPLAN Conf. Prog. Lang. Design and Impl. (PLDI'95)*, volume *30*,6 of *ACM SIGPLAN Not.*, pages 233 – 245, 1995. 279

20. J. Knoop, O. Rüthing, and B. Steffen. Code motion and code placement: Just synomyms? In *Proc. 7th European Symp. on Programming (ESOP'98)*, LNCS 1381, pages 154 – 169. Springer-V., 1998. 263, 264

21. S. A. Mahlke, D. C. Lin, W. Y. Chen, R. E. Hank, and R. A. Bringmann. Effective compiler support for predicated execution using the hyperblock. In *Proc. 25th Int. Symp. on Microarchitecture (MICRO-25)*, volume 23:1&2, pages 45 – 54, 1992. 268

22. E. Morel and C. Renvoise. Global optimization by suppression of partial redundancies. *Comm. ACM*, 22(2):96 – 103, 1979. 263, 264, 268, 272

23. S. S. Muchnick. *Advanced Compiler Design and Implementation*. Morgan Kaufmann, San Francisco, CA, 1997. 276

24. B. K. Rosen, M. N. Wegman, and F. K. Zadeck. Global value numbers and redundant computations. In *Conf. Rec. 15th Symp. Principles of Prog. Lang. (POPL'88)*, pages 2 – 27. ACM, NY, 1988. 264

25. O. Rüthing, J. Knoop, and B. Steffen. Sparse code motion. In *Conf. Rec. 27th Symp. Principles of Prog. Lang. (POPL 2000)*, pages 170 – 183. ACM, NY, 2000. 264, 268

26. B. Steffen, J. Knoop, and O. Rüthing. The value flow graph: A program representation for optimal program transformations. In *Proc. 3rd Europ. Symp. Programming (ESOP'90)*, LNCS 432, pages 389 – 405. Springer-V., 1990. 264

27. N. J. Warter, S. A. Mahlke, Wen-Mei Hwu, and B. R. Rau. Reverse if-conversion. In *Proc. ACM SIGPLAN Conf. Prog. Lang. Design and Impl. (PLDI'93)*, volume *28*,6 of *ACM SIGPLAN Not.*, pages 290–299, 1993. 263

TVLA: A System for Implementing Static Analyses*

Tal Lev-Ami and Mooly Sagiv

Department of Computer Science, Tel-Aviv University, Israel
{tla,sagiv}@math.tau.ac.il

Abstract. We present TVLA (Three-Valued-Logic Analyzer). TVLA is a "YACC"-like framework for automatically constructing static-analysis algorithms from an operational semantics, where the operational semantics is specified using logical formulae. TVLA has been implemented in Java and was successfully used to perform shape analysis on programs manipulating linked data structures (singly and doubly linked lists), to prove safety properties of Mobile Ambients, and to verify the partial correctness of several sorting programs.

1   Introduction

The abstract-interpretation technique [5] for static analysis allows one to summarize the behavior of a statement on an infinite set of possible memory states. This is sometimes called an *abstract semantics* for the statement. With this methodology it is necessary to show that the abstract semantics is *conservative*, i.e., it summarizes the (*concrete*) *operational semantics* of the statement for every possible memory state. Intuitively speaking, the operational semantics of a statement is a formal definition of an interpreter for this statement. This operational semantics is usually quite natural. However, designing and implementing sound and reasonably precise abstract semantics is quite cumbersome (the best induced abstract semantics defined in [5] is usually not computable). This is particularly true in problems like shape analysis and pointer analysis (e.g., see [6,17,15]), where the operational semantics involves destructive memory updates.

In this paper, we present TVLA (**T**hree-**V**alued-**L**ogic **A**nalyzer), a system for automatically generating a static-analysis algorithm from the operational semantics of a given program. The operational semantics is written in a special form, based on first-order predicate logic with transitive closure. An additional input to TVLA is an abstract representation of all the possible memory states at the beginning of the analyzed program. TVLA automatically generates the abstract semantics, and, for each program point, produces a conservative abstract representation of the memory states at that point.

---

* Supported, in part, by a grant from the Academy of Science, Israel.

J. Palsberg (Ed.): SAS 2000, LNCS 1824, pp. 280–302, 2000.

1.1 Main Results

TVLA is intended as a proof of concept for intra-procedural shape analysis, and other static-analysis algorithms. It is a test-bed in which it is quite easy to try out new ideas. The theory behind TVLA is based on [16,17] (see Sect. 5.2). The system is publicly available from http://www.math.tau.ac.il/~tla.

TVLA was implemented in Java and has been successfully used to perform shape analysis on programs manipulating linked data structures (singly and doubly linked lists), to prove safety properties of Mobile Ambients, and to verify partial correctness of several programs. We also report on some programs that are too complex for the current system. The system was tested on a Pentium II 400 MHz running Linux with JDK 1.2. All the timing information about the system refers to this computer[1].

Applications TVLA has been utilized to analyze a variety of small but intricate programs from the groups described below.

Singly Linked Lists. We performed shape analysis on the set of programs manipulating singly linked lists used in [7], including ones for searching, element insertion, and element deletion. These programs perform destructive updating. Some of these programs are (deliberately) semantically incorrect, and we are able to locate the bugs in them. The analysis times are reported in AppendixA.

Doubly Linked Lists. Doubly linked lists are more challenging than singly linked lists because they create shared memory cells and cycles. We have analyzed a program that inserts a new element into an arbitrary place in a doubly linked list, and the analysis was able to conclude that the insertion results in a doubly linked list.

Sorting Programs. A different kind of application of TVLA is for program verification (see [11]). We applied TVLA to several implementations of sorting algorithms, and proved that, given a possibly unsorted linked list as input, we always end up with a sorted list. This is proven without the need for programmer-specified loop invariants. Instead, the operational semantics also keeps track of inequalities between the list elements. We are encouraged by the fact that we have successfully verified both insert sort and bubble sort on singly linked lists.

Mobile Ambients. We implemented the analysis of [13] and found out that it is imprecise and quite slow. This motivated us to generalize the techniques presented in [16,17] in order to guarantee that only a constant number of structures arise at each program point (see Sect. 3.4). With this extension, TVLA was able to successfully analyze a slight variant of the original specification used in [13]. This took 336 CPU seconds and the analysis proved the necessary properties (uniqueness of ambient instance and mutual exclusion) precisely.

---

[1] Our experience indicates that using JVM on Windows, the system runs about 20% faster.

1.2   Outline of the Paper

The rest of the paper is organized as follows. In Sect. 2, we give a primer on the use of 3-valued logic in static analysis. Sect. 3 contains an overview of the TVLA system and its capabilities. Sect. 4 gives a description of the analyses done with the system. We conclude by summarizing related work and further research directions (Sect. 5). Appendix A presents the empirical results for test runs of the system. Appendix B presents an operational semantics for statements manipulating nodes of singly linked lists. For other aspects of TVLA, including algorithms, proofs, description of other features, additional examples, and a user's manual, we refer the reader to [10].

A program that destructively reverses a singly linked list is shown in Fig. 1. The shape analysis of this program serves as a running example in this paper.

```
                                /* reverse.c */
                                #include "list.h"
                                L reverse(L x) {
                                  L y, t;
        /* list.h */              y = NULL;
        typedef struct node        while (x != NULL) {
        {                            t = y;
          struct node *n;            y = x;
          int data;                  x = x->n;
        } *L;                        y->n = t;
                                     t = NULL;
                                   }
                                   return y;
                                 }
              (a)                           (b)
```

Fig. 1. (a) Declaration of a linked-list data type in C. (b) A C function that uses destructive updates to reverse the list pointed to by parameter x.

2   A Primer on 3-Valued-Logic-Based Analysis

Kleene's 3-valued logic is an extension of ordinary 2-valued logic with the special value of $1/2$ (unknown) for cases that can be either 1 or 0. Kleene's interpretation of the propositional operators is given in Table 1. We say that the values 0 and 1 are *definite values* and that $1/2$ is an *indefinite value*.

Table 1. Kleene's 3-valued interpretation of the propositional operators.

$\wedge$	0	1	1/2		$\vee$	0	1	1/2		$\neg$	
0	0	0	0		0	0	1	1/2		0	1
1	0	1	1/2		1	1	1	1		1	0
1/2	0	1/2	1/2		1/2	1/2	1	1/2		1/2	1/2

2.1   Representing Memory States via Logical Structures

Our vocabulary includes a set of predicate symbols partitioned into two disjoint sets: *core* and *instrumentation* predicates. Instrumentation predicates are used to observe derived properties based on core predicates.

A 2-*valued logical structure* S is comprised of a set of individuals (nodes) called a universe, denoted by U^S, and an interpretation over that universe for a set of predicate symbols. The interpretation of a predicate symbol p in S is denoted by p^S. For every (core and instrumentation) predicate p of arity k, p^S is a function $p^S : (U^S)^k \rightarrow \{0, 1\}$. 2-valued structures are used to represent memory states used in the operational semantics of the program.

TVLA makes an explicit assumption that the set of predicate symbols used throughout the analysis is fixed. (The number of individuals in structures can vary throughout the analysis.)

TVLA only supports predicates of arity ≤ 2; such logical structures can be thought of as directed graphs. A directed edge labeled by p from u_1 to u_2 denotes that $p^S(u_1, u_2) = 1$. Also, we draw p inside a node u when $p^S(u) = 1$.

Table 2. The core predicates used in the analysis of the running example.

Predicate	Intended Meaning
$x(v)$	Is v pointed to by variable x?
$y(v)$	Is v pointed to by variable y?
$t(v)$	Is v pointed to by variable t?
$n(v_1, v_2)$	Does the n-field of v_1 point to v_2?

Example 1. In the running example, a 2-valued structure represents a memory state (also called a *store*); an individual corresponds to a list element. The intended meaning of the core predicates is given in Table 2, and the intended meaning of the instrumentation predicates is given in Table 3 (for the moment ignore the third column). The store in Fig. 2 is represented by the 2-valued structure S_3 shown in Fig. 3. The structure S_3 has four nodes, u_0, u_1, u_2, and u_3 representing the four list elements. This representation intentionally ignores the values of the data field, which are usually immaterial for the analysis.

Table 3. The instrumentation predicates used in the analysis of the running example and their meaning. Similar instrumentation predicates are used in all of our shape analyses for singly linked lists. The defining formulae are explained in Sect. 2.3.

Predicate	Intended Meaning	Defining Formula
$r[n,x](v)$	Is v reachable from program variable x using field n?	$\exists v_1 : (x(v_1) \wedge n^*(v_1, v))$
$r[n,y](v)$	Is v reachable from program variable y using field n?	$\exists v_1 : (y(v_1) \wedge n^*(v_1, v))$
$r[n,t](v)$	Is v reachable from program variable t using field n?	$\exists v_1 : (t(v_1) \wedge n^*(v_1, v))$
$c[n](v)$	Does v reside on a directed cycle via dereferences along n-fields?	$n^+(v, v)$
$is[n](v)$	Is v pointed to by more than one n-field	$\exists v_1, v_2 : n(v_1, v) \wedge n(v_2, v) \wedge v_1 \neq v_2$

Pointer variables are represented by unary predicates (i.e., $x^S(u) = 1$ if the variable x points to the list element represented by u). In Fig. 3, the variable x is represented by the unary predicate x, which is 1 only for u_0. Notice that TVLA allows the user to specify that a unary predicate is drawn as a box with an arrow into each node for which it holds. In Fig. 3, x is drawn as a box and has an arrow to u_0. Pointer fields within the list elements are represented as binary predicates (i.e., $n^S(u_1, u_2) = 1$ if the n-field of u_1 points to u_2).

The instrumentation predicate $r[n,x]$ holds for list elements that are reachable from program variable x, possibly using a sequence of accesses through the n-field. The structure S_3 in Fig. 3 has $r[n,x]^{S_3}$ set to 1 for all the nodes because they are all reachable from x. An important aspect of explicitly storing $r[n,x]$ is that we can incrementally compute the appropriate values for the predicates after execution of the program statement (see [17, Sect. 6.1]). For example, for the statement y = x, the nodes reachable from y after the statement executes are the same as the nodes reachable from x.

The instrumentation predicate $is[n]$ holds for nodes shared by n-fields (a node is *shared* by n-fields, if it is pointed to by more than one list element using the field n). In Fig. 3, all the elements of the list are unshared, and thus $is[n]^{S_3}$ is 0 for all of them.

The instrumentation predicate $c[n]$ holds for nodes on a cycle of accesses along n-fields. We use the cyclicity instrumentation to avoid performing a transitive-closure operation when updating the reachability information. In Fig. 3, the list is acyclic, and thus $c[n]^{S_3}$ is 0 for all of the nodes.

In fact, throughout the analysis of the running example, $is[n]^S$ and $c[n]^S$ are 0 for all of the nodes.

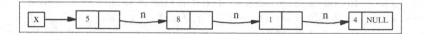

Fig. 2. A possible store for the running example.

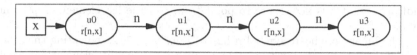

Fig. 3. A logical structure S_3 representing the store shown in Fig. 2 in a graphical representation.

2.2 Conservative Representation of Sets of Memory States via 3-valued Structures

Like 2-valued structures, a 3-*valued logical structure* S is also comprised of a universe U^S, and an interpretation p^S for every predicate symbol p. But, for every predicate p of arity k, p^S is a function $p^S : (U^S)^k \rightarrow \{0, 1, 1/2\}$, where $1/2$ explicitly captures unknown predicate values.

3-valued logical structures are also drawn as directed graphs. Definite values are drawn as in the 2-valued structures. Binary indefinite ($1/2$) predicate values are drawn as dotted directed edges. Unary indefinite predicate values are drawn inside the nodes and marked as indefinite (this does not occur in the running example).

Let $S^\natural$ be a 2-valued structure, S be a 3-valued structure, and $f : U^{S^\natural} \rightarrow U^S$ such that f is surjective. We say that f *embeds* $S^\natural$ *into* S if for every predicate p of arity k and $u_1, u_2, \ldots, u_k \in U^{S^\natural}$, either $p^{S^\natural}(u_1, u_2, \ldots, u_k) = p^S(f(u_1), f(u_2), \ldots, f(u_k))$ or $p^S(f(u_1), f(u_2), \ldots, f(u_k)) = 1/2$. We say that S *conservatively represents all the 2-valued structures that can be embedded into it with some function* f. Thus, S can compactly represent many structures.

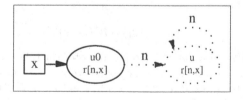

Fig. 4. A 3-valued structure S_4 representing lists of length 2 or more that are pointed to by program variable x(e.g., S_3).

Example 2. In the running example, the 3-valued structure S_4 shown in Fig. 4 represents the 2-valued structure S_3 for $f(u_0) = u_0$ and $f(u_1) = f(u_2) = f(u_3) = u$. In fact, the structure shown in Fig. 4 represents all the lists with two or more elements.

The unary predicate symbol x has $x^{S_4}(u_0) = 1$, indicating that the program variable x is known to point to the list element represented by u_0, and $x^{S_4}(u)=0$, indicating that x is known not to point to any of the list elements represented by u.

The binary predicate symbol n has $n^{S_4}(u_0, u) = 1/2$, indicating that the n-field of the list element represented by u_0 may point to a list element represented by u — namely the second list element (u_1 in Fig. 3) — but does not point to all the list elements represented by u (e.g. u_2 in Fig. 3). Also, $n^{S_4}(u, u) = 1/2$, indicating that the n-field of a list element represented by u may point to another list element represented by u or even to itself but does not point to all the list elements represented by u (e.g., in Fig. 3 the n-field of u_2 points to u_3, but not to u_1).

Summary nodes Nodes in a 3-valued structure that may represent more than one individual from a given 2-valued structure are called *summary nodes*. For example, in the structure shown in Fig. 3, the nodes u_1, u_2, and u_3 are represented by the single node u in Fig. 4.

TVLA uses a special designated unary predicate sm to maintain summary-node information. Such a summary node w has $sm^S(w) = 1/2$, indicating that it may represent more than one node in the embedded 2-valued structures. These nodes are graphically drawn as dotted ellipsis. In contrast, if $sm^S(w) = 0$ then w is known to represent a unique node. Only nodes with $sm^S(w) = 1/2$ can have more than one node mapped to them by the embedding function.

The exact choice of which nodes should be summarized is crucial for the precision of the analysis and is discussed in Sect. 3.2.

2.3   Formulae

Properties of structures can be extracted by evaluating formulae. We use first-order logic with transitive closure and equality, but without function symbols and constant symbols. For example, the formula

$$\exists v_1 : (x(v_1) \land n^*(v_1, v)) \tag{1}$$

extracts reachability information. Here, n^* denotes the reflexive transitive closure of the predicate n. Therefore, in every structure S, $x(v_1)$ evaluates to 1 if v_1 is the node pointed to by x and $n^*(v_1, v)$ evaluates to 1 in S if there exists a path of zero or more n-edges from v_1 to v. The third column of Table 3 displays the defining formula of all the instrumentation predicates used in the running example.

We say that a formula φ is potentially satisfied on a structure S if there exists an assignment that evaluates φ to 1 or 1/2 on S.

The Embedding Theorem. The Embedding Theorem (see [16, Theorem 3.7]) states that any formula that evaluates to a definite value in a 3-valued structure evaluates to the same value in all the 2-valued structures embedded into that structure. The Embedding Theorem is the foundation for the use of 3-valued logic in static-analysis: it ensures that it is sensible to reinterpret on the 3-valued structures the formulae, that when interpreted in 2-valued logic, define the operational semantics.

TVLA requires each instrumentation predicate to be associated with a formula over the core predicates defining its meaning. For example, evaluating formula (1) on the 3-valued structure shown in Fig. 4, yields 1 for $v \mapsto u_0$, which indicates that the list element represented by u_0 is reachable from variable x, and 1/2 for $v \mapsto u$, which indicates that the list elements represented by u may or may not be reachable from program variable x. Notice that $r[n, x]^{S_4}(u) = 1$, which is more precise. This is a general principle with instrumentation predicates (referred to as the *instrumentation principle* in [16]). The stored information can be more precise than the result of evaluating the corresponding formula.

3   System Description

The input to TVLA consists of two files: (i) a TVS (Three Valued logical Structure) file containing a textual representation of the input structures (see Fig. 5), and (ii) a TVP (Three Valued Program) file, which includes the operational semantics and the association of the operational semantics with the edges of the control flow graph (CFG) of the analyzed program (see Figs. 6 and 7). To simplify the specification, we allow the operational semantics to be specific to the analyzed data type (e.g., singly linked lists in the running example). In the conversion of a C program into a TVP file, some normalizing transformations are applied (see [4,15]). For example, the assignment y->n=t is broken into two statements: (i) y->n=NULL, followed by (ii) y->n=t assuming that y->n==NULL. The full operational semantics for programs manipulating singly-linked-lists of type L is given in Appendix B.

$$
\begin{aligned}
\%n &= \{u, u0\} \\
\%p &= \left\{ \begin{array}{ll}
sm & = \{u : 1/2\} \\
n & = \{u \to u : 1/2, u0 \to u : 1/2\} \\
x & = \{u0 : 1\} \\
r[n, x] & = \{u : 1, u0 : 1\}
\end{array} \right\}
\end{aligned}
$$

Fig. 5. A TVS structure describing a singly linked list pointed to by x(cf. Fig. 4).

3.1   TVP

There are two challenging aspects to writing a good TVP specification: one is the design of the instrumentation predicates, which is important for the precision of the analysis; the other is writing the operational semantics manipulating these predicates.

An important observation is that the TVP specification should always be thought of in the terms of the concrete 2-valued world rather than the abstract 3-valued world: the Embedding Theorem guarantees the soundness of the reinterpretation of the formulae in the abstract world. This is an application of the well-known credo of Patrick and Radhia Cousot that the design of a static analysis always starts with a concrete operational semantics.

```
/* Declarations */
%s PVar {x, y, t} // The set of program variables
#include "pred.tvp" // Core and Instrumentation Predicates
%%
/* An Operational Semantics */
#include "cond.tvp" // Operational Semantics of Conditions
#include "stat.tvp" // Operational Semantics of Statements
%%
/* The program's CFG and the effect of its edges */
n₁ Set_Null_L(y) n₂            // y = NULL;
n₂ Is_Null_Var(x) exit         // x == NULL
n₂ Is_Not_Null_Var(x) n₃       // x != NULL
n₃ Copy_Var_L(t, y) n₄         // t = y;
n₄ Copy_Var_L(y, x) n₅         // y = x;
n₅ Get_Next_L(x, x) n₆         // x = x->n;
n₆ Set_Next_Null_L(y) n₇       // y->n = NULL;
n₇ Set_Next_L(y, t) n₈         // y->n = t;
n₈ Set_Null_L(t) n₂            // t = NULL;
```

Fig. 6. The TVP file for the running example shown in Fig. 1. Files pred.tvp, cond.tvp, and stat.tvp are given in Figures 7, 11, and 12 respectively.

The TVP file is divided into sections separated by %%, given in the order described below.

Declarations The first section of the TVP file contains all the declarations needed for the analysis.

Sets. The first declaration in the TVP file is the set *PVar*, which specifies the variables used in the program (here x, y, and t). In the remainder of the specification, set notation allows the user to define the operational semantics for all programs manipulating a certain data type, i.e., it is parametric in *PVar*.

Predicates. The predicates for manipulating singly linked lists as declared in Fig. 1(a) are given in Fig. 7. The **foreach** clause iterates over all the program variables in the set *PVar* and for each of them defines the appropriate core predicate — the unary predicates x, y, and t (**box** tells TVLA to display the predicate as a box). The binary predicate n represents the pointer field **n**.

For readability, we use some mathematical symbols here that are written in C-like syntax in the actual TVP file (see [10, Appendix B]).

The second **foreach** clause (in Fig. 7) uses *PVar* to define the reachability instrumentation predicates for each of the variables of the program (as opposed to Table 3, which is program specific). Thus, to analyze other programs that manipulate singly linked lists the only declaration that is changed is that of *PVar*.

The fact that the TVP file is specific for the data type L declared in Fig. 1(a) allows us to explicitly refer to n.

```
/* pred.tvp */
foreach (z in PVar) {
    %p z(v₁) unique box // Core predicates corresponding to program variables
}
%p n(v₁, v₂) function // n-field core predicate
%i is[n](v) = ∃v₁, v₂ : (n(v₁, v) ∧ n(v₂, v) ∧ v₁ ≠ v₂) // Is shared instrumentation
foreach (z in PVar) {
    %i r[n, z](v) = ∃v₁ : (z(v₁) ∧ n*(v₁, v)) // Reachability instrumentation
}
%i c[n](v) = ∃v₁ : n(v, v₁) ∧ n*(v₁, v) // Cyclicity instrumentation
```

Fig. 7. The TVP predicate declarations for manipulating linked lists as declared in Fig. 1 (a). The core predicates are taken from Table 2. Instrumentation predicates are taken from Table 3.

Functional properties. TVLA also supports a concept of *functional properties* borrowed from the database community. Since program variables can point to at most one heap cell at a time, they are declared as **unique**. The binary predicate n represents the pointer field **n**; the n-field of each list element can only point to at most one target list element, and thus n is declared as a (partial) **function**.

Actions In the second section of the TVP file, we define *actions* that specify the operational semantics of program statements and conditions. An action defines a 2-valued structure transformer. The actions are associated with CFG edges in the third section of the TVP file.

An action specification consists of several parts, each of which is optional (the meaning of these constructs is explained in Sect. 3.2). There are three major parts to the action: (i) Focus formulae (explained in Sect. 3.2), (ii) precondition formula specifying when the action is evaluated, and (iii) update formulae specifying the actual structure transformer. For example, the action Is_Null_Var(x1) (see Fig. 11) specifies when the true branch of the condition x1 == NULL, is enabled by means of the formula $\neg \exists v : x1(v)$, which holds if x1 does not point to any list element. Since this condition has no side effects there are no update formulae associated with this action and thus the structure remains unchanged. As another example, the action Copy_Var_L(x1, x2) (see Fig. 12) specifies the semantics the statement x1 = x2. It has no precondition, and its side effect is to set the $x1$ predicate to $x2$ and the $r[n, x1]$ predicate to $r[n, x2]$.

CFG The third section of the TVP specification is the CFG with actions associated with each of its edges. The edges are specified as **source action target**. The first CFG node that appears in the specification is the entry node of the CFG. The CFG specification for the running example, is given in Fig. 6.

3.2 Process

This section presents a more detailed explanation, using the example shown in Fig. 8, of how the effect of an action associated with a CFG edge is computed. To complete the picture, an iterative (fixed-point) algorithm to compute the result of static-analysis is presented in Sect. 3.3.

Focus First, the Focus operation converts the input structure into a more refined set of structures that represents the same 2-valued structures as the input structure. Given a formula, Focus guarantees that the formula never evaluates to 1/2 in the focused structures. Focus (and Coerce) are semantic reductions (see [5]), i.e., they transfer a 3-valued structure into a set of 3-valued structures representing the same memory states. An algorithm for Focus of a general formula is given in [10]. In the running example, the most interesting focus formula is $\exists v_1 : x(v_1) \wedge n(v_1, v)$, which determines the value of the variable x after the Get_Next_L(x, x) action (which corresponds to the statement x = x->n). Focusing on this formula ensures that $x^S(u)$ is definite at every node u in every structure S after the action. Fig. 8 shows how the structure S_{in} is focused for this action. Three cases are considered in refining S_{in}: (i) The n-field of u_0 does not point to any of the list elements represented by u (S_{f0}); (ii) The n-field of u_0 points to all of the list elements represented by u (S_{f1}); and (iii) The n-field of u_0 points to only some of the list elements represented by u (S_{f2}): u is bifurcated into two nodes — nodes pointed to by the n-field of u_0 are represented by $u.1$, and nodes not pointed to by the n-field of u_0 are represented by $u.0$.

As explained later, the result can be improved (e.g., S_{f0} can be discarded since u is not reachable from x, and yet $r[n, x]^{S_{f0}}(u) = 1$). This is solved by the Coerce operation, which is applied after the abstract interpretation of the statement (see Sect. 3.2).

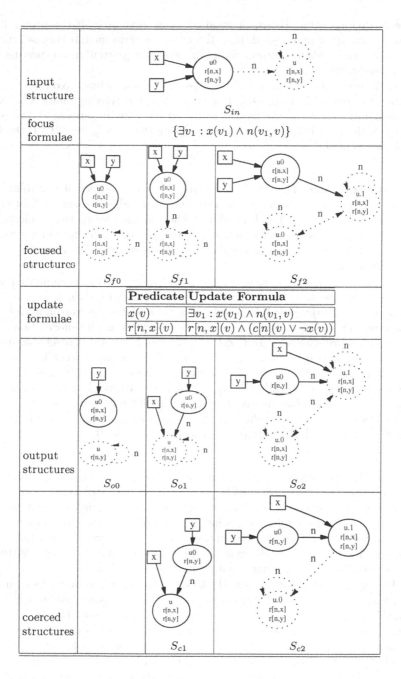

Fig. 8. The first application of abstract interpretation for the statement x = x->n in the reverse function shown in Fig. 1.

Preconditions After Focus, preconditions are evaluated. If the precondition formula is potentially satisfied, then the action is performed; otherwise, the action is ignored. This mechanism comes in handy for (partially) interpreting program conditions.

In the running example, the loop while (x != NULL) has two outgoing edges in the CFG: one with the precondition $\neg(\exists v : x(v))$, specifying that if x is NULL the statement following the loop is executed (the exit in our case). The other edge has the precondition $\exists v : x(v)$, specifying that if x is not NULL the loop body is executed.

Update Formulae The effect of the operational semantics of a statement is described by a set of update formulae defining the value of each predicate after the statement's action. The Embedding Theorem enables us to reevaluate the formulae on the abstract structures and know that the result provides a conservative abstract semantics. If no update formula is specified for a predicate, it is left unchanged by the action.

In Fig. 8, the effect of the Get_Next_L action (x = x->n) is computed using the following update formulae: (i) $x(v) = \exists v_1 : x(v_1) \land n(v_1, v)$, (ii) $r[n, x](v) = r[n, x](v) \land (c[n](v) \lor \neg x(v))$. The first formula updates the xvariable to be the n-successor of the original x. The second formula updates the information about which nodes are reachable from xafter the action: A node is reachable from x after the action if it is reachable from xbefore the action, except for the node directly pointed to by x(unless xappears on an n-cycle, in which case the node pointed to by xis still reachable even though we advanced to its n-successor). For S_{f2}, the update formula for x evaluates to 1 for $v \mapsto u.1$ and to 0 for all nodes other than $u.1$. Therefore, after the action, the resulting structure S_{o2} has $x^{S_{o2}}(u.1) = 1$ but $x^{S_{o2}}(u.0) = 0$ and $x^{S_{o2}}(u_0) = 0$.

Coerce The last stage of the computation is the Coerce operation, which uses a set of consistency rules (defined in [16,17,10]) to make structures more precise by removing unnecessary indefinite values and discarding infeasible structures. The set of consistency rules used is independent of the current action being performed. See [10] for a detailed description of the Coerce algorithm used in TVLA and how TVLA automatically generated consistency rules from the instrumentation predicates and the functional properties of predicates.

For example, Fig. 8 shows how the Coerce operation improves precision. The structure S_{o0} is infeasible because the node u must be reachable from y (since $r[n, y]^{S_{o0}}(u) = 1$) and this is not the case in S_{o0}. In the structure S_{o1}, u is no longer a summary node because x is **unique**; u's self-loop is removed because u already has an incoming n-field and it does not represent a shared list element $(is[n]^{S_{o1}}(u) = 0)$. For the same reason, in S_{o2}, $u.1$ is no longer a summary node; Also, the list element represented by $u.1$ already has an incoming n-field and it is not shared $(is[n]^{S_{o2}}(u.1) = 0)$, and thus $u.1$'s self-loop is removed. For a similar reason, the indefinite n-edge from $u.0$ to $u.1$ is removed.

Blur To guarantee that the analysis terminates on programs containing loops, we require the number of potential structures for a given program to be finite.

Toward this end, we define the concept of a *bounded structure*. For each analysis, we choose a set of unary predicates called the *abstraction predicates*.[2] In the bounded structure, two nodes u_1, u_2 are merged if $p^S(u_1) = p^S(u_2)$ for each abstraction predicate p. When nodes are merged, the predicate values for their non-abstraction predicates are joined (i.e., the result is $1/2$ if their values are different). This is a form of widening (see [5]). The operation of computing this kind of bounded structure is called *Blur*. The choice of abstraction predicates is very important for the balance between space and precision. TVLA allows the user to select the abstraction predicates. By default, all the unary predicates are abstraction predicates, as in the running example.

Example 3. In Fig. 4, the nodes u_0 and u are differentiated by the fact that $x^{S_4}(u_0) = 1$, whereas $x^{S_4}(u) = 0$. (All other predicates are 0.) If x was not an abstraction predicate, then the appropriate bounded structure S'_4 would have had a single node, say u, with $x^{S'_4}(u) = 1/2$ and $n^{S'_4}(u, u) = 1/2$.

After the action is computed and Coerce applied, the Blur operation is used to transform the output structures into bounded structures, thereby generating more compact, but potentially less precise structures.

3.3 Output

Now that we have a method for computing the effect of a single action, what remains is to compute the effect of the whole program, i.e., to compute what structures can arise at each CFG node if the program was used on the given input structures. We use a standard iterative algorithm (e.g., see [12]) with a set of bounded structures as the abstract elements. A new structure is added to the set if the set does not already contain a member that is isomorphic to the new structure. In the running example, the analysis terminates when the structures created in the fourth iteration are isomorphic to the ones created in the third iteration (see Fig. 9). We can see that the analysis precisely captures the behavior of the reverse program.

3.4 Additional Features

One of the main features of TVLA is the support of single structure analysis. Sometimes when the number of structures that arise at each program point is too large, it is better to merge these structures into a single structure that represents at least the same set of 2-valued structures. TVLA enhances this feature even more by allowing the user to specify that some chosen constant number of structures will be associated with each program point.

---

[2] In [16,17] the abstraction predicates are all the unary predicates.

294   Tal Lev-Ami and Mooly Sagiv

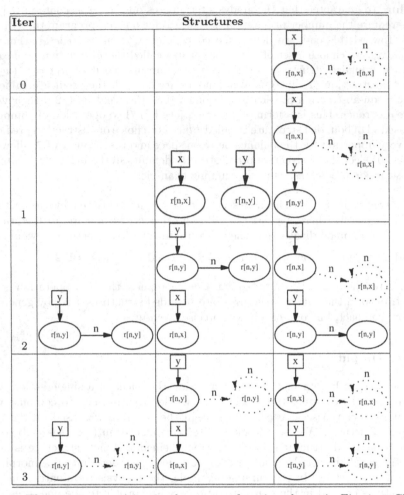

Fig. 9. The structures arising in the reverse function shown in Fig. 1 at CFG node n_2 for the input structure shown in Fig. 4.

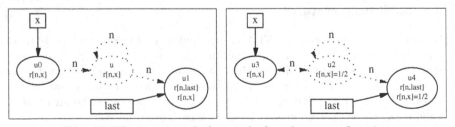

Fig. 10. The structure before and after the rotate function.

More specifically, nullary predicates (i.e., predicates of 0-arity) are used to discriminate between different structures. For example, for linked lists we use the predicate $nn[x]() = \exists v : x(v)$ which discriminates between structures in which x actually points to a list element from structures in which it does not. For example, consider a structure S_1 in which both x and y point to list elements, and another structure S_2 in which both x and y are NULL. Merging S_1 and S_2 will loose the information that x and y are simultaneously allocated or not allocated. Notice that S_1 has $nn[x] = nn[y] = 1$ and S_2 has $nn[x] = nn[y] = 0$ therefore S_1 and S_2 will not be merged together.

In some cases (such as safety analysis of Mobile Ambients, see [13]) this option makes an otherwise infeasible analysis run in a reasonable time. However, there are other cases in which the single-structure method is less precise or even more time consuming than the usual method, which uses sets of structures.

TVLA also supports modeling statements that handle dynamically allocated and freed memory.

4 A Case Study - Singly Linked Lists

We used the functions analyzed in [7] with sharing and reachability instrumentation predicates (see Appendix A). The same specification for the operational semantics of pointer-manipulating statements was used for each of the functions was written once and used with each of the CFGs.

Most of the analyses were very precise, and running times were no more than 8 seconds for even the most complex function (merge).

The **rotate** function performs a cyclic shift on a linked-list. The analysis of this example is not as precise as possible (see Fig. 10). The indefinite edge from u_2 to u_3 is superfluous and all the list elements should be known to be reachable from x. The imprecision arises because the list becomes cyclic in the process, and the 3-valued evaluation of the reachability update-formula in the action Set_Next_Null_L (see Fig. 12) is not very precise in the case of cyclic lists. A simple rewriting of the program to avoid the temporary introduction of a cycle state would have solved the problem.

The **merge** function, which merges two ordered linked-lists, is a good example of how extra instrumentation (reachability) can improve the space consumption of the analysis. Analyzing the merge function without the reachability predicate creates tens of thousands of graphs and takes too much space. Adding the reachability predicate as an instrumentation reduces the number of graphs to 327 and the time to about 8 seconds.

5 Conclusion

The method of 3-valued-logic-based static analysis can handle a wider class of problems than shape analysis. We have successfully analyzed Mobile Ambients [13] even though it is a completely different sort of language for specifying computation. We can also show partial correctness of algorithms such as sorting programs [11].

However, it is clear that some analyses go beyond the scope of TVLA, and it is not obvious whether TVLA can or should be extended to support them. Specifically, the operational semantics must be expressible using first-order logic with transitive closure; in particular, no explicit arithmetic is currently supported, although it can be defined using predicate symbols. Also, the set of predicate symbols is fixed.

The system was implemented in Java, which is an Object-Oriented imperative language. The use of libraries, such as the Collections library, enabled us to incorporate fairly complex data structures without using a more high-level language, such as ML.

Static-analysis algorithms are hard to design, prove correct, and implement. The concept of 3-valued-logic-based analysis greatly simplifies the problem, because it allows us to work with the concrete operational semantics instead of the abstract semantics. The use of 3-valued logic guarantees that the transition to the abstract semantics is sound. TVLA introduces two major contributions toward the simplification of the problem. First, it provides a platform on which one can easily try new algorithms and observe the results. Second, it contains system and algorithmic support for instrumentation information.

5.1   The Essence of Instrumentation

Our experience indicates that instrumentation predicates are essential to achieving efficient and useful analyses. First, they are helpful in debugging the operational semantics. The instrumentation predicates are updated separately from the core predicates, and any discrepancy between them is reported by the system. Our experience indicates that in many cases this reveals bugs in the operational semantics.

The conventional wisdom in static analysis is that there is a trade-off between the time of analysis and its precision (i.e., that a more precise analysis is more expensive). In case of 3-valued-logic-based analysis, this is not always true. Often it happens that an analysis that uses more instrumentation predicates creates fewer unneeded structures, and thus runs faster. A good example of this is the merge function (see Sect. 4) where adding the reachability information drastically reduces both the space and the time needed for the analysis.

In general, the introduction of instrumentation predicates is a very good tool for improving precision, and has a very low cost. If a property holds for many but not all nodes of the structures that arise in a program, then we can use an instrumentation predicate to track at which program points and for which nodes the property holds. This allows us to use the implications of the property without limiting ourselves to programs where the property holds . For example, we use cyclicity instrumentation to update the reachability information. If a singly linked list is acyclic, updating the reachability information can be done more precisely. The use of cyclicity instrumentation allows us to take advantage of this property without limiting the analysis to programs in which lists are always acyclic. Of course, in some programs, such as `rotate`, where cyclicity is temporarily introduced, we may lose precision when evaluating formulae in 3-valued logic. This is in line with the inherent complexity of these problems. For example, updating reachability in general directed graphs is a difficult problem.

Formally, instrumentation predicates allow us to narrow the set of 2-valued structures represented by a 3-valued structure, and thereby avoid making overly conservative assumptions in the abstract interpretation of a statement. For example, the structure shown in Fig. 4 represents an acyclic singly linked list, which means that all of the list elements represented by u are not shared. Thus, $is[n]^S 4(u) = 0$. The same holds for u_0. Without the sharing information, the structure might also represent 2-valued structures in which the linked list ends with a cycle back to itself.

For unary instrumentation predicates, we can fine-tune the precision of an analysis by varying the collection of predicates used as abstraction predicates. The more abstraction predicates used, the finer the distinctions that are made, which leads to a more precise analysis. For example, the fact that is is an abstraction predicate allow us to distinguish between shared and unshared list elements in programs such as the `swap` function, where a list element is temporarily shared. Of course, this may also increase the cost of the analysis.

5.2 Theoretical Contributions

Space precludes us from a comprehensive comparison with [17]. The Coerce algorithm was optimized to avoid unnecessary recomputations by using lazy evaluation, imposing an order of constraint evaluation and using relational database query optimization techniques (see [19]) to evaluate formulae. The Focus algorithm was generalized to handle an arbitrary formula. This was crucial to support the formulae used for analyzing sorting programs. In addition, the Focus algorithm in TVLA was also optimized to take advantage of functional properties of the predicates.

The worst-case space of the analysis was improved from doubly exponential to singly exponential by means of the option in which all the structures with the same nullary predicate values are merged together. Thus, the number of potential structures becomes independent of the number of nodes in the structure. Interestingly, in most of the cases analyzed to date the analysis remains rather precise. However, in some cases it actually increases the space needed for the analysis due to decreased precision.

5.3 Other Analysis Engines

The main advantages of TVLA over existing systems, such as [1,18,2], are: (i) quick prototyping of non-trivial analyses (e.g., sorting); (ii) good control over precision through instrumentation predicates; (iii) good separate control over space requirements through abstraction predicates and the single-structure option; and (iv) the abstract semantics is automatically derived from the concrete operational semantics (i.e., there is no need to specify the abstract semantics directly, which is quite complicated for shape-analysis). However, TVLA currently is intra-procedural only, there is an ongoing research to extend TVLA to handle recursive procedures (see [14]).

5.4   Further Work

The system is very useful in the analysis of small programs. However, there are many theoretical and implementation issues that need to be solved before the analysis can scale to larger programs.

An operational semantics of the instrumentation predicates needs to be specified for all programming language constructs, which can be error-prone. In the future, it may be possible to generate such update formulae for a subset of first-order logic.

The choice of the abstraction predicates is very important for the space/precision trade-off. We lack a good methodology for selecting these predicates.

The major problem in terms of scalability of the system is the space needed for the analysis. We have devised some techniques to alleviate the problem, but they are not enough. A possible solution to the problem may be to use Binary Decision Diagrams (BDDs) to represent logical structures ([3]). Another possible solution is the use of secondary storage.

Acknowledgements

We are grateful for the helpful comments and contributions of N. Dor, M. Fähndrich, G. Laden, F. Nielson, H.R. Nielson, T. Reps, N. Rinetskey, R. Shaham, O. Shmueli, R. Wilhelm, and A. Yehudai.

References

1. M. Alt and F. Martin. Generation of efficient interprocedural analyzers with PAG. In *SAS'95, Static Analysis Symposium*, LNCS 983, pages 33–50. Springer, September 1995. 297
2. U. Aßmann. *Graph Grammar Handbook*, chapter OPTIMIX, A Tool for Rewriting and Optimizing Programs. Chapman-Hall, 1998. 297
3. R. E. Bryant. Symbolic boolean manipulation with ordered binary decision diagrams. *Computing Surveys*, 24(3):293–318, September 1992. 298
4. D.R. Chase, M. Wegman, and F. Zadeck. Analysis of pointers and structures. In *SIGPLAN Conf. on Prog. Lang. Design and Impl.*, pages 296–310, New York, NY, 1990. ACM Press. 287
5. P. Cousot and R. Cousot. Systematic design of program analysis frameworks. In *Symp. on Princ. of Prog. Lang.*, pages 269–282, New York, NY, 1979. ACM Press. 280, 290, 293
6. A. Deutsch. Interprocedural may-alias analysis for pointers: Beyond k-limiting. In *SIGPLAN Conf. on Prog. Lang. Design and Impl.*, pages 230–241, New York, NY, 1994. ACM Press. 280

7. N. Dor, M. Rodeh, and M. Sagiv. Checking cleanness in linked lists. In *SAS'00, Static Analysis Symposium*, 2000. 281, 295

8. D. Evans. Static detection of dynamic memory errors. In *SIGPLAN Conf. on Prog. Lang. Design and Impl.*, 1996. 300

9. J.L. Jensen, M.E. Joergensen, N.Klarlund, and M.I. Schwartzbach. Automatic verification of pointer programs using monadic second-order logic. In *SIGPLAN Conf. on Prog. Lang. Design and Impl.*, 1997. 300

10. T. Lev-Ami. TVLA: A framework for Kleene based static analysis. Master's thesis, Tel-Aviv University, 2000. Available at http://www.math.tau.ac.il/~tla. 282, 289, 290, 292

11. T. Lev-Ami, T. Reps, M. Sagiv, and R. Wilhelm. Putting static analysis to work for verification: A case study. In *International Symposium on Software Testing and Analysis*, 2000. Available at http://www.cs.wisc.edu/~reps. 281, 296

12. S.S. Muchnick. *Advanced Compiler Design and Implementation*. Morgan & Kaufmann, third edition, 1999. 293

13. F. Nielson, H.R. Nielson, and M. Sagiv. A kleene analysis of mobile ambients. In *Proceedings of the 2000 European Symposium On Programming*, March 2000. 281, 295

14. N. Rinetskey and M. Sagiv. Interprocedual shape analysis for recursive programs. Available at http://www.cs.technion.ac.il/~maon, 2000. 298

15. M. Sagiv, T. Reps, and R. Wilhelm. Solving shape-analysis problems in languages with destructive updating. *Trans. on Prog. Lang. and Syst.*, 20(1):1–50, January 1998. 280, 287

16. M. Sagiv, T. Reps, and R. Wilhelm. Parametric shape analysis via 3-valued logic. In *Symp. on Princ. of Prog. Lang.*, 1999. 281, 287, 292, 293

17. M. Sagiv, T. Reps, and R. Wilhelm. Parametric shape analysis via 3-valued logic. Tech. Rep. TR-1383, Comp. Sci. Dept., Univ. of Wisconsin, Madison, WI, March 2000. Submitted for publication. Available at "http://www.cs.wisc.edu/wpis/papers/tr1383.ps". 280, 281, 284, 292, 293, 297

18. S.W.K. Tjiang and J. Hennessy. Sharlit—a tool for building optimizers. In *SIGPLAN Conf. on Prog. Lang. Design and Impl.*, pages 82–93, June 1992. 297

19. J. D. Ullman. *Principles of Database and Knowledge-Base Systems, Volume II: The New Technologies*. Comp. Sci. Press, Rockville, MD, 1989. 297

A   Empirical Results

The system was used to analyze on a number of examples (see Sect. 4). The timing information for all the functions analyzed is given in Table 4.

Table 4. Description of the singly-linked-list programs analyzed and their timing information. These programs are collections of interesting programs from LCLint [8], [9], Thomas Ball, and from first-year students. They are available at http://www.math.tau.ac.il/~nurr.

Program	Description	Time (seconds)	Number of Structures
search	searches for an element in a linked list	40	0.708
null_deref	searches a linked list, but with a typical error of not checking for the end of the list	48	0.752
delete	deletes a given element from a linked list	145	2.739
del_all	deletes an entire linked list	11	0.42
insert	inserts an element into a sorted linked list	140	2.862
create	prepends a varying number of new elements to a linked list	21	0.511
merge	merges two sorted linked lists into one sorted list	327	8.253
reverse	reverses a linked list via destructive updates	70	1.217
fumble	an erroneous version of reverse that loses the list	81	1.406
rotate	performs a cyclic rotation when given pointers to the first and last elements	25	0.629
swap	swaps the first and second elements of a list, fails when the list is 1 element long	31	0.7
getlast	returns the last element of the list	40	0.785
insert_sort	sorts a linked list using insertion sort	3773	160.132
bubble_sort	sorts a linked list using bubble sort	3946	186.609

B   A TVP File for Shape Analysis on Programs Manipulating Singly Linked Lists

The actions for handling program conditions that consists of pointer equalities and inequalities are given in Fig. 11.

The actions for manipulating the **struct node** declaration from Fig. 1(a) are given in Fig. 12. The actions Set_Next_Null_L and Set_Next_L model destructive updating (i.e., assignment to x1->n), and therefore have a nontrivial specification.

We use the notation $\varphi_1?\varphi_2 : \varphi_3$ for an if-then-else clause. If φ_1 is 1 then the result is φ_2, if φ_2 is 0 then the result is φ_3. If φ_1 is 1/2 then the result is $\varphi_2 \sqcup \varphi_3$. We use the notation $TC(v_1, v_2)(v_3, v_4)$ for the transitive-closure operator. The

```
/* cond.tvp */
%action Is_Not_Null_Var(x1) { %t  x1 + " != NULL"
    %f { x1(v) } %p ∃v : x1(v)
}
%action Is_Null_Var(x1) { %t  x1 + " == NULL"
    %f { x1(v) } %p ¬(∃v : x1(v))
}
%action Is_Eq_Var(x1, x2) { %t x1 + " == " + x2
    %f { x1(v), x2(v) }
    %p ∀v : x1(v) ⇔ x2(v)
}
%action Is_Not_Eq_Var(x1, x2) { %t x1 + " != " + x2
    %f { x1(v), x2(v) }
    %p ¬∀v : x1(v) ⇔ x2(v)
}
```

Fig. 11. An operational semantics in TVP for handling pointer conditions.

variables v_3 and v_4 are the free variables of the sub-formula over which the transitive closure is performed, and v_1 and v_2 are the variables used on the resulting binary relation.

```
/* stat.tvp */
%action Set_Null_L(x1) { %t  x1 + " = NULL"
    { x1(v) = 0    r[n, x1](v) = 0}
}

%action Copy_Var_L(x1, x2) { %t  x1 + " = " + x2
    %f { x2(v) }
    { x1(v) = x2(v)    r[n, x1](v) = r[n, x2](v)}
}

%action Malloc_L(x1) { %t x1 + " = (L) malloc(sizeof(struct node))) "
    %new
    { x1(v) = isNew(v)    r[n, x1](v) = isNew(v) }
}

%action Free_L(x1) { %t "free(x1)"
    %f {x1(v)}
    %message ∃v₁, v₂ : x1(v₁) ∧ n(v₁, v₂) ->
                "Internal error! assume that " + x1 + "->" + n + "==NULL"
    %retain ¬x1(v)
}

%action Get_Next_L(x1, x2) { %t  x1 + " = " + x2 + "->" + n
    %f { ∃v₁ : x2(v₁) ∧ n(v₁, v)}
    { x1(v) = ∃v₁ : x2(v₁) ∧ n(v₁, v)
      r[n, x1](v) = r[n, x2](v) ∧ (c[n](v) ∨ ¬x2(v))}
}

%action Set_Next_Null_L(x1) { %t  x1 + "->" + n + " = NULL"
    %f { x1(v) }
    { n(v₁, v₂) = n(v₁, v₂) ∧ ¬x1(v₁)
      is[n](v) = is[n](v) ∧ (¬(∃v₁ : x1(v₁) ∧ n(v₁, v))∨
                    ∃v₁, v₂ : (n(v₁, v) ∧ ¬x1(v₁)) ∧ (n(v₂, v) ∧ ¬x1(v₂)) ∧ v₁ ≠ v₂)
      r[n, x1](v) = x1(v)
      foreach(z in PVar-{x1}) {
          r[n, z](v) =(c[n](v) ∧ r[n, x1](v)?
                    z(v) ∨ ∃v₁ : z(v₁) ∧ TC(v₁, v)(v₃, v₄)(n(v₃, v₄) ∧ ¬x1(v₃)) :
                    r[n, z](v) ∧ ¬(r[n, x1](v) ∧ ¬x1(v) ∧ ∃v₁ : r[n, z](v₁) ∧ x1(v₁)))
      }
      c[n](v) = c[n](v) ∧ ¬(∃v₁ : x1(v₁) ∧ c[n](v₁) ∧ r[n, x1](v))}
}

%action Set_Next_L(x1, x2) { %t  x1 + "->" + n + " = " + x2
    %f { x1(v), x2(v) }
    %message ∃v₁, v₂ : x1(v₁) ∧ n(v₁, v₂) ->
                "Internal error! assume that " + x1 + "->" + n + "==NULL"
    { n(v₁, v₂) = n(v₁, v₂) ∨ x1(v₁) ∧ x2(v₂)
      is[n](v) = is[n](v) ∨ ∃v₁ : x2(v) ∧ n(v₁, v)
      foreach(z in PVar) {
          r[n, z](v) = r[n, z](v) ∨ r[n, x2](v) ∧ ∃v₁ : r[n, z](v₁) ∧ x1(v₁)
      }
      c[n](v) = c[n](v) ∨ (r[n, x2](v) ∧ ∃v₁ : x1(v₁) ∧ r[n, x2](v₁))}
}
```

Fig. 12. An operational semantics in TVP for handling the pointer-manipulation statements of linked lists as declared in Fig. 1(a).

Tree Schemata and Fair Termination

Laurent Mauborgne

LIENS – DMI, École Normale Supérieure
45 rue d'Ulm, 75 230 Paris cedex 05, France
Tel: +33 (0) 1 44 32 20 66
Laurent.Mauborgne@ens.fr
http://www.dmi.ens.fr/~mauborgn/

Abstract. We present a new representation for possibly infinite sets of possibly infinite trees. This representation makes extensive use of sharing to achieve efficiency. As much as possible, equivalent substructures are stored in the same place. The new representation is based on a first approximation of the sets which has this uniqueness property. This approximation is then refined using powerful representations of possibly infinite relations. The result is a representation which can be used for practical analysis using abstract interpretation techniques. It is more powerful than traditional techniques, and deals well with approximation strategies. We show on a simple example, fair termination, how the expressiveness of the representation can be used to obtain very simple and intuitive analysis.

1   Introduction

1.1   Trees and Static Analysis

Trees are one of the most widespread structures in computer science. And as such, it is not surprising that sets of trees appear in many areas of static analysis. One of the first practical use of sets of trees in an analysis was presented by Jones and Muchnick in [15], using regular tree grammars to represent sets of trees. The problem was with tree grammars, which are far from ideal, mainly because of the use of set variables. Computing the intersection of two sets, for example, requires the introduction of a quadratic number of variables [1].

In fact, the use of sets of trees have been proposed many times (see [20,2,22], and recently all the developments around set based analysis [13]). But all these applications suffer from the same drawbacks, namely the inadequacy of the representation. Practical implementations have been exhibited using tree automata instead of grammars (or sets constraints) [10]. But even tree automata have been introduced at the origin as a theoretical tool for decision problems [23], and they are quite complex to manipulate (see [4,14,3] for useful investigations on implementations). Tree automata are also limited in their expressiveness, in that we cannot express sets of trees with real relationship between subtrees, such as sets of the form $\{f(a^n, b^n, c^n)|n \in \mathbb{N}\}$. They become very complex when we

J. Palsberg (Ed.): SAS 2000, LNCS 1824, pp. 302–319, 2000.
© Springer-Verlag Berlin Heidelberg 2000

want to add infinite trees, whereas considering infinite behaviors is known to be important in static analysis [21,24,6].

When we look closely at those analysis, we see that, due to some lack of expressiveness in the representations, the actual behavior of programs is always approximated in practice. We know a theory to deal smartly with approximations, namely abstract interpretation [7,8]. And in this framework, we do not need too much from the representations we work with. In particular, there is no need that the sets we can represent be closed by boolean operations, as long as we can *approximate* these operations. What we propose is an entirely new representation for sets of trees —tree schemata—, which is practical and more expressive than traditional techniques (which means finer analysis), taking advantage of the possibilities offered by abstract interpretation.

1.2   How to Read the Paper

Tree schemata cannot be extensively described in the frame of one paper. It is the reason why the main ideas leading to these structures have been published in three papers, the present one being the final synthesizing one. The main idea of tree schemata is the use of a first raw approximation, the skeleton, which is then refined by the use of relations. The first approximation is called *skeletons*, and is described in [18]. A short summary of what a skeleton is can be found in this paper in section 2. The relations used in tree schemata may need to relate infinitely many sets, which is why new structures where developed and presented in [16]. These new representations for infinite structures are also described section 3.3.

The rest of the paper is organized as follows: after some basic definitions and the description of skeletons, we show in section 3 how we can enhance them with relations, and still have an incremental representation. The next section describes the expressiveness and some properties of tree schemata, and how they fit in the abstract interpretation framework. Section 5 describes an example of simple analysis exploiting a little bit of the expressiveness of tree schemata.

1.3   Basic Definitions and Notations

The trees we consider in this article are possibly infinite trees labeled over a finite set of labels F of fixed arity. A path of the tree is a finite word over $\mathbb{N}$. We write $\prec$ for the prefix relation between paths. The subtree of a tree t at position p is denoted $t_{[p]}$. A tree is said to be *regular* when it has a finite number of non-isomorphic subtrees. In this case, we can draw it as a finite tree plus some looping arrows.

We will write $\underset{t_0 \, \cdots \, t_{n-1}}{\overset{f}{\swarrow \searrow}}$ for a generic tree. The label of its root is f of arity n, and its children are the t_i's.

We will also consider n-ary relations and infinite relations. An n-ary relation is defined as a subset of the cartesian product of n sets. The *entry* number i in such a relation corresponds to the ith position (or set) in the relation. An infinite relation is a subset of an infinite cartesian product.

We will usually use a, b, f, g... for labels, t, u, v... for trees, x, y, z for variables and capitalized letters for sets of trees or structures representing sets of trees.

2   Skeletons

Skeletons (see Fig 1) were introduced in [18] as an efficient, yet limited, representation of sets of trees. This representation is based on a canonical representation of infinite regular trees which allows constant time equality testing and very efficient algorithms.

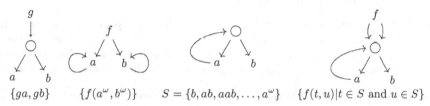

$$\{ga, gb\} \qquad \{f(a^\omega, b^\omega)\} \qquad S = \{b, ab, aab, \ldots, a^\omega\} \qquad \{f(t,u) | t \in S \text{ and } u \in S\}$$

Fig. 1. Examples of skeletons

2.1   Set Represented by a Skeleton

A skeleton is a regular tree —possibly infinite— with a special label, $\bigcirc$, which stands for a kind of union node.

Let F be a finite set of labels of fixed arity ($\bigcirc \notin F$). A skeleton $\overset{\bigcirc}{\underset{S_0 \,\cdots\, S_{n-1}}{\swarrow\;\searrow}}$ will represent the union of the sets represented by the S_i, and $\overset{f}{\underset{S_0 \,\cdots\, S_{n-1}}{\swarrow\;\searrow}}$ will represent the set of trees starting by an f and such that its child number i is in the set represented by S_i. This definition of the set represented by a skeleton is recursive. In fact, it defines a fixpoint equation. We have two natural ways of interpreting this definition: either we choose the least fixpoint (for set inclusion) or the greatest fixpoint. In the least fixpoint interpretation, a skeleton represents any finite tree that can be formed from it. In the greatest fixpoint interpretation, we add also the infinite tree. As we want the skeletons to be a first approximation to be refined, we choose the *greatest fixpoint*.

2.2   Uniqueness of the Representation

In order to have an efficient and compact representation, skeletons are unique representations of sets of trees. It means that if two sets of trees are equal, they will be stored in the same memory location, making reuse of intermediate results very easy.

In order to achieve this uniqueness, as skeletons are infinite regular trees, we use a representation with this property for infinite regular trees [18]. But we don't have a unique representation for sets of trees yet. We need to restrict skeletons to regular trees labeled by $F \cup \{\bigcirc\}$ and even more:

- in a skeleton, no subtree is the empty skeleton[1] unless the skeleton is the empty skeleton,
- a choice node has either 0 or at least two children,
- a choice node cannot be followed by a choice node,
- each subtree of a choice node starts with a different label. In this way, the choices in the interpretation of a skeleton are deterministic. As a consequence, in addition to common subtrees, we also share common prefixes of the trees, for a greater efficiency.

With these restrictions, skeletons have the uniqueness property, and they are indeed easy to store and manipulate. But the last two rules imply that not every set of trees can be represented by a skeleton. The limitation is that we cannot have any kind of relation between two sets of brother subtree. For example,

in the set $\left\{ \begin{array}{cc} f & f \\ \swarrow \searrow & \swarrow \searrow \\ a \quad b & c \quad d \end{array} \right\}$, the presence of the subtree b is related to the right

subtree a, but with a skeleton, the best we can do is $\begin{array}{c} f \\ \swarrow \searrow \\ \bigcirc \quad \bigcirc \\ \swarrow \searrow \ \swarrow \searrow \\ a \ c \ b \ d \end{array}$. If we did

not have infinite trees, the expressive power would be the same as top down deterministic tree automata.

3 Links

3.1 Choice Space of a Skeleton

Skeletons can be used to give a first upper approximation of the sets we want to represent. Then, we can enrich the skeletons to represent finer sets of trees. A first step towards the understanding of what that means is to define what is the set of possible restrictions we can impose on a skeleton.

The only places in the skeletons where we have any possibility of restriction are choice nodes. Let us consider a choice node with n children. The restrictions we can make are on some of the choices of this node, forbidding for example the second child. So the choice space of a choice node will be the set $\{0, 1, \ldots, n-1\}$. Now, let S be a skeleton. We can make such a restriction for every path of S leading to a choice, and each such restriction can depend on the others.

Thus, the choice space of a skeleton is the cartesian product of all the choice spaces of its choice nodes. Indeed, it gives a new vision of skeletons: we can now

---

[1] The empty skeleton is the tree $\bigcirc$, which is a choice with no child.

see them as a function from their choice space to trees. Each value (which is a vector) in the choice space corresponds to a commitment of every choice nodes in the skeleton to a particular choice.

Example 1. Let S be the skeleton
. Then the choice space of S is $\{0,1\} \times \{0,1\}$. And if we consider S as a function from its choice space, $S(01) =$
.

3.2   Links Are Relations

Now we can see clearly what is a restriction of a skeleton: it is a subset of the set of trees it represents which can be defined by choosing a subset of its choice space. And a subset of a cartesian product is merely a relation. So we have our first definition of tree schemata: a tree schema is a skeleton plus a relation on its choice space.

But this definition raises some problems. First of all, how do we represent the relation? Second, this definition is not *incremental*. A representation is incremental when you do not need to build again the entire representation each time you make a tiny little change in the data. Changes can be made locally, in general. For example, tree automata are not incremental, especially when they are kept minimal, because for each modification of the set, you have to run the minimization algorithm on the whole automaton again. Skeletons are incremental [18]. The advantage of incrementality is clear for the implementation, so we would like to keep tree schemata as incremental as possible. The problem with tree schemata as we have defined them so far is that the relation which binds everything together is global. To change the relation into more local objects, we address two problems: the entries in the relation should not be the paths starting from the root of the tree schema, and the relation should be split if possible. These problems are solved by the notion of links in the tree schema.

A *link* is a relation with entry names (or variables) [16] plus a function from entry names to sets of choice nodes of the tree schema (formally, a couple (relation, function)). The splitting of the global relation is performed by means of *independent decomposition*. A relation R is independently decomposed in R_1 and R_2 if: the entries of R_1 and R_2 partition the entries of R, and $R(e)$ is true if and only if $R_1(e_1)$ and $R_2(e_2)$ are true, where e_i is the subvector of e on the entries of R_i. The idea is that the global relation is true for a given element of the choice space if and only if it is true on every link. Each choice node is associated with at most one link, and one entry name of that link.

Example 2. Consider the following skeleton:

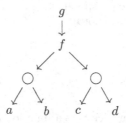

Its choice space is $\{0,1\}_{00} \times \{0,1\}_{01}$ (we use subscripts to denote the entries in the relation, which is the path from the root to the choice node). A possible restriction would be to consider the set $\left\{ \begin{smallmatrix} g \\ \downarrow \\ f \\ \swarrow\searrow \\ a \quad c \end{smallmatrix} , \begin{smallmatrix} g \\ \downarrow \\ f \\ \swarrow\searrow \\ a \quad d \end{smallmatrix} , \begin{smallmatrix} g \\ \downarrow \\ f \\ \swarrow\searrow \\ b \quad d \end{smallmatrix} \right\}$. The associated global relation would be $\{0_{00}0_{01}, 0_{00}1_{01}, 1_{00}1_{01}\}$. In order to define the local link, let us call $\square_1$ and $\square_2$ the memory locations of the left and right choice nodes respectively. The local link l would be $(R, x \to \{\square_1\}, y \to \{\square_2\})$, where R is the relation $\{0_x0_y, 0_x1_y, 1_x1_y\}$. In the tree schema, the first choice node would be associated with (x, l) and the second one with (y, l). If we represent the relation by a Binary Decision Diagram (BDD) [5], the tree schema can be depicted this way:

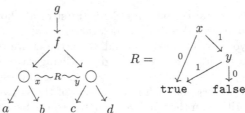

Note that in this example, the letter R appears just for graphical conventions, in tree schemata, links are named just by the representation of their relations and the function from entry names to choice nodes that are associated with them.

3.3   Representation of Relations

The last problem concerns the representation of the independent relations. Binary Decision Diagrams [5] having entry names (variables) seem to be a good candidate, as long as the relations are finite! Because the skeleton is an infinite tree, we may have an infinite number of paths leading to choice nodes, and it may be useful to link them together. To achieve this, we need to represent infinite relations, which raise some problems. Those problems have been studied, and a possible solution is presented in [16], which we briefly summarize here. Note that the actual representation of relations is but a *parameter* of tree schemata, and one could choose different representations to change the balance between efficiency and precision, or expressiveness.

Entry Names One problem which is common to all representations of infinite relation is that we have an infinite number of entries in the relations, and each of them should be named in order to perform operations such as restrictions. In BDDs, entry names are the variables, one for each entry in the relation. For infinite relations we can use the notion of *equivalent entries*: two entries i and j are equivalent if for every vector v in the relation, the vector obtained by exchanging its values on the entries i and j is also in the relation. In this case, we show that we can use the same name for i and j. This allows the use of a finite number of names, if the relation is regular enough.

Binary Decision Graphs In [16], a new class of infinite relations is defined, the set of *omega*-deterministic relations. Intuitively, we can see in relations a finite behavior part, which deals with the prefixes of the vectors, and an infinite behavior. The idea is that for *omega*-deterministic relations, the finite behavior is regular, and at any point in the decision process, there at most one infinite regular behavior.

The representation of such relations is an extension of BDDs: instead of having just DAGs (directed acyclic graphs), we allow cycles in the representation (which are uniquely represented, thanks to the techniques developed in [18]), and we add a special arrow, $\longrightarrow\!\!\!\!\!\times$, which signals the beginning of a new infinite behavior. One can read those graphs as follows (see examples of Fig 2): to accept a vector in the relation, we must follow the decisions in the graph, and count a infinite number of **true**. Each time we encounter a $\longrightarrow\!\!\!\!\!\times$, we reset our count, and each time we encounter a **true**, we start again at the last encountered $\longrightarrow\!\!\!\!\!\times$ (or the beginning of the graph if none was encountered yet). Finite BDDs correspond to the graphs with no cycle and a $\longrightarrow\!\!\!\!\!\times$ before the **true**.

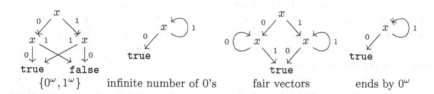

Fig. 2. Examples of Binary Decision Graphs

This class of relations is closed by intersection, and has a best (in the sense of relation inclusion) representation property for all boolean operations. Also, the representation is canonical, which gives the constant time equality testing, as with BDDs. It is possible also to represent a bigger class of infinite relations, the class of *regular* relations, which is closed under all boolean operations, but with far less efficient data structures.

3.4 A Pseudo-Decision Procedure

In order to help reading tree schemata, we give a pseudo[2] decision procedure to decide whether a tree is in the set represented by a tree schema. This procedure is performed by going through the tree and the tree schema at the same time. We call t the current subtree, and T the current subtree of the tree schema.

- If $T = \begin{array}{c} \overset{x}{\bigcirc \sim} R \\ \swarrow \searrow \\ T_0 \cdots T_n \end{array}$ then

  - if no T_i has the same label as t, then the tree is not in the tree schema;
  - otherwise, let i be the index corresponding to the label of t. If $R(x = i) = \texttt{false}$ then the tree is not in the tree schema. Else proceed on T_i and t, while keeping the fact that R is partially evaluated on x with value i.

- $T = \begin{array}{c} f \\ \swarrow \searrow \\ T_0 \cdots T_{n-1} \end{array}$ and $t = \begin{array}{c} g \\ \swarrow \searrow \\ t_0 \cdots t_{n-1} \end{array}$

  - if $f \neq g$ then the tree is not in the tree schema,
  - else proceed with each (T_i, t_i).

If in this procedure, we need to evaluate a relation on an entry which is already evaluated, we stack a new version of the relation. The procedure is a success if we can go through the entire tree t in this way without failing, and the infinite valuations of relations are accepted. Note that if a relation is not entirely evaluated and there is a possibility of evaluation accepted by the relation, then the process is still a success.

3.5 Restrictions on the Links

Just as not every regular tree labeled on $F \cup \{\bigcirc\}$ is a skeleton, not every skeleton with any link is a valid tree schema. There are two main reasons for that: the whole thing must be kept finite (it is a constraint on the representation of the relations only), and we want only one possible representation for the empty set and no infinitely increasing (for the size of the representation) chain of tree schemata representing the same tree.

Concerning the second constraint, the first thing we need to fix is the skeleton on which the tree schema is based. Because the tree schema represents a subset of the set represented by the skeleton, this skeleton could be any one approximating the set we want to represent. If the set we want to represent admits a best skeleton approximation, it is natural that we choose this skeleton, because the better the first approximation (the skeleton), the more efficient the algorithms. So we choose to put as much information as possible in the skeleton, which corresponds to the arborescent backbone of the set of trees, sharing every possible prefixes and subtrees. In this article, we will restrict tree schemata to such sets

---

[2] We call this procedure a "pseudo decision" procedure because the trees and tree schemata being infinite, it cannot end.

of trees, although it is possible to represent sets of trees with no best skeleton approximation, such as $\{a^n b^n c | n \in \mathbb{N}\}$. The reader is referred to [17] for further description.

To restrict the sets we represent to sets with best skeleton approximation, and to keep the skeleton of a tree schema be that best skeleton, we just need to enforce the following two local properties:

Property 1. Whatever the link l between two choice nodes C_1 and C_2, either there is no path from one choice node to the other, or if there is one from C_1 to C_2, then the choice leading to that path from C_1 does not restrict the choices in C_2.

Property 2. Whatever the link l in a tree schema, the relation of the link is *full*, that is for every entry in the relation and for every possible value at that entry, there is always a vector in the relation with that value on that entry.

A tree schema respecting those properties is said to be valid. In the sequel, we will only consider valid tree schemata.

Corollary 1. *Whatever the valid tree schema T based on the skeleton S, S is the best (for set inclusion) skeleton approximation for the set represented by T.*

Proof. Suppose there is a skeleton S' such that $S' \neq S$ and the set represented by S' is included in the set represented by S, but still contains the set represented by T. It means that there is a path p in S such that $S_{[p]}$ is a choice node and there is a choice i which is not possible in S'. The choice node $T_{[p]}$ is associated with the link l. If there is no other choice node in p linked to l, we know by property 2 that there is a vector v such that v is admitted by l and the value of v on the choice node is i. Because of the independence of the other links with l, there is a tree in T which corresponds to the choice i in p, and necessarily this tree is not in S'. If there is a choice node in p linked to l, say at path q. There is a j such that $qj \preceq p$. By induction on the number of choice nodes linked to l along p, and by the same argument as above, we show that there is an element of the choice space that leads to q and allows the choice j. But then, by property 1, such a choice allows the choice of i at p. Once again, we have a tree in T which is not in S'. $\square$

4   Tree Schemata and Abstract Interpretation

Tree schemata were designed to be used in abstract interpretation. In this section, we show what is gained by this choice, and how abstract interpretation can deal with tree schemata.

4.1   Properties of Tree Schemata

Expressiveness One of the interesting properties of tree schemata is that they are more expressive than their most serious opponents, tree automata. Of course, tree schemata can easily express sets containing infinite trees, and even complex ones, but even when restricted to finite trees, the second example of Fig 3 shows that tree schemata can express some sets of trees which cannot be represented by tree automata.

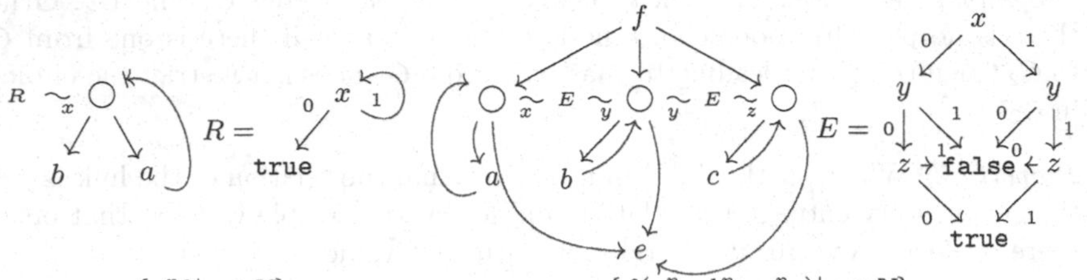

Fig. 3. Examples of Tree Schemata

With the appropriate representation for relations, we can also represent any regular set of trees with a tree schema. We give hereafter an idea of the construction. Let L be the set of binary trees accepted by the finite top-down non-deterministic tree automaton, $\mathcal{A} = (Q, A, q_0, \Delta, F)$ (see [12] for a definition). To build the tree schema representing L, the first step is to build a non valid tree schema based on a non valid skeleton, but which represents L, and then to apply some rules that give a valid tree schema, without changing its meaning. The first graph is built using the rules of Fig 4 and connecting the states together. For the final states, we just add the labels of arity 0 to the first choice.

For any tree $\begin{smallmatrix} & f & \\ \swarrow & & \searrow \\ t_0 & & t_1 \end{smallmatrix}$ recognized by the automaton starting at q, there is a rule $(q, f, q^0, q^1) \in \Delta$ such that each t_i is recognized by the automaton starting at q^i. According to the pseudo decision procedure, it means that the tree is accepted by the tree schema starting at the choice node pointed by q, and the converse holds because of the relations $=$ which force a valid (q^0, q^1) to be taken.

In order to simplify the skeleton on which the non valid tree schema is built, we can suppress choice nodes everywhere there is only one outgoing edge, but we still have some possible cascading choices, one of them with a relation, which cannot so easily be simplified. Fig 5 shows how this case can be reduced, by choosing the set of S^0's and S^1's to be exactly the sets of T^0's and T^1's, but without repetitions, and the relation R to be $\{(a, b)|\exists c, d, e$ such that $S_a^0 = T_{c,d}^0$ and $S_b^1 = T_{c,e}^1\}$. The relation R is finite, and so easy to represent with the techniques of [16]. The last step will combine the relations to make the skeleton deterministic: for each choice node such that there is an S_i and an S_j starting with the same label, we must merge the two schemata and incorporate

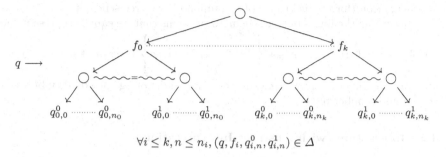

$$\forall i \leq k, n \leq n_i, (q, f_i, q_{i,n}^0, q_{i,n}^1) \in \Delta$$

Fig. 4. Rules to build the non valid tree schema

their choice nodes in R. The immediate looping in the schema will result in the construction of infinite relations.

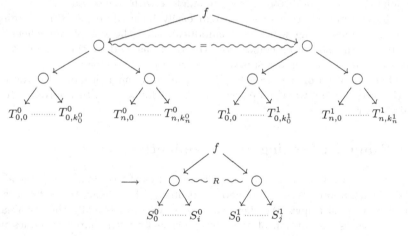

Fig. 5. Simplification rule to eliminate cascading choices

Other Properties Deciding the inclusion of tree schemata can be efficiently implemented. If the relations used in tree schemata are closed by union intersection and projection, then tree schemata are closed by union, intersection and projection. See [17] for proofs and algorithms. It seems that BDGs are the best suited so far to represent relations in tree schemata, and we will use them in the example of section 5. But as BDGs are not closed by union, tree schemata using BDGs are not closed by union, although we can indeed compute a best approximation (for set inclusion) of the union of two tree schemata.

Concerning the limits of tree schemata, it seems that we cannot represent the set of balanced trees, or the set $\left\{ \begin{array}{c} C\!\!\!\!\!\!\nearrow f \\ \searrow \\ t \end{array} \middle| t \text{ is a tree} \right\}$ because it would require an infinite number of entry names in the relation denoting the equality between the infinite number of trees.

4.2   Interactions with Abstract Interpretation

Abstract interpretation deals with concrete and abstract domains to describe different semantics of programs. The semantics is generally computed via the resolution of a fixpoint equation. Such equations can be expressed with formal language transformers [9] using unions and projection (which subsumes intersection). The fixpoint can then be computed by an iteration sequence, possibly with widening. Such iteration can be computed with tree schemata, where the approximation for union can be seen as a widening. One of the most common operations is the inclusion testing to decide whether we have reached a post-fixpoint. And inclusion testing is quite efficient with tree schemata.

The structure of tree schemata can easily be used to perform meaningful approximations (using widening techniques) when the size of the schemata is too big, as this size often comes from the relations, and we can choose to relax some relations. We can also simplify the skeletons if necessary.

One limitation of tree schemata is the finite number of labels for the trees. In the next section, we will see how an infinite domain can be approximated by a finite partition.

5   Example: Proving Fair Termination

In order to show the interests of one of the features of tree schemata —the ability to deal with infinite trees—, we chose a problem where using tree schemata can simplify a lot of things. We show how to prove automatically the termination under fairness assumption of concurrent processes with shared variables using abstract interpretation.

5.1   Semantics of the Shared Variables Language

We choose a simple language originated from [19] to describe concurrent processes sharing their variables. A program will be of the form $P := I; [P_1|| \ldots ||P_n]; T$, where I, P_i and T are sequential deterministic programs composed of assignments of integers or booleans, if-then-else branching and while loops. In addition, the parallel processes P_i have an await instruction of the form await B then S end where B is a boolean expression and S a sequential program without await instruction.

Informally the semantics of the program uses a global state. It executes I, and when I ends each P_i are executed in parallel with a notion of atomic actions which cannot interact (no simultaneous assignment to the same variable). The effect of the `await` instruction is to execute its program as an atomic action starting at a time when the boolean expression is true. The boolean expression is guaranteed to be true when the sequential program starts. Finally, when every parallel program has terminated, the program executes T.

We give the notion of atomic actions through a relation $\rightarrow$ defined by structural induction (following [11]). The definition is described in figure 6 using a special empty program E. Based on this relation, we can define a semantics

$$\langle x\,{:}{=}e, \sigma \rangle \rightarrow \langle E, \sigma[e/x] \rangle \qquad\qquad E; S = S; E = S$$

$$\frac{\sigma \models B}{\langle \texttt{while } B \texttt{ do } S, \sigma \rangle \rightarrow \langle S; \texttt{while } B \texttt{ do } S, \sigma \rangle} \qquad \frac{\sigma \models \neg B}{\langle \texttt{while } B \texttt{ do } S, \sigma \rangle \rightarrow \langle E, \sigma \rangle}$$

$$\frac{\sigma \models B \text{ and } \langle S, \sigma \rangle \rightarrow^* \langle E, \tau \rangle}{\langle \texttt{await } B \texttt{ then } S \texttt{ end}, \sigma \rangle \rightarrow \langle E, \tau \rangle} \qquad \frac{\langle S_1, \sigma \rangle \rightarrow \langle S_2, \tau \rangle}{\langle S_1; S, \sigma \rangle \rightarrow \langle S_2; S, \tau \rangle}$$

$$\frac{\langle P_i, \sigma \rangle \rightarrow \langle P_i', \tau \rangle}{\langle [P_1 || \ldots || P_n], \sigma \rangle \rightarrow \langle [P_1 || \ldots || P_{i-1} || P_i' || P_{i+1} || \ldots || P_n], \tau \rangle}$$

Fig. 6. Definition of the Transition Relation $\rightarrow$

based on interleaving traces. We incorporate a notion of program points in the states. The program points of the parallel programs are the vectors of their program points. We have the following definition of the semantics $\mathcal{T}(\langle i : S, \sigma \rangle)$ of a program point i with expression S and environment σ:

$$\mathcal{T}(\langle i : S, \sigma \rangle) \stackrel{\text{def}}{=} \left\{ \begin{array}{c} \langle i, \sigma \rangle \\ \downarrow \\ t \end{array} \middle| \; t \in \mathcal{T}(\langle j : P, \tau \rangle) \text{ and } \langle S, \sigma \rangle \rightarrow \langle P, \tau \rangle \right\}$$

$$\mathcal{T}(\langle i : S, \sigma \rangle) \stackrel{\text{def}}{=} \langle i, \sigma \rangle \text{ if there is no state reachable from } \langle S, \sigma \rangle$$

A program P is said to be *terminating* if and only if for every σ $\mathcal{T}(\langle P, \sigma \rangle)$ does not contain any infinite trace. We can also define a deadlock as the end of a trace with index different from the last index of the program. We define $\mathcal{T}(P)$ as the union of the $\mathcal{T}(\langle P, \sigma \rangle)$ for all environment σ. The elements of $\mathcal{T}(P)$ are called the traces of P.

5.2   Expressing Program Properties as Sets of Traces

It is possible to express many program properties using just sets of traces. For example, termination is expressed as the set of all finite traces. To check that the program terminates, we just have to check that its set of traces is included in the termination property. In the same way, we can express termination without deadlock.

We can also express different kinds of fairness to decide whether a given trace of the program satisfies the fairness property. Every fairness property contains all finite traces. If it is an unconditional fairness [11] property then it contains also the infinite traces either with a finite passage in the concurrent part of the program, or such that each concurrent program that is not terminated progresses infinitely often.

We can prove that a program fairly terminates by proving that its set of traces intersected with the set of fair traces is included in the set of terminating traces.

Example 3. Consider the program

$$P =_0 b\text{:=}\mathtt{true}[_0\mathtt{while}\ b\ \mathtt{do}\ _1\mathtt{skip}_2||_0 b\text{:=}\mathtt{false}_1]_1$$

The set of traces of P can be described by the following tree schema (we omit the beginning, which is not important):

$$\mathcal{T}(P) =$$

The termination property is expressed as:

$$\mathrm{Term} = \qquad \qquad \qquad \qquad \text{where}\ \mathtt{Fin} =$$

To express the fairness property, we first describe the infinite fair traces, then we add the finite traces[3]:

$$\mathrm{Fair}_\omega = \qquad \qquad \qquad \text{where}\ \mathtt{Fai} =$$

_____

[3] We use this presentation just for the clarity of the schemata, we could just as well define Fair directly.

$$\text{Fair} = \text{Fair}_\omega \cup \text{Term}$$

Then, to prove the fair termination of the program P, we just have to compute $\text{Fair} \cap \mathcal{T}(P)$ and verify that it is included in Term.

5.3   Abstraction of the Set of Traces

One of the limitations of tree schemata (necessary for a finite representation) is that we need a finite set of labels. Choosing the states to be the labels, we can have infinite sets of labels. To cope with this difficulty, we define an abstract semantics which approximates the concrete one described above, using the techniques of abstract interpretation.

Because we are interested in the control flow of the program, we just need to distinguish between states that evaluate differently on the boolean expressions in the program we analyze. We define abstract states to be each such partition of the set of states. We write $\text{states}^\sharp$ to denote this set of states. We define now abstract traces as traces labeled by $\text{states}^\sharp$. The concrete semantics is a set of concrete traces, the abstract semantics is a set of abstract traces. There is a Galois connection (for set of traces inclusion) [7] between those two semantics. Let trace be the set of sets of concrete traces, and $\text{trace}^\sharp$ be the set of sets of abstract traces. The concretisation of a trace $t^\sharp$ is the set of traces obtained by replacing every abstract state by a concrete state in the set of states it defines. The concretisation of a set of abstract traces is the union of the concretisations of its elements.

Sets of abstract traces are represented as tree schemata, but for our analysis to be ready, we need also to translate the properties into sets of abstract traces which will then be represented by tree schemata. The problem is that, whereas the fairness property can safely be over-approximated, we cannot over-approximate the termination property. The good news is that we can always represent this property *exactly*. Because of the way we chose the abstract states, the set of states with no successor for $\to$ is represented exactly by the set of abstract state with no successor. Thus the concretisation of the set of finite abstract traces is exactly the set of finite concrete traces. The set of finite abstract traces can easily be represented by a tree schema, the general method is the same as in the previous example.

For more powerful results, we need also to take into account the decreasing chains of integers in the states. For our purpose, such decreasing chains can be seen as a further constraint that some loop can only be taken finitely often, a fact that can be exactly expressed with tree schemata.

Of course, even with that analysis, we still manipulate abstractions of the sets of traces, so there will be some programs fairly terminating and not proved by this technique. This is inherent to approximation techniques, and unavoidable anyway when dealing with termination.

Example 4. Let P be the following program:

$$P = {}_0x\!:=\!?_1; b\!:=\!\texttt{true}; [{}_0\texttt{while } b \texttt{ do } {}_1x\!:=\!x-1_2\|$$
$${}_0\texttt{await } x < 0 \texttt{ then } {}_1b\!:=\!\texttt{false end}_2]$$

In this example, the set of abstract states is $\{(x \geq 0, \mathtt{t}), (x \geq 0, \mathtt{f}), (x < 0, \mathtt{t}),$ $(x < 0, \mathtt{f})\}$ to which we add the indexes of the program. The abstract state corresponding to the set of all the sets which are terminating is $(22, x < 0, \mathtt{f})$.

Due to this approximation, the two possible states following $(10, x \geq 0, \mathtt{t})$ are $(20, x \geq 0, \mathtt{t})$ and $(20, x < 0, \mathtt{t})$. The first state leads to a loop towards $(00, x \geq 0, \mathtt{t})$. It is a very simple analysis that reveals that in this loop we have a decreasing chain, so this loop cannot be taken for ever. By adding this constraint we can perform the same analysis as in the previous example and still conclude that the program fairly terminates.

6   Conclusion

We presented a new representation for sets of trees. This representation has been developed with tractability in mind. It is based on a structure, the skeleton, which is an upper approximation of the set we represent. Tree schemata benefit from the great efficiency of the operations on skeletons. The skeletons are enriched with possibly infinite relations. With them, they are more powerful than tree automata, while more adapted to approximation techniques.

The example of fair termination showed that with such expressiveness it is possible to model very easily the behavior of programs. There was no need for complicated program transformations, introduction of variables or deep proofs. It is to be noted that the full power of tree schemata have not been used in this example, as no relation between distinct traces occurs.

The main drawbacks of this representation is that it is not fully tested yet. But the algorithms presented in [17] show that it is very promising, due to the unique representation of many elements of tree schemata. Moreover, the canonical decomposition of sets of trees in a tree structure and relations, allows for a very natural introduction of counters which can be very useful in analysis, especially if some of these counters are related to the programs we analyze.

Acknowledgments

I would like to thank the anonymous referees for their encouraging comments and their constructive remarks which helped a lot in the improvement of this paper.

References

1. Alexander Aiken and Brian R. Murphy. Implementing regular tree expressions. In J. Hughes, editor, *Functional Programming Languages and Computer Architecture*, volume 523 of *Lecture Notes in Computer Science*, pages 427–446. Springer-Verlag, 1991. 302
2. Nils Andersen. Approximating term rewriting systems with tree grammars. Technical Report 86/16, Institute of Datalogy, University of Copenhagen, 1986. 302

3. Morten Biehl, Nils Klarlund, and Theis Rauhe. Algorithms for guided tree automata. In *First International Workshop on Implementing Automata*, volume 1260 of *Lecture Notes in Computer Science*, 1997. 302
4. Jürger Börstler, Ulrich Möncke, and Reinhard Wilhelm. Table compression for tree automata. *ACM Transactions on Programming Languages and Systems*, 13(3):295–314, July 1991. 302
5. Randal E. Bryant. Graph based algorithms for boolean function manipulation. *IEEE Transactions on Computers*, C-35:677–691, August 1986. 307
6. Witold Charatonik and Andreas Podelski. Co-definite set constraints. In T. Nipkow, editor, *9th International Conference on Rewriting Techniques and Applications*, volume 1379 of *Lecture Notes in Computer Science*, pages 211–225. Springer-Verlag, March-April 1998. 303
7. Patrick Cousot. *Méthodes itératives de construction et d'approximation de points fixes d'opérateurs monotones sur un treillis, analyse sémantique des programmes*. PhD thesis, Université de Grenoble, March 1978. 303, 316
8. Patrick Cousot and Radhia Cousot. Abstract interpretation: a unified lattice model for static analysis of programs by construction of approximation of fixpoints. In *4th ACM Symposium on Principles of Programming Languages (POPL '77)*, pages 238–252, 1977. 303
9. Patrick Cousot and Radhia Cousot. Formal languages, grammar and set-constraint-based program analysis by abstract interpretation. In *Conference on Functional Programming and Computer Architecture (FPCA '95)*, pages 170–181, June 1995. 313
10. P. Devienne, JM. Talbot, and Sophie Tison. Solving classes of set constraints with tree automata. In G. Smolka, editor, *3th International Conference on Principles and Practice of Constraint Programming*, volume 1330 of *Lecture Notes in Computer Science*, pages 62–76. Springer-Verlag, October 1997. 302
11. Nissim Francez. *Fairness*. Texts and Monographs in Computer Science. Springer-Verlag, 1986. 314, 315
12. F. Gécseg and M. Steinby. *Tree Automata*. Akadémia Kiadó, 1984. 311
13. Nevin Heintze. *Set Based Program Analysis*. PhD thesis, School of Computer Science, Carnegie Mellon University, October 1992. 302
14. Jesper G. Henriksen, Jakob Jensen, Michael Jørgensen, Nils Klarlund, Robert Paige, Theis Rauhe, and Anders Sandholm. Mona: Monadic second-order logic in practice. In *Tools and Algorithms for the Construction and Analysis of Systems*, volume 1019 of *Lecture Notes in Computer Science*, 1996. 302
15. N. D. Jones and S. S. Muchnick. Flow analysis and optimization of LISP-like structures. In *6th ACM Symposium on Principles of Programming Languages (POPL '79)*, pages 244–256. ACM Press, January 1979. 302
16. Laurent Mauborgne. Binary decision graphs. In A. Cortesi and G. Filé, editors, *Static Analyis Symposium (SAS'99)*, volume 1694 of *Lecture Notes in Computer Science*, pages 101–116. Springer-Verlag, 1999. 303, 306, 307, 308, 311
17. Laurent Mauborgne. *Representation of Sets of Trees for Abstract Interpretation*. PhD thesis, École Polytechnique, Palaiseau, France, November 1999. 310, 312, 317
18. Laurent Mauborgne. Improving the representation of infinite trees to deal with sets of trees. In *European Symposium on Programming (ESOP 2000)*, volume to appear of *Lecture Notes in Computer Science*. Springer-Verlag, 2000. 303, 304, 305, 306, 308
19. S. Owicki and D. Gries. Verifying properties of parallel programs: an axiomatic approach. *CACM*, 19(5):279–286, August 1976. 313

20. J. Reynolds. Automatic computation of data set definitions. In *Information Processing '68*, pages 456–461. Elsevier Science Publisher, 1969. 302
21. Michael I. Schwartzbach. Infinite values in hierarchical imperative types. In A. Arnold, editor, *15th Colloquium on Trees in Algebra and Programming (CAAP '90)*, volume 431 of *Lecture Notes in Computer Science*, pages 254–268. Springer-Verlag, May 1990. 303
22. Morten Heine Sørensen. A grammar-based data-flow analysis to stop deforestation. In Sophie Tison, editor, *Trees in Algebra and Programming — CAAP '94*, volume 787 of *Lecture Notes in Computer Science*, pages 335–351. Springer-Verlag, April 1994. 302
23. J. W. Thatcher and J. B. Wright. Generalized finite automata with an application to a decision problem of second-order logic. *Mathematical Systems Theory*, 2:57–82, 1968. 302
24. Moshe Y. Vardi. Nontraditional applications of automata theory. In Masami Hagiya and John C. Mitchell, editors, *Theoretical Aspects of Computer Software*, volume 789 of *Lecture Notes in Computer Science*, pages 575–597. Springer-Verlag, April 1994. 303

Abstract Interpretation of Probabilistic Semantics

David Monniaux

LIENS
45 rue d'Ulm, 75230 Paris cedex 5, France
http://www.di.ens.fr/ monniaux

Abstract. Following earlier models, we lift standard deterministic and nondeterministic semantics of imperative programs to probabilistic semantics. This semantics allows for random external inputs of known or unknown probability and random number generators.

We then propose a method for analysing programs according to this semantics, in the general framework of abstract interpretation. This method lifts an "ordinary" abstract lattice, for non-probabilistic programs, to one suitable for probabilistic programs.

Our construction is highly generic. We discuss the influence of certain parameters on the precision of the analysis, basing ourselves on experimental results.

1 Introduction

In this paper, we give both a theoretical framework for abstract semantics of probabilistic computer programs and practical methods of analysis. Our analyses are set in the general field of abstract interpretation.

1.1 Abstract Interpretation

A well-known fact of computer science is that properties of the denotational semantics of programs in Turing-complete languages cannot be decided mechanically. Automatic methods of analysis thus have to forget completeness, while still yielding interesting results on realistic programs.

The basic idea behind abstract interpretation [1,2] is to replace computations on sets that are non recursive or too complex to handle by computations on supersets of them (or subsets; what is important is we know whether we are handling a superset or a subset). For instance, instead of handling sets of integers, one might want to upper-approximate them using an interval. If all computations are done monotonically, the result interval is necessarily a superset of the exact set of possible values at the end of execution.

Intervals are just one of many possible abstract domains. For tuples of numerical values, polyhedra can be used [3]. Tuples of integers can be abstracted using congruences, interval congruences [13] or systems of linear congruential equations [6]. Appropriate domains can be used to discover data structure configurations [4].

J. Palsberg (Ed.): SAS 2000, LNCS 1824, pp. 322–340, 2000.

1.2 Probabilistic Semantics

One of the drawbacks of such analysis methods is that they do not distinguish between what is possible (even with extremely low probability) and what is likely (possible with a non-negligible probability). This is especially important in the analysis of reactive systems.

Let us take a real-life example: the monitoring program of a copy machine system is a reactive program taking inputs for sensors and giving orders to servo-motors. Each sensor has a probability of failure, from mechanical or electric wearing, scraps of papers etc... Sensors are redundant, with the idea that if a moderate amount of sensors are failing, the system will diagnosis the sensor failure instead of getting a false idea of what is going on in the machine. It is possible that failure of several sensors can make the system err. The reliability of the system can be improved by increasing the number of sensors, which is not always economically and mechanically possible. It is interesting, given a description of the system, to get upper bounds on the probability of failure.

Another field of possible use of analysis is randomized algorithms. Randomized algorithms have enjoyed considerable interest [9]. While it is of course impossible to derive automatically the most advanced properties of some of these algorithms, it is still interesting to be able to deal with such programs in a more precise way than just considering them as nondeterministic.

It is required that the analysis method should not constrain the analyzed programs in a class of well-studied algorithms. Also, we must allow all usual flow-control constructs, including tests and loops.

1.3 Comparison to Other Works

The concrete semantics we consider is essentially equivalent to the one proposed by Kozen [10,11, second semantic]; we do not consider structures as complex as those proposed by Jones [9]. We extend this semantics to nondeterministic probabilistic cases [12,8].

Contrary to some other works [8,12,14,15], our goal is not to propose rules to reason on à la Dijkstra weakest precondition semantics and prove refinements. These methods are adequate for computer-aided program design and verification, but of course cannot deal automatically with loop invariants. We rather propose a natural extension of abstract interpretation [1,2] to probabilistic semantics. The analyses described here are meant to be fully automatic, even though some heuristics need some tuning guided by experience.

Some automatic program analysis techniques with a view on improving optimizing compilers have been developed [17]. These techniques are essentially ad hoc and imprecise; only the control flow is considered, the probability of tests being taken or not being estimated from crude syntactic criteria (such as: a branch whose condition is a conjunction is less likely to be taken than a branch whose condition is atomic, tests checking for null pointers are not likely to be taken...). While such techniques are interesting in heuristics for compilers, they are not suitable to get any precise result on programs.

1.4 Notations

$\mathcal{P}(X)$ shall be the set of parts of X. Y^C shall be the complement of X if there is no ambiguity as to the superset.

1.5 Structure of the Article

In section 2, we shall define denotational semantics for probabilistic programs. In section 3, we shall see how to abstract this semantics, and more particularly we shall explain how to deal with loops (fixpoints). In section 4 we shall define a parametric abstract domain and in section 5 we shall review some implementation issues and experimental results.

2   Probabilistic Concrete Semantics

Throughout this paper, we shall define compositionally several semantics and expose relationships between them. We shall use as an example some simple Pascal-like imperative language, but we do not mean that our analysis methods are restricted to such languages.

2.1 Summary of Non-probabilistic Concrete Semantics

We shall here consider denotational semantics for programs. (equivalent operational semantics could be easily defined, but we shall mostly deal with denotational ones for concision).

The language is defined as follows: the compound program instructions are

instruction ::= *elementary*
            instruction ; *instruction*
            if *boolean_expr* then *instruction* else *instruction* endif
            while *boolean_expr* do *instruction* done

and the boolean expressions are defined as

boolean_expr ::= *boolean_atomic*
            boolean_expr and *boolean_expr*
            boolean_expr or *boolean_expr*
            not *boolean_expr*

elementary instructions are deterministic, terminating basic program blocks like assignments and simple expression evaluations. *boolean_atomic* boolean expressions, such as comparisons, have semantics as sets of "acceptable" environments. For instance, a *boolean_atomic* expression can be x < y + 4; its semantics is the set of execution environments where variables x and y verify the above comparison. If we restrict ourselves to a finite number n of integer variables, an environment is just a n-tuple of integers.

The denotational semantics of a code fragment c maps the set X of possible execution environments before the instruction into the set Y of possible environments after the instruction. Let us take an example: environments are elements of $\mathbb{Z}^3$, representing the values of three integer variables x, y and z, then $[\![\texttt{x:=y+z}]\!]$ is the function $\langle x, y, z \rangle \mapsto \langle y + z, y, z \rangle$. Semantics of basic constructs (assignments, arithmetic operators) can be easily dealt with this way; we shall now see how to deal with flow control.

The semantics of a sequence is expressed by simple composition

$$[\![e_1;\ e_2]\!] = [\![e_2]\!] \circ [\![e_1]\!]$$

Tests get expressed easily, using as the semantics $[\![c]\!]$ of a boolean expression c the set of environments it matches:

$$[\![\texttt{if } c \texttt{ then } e_1 \texttt{ else } e_2]\!](x) = \text{if } x \in [\![c]\!] \text{ then } [\![e_1]\!](x) \text{ else } [\![e_2]\!](x)$$

and loops get the usual least-fixpoint semantics (considering the point-wise extension of the Scott flat ordering on partial functions)

$$[\![\texttt{while } c \texttt{ do } f]\!] = \text{lfp } \lambda\phi.\lambda x.\text{if } x \in [\![c]\!] \text{ then } \phi \circ [\![f]\!](x) \text{ else } x.$$

Non-termination shall be noted by $\perp$.

2.2   Our Framework for Probabilistic Concrete Semantics

We shall express probabilities using **measures** [16, §1.18]. We shall begin by a few classical mathematical definitions.

Measures The basic objects we shall operate on are measures.

- A **σ-algebra** is a set of subsets of a set X that contains $\emptyset$ and is stable by countable union and complementation (and thus contains X and is stable by countable intersection). For technical reasons, not all sets can be measured (that is, given a probability) and we have to restrict ourselves to some sufficiently large σ-algebras, such as the Borel or Lebesgue sets [16].
- A set X with a σ-algebra σ_X defined on it is called a **measurable space** and the elements of the σ-algebra are the **measurable subsets**. We shall often mention measurable spaces by their name, omitting the σ-algebra, if no confusion is possible.
- If X and Y are measurable spaces, $f : X \to Y$ is a **measurable function** if for all W measurable in Y, $f^{-1}(W)$ is measurable in X.
- A **positive measure** is a function μ defined on a σ-algebra σ_X whose range is in $[0, \infty]$ and which is countably additive. μ is countably additive if, taking $(A_n)_{n \in \mathbb{N}}$ a disjoint collection of elements of σ_X, then $\mu(\cup_{n=0}^{\infty} A_n) = \sum_{n=0}^{\infty} \mu(A_n)$. To avoid trivialities, we assume $\mu(A) < \infty$ for at least one A. The **total weight** of a measure μ is $\mu(X)$. μ is said to be **concentrated** on $A \subseteq X$ if for all B, $\mu(B) = \mu(B \cap A)$. We shall note $\mathcal{M}_+(X)$ the positive measures on X.

- A **probability measure** is a positive measure of total weight 1; a **sub-probability measure** has total weight less or equal to 1. We shall note $\mathcal{M}_{\leq 1}(X)$ the sub-probability measures on X.
- Given two sub-probability measures μ and μ' (or more generally, two σ-finite measures) on X and X' respectively, we note $\mu \otimes \mu'$ the product measure [16, definition 7.7], defined on the product σ-algebra $\sigma_X \times \sigma_{X'}$. The characterizing property of this product measure is that $\mu \otimes \mu'(A \times A') = \mu(A).\mu'(A')$ for all measurable sets A and A'.

Our semantics shall be expressed as continuous linear operators between measure spaces, of norm less than 1, using the Banach norm of total variation on measures. This is necessary to ensure the mathematical well-formedness of certain definitions, such as the concrete semantics of loops. As the definitions for these concepts and some mathematical proofs for the definition of the concrete semantics are quite long and not relevant at all to the analysis, we shall omit them from this paper and refer the reader to an extended version. As a running example for the definitions of the semantics, we shall use a program with real variables x, y and z; the set of possible environments is then $\mathbb{R}^3$.

General Form Let us consider an elementary program statement c so that $[\![c]\!] : X \to Y$, X and Y being measurable spaces. We shall also suppose that $[\![c]\!]$ is measurable. Let us first remark that this condition happens, for instance, for any continuous function from X and Y if both are topological spaces and σ_Y is the Borel σ-algebra [16, §1.11]. $[\![x := y+z]\!] = \langle x, y, z \rangle \mapsto \langle y + z, y, z \rangle$ is continuous.

To $[\![c]\!]$ we associate the following linear operator $[\![c]\!]_p$:

$$[\![c]\!]_p : \left| \begin{array}{l} \mathcal{M}_{\leq 1}(X) \to \mathcal{M}_{\leq 1}(Y) \\ \mu \qquad \mapsto \lambda W.\mu([\![c]\!]^{-1}(W)) \end{array} \right. .$$

We shall see that all flow control constructs "preserve" measurability; i.e., if all sub-blocks of a complex construct have measurable semantics, then the construct shall have measurable semantics. We shall then extend the framework to programs containing **random**-like operators; their semantics will be expressed as linear operators of norm less than 1 on measure spaces.

Random Inputs or Generators An obvious interest of probabilistic semantics is to give an accurate semantics to assignment such as x:=random();, where random() is a function that, each time it is invoked, returns a real value equidistributed between 0 and 1, independently of previous calls.[1] We therefore have to

---

[1] Of course, functions such as the POSIX C function drand48() would not fulfill such requirements, since they are pseudo-random generators whose output depends on an internal state that changes each time the function is invoked, thus the probability laws of successive invocations are not independent. However, ideal random generators are quite an accurate approximation for most analyses.

give a semantics to constructs such as `x:=random();`, where `random` returns a value in a measured space R whose probability is given by the measure μ_R and is independent of all other calls and previous states.

We decompose this operation into two steps:[2]

$$X_p \xrightarrow[\ [\![\rho:=\mathtt{random}()]\!]\ ]{} (X \times R)_p \xrightarrow[\ [\![\mathtt{x}:=\rho]\!]\ ]{} X_p$$

with the arc labelled $[\![\mathtt{x}:=\mathtt{random}()]\!]$ over the top.

The second step is a simple assignment operator, addressed by the above method. The first step boils down to measure products:

$$[\![\rho:=\mathtt{random}()]\!] : \left| \begin{array}{l} X_p \to (X \times R)_p \\ \mu \mapsto \mu \otimes \mu_R \end{array} \right. .$$

Tests and Loops We restrict ourselves to test and loop conditions b so that $[\![b]\!]$ is measurable. This condition is fulfilled if all the *boolean_atomic* sets are measurable since the σ-algebra is closed by finite union and intersection. For instance, $[\![\mathtt{x} < \mathtt{y}]\!] = \{\langle x, y, z\rangle \mid x < y\}$ is measurable.

The deterministic semantics for tests are:

$$[\![\mathtt{if}\ c\ \mathtt{then}\ e_1\ \mathtt{else}\ e_2]\!](x) = \mathtt{if}\ x \in [\![c]\!]\ \mathtt{then}\ [\![e_1]\!](x)\ \mathtt{else}\ [\![e_2]\!](x).$$

Let us first compute

$$[\![\mathtt{if}\ c\ \mathtt{then}\ e_1\ \mathtt{else}\ e_2]\!]^{-1}(W) = ([\![e_1]\!]^{-1}(W) \cap [\![c]\!]) \cup ([\![e_2]\!]^{-1}(W) \cap [\![c]\!]^C).$$

$[\![c]\!]$ is the set of environments matched by condition c. It is obtained inductively from the set of environment matched by the atomic tests (e.g. comparisons):

- $[\![c_1\ \mathtt{or}\ c_2]\!] = [\![c_1]\!] \cup [\![c_2]\!]$
- $[\![c_1\ \mathtt{and}\ c_2]\!] = [\![c_1]\!] \cap [\![c_2]\!]$
- $[\![\mathtt{not}\ c]\!] = [\![c]\!]^C$

Using our above framework to lift deterministic semantics to probabilistic ones, we obtain

$$[\![\mathtt{if}\ c\ \mathtt{then}\ e_1\ \mathtt{else}\ e_2]\!]_p(\mu) = X \mapsto \mu([\![\mathtt{if}\ c\ \mathtt{then}\ e_1\ \mathtt{else}\ e_2]\!]^{-1}(X))$$
$$= X \mapsto \mu(([\![e_1]\!]^{-1}(X) \cap [\![c]\!]) \cup ([\![e_2]\!]^{-1}(X) \cap [\![c]\!]^C)$$
$$= X \mapsto \mu([\![e_1]\!]^{-1}(X) \cap [\![c]\!]) + \mu([\![e_2]\!]^{-1}(X) \cap [\![c]\!]^C)$$
$$= [\![e_1]\!]_p \circ \phi_{[\![c]\!]}(\mu) + [\![e_2]\!]_p \circ \phi_{[\![c]\!]^C}(\mu) \quad (1)$$

where $\phi_W(\mu) = \lambda X.\mu(X \cap W)$.

---

[2] Another equivalent way, used by Kozen [10,11], is to consider random values as countable streams in the input environment of the program.

We lift in the same fashion the semantics of loops (we note $\sqcup$ an union of pairwise disjoint subsets of a set):

$$[\![\text{while } c \text{ do } e]\!]^{-1}(X)$$
$$= (\text{lfp } \lambda\phi.\lambda x.\text{if } x \in [\![c]\!] \text{ then } \phi \circ [\![e]\!](x) \text{ else } x)^{-1}(X)$$
$$= \bigsqcup_{n \in \mathbb{N}} (\lambda Y.[\![e]\!]^{-1}(Y) \cap [\![c]\!])^n (X \cap [\![c]\!]^C)$$

(2)

We therefore derive the form of the probabilistic semantics of the while loop:

$$[\![\text{while } c \text{ do } e]\!]_p(\mu) = \lambda X.\mu \left(\bigsqcup_{n \in \mathbb{N}} (\lambda Y.[\![e]\!]^{-1}(Y) \cap [\![c]\!])^n (X \cap [\![c]\!]^C) \right)$$

$$= \lambda X. \sum_{n \in \mathbb{N}} \mu \left((\lambda Y.[\![e]\!]^{-1}(Y) \cap [\![c]\!])^n (X \cap [\![c]\!]^C) \right)$$

$$= \sum_{n=0}^{\infty} \phi_{[\![c]\!]^C} \circ ([\![e]\!]_p \circ \phi_{[\![c]\!]})^n (\mu)$$

$$= \phi_{[\![c]\!]^C} \left(\sum_{n=0}^{\infty} ([\![e]\!]_p \circ \phi_{[\![c]\!]})^n (\mu) \right)$$

$$= \phi_{[\![c]\!]^C} \left(\lim_{n \to \infty} (\lambda\mu'.\mu + [\![e]\!]_p \circ \phi_{[\![c]\!]}(\mu'))^n (\lambda X.0) \right)$$

(3)

Limits and infinite sums are taken according to the set-wise topology. We refer the reader to an extended version of this paper for the technical explanations on continuity and convergence.

2.3   Probabilities and Nondeterminism

It has been pointed out [12,8] that we must distinguish deterministic and non-deterministic probabilistic semantics. Deterministic, non-probabilistic semantics embed naturally into the above probabilistic semantics: instead of a value $x \in X$, we consider the Dirac measure $\delta_x \in \mathcal{M}_{\leq 1}(X)$ defined by $\delta_x(X) = \begin{cases} 1 & \text{if } x \in X \\ 0 & \text{otherwise.} \end{cases}$

How can we account for nondeterministic non-probabilistic semantics?

We move from deterministic to nondeterministic semantics by lifting to power-sets. It is possible to consider nondeterministic probabilistic semantics: the result of a program is then a set of probability measures. Of course, non-deterministic non-probabilistic semantics get embedded naturally: to $A \in \mathcal{P}(X)$ we associate $\{\delta_a \mid a \in A\} \in \mathcal{P}(\mathcal{M}_+(X))$. We therefore consider four semantics:

determinism	nondeterminism
probabilistic	nondeterministic probabilistic

The advantage of probabilistic nondeterminism is that we can consider programs whose inputs are not all distributed according to a distribution, or whose distribution is not exactly known. Our analysis is based on probabilistic nondeterminism and thus handles all cases.

3   Abstract Semantics

We shall first give the vocabulary and notations we use for abstractions in general. We shall then proceed by giving an example of an domain that abstracts probabilistic semantics as defined in the previous section. This domain is parametric in multiple ways, most importantly by the use of an abstract domain for the non-probabilistic semantics of the studied system.

3.1   Summary of Abstraction

Let us consider a preordered set $X^\sharp$ and a monotone function $\gamma_X : X^\sharp \to \mathcal{P}(X)$. $x^\sharp \in X^\sharp$ is said to be an **abstraction** of $x^\flat \subset X$ if $x^\flat \subseteq \gamma_X(x^\sharp)$. γ_X is called the **concretization function**. The triple $\langle \mathcal{P}(X), X^\sharp, \gamma_X \rangle$ is called an **abstraction**. $\mathcal{P}(X)$ is the **concrete domain** and $X^\sharp$ the **abstract domain**. Such definitions can be extended to any preordered set $X^\flat$ besides $\mathcal{P}(X)$.

Let us now consider two abstractions $\langle \mathcal{P}(X), X^\sharp, \gamma_X \rangle$ and $\langle \mathcal{P}(Y), Y^\sharp, \gamma_Y \rangle$ and a function $f : X \to Y$. $f^\sharp$ is said to be **an abstraction of f** if

$$\forall x^\sharp \in X^\sharp \ \forall x \in X \ \ x \in \gamma_X(x^\sharp) \Rightarrow f(x) \in \gamma_Y(f^\sharp(x^\sharp)) \tag{4}$$

More generally, if $\langle X^\flat, X^\sharp, \gamma_X \rangle$ and $\langle Y^\flat, Y^\sharp, \gamma_Y \rangle$ are abstractions and $f^\flat : X^\flat \to Y^\flat$ is a monotone function, then $f^\sharp$ is said to be **an abstraction of $f^\flat$** if

$$\forall x^\flat \in X^\flat \ \forall x^\sharp \in X^\sharp \ \ x^\flat \sqsubseteq \gamma_X(x^\sharp) \Rightarrow f^\flat(x^\flat) \sqsubseteq \gamma_X(f^\sharp(x^\sharp)) \tag{5}$$

Algorithmically, elements in $X^\sharp$ will have a machine representation. To any program construct c we shall attach an effectively computable function $[\![c]\!]^\sharp$ so that $[\![c]\!]^\sharp$ is an abstraction of $[\![c]\!]$. Given a machine description of a superset of the inputs of the programs, the abstract version yields a superset of the outputs of the program. If a state is not in this superset, this means that, for sure, the program cannot reach this state.

Let us take an example, the **domain of intervals**: if $X^\sharp = Y^\sharp = T^3$ where $T = \{(a,b) \in \mathbb{Z} \cup \{-\infty, +\infty\} \mid a \le b\} \cup \{\bot\}$, $\gamma(a,b) = \{c \in \mathbb{Z} \mid a \le c \le b\}$ and γ induces a preorder $\sqsubseteq_T$ over T and, pointwise, over $X^\sharp$, then we can take $[\![\mathtt{x:=y+z}]\!]^\sharp((a_\mathtt{x}, b_\mathtt{x}), (a_\mathtt{y}, b_\mathtt{y}), (a_\mathtt{z}, b_\mathtt{z})) = ((a_\mathtt{y} + a_\mathtt{z}, b_\mathtt{y} + b_\mathtt{z}), (a_\mathtt{y}, b_\mathtt{y}), (a_\mathtt{z}, b_\mathtt{z}))$.

3.2   Probabilistic Abstraction

The concrete probabilistic domains given in 2.2 can be abstracted as in the previous definition. Interesting properties of such an abstraction would be, for instance, to give an upper bound on the probability of some subsets of possible environments at the end of a computation.

3.3 Turning Fixpoints of Affine Operators into Fixpoints of Monotone Set Operators

Equation 3 shows that the semantics of loops are given as infinite sums or, equivalently, as fixpoints of some affine operators. In non-probabilistic semantics, the semantics of loops is usually the fixpoint of some monotone operator on the concrete lattice, which get immediately abstracted as fixpoints on the abstract lattice. The approximation is not so evident in the case of this sum; we shall nevertheless see how to deal with it using fixpoints on the abstract lattice.

Defining μ_n recursively, as follows: $\mu_0 = \lambda X.0$ and $\mu_{n+1} = \psi \mu_n$, with $\psi(\nu) = \mu + [\![e]\!]_p \circ \phi_{[\![c]\!]}(\nu)$, we can rewrite equation 3 as $[\![\text{while } c \text{ do } e]\!]_p(\mu) = \phi_{[\![c]\!]^C}(\lim_{n \to \infty} \mu_n)$. We wish to approximate this limit in the measure space by an abstract element.

We shall use the following method: to get an approximation of the limit of a sequence $(u_n)_{n \in \mathbb{N}}$ defined recursively by $u_{n+1} = f(u_n)$, we can find a closed set S stable by f so that $u_N \in S$ for some N; then $\lim_{n \to \infty} u_n \in S$. Let us note than finding such a set does not prove that the limit exists; we have to suppose that f is such that this limit exists. In our case, this condition is necessarily fulfilled.

Let us take $\mu^\sharp$ and $\mu^\sharp_0$ respective abstractions of μ. Let us call $\psi^\sharp(\nu^\sharp) = \mu^\sharp +^\sharp [\![e]\!]_p^\sharp \circ \phi^\sharp_{[\![c]\!]}(\nu^\sharp)$. Let us take a certain $N \in \mathbb{N}$ and call $L^\sharp = \text{lfp } \lambda \nu^\sharp . \psi^{\sharp N}(\mu_0^\sharp) \sqcup \psi^\sharp(\nu^\sharp)$; then by induction, for all $n \geq N$, $\mu_n \in \gamma(L^\sharp)$. As $\gamma(L^\sharp)$ is topologically closed, $\lim n \to \infty \in \gamma(L^\sharp)$. Therefore $L^\sharp$ is an approximation of the requested limit.

Let us suppose that we have an "approximate least fixpoint" operation $\text{lfp}^\sharp :$ $(X^\sharp \xrightarrow{\text{monotonic}} X^\sharp) \to X^\sharp$. By "approximate least fixpoint" we mean that if $f^\sharp : X^\sharp \to X^\sharp$ is monotonic, then, noting $x_0^\sharp = \text{lfp}^\sharp(f)$, $f^\sharp(x_0^\sharp) \sqsubseteq x_0^\sharp$. The justification of our appellation, and the interest of such a function, lies in the following well-known result:

Lemma 1. *If* $f^\sharp : X^\sharp \to X^\sharp$ *is an abstraction of* $f^\flat : \mathcal{P}(X) \to \mathcal{P}(X)$ *and* $f^\sharp(x_0^\sharp) \sqsubseteq x_0^\sharp$, *then* $\text{lfp } f^\flat \subseteq \gamma_X(x_0^\sharp)$.

Of course, building such an operation is not easy. Trying the successive iterations of $f^{\sharp n}$ until reaching a fixpoint does not necessarily terminate. One has to use special tricks and widening operators to build such a function (see 5.3).

Provided we have such an operation, abstraction follows directly:

$$[\![\text{while } c \text{ do } e]\!]^\sharp(W^\sharp) = \phi^\sharp_{[\![c]\!]^C}(\text{lfp}^\sharp X^\sharp \mapsto W^\sharp \sqcup [\![e]\!]^\sharp(\phi^\sharp_{[\![c]\!]}(X))).$$

As usual in abstract interpretation, it might be wise to do some semantics-preserving transformations on the program, such as unrolling the first few turns of the loop, before applying this abstraction. This is likely to yield better results.

4   A Probabilistic Abstract Domain

As considerable effort has been put into the design and implementation of non-probabilistic abstract domains (see §1.1 for examples), it would be interesting to be able to create probabilistic abstract domains from these. In the this section, we shall give such a generic construction.

4.1   The Intuition Behind the Method

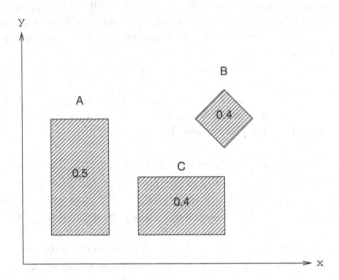

Fig. 1. An abstract value representing measures μ so that $\mu(A) \leq 0.5$, $\mu(B) \leq 0.4$ and $\mu(C) \leq 0.4$.

A finite sequence A_i of disjoint measurable subsets of X and corresponding coefficients $\alpha_i \in \mathbb{R}_+$, represent the set of measures μ so that:

- μ is concentrated on $\bigcup A_i$
- for all i, $\mu(A_i) \leq \alpha_i$.

For practical purposes, the A_i are concretizations of abstract elements, polyhedra for instance (Fig. 1).

This abstraction is intuitive, but lifting operations to it proves difficult: the constraint that sets must be disjoint is difficult to handle in the presence of non injective semantics $[\![c]\!]$. This is the reason why we rather consider the following definition: a finite sequence A_i of (non-necessarily disjoint) measurable subsets of X and corresponding coefficients $\alpha_i \in \mathbb{R}_+$ represent the set of measures μ so that there exist measures μ_i so that:

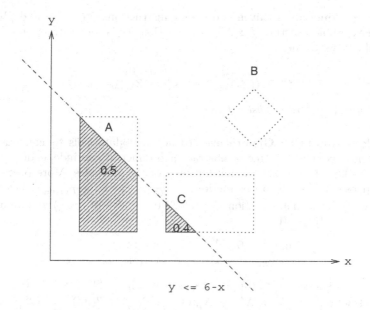

Fig. 2. The abstract value of Fig. 1 after going into the first branch of a `if`
`y<=6-x...` test.

- $\mu = \sum \mu_i$;
- for all i, μ_i is concentrated on A_i;
- for all i, $\mu(A_i) \leq \alpha_i$.

We shall see how to formalize this definition and how program constructs act on
such abstract objects.

4.2   Theoretical Construction

Let us take an indexing set Λ, an abstraction (see §3.1) $\Gamma_X = \langle \sigma_X, X^\sharp, \gamma_X \rangle$ and
an abstraction $\Gamma_W = \langle \mathcal{P}([0,1]^\Lambda), W^\sharp, \gamma_W \rangle$. We define an abstraction $\Gamma_{\Lambda,\Gamma_X,\Gamma_W} = \langle \mathcal{C}(X_p), S_{\Lambda,\Gamma_X,\Gamma_W}, \gamma_{\Lambda,\Gamma_X,\Gamma_W} \rangle$. $\mathcal{C}(X_p)$ is the set of closed sets of the topological
space X_p for the set-wise topology [5, §III.10] — this is a technical requirement
that is easy to fulfill. We wish to define compositionally abstract semantics for
our language (defined in §2.1). We shall omit the $\Lambda, \Gamma_X, \Gamma_W$ subscript if there is
no ambiguity.

Domain   Let $S_{\Lambda,\Gamma_X,\Gamma_W} = X^{\sharp \Lambda} \times W^\sharp$ be our abstract domain. We then define
$\gamma_{\Lambda,\Gamma_X,\Gamma_W} : S_{\Lambda,\Gamma_X,\Gamma_W} \to \mathcal{P}(X_p)$ so that $((Z_\lambda)_{\lambda \in \Lambda}, w)$ maps to the set of measures
$\mu \in \mathcal{M}_{\leq 1}(X)$ so that there exist measures $(\mu_\lambda)_{\lambda \in \Lambda}$ so that

- for each $\lambda \in \Lambda$, μ_λ is concentrated on $\gamma_X(Z_\lambda)$;
- the family $(\int d\mu_\lambda)_{\lambda \in \Lambda}$ of total weights of those measures is in $\gamma_W(w)$.

Regular Constructs Given two such constructions $\Gamma_{\Lambda,\Gamma_X,\Gamma_W}$ and $\Gamma_{\Lambda,\Gamma_Y,\Gamma_W}$ and measurable function $f : X \to Y$ so that $f^{\sharp}$ is an abstraction of f (see formula 4), we define

$$f_p{}^{\sharp} : \left| \begin{array}{l} S_{\Lambda,\Gamma_X,\Gamma_W} \quad \to S_{\Lambda,\Gamma_Y,\Gamma_W} \\ ((Z_\lambda)_{\lambda \in \Lambda}, w) \mapsto ((f^{\sharp}(Z_\lambda))_{\lambda \in \Lambda}, w). \end{array} \right.$$

Theorem 1. $f_p{}^{\sharp}$ is an abstraction of f_p.

Random Inputs or Generators To accommodate calls to `random`-like instructions, we must be able to abstract a product of two independent random variables knowing an abstraction for each of the variables. More precisely, let us suppose we have two abstractions $S_{\Lambda,\Gamma_X,\Gamma_W}$ and $S_{\Lambda',\Gamma_{X'},\Gamma_{W'}}$. Let us also suppose we have an abstraction $\Gamma_{W_p} = \langle \mathcal{P}([0,1]^{\Lambda \times \Lambda'}), W_p, \gamma_{W_p} \rangle$ and an abstraction $p^{\sharp} : W \times W' \to W_p$ of

$$p : \left| \begin{array}{l} [0,1]^{\Lambda} \times [0,1]^{\Lambda'} \quad \to [0,1]^{\Lambda \times \Lambda'} \\ ((w_\lambda)_{\lambda \in \Lambda}, (w_{\lambda'})_{\lambda' \in \Lambda'}) \mapsto (w_\lambda.w_{\lambda'})_{(\lambda,\lambda') \in \Lambda \times \Lambda'}. \end{array} \right.$$

Let us also suppose we have an abstraction $\Gamma_{\Pi} = \langle \mathcal{P}(X \times X'), \Pi^{\sharp}, \gamma_{\Pi} \rangle$ and an abstraction $\times^{\sharp} : X^{\sharp} \times X'^{\sharp} \to X_p$ of $\times : \mathcal{P}(X) \times \mathcal{P}(X') \to \mathcal{P}(X \times X')$ (see formula 5). Let us take abstract elements $A = ((Z_\lambda)_{\lambda \in \Lambda}, w) \in S_{\Lambda,\Gamma_X,\Gamma_W}$ and $A' = ((Z'_{\lambda'})_{\lambda' \in \Lambda'}, w') \in S_{\Lambda',\Gamma_{X'},\Gamma_{W'}}$ then we define

$$A \otimes^{\sharp} A' = ((Z_\lambda \times^{\sharp} Z'_{\lambda'})_{(\lambda,\lambda') \in \Lambda \times \Lambda'}, p^{\sharp}(W, W'))$$

Theorem 2. $(A^{\sharp}, A'^{\sharp}) \mapsto A^{\sharp} \otimes^{\sharp} A'^{\sharp}$ is an abstraction of $(\mu, \mu') \mapsto \mu \otimes \mu'$. That is, if $\mu \in \gamma_{\lambda,\Gamma_X,\Gamma_W}(A^{\sharp})$ and $\mu' \in \gamma_{\Gamma_{X'},\Gamma_{W'}}(A'^{\sharp})$ then $\mu \otimes \mu' \in \gamma_p(A^{\sharp} \otimes^{\sharp} A'^{\sharp})$.

Tests Lifting equation 1 to powersets yields the concrete semantics:

$$[\![\text{if } c \text{ then } e_1 \text{ else } e_2]\!]_p{}^{\flat}(W) = [\![e_1]\!]_p{}^{\flat} \circ \phi^{\flat}{}_{[\![c]\!]}(W) +^{\flat} [\![e_2]\!]_p{}^{\flat} \circ \phi^{\flat}{}_{[\![c]\!]^c}(W)$$

which can be abstracted right away by replacing $\flat$'s by $\sharp$'s. All that is therefore needed are suitable $\phi^{\sharp}{}_{[\![c]\!]}(W)$ and $+^{\sharp}$.

We define

$$((Z_\lambda)_{\lambda \in \Lambda}, w) +^{\sharp} ((Z'_\lambda)_{\lambda' \in \Lambda'}, w') = ((Z_\lambda)_{\lambda \in \Lambda \amalg \Lambda'}, w \oplus^{\sharp} w')$$

where $\oplus^{\sharp}$ is an abstraction of the canonical bijection between $[0,1]^{\Lambda} \times [0,1]^{\Lambda'}$ and $[0,1]^{\Lambda \amalg \Lambda'}$ where $\Lambda \amalg \Lambda'$ is the disjoint union of Λ and Λ'. It is easy to see that such a $+^{\sharp}$ is an abstraction of $+^{\flat}$.

Let us suppose we have a suitable abstraction $I^{\sharp}{}_{[\![c]\!]} : X^{\sharp} \to X^{\sharp}$ of the intersection function $W^{\flat} \mapsto W^{\flat} \cap [\![c]\!]$. We also require that $\forall x^{\sharp} \in X^{\sharp}$ $I^{\sharp}{}_{[\![c]\!]}(x^{\sharp}) \sqsubseteq x^{\sharp}$.[3] Then we can define

$$\phi^{\sharp}{}_{[\![c]\!]}((Z_\lambda)_{\lambda \in \Lambda}, w) = ((I^{\sharp}{}_{[\![c]\!]}(Z_\lambda))_{\lambda \in \Lambda}, d^{\sharp}(w))$$

---

[3] One possible construction for this function is $W^{\sharp} \mapsto W^{\sharp} \cap^{\sharp} [\![c]\!]^{\sharp}$ using an approximation $[\![c]\!]^{\sharp}$ of the set of environments matched by c and an approximation $\cap^{\sharp}$ of the

Theorem 3. $\phi^{\sharp}{}_{[\![c]\!]}$ *is an abstraction of* $\phi^{\flat}{}_{[\![c]\!]}$.

Loops Using the $\phi^{\sharp}{}_{[\![c]\!]}$ functions defined in the preceding paragraph and the framework of §3.3, it is easy to build an abstract semantics for loops provided we have suitable widening operators. The heuristic design of such operators will be discussed in §5.3.

4.3   Multiplicity of Representations and Coalescing

The reader might have been surprised we consider a preorder on the abstract values, not an order. The reason is that we want to talk of algorithmic representations, and a same concrete set can be represented in several ways. For instance, rational languages can be represented by an infinity of finite automata. Of course, an interesting property is that there is a minimal automaton and thus a canonical form. Yet we point out that this minimal automaton is defined up to state renaming, thus it has several representations.

We propose two **coalescing operations** to simplify representations without loss of precision:

1. If there is a certain Z_0 so that several λ are so that $Z_\lambda = Z_0$, and our numerical lattice enables us to represent exactly a sum, then one could replace all the entries for all these λ's by a single one.
2. Similarly, if Z_{λ_1} and Z_{λ_2} are so that there exists W so that $\gamma_X(Z_{\lambda_1}) \cup \gamma_X(Z_{\lambda_2}) = \gamma_X(W)$, then one can coalesce Z_{λ_1} and Z_{λ_2} into W, with probability $\min(w_{\lambda_1} + w_{\lambda_2}, 1)$.

5   Practical Constructions

In the previous section, we have given a very parametric construction, depending on parameters and assuming the existence of some operators. In this section we shall give examples of instances of suitable parameters and experimental results on a simple example.

5.1   Abstract Domain

We shall first define a narrower class of abstract domains for probabilistic applications, for which we shall give algorithms for some operations.

---

greatest lower bound. This does not in general yield optimal results, and it is better to compute $I^{\sharp}{}_{[\![c]\!]}(W^{\sharp})$ by induction on the structure of c if c is a boolean expression. An example of suboptimality is the domain of integer intervals on one variable, with $W = [0, +\infty[$ and boolean expression $(\mathbf{x} > 2) \vee (\mathbf{x} < -2)$. The abstraction of the domain matched by the expression is $\top$, which gives us the approximate intersection $[0, +\infty[$ while recursive evaluation yields $[2, +\infty[$. Further precision can be achieved by local iterations [7].

Finite Sequences Let us suppose that $X^\sharp$ has a minimum element $\perp_{X^\sharp}$. We then take $\Lambda = \mathbb{N}$. We note $X^{\sharp(\mathbb{N})}$ the set of sequences with finite support; that is, those that are stationary on the value $\perp_{X^\sharp}$. We shall restrict ourselves to such abstract sequences.

As for the set of numeric constraints, one can for example use polyhedric constraints. Such constraints have the following nice property:

Theorem 4. *Let us suppose that:*

- *the numeric constraints are expressed as convex polyhedra, and the inclusion of two such polyhedra is decidable;*
- *the intersection test over $X^\sharp$ is computable.*

Then the preorder test on $S(X^\sharp)$ (i.e. the function that, taking $(a,b) \in S(X^\sharp)^2$ as parameter, returns 1 if and only if $a \sqsubseteq_{S(X^\sharp)} b$ and 0 otherwise) is computable.

Proof. Let $a = ((Z_i)_{i<N}, w)$ and $b = ((Z'_i)_{i<N'}, w')$. Let us call $\alpha_i = \mu_i(Z_i)$ and $\alpha'_i = \mu_i(Z'_i)$. Let $(\Xi_i)_{i<M}$ be the set of all nonempty intersections of elements of the sequences Z and Z_i. Let E be the system of equations of the form $\alpha_i = \sum \xi_j$ taking only the ξ_j so that $\Xi_j \subseteq Z_i$, E' the system of equations of the form $\alpha'_i = \sum \xi_j$ taking only the xi_j so that $\Xi_j \subseteq Z_i$. F the system of linear inequations yielded by $(\alpha_i)_{i<N} \in w$ and F' the system of linear inequations yielded by $(\alpha'_i)_{i<N} \in w'$. Given a system of (in)equations σ, we call $\mathcal{S}(\sigma)$ the set of solutions of σ. We claim that

$$a \sqsubseteq_{S(X^\sharp)} b \iff \mathcal{S}(E \cup E' \cup F) \subseteq \mathcal{S}(E \cup E' \cup F').$$

The right-hand side of the equivalence is decidable by hypothesis.

Our claim is the consequence of the following lemma:

Lemma 2. *If Z is a nonempty measurable set and $c \in \mathbb{R}_+$, then there exists $\mu \in \mathcal{M}_+(Z)$ so that $\mu(Z) = c$.*

Proof. Let $z_0 \in Z$. Then we define $\mu(A)$ to be equal to c if $z_0 \in A$ and to 0 otherwise.

Simple Constraints We propose a very restricted class of polyhedric constraints, given by finite sequences $(c_n)_{n \in \mathbb{N}} \in [0,1]^{(\mathbb{N})}$, so that

$$(\alpha_n)_{n \in \mathbb{N}} \in \gamma_W((c_n)_{n \in \mathbb{N}}) \iff \forall n \in \mathbb{N} \; \alpha_n \le c_n.$$

An abstract element is thus stored a finite sequence (Z_n, c_n) of pairs in $X^\sharp \times [0,1]$. Similar **convex hulls** have already been proposed for rules operating on concrete semantics [8].

It is very easy in such a framework to get an upper approximation of the probability of a set W, if we have a function $\tau_W : X^\sharp \to \{\text{true}, \text{false}\}$ so that $\tau_W(X^\sharp) = \text{true} \iff W \cap \gamma_X(X^\sharp) \ne \emptyset$: just take $\sum_{n \in \{n \in \mathbb{N} | \tau_W(Z_n) = \text{true}\}} c_n$.

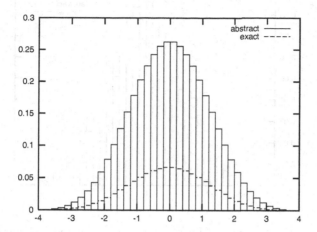

Fig. 3. Experimental results: $X_1 + X_2 + X_3 + X_4$ where the X_i are independent random variables equidistributed in $[-1, 1]$. The approximate simulation divided $[-1, 1]$ into 10 sub-segments each of maximal probability 0.1. Estimates on segments of length 0.2.

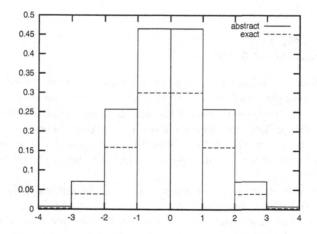

Fig. 4. Same computations as Fig. 3. Approximations on segments of length 1 give more accurate results than approximations on smaller segments.

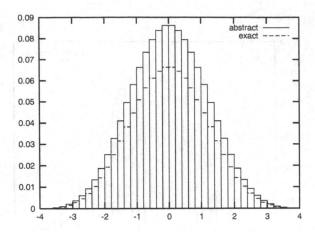

Fig. 5. Same computation as Fig. 3, but the approximate simulation divided $[-1, 1]$ into 100 sub-segments each of maximal probability 0.01. The sampled segments are of length 0.2. As with Fig. 4, precision is improved is sampling segments are bigger than the segments used in the computation.

5.2   Experiments

Using our framework, we analyzed the following C program:

```
double x=0.0;
int i;
for (i=0; i<4; i++)
  x += drand48()*2.0-1.0;
```

The `drand48()` function returns a `double` number equidistributed in $[0, 1[$. We chose such a simple program so as to have an easy exact computation.

As an accurate representation of the `double` type would be complex and dependent on the particular C implementation, we rather chose to use an idealized version of this type as the real numbers. Figures 3, 4 and 5 show results of the experiments with different parameters, comparing abstract samples and exact computations.

In those tests, `drand48()` is supposed to return an uniformly distributed real number in $[0, 1]$. It is abstracted as $([n/N, (n+1)/N], 1/N)_{0 \le n < N}$ where N is a parameter. The "samples" are segments $[\alpha, \beta]$; for each sample segment W, both an upper bound and an exact results of $\mu(W)$ are computed, where μ is the distribution of the final value of x in the above program. The upper bound is is computed from the abstract result, by the method described in 5.1. The bars displayed in the figure are the chosen segments $[\alpha, \beta]$ in x and their exact and approximate probabilities in y.

Those figures illustrate the following phenomenon: as computations go, the abstract areas Z_n grow bigger. If the samples are not enough bigger than those areas, the approximation are bad (Fig. 3). Results improve if N is increased (Fig. 5) or the sample size is increased (Fig. 4). An intuitive vision of this somewhat paradoxical behavior is that our abstract domain represents masses quite exactly, but loses precision on their exact location. If we ask our analysis to provide information on the probability of a very small area of the output domain (small compared to the precision of the input distribution and of the complexity of the transfer function), it tends to overestimate it (Fig. 3) because lots of masses could be located at that point. If we ask on a wider area, the error on the locations of the masses compared to the area becomes small and thus the error on the result becomes acceptable (Fig. 4).

5.3 Widenings

The crucial problem of the abstract domains not satisfying the ascending chain condition is the "widening" to choose. By widening, we mean some kind of over-approximation that jumps higher in the abstract domain to allow for convergence in finite time even if the abstract domain does not enjoy the property that every ascending sequence is stationary. Let us take a simple example on a nonprobabilistic program, with the domain of intervals: if successive abstract values are $[1,1]$, $[1,2]$, $[1,3]$, $[1,4]$, the system might try jumping to $[1,+\infty[$ for the next iteration. As this overestimates the set, it is safe.

The design of widenings is experimental in order to find a satisfying balance between cost and precision. While it is always possible to give a widening in all abstract domains with a maximum element (just jump to $\top$), it is quite difficult to design widenings giving interesting results. Here, we shall propose a few ideas:

- Let us suppose we have a widening operator in $X^\sharp$. When successive abstract values in an iteration are $(Z_n, c_n)_{n \leq N}$ so that both Z_n and c_n increase, then try the next iteration with (Z, c_N) where Z is the result of the widening in $X^\sharp$.
- We can also apply widenings on the numerical coefficients c_n. For instance, if we have an increasing sequence $(Z, c_n)_{n \leq N}$, we can jump to (Z, c) where c is slightly above c_N, possibly 1.

Both approaches can be combined.

Another important area is simplification. Each call to **random**-like functions yields a product of measures and multiplies the number of length of the sequence making up the abstract environment by the length of the sequence approximating the measure of the function. This of course can mean fast explosion. While coalescing (see 4.3) can help, we might have to consider more energic steps. A possibility is to coalesce several abstract sets that have high probability (let us say, > 0.8) and are "close enough", such as $[0,2]$ and $[1,3]$.

We are currently working on designing on implementing such strategies and testing them on realistic examples.

6   Conclusions and Prospects

We have given simple probabilistic semantics to a deterministic language supplementing the usual constructions by functions returning random values of known distributions. We have a generic construct to lift usual (that is, non-probabilistic) abstract analyses to probabilistic analyses. The analysis we propose can be used to get upper bounds on the probability of certain events at certain points of a program. We have tested it on some simple examples where an exact computation of the probabilities was possible, so as to have early experimental results of the influence of certain parameters over the quality of approximation.

We have proposed heuristics for some operators needed to handle large programs or loops. We expect to be able soon to propose results as to efficient heuristics on certain classes of problems.

Acknowledgements

We wish to thank the referees, as well as Patrick and Radhia Cousot, Jérôme Feret for their comments and proofreading.

References

1. Patrick Cousot. *Méthodes itératives de construction et d'approximation de points fixes d'opérateurs monotones sur un treillis, analyse sémantique de programmes.* Thèse d'état ès sciences mathématiques, Université scientifique et médicale de Grenoble, Grenoble, France, 21 mars 1978. 322, 323
2. Patrick Cousot and Radhia Cousot. Abstract interpretation and application to logic programs. *J. Logic Prog.*, 2-3(13):103–179, 1992. 322, 323
3. Patrick Cousot and Nicolas Halbwachs. Automatic discovery of linear restraints among variables of a program. In *Proceedings of the Fifth Conference on Principles of Programming Languages.* ACM Press, 1978. 322
4. Alain Deutsch. Semantic models and abstract interpretation techniques for inductive data structures and pointers. In *Proceedings of the ACM SIGPLAN Symposium on Partial Evaluation and Semantics-Based Program Manipulation*, pages 226–229, La Jolla, California, June 21–23, 1995. 322
5. J.L. Doob. *Measure Theory*, volume 143 of *Graduate Texts in Mathematics.* Springer-Verlag, 1994. 332
6. Philippe Granger. Static analysis of linear congruence equalities among variables of a program. In *Proceedings of TAPSOFT '91*, volume 493 of *Lecture Notes in Computer Science*, pages I. 169–172. Springer-Verlag, 1991. 322
7. Philippe Granger. Improving the results of static analyses programs by local decreasing iteration. In R. K. Shyamasundar, editor, *Foundations of Software Technology and Theoretical Computer Science, 12th Conference, New Delhi, India*, volume 652 of *Lecture Notes in Computer Science*, pages 68–79. Springer-Verlag, December 1992. 334
8. Jifeng He, K. Seidel, and A. McIver. Probabilistic models for the guarded command language. *Science of Computer Programming*, 28(2–3):171–192, April 1997. Formal specifications: foundations, methods, tools and applications (Konstancin, 1995). 323, 328, 335

9. Claire Jones. *Probabilistic Non-Determinism*. PhD thesis, University of Edinburgh, 1990. 323
10. D. Kozen. Semantics of probabilistic programs. In *20th Annual Symposium on Foundations of Computer Science*, pages 101–114, Long Beach, Ca., USA, October 1979. IEEE Computer Society Press. 323, 327
11. D. Kozen. Semantics of probabilistic programs. *Journal of Computer and System Sciences*, 22(3):328–350, 1981. A novel attempt at defining the semantics of probabilistic programs. Two equivalent semantics are presented. 323, 327
12. Gavin Lowe. Representing nondeterminism and probabilistic behaviour in reactive processes. Technical Report TR-11-93, Oxford University, 1993. 323, 328
13. François Masdupuy. Semantic analysis of interval congruences. In *Formal methods in programming and their applications*, volume 735 of *Lecture Notes in Computer Science*, Novosibirsk, Russia, June/july 1993. Springer-Verlag. 322
14. Carroll Morgan, Annabelle McIver, Karen Seidel, and J. W. Sanders. Probabilistic predicate transformers. Technical Report TR-4-95, Oxford University, February 1995. 323
15. Carroll Morgan, Annabelle McIver, Karen Seidel, and J. W. Sanders. Refinement-oriented probability for CSP. *Formal Aspects of Computing*, 8(6):617–647, 1996. 323
16. Walter Rudin. *Real and Complex Analysis*. McGraw-Hill, 1966. 325, 326
17. Tim A. Wagner, Vance Maverick, Susan L. Graham, and Michael A. Harrison. Accurate static estimators for program optimization. *ACM SIGPLAN Notices*, 29(6):85–96, June 1994. 323

Code Specialization Based on Value Profiles*

Robert Muth, Scott Watterson, and Saumya Debray

Department of Computer Science
University of Arizona
Tucson, AZ 85721
{muth,saw,debray}@cs.arizona.edu

Abstract. It is often the case at runtime that variables and registers in programs are "quasi-invariant," i.e., the distribution of the values they take on is very skewed, with a small number of values occurring most of the time. Knowledge of such frequently occurring values can be exploited by a compiler to generate code that optimizes for the common cases without sacrificing the ability to handle the general case. The idea can be generalized to the notion of *expression profiles*, which profile the runtime values of arbitrary expressions and can permit optimizations that may not be possible using simple value profiles. Since this involves the introduction of runtime tests, a careful cost-benefit analysis is necessary to make sure that the benefits from executing the code specialized for the common values outweigh the cost of testing for these values. This paper describes a static cost-benefit analysis that allows us to discover when such specialization is profitable. Experimental results, using such an analysis and an implementation of low-level code specialization based on value and expression profiles within a link-time code optimizer, are given to validate our approach.

1 Introduction

Knowledge that an expression in a program can be guaranteed to evaluate to some particular constant at compile time can be profitably exploited by compilers via the optimization known as constant folding [17]. This is an "all-or-nothing" transformation, however, in the sense that unless the compiler is able to guarantee that the expression under consideration evaluates to a compile-time constant, the transformation cannot be applied. A similar situation holds in partial evaluation, where a variable has to be static in order to permit specialization [15]. In practice, it is often the case that an expression at a point in a program "almost always" takes on a particular value [6]. As an example, in the SPEC-95 benchmark *perl*, the function *memmove* is called close to 24 million times. The argument giving the size of the memory region to be processed has the value 1 in 70% of these calls. We can take advantage of this fact to direct such calls to an optimized version of the function that is significantly simpler and faster. As another example, in the SPEC-95 benchmark *li*, a very frequently called function,

---

* This work was supported in part by the National Science Foundation under grants CDA-9500991, CCR-9711166, and ASC-9720738.

J. Palsberg (Ed.): SAS 2000, LNCS 1824, pp. 340–361, 2000.

livecar, contains a `switch` statement where one of the case labels, corresponding to the type LIST, occurs over 80% of the time. Knowledge of this fact allows the code to be restructured so that this common case can be tested separately first, and so does not have to go through the jump table, which is relatively expensive. As these examples suggest, if we know that certain values occur very frequently at certain program points, we may be able to take advantage of this information to improve the performance of the program. Information about the relative frequency of occurrence is given by *value profiles*: a value profile for a variable or register x at a program point p is a (partial) probability distribution on the values taken on by x when control reaches p during program execution. This idea can be generalized to the notion of *expression profiles*, which profile the runtime values of arbitrary expressions and can permit optimizations that may not be possible using simple value profiles. Unfortunately, classical compiler techniques cannot take advantage of knowledge of the distribution of values, and optimize for the common case, in situations where a variable may take on multiple values at runtime. The idea behind value-profile-based code specialization is to allow such optimization.

From a semantic perspective, the transformation we use is very simple. To specialize a code fragment C for a value v of a register r,[1] we simply replace C by the equivalent code 'if $(r == v)$ then C else C.' Once this has been done, "ordinary" specializing and optimizing transformations suffice to specialize the *true*-branch of this conditional to the value v of r. The resulting code has the structure

if (r == v) **then** $\langle C \rangle_{\mathbf{r}=v}$ **else** C

where $\langle C \rangle_{\mathbf{r}=v}$ represents the residual code of C after it has been specialized to the value v of $\mathbf{r}$. The runtime test 'if $(r == v)$ ...' is required since we cannot guarantee that r will take on only the value v at that point. This idea can be generalized to multiple values: given a probability distribution on these values, we can use a collection of tests such as that above, organized as an optimal binary search tree, to choose between the specialized versions. For simplicity of discussion, we focus on specialization for a single value in this paper, since this illustrates the technical issues that arise.

Notice that this transformation is obviously semantics-preserving, can be applied anywhere, to any variable or register and any value (subject to any applicable type constraints), without requiring, for example, a binding-time analysis. This is the primary strength of our approach, and it allows optimizations that would not be possible otherwise; it is also our biggest weakness, because we have so little to guide us in exercising the tremendous freedom that we are given. For example, notice that due to the runtime test that has been introduced, the code resulting from specialization, shown above, is actually less efficient than the original for values of $\mathbf{r}$ other than v. Thus, value-profile-based specialization reduces

---

[1] In general, specialization can be carried out based on the value of a register, variable, or memory location, or relationships between such values. To simplify the discussion, and because our current implementation carries out specialization based on register values, we refer to register values when discussing specialization.

cost of some execution paths, but the cost of other paths increases. If this tradeoff is not assessed carefully, it can result in significant performance degradation. In general, the technical issues that have to be addressed during value-profile-based code specialization are as follows:

1. we have to determine the program point[2] p where the specialization should begin (this corresponds to the point where runtime tests on values have to be inserted, as discussed above);
2. we have to identify the register r whose values we are interested in, and the particular value(s) v of this register that we specialize for;
3. we have to determine the actual code fragment C that is to be subjected to specialization.

The primary contribution of this paper is a low-level static cost-benefit analysis that allows us to evaluate the runtime tradeoff mentioned above—where specialization can reduce the runtime cost of some execution paths but increase the cost of others—and guide the specialization process. This analysis is crucial, since specializing a piece of code for too many different values, or specializing code where the benefits of specialization are not high enough, can lead to a performance degradation. We then describe details of how the analysis, specialization, and subsequent code optimization have been automated and integrated into a link-time code optimizer (*alto*), and give experimental results to validate our ideas.

2   Code Specialization

Value-profile-based code specialization is a three-step process:

1. identify program points and registers where specialization may be profitable using basic block profiles;
2. obtain value and expression profiles for those program points;
3. use these profiles to carry out specialization for those program points where this is deemed profitable

A *specialization triple* is a triple of the form (p, r, v), where p is a program point, r is a register, and v is a value for that register. These triples identify the runtime tests that have to be inserted in the context of value-profile-based specialization and the program points where they must be inserted. The *specialization region* of a triple (p, r, v) refers to the region of code that is chosen for specialization; this identifies the code fragments that appear in the **then-** and **else**-branches of the runtime test corresponding to that triple.

Section 2.1 describes a benefit analysis that is fundamental to our approach. In Sections 2.2 through 2.4 we discuss the three steps mentioned above. Section 2.5 provides an example illustrating our approach.

---

[2] For our purposes a "program point" refers to the points immediately before or after an instruction; this includes the entry and exit points of basic blocks.

2.1 Estimating Benefits of Specialization

Our value profiling and specialization decisions are guided by estimates of the benefit that would be obtained from code specialization given the knowledge that the value of a register r is known at a program point p. This estimate is denoted by $\mathsf{Benefit}(p, r)$. There are two components to the computation of benefits:

(i) For each instruction I that uses the value of r available at p, there may be some benefit to knowing this value. The magnitude of this benefit will depend on the type of I, and is denoted by $\mathsf{Savings}(I, r)$.

(ii) It may happen that knowing the value of an operand register r of an instruction I allows us to determine the value computed by I. In this case, I is said to be *evaluable* given r, written $\mathsf{Evaluable}(I, r)$. If I is evaluable given r, the benefits obtained from specializing other instructions that use the value computed by I for a particular value of r can also be credited to knowing the value of r at p. The indirect benefits so obtained from knowing the value of r in instruction I are denoted by $\mathsf{IndirBenefit}(I, r)$.

If we know the values of all operands to an instruction, we can compute the result v of the instruction, and propagate this value to all instructions that use v. There is therefore no need to execute this instruction at run-time. The savings obtained from knowing the operand values for an individual instruction is essentially the latency of that instruction (i.e., the number of cycles it takes to execute), if knowing the operand values allows us to determine the value computed by that instruction, and thereby eliminate that instruction entirely[3] (our implementation uses latency figures for various classes of operations based on data from the Alpha 21164 hardware reference manual):

$$\mathsf{Savings}(I, r) = \textbf{if } \mathsf{Evaluable}(I, r) \textbf{ then } \mathsf{Latency}(I) \textbf{ else } 0.$$

Let $\mathsf{Uses}(p, r)$ denote the set of all instructions that use the value of register r that is available at program point p. Then the benefit of knowing the value of a register r at program point p is given by the following:

$$\mathsf{Benefit}(p, r) \quad = \sum_{I \in \mathsf{Uses}(p, r)} (\mathsf{Freq}(I)^4 \times \mathsf{Savings}(I, r) + \mathsf{IndirBenefit}(I, r))$$

$$\mathsf{IndirBenefit}(I, r) = \textbf{if } \mathsf{Evaluable}(I, r) \textbf{ then } \mathsf{Benefit}(p', ResultReg(I)) \textbf{ else } 0.$$

Here p' is the program point immediately after I, and $ResultReg(I)$ the register into which I computes its result.

These equations for computing benefits propagate information from the uses of a register to its definitions. They can be recursive in general, corresponding

---

[3] The benefit estimation can be improved to take into account the fact that for some instructions, knowing some of the operands of the instruction may allow us to strength-reduce the instruction to something cheaper even if its computation cannot be eliminated entirely. While our implementation uses such information in its benefit estimation, we do not pursue the details here due to space constraints.

[4] $\mathsf{Freq}(I)$ refers to the dynamic execution frequency of the instruction.

to a cycle in the use-definition chain. The usual approach to solving recursive equations in the context of program analysis is to use an iterative fixpoint computation (e.g., see [9]). In our case, however, it is not obvious from a pragmatic standpoint that this is the right thing to do. The reason for this is that propagating benefit information around a cycle is meaningful only if we know, *a priori*, that the loop will be unrolled later (otherwise we cannot specialize the loop body for values encountered on different iterations of the loop). When carrying out loop unrolling, however, it is essential to take into account machine-level resources such as registers and the instruction cache: excessive unrolling that does not consider these factors can result in severe performance degradation (e.g., see [11]). For this reason, the decision as to whether the loop should actually be unrolled is not made at the time of the cost-benefit computation, but later, based in part on information obtained from value and expression profiling (see Section 3). If benefit information is propagated around the loop but the loop subsequently is not unrolled (e.g., due to cache considerations), we can get wildly optimistic benefit values. These values can mislead the cost-benefit estimation and lead to the introduction of useless runtime tests, thereby degrading performance.

We therefore have a chicken-and-egg problem: propagating information around cycles when identifying candidates for value profiling requires knowledge of whether or not loops will be unrolled; but the decision of whether or not to unroll a loop depends upon, among other things, knowledge of value profiles. As a practical matter, it happens that complex low-level analyses of machine code programs (as in our implementation) and determination of value profiles are both quite expensive; this greatly limits our choices in dealing with this circular dependence. The approach we take, therefore, is one where we attempt to "do no harm:" we conservatively assume that loops will not be unrolled when carrying out our benefit analysis, and therefore do not propagate information along loop back edges. This has the drawback that it can sometimes cause us to underestimate the benefit that might actually have been obtained if cycles had been taken into account; as a result we could miss some opportunities for optimization. Note, however, that this is conservative, in the sense that it will not insert runtime tests or specialize code that is not worth specializing.

Our approach, therefore, is to obtain approximate solutions to the benefit equations given above, where the approximation occurs in the handling of loops as discussed above. This is done as follows. First, let the *defining instruction* of an instruction I, written $defInst(I)$, be the (single) instruction J such that knowing the value computed by J into its destination register allows us to determine the value computed by I; if there is not a single such instruction, the defining instruction is undefined, denoted by $\perp$.[5] Use-definition chains are used

---

[5] Our implementation introduces, at the entry to each basic block that has more than one predecessor, a pseudo-instruction, similar to a SSA ϕ-function, that defines each register that is live at that point and has more than one definition reaching it. The notion of defining instructions extends to such pseudo-instructions in the obvious way.

to compute the defining instruction for an instruction $I \equiv {}'r_c = r_a \oplus r_b'$ as follows:

(i) if the values of both r_a and r_b are statically known, $defInst(I) = \perp$;

(ii) otherwise, if the value of one of the operand registers is statically known, and there is a single definition J for the other operand register that reaches I, then $defInst(I) = J$;

(iii) otherwise, if $r_a = r_b$ and there is a single definition J for r_a that reaches I, then $defInst(I) = J$;

(iv) otherwise $defInst(I) = \perp$.

In case (i), all of the operands of an instruction I are known statically. This instruction will be specialized without relying on value profiles at all. For the purpose of value profile based specialization, therefore, we do not consider such instructions. A convenient way to do this is by setting $defInst(I)$ to $\perp$. In case (iv), neither of the operands of an instruction are known statically. We do not wish to propagate benefit from case (iv) instructions since they cannot be evaluated after knowing the value of a single defining instruction.

The benefit for each instruction can now be computed as follows. Let $Benefit(I)$, where I is an instruction, denote the value $\mathsf{Benefit}(p, r)$, where p is the program point immediately after I and r is the destination register of I. First, we mark all instructions in the program as *unprocessed*, and set $Benefit(I) = 0$ for each instruction I. The following is then repeated until no new instruction can be marked as *processed*:

```
for each unprocessed instruction I do
    /* memory operations are not specialized away */
    if I is not a memory operation then
    J = defInst(I);
    if J ≠ ⊥ and all instructions dependent on I have been processed then
        Benefit(J) += Benefit(I) + Savings(I, r),
            where r is the destination register of J;
        mark I as processed;
    fi
    fi
od
```

This algorithm will not process any instruction that is involved in such a cycle, since $Benefit(I)$ is added to $Benefit(J)$ only after all of the instructions dependent on I have been processed, i.e., after the value of $Benefit(I)$ has stabilized. This will cause benefit information to not be propagated around loops, for the reasons discussed above. An added benefit of such an approach is that of efficiency: disallowing information propagation around cycles makes the code for estimating benefits simpler and faster.

2.2 Identifying Candidates for Specialization

In order to reduce the time and space overheads for value profiling as far as possible, we attempt to identify candidate (*program point*, *register*) pairs for which specialization could conceivably yield a performance improvement if we had a sufficiently skewed runtime distribution of values. Once the benefits associated with each instruction have been computed as described above, we only consider those instructions whose benefit is equivalent to the elimination of at least a single instruction from a "hot" basic block. The intent is to avoid the overheads associated with value profiling, and perhaps specializing, instructions where this is unlikely to lead to a noticeable improvement in performance. Notice that this does not mean that instructions considered for specialization must actually cause the elimination of instructions in hot basic blocks, but simply that the savings incurred from specialization be large enough to be comparable to the elimination of at least one instruction from a hot block. Employing this cost-benefit analysis reduces the overhead of profiling significantly. We discuss this in more detail in Section 4

Alto uses a two-stage profiling scheme where basic block profiles are first generated, and these are used to determine which value profiles to compute. At this point, therefore, we have basic block execution counts. To determine the basic blocks that are "hot," i.e., executed sufficiently frequently, we start with a value ϕ in the interval $(0,1]$ and determine the largest execution frequency threshold N such that the set of basic blocks that have execution frequencies exceeding N together account for at least the fraction ϕ of the total number of instructions executed by the program (as indicated by its basic block execution profile). For the purposes of value-profile-based specialization, we use an empirically derived value of $\phi = 0.50$, i.e., the hot basic blocks consist of those that allow us to account for at least 50% of the instructions executed at runtime.

2.3   Value Profiling

Given a set of (*program point, register*) pairs to be value-profiled, we use a scheme based on that of Calder *et al.* [6] for obtaining value profiles. As mentioned earlier, our implementation of value profiling obtains profiles for registers only, not for memory locations. The actual profiling is carried out by a function created for this purpose. This function, which is added to the program as part of the instrumentation code and invoked at the profiling points, compares the value of the register in question with the contents of a fixed-size table of previously encountered values. If the current value is already in the table, the count of that value is incremented. Otherwise, if the table is not full, the value is added to the table and its count initialized to 1. If the table is full the value is ignored. Periodically, the table is cleaned by evicting the least frequently used values from the table: this allows new values to enter the table. We also keep track of the total number of times execution passes through the point p by incrementing a counter associated with that point.

2.4   Carrying Out the Specialization

Code specialization involves two steps: (1) identification of the particular specialization triples, and the corresponding specialization regions, that should be specialized; and (2) transforming the program appropriately.

The benefit computation described in Section 2.1 is used to identify the specialization triples for which code specialization is worthwhile. Once the actual value profile has been obtained, we know the distribution of the values taken on at the points that have been profiled and can determine the probability $\mathsf{prob}(v)$ with which a value v occurs. The benefits of specialization have to be weighed against the costs incurred due to runtime tests. The cost of such a test depends on the register and value being tested: e.g., testing for the value 0 is usually fairly cheap, while testing for a non-zero floating point constant may incur a load from memory. The cost of testing whether a register r has a value v is denoted by $\mathsf{TestCost}(r, v)$. Specializing at a program point p for a value v of a register r is then worthwhile only if the marginal benefit, given by

$$\mathsf{Benefit}(p, r) \times \mathsf{prob}(v) - \mathsf{TestCost}(r, v) \times \mathsf{Freq}(p),$$

is equivalent to at least one hot instruction (cf. the discussion in Section 2.2).

Once we have identified the set of specialization triples for which specialization is worthwhile, we have to choose which of these should actually be specialized. An issue that must be addressed here is that the specialization regions for different such triples may overlap. This is illustrated by the following instruction sequence:

```
ld   r5, 0(r4)        # r5 := load from 0(r4)
and  r5, 0xff, r6     # r6 := r5 & 0xff
```

Suppose that we have value profiled register r5 after the ld instruction and register r6 after the and instruction, and that based on the cost benefit analysis, both of these instructions are candidates for specialization. However, the program points are dependent—r6 is computed from r5—and their specialization regions overlap. Depending on the circumstances, it might be better to specialize based on the ld instruction because more instructions use the result of this instruction; in other situations, it might be better to specialize based on the and instruction because its value distribution might be more skewed. In such cases, we specialize only the more promising one, based on the cost benefit analysis; in the case of a tie, the program point that dominates the other is chosen (as discussed below, overlaps are not possible unless one of the points dominates the other).

Given a set of specialization triples, we have to determine the specialization region associated with each of them. The basic intuition is that given a triple (p, r, v), we want to identify the instructions that, directly or indirectly, use the value of r available at p, and so might potentially benefit from specialization. We first make precise the notion of an instruction using a value "directly or indirectly." Given a program point p and register r, we say that (p, r) *influences* an instruction I if (i) I uses the value of r at p; or (ii) there is an instruction J at a program point p' such that: J defines a register r'; (p, r) influences J; and (p', r') influences I. Then, given a triple (p, r, v), the specialization region for this triple is defined to be the smallest set of basic blocks R such that

- R contains the basic block B_p containing p is in R;
- if (p, r) influences an instruction I occurring in a basic block B_I, and p dominates B_I, then B_I is in R; and
- if B is in R, $B \neq B_p$, and B' is a (immediate) intra-procedural predecessor of B in the control flow graph of the program, then B' is in R.

It is not hard to see that, given a specialization triple (p, r, v), the basic block B_p containing p dominates every block in the specialization region of this triple. This is necessary for correctness: we have to ensure that any execution path that can reach the specialization region of this triple must pass through the test inserted at p.

There are two issues that are not addressed by this definition of specialization regions. The first is that, given a triple (p, r, v), it may happen that (p, r) influences an instruction I but the basic block B_I containing I is not in the specialization region of this triple because p does not dominate B_I. This problem can be remedied by duplicating code so as to make p dominate B_I. This is an issue that is, by and large, orthogonal to the main focus of this paper, and so is not pursued further here. The second is that, as given, this definition does not take into account the size of a specialization region relative to the benefits obtained from its specialization. It may happen that an instruction I in a block B_I that is very far away from the point p is influenced by the value of a register r at p. If we include B_I in the specialization region, it is necessary to also include all of the blocks between p and B_I, even though these blocks may not benefit from specialization. This could, in extreme cases, give rise to large specialization regions in order to include distant influenced instructions. This can be handled using a notion of *density* of influenced instructions, analogous to the notion of density of case labels used for code generation for switch statements [5], to limit the specialization regions to code that contains a sufficiently high proportion of instructions that would benefit from the specialization. Our current implementation does not address this issue.

The final step is to actually carry out the code transformations for specialization. The transformations that are effected during specialization can be quite involved. Since much of this functionality is already available elsewhere in our system in the routines that implement various analyses and optimizations, we attempt to have as little code as possible for transformations specifically geared towards value-profile-based specialization. Our goal is to transform the code just enough, at this point, that the desired specialization will subsequently happen in the course of "ordinary" optimizations. We have only two transformations specific to value-profile-based specialization:

1. The basic transformation, aimed at transferring control to specialized code when a register has the appropriate value, is implemented as follows. When specializing for a triple (p, v, r), we simply create a copy C' of the specialization region C for that triple and insert a test at program point p that tests r and branches to the copy if r's value is v.
2. When value profiling indicates that the iteration count of a (hot) loop C has a sufficiently skewed distribution, we may generate a specialized version C'

of that loop that has been unrolled some number of times. The specific number of unrollings is based on the sizes of the bodies of the loop under consideration as well as those of any loops in which it is nested, together with the size of the instruction cache, so as to avoid excessive unrolling that could adversely affect the i-cache utilization of the program (e.g., see [11]). Control is transferred to the unrolled loop by testing the register r controlling the number of iterations against a particular value v, as for the basic transformation above.

Once the code has been transformed as described, the information that r has the value v when control reaches the cloned region C', but not the original code fragment C, is propagated during the course of conditional constant propagation [19]; The actual specialization of the code then takes place in the course of normal optimizations, which exploit the additional information that is available about the value of r—and, possibly, other computations that use the value of r—to effect a variety of optimizing transformations. Using this approach we are able to reuse much of the optimization infrastructure of our system for value-profile-based specialization, leading to a simpler system that is easier to implement, debug, and maintain.

Given a specialization triple (p, r, v), a variety of idioms may be used to implement the test inserted at the program point p, depending on the magnitude of the value v and whether or not there is a free register available. If a free register r' is available, we simply compute the difference of r and v into r', then conditionally branch to the cloned code if r' is zero. If there are no free registers available, if v is small enough to be an immediate operand the following pair of instructions is inserted:

```
subq r, v, r    # r := r - v
beq  r, B_clone # if (r = 0) goto  B_clone;
                # else fall through to original code
```

To compensate for the effect of the subq instruction, we add the instruction 'addq r, v, r' at the entry to both the original specialization region and its clone. If v is too big to be an immediate operand, one or more instructions may be needed to compute it into a register; however, the cost of doing so will have been taken into account in TestCost(r, v).

2.5 An Example

As an example illustrating our approach, we consider the function *memmove()*, from the SPEC-95 benchmark *perl*. The frequently executed portion of its control flow graph is shown in Figure 1(a), with the execution count of each basic block shown in parentheses on the right of the block. Instructions that (directly or indirectly) use the value of the third argument, passed in register $18, are shown in italics. The distribution of values for this register is shown in Figure 1(b): notice that over 70% of the time, this register has the value 1.[6] The instructions along

---

[6] The basic block execution counts given in Figure 1(a), as well as the value distribution shown in Figure 1(b), correspond to the training inputs of the SPEC-95

the critical path of the function that are influenced by the value of register $18
are shown in italics in Figure 1. We focus on the transformations that occur
along the critical path of this function in the course of specialization, since these
have the largest impact on performance:

- [+2 instructions] The most commonly occurring value for this register is 1,
  and value-profile-based specialization introduces a test for this value in block
  B0 (see Figure 1(c)).
- [−3 instructions] Constant propagation then causes the elimination of the
  following instructions: 'beq $18, ...' from block B1; and the
  pair 'cmpule $1, 0x08, $1', 'beq $1, ...' from block B4 (a similar pair
  is eliminated from block B7).
- [−2 instructions] The elimination of the 'beq $1, ...' instruction from
  block B4 causes the deletion of the control flow edge out of B4 away from the
  critical path (i.e., into the oval marked "[14 basic blocks]"). This has two
  effects. First, it causes register $20 to become dead at the end of block B4,
  which allows the deletion of the instruction 'addq $17, $18, $20' in B4.
  Second, it causes the instruction 'and $16, 0x07, $2' to become partially
  dead in block B3; partial dead code elimination then moves it out of B3, and
  hence out of the critical path.
- [−1 instruction] For the instruction pair 'cmpult $1, $18, $6', 'beq $6,
  ...' in block B2, given that the value of register $18 is 1, the instruction
  'cmpult $1, $18, $6', which does an unsigned comparison of registers $1
  and $18, will yield a value of 1 only if register $1 is 0. The optimizer rec-
  ognizes this and replaces this pair of instructions by the single instruction
  'beq $1, ...'.
- [−1 instruction] Constant propagation of the value of register $18 also
  succeeds in deleting a mskql instruction (a bit mask instruction used in byte
  manipulations) from block B5.

The resulting code is also subjected to other transformations, such as code hoisting and basic block fusion, that are enabled by the transformations described
above. The resulting code is shown in Figure 1(c). The overall effect of these
transformations is to reduce the length of the critical path through this function
from 37 instructions to 32 instructions, a reduction of 13.5%.

3   Expression Profiling

The idea of value profiling can be generalized to that of *expression profiling*,
where we profile the distribution of values for an arbitrary expression, not just
a variable or register, at a given program point. Examples include arithmetic
expressions, such as "the difference between the contents of registers r_a and r_b"
and boolean expressions such as "is the value of register r_a different from that of
register r_b?" In general, as shown below, the expressions profiled may not even
occur in the program, either at the source or executable level.

---

benchmarks, since that is what a compiler would use to reason about the program.
Those mentioned in Section 1 refer to the SPEC reference inputs.

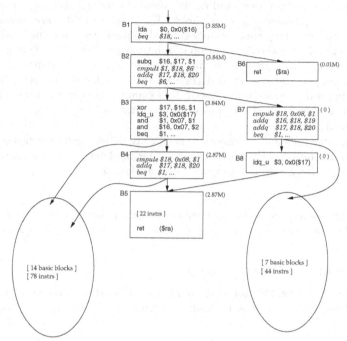

(a) (Frequently executed portions of) the control flow graph

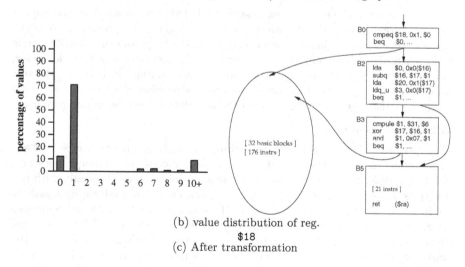

(b) value distribution of reg.
$18
(c) After transformation

Fig. 1. A specialization example: the function *memmove()* (from the SPEC-95 benchmark *perl*)

Expression profiles are not simply summaries of value profiles: e.g., given value profiles for registers r_a and r_b, we cannot in general reconstruct how often the boolean expression $r_a \text{ == } r_b$ holds. Expression profiles are important for two reasons. First, they conceptually generalize the notion of value profiles by allowing us to capture the distribution of relationships between different program entities. Second, an expression profile may have a skewed distribution, and therefore enable optimizations, even if the value profiles for the constituents of the expression profile are not very skewed: for example, a boolean expression $r_a \neq r_b$ may be true almost all of the time even if the values in r_a and r_b do not have a very skewed distribution.

The expressions that we choose to profile are determined by considerations of the optimizations that they might enable. Our implementation currently targets two optimizations: *loop unrolling* and *load avoidance*.

3.1   Loop Unrolling

Here we try to determine the distribution of the number of iterations of the loop. In simple cases, this may be just the value of a variable: e.g., in a loop of the form

```
for (i = n; i > 0; i--) { ... }
```

In general, however, the iteration count may depend on more complex expressions whose value may not be known at compile time: e.g., in a loop of the form

```
for (i = m; i < n; i++) { ... }
```

iteration count is given by the expression n-m. This expression does not appear in the source code. If the iteration count of a loop can be predicted given the value of an expression prior to the execution of the loop, and this distribution is sufficiently skewed, we may choose to generate, subject to i-cache considerations, an unrolled version of the loop based on that information. Notice that the test to decide whether or not to execute the unrolled version of a loop is made by a single test that is outside the loop, so the associated overhead is not very high.

3.2   Load Avoidance

The goal here is to use expression profiling to determine relationships between memory access operations, and thereby avoid unnecessary memory operations where possible. Suppose we have a sequence of operations (typically within a loop) as shown in Figure 2(a). Let $k(r)$ represent the address obtained by adding k to the contents of register r. If we can guarantee that the addresses $A(r_a)$ and $B(r_b)$ will never overlap, we can eliminate the second load operation in the sequence shown. However, in practice, it is very difficult to prove that the two instructions will never overlap. We use expression profiling to determine how often the two instructions overlap at runtime, and use this information to optimize the code.

We first identify the instructions that define the index registers r_a and r_b and attempt to determine the rate at which these registers change within the

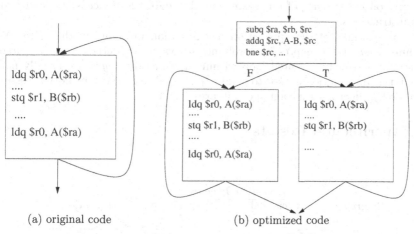

(a) original code   (b) optimized code

Fig. 2. Load Avoidance Example

loop; if either register is defined by a load operation from a fixed location, we attempt to determine the rate at which the value at that location changes. If we can obtain constant rates of change δ_a and δ_b for these registers, respectively, we consider the following cases:

$(\delta_a = \delta_b)$: Here, it suffices to test whether $A(r_a) \neq B(r_b)$ at entry to the loop; the expression profiled in this case is essentially this expression, simplified as far as possible to reduce runtime overheads.

$(\delta_a \neq \delta_b)$: Assume that $\delta_a > \delta_b$ and both rates are non-negative (the other cases are analogous). There is no conflict between the two addresses if, at entry to the loop, either $m_a(r_a) > m_b(r_b)$ or $(m_a(r_a) + n \times \delta_a) < m_b(r_b)$, where n is the iteration count of the loop. In this case we profile these two expressions separately.

In our example, r_a and r_b are unchanged within the loop. Therefore, we profile the expression $A(r_a) \neq B(r_b)$. If expression profiling determines that at runtime the above expression is true sufficiently frequently, we optimize the code. The specialized code from our example is shown in Figure 2(b). Again, in the specialized code the expression is tested once outside the loop and so is not very expensive. Note that the aliasing test is not present in either the source code or the original executable.

3.3 Transformation

Expression-profile-based code transformations are nearly identical to those performed for value-profile-based code specialization. A clone of the affected blocks is created, and a test is inserted to choose between the specialized code and the original code. Additionally, information about (non-)aliasing between pointers, obtained from expression profiling, is attached to the relevant basic blocks. We then rely on other parts of our system to eliminate the unnecessary load and store instructions.

As an example of the application of expression profiling, in the SPEC-95 benchmark *m88ksim*, expression profiling allows us to determine that three pointers in a heavily executed loop within the function *alignd* are usually not aliased; this information is used to eliminate several redundant memory accesses and thereby effect a significant speed improvement.

4 Experimental Results

| Program | Execution Time (secs) | | T_{spec}/T_{nospec} |
	unspecialized (T_{nospec})	specialized (T_{spec})	
compress	260.75±0.02%	254.25±0.30%	0.975
gcc	220.45±0.16%	221.58±0.08%	1.005
go	309.43±0.81%	301.57±0.26%	0.975
ijpeg	327.24±0.02%	320.95±0.41%	0.981
li	249.59±0.03%	237.97±0.04%	0.953
m88ksim	220.21±0.08%	189.19±0.06%	0.859
perl	178.96±1.91%	169.54±0.51%	0.947
vortex	301.22±1.09%	297.35±0.05%	0.987

Table 1. Impact of Value-Profile-based Specialization on Execution Time

We have implemented the ideas described here within the *alto* link-time optimizer [18]. The programs used were the 8 integer programs from the SPEC-95 benchmark suite. The programs were compiled with the vendor-supplied C compiler V5.2-036, invoked as `cc -O4`, with additional linker options to retain relocation information and produce statically linked executables.[7] Both the initial execution frequency profiles as well as the value profiles for each program were obtained using the SPEC training inputs; the execution times reported were then obtained using the SPEC reference inputs.

The results of our experiments are shown in Table 1. The second column of this table, with heading "unspecialized", gives the execution time for the executables using all optimizations within *alto* except for value-profile-based specialization, while the third column, with heading "specialized", gives the execution times when value-profile-based specialization is carried out as well. The last column gives the ratio of the execution times with and without specialization. The timings were obtained on a lightly loaded DEC Alpha workstation (i.e., with no

---

[7] We use statically linked executables because *alto* relies on the presence of relocation information for its control flow analysis. The Digital Unix linker `ld` refuses to retain relocation information for non-statically-linked executables.

other active processes) with a 300 MHz Alpha 21164 processor with a split primary cache (8 Kbytes each of instruction and data cache), 96 Kbytes of on-chip secondary cache, 2 Mbytes of off-chip backup cache, and 512 Mbytes of main memory, running Digital Unix 4.0. In each case, we ran the program 10 times and discarded the biggest and smallest execution times; for the remaining runs, we computed the mean as well as the maximum deviation of any run from the mean. Our results are given in Table 1, with the maximum deviation expressed as a percentage of the mean.

It can be seen from these numbers that automatic value-profile-based specialization can yield noticeable performance improvements for nontrivial programs. Most of our benchmarks experience speedups, with *m88ksim* and *perl* experiencing the largest speedups of 14.1% and 5.6% respectively. Due to space constraints, a description of the reasons for the performance improvements in the various benchmarks is relegated to Appendix A. We have not yet determined the reasons for the slowdown in the *gcc* benchmark: sometimes, as shown here, the specialized code is slower than the unspecialized code, while at other times the specialized code is faster; we are currently investigating this problem. A detailed examination of the low-level performance of the specialized programs, using hardware performance counters, indicates that the performance of the specialized programs suffers from deficiencies in other parts of our system that we believe will not be difficult to rectify. For example, several of the specialized benchmarks suffer from an increase in mispredicted branches (*compress* by about 7%, *perl* by about 4%), which we suspect may be due to the layout of the code. The number of i-cache misses also goes up in some programs (*m88ksim* by 6%; *compress* by 16%, though in this case the miss rate is so low that it is not clear that this has a significant effect), again pointing to code layout as a possible culprit. We expect to be able to address these problems soon.

Program	No. of Program Points		
	Total	Profiled	Optimized
compress	16749	74	0+1
gcc	271899	7231	196+0
go	65328	1352	4+0
ijpeg	49650	243	5+1
li	32221	171	7+0
m88ksim	40867	253	16+0
perl	82462	501	14+0
vortex	113236	322	15+0

Table 2. Extent of Profiling and Specialization

Table 2 compares, for each benchmark, the total number of program points that could have been profiled/specialized (column 2) with the number that were actually profiled (column 3) and the number that were then optimized (col-

Program	Code Size (Instructions)		I_{spec}/I_{nospec}
	unspecialized (I_{nospec})	specialized (I_{spec})	
compress	17381	17529	1.009
gcc	279429	281584	1.007
go	71046	71169	1.002
ijpeg	51045	52385	1.026
li	29106	29131	1.001
m88ksim	40865	41237	1.009
perl	82167	82304	1.002
vortex	103660	103743	1.001

Table 3. Impact of Value-Profile-based Specialization on Code Size

umn 4); the last of these entries are given in the form $m + n$, where m is the number of program points that were specialized and n the number of loops that were unrolled. This indicates that the our computation of the cost/benefit trade-offs is highly selective: for most of the benchmarks fewer than 1% of the potential candidates for profiling are actually chosen for profiling (*gcc* comes in highest with a little under 2.5% of the candidates actually profiled). Table 3 shows, for each benchmark, the code growth that results from specialization. The small number of points chosen for profiling keeps the value profiling overhead under control, while of the small number of points chosen for specialization keeps the code growth modest. As mentioned previously in Section 2.2, our profiling over-head is considerably reduced by applying our benefit analysis before performing the value profiling. Calder *et al.* [7] report a 33x average slowdown for full value profiling on the SPEC-95 benchmarks. *Alto*, in contrast, produced 3x-9.5x slow-downs (6.3x on average) for value and expression profiling.

Figure 3 illustrates the overheads associated with value-profile-based special-ization. It shows, relative to the time taken by *alto* to optimize an executable program without either value profiling or specialization, the following quanti-ties: (i) the time taken to instrument the code for value profiling, i.e., to read in an executable file, identify candidates for value profiling, insert instrumentation code, and write out the instrumented binary (Section 2.2); and (ii) the time taken to specialize the program using value profiles, i.e., read in the program as well as the profile data, carry out all optimizations including value-profile-based specialization, and write out the optimized executable (Section 2.4). The initial cost-benefit computation to identify profiling candidates, together with the instrumentation overhead, results in overheads in the range of 20%–80% (about 44% on the average) compared to the time for ordinary processing by alto. Specialization based on value profiles incurs overheads of factors ranging from 1.6x to 2.1x (about 1.87x on the average).

5   Related Work

There is a considerable body of work on program specialization within the partial evaluation community: Jones *et al.* give an extensive discussion and bibliogra-

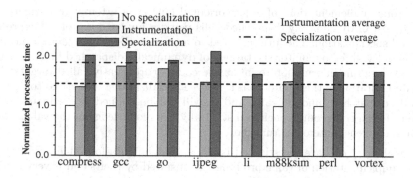

Fig. 3. Overhead of Value-Profile-Based Code Specialization

phy [15]. This work focuses largely on code specialization starting with known values for some or all of a program's inputs. Specialization based on value profiles, where we reason about the runtime distribution of values taken on by a variable, is not considered.

In some ways, our approach to specialization is reminiscent of a transformation referred to as "the trick" in the partial evaluation literature (e.g., see [15]). There are two main differences between these transformations. The first is that "the trick" is applied to variables of *bounded static variation*, i.e., which take on values from a finite, statically known, set, while our approach does not have such a restriction (e.g., in the example discussed in Section 2.5, the variable that is specialized ranges over the set of integers). Furthermore, "the trick" offers no guidance regarding which values are worth specializing and which are not: because of this, automatic application of this transformation can be problematic if the candidate variable is of bounded static variation but ranges over a very large, albeit finite, set. The analysis we describe is intended to address precisely this problem. As such, it can be a useful complement to standard partial evaluation techniques.

Also related to our cost-benefit analysis is the work on speedup analysis in partial evaluation [2,15]. This analysis starts with a binding-time annotated program, where variables whose values are statically known are marked as such. Speedup analysis estimates the asymptotic speedup that partial evaluation of the program would yield. By contrast to this work, we cannot assume that we have a binding-time annotated program—indeed, the whole point of our analysis is to take variables whose values cannot be statically predicted, and determine which if any, of the (possibly unboundedly many) values taken on by such variables might yield performance improvements. Another important difference is that we are concerned not with asymptotic speedups but rather with concrete improvements in speed, and therefore pay careful attention to low level issues such as the effects of specialization on instruction cache utilization (as discussed, for example, in Section 2.4 in the context of loop unrolling).

Some implementations of object-oriented languages attempt to mitigate the high cost of dynamically dispatched calls using a limited form of value-profile-based specialization. The idea, referred to as *type feedback* or *receiver class prediction* [1,14], is to monitor the targets of dynamically dispatched function calls, and to use this information to inline the code for frequently called targets. The main limitation of this approach is that the specialization is restricted to dynamically dispatched function calls, and so will not be applied to "ordinary" code even if such code could benefit substantially from knowledge of the values most commonly encountered at runtime.

Calder *et al.* have investigated issues and techniques for value profiling [6]. Our implementation of value profiling was inspired by theirs and is very similar to it. While Calder *et al.* consider profiling both registers and memory locations, we only profile registers. We use a two-stage profiling process in order to reduce the time and space overheads. The idea is to first profile the application using a simple basic-block profiler such as pixie, and then use the execution frequency information so obtained to identify candidates for value profiling and specialization. In a different paper, Calder *et al.* discuss value-profile-based optimization [7]: they use hand-transformed examples to show that value-profile-based specialization can yield significant speed improvements. By contrast, our work describes value-profile-based specialization that is fully automatic and that has been integrated into a link-time optimizer.

Systems for dynamic code generation and optimization [4,8,12] are also confronted with tradeoffs between the cost of generating specialized code and the savings obtained from the execution of this code. The problem, while qualitatively similar to ours, is considerably more complicated in practice because the runtime costs include the cost of generating the specialized code, which can be difficult to estimate precisely. Systems that extend existing source languages with facilities for dynamic code generation, such as Tempo [8] and DyC [12], generally require users to annotate the program fragments that should be subjected to runtime code generation and specialization, effectively moving the burden of analyzing the cost-benefit tradeoff to them. Systems for dynamic optimization of conventionally optimized programs, such as Dynamo [4], rely on simple heuristics to determine whether a code fragment is worth optimizing: programs where these heuristics are inadequate can suffer noticeable performance degradation.

The work that is conceptually closest to that described here is some recent work towards automating the cost-benefit analysis for DyC [16]. The goals of this work are considerably more ambitious—and also more difficult—than ours. A direct comparison of the efficacy of the two systems is difficult, partly because they take very different approaches towards specialization (one is static, the other dynamic), and partly because the benchmarks used by the authors are mostly different from ours; of the benchmarks considered for DyC [13], the only one that is also considered by us is *m88ksim*. For this program, Grant *et al.* report an overall speedup of 5%, whereas we obtain a speedup of a little over 13%. Other studies by the authors of DyC suggest that, assuming that the cost-benefit tradeoff assessment can be made properly, runtime specialization can yield significant asymptotic speedups, albeit sometimes with fairly high break-even points [3].

6   Conclusions

This paper describes an implementation of low level code specialization based on value profiles. Fundamental to our approach is a low-level cost-benefit analysis that is used both to reduce the overheads due to value profiling and also to identify the code to be specialized. Experimental results indicate that the cost-benefit analysis is effective in filtering out unpromising candidates, and that several non-trivial programs experience noticeable performance improvements due to value-profile-based specialization.

Acknowledgements

We are grateful to Brad Calder for very helpful discussions as well as comments on an earlier version of this paper.

References

1. G. Aigner and U. Hölzle, "Eliminating Virtual Function Calls in C++ Programs", *Proc. ECOOP '96*, Springer Verlag LNCS vol. 1098, pp. 142–166. 358
2. L. O. Andersen and C. K. Gomard, "Speedup Analysis in Partial Evaluation (Preliminary Results)", *Proc. ACM SIGPLAN Workshop on Partial Evaluation and Semantics-Based Program Manipulation*, June 1992, pp. 1–7. (Also available as Research Report YALEU/DCS/RR-909, Department of Computer Science, Yale University, New Haven, CT.) 357
3. J. Auslander, M. Philipose, C. Chambers, S. J. Eggers, and B. N. Bershad, "Fast, Effective Dynamic Compilation", *Proc. SIGPLAN '96 Conference on Programming Language Design and Implementation*, June 1996, pp. 149–159. 359
4. V. Bala, E. Duesterwald, and S. Banerjia, "Transparent Dynamic Optimization: The Design and Implementation of Dynamo", Technical Report *HPL-1999-78*, Hewlett-Packard Laboratories, Cambridge, Mass., June 1999. 358
5. R. L. Bernstein, "Producing Good Code for the Case Statement", *Software—Practice and Experience* vol. 15 no. 10, Oct. 1985, pp. 1021–1024. 348
6. B. Calder, P. Feller, and A. Eustace, "Value Profiling", *Proc. 30th International Symposium on Microarchitecture*, Dec. 1997, pp. 259–269. 340, 346, 358
7. B. Calder, P. Feller, and A. Eustace, "Value Profiling and Optimization", *Journal of Instruction-Level Parallelism* 1 (1999), 1–6. 356, 358
8. C. Consel and F. Noël, "A General Approach for Run-time Specialization and its Application to C", *Proc. 23rd Annual ACM Symposium on Principles of Programming Languages*, Jan. 1996, pp. 145–156. 358
9. P. Cousot and R. Cousot, "Abstract Interpretation: A Unified Lattice Model for Static Analysis of Programs by Construction or Apporoximation of Fixpoints", *Proc. Fourth ACM Symposium on Principles of Programming Languages*, 1977, pp. 238-252. 344
10. J. Davidson and S. Jinturkar, "Memory Access Coalescing: A Technique for Eliminating Redundant Memory Accesses", *Proc. SIGPLAN 94 Symposium on Programming Language Design and Implementation*, June 1994, pp. 186-195. 360

11. J. W. Davidson and S. Jinturkar, "Aggressive Loop Unrolling in a Retargetable Optimizing Compiler", in *Proc. CC'96: Compiler Construction*, April 1996. 344, 349

12. B. Grant, M. Mock, M. Philipose, C. Chambers, and S. J. eggers, "DyC: An Expressive Annotation-Directed Dynamic Compiler for C", Technical Report UW-CSE-97-03-03, Jan. 1998 (updated May 1999). 358

13. B. Grant, M. Philipose, M. Mock, C. Chambers, S.J. Eggers, "An Evaluation of Staged Run-time Optimizations in DyC", *Proc. SIGPLAN '99 Conference on Programming Language Design and Implementation*, May 1999, pp. 293–304. 358

14. U. Hölzle and O. Agesen, "Dynamic vs. Static Optimization Techniques for Object-Oriented Languages", *Theory and Practice of Object Systems* 1(3), 1996. 358

15. N. D. Jones, C. K. Gomard and P. Sestoft, *Partial Evaluation and Automatic Program Generation*, Prentice Hall, 1993. 340, 357

16. M. Mock, M. Berryman, C. Chambers, and S. J. Eggers, "Calpa: A Tool for Automating Dynamic Compilation", *Proc. 2nd. ACM Workshop on Feedback-Directed Optimization*, Nov. 1999. Available as http://www-cse.ucsd.edu/users/calder/fdo/fdo2-mock.ps. 358

17. S. S. Muchnick, *Advanced Compiler Design and Implementation*, Morgan Kaufman, 1997. 340

18. R. Muth, S. K. Debray, S. Watterson, and K. De Bosschere, "alto : A Link-Time Optimizer for the DEC Alpha", Technical Report 98-14, Dept. of Computer Science, The University of Arizona, December 1998. 354

19. M. N. Wegman and F. K. Zadeck, "Constant Propagation with Conditional Branches", *ACM Transactions on Programming Languages and Systems* vol. 13 no. 2, April 1991, pp. 181–210. 349

Appendix A   Sources of Improvements

The sources of performance improvements for these benchmarks are discussed below. There is, however, one caveat. In our system, value-profile-based specialization is carried out after function inlining. Because of this, the code structure encountered during specialization, and the functions associated with the specialized code fragments, may not always correspond to those of the source program. Due to space constraints we only report most important sources for improvements.

compress : Expression profiling is used to unroll a loop and identify non-conflicting memory operations. This information allows memory access coalescing [10].

gcc : Most of the improvement comes from knowing that one of the values in the function *note_stores* has the value 34 over 80% of the time, and from knowing that 70% of the time the third argument to the function *simplify_binary_operation* is 34.

go : Roughly half of the improvement comes from specializing a value in the function *j2more* to 0, which causes several conditionals to be eliminated. Most of the rest of the speedup comes from specializing a value in the function *playnextto* to 0.

ijpeg : Expression profiling is used to unrol a loop and simplify the code in the unrolled loop.

li : Sequences of independent conditionals in functions *xleval* and *sweep* are transformed so that the common case is tested first. A `switch` statement in the function *livecar* is transformed so that the common case did not have to go through a jump table.

m88ksim : Expression profiling is used to determine that three pointers in the function *alignd* are unaliased in the common case, allowing the elimination of several load and store instructions in that function. The function *killtime* is specialized for an argument of 1.

perl : The function *memmove* is specialized for the single byte move. The (internal) function *OtsDivide64Unsigned*, which emulates integer divison (since the Alpha does not have an integer division instruction), is specialized for the divisor 16.

vortex : Most of the improvement comes from knowing that a value in the function *Mem_GetWord* takes on the value -1 nearly 100% of the time.

Flattening Is an Improvement
(Extended Abstract)

James Riely[1] and Jan Prins[2]

[1] DePaul University
[2] University of North Carolina at Chapel Hill

Abstract. Flattening is a program transformation that eliminates nested parallel constructs, introducing flat parallel (vector) operations in their place. We define a sufficient syntactic condition for the correctness of flattening, providing a static approximation of Blelloch's "containment". This is acheived using a typing system that tracks the control flow of programs. Using a weak improvement preorder, we then show that the flattening transformations are intensionally correct for all well-typed programs.

1 Introduction

The study of program transformations has largely been concerned with functional correctness, *i.e.* whether program transformations preserve program meaning. However, if we include an execution cost-model as part of the programming language semantics, then we can ask whether program transformations additionally preserve or "improve" program performance. One program *improves* another if, for every binding of variables, it evaluates to the same answer in fewer steps. Sands has initiated a formal study of improvement for source-to-source transformation of sequential programs [30,29]. In this paper we study improvement for source-to-target transformation of parallel programs. Our source language is equipped with a natural parallel semantics, including a cost model, but lacks a direct parallel implementation. Our target is (almost) a subset of the source language that is directly implementable on parallel machines within the bounds of our cost model. We are interested in showing that a transformed program improves execution cost, *i.e.* that its performance is approximately the same as that prescribed for the source program. This gives our work a different flavor from that of Sands.

We study Blelloch and Sabot's *flattening* transformations [7], used to implement a nested data-parallel programming language in terms of a vector-based sublanguage. Nested parallelism allows the simple expression of parallel algorithms over irregular structures, such as nested lists. For examples, including many divide-and-conquer algorithms, see [3].

The flattening transformations remove instances of a second order parallel "map" functional, introducing vector operations in the process. We write parallel maps using the *iterator* construct. The syntax is similar to that normally used for list comprehensions [14], although the semantics is quite different. For example, the iterator

$$[x \Leftarrow xs, y \Leftarrow ys\colon \mathsf{plus}(x, \mathsf{mult}(y, 2))] \tag{$*$}$$

specifies the evaluation of '$\mathsf{plus}(x, \mathsf{mult}(y, 2))$)' for each binding of (x, y), drawn from $\mathsf{zip}(xs, ys)$. If xs is $\langle 1, 2 \rangle$ and ys is $\langle 5, 7 \rangle$, then $(*)$ evaluates to $\langle 11, 16 \rangle$. The expression

J. Palsberg (Ed.): SAS 2000, LNCS 1824, pp. 360-376, 2000.

has a natural parallel interpretation.[1] The *step-count* of an iterator is the maximum of the step-counts of the subevaluations. The *work-count* of an iterator is the sum of the work-counts of the subevaluations. Thus (∗) takes a constant number of steps and takes work proportional to the length of *xs* and *ys*.

Using the flattening transformations, (∗) can be rewritten to:

$$\text{let } twos \Leftarrow \text{prom}(xs, 2) \text{ in plus}^1(xs, \text{mult}^1(ys, twos)) \qquad (†)$$

Here, prom is a primitive that "promotes" its second argument by copying it to match the length of its first argument; if *xs* is $\langle 1, 2, 3 \rangle$ then prom(*xs*, 2) evaluates to $\langle 2, 2, 2 \rangle$. plus[1] and mult[1] are respectively vector addition and vector multiplication. prom and the vector operators each execute in one parallel step.

Note that in translating from (∗) to (†), the nesting of parallel and sequential constructs has been inverted. (∗) specifies the parallel execution of a sequential expression involving scalar addition and multiplication, whereas (†) specifies the sequential execution of vector addition and vector multiplication. In both expressions the step-count is constant and the work-count is proportional to the length of *xs* and *ys*. In general, however, nesting inversion creates problems, particularly for conditional expressions.

We say that a transformation is *correct* if, for any program, applying the transformation results in a weak improvement. *Weak improvement* allows that program *P* may improve *Q* even if *P* is slower by a constant factor. Weak improvement is a permissive condition; nonetheless, the flattening transformations fail to satisfy it. Although flattening does not change the results computed by an expression, it may serialize certain parallel computations, increasing the step-count drastically. This lead Blelloch [1] to define a semantic condition, known as *containment*, that identifies iterator-based programs that are suitable for implementation using only parallel vector operations. Contrary to folklore, however, containment is not sufficient to guarantee that flattening results in weak improvement; we present a counterexample in Section 5.

In order to specify a subset of programs for which flattening *does* imply weak improvement, we introduce a typing system that divides expressions into three categories. Roughly described, these are: cnst, expressions that evaluate in a constant number of parallel steps; flat, a subset of contained expressions; and exp, all expressions. Using this typing system, we are able to prove that, for flat expressions, flattening is correct. We believe that ours is the first proof of the correctness of flattening.

The paper is organized as follows: We first introduce the programming language and its semantics and the flattening transformations. In Section 5, we show that the transformations do not imply weak improvement, even for contained programs. The

---

[1] The cost of a parallel program is typically described using two metrics, *steps*, which are computed assuming that all available parallelism is realized, and *work*, which is computed assuming that no available parallelism is realized. Terms in our target language can be mapped to the Vector Random Acccess Machine (VRAM) [1] in a straightforward way that preserves both steps and work. The VRAM, in turn, can be related to other models of computation [8]. An expression in our target language that has step-count *t* and work-count *w* can be executed on a *p*-processor PRAM in $O(w/p + t \log p)$ time [1]. When $w \gg p \log p$, the PRAM running time is a good estimate of actual running times on uniform-access shared-memory machines with high-bandwidth memory systems, such as vector machines or the Tera MTA [4,23].

Table 1 Source, Intermediate and Target Expressions

$A,B,C,D,E ::=$	Expressions	Sublanguage
a	Value	S/I/T
x	Variable	S/I/T
p	Primitive	S/I/T
$B(A_1, .., A_\ell)$	Application	S/I/T
if B then A else C	Conditional	S/I/T
let $x \Leftarrow B$ in A	Sequencing	S/I/T
letrec $f \Leftarrow (x_1, .., x_\ell)\,D,E$ in A	Function definition	S/I/T
$[x_1 \Leftarrow B_1, .., x_\ell \Leftarrow B_\ell : A]$	Iterator	S/I
$\langle x_1 \Leftarrow xs_1, .., x_\ell \Leftarrow xs_\ell : A\rangle$	Evaluated iterator	I
$B^1(A_1, .., A_\ell)$	Parallel application	I/T

typing system is defined in Section 6. In the following section we sketch the correctness proof. The details are omitted for lack of space; interested readers are referred to [27]. We conclude with a discussion of related work.

2   A Nested-Sequence Language

Source Language. The language is strict, functional, and first-order. The datatypes include sequences and integer and boolean scalars. We use two notations for sequence values, angle brackets and overlines; thus, $\langle 1,2,3 \rangle$ and $\overline{123}$ both represent the three-element sequence whose i^{th} element is the integer i. The empty sequence is written $\langle\rangle$ or $\bullet$.

The basic constructors for sequences are a family of primitives build_ℓ that build an ℓ-element list from ℓ arguments; for example, $\text{build}_2(1,2) = \langle 1,2 \rangle$. The basic destructor is the elt primitive, which selects an element from a sequence; for example, $\text{elt}(2, \langle 5,6,7 \rangle) = 6$. Other important primitives include rstr, which restricts a sequence based on a sequence of booleans, merge, which merges two sequences based on a sequence of booleans, flat, which "flattens" a nested sequence, and part, which partitions a sequence according to the structure of a different sequence. Let t and f be the boolean values true and false respectively, and let a through e be arbitrary values, then:

$$\text{rstr}\,(\overline{\text{tft}}, \overline{123}) = \overline{13} \qquad\qquad \text{flat}\,\overline{12\ 345} = \overline{12345}$$

$$\text{merge}\,(\overline{123}, \overline{\text{ftfft}}, \overline{89}) = \overline{18239} \qquad \text{part}(\overline{ab\ cde}, \overline{12345}) = \overline{12\ 345}$$

The primitives satisfy the following equations. Let i be a natural number between 1 and ℓ. Let as be a sequence and let bs be a boolean sequence of equal length, with $\widehat{bs}$ its elementwise logical complement. Let ass be a sequence of sequences.

$$\text{elt}\,(i, \text{build}_\ell\,(a_1, .., a_\ell)) = a_i$$
$$\text{merge}\,(\text{rstr}(\widehat{bs}, as), bs, \text{rstr}(bs, as)) = as$$
$$\text{part}\,(ass, \text{flat}\ ass) = ass$$

The syntax is parameterized with respect to sets *Prim*, of *primitive names*, ranged over by p, and *Var*, of *variable names*, ranged over by f, x, y, z, xs, xss, etc. Let h through n range over integers, bv over booleans, and a, b, as, bs, etc. over arbitrary values.

Thesyntaxof*expressions*,or*terms,A,B*,etc.isgiveninTable 1. A term is *source* term if it contains no evaluated iterators or parallel applications. A term is *target* term if it contains no iterators or evaluated iterators. We sometimes refer to arbitrary terms as *intermediate* terms.

Parallelism. Most of the constructs of the language are sequential; thus step-count and work-count are computed the same way. For example, the step-count of 'let $x \Leftarrow B$ in A' is the sum of the step-counts for the subexpressions A and B; the work-count is the sum of the work-counts for A and B.

Parallelism is expressed in the source language using reduction primitives and the iterator construct. For example, the key step in the parallel *quicksort* of a sequence xs (with no duplicate values) can be written, with some syntactic sugar, as follows [3]:

$$\text{let } les = [x \Leftarrow xs \mid x < \text{elt}(1,xs) : x]$$
$$gtr = [x \Leftarrow xs \mid x \geq \text{elt}(1,xs) : x]$$
$$\text{in flat } [ys \Leftarrow \text{build}_2(les, gtr) : quicksort(ys)]$$

If n is the length of xs, then the expected step-count is $O(\log n)$ and the expected work is $O(n \log n)$. Like all other primitives, reductions are assigned a constant number of steps. Thus 'sum $\langle 1,2,3,4,5 \rangle$' evaluates to 15 with step-count 1. We formalize the notions of step and work complexity in Section 4.

Execution of the nested data-parallelism expressed in this simple algorithm is quite challenging, as the subproblems created by recursive invocations vary in size, and the quicksort call tree varies in depth. The correctness of the flattening transformations established in this paper guarantee that the flattened quicksort combines all these separate pieces of work in the form of an expected $O(\log n)$ vector operations of size $O(n)$.

Intermediate Constructs. The flattening transformations eliminate iterators. To simplify the expression of the transformation rules, we introduce an intermediate construct, called the *evaluated iterator* or *e-iterator*. Semantically, e-iterators are similar to iterators.

In the target language, parallelism is expressed using parallel implementations of the primitives. Thus '$[x \Leftarrow xs : \text{plus}(x,x)]$' in the source language becomes '$\text{plus}^1(xs,xs)$' in the target. We require that each primitive p have a parallel implementation p^1. The target language also allows for parallel application of user-defined functions. Thus '$[x \Leftarrow xs : f x]$' in the source language becomes '$f^1 xs$' in the target. Here, however, the body of f^1 must be provided explicitly. In the expression 'letrec $f \Leftarrow \tilde{x} D, E$ in A', the expressions D and E give definitions for f. Essentially D gives the sequential implementation of f, whereas E gives the parallel implementation of f^1. In practice, only the sequential definition need be provided by a programmer, the parallel definition can be derived automatically, as $E \stackrel{def}{=} \langle \tilde{y} \Leftarrow \tilde{x} : D\{\tilde{y}/\tilde{x}\}\rangle$. In examples, we usually write function declarations simply as 'letrec $f \Leftarrow \tilde{x} D$ in A' or equivalently 'letrec $f\tilde{x} \Leftarrow D$ in A'.

Notation. The notation for iterators is sometimes cumbersome. We often write '$[x_1 \Leftarrow B_1, .., x_\ell \Leftarrow B_\ell : A]$' as '$[\tilde{x} \Leftarrow \tilde{B} : A]$'. In examples, we also use a notation for *filters*, which can be coded using the rstr primitive. For example, '$[x \Leftarrow \langle 1,2,3,4,5,6 \rangle \mid \text{odd} x : \text{square} x]$' evaluates to the sequence $\langle 1,9,25 \rangle$. Here, '$\text{odd} x$' is an expression that filters the values over which the iterator is applied.

Table 2 Transformations: Context and Let Rules

(X-CTXT$_A$)	$B\tilde{A} \leadsto B'\tilde{A}$	if $B \leadsto B'$
(X-CTXT$_{L1}$)	let $x \Leftarrow B$ in $A \leadsto$ let $x \Leftarrow B'$ in A	if $B \leadsto B'$
(X-CTXT$_{L2}$)	let $x \Leftarrow B$ in $A \leadsto$ let $x \Leftarrow B$ in A'	if $A \leadsto A'$
(X-CTXT$_{C1}$)	if B then A else $C \leadsto$ if B then A' else C	if $A \leadsto A'$
(X-CTXT$_{C2}$)	if B then A else $C \leadsto$ if B then A else C'	if $C \leadsto C'$
(X-CTXT$_{R1}$)	letrec $f \Leftarrow \tilde{x}D,E$ in $A \leadsto$ letrec $f \Leftarrow \tilde{x}D',E$ in A	if $D \leadsto D'$
(X-CTXT$_{R2}$)	letrec $f \Leftarrow \tilde{x}D,E$ in $A \leadsto$ letrec $f \Leftarrow \tilde{x}D,E'$ in A	if $E \leadsto E'$
(X-CTXT$_{R3}$)	letrec $f \Leftarrow \tilde{x}D,E$ in $A \leadsto$ letrec $f \Leftarrow \tilde{x}D,E$ in A'	if $A \leadsto A'$
(X-ELET)	let $x \Leftarrow y$ in $A \leadsto A\{\!\!\{y/x\}\!\!\}$	
(X-ILET$_A$)	$B\ (A_1,..,A_i,..,A_\ell) \leadsto$ let $x \Leftarrow A_i$ in $B\ (A_1,..,x,..,A_\ell)$	if $A_i \notin Var$
(X-ILET$_P$)	$B^1(A_1,..,A_i,..,A_\ell) \leadsto$ let $x \Leftarrow A_i$ in $B^1(A_1,..,x,..,A_\ell)$	if $A_i \notin Var$
(X-ILET$_C$)	if B then A else $C \leadsto$ let $x \Leftarrow B$ in if x then A else C	if $B \notin Var$
(X-ILET$_I$)	$\left[x_1 \Leftarrow B_1,..,x_i \Leftarrow B_i,..,x_\ell \Leftarrow B_\ell : A\right]$	if $B_i \notin Var$
	$\leadsto$ let $xs_i \Leftarrow B_i$ in $\left[x_1 \Leftarrow B_1,..,x_i \Leftarrow xs_i,..,x_\ell \Leftarrow B_\ell : A\right]$	

The variable x is bound in 'let $x \Leftarrow B$ in A', the scope is A. The variable f is bound in the definition 'letrec $f \Leftarrow \tilde{x}D,E$ in A', the scope is D, E and A; the variables x_i are also bound in the definition 'letrec $f \Leftarrow \tilde{x}D,E$ in A', the scope is D and E. The variables x_i are bound in the iterator '$[\tilde{x} \Leftarrow \tilde{B}: A]$', the scope is A. The variables x_i are bound in the e-iterator '$\langle\tilde{x} \Leftarrow \widetilde{xs}: A\rangle$', the scope is A. Let $fv(A)$ be the set of free variables occuring in A. We identify expressions up to renaming of bound variables. In every binding construct, the variables x_i must be unique. In every e-iterator $\langle\tilde{x} \Leftarrow \widetilde{xs}: A\rangle$, A must be a source term.

3   The Transformations

Flattening was introduced in [7] and is an important implementation strategy for NESL [6] and Proteus [24,20]. Blelloch and Sabot described flattening as a set of transformations. A typical rule is the following rule for let-expressions. Given that variable zs does not occur free in A, '$[x \Leftarrow xs:$ let $z \Leftarrow B$ in $A]$' rewrites to:

$$\text{let } zs \Leftarrow [x \Leftarrow xs: B] \text{ in } [x \Leftarrow xs, z \Leftarrow zs: A]$$

As the example implies, the basic strategy is to "push" the iterator expressions through the abstract syntax until it can be replaced, either by a variable or a promoted constant. The elimination rules allow '$[x \Leftarrow xs: x]$' to be rewritten simply as 'xs' and '$[x \Leftarrow xs: A]$' to be rewritten as 'prom(xs,A)' as long as x does not appear free in A. The transformation of conditionals specifies that if z does not appear free in A or C, then '$[z \Leftarrow zs, x \Leftarrow xs:$ if z then A else $C]$' rewrites to:

$$\text{merge}\left([x \Leftarrow \text{rstr}(zs,xs): A], \text{not}^1 zs, [x \Leftarrow \text{rstr}(\text{not}^1 zs,xs): C]\right)$$

We formalize the flattening transformations as a relation $A \leadsto A'$ on expressions. The relation is defined in two tables. The context rules and the transformations for let introduction and elimination are given in Table 2. The main rules are in Table 3. In all of the rules, variables introduced on the right-hand-side of the transformation must be

Table 3 Transformations: Iterator Rules

(X-IIT)	$[\widetilde{x} \Leftarrow \widetilde{xs} : A]$ $\boxed{\begin{array}{l} fv(A) \setminus \widetilde{x} = \{y_1, .., y_\ell\} \\ A \text{ is a source term} \end{array}}$	$\rightsquigarrow$ if empty xs_h then $\langle\rangle$ else let $ys_1 \Leftarrow \mathsf{prom}(xs_h, y_1)$ $\quad\vdots$ let $ys_\ell \Leftarrow \mathsf{prom}(xs_h, y_\ell)$ in $\langle \widetilde{x} \Leftarrow \widetilde{xs}, \widetilde{y} \Leftarrow \widetilde{ys} : A \rangle$
(X-EIT)	$\langle \widetilde{y} \Leftarrow \widetilde{ys}, x \Leftarrow xs, \widetilde{z} \Leftarrow \widetilde{zs} : A \rangle$	$\rightsquigarrow \langle \widetilde{y} \Leftarrow \widetilde{ys}, \widetilde{z} \Leftarrow \widetilde{zs} : A \rangle \qquad \boxed{x \notin fv(A)}$
(X-CONST)	$\langle x \Leftarrow xs : A \rangle$	$\rightsquigarrow \mathsf{prom}(xs, A) \qquad\qquad\qquad \boxed{x \notin fv(A)}$
(X-VAR)	$\langle x \Leftarrow xs : x \rangle$	$\rightsquigarrow xs$
(X-APP)	$\langle \widetilde{x} \Leftarrow \widetilde{xs} : B(x_{i_1}, .., x_{i_\ell}) \rangle$	$\rightsquigarrow B^1(xs_{i_1}, .., xs_{i_\ell})$
(X-LETREC)	$\langle \widetilde{x} \Leftarrow \widetilde{xs} : \mathsf{letrec}\, f \Leftarrow \widetilde{y}D, E \text{ in } A \rangle$	$\rightsquigarrow \mathsf{letrec}\, f \Leftarrow \widetilde{y}D, E \text{ in } \langle \widetilde{x} \Leftarrow \widetilde{xs} : A \rangle$
(X-LET)	$\langle \widetilde{x} \Leftarrow \widetilde{xs} : \mathsf{let}\, z \Leftarrow B \text{ in } A \rangle$	$\rightsquigarrow \mathsf{let}\, zs \Leftarrow \langle \widetilde{x} \Leftarrow \widetilde{xs} : B \rangle \text{ in } \langle \widetilde{x} \Leftarrow \widetilde{xs}, z \Leftarrow zs : A \rangle$
(X-IF)	$\langle \widetilde{x} \Leftarrow \widetilde{xs} : \mathsf{if}\, x_h \text{ then } A \text{ else } C \rangle$ $\boxed{\begin{array}{l} fv(A) = \{x_{i_1}, .., x_{i_\ell}\} \neq \emptyset \\ fv(C) = \{x_{j_1}, .., x_{j_k}\} \neq \emptyset \end{array}}$	$\rightsquigarrow$ if all xs_h then $\langle \widetilde{x} \Leftarrow \widetilde{xs} : A \rangle$ else if not some xs_h then $\langle \widetilde{x} \Leftarrow \widetilde{xs} : C \rangle$ else let $ys_1 \Leftarrow \mathsf{rstr}(xs_h, xs_{i_1})$ $\qquad\vdots$ let $ys_{i_\ell} \Leftarrow \mathsf{rstr}(xs_h, ys_{i_\ell})$ let $zs_{j_1} \Leftarrow \mathsf{rstr}(\mathsf{not}^1 xs_h, xs_{j_1})$ $\qquad\vdots$ let $zs_{j_k} \Leftarrow \mathsf{rstr}(\mathsf{not}^1 xs_h, xs_{j_k})$ in $\mathsf{merge}(\langle \widetilde{y} \Leftarrow \widetilde{ys} : A \rangle, \mathsf{not}^1 xs_h, \langle \widetilde{z} \Leftarrow \widetilde{zs} : C \rangle)$
(X-IT)	$\langle \widetilde{x} \Leftarrow \widetilde{xs} : [y_1 \Leftarrow x_{i_1}, .., y_{m'} \Leftarrow x_{i_{m'}} : A] \rangle$ $\boxed{\begin{array}{l} fv(A) = \{x_{k_1}, .., x_{k_p}\} \\ \cup \{y_{k'_1}, .., y_{k'_q}\} \\ \neq \emptyset \end{array}}$	$\rightsquigarrow$ if all empty$^1 xs_h$ then $\mathsf{prom}(xs_h, \langle\rangle))$ else let $xs'_{k_1} \Leftarrow \mathsf{flat}(\mathsf{prom}^1(xs_{i_{k'}}, xs_{k_1}))$ $\qquad\vdots$ let $xs'_{k_p} \Leftarrow \mathsf{flat}(\mathsf{prom}^1(xs_{i_{k'}}, xs_{k_p}))$ let $ys'_{k'_1} \Leftarrow \mathsf{flat}(xs_{i_{k'_1}})$ $\qquad\vdots$ let $ys'_{k'_q} \Leftarrow \mathsf{flat}(xs_{i_{k'_q}})$ in $\mathsf{part}(xs_{i_{h'}}, \langle \widetilde{x} \Leftarrow \widetilde{xs}', \widetilde{y} \Leftarrow \widetilde{ys}' : A \rangle)$

fresh, that is, they may not appear free in any subexpression given anywhere in the rule. We write $\overset{*}{\rightsquigarrow}$ for the reflexive and transitive closure of $\rightsquigarrow$.

The general transformation strategy is as follows. The context and let introduction rules are used to isolate an iterator expression. Once an iterator expression is found, the let introduction rule (X-ILET$_I$) is applied until the iteration space of the iterator is described entirely by variables. Note that '$\widetilde{x} \Leftarrow \widetilde{xs}$' is shorthand for '$x_1 \Leftarrow xs_1, .., x_h \Leftarrow xs_h,$ $.., x_m \Leftarrow xs_m$'; thus, on the right-hand side of the rule, h can be bound to any integer between 1 and m.

At this point (X-IIT) is used to remove the iterator construct, replacing it with an e-iterator. The remaining rules of Table 3 are then used to "push" the e-iterator through the syntax until it can be removed using (X-CONST), (X-VAR) or (X-APP). The rules (X-ELET) and (X-EIT) allow for the elimination of useless let and e-iterator binders.

The rule (X-IIT) enforces two properties of e-iterators. First, it guarantees that e-iterators are only invoked dynamically on non-empty sequences. Second, it guarantees that e-iterators have no free variables. All free variables in an iterator are explicitly bound before the iterator is replaced with an e-iterator. The rules for conditionals and iterators are designed to preserve these properties. The transformation rules (X-IF) and (X-IT) require that A and C contain at least one free variable. Variants of these rules must be used in the case that $fv(A)$ or $fv(C)$ are empty; the variants are straightforward and have been elided. The soundness of (X-LETREC) is ensured by the typing rules, presented in Section 6.

4   A Reference-Based Semantics

We present the semantics of the intermediate language, and thus also the source and target languages. The semantics gives a formal defintion of the steps and work used in the evaluation of an expression. We sketch a reference-based implementation of the target language that meets the constraints imposed by the semantics and discuss other alternatives.

The semantics of expressions is defined in Table 4 using judgments of the form '$\sigma \vdash A \xrightarrow{t}_{w} a$', which is read, "given environment σ, expression A evaluates to a with t steps and w work." We occasionally drop the annotations t and w when they are not of interest. Here σ is a runtime environment which maps variables to values and function definitions; formally,

$$\sigma ::= \emptyset \mid f \Leftarrow \tilde{x}D,E \mid x \Leftarrow a \mid \sigma_1,\sigma_2$$

where σ_1 and σ_2 have disjoint domains. Intuitively, the evaluation of an expression is an operation on a computer store. Given a store σ, the evaluation '$\sigma \vdash A \xrightarrow{t}_{w} a$' models the execution of A to produce a value a stored in memory. In particular, I/O costs are not taken into account. This leads us to the axiom '$\sigma \vdash x \xrightarrow{0}_{0} \sigma(x)$', which states that variable x can be evaluated with no computation whatsoever; the value of x is already in σ and therefore need not be computed.

The evaluation of a value takes time proportional to the cost of copying the value into the store. Copying a value a takes steps proportional to its *depth* $(\mathcal{D}\ a)$ and work proportional to its *size* $(\mathcal{S}\ a)$. For example, the depth of $\langle\langle 1\rangle,\langle 2,3,4\rangle,\langle 5,6\rangle\rangle$, is 2; its size is 10.

Explicit sequencing, via the let construct, incurs no cost. This ensures the validity of the let-introduction rules given in Table 2. For example, the semantics validates the equation '$fA = \mathsf{let}\ x \Leftarrow A\ \mathsf{in}\ fx$'. In order to compute fA, one must first compute A. In let $x \Leftarrow A$ in fx the sequence of events is simply made explicit, it is not changed.

Function declaration also incurs no cost. This interpretation is justified by the typing rules given in the next chapter. Roughly, functions must be fully parameterized; therefore, function declarations can be processed statically, with no runtime cost.

The rules (E-IT) and (E-EIT) formalize the interpretation of iterators outlined in the Introduction. In $\left[\tilde{x} \Leftarrow \tilde{B}: A\right]$, the expressions B_i are evaluated sequentially to produce sequences $\langle b_{ji}\rangle_{j=1}^{n}$, then A is evaluated in parallel for each of the n bindings of b_{ji} to x_i. The work of an iterator includes a constant charge for each parallel subevaluation; this ensures, e.g., that $[x \Leftarrow xs: y]$ has work proportional to the length of xs.

The rule (E-APPP) appeals to an evaluation relation for primitives. The judgment '$p\ \tilde{a} \xrightarrow{t}_{w} d$' states that given parameters a_i, p evaluates to d with t steps and w work. We elide the definition for lack of space; a few examples are given at the end of this section.

Table 4 The Evaluation Relation

(E-LET)

$$\sigma \vdash B \xrightarrow[w_B]{t_B} b$$

(E-VAR)   (E-VAL) $$\sigma, x \Leftarrow b \vdash A \xrightarrow[w_A]{t_A} a$$ (E-LETREC)

$$\sigma \vdash x \xrightarrow[0]{0} \sigma(x) \qquad \sigma \vdash a \xrightarrow[\mathcal{S}a]{\mathcal{D}a} a \qquad \sigma \vdash \text{let } x \Leftarrow B \text{ in } A \xrightarrow[w_B+w_A]{t_B+t_A} a \qquad \sigma \vdash \text{letrec } f \Leftarrow \tilde{x}D, E \text{ in } A \xrightarrow[w_A]{t_A} a$$

(E-IF$_T$)

$$\frac{\sigma \vdash B \xrightarrow[w_B]{t_B} \mathsf{t} \quad \sigma \vdash A \xrightarrow[w_A]{t_A} a}{\sigma \vdash \text{if } B \text{ then } A \text{ else } C \xrightarrow[1+w_B+w_A]{1+t_B+t_A} a}$$

(E-IF$_F$)

$$\frac{\sigma \vdash B \xrightarrow[w_B]{t_B} \mathsf{f} \quad \sigma \vdash C \xrightarrow[w_C]{t_C} c}{\sigma \vdash \text{if } B \text{ then } A \text{ else } C \xrightarrow[1+w_B+w_C]{1+t_B+t_C} c}$$

(E-IT)

$$\frac{\left\{ \begin{array}{l} \sigma \vdash B_i \xrightarrow[w_i]{t_i} \langle b_{ji} \rangle_{j=1}^n \end{array} \right\}_{i=1}^\ell}{\left\{ \sigma, \tilde{x} \Leftarrow \tilde{b}_j \vdash A \xrightarrow[w_j]{t_j} a_j \right\}_{j=1}^n}{\sigma \vdash \left[\tilde{x} \Leftarrow \tilde{B} : A \right] \xrightarrow[1+n+(\Sigma w_i)+(\Sigma w_j)]{1+(\Sigma t_i)+(\max t_j)} \langle a \rangle_{j=1}^n}$$

(E-EIT)

$$\frac{\left\{ \sigma \vdash x s_i \xrightarrow[0]{0} \langle b_{ji} \rangle_{j=1}^n \right\}_{i=1}^\ell}{\left\{ \sigma, \tilde{x} \Leftarrow \tilde{b}_j \vdash A \xrightarrow[w_j]{t_j} a_j \right\}_{j=1}^n} \quad n \geq 1}{\sigma \vdash \langle \tilde{x} \Leftarrow \tilde{x}s : A \rangle \xrightarrow[n+\Sigma w_j]{1+\max t_j} \langle a_j \rangle_{j=1}^n}$$

(E-APP$_P$)

$$\frac{\left\{ \sigma \vdash A_i \xrightarrow[w_i]{t_i} a_i \right\}_{i=1}^\ell}{p\tilde{a} \xrightarrow[w_p]{t_p} d}{\sigma \vdash p\tilde{A} \xrightarrow[1+(\Sigma w_i+1)+w_p]{1+(\Sigma t_i+1)+t_p} d}$$

(E-PAPP$_P$)

$$\frac{\left\{ \sigma \vdash A_i \xrightarrow[w_i]{t_i} \langle a_{ji} \rangle_{j=1}^n \right\}_{i=1}^\ell}{\left\{ p\tilde{a}_j \xrightarrow[w_j]{t_p} d_j \right\}_{j=1}^n} \quad n \geq 1}{\sigma \vdash p^1\tilde{A} \xrightarrow[1+(\Sigma w_i+1)+\Sigma w_j]{1+(\Sigma t_i+1)+t_p} \langle d_j \rangle_{j=1}^n}$$

(E-APP$_F$)

$$\frac{\left\{ \sigma \vdash A_i \xrightarrow[w_i]{t_i} a_i \right\}_{i=1}^\ell}{\sigma, \tilde{x} \Leftarrow \tilde{a} \vdash D \xrightarrow[w_D]{t_D} d}{\sigma \vdash f\tilde{A} \xrightarrow[1+(\Sigma w_i+1)+w_D]{1+(\Sigma t_i+1)+t_D} d} \quad \sigma(f) = \tilde{x}D, E$$

(E-PAPP$_F$)

$$\frac{\left\{ \sigma \vdash A_i \xrightarrow[w_i]{t_i} a_i \right\}_{i=1}^\ell}{\sigma, \tilde{x} \Leftarrow \tilde{a} \vdash E \xrightarrow[w_E]{t_E} e}{\sigma \vdash f^1\tilde{A} \xrightarrow[1+(\Sigma w_i \mid 1)+w_E]{1+(\Sigma t_i+1)+t_E} e} \quad \sigma(f) = \tilde{x}D, E$$

In both primitive and function application, charges are assessed for storing the return value, as well as for each parameter passed. Note that (E-APP$_F$) and (E-PAPP$_F$) differ only in which definition, D or E, is executed.

In Section 7 we prove that the typed version of the source language can be implemented in terms of the target language and that the translation respects the step and work complexities of the source semantics. There remains the question of whether the target language can be implemented on any actual machine. We treat this issue informally, by sketching an implementation of the target language on the VRAM [1].

In implementing the target language on the VRAM, one is confronted with two main difficulties: representing nested sequences in terms of vectors, and implementing the primitives. Implementations of the other constructs of the target language — function definition and application, let expressions and conditionals — are simple and direct.

The representation for sequences is crucial, as this sets a lower bound on the steps and work required to implement the primitives; this, in turn, affects the implementability of the source language. Blelloch and Sabot introduced the *segment-vector* encoding of sequences [7]. In this encoding, a depth-d sequence is represented as a tuple of d vectors: one to describe the data and $d-1$ to describe the nesting structure that contains it. Using segment vectors, the prom(as, b) primitive must create n copies of b, where

n is the length of as; this operation requires a minimum work of $n \cdot \mathcal{S}\ b$. Unfortunately, this means that our transformation rule for constant expressions is invalid. Consider the iterator '$[x \Leftarrow xs\colon y]$', which (X-CONST) translates to 'prom(xs,y)'. Suppose the length of xs is n. Looking at the source term, '$[x \Leftarrow xs\colon y]$' takes work proportional n. However, 'prom(xs,y)' takes work proportional to n times the size of y. If y refers to a non-scalar value, its size may easily dominate n. More important, the size of y depends on the environment; thus we cannot bound the work of the target expression with respect to the work of the source expression, not even asymptotically.

A solution adopted by Blelloch [2, appendix], is to change the costing of iterators to include the size of free variables. This change creates an unintuitive cost model for programmers that discourages the use of iterators. Here, we adopt a different strategy, representing nested sequences as vectors of references. Using this representation, prom(xs,y) takes work proportional n, creating n references to y.

This representation allows us to prove the transformations correct with respect to the natural high-level metric. However, it also leads to a greater number of concurrent reads, when compared to the segment vector representation, and hence greater memory contention at runtime. We believe that a reference-based implementation can perform well using techniques from [21], but we have no experimental results as of yet.

In [27], we present a semantics which captures the work/step model used in the implementation of NESL [6]. By adapting the techniques presented here, [27] provides the first proof of the correctness of flattening for NESL.

5   Improvement

To demonstrate the extensional correctness of the transformations, one can show:

$$\text{if } D \overset{*}{\leadsto} D' \text{ then } \sigma \vdash D \longrightarrow d \text{ iff } \sigma \vdash D' \longrightarrow d$$

This states that transformation preserves the extensional meaning of programs. We wish to show something stronger, however. Our goal is to show that the transformations preserve computational cost, in some sense, not just extensional meaning. We wish to show that $D \overset{*}{\leadsto} D'$ implies $D \succ D'$, for some relation $\succ$ that captures the intuition that if D reduces to a value, then D' reduces to the same value and does so as fast or faster. As a first attempt, we might say that $D \succ E$ if for all σ,

$$\sigma \vdash D \xrightarrow[w]{t} d \text{ implies } \sigma \vdash E \xrightarrow[\leq w]{\leq t} d$$

where "$\sigma \vdash D \xrightarrow[\leq w]{\leq t} d$" abbreviates "there exists $t' \leq t$ and $w' \leq w$ such that $\sigma \vdash D \xrightarrow[w']{t'} d$." This relation is known as *strong improvement*; however, this relation is too strong to be useful directly. The transformations do not imply strong improvement, as one can easily see by looking at, *e.g.*, (X-CONST), (X-IF$_2$) or (X-IT$_2$).

While we cannot prove that flattening strictly improves performance with respect to our operational semantics, we can prove that it does so *up to a constant factor* (in some cases). Formally, we will define $D \succ E$ if there exist constants u and v such that for all σ:

$$\sigma \vdash D \xrightarrow[w]{t} d \text{ implies } \sigma \vdash E \xrightarrow[\leq v \cdot w]{\leq u \cdot t} d$$

This relation is called *weak improvement*.

Unfortunately, there are programs in our language for which flattening does not imply even weak improvement. Suppose that $f(x)$ is defined as follows:

$$f(x) \Leftarrow \text{ if } x \le 1 \text{ then } 1 \text{ else } (\text{if even} x \text{ then } f(x/2) \text{ else} f(x/2))$$

Then $f(2^n)$ evaluates to 1 in $O(n)$ steps. If xs is the sequence $\langle 2^n, 2^n + 1, .., 2^{(n+1)} \rangle$ of 2^n values, then $[x \Leftarrow xs : f\,x]$ also evaluates in $O(n)$ steps. The transformations sequentialize the branches of the conditional so that the two recursive calls to f are performed one after the other. The result is that after the transformations, $f^1(xs)$ takes $O(n^2)$ steps, destroying any hope that the transformation of f might result in even a weak improvement.

As we stated in the introduction, it has long been known that flattening is not correct for all expressions, leading Blelloch to define containment [1]. Roughly stated, a recursive function such as f is *contained* if it always evaluates in the same way, calling the same functions and primitives in the same order, regardless of its actual parameters. According to Blelloch's definition, f is contained, although it is not correctly flattened by the standard transformations. This apparent anomaly can be explained by looking more closely at Blelloch's results. His *containment theorem* does not address flattening, but rather uses an entirely different simulation technique which appeals to the semantics, rather than the syntax, of expressions.

One of the main contributions of this work is to move containment from a semantic criterion to a syntactic one, thus allowing us to precisely characterize a set of programs for which flattening is correct. This is achieved using a typing system, presented next.

6   A Typing System for Containment

We introduce a typing system that captures the essential properties of containment using three *complexity annotations*:

$$\Phi ::= \text{cnst} \mid \text{flat} \mid \text{exp}$$

The complexity annotation cnst refers to constant-step (although not necessarily terminating) expressions, flat refers to (a subset of) contained expressions, and exp refers to all expressions. Every constant-step expression is contained, and every contained expression is an expression. This gives rise to a natural ordering on complexity annotations and, by extension, to types.

The syntax of types is parameterized with respect to a set *TVar* of *type variable names*, α, β. The type language is stratified between value types U, V and types S, T. The latter include function types:

$$V ::= \alpha \mid \text{int} \mid \text{bool} \mid V^1 \qquad\qquad T ::= V \mid (U_1, .., U_\ell) \to \Phi\,V$$

For function types, we require that $fv(V) \subseteq \bigcup_i fv(U_i)$. Functions are constrained to act over values. Additionally, the function body is constrained to be an expression with complexity Φ; thus, a function's type tells us something of how it evaluates.

The *subcomplexity* relation (notation $\Phi <: \Psi$) is defined to be the smallest preorder on complexity annotations such that cnst $<:$ flat and flat $<:$ exp. The *subtype*

Table 5 Typing Rules: Part I

(VAL-INT)	(VAL-BOOL)	(VAL-SEQ)

$$\frac{}{\Gamma \vdash n : \text{cnst int}} \qquad \frac{}{\Gamma \vdash bv : \text{cnst bool}} \qquad \frac{\Gamma \vdash a_j : \text{cnst V} \ (\forall j)}{\Gamma \vdash \langle a_1, .., a_n \rangle : \text{cnst V}^1}$$

(EXP-SUB)   (EXP-VAR)   (EXP-PRIM)

$$\frac{\Gamma \vdash A : \Phi S \quad \Phi <: \Psi}{\Gamma \vdash A : \Psi T} \ S <: T \qquad \frac{\Gamma(x) = T}{\Gamma \vdash x : \text{cnst T}} \qquad \frac{\delta(p) = T}{\Gamma \vdash p : \text{cnst T}}$$

(EXP-LETREC)   (EXP-LET$_E$)   (EXP-IT$_E$)

$$\frac{\Gamma, f : \widetilde{U} \to \Phi V \vdash f \Leftarrow \tilde{x}D, E \quad \Gamma, f : \widetilde{U} \to \Phi V \vdash A : \Psi W}{\Gamma \vdash \text{letrec} f \Leftarrow \tilde{x}D, E \text{ in } A : \Psi W}$$

$$\frac{\Gamma \vdash B : \text{exp U} \quad \Gamma, x : U \vdash A : \text{exp V}}{\Gamma \vdash \text{let } x \Leftarrow B \text{ in } A : \text{exp V}}$$

$$\frac{\Gamma \vdash B_i : \text{exp U}_i \ (\forall i) \quad \Gamma, \tilde{x} : \widetilde{U} \vdash A : \text{flat V}}{\Gamma \vdash [\tilde{x} \Leftarrow \widetilde{B} : A] : \text{exp V}}$$

(EXP-IF$_E$)

$$\frac{\Gamma \vdash B : \text{exp bool} \quad \Gamma \vdash A : \text{exp V} \quad \Gamma \vdash C : \text{exp V}}{\Gamma \vdash \text{if } B \text{ then } A \text{ else } C : \text{exp V}}$$

(EXP-APP$_E$)   (EXP-PAPP$_E$)

$$\frac{\Gamma \vdash B : \text{exp} \ (\widetilde{U} \to \text{exp V}) \quad \Gamma \vdash A_i : \text{exp} \ (U_i \pi) \ (\forall i)}{\Gamma \vdash B\widetilde{A} : \text{exp} \ (V\pi)}$$

$$\frac{\Gamma \vdash B : \text{exp} \ (\widetilde{U} \to \text{exp V}) \quad \Gamma \vdash A_i : \text{exp} \ (U_i^1 \pi) \ (\forall i)}{\Gamma \vdash B^1\widetilde{A} : \text{exp} \ (V^1 \pi)}$$

(ENV-FUN$_E$)

(ENV-0)   (ENV-VAL)   (ENV-UNION)

$$\frac{}{\Gamma \vdash \emptyset} \qquad \frac{\Gamma \vdash x : \text{cnst V} \quad \Gamma \vdash a : \text{cnst V}}{\Gamma \vdash x \Leftarrow a} \qquad \frac{\Gamma \vdash \sigma \quad \Gamma \vdash \rho}{\Gamma \vdash \sigma, \rho}$$

$$\frac{\Gamma \vdash f : \text{cnst} \ (\widetilde{U} \to \Phi V) \quad (\Gamma \backslash_{\mathcal{F}}), \tilde{x} : \widetilde{U} \ \vdash D : \Phi V \quad (\Gamma \backslash_{\mathcal{F}}), \tilde{x} : \widetilde{U}^1 \vdash E : \Phi V^1 \quad C \overset{\star}{\leadsto} D \quad \langle \tilde{y} \Leftarrow \tilde{x} : C \{\!| \tilde{y}/\tilde{x} |\!\} \rangle \overset{\star}{\leadsto} E}{\Gamma \vdash f \Leftarrow \tilde{x}D, E}$$

relation (notation S <: T) is defined to be the smallest preorder on types such that $\Phi <: \Psi$ implies $\widetilde{U} \to \Phi V <: \widetilde{U} \to \Psi V$.

The typing rules are given in Tables 5 and 6. We prove that evaluation and transformation preserve typing. We also prove an important property of cnst expressions, described below. The significance of flat expressions is made clear in the proofs of Proposition 6.1c and Theorem 7.2 where the typing rules for flat are used in conjunction with Proposition 6.1a to prove the flattening transformations correct.

The judgments of the type system have the form:

$\Gamma \vdash a : \text{cnst V}$ Value a has type V.

$\Gamma \vdash A : \Phi T$ Expression A has type T and complexity Φ.

$\Gamma \vdash \sigma$ Environment σ is well typed.

Here Γ is a type environment that maps type variables to types. Let us first look at Table 5, which gives the rules for values, exp expressions and environments. The three rules for values are given on the first line of the table. Ignoring the complexity annotations, these are standard rules for monomorphic sequences. The rule (VAL-SEQ), for example, states that in order for a sequence value to have type V^1, every element of the sequence must have type V. The complexity annotation cnst indicates that the construction of a literal value takes a constant number of steps (independent of the runtime environment).

Table 6 Typing Rules: Part II

(EXP-EIT_C)

$fv(A) \subseteq \tilde{x}$

$\Gamma \vdash xs_i : \text{cnst } U_i \;\; (\forall i)$

$\Gamma, \tilde{x} : \tilde{U} \vdash A : \text{cnst } V$

$\overline{\Gamma \vdash \langle \tilde{x} \Leftarrow \tilde{xs} : A \rangle : \text{cnst } V}$

(EXP-EIT_{F1})

$fv(A) \subseteq \tilde{x}$

$\Gamma \vdash xs_i : \text{cnst } U_i \;\; (\forall i)$

$\Gamma, \tilde{x} : \tilde{U} \vdash A : \text{flat } V$

$\overline{\Gamma \vdash \langle \tilde{x} \Leftarrow \tilde{xs} : A \rangle : \text{flat } V}$

(EXP-LET_C)

$\Gamma \vdash B : \text{cnst } U$

$\Gamma, x : U \vdash A : \text{cnst } V$

$\overline{\Gamma \vdash \text{let } x \Leftarrow B \text{ in } A : \text{cnst } V}$

(EXP-LET_{F1})

$\Gamma \vdash B : \text{cnst } U$

$\Gamma, x : U \vdash A : \text{flat } V$

$\overline{\Gamma \vdash \text{let } x \Leftarrow B \text{ in } A : \text{flat } V}$

(EXP-LET_{F2})

$\Gamma \vdash B : \text{flat } U$

$\Gamma, x : U \vdash A : \text{cnst } V$

$\overline{\Gamma \vdash \text{let } x \Leftarrow B \text{ in } A : \text{flat } V}$

(EXP-APP_{F2})

$\Gamma \vdash B : \text{cnst } (\tilde{U} \to \text{cnst } V)$

$\Gamma \vdash A_i : \text{cnst } (U_i \pi) \;\; (\forall i \neq h)$

$\Gamma \vdash A_h : \text{flat } (U_h \pi)$

$\overline{\Gamma \vdash B\tilde{A} : \text{flat } (V\pi)}$

(EXP-APP_C)

$\Gamma \vdash B : \text{cnst } (\tilde{U} \to \text{cnst } V)$

$\Gamma \vdash A_i : \text{cnst } (U_i \pi) \;\; (\forall i)$

$\overline{\Gamma \vdash B\tilde{A} : \text{cnst } (V\pi)}$

(EXP-APP_{F1})

$\Gamma \vdash B : \text{cnst } (\tilde{U} \to \text{flat } V)$

$\Gamma \vdash A_i : \text{cnst } (U_i \pi) \;\; (\forall i)$

$\overline{\Gamma \vdash B\tilde{A} : \text{flat } (V\pi)}$

(EXP-PAPP_{F2})

$\Gamma \vdash B : \text{cnst } (\tilde{U} \to \text{cnst } V)$

$\Gamma \vdash A_i : \text{cnst } (U_i^1 \pi) \;\; (\forall i \neq h)$

$\Gamma \vdash A_h : \text{flat } (U_h^1 \pi)$

$\overline{\Gamma \vdash B^1\tilde{A} : \text{flat } (V^1 \pi)}$

(EXP-PAPP_C)

$\Gamma \vdash B : \text{cnst } (\tilde{U} \to \text{cnst } V)$

$\Gamma \vdash A_i : \text{cnst } (U_i^1 \pi) \;\; (\forall i)$

$\overline{\Gamma \vdash B^1\tilde{A} : \text{cnst } (V^1 \pi)}$

(EXP-PAPP_{F1})

$\Gamma \vdash B : \text{cnst } (\tilde{U} \to \text{flat } V)$

$\Gamma \vdash A_i : \text{cnst } (U_i^1 \pi) \;\; (\forall i)$

$\overline{\Gamma \vdash B^1\tilde{A} : \text{flat } (V^1 \pi)}$

(EXP-IT_C)

$\Gamma \vdash B_i : \text{cnst } U_i \;\; (\forall i)$

$\Gamma, \tilde{x} : \tilde{U} \vdash A : \text{cnst } V$

$\overline{\Gamma \vdash \left[\tilde{x} \Leftarrow \tilde{B} : A \right] : \text{cnst } V}$

(EXP-IT_{F1})

$\Gamma \vdash B_i : \text{cnst } U_i \;\; (\forall i)$

$\Gamma, \tilde{x} : \tilde{U} \vdash A : \text{flat } V$

$\overline{\Gamma \vdash \left[\tilde{x} \Leftarrow \tilde{B} : A \right] : \text{flat } V}$

(EXP-IT_{F2})

$\Gamma \vdash B_i : \text{flat } U_i \;\; (\forall i)$

$\Gamma, \tilde{x} : \tilde{U} \vdash A : \text{cnst } V$

$\overline{\Gamma \vdash \left[\tilde{x} \Leftarrow \tilde{B} : A \right] : \text{flat } V}$

(EXP-IF_{F1})

$\Gamma \vdash B : \text{flat bool}$

$\Gamma \vdash A : \text{cnst } V$

$\Gamma \vdash C : \text{cnst } V$

$\overline{\Gamma \vdash \text{if } B \text{ then } A \text{ else } C : \text{flat } V}$

(EXP-IF_{F2})

$\Gamma \vdash B : \text{cnst bool}$

$\Gamma \vdash A : \text{flat } V$

$\Gamma \vdash C : \text{cnst } V$

$\overline{\Gamma \vdash \text{if } B \text{ then } A \text{ else } C : \text{flat } V}$

(EXP-IF_{F3})

$\Gamma \vdash B : \text{cnst bool}$

$\Gamma \vdash A : \text{cnst } V$

$\Gamma \vdash C : \text{flat } V$

$\overline{\Gamma \vdash \text{if } B \text{ then } A \text{ else } C : \text{flat } V}$

(EXP-SUB) is a standard rule for subsumption; the side conditions specify constraints on Ψ and T. The rule for primitives (EXP-PRIM) makes use of the function δ which maps primitive names to types; the definition is elided. Both primitive and variable occurrences can be resolved dynamically in a constant number of steps and therefore are assigned complexity cnst.

The rule (EXP-LETREC) relies on the environment rule (ENV-FUN), described below. In (EXP-LETREC), also note that the complexity and type of the expression A need not be the same as the complexity or type of the function being defined. The rules for let-expressions (EXP-LET$_E$) and conditionals (EXP-COND$_E$) are standard. Note that using subsumption, these rules can be applied even if a subexpression is in cnst or flat. The iterator rule (EXP-IT$_E$) is similar to the let-rule in its treatment of binders, as should be expected. Here, however, the bound expression A is required to be flat. This is an essential aspect of the typing system; the main purpose of the type system, after all, is to ensure that iterator expressions are correctly flattenable.

The rules for application and parallel application allow for the instantiation of type variables via a type substitution π. Note the difference between these rules. If B has type $\tilde{U} \to \exp V$, then $B\tilde{A}$ has type V, whereas $B^1\tilde{A}$ has type V^1.

The rules for runtime environments are presented in the bottom row of the table. These are straightforward, but for (ENV-FUN). Note the difference in the treatment of two function bodies, D and E. Whereas D must evaluate to a value of type V, E must evaluate to a value of type V^1; the types of the input parameters are adjusted accordingly. The unusual side conditions enforce a syntactic relation between the two function bodies, formalizing the intuition that E and D must be derived from a common source C. The conditions are not onerous; in practice E is automatically generated from D. We write $(\Gamma\backslash_{\mathcal{F}})$ for the type environment derived by removing all value-typed variables from Γ. Thus the type rules require that function declarations be fully parameterized; i.e. D and E cannot refer to free value variables.

We now turn to Table 6. Here we find the first rule for e-iterators; the rule has a side condition requiring that all variables in the iterator expression be bound.

The table is best read in columns. The first column gives rules for cnst expressions. The exception is the conditional. Expressions that include a conditional may take a varying number of steps depending on the value of the condition, which may in turn depend on the runtime environment; therefore, no conditional expression is in cnst. Note that cnst expressions can be recursive, although in this case the typing rules guarantee that they are nonterminating, since no conditionals are allowed in cnst expressions.

The second and third columns give rules for flat expressions. These require that at most one subexpression is flat, all others are cnst, ensuring that at most one sequential component is recursive. This is a sufficient condition for containment.

It is important to emphasize that our typing system is not overly conservative. For example, all but one of the programs on the Scandal website `http://www.cs.cmu.edu/~scandal/` can be typed using our system (although some require trivial rewriting). Potential improvements are discussed in Section 8.

Proposition 6.1. (a) *Suppose that* $\Gamma \vdash \sigma$ *and* $\Gamma \vdash \rho$ *and that* σ *and* ρ *differ only in their value bindings. If* $\Gamma \vdash D : \mathsf{cnst}\ V$, $\sigma \vdash D \xrightarrow{t}_{w} d$ *and* $\rho \vdash D \xrightarrow{t'}_{w} d'$, *then* $t = t'$.
(b) *If* $\Gamma \vdash \sigma$ *and* $\Gamma \vdash D : \Phi T$ *and* $\sigma \vdash D \xrightarrow{t}_{w} d$, *then* $\Gamma \vdash d : \mathsf{cnst}\ T$.
(c) *If* $\Gamma \vdash D : \Phi T$ *and* $D \rightsquigarrow D'$, *then* $\Gamma \vdash D' : \Phi T$. $\square$

7 Correctness of the Reference Implementation

We can now state the main result.

Definition 7.1. D *is weakly improved by* E *under* Γ *(notation* $D \succsim_{\Gamma} E$*) if* $\Gamma \vdash D$, $\Gamma \vdash E$, and there exist constants u and v such that for all σ such that $\Gamma \vdash \sigma$,

$$\sigma \vdash D \xrightarrow{t}_{w} d \text{ implies } \sigma \vdash E \xrightarrow{\leq u \cdot t}_{\leq v \cdot w} d \qquad\qquad \square$$

Theorem 7.2. *If* $\Gamma \vdash A$ *and* $A \xrightarrow{*} B$ *then* $A \succsim_{\Gamma} B$. $\square$

This theorem is very hard to prove directly. Weak improvement has some nice properties; for example it is a preorder. However, it is not substitutive. In light of the context rules given in Table 2, this makes it very difficult to prove the transformations correct directly.

To prove Theorem 7.2, we define an alternative, *costed* semantics, and, using this, a *strong improvement* relation $\succsim_\Gamma$. Strong improvement is a congruence that allows us to establish the following results, which together prove Theorem 7.2.

$$A \succsim_\Gamma B \text{ implies } A \gtrsim_\Gamma B$$
$$\Gamma \vdash A \text{ and } A \xrightarrow{*} B \text{ imply } A \succsim_\Gamma B$$

The close relation between standard evaluation and costed evaluation (denoted $\longmapsto$) is given by a costing function $\mathcal{C}$, which is determined by the syntax of a term. We have:

$$\sigma \vdash D \overset{t}{\underset{w}{\longmapsto}} d \text{ implies } \sigma \vdash D \xrightarrow[\leqslant w]{\leqslant t} d$$
$$\sigma \vdash D \overset{t}{\underset{w}{\longrightarrow}} d \text{ implies } \sigma \vdash D \overset{\leqslant \mathcal{C}(\sigma \vdash D) \cdot t}{\underset{\leqslant \mathcal{C}(\sigma \vdash D) \cdot w}{\longmapsto}} d$$

Our proof technique is similar to Sands' use of the tick algebra [29]. We introduce "ticks" in the costed semantics in order to account for the costs introduced later by the transformations. There are differences, however; for example, our "ticks" depend on the nesting depth of iterators and conditionals. Unfortunately, a detailed discussion is beyond the scope of this extended abstract.

8 Related and Future Work

This paper is derived from [27] which closes many problems left open in [28], where we first outlined our approach. The techniques and results in this paper are all new; in particular, [28] does not mention the typing system, the costed semantics, strong improvement, nor the counterexample for the adequacy of containment.

Several other authors have considered the implementation of nested parallelism via flattening transformations. Steele and Hillis [32] presented a set of laws for relating expressions that include an apply-to-each operator. Blelloch and Sabot [7] picked up on this theme to define a flattening compiler for Paralation-LISP, which became the basis for NESL. Prins and Palmer [24] presented a different form of flattening using program transformations; this approach was further refined in [21,20] and here. The thread-based execution model of nested parallelism has been shown to respect the step and work complexities of the source-level metrics [9,5]. However, overheads and space requirements in the realization of this model require careful run-time scheduling [4], fast synchronization [25], and granularity control (in the sense of [10]) to make it practical. Blelloch [1] and Suciu and Tannen [34,33], have presented nested parallel languages and have argued that these languages can be implemented on the VRAM with the correct step/work complexity. However, these results are based on simulation techniques rather than explicit source-to-target translations.

Skillicorn and Cai [31] presented a cost calculus for parallel programs using the Bird-Meertens formalism. This approach has been developed further by Jay [16,15], using shape analysis. Another promising direction is that of Keller, who develops transformations that take distribution into account [17]. In this setting, flattening can profitably be combined with deforestation and related techniques [35,18,11].

Nested data-parallelism may be seen as a particular form of the more general and-parallelism found in logic programs [13]. Research on the parallel execution of logic programs has explored ideas similar to flattening to reduce communication [26] and scheduling overheads [13,22] for restricted nested and-parallel constructs. These are presented as optimizations but there are no formal performance guarantees. A source-level cost semantics is used in [10] to control the compilation and run-time execution of parallel logic programs.

Our notion of weak improvement is similar that developed in [19,12]. There, however, the relation is a congruence by construction; it is the least congruence contained in our (stronger) relation. In our setting, little is gained by forcing weak improvement to be a congruence; therefore, we use the simpler definition.

There are several possibilities for further work. We believe it is possible to weaken the typing system to allow for sequential composition of flat expressions. Currently we require that for 'let $x \Leftarrow A$ in B' to be in flat, either A or B must be in cnst. It appears that both A and B could be in flat; however, we have not yet been able to establish a correctness proof in this case. We plan to implement our reference-based semantics with the intention of deriving an experimental measure of its performance. We would also like to adapt our results to the "construct-results" costing function outlined in [28]; this costing function allows the use of the segment-vector representation of nested sequences without the compromising the usability of the semantics.

Acknowledgements

We thank the referees and the DePaul Foundations of Programming Languages group for useful comments and references to related work. The work reported here began while the first author was a student at the University of North Carolina and was completed during an appointment at North Carolina State University. I would like to thank both institutions, and Rance Cleaveland who supervised me at NCSU, for their support.

References

1. G. E. Blelloch. *Vector Models for Data-Parallel Computing*. MIT Press, 1990.
2. G. E. Blelloch. NESL: A nested data-parallel language (version 3.0). Technical report, Carnegie-Mellon University, Department of Computer Science, 1994.
3. G. E. Blelloch. Programming parallel algorithms. *Communications of the ACM*, 39(3), 1996.
4. G. E. Blelloch, P. B. Gibbons, Y. Matias, and M. Zagha. Accounting for memory bank conetention and delay in high-bandwidth multiprocessors. In *Proceedings of the ACM Symposium on Parallel Algorithms and Architectures*, pages 84–94, Santa Barbara, CA, July 1995. ACM Press.
5. G. E. Blelloch and J. Greiner. A provable time and space efficient implementation of NESL. In *International Conference on Functional Programming*, 1996.
6. G. E. Blelloch, J. C. Hardwick, J. Sipelstein, M. Zagha, and S. Chatterjee. Implementation of a portable nested data-parallel language. *Journal of Parallel and Distributed Computing*, 21(1):4–14, Apr. 1994.
7. G. E. Blelloch and G. W. Sabot. Compiling collection-oriented languages onto massively parallel computers. *Journal of Parallel and Distributed Computing*, 8:119–134, 1990.
8. R. P. Brent. The parallel evaluation of generic arithmetic expressions. *Journal of the ACM*, 21(2):201–206, 1974.

9. D. Engelhardt and A. Wendelborn. A partitioning-independent paradigm for nested data parallelism. *International Journal of Parallel Programming*, 24(4):291–317, Aug. 1996.

10. P. L. Garcia, M. Hermenegildo, and S. K. Debray. A methodology for granularity based control of parallelism in logic programs. *J. of Symbolic Computation*, 22:715–734, 1998.

11. A. M. Ghuloum and A. L. Fisher. Flattening and parallelizing irregular, recurrent loop nests. In *Proceedings of the Symposium on Principles and Practice of Parallel Programming*, pages 58–67, Santa Barbara, July 1995.

12. J. Gustavsson and D. Sands. A foundation for space-safe transformations of call-by-need programs. In A. D. Gordon and A. M.Pitts, editors, *The Third International Workshop on Higher Order Operational Techniques in Semantics*, volume 26 of *Electronic Notes in Theoretical Computer Science*. Elsevier, 1999.

13. M. Hermenegildo and M. Carro. Relating data-parallelism and (and-)parallelism in logic programs. *The Computer Languages Journal*, 22(2/3):143–163, July 1996.

14. P. Hudak, S. Peyton Jones, and P. Wadler. Report on the programming language Haskell version 1.2. *ACM SIGPLAN notices*, 27(5), May 1992.

15. C. Jay. The FISh language definition. http://www-staff.socs.uts.edu.au/~cbj/Publications/fishdef.ps.gz, 1998.

16. C. Jay. Costing parallel programs as a function of shapes. *Science of Computer Programming*, 1999.

17. G. Keller. *Transformation-Based Implementation of Nested Data-Parallelism for Distributed Memory Machines*. PhD thesis, TU Berlin, 1999.

18. J. Launchbury and T. Sheard. Warm fusion: deriving build-catas from recursive definitions. In *Proceedings of the Conference on Functional Programming Languages and Computer Architecture*, pages 314–323, La Jolla, CA, June 1995.

19. A. K. Moran and D. Sands. Improvement in a lazy context: An operational theory for call-by-need. In *Conference Record of the ACM Symposium on Principles of Programming Languages*, pages 43–56, San Antonio, Jan. 1999. ACM Press.

20. D. W. Palmer. *Efficient Execution of Nested Data Parallel Programs*. PhD thesis, University of North Carolina, 1996.

21. D. W. Palmer, J. F. Prins, and S. Westfold. Work-efficient nested data-parallelism. In *Frontiers '95*, 1995.

22. E. Pontelli and G. Gupta. Nested parallel call optimization. In *International Parallel Processing Symposium*. IEEE Computer Society Press, 1996.

23. J. Prins, M. Ballabio, M. Boverat, M. Hodous, and D. Maric. Fast primitives for irregular computations on the nec sx-4. *Crosscuts*, 6(4), 1997.

24. J. F. Prins and D. W. Palmer. Transforming high-level data-parallel programs into vector operations. In *Proceedings of the Symposium on Principles and Practice of Parallel Programming*, pages 119–128, San Diego, May 1993. (ACM SIGPLAN Notices, 28(7), , 1993).

25. V. Ramakrishnan, I. Sherson, and R. Subramanian. Efficient techniques for fast nested barrier synchronization. In *ACM Symposium on Parallel Algorithms and Architectures*, 1995.

26. B. Ramkumar and L. Kale. Compiled execution of the reduced-or process model on multi-processors. In *North American Conference on Logic Programming*. MIT Press, 1989.

27. J. Riely. *Applications of Abstraction for Concurrent Programs*. PhD thesis, University of North Carolina at Chapel Hill, 1999.

28. J. Riely, J. Prins, and S. Iyer. Provably correct vectorization of nested-parallel programs. In *Programming Models for Massively Parallel Computers (MPPM'95)*, Berlin, Dec. 1995.

29. D. Sands. Proving the correctness of recursion-based automatic program transformations. *Theoretical Computer Science*, 167(10), Oct. 1996.

30. D. Sands. Total correctness by local improvement in the transformation of functional programs. *ACM Transactions on Programming Languages and Systems*, 18(2):175–234, 1996.

31. D. B. Skillicorn and W. Cai. A cost calculus for parallel functional programming, 1994. Queens University Department of Computer Science TR-93-348.
32. G. L. Steele and W. D. Hillis. Connection machine Lisp: Fine-grained parallel symbolic processing. In *Proceedings of the ACM Conference on LISP and Functional Programming*, pages 279–297, Cambridge, MA, Aug. 1986. ACM Press.
33. D. Suciu. *Parallel Programming Languages for Collections*. PhD thesis, University of Pennsylvania, 1995.
34. D. Suciu and V. Tannen. Efficient compilation of high-level data parallel algorithms. In *Proceedings of the ACM Symposium on Parallel Algorithms and Architectures*. ACM Press, June 1994.
35. P. Wadler. Deforestation: Transforming programs to eliminate trees. *Theoretical Computer Science*, 73:231–248, 1990.

Model Checking Guided Abstraction and Analysis*

Hassen Saïdi

System Design Laboratory
SRI International
Menlo Park, CA 94025, USA
Tel: (+1) (650) 859-3810, Fax: (+1) (650) 859-2844
saidi@sdl.sri.com

Abstract. The combination of abstraction and state exploration techniques is the most promising recipe for a successful verification of properties of large or infinite state systems. In this work, we present a general, yet effective, algorithm for computing automatically boolean abstractions of infinite state systems, using decision procedures. The advantage of our approach is that it is not limited to particular concrete domains, but can handle different kinds of infinite state systems. Furthermore, our approach provides, through the use of model checking as a tool for the exploration of the state-space of the abstract system, an automatic way of refining the abstraction until the property of interest is verified or a counterexample is exhibited. We illustrate our approach on some examples and discuss its implementation.

1 Introduction

The combination of abstraction and state exploration techniques is probably the most promising recipe for a successful verification of properties of large or infinite state systems. It is now widely accepted that abstraction techniques are not only useful, but even necessary for a successful verification [19,6,21,13,12,9,14] in order to avoid the limiting factor of using model checking by reducing all the behaviors of a program to a simplified description on which the property of interest can be verified using model checking. While the theoretical frameworks for defining property preserving abstractions such as abstract interpretation [8] have been widely studied in the literature, the *automatic* construction of useful and accurate abstractions preserving useful properties is in an early stage of investigation. Abstract models are usually provided manually, and theorem proving is used to check that the provided abstract mapping preserves the properties. Once the preservation property is established, the abstract model is analyzed by model checking. Recently [14,7,1,25,11], novel techniques based on abstract interpretation have been proposed in the context of the verification of temporal

---

* This research was supported by DARPA contract F30602-97-C-0040.

J. Palsberg (Ed.): SAS 2000, LNCS 1824, pp. 377–396, 2000.

properties where theorem proving is used to compute automatically finite abstractions. These techniques are quite effective, but require heavy use of theorem proving and decision procedures.

The most general and yet simple and effective abstraction scheme consists of constructing
boolean abstractions following the scheme introduced in [14]. Boolean abstractions consist in using predicates over concrete variables as boolean abstract variables. In this abstraction, certain predicates at the concrete level (that might be used in guards, expressions, or properties) can be replaced by boolean variables at the abstract level. An abstract version of the infinite-state transition system is a transition system where the set $\{B_1, \cdots, B_k\}$ of abstract variables is a set of boolean variables corresponding to predicates $\{\varphi_1, \cdots, \varphi_k\}$ over the concrete variables. An abstract state in this transition system is therefore a truth assignment to these boolean variables. Boolean abstractions have very nice properties. In fact, any abstraction mapping that maps an arbitrary system to a finite state system can be expressed as a boolean abstraction. Furthermore, the abstract system can be represented symbolically using Binary Decision Diagrams (BDDs) and therefore can be analyzed using symbolic model checking, allowing an efficient exploration of abstract systems with a large state space. The techniques we developed for the automatic construction of boolean abstractions do not require a preservation check, and ensure that the constructed abstraction indeed preserves various temporal logics properties, including safety properties. Furthermore, boolean abstraction is an efficient and more powerful alternative to static analysis techniques dedicated to the automatic generation of various properties such as invariants like the ones presented in [3,2,24].

The drawback of using abstraction followed by model checking as a verification and analysis technology consists in the fact that abstractions are approximations of the original systems that induce false negative results. For instance, a model checker may exhibit an error trace that corresponds to an execution of the abstract program that violates the desired properties. However, this error trace may not correspond to an execution trace in the concrete program. This situation indicates that the abstraction is too coarse, and that the results of model checking the abstract system are not conclusive. That is, too many details were abstracted and the abstraction needs to be refined. The contribution of our work can be summarized as follows:

- We propose an efficient algorithm for the automatic construction of boolean abstractions that requires fewer calls to decision procedures and subsumes the previous and recent work [14,7,1,11] in this topic.

- In all the recent work on the automatic construction of finite abstractions, parallel programs are considered. However, each component are abstracted separately. In our work, the abstraction of a component takes into account its interaction with the environment, allowing the construction of more precise abstractions.

- We propose to use the error trace generated by model checking to automatically refine the abstraction, even more. This methodology consists in successively refining a first abstraction until the property is proved or a concrete error trace violating the property is exhibited. The refinement algorithm generates new predicates that will be used to enrich the abstract state-space.

- The refinement procedure may not always terminate. However, at any refinement step, the reachable states of the constructed abstract system represent an invariant and a new more precise control structure of the concrete system that can be exploited for further analysis. In [20], we use the newly generated predicates to construct a more precise control structure of parameterized systems. Similar ideas are used in [18] for the generation of control structure in the particular case of synchronous linear systems.

Our verification methodology based on abstraction followed by successive model checking guided refinement steps is implemented in a verification environment that combines deduction and state-exploration techniques. We successfully used our methodology to prove safety properties of several systems, including a data-link protocol used by Philips Corporation in one of its commercial products. The original proofs [15,17,16] of the protocol required two to six months of work and were entirely done using theorem provers. A boolean abstraction of the protocol can be automatically generated using the predicates appearing in the description of the protocol in about a hundred seconds with the help of the PVS theorem prover [23] and its new efficient implementation of decision procedures. The abstract protocol is then analyzed in a few seconds to check that all the safety properties hold.

This paper is organized as follows: in Section 2, we present the model in which systems are described, and give some basic definitions. In Section 3, we define boolean abstractions in the general framework of abstract interpretation using Galois connections. In Section 4, we show how boolean abstractions can be constructed in an efficient way using decision procedures and compositional reasoning. In Section 5, we show how model checking is used to prove properties on abstract systems and how it can be used as a guide to the automatic refinement of already constructed abstractions. In Section 6, we describe our refinement algorithms. Finally, in Section 7, we describe a tool implementing our methodology.

2   Preliminaries

We consider systems that are parallel compositions of sequential processes, where each process is modeled as a transitions system.

Definition 1 (transition system).
A transition system S is a tuple $S = \ <\mathcal{V}, \mathcal{T} = \{\tau_1, \cdots, \tau_n\}, \mathcal{L}, Init>$, where

- *$\mathcal{V}$ is a set of system variables including a program counter pc.*
- *$\mathcal{T}$ is a set of transitions.*
- *$\mathcal{L}$ is a set of control locations, that is, the possible values of pc.*
- *$Init$ is a predicate characterizing the set of initial states.*

Each transition τ is a guarded command

$$l_i : \quad guard \longrightarrow v_1 ::= e_1, \cdots, v_n ::= e_n \ \text{goto} \ l_j$$

where $\{v_1, \cdots, v_k\} \subseteq \mathcal{V}$ and $\{l_i, l_j\} \subseteq \mathcal{L}$. The boolean expression $guard$ is the guard of the transition τ. Each variable v_i is assigned with an expression e_i of a compatible type. Locations l_i and l_j are, respectively, the source and target locations of transition τ_i. A state of a system S is a valuation of the system variables of $\mathcal{V}$. A system can be a parallel composition of components described as transition systems. The system can be described as a single transition system where the set of variables is the union of the set of variables of each component, the set of transitions is the union of all the transitions of all components, the program counter is a tuple formed by the program counters of all components, and the initial state is the conjunction of the initial states of each component.

Figure 1 shows the description of the Bakery protocol in our specification lan-

```
bakery : SYSTEM
  BEGIN
    process_1 : PROGRAM
      y1 : VAR nat
      BEGIN
        p1_Try 1: TRUE              → y1 := y2+1 GOTO  2
        p1_In   2: y2 = 0 ∨ y1 ≤ y2 →  SKIP      GOTO  3
        p1_Out 3: TRUE              → y1 := 0     GOTO  1
      END process_1
  ||
    process_2 : PROGRAM
      y2 : VAR nat
      BEGIN
        p2_Try 1: TRUE              → y2 := y1+1 GOTO  2
        p2_In   2: y1 = 0 ∨ y2 < y1 →  SKIP      GOTO  3
        p2_Out 3: TRUE              → y2 := 0     GOTO  1
      END process_2
    INITIALLY : y1 = 0 ∧ y2 = 0 ∧ pc2 = 1 ∧ pc1 = 1
  END bakery
```

Fig. 1. Bakery transition system (version A)

guage. The algorithm is called the Bakery algorithm, since it is based on the idea that customers, as they enter a bakery, pick numbers that form an ascending sequence. Then a customer with a lower number has higher priority in accessing its critical section, which in this case is control location 3. Each process process_i modifies its local variable yi, and can read the other's variable.

We also recall the definitions of predicate transformers over transition systems. The predicate transformers $post$ and pre expressing, respectively, the strongest postcondition and precondition by a transition τ of a predicate P over the state variables of $\mathcal{V}$ are defined as follows:

$$post[\tau](P) = \exists \mathcal{V}'.action_\tau(\mathcal{V}',\mathcal{V}) \wedge P(\mathcal{V}')$$
$$pre[\tau](P) = \exists \mathcal{V}'.action_\tau(\mathcal{V},\mathcal{V}') \wedge P(\mathcal{V}')$$

where $action_\tau(\mathcal{V},\mathcal{V}')$ is defined as the relation between the current state and next state, that is, the expression

$$pc = l_i \wedge guard \wedge \bigwedge_{i=1}^{k} v_i' = e_i,\ pc' = l_j$$

Defining the transition relation of a system as a relational predicate for each transition is a more general alternative to the use of guarded commands. The semantics of a transition system S is given by its computational model $K_S = (Q, \mathcal{T}, R)$, where Q is the set of valuations of the program variables $\mathcal{V}$, and $R \subseteq Q \times \mathcal{T} \times Q$ a transition relation. A set of states of a program can be represented by its corresponding predicate over the state variables of $\mathcal{V}$.

3   Boolean Abstractions

Boolean abstraction is a simple abstraction scheme defined in [14] that consists of using predicates over concrete variables as boolean abstract variables. In an abstract version of the infinite-state transition system, the set $\{B_1, \cdots, B_k\}$ of abstract variables is a set of boolean variables corresponding to predicates $\{\varphi_1, \cdots, \varphi_k\}$ over the concrete variables. An abstract state in this transition system is therefore a truth assignment to these boolean variables. Since the set of boolean variables is finite, so is the set of abstract states. Boolean abstractions can easily be defined in the framework of abstract interpretation using Galois connections.

Definition 2 (Galois connection). *A pair of monotonic functions (α, γ) defining a mapping between a concrete domain lattice $\wp(\mathcal{Q}, \subseteq)$ and an abstract domain lattice $\wp(\mathcal{Q}^a, \sqsubseteq)$, is a Galois connection if and only if*

$$\forall (P, P^a) \in \wp(\mathcal{Q}) \times \wp(\mathcal{Q}^a).\ \alpha(P) \sqsubseteq P^a \Leftrightarrow P \subseteq \gamma(P^a)$$

Sets of states in $\wp(\mathcal{Q})$ and $\wp(\mathcal{Q}^a)$ are represented by their corresponding predicates. Thus, $\wp(\mathcal{Q})$ and $\wp(\mathcal{Q}^a)$ correspond to lattices of concrete and abstract predicates ordered by the logical implication. A boolean abstraction can be expressed as a Galois connection as follows:

- $\alpha(P) = \bigwedge\{B^a \mid P \Rightarrow \gamma(B^a)\} = P^a$, where B^a is any boolean expression over the set $\{B_1, \cdots, B_k\}$.
- γ is defined as a substitution function. That is, $\gamma(P^a) = P^a[\varphi_1/B_1, \cdots, \varphi_k/B_k]$,

where each boolean variable B_i is substituted by its corresponding concrete predicate φ_i.

Thus, the abstraction of a concrete set of states represented by a predicate P over concrete variables is defined as the smallest boolean formula P^a over the abstract variables B_i. That is, an overapproximation of P. In [25], we presented an efficient algorithm for computing the most precise boolean abstraction with respect to a set of predicates, for systems where the transition relation is given as a relational predicate. The algorithm consists of an efficient enumeration of all boolean combinations B^a to test the assertion $P \Rightarrow \gamma(B^a)$. The algorithm abstracts systems where the transition relation is given as a predicate. Each implication $P \Rightarrow \gamma(B^a)$ is submitted to the decision procedure to test its validity. In [25], we proved that in order to compute P^a it is not necessary to consider all the possible B^a, that is 2^{2^k} expressions, but at most $3^k - 1$. However, this is still a high price to pay for the construction of an abstract system. Notice that any approximation of P^a is a valid abstraction of P.

```
bakery : SYSTEM
B3 : VAR bool
  BEGIN
    process_1 : PROGRAM
      B1 : VAR bool
      BEGIN
      p1_Try 1 : TRUE      → B1 := F, B3 := F GOTO 2
      p1_In   2 : B2 ∨ B3 →  SKIP              GOTO 3
      p1_Out 3 : TRUE      → B1 := T, B3 := T GOTO 1
      END process_1
  ||
    process_2 : PROGRAM
      B2 : VAR nat
      BEGIN
      p2_Try 1 : TRUE      → B2 := F, B3 := T            GOTO 2
      p2_In   2 : B1 ∨ ¬B3 →  SKIP                       GOTO 3
      p2_Out 3 : TRUE      → B2 := T,
                             B3 := if  B1
                                   then  T
                                   else if  (¬B1 ∨ ¬B3)
                                        then  F
                                        else  ?
                                                          GOTO 1
      END process_2
    INITIALLY :  B1 ∧ B2 ∧ B3 ∧ pc2 = 1 ∧ pc1 = 1
  END bakery
```

Fig. 2. Abstract version of Bakery transition system (version A)

Thus, in order to compute for a concrete system S, an abstract system S^a, it is sufficient to abstract the initial state $Init$ by computing $\alpha(Init)$, and to abstract each transition τ as follows:

$$\tau^a = \alpha(\tau) = \alpha(action_\tau(\mathcal{V}, \mathcal{V}')) = \bigwedge\{(B^a, B^{a'})| \vdash post[\tau](\gamma(B^a)) \Rightarrow \gamma(B^{a'})\}$$

that is, the pair $(B^a, B^{a'})$ characterizing the abstraction of the set of possible predecessors by τ and the abstraction of the set of possible successors by τ. In this case, the complexity of the computation of τ^a is $(3^k - 1) * (3^k - 1)$ calls to the decision procedure, $(3^k - 1)$ calls to test the successors, and $(3^k - 1)$ calls to test the potential predecessors.

The preservation of properties expressed in temporal logic is widely studied in [21,10,5]. Preservation results are established via equivalences and preorders between the concrete and abstract models. The following theorem establishes the preservation of safety properties expressed in the logic CTL^* via simulation.

Theorem 1 (weak preservation). *Let S be a concrete system, and let S^a be a boolean abstraction of S using any set of predicates. We have*

$$S^a \models \alpha(\varphi) \quad \Rightarrow \quad S \models \varphi$$

for each formula $\varphi \in \forall CTL^*$, that is, temporal formulas with universal quantification over paths, including safety properties such as invariants.

Proof. This result can be established by proving that S^a simulates S. This can be done by proving that the following holds for each transition τ of S:

$$\forall P. \ post[\tau](P) \quad \Rightarrow \quad \gamma(post[\alpha(\tau)](\alpha(P)))$$

that is, each set of successor states by an abstract transition is an overapproximation of the corresponding set of states of the concrete system.

Intuitively, $\forall CTL^*$ properties hold in all execution paths. Since S^a simulates S, that is, all the executions of S are executions of S^a, then if a property holds along all execution paths of S^a, it holds in all execution paths of S. Theorem 1 indicates that when a property is established in the abstract system, its corresponding concrete property holds in the concrete system. However, nothing can be concluded when the property does not hold in the abstract system. Strong preservation results can be applied in this case under some conditions.

Theorem 2 (strong preservation). *Let S be a concrete system, and let S^a be a boolean abstraction of S using any set of predicates that includes all the literals appearing in the guards of S and in the property φ. If S^a is deterministic, we have*

$$S^a \models \alpha(\varphi) \quad \Leftrightarrow \quad S \models \varphi$$

That is, S^a and S are equivalent.

Proof. By construction S^a simulates S. Thus, it is sufficient to prove now that S simulates S^a. To show this, it is sufficient to prove that for each pair of abstract states s_1^a and s_2^a, if s_2^a is a successor of s_1^a by τ^a in the abstract system, then, for every pair s_1 and s_2 of states in the concretization of s_1^a and s_2^a, s_2 is the successor of s_1 by τ in the original system. Every concrete state s_1 in the concretization of s_1^a satisfies the guard of τ, and every successor s_2 of s_1 is in the concretization of s_2^a. Thus, S simulates S^a.

The strong preservation result allows us to avoid false negative results by mapping abstract error traces to concrete executions violating the property. However, the condition for strong preservation requires that S^a be deterministic. This is usually not the case. However, we will see later how we exploit Theorem 2 to generate boolean abstractions to verify properties, and also to generate counterexamples when a formula is not a property of the concrete system. As we mentioned earlier in the introduction, boolean abstraction subsumes abstractions where the abstract domain is finite.

Theorem 3 (generality). *Let S be a system and let α be an abstraction function where the abstract domain is finite. Then, α can be expressed as a boolean abstraction.*

Proof. The proof is based on the fact that a finite domain can be encoded by a set of boolean variables. Each abstract state is then a conjunction of a subset of the set of boolean variables. The concretization of an abstract state is a set of concrete states that can be represented as a predicate.

Figure 2 shows the abstraction of the Bakery protocol using predicates $y1 = 0$, $y2 = 0$, and $y1 \leq y2$ appearing in the guards. Notice that all the assignments are deterministic except the assignment for the variable $B3$ in the transition **p2_Out**.

4   Automatic Construction of Boolean Abstractions

Decision procedures can be used for the automatic construction of a boolean abstraction of a concrete, infinite state system described as a transition system. The abstraction of a concrete system $S = \ <\mathcal{V}, \mathcal{T} = \{\tau_1, \cdots, \tau_n\}, \mathcal{L}, Init>$ is an abstract system $S^a = \ <\mathcal{V}^a, \mathcal{T}^a = \{\tau_1^a, \cdots, \tau_n^a\}, \mathcal{L}, Init^a>$ such that

- $\mathcal{V}^a$ is the set $\{B_1, \cdots, B_k, pc\}$.
- $\mathcal{T}^a$ is a set of abstract transitions.
- $Init^a$ is the abstract initial state computed as $\alpha(Init)$.

The abstraction algorithm consists in computing $Init^a$ and for each concrete transition τ

$$l_i : \quad guard \ \longrightarrow \ v_1 ::= e_1, \cdots, v_n ::= e_n \ \ goto \ l_j$$

a corresponding abstract transition τ^a

$$l_i: \quad guard^a \quad \longrightarrow \quad B_1 ::= b_1, \cdots, B_k ::= b_k \ \ goto \ l_j$$

such that:

- The abstract guard $guard^a$ is computed as $\alpha(guard)$. When using the literals of the guards as abstract boolean variables, $\alpha(guard)$ is an *exact* abstraction, where each literal of $guard$ is substituted by its corresponding abstract boolean variable. - Each assignment $B_i := b_i$ is defined as follows:

$$B_i := \begin{cases} \mathbf{T} \text{ if} & post[\tau](true) \Rightarrow \gamma(B_i) \ \ (1) \\ \mathbf{F} \text{ if} & post[\tau](true) \Rightarrow \neg\gamma(B_i) \ (2) \\ ? \ \ \text{otherwise} \end{cases}$$

that is, for each abstract variable B_i, the strongest postcondition by τ of any arbitrary state is in $\gamma(B_i)$ or $\neg\gamma(B_i)$, that is, in φ_i or $\neg\varphi_i$. When neither of the above implications is valid, the variable is nondeterministically assigned the value ?.

- The variable pc is not abstracted since it is of a finite type.

When a variable is assigned the value ?, it is possible to compute a more refined assignment by taking into account the dependencies between the abstract variables. Thus, the assignment $B_i :=?$ can be redefined as follows:

$$B_i := if \ b_i^{\mathbf{T}}$$
$$then \ \mathbf{T}$$
$$else \ if \ b_i^{\mathbf{F}}$$
$$then \ \mathbf{F}$$
$$else \ ?$$

where $b_i^{\mathbf{T}}$ and $b_i^{\mathbf{F}}$ are defined as follows:

$$b_i^{\mathbf{T}} \equiv \bigvee \{B^a \mid post[\tau](\gamma(B^a)) \Rightarrow \gamma(B_i)\}$$

$$b_i^{\mathbf{F}} \equiv \bigvee \{B^a \mid post[\tau](\gamma(B^a)) \Rightarrow \neg\gamma(B_i)\}$$

That is, $b^{\mathbf{T}}$ and $b^{\mathbf{F}}$ are, respectively, the smallest boolean combination over the abstract variables $\{B_1, \cdots, B_k\}$ that defines the abstract state from which, if the transition τ is executed, the variable B_i gets either the value $\mathbf{T}$ or $\mathbf{F}$. In the worst case, both $b_i^{\mathbf{T}}$ and $b_i^{\mathbf{F}}$ are equivalent to true. Thus, the variable B_i is assigned with the value ?.

In [25], the complexity of the abstraction algorithm for a transition is $3^k - 1 * 3^k - 1$. In our case, this is reduced to at most $3^k - 1 * 2 * k$.

Theorem 4 (complexity). *The complexity of the abstraction of a transition τ using k predicates $\{\varphi_1, \cdots, \varphi_k\}$ requires checking the validity of $3^k - 1 * 2 * k$ implications.*

Proof. For each abstract variable B_i assigned in the abstraction of τ, The boolean expressions $b_i^{\mathbf{T}}$ and $b_i^{\mathbf{F}}$ are computed. Thus $2 * k$ implications have to be proved. For each of the expressions $b_i^{\mathbf{T}}$ and $b_i^{\mathbf{F}}$, all possible boolean expressions B^a over $\{B_1, \cdots, B_k\}$ have to be considered. There are $3^k - 1$ possible expressions as illustrated in the following Figure with $k = 2$. The elements of the set of possible

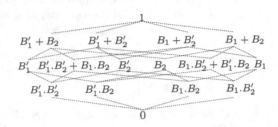

Fig. 3. Boolean algebra for 2 boolean variables B_1 and B_2

boolean expressions B^a are the elements of the boolean algebra defined by the k boolean variables, that is, 2^{2^k} expressions. However, the expression B^a appears on the left hand side of an implication. Thus, it is necessary to consider only expressions that are conjunctions of boolean variables. That is is only $3^k - 1$ possible expressions that can be tested incrementally by first testing each boolean variable B_i and its negation, and then testing conjunctions of the set of variables for which both tests fail.

The results in [25], shows that the enumeration of $3^k - 1$ expressions subsumes the enumeration of the possible 2^{2^k} expressions. However, the enumeration of the possible B^a satisfying the above implications can be done only for the expressions B^a such that

$$FV(post[\tau](\gamma(B^a))) \cap FV(\gamma(B_i)) \neq \emptyset$$

where $FV(P)$ is the set of free variables of the predicate P.

5   Model Checking Guided Analysis

Once an abstract system is constructed, model checking is used to explore its state-space. We use both symbolic and explicit-state model checking techniques. Figure 4 shows the reachable abstract states of the Bakery protocol. It is easy to show that the protocol does guarantee mutual exclusion for both processes since there is no reachable state where both control variables $pc1$ and $pc2$ have the value 3.

The advantage of model checking over other verification techniques is its ability to generate counterexamples when a property is violated. The error trace

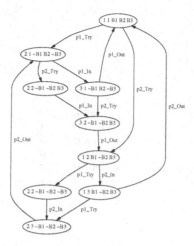

Fig. 4. Abstract state graph for the Bakery protocol

is a sequence of states and transitions starting from the initial state of the system leading to a state violating the property. Error traces of an abstract system can be mapped to executions of a concrete system since each abstract transition corresponds to a single concrete one with the same label.

Figure 5 shows a more complex version of the Bakery protocol (known as *Bakery_C*) where the critical section corresponds to control location 7. This version was proposed to avoid the long wait of one process at location 2 in the previous version (known as *Bakery_A*) before the process enters its critical section. The abstraction of the protocol with respect the guards $y1 = 0$, $y2 = 0$, $y1 \leq y2$, $x1 = 0$, and $x2 = 0$ is given in Figure 6. Figure 7 shows an error trace from the initial abstract state 0 to abstract state 30 violating the mutual exclusion property, where for both processes the program counter has value 7. The simulation of the error trace on the concrete system indicates that it does not correspond to an execution of the concrete system. However, this does not rule out the possibility that the property is violated. In the next section, we show how model checking can guide the automatic refinement of an abstract system until the property is verified or a counterexample corresponding to a concrete execution violating the property is generated.

6   Automatic Refinement of Abstractions

Unlike current model checking tools, the error trace we generate is a tree indicating the states where abstract variables are nondeterministically assigned. In Figure 7, states 9 and 12 indicate loss of information on, respectively, the abstract variables B_1, B_3, and B_2. The concrete system is deterministic. Thus,

```
bakery : SYSTEM
BEGIN
process_1 : PROGRAM
y1, x1, t1 : VAR nat
BEGIN
p1_init_x1 1:  TRUE                    → x1 := 1     : 2
p1_init_t   2:  TRUE                    → t1 := y2+1 : 3
p1_init_y   3:  TRUE                    → y1 := t1    : 4
p1_init_x0 4:  TRUE                    → x1 := 0     : 5
p1_Wait     5:  x2 = 0                  → SKIP        : 6
p1_In        6:  y2=0 ∨ y1 ≤ y2 → SKIP        : 7
p1_Out      7:  TRUE                    → y1 := 0     : 1
END process_1
   ‖
process_2 : PROGRAM
y2, x2, t2 : VAR nat
BEGIN
p2_init_x1 1:  TRUE                    → x2 := 1     : 2
p2_init_t   2:  TRUE                    → t2 := y1+1 : 3
p2_init_y   3:  TRUE                    → y2 := t2    : 4
p2_init_x0 4:  TRUE                    → x2 := 0     : 5
p2_Wait     5:  x1 = 0                  → SKIP        : 6
p2_In        6:  y1=0 ∨ y2 < y1 → SKIP        : 7
p2_Out      7:  TRUE                    → y2 := 0     : 1
END process_2
INITIALLY : y1=0 ∧ y2=0 ∧ x1=0 ∧ x2=0 ∧ t1=0 ∧ t2=0 ∧ pc1=1 ∧ pc2=1
END bakery
```

Fig. 5. Bakery transition system (version C)

in an execution of the concrete system, each abstract state s, such as the abstraction of s is state 9, has only one successor by the transition **p1_init_y**. Also, each state s such as the abstraction of s is state 12, has only one successor by the transition **p2_init_y**. However, if the error trace is a sequence and not a tree, that is all assignments in the sequence are deterministic, the following theorem allows us to conclude that the error trace corresponds to a sequence of concrete transitions violating the property. The theorem is a corollary of Theorem 2.

Theorem 5. *Let Let S be a concrete system, and let S^a be a boolean abstraction of S using any set of predicates that includes all the literals appearing in the guards of S and in the property φ. every sequence of transitions in S^a where all assignments are deterministic is a sequence of transitions of S. We call such a sequence a deterministic trace.*

Our refinement methodology consists in computing a new abstract system with more abstract variables. This is done by enriching the current abstract state by adding additional predicates, and therefore additional abstract boolean variables.

bakery : SYSTEM
$B3$: VAR bool
BEGIN
process_1 : PROGRAM
$B1$, $B4$: VAR bool
BEGIN

p1_init_x1	1:	TRUE	$\rightarrow B4 := \mathbf{F}$	: 2
p1_init_t	2:	TRUE	$\rightarrow SKIP$	: 3
p1_init_y	3:	TRUE	$\rightarrow B1 :=?, B3 :=?$	: 4
p1_init_x0	4:	TRUE	$\rightarrow B4 := \mathbf{T}$	: 5
p1_Wait	5:	$B5$	$\rightarrow SKIP$	: 6
p1_In	6:	$B2 \vee B3 \rightarrow SKIP$		: 7
p1_Out	7:	TRUE	$\rightarrow B1 := \mathbf{T}, B3 := \mathbf{T}$	: 1

END process_1
    ||
process_2 : PROGRAM
$B2$, $B5$: VAR bool
BEGIN

p2_init_x1	1:	TRUE	$\rightarrow B5 := \mathbf{F}$	: 2
p2_init_t	2:	TRUE	$\rightarrow SKIP$	: 3
p2_init_y	3:	TRUE	$\rightarrow B2 :=?,$	
			$B3 := if\ B1\ then\ \mathbf{T}\ else\ ?$	: 4
p2_init_x0	4:	TRUE	$\rightarrow B5 := \mathbf{T}$	: 5
p2_Wait	5:	$B4$	$\rightarrow SKIP$	: 6
p2_In	6:	$B1 \vee \neg B3 \rightarrow SKIP$		: 7
p2_Out	7:	TRUE	$\rightarrow B2 := \mathbf{T},$	
			$B3 := if\ B1$	
			$then\ \mathbf{T}$	
			$else\ if\ \neg B1 \vee \neg B3\ then\ \mathbf{F}\ else\ ? : 1$	

END process_2
INITIALLY : $B1 \wedge B2 \wedge B3 \wedge B4 \wedge B5 \wedge pc1=1 \wedge pc2=1$
END bakery

Fig. 6. Abstract version of Bakery transition system (version C)

We use Theorem 5 in order to construct a new abstract system that may produce more error traces that are deterministic. That is, by eliminating the nondeterminism in the current error traces. This is done by computing the constraints under which the system may execute one of the nondeterministic transitions. These constraints are captured as preconditions and computed using the predicate transformer *pre*. We use the following lemma, allowing an efficient computation of preconditions for assignments.

Lemma 1. *Let τ be a transition. If $guard(\tau)$ is equivalent to true, then*

$$\forall P.\ pre[\tau](P) \equiv \neg pre[\tau](\neg P)$$

This lemma indicates that when computing a precondition for assignments, it is not necessary to compute it for both the predicate and its negation. Let us consider the case of the Bakery protocol. The error trace indicates that nondeterminism is created for transitions **p1_init_y** and **p2_init_y** at, respectively, states 9 and 12. The refinement technique is applied to each of these states by computing the preconditions for each boolean variable that is assigned the value ? as follows:

- refining state 9:

$$pre[\textbf{p1\_init\_y}](y1 = 0) \equiv t1 = 0$$

$$pre[\textbf{p1\_init\_y}](y1 \leq y2) \equiv t1 \leq y2$$

- refining state 12:

$$pre[\textbf{p2\_init\_y}](y2 = 0) \equiv t2 = 0$$

Three new predicates $t1 = 0$, $t2 = 0$ and $t1 \leq y2$ corresponding to the new abstract variables $B6$, $B7$, and $B8$ are generated. Each transition where a variable is not assigned with the value **T** or **F** is refined. The refinement of the transition **p1_init_y**

$$3: \text{TRUE} \rightarrow B1 :=?,\ B3 :=? : 4$$

where $B1$ and $B3$ correspond to $y1 = 0$ and $y1 \leq y2$ is the transition

$$3: \text{TRUE} \rightarrow B1 := if\ B6\ then\ \textbf{T}\ else\ if\ \neg B6 \vee \neg B8\ then\ \textbf{F}\ else\ ?,$$
$$B3 := if\ B6\ then\ \textbf{T}\ else\ ? \qquad\qquad : 4$$

The refinement algorithm uses a refined way of computing the values $b_i^{\textbf{T}}$ and $b_i^{\textbf{F}}$

$$b_i^{\textbf{T}} \equiv \bigvee \{B^a \mid \gamma(\mathcal{R}_\tau^a) \wedge post[\tau](\gamma(B^a)) \Rightarrow \gamma(B_i)\}$$

$$b_i^{\textbf{F}} \equiv \bigvee \{B^a \mid \gamma(\mathcal{R}_\tau^a) \wedge post[\tau](\gamma(B^a)) \Rightarrow \neg\gamma(B_i)\}$$

where $\mathcal{R}_\tau^a$ is a boolean expression representing the set of reachable states of the already constructed abstract system at the source location of τ. For instance, $\mathcal{R}_{\textbf{p1\_Try}}^a$ of $Bakery\_A$ is equal to $B_1 \vee B_2$. The expression B^a is any expression over the union of the new set of variables and set of the old one that satisfy the invariant $\mathcal{R}_\tau^a$. Thus, each refinement step uses the results of model checking the

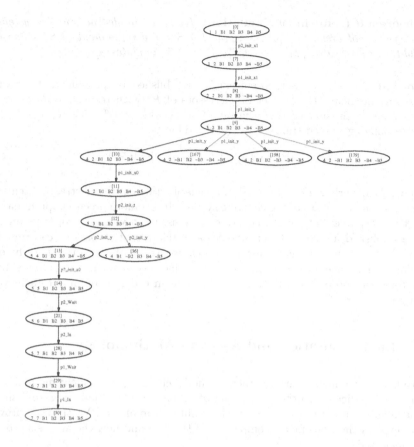

Fig. 7. Error trace for the Bakery Protocol

constructed abstract system to generate new abstract variables and to reduce the cost of the refinement algorithm. Furthermore, the invariant $\mathcal{R}_\tau^a$ refers to variables written by the component where τ belongs and to variables that are modified by other components that form its environment. The new generated predicates are used as new abstract boolean variables to compute a refined abstract system. The new abstract system is then analyzed and a new error trace indicates that mutual exclusion is violated. However, the trace is not deterministic, and a new refinement step is performed where two new predicates $y1 \leq t2$ and $t1 \leq t2$ corresponding to the new boolean variables $B9$ and $B10$ are generated. A new abstract system is then generated and analyzed, and the property is proved to be a property of the abstract system. Thus by Theorem 1, it is a property of the Bakery protocol.

In general, the an abstract system obtained after refinement is a more precise an accurate abstraction of the corresponding original system.

Theorem 6 (refinement simulation). *Let S^a be an abstraction of a system S using a set of predicates $\{\varphi_1, \cdots, \varphi_k\}$. Let S_r^a be a refinement of S^a using the additional predicates $\{\varphi_{k+1}, \cdots, \varphi_j\}$. Then, S^a simulates S_r^a.*

Proof. The proof of the theorem can be established by proving that for each abstract predicate P^a, the set of successors of P^a with respect to an abstract transition τ^a is smaller that the set of successors of P^a with respect to the corresponding refined transition τ_r^a of S_r^a. That is:

$$\forall P^a. \; post[\tau_r^a](P^a) \;\Rightarrow\; post[\tau^a](P^a)$$

Thus, the concretization of the set of reachable states of the abstract system is a more refined invariant of the concrete system. It is a more precise approximation of the reachable state of the concrete systems. Even when a property can not be established after a number of successive refinement steps, one can use this invariant as a starting point for a more elaborate proof and analysis technique using for instance a theorem prover. It is in fact necessary for even very simple systems and property to provide an invariant in order to be able to achieve a correctness proof.

7   Implementation and Analysis Methodology

We have implemented the abstraction/model checking/refinement methodology in a tool dedicated to the verification of infinite state systems. Figure 8 shows the architecture of the tool. Our tool is built on top of the PVS theorem prover. We explain the role of each component of the tool and how the analysis process is organized.

Syntax: Systems can be described in a Simple Programming Language (SPL), close to the one used in [22], but with the rich data types and expression definition mechanism available in PVS. Our SPL language includes common algorithmic constructions such as single and multiple assignment statements, conditionals If-Then-Else, and loop statements. We also allow parallel composition by interleaving and synchronization by shared variables as in Unity [4]. Systems described in SPL are translated automatically into guarded commands with explicit control. Program variables can be of any type definable in PVS, and can be assigned by any definable PVS expression of a compatible type. It is possible to import any defined PVS theory. The examples in this paper are presented in the automatically generated LATEX format for guarded commands.

Internal representation: Pvs is implemented in LISP. Every object manipulated in Pvs such as a theory, a theorem, or a proof is represented as an instance of a predefined object class. We have defined for transition systems a representation that is also a class. An important aspect of such a structure is that it is

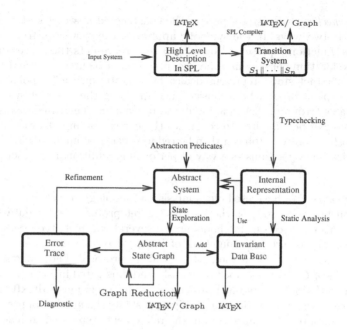

Fig. 8. Analysis methodology

independent of the PVS internal structure, and makes our implementation independent of the possible changes in the PVS internal representation. However, the expression manipulated and the verification condition generated are represented as PVS expressions and PVS obligations. This is necessary for the automatic interaction with the decision procedures.

Static analysis: We use the techniques developed in [24] to generate useful invariants of the concrete system. Static analysis consists in a set of techniques for the automatic generation of such invariants. These techniques are based on propagation of guards and assignments through program control points. The techniques we use computes invariants for each component and are composed using a novel composition rule presented in [24] to form invariants of the global system. These invariants are used to weaken all the implications that are generated when an abstraction is computed. When used, the allow a more efficient construction of abstractions. That is, one can decide with the help of these invariants that a variable is not assigned the value ? but either **T** or **F**, and thus, allows to generate less implications.

Automatic abstraction: The abstraction module takes a transition system and builds a first abstraction using the predicates appearing in the guards and the property to verify, and then submits the abstract system to our model checker. This module is also used for automatic refinement.

Model checking: The state-space of the constructed abstract system can be explored in two ways. In the symbolic approach, the system is translated into a boolean function represented by a BDD that represents the successor function. The exploration consists in applying the function recursively starting from the initial abstract state, represented also by a BDD until a fix point is reached. In the explicit approach, it consists in translating the abstract system into an executable form and then running it and by hashing the visited states. Both approaches can be exploited to construct the corresponding abstract state graph. The abstract state graph can then be reduced using simulation and bisimulation minimization algorithms as a way of performing additional abstractions.

Experiments: We have used our analysis methodology to verify several communication protocols such as the alternating bit protocol and a data link protocol. We also applied our methodology on several parametrized systems that are compositions of arbitrary numbers of identical processes. Figure 7 shows our experiments with three versions of the Bakery protocol. The versions *Bakery_A* and *Bakery_C* were described previously and illustrated in Figures 1 and 5. The version *Bakery_B* is obtained by removing the transitions **init_x0** and **Init_x1** from the description of *Bakery_C*. Figure 7 shows the number of predicates used in the compute a first abstraction, the refinement steps used to reach a conclusive result, that is either the property is verified, or to generate a deterministic error trace. It shows, the number of predicates computed each refinement step. It shows the numbers of implications generate and proved for each abstraction/refinement step, and the duration of each step. It also shows a comparison with our previous work in [25] where transitions systems are given as relational predicates, and where the numbers of implications is much higher as shown by Theorem 4. Notice that in general the complexity of each refinement step is less than the complexity of the computation of the first abstraction. The version *Bakery_B* is shown to violate the mutual exclusion property, and a deterministic error trace is generated after two refinements steps.

	#of initial predicates	#of refinements steps	#of new predicates	#of calls to the decision procedure	comparison with [25]	time (s)
Bakery_A	3	0	–	27	33	1.8
Bakery_B	3	2	–	72	100	5.1
			3	32	178	3.3
			4	134	366	15.5
Bakery_C	5	2	–	120	168	12
			3	35	94	3.2
			2	32	136	3.4

Fig. 9. Experiments results for 3 versions of the Bakery protocol

8 Conclusion and Future Work

We presented a general, yet effective, methodology for the verification of large systems, based on abstraction followed by model checking. The novelty of our methodology consists of an efficient algorithm for the automatic construction of boolean abstractions and an efficient algorithm for automatically refining a coarse abstraction when model checking the abstract system fails. This methodology also allows in many cases the generation of counterexamples, that is executions violating the property of interest. Our abstraction algorithm can be used to compute abstraction for any abstract domain which is a boolean algebra. Our verification tool represents the core of a verification and analysis technology for large software. The first step will be to translate source code into transition systems. For large programs, thousands of calls to the decision procedure are necessary. This can be done in few minutes or at most few hours.

References

1. S. Bensalem, Y. Lakhnech, and S. Owre. Computing abstractions of infinite state systems compositionally and automatically. In *Proceedings of the 9th Conference on Computer-Aided Verification, CAV'98*, LNCS. Springer Verlag, June 1998. 377, 378
2. S. Bensalem, Y. Lakhnech, and Hassen Saïdi. Powerful techniques for the automatic generation of invariants. In Rajeev Alur and Thomas A. Henzinger, editors, *Computer-Aided Verification, CAV '96*, number 1102 in Lecture Notes in Computer Science, pages 323–335, New Brunswick, NJ, July/August 1996. Springer-Verlag. 378
3. Nikolaj Bjorner, Anca Browne, and Zohar Manna. Automatic Generation of Invariants and Intermediate Assertions. *Theoretical Computer Science*, 1997. 378
4. K. Mani Chandy and Jayadev Misra. *Parallel Program Design*. Addison-Wesley, Reading, Massachusetts, 1988. 392
5. Ching-Tsun Chou. Simple proof techniques for property preservation via simulation. *Information Processing Letters*, 60(3):129–134, 1996. 383
6. E.M. Clarke, O. Grumberg, and D.E. Long. Model checking and abstraction. *ACM Transactions on Programming Languages and Systems*, 16(5):1512–1542, September 1994. 377
7. Michael Colon and Thomas Uribe. Generating finite-state abstractions of reactive systems using decision procedures. In *Proceedings of the 9th Conference on Computer-Aided Verification, CAV'98*, LNCS. Springer Verlag, June 1998. 377, 378
8. P. Cousot and R. Cousot. Abstract interpretation: a unified lattice model for static analysis of programs by construction or approximation of fixpoints. In *4th POPL*, January 1977. 377
9. D. Dams. *Abstract interpretation and partition refinement for model checking*. PhD thesis, Technical University of Eindhoven, July 1996. 377
10. D. Dams, O. Grumberg, and R. Gerth. Abstract interpretation of reactive systems: Abstractions preserving ∀CTL*, ∃CTL* and CTL*. In Ernst-Rudiger Olderog, editor, *IFIP Conference PROCOMET'94*, pages 561–581, 1994. 383

11. S. Das, D. L. Dill, and S. Park. Experience with predicate abstraction. *Lecture Notes in Computer Science*, 1633:160–??, 1999. 377, 378
12. J. Dingel and Th. Filkorn. Model checking for infinite state systems using data abstraction, assumption-commitment style reasoning and theorem proving. In *Proc. of 7th CAV 95, Liège*. LNCS 939, Springer Verlag, 1995. 377
13. S. Graf. Characterization of a sequentially consistent memory and verification of a cache memory by abstraction. *Distributed Computing*, 1995. 377
14. S. Graf and H. Saïdi. Construction of abstract state graphs with PVS. In *Conference on Computer Aided Verification CAV'97*, LNCS 1254, Springer Verlag, 1997. 377, 378, 381
15. J.F. Groote and J. van de Pol. A bounded retransmission protocol for large data packets. Technical report, Department of Philosophy, October 1993. 379
16. Klaus Havelund and N. Shankar. Experiments in theorem proving and model checking for protocol verification. In *Formal Methods Europe FME '96*, number 1051 in Lecture Notes in Computer Science, pages 662–681, Oxford, UK, March 1996. Springer-Verlag. 379
17. L. Helmink, M.P.A. Sellink, and F.W. Vaandrager. Proof-checking a data link protocol. Technical report, Department of Philosophy, Utrech University, The Netherlands, March 1994. 379
18. Bertrand Jeannet, Nicolas Halbwachs, and Pascal Raymond. Dynamic partitioning in analyses of numerical properties. In Agostino Cortesi and Gilberto Filé, editors, *Static Analysis*, volume 1694 of *Lecture Notes in Computer Science*, pages 39–50. Springer, 1999. 379
19. R.P. Kurshan. *Computer-aided verification of coordinating processes, the automata theoretic approach*. Princeton Series in Computer Science. Princeton University Press, 1994. 377
20. David Lesens and Hassen Saïdi. Automatic verification of parameterized networks of processes by abstraction. In Faron Moller, editor, *2nd International Workshop on Verification of Infinite State Systems: Infinity '97*, volume 9 of *Electronic Notes in Theoretical Computer Science*, Bologna, Italy, July 1997. Elsevier. 379
21. C. Loiseaux, S. Graf, J. Sifakis, A. Bouajjani, and S. Bensalem. Property preserving abstractions for the verification of concurrent systems. *Formal Methods in System Design, Vol 6, Iss 1, January 1995*, 1995. 377, 383
22. Zohar Manna and Amir Pnueli. *The Temporal Verification of Reactive Systems: Safety*. Springer-Verlag, 1995. 392
23. S. Owre, N. Shankar, and J. M. Rushby. A tutorial on specification and verification using pvs. Technical report, Computer Science Laboratory, SRI International, February 1993. 379
24. H. Saïdi. Modular and incremental analysis of concurrent software systems. In *14th IEEE International Conference on Automated Software Engineering*, pages 92–101, Cocoa Beach, FL, October 1999. IEEE Computer Society Press. 378, 393
25. Hassen Saïdi and Natarajan Shankar. Abstract and model check while you prove. In *Computer-Aided Verification, CAV '99*, Trento, Italy, July 1999. 377, 382, 385, 386, 394

Abstract Domains for Sharing Analysis by Optimal Semantics

Francesca Scozzari*

Dipartimento di Informatica
Università di Pisa
Corso Italia 40, 56125 Pisa, Italy
scozzari@di.unipi.it

Abstract. We propose a new technique for transforming abstract domains for logic program analysis in the theory of abstract interpretation. The basic idea is to exploit the notion of optimal semantics in order to improve the precision of a given analysis, with respect to a fixed property of interest. We show an application of our technique to the analysis of variable sharing. We propose a new domain for detecting pairs of independent variables which is obtained by transforming the Jacobs and Langen's domain for sharing analysis. The new domain has the advantage of being strictly more powerful than the original domain in detecting pair-sharing information and, at the same time, smaller in size.

1 Introduction

This work presents a new technique for transforming abstract domains for program analysis, in the theory of abstract interpretation [7]. Abstract interpretation is a general theory for describing both approximated semantics and program analyses. On the semantics side, it allows us to compare semantics at different levels of abstraction and to order them in a suitable hierarchy, which reflects the approximation order. From the analysis point of view, abstract domains proved to be a powerful and elegant method to formally describe and compare static analyses for a variety of programming languages.

In this paper we face with the problem of improving the precision of abstract domains for static analysis of logic programs. We propose a new methodology for transforming an abstract domain in order to improve its precision in computing some fixed property of interest. The basic idea is to exploit the notion of *optimal semantics* [10,11] as a guideline for the definition of the transformation. An optimal semantics can be thought of as a semantics which is neither too concrete nor too abstract for characterizing a given property of interest. We consider as a starting point the semantics of computed answers substitutions, the so-called s-semantics [9]. As shown in [11], given any property of interest π (e.g., groundness, sharing), it always exists the most abstract semantics σ^π where the property π

---

* Part of this work was carried out while the author was at the *Laboratoire d'Informatique, École Polytechnique*, Palaiseau, France.

J. Palsberg (Ed.): SAS 2000, LNCS 1824, pp. 397–412, 2000.
© Springer-Verlag Berlin Heidelberg 2000

is observable without approximation errors. In abstract interpretation, it is often the case that the actual domain used for performing the analysis is not π, but a more complex domain, which contains π and, in addition, some other information which improves the precision of the analysis. For instance, this is the case for the basic property of groundness, where the more complex domains Def [1] and Pos [16,5,1] are used instead of the basic domain G by Jones and Søndergaard ([14]) which merely describes the property of groundness. Another example is the property of variable sharing, where the abstract domain Sh by Jacobs and Langen [12,13], and even more complex domains which keep track of linearity and freeness information, are used for sharing analyses.

Our idea is to exploit the optimal semantics of a given property π for enriching any abstract domain for the analysis of π. Let A be an abstract domain for detecting the property π, i.e., which contains π. The idea is to substitute each abstract object $a \in A$ with the object $\sigma^\pi(a)$, where σ^π is the closure corresponding to the optimal semantics for π, and to consider the most abstract domain B which contains all these objects, for all $a \in A$. The new domain that we obtain is therefore the most abstract domain which contains the set $\{\sigma^\pi(a) \mid a \in A\}$. As a remarkable point of this construction, the new domain B turns out to be, at least, as precise as A in computing the property π and, when B is different from A, it is strictly more precise than A. It is worth noting that the new domain we set up can be unrelated to the original domain A, when the common order for comparing abstract domains is used. In other words, B can be neither an abstraction nor a concretization of A. Therefore, the method we propose is not a refinement, nor a widening operator on the domain A.

As an application, we consider the pair-sharing property ([2]), whose aim is to detect which pairs of variables are definitely independent. One of the most commonly used domain for pair-sharing analysis is the domain Sh [12,13]. We fix the pair-sharing property and we apply our transformation technique to the abstract domain Sh. The result is quite surprising, since the domain we obtain is strictly more powerful than Sh in detecting pair-sharing information and, at the same time, is smaller in size. It is worth noting that the domain we obtain is incomparable to Sh, i.e., it is neither an abstraction nor a concretization of Sh. Moreover, it clarifies how groundness information helps in pair-sharing analysis.

2   Basic Notions

Abstract interpretations. In the abstract interpretation theory [7,8], abstract domains can be equivalently specified either by Galois connections, i.e., adjunctions, or by upper closure operators (uco). In the first case, the concrete domain C and the abstract domain A (both assumed to be complete lattices) are related by a pair of adjoint functions of a Galois connection (α, C, A, γ). Also, it is generally assumed that (α, C, A, γ) is a Galois insertion, i.e., α is onto or, equivalently, γ is 1-1. In the latter case, an abstract domain is specified as an uco on the concrete domain C, i.e., a monotone, idempotent and extensive operators on C. These two approaches are equivalent, modulo isomorphic representation of domain's objects. When $\langle C, \leq, \vee, \wedge, \top, \bot \rangle$ is a complete lattice, the poset of all uco's $\langle uco(C), \sqsubseteq, \sqcup, \sqcap, \lambda x.\top, \lambda x.x \rangle$ is a complete lattice as well. Hence, we will identify $uco(C)$ with the lattice of abstract interpretations of C, i.e., the complete lattice of all possible abstract domains of the concrete domain C. For an abstract domain A of C, $\alpha_A : C \mapsto A$ and $\gamma_A : A \mapsto C$ will denote, respectively, the abstraction and concretization functions. When A is specified by a Galois connection, then $\rho_A = \gamma_A \circ \alpha_A \in uco(C)$ denotes the corresponding uco. Let us recall that each $\rho \in uco(C)$ is uniquely determined by the set of its fixpoints, which is its image, i.e., $\rho(C) = \{x \in C \mid \rho(x) = x\}$, and that, for $\rho, \eta \in uco(C)$, $\rho \sqsubseteq \eta$ iff $\eta(C) \subseteq \rho(C)$. A subset $X \subseteq C$ is the set of fixpoints of an uco iff X is meet-closed, i.e., $X = \lambda(X) = \{\wedge Y \mid Y \subseteq X\}$. Hence, often, we will identify closures with their sets of fixpoints. This does not give rise to ambiguity, since one can distinguish their use as functions or sets according to the context. The ordering on $uco(C)$ corresponds to the standard order used to compare abstract domains: A_1 is *more concrete* than A_2 (or, equivalently, A_2 is *more abstract* than A_1) iff $A_1 \sqsubseteq A_2$ in $uco(C)$. The *lub* and *glb* on $uco(C)$ have therefore the following meaning as operators on domains. Suppose $\{A_i\}_{i \in I} \subseteq uco(C)$: (i) $\sqcup_{i \in I} A_i$ is the most concrete among the domains which are abstractions of all the A_i's, i.e., it is their least common abstraction; (ii) $\sqcap_{i \in I} A_i$ is the most abstract among the domains (abstracting C) which are more concrete than every A_i; this domain is also known as *reduced product* of all the A_i's.

Logic programming. Let $\mathcal{V}$ be an infinite, recursively enumerable (r.e.) set of variables. *Term* denotes the set of terms with variables in $\mathcal{V}$. A *substitution* is a finite mapping from $\mathcal{V}$ to *Term*. If s is any syntactic object and σ and θ are substitutions, then $\sigma(s)$ denotes the application of σ to s, $\sigma \circ \theta$ denotes the standard composition of σ and θ (i.e., $\sigma \circ \theta = \lambda x.\sigma(\theta(x))$), $vars(s)$ denotes the set of variables occurring in s. A term t is ground if $vars(t) = \emptyset$. The set of *idempotent* substitutions modulo renaming (i.e., $\theta \sim \sigma$ if and only if there exist β and δ such that $\theta = \beta \circ \sigma$ and $\sigma = \delta \circ \theta$) is denoted by *Sub*. *Sub* is partially ordered by instantiation, denoted by $\preceq$, i.e., $\sigma \preceq \theta$ iff $\exists \delta \in Sub. \sigma = \delta \circ \theta$. By adding to *Sub* an extra object τ as least element, one gets a complete lattice $\langle Sub^\tau, \preceq, \vee, \wedge, \epsilon, \tau \rangle$, where $\vee$ is the least general anti-instance, $\wedge$ is the standard unification and ϵ is the empty substitution (see [18,15] for more details). Our basic semantic structure is the algebra $\langle \wp(Sub), \subseteq, \otimes \rangle$, where $\langle \wp(Sub), \subseteq \rangle$ is a complete lattice, $\otimes : \wp(Sub) \times \wp(Sub) \mapsto \wp(Sub)$ is the obvious lifting of unification $\wedge$ to sets of substitutions, defined as:

$$X \otimes Y \stackrel{\text{def}}{=} \{x \wedge y \mid x \wedge y \neq \tau, x \in X, \ y \in Y\}.$$

In the following, we will slightly abuse the notation by applying the operation $\otimes$ also to substitutions. Since $\otimes$ is additive on both arguments, commutative and associative, given any $c \in \wp(Sub)$, the unary function $\lambda x.c \otimes x$ is still additive. Thus it admits a right adjoint given by $\lambda x. \bigcup \{d \in \wp(Sub) \mid c \otimes d \subseteq x\}$. In the following, we denote by $y \multimap x$ the object $\bigcup \{d \in \wp(Sub) \mid y \otimes d \subseteq x\}$.

3 Optimal Semantics

An optimal semantics can be thought of as a semantics which is neither too concrete nor too abstract for characterizing a given property of interest. We briefly recall from [11] the definition and the main results concerning optimal semantics for logic programs. Given a program P, let $T_P^s : \wp(Sub) \mapsto \wp(Sub)$ be the immediate consequences operator for computed answer substitutions [9], and let us define the semantics of a program P as the least fixpoint of T_P^s, i.e., $[\![P]\!]^s = lfp(T_P^s)$. Let $\pi \in uco(\wp(Sub))$ be the abstract domain describing the property of interest. We say that π is *decidable* when each set $a \in \pi$ is a r.e. set. In [11] it is proved that, for decidable domains, there exists the most abstract domain $\sigma^\pi \in uco(\wp(Sub))$ such that π is still observable in σ^π without introducing approximation errors, as shown in the next theorem.

Theorem 1 ([11]). *Let $\pi \in uco(\wp(Sub))$ be a decidable domain and let $\sigma^\pi : \wp(Sub) \mapsto \wp(Sub)$ be defined as follows, for any $x \in \wp(Sub)$:*

$$\sigma^\pi(x) \stackrel{def}{=} \bigcap \{\theta \multimap a \mid \theta \in Sub, a \in \pi, x \subseteq \theta \multimap a\}.$$

Then it holds $\pi(lfp(T_P^s)) = \pi(lfp(\sigma^\pi \circ T_P^s))$. Moreover, σ^π is the most abstract domain in $uco(\wp(Sub))$ which enjoys this property.

This theorem ensures us that the result of any abstract computation on the domain σ^π (i.e., $lfp(\sigma^\pi \circ T_P^s)$) is equal to the result on the concrete domain $\wp(Sub)$ (i.e., $lfp(T_P^s)$) when they are observed on the abstract domain π. Therefore, the domain σ^π can be freely used instead of the concrete domain without introducing approximation errors. Moreover, σ^π is the most abstract domain (abstracting $\wp(Sub)$) for which this property holds. Thus, σ^π can be rightfully considered as the optimal semantics for the property π. It is worth noting that being a decidable domain is a very weak notion and practically all the common domains used in practice are decidable domains. In fact, an abstract domain π is not decidable when there exists an abstract object $a \in \pi$ such that a is not r.e., i.e., one cannot decide when a substitution θ belongs to a. Therefore, the property π is not decidable even for single substitutions, and the abstraction function $\alpha_\pi : \wp(Sub) \mapsto \pi$ cannot be effectively computed. In the following, we will always assume that the property of interest is representable by a decidable domain $\pi \in uco(\wp(Sub))$ and we will denote by σ^π the optimal semantics for π. The abstraction σ^π can be equivalently defined as follows (see [11,19] for more details):

- σ^π is the most abstract domain which contains π (i.e., $\sigma^\pi \sqsubseteq \pi$) and is complete for $\otimes$, i.e., for any $a, b \in \wp(Sub)$, it holds:

$$\sigma^\pi(a \otimes b) = \sigma^\pi(\sigma^\pi(a) \otimes \sigma^\pi(b));$$

- for any $x \in \wp(Sub)$:

$$\sigma^\pi(x) = \{\theta \in Sub \mid \forall c, d \in \wp(Sub)\ x \otimes c \subseteq \pi(d) \Rightarrow \theta \otimes c \subseteq \pi(d)\}.$$

The first characterization of σ^π shows the strict connection between the immediate consequences operator T_P^s and the unification operation $\otimes$. In fact, [11] showed that an abstract domain ρ is complete for T_P^s (i.e., $\rho \circ T_P^s \circ \rho = \rho \circ T_P^s$) if and only if ρ is complete for $\otimes$ (i.e., $\rho \circ \otimes \circ \langle \rho, \rho \rangle = \rho \circ \otimes$). According to this result, one can disregard the other operations involved in the computation of the T_P^s, namely union and variable projecting, in order to prove completeness properties for the semantics of computed answer substitutions.

The latter characterization of σ^π is particularly interesting, since it precisely describes the way optimal semantics behave. For any $x \in \wp(Sub)$, it states that a substitution θ belongs to $\sigma^\pi(x)$ if and only if the following property holds:

$$\forall c, d \in \wp(Sub) \ \ x \otimes c \subseteq \pi(d) \Rightarrow \theta \otimes c \subseteq \pi(d). \tag{1}$$

According to this property, the optimal semantics enriches the set x with all and only the substitutions θ such that the unification of θ with any object c cannot be distinguished from the unification of x with c, when they are observed in π. This property also explains in which sense σ^π is optimal. In fact, for any substitution θ which is not in $\sigma^\pi(x)$, there always exist two objects $c, d \in \wp(Sub)$ such that $x \otimes c \subseteq \pi(d)$ but $\theta \otimes c \nsubseteq \pi(d)$. As a consequence, we have that $\theta \otimes c \nsubseteq \pi(x \otimes c)$ and thus Property (1) can be rephrased in a more compact way as follows:

$$\forall c \in \wp(Sub) \ \ \theta \otimes c \subseteq \pi(x \otimes c).$$

This last characterization gives us a precise upper bound to the set of substitutions which can be added still preserving the property π in the unification operation.

4 Abstract Domains by Optimal Semantics

In abstract interpretation, it is often the case that the abstract domain π, which encodes the property of interest, is not actually used for the analysis. Instead of π, some more complex domain α (which contains π) is used, in order to improve the precision of the analysis. For instance, this is the case for the domains Def [1] and Pos [16,5,1], which are commonly used instead of the basic domain G by Jones and Søndergaard ([14]), encoding the property of groundness.

Let $\pi \in uco(\wp(Sub))$ be a fixed property of interest and let us consider some domain $\alpha \in uco(\wp(Sub))$ such that $\alpha \sqsubseteq \pi$. Our idea is to consider, instead of the domain α, the abstract domain α^π obtained by abstracting each element $a \in \alpha$ by σ^π. The domain α^π is formally defined as follows:

$$\alpha^\pi \overset{def}{=} \bigwedge(\sigma^\pi(\alpha)) = \bigwedge(\{\sigma^\pi(a) \mid a \in \alpha\}).$$

By Property (1), $\sigma^\pi(a)$ is obtained by enriching a with all and only the substitutions which behave like a when the result of the unification is observed in π. Let us first show some properties of α^π.

Proposition 1. *Let* $\alpha, \pi \in uco(\wp(Sub))$ *with* $\alpha \sqsubseteq \pi$. *Then* α^π *enjoys the following properties.*

1. $\sigma^\pi \sqsubseteq \alpha^\pi \sqsubseteq \pi$
2. $\alpha^\pi \circ \alpha = \sigma^\pi \circ \alpha$
3. α^π *is complete for* $\otimes$ *w.r.t.* α, *i.e., for all* $a, b \in \alpha$, *it holds:*

$$\alpha^\pi(a \otimes b) = \alpha^\pi(\alpha^\pi(a) \otimes \alpha^\pi(b)).$$

4. $lfp(\alpha^\pi \circ T_P^s) \leq \alpha^\pi(lfp(\alpha \circ T_P^s))$

Note that, consistently with Point 3, it may well happen that α^π is complete for $\otimes$ w.r.t. α, even if α^π and α are possibly unrelated domains. In particular, it is not required for α^π to be an abstraction of α. When α is more concrete than α^π, this notion boils down to the standard notion of completeness. Point 4 is a direct consequence of Point 3 and ensures us that abstract computations on the domain α^π are more precise than abstract computations on α when the result is observed in α^π. Since $\alpha^\pi \sqsubseteq \pi$, as a consequence α^π is, at least, as precise as α when we are interested in observing the property π. Moreover, the domain α^π still enjoys Property (1) for any abstract object $a \in \alpha$, as stated in the next proposition.

Proposition 2. *Let* $\alpha, \pi \in uco(\wp(Sub))$ *with* $\alpha \sqsubseteq \pi$. *Then, for all* $x \in \wp(Sub)$, $\alpha^\pi(\alpha(x))$ *enjoys Property* (1), *i.e.,* $\forall \theta \in Sub$, *it holds:*

$$\theta \in \alpha^\pi(\alpha(x)) \iff \forall c, d \in \wp(Sub) \; \alpha(x) \otimes c \sqsubseteq \pi(d) \Rightarrow \theta \otimes c \sqsubseteq \pi(d).$$

Proposition 1 states that the new domain α^π is a concretization of the property of interest π and, more importantly, it is complete for the unification with objects of α. This means that α^π is at least as precise as α in computing the operation of unification. These two properties are obviously the fundamental requirements for any domain candidate for improving the precision of α. It is worth noting that many other domains enjoy these properties, for instance σ^π and α itself. Let us denote by $C(\alpha, \pi)$ the collection of all the abstractions of π which are complete for $\otimes$ w.r.t. α, i.e., :

$$C(\alpha, \pi) \stackrel{\text{def}}{=} \{\beta \in uco(\wp(Sub)) \mid \beta \sqsubseteq \pi, \beta \text{ complete for } \otimes \text{ w.r.t. } \alpha\}.$$

According to the above definition, for all $\beta \in C(\alpha, \pi)$ it holds:

$$\forall c, d \in \wp(Sub) \; \beta(\beta(\alpha(c)) \otimes \beta(\alpha(d))) = \beta(\alpha(c) \otimes \alpha(d))$$

which, in turn, implies the following property:

$$\forall c, d \in \wp(Sub) \; \beta(\beta(c) \otimes \beta(d)) \leq \beta(\alpha(\alpha(c) \otimes \alpha(d))).$$

The latter property precisely says that, given any two objects $c, d \in \wp(Sub)$, the result of any abstract computation on the domain β (i.e., $\beta(\beta(c) \otimes \beta(d))$) is more precise than the corresponding computation on the domain α (i.e.,

$\alpha(\alpha(c) \otimes \alpha(d)))$ when the result is observed in β. This property, combined with the assumption that $\beta \sqsubseteq \pi$, ensures us that the domain β is, at least, as precise as α in computing the operation of unification, when we are interested in observing the property π only. It is worth remarking that we do not require that $\beta(\beta(c) \otimes \beta(d)) \leq \alpha(\alpha(c) \otimes \alpha(d))$, since we are not interested in directly comparing the absolute precision of the two domains α and β.

In general, given two closures $\beta_1, \beta_2 \in C(\alpha, \pi)$, the closure $\beta_1 \sqcup \beta_2$ may not be in $C(\alpha, \pi)$ and, in particular, $\sqcup C(\alpha, \pi)$ may not be in $C(\alpha, \pi)$. For instance, it easy to see that both α and α^π belong to $C(\alpha, \pi)$, but, in general, $\alpha \sqcup \alpha^\pi$ is not in $C(\alpha, \pi)$ (see Section 6.1 for a counterexample). The idea is to restrict our attention to those domains $\beta \in C(\alpha, \pi)$ which satisfy Property (1) on the abstract objects. In other words, we require that for any $a \in \alpha$, it holds: $\theta \in \beta(a)$ if and only if Property (1) holds. This ensures us that β has been designed by adding to each abstract object $a \in \alpha$ the greatest amount of substitutions, still preserving the observable property π. The next proposition proves that α^π is indeed the most abstract element in $C(\alpha, \pi)$ which satisfies Property (1) for all abstract objects.

Proposition 3. *Let* $\alpha, \pi \in uco(\wp(Sub))$ *with* $\alpha \sqsubseteq \pi$. *Then* α^π *is the most abstract domain in* $C(\alpha, \pi)$ *which enjoys Property* (1) *for all* $a \in \alpha$.

The above result implies that, for any domain $\beta \in C(\alpha, \pi)$, β is complete for $\otimes$ w.r.t. α^π if and only if it is a concretization of α^π, as the next theorem shows.

Theorem 2. *Let* $\alpha, \pi \in uco(\wp(Sub))$ *with* $\alpha \sqsubseteq \pi$. *For any* $\beta \in C(\alpha, \pi)$, *it holds:*

$$\beta \text{ is complete for } \otimes \text{ w.r.t. } \alpha^\pi \iff \beta \sqsubseteq \alpha^\pi.$$

This theorem says that any domain which is at least as precise as α^π must be a concretization of α^π. Thus, the domain α^π cannot be further reduced without loosing precision. It is worth remarking that in the previous theorem, α^π is not compared to its proper abstractions only, but to any domain in $C(\alpha, \pi)$, i.e., to all the domains which contain π and which are complete for $\otimes$ w.r.t. α. Hence, this result is much stronger then a mere result of completeness, where the domain is compared to its abstractions/concretizations only.

5   An Application to Pair-Sharing Analysis

In this section, we show an application of our construction to the property of variable independence. In particular, we are interested in observing *pair-independence*, i.e., independence of pairs of variables. We say that two variables are independent if the terms they are bound to, have no variable in common. In other words, two variables are independent if they are bound to terms which do not share any variable. Information about pair-independence is typically used in order to exploit the so-called AND-parallelism [13,17], i.e., to allow a parallel execution of different atoms in the same goal, and for the safe elimination of the occur-check [21], in order to speed-up the unification algorithm.

Variable independence analysis is strictly related to sharing analysis. In fact, many domains for sharing analyses in the literature (e.g., Sh [12,13] and ASub [21]) actually are concerned with *possible* sharing of variables, i.e., the property of interest is to determine when variables are allowed to share. The information they encode is not that a set of variables definitely share, but, instead, that a set of variables possibly share. This duality has lead to a non-uniform (and quite confusing) terminology in the literature for the different properties of (definite) variable independence and (possible) variable sharing. With a slight abuse of terminology (and adopting the current name in the literature) we will refer to the property of (definite) independence of pairs of variables as pair-sharing, which has to be intended as *possible* pair-sharing.

Even if many different domains for sharing analysis have been proposed, the abstract domain Sh by Jacobs and Langen [12,13] is undoubtly the most popular and more frequently used for sharing analysis. The increasing amount of results concerning this domain has contributed to confirm the adequacy and efficiency of Sh. Hence, in the following, we apply our results to the domain Sh, where the property of interest is pair-sharing. We proceed as follows. First, we formally define the abstract domain PSh encoding the property of interest (which turns out to be isomorphic to the domain for pair-sharing analysis described in [2]) and the optimal semantics for PSh, denoted by σ^{PSh}.

In order to compute $Sh^{PSh} = \lambda(\sigma^{PSh}(Sh))$ we proceed modularly[1]. It is well-known that the domain Sh can be decomposed into two parts, namely Sh^+ and Def ([4]). We compute separately $\sigma^{PSh}(Sh^+)$ and $\sigma^{PSh}(Def)$, which happen to be both abstract domains. Then we show that Sh^{PSh} is the reduced product of $\sigma^{PSh}(Sh^+)$ and $\sigma^{PSh}(Def)$. Finally, we show that Sh^{PSh} is smaller in size than Shand, at the same time, it is strictly more powerful in detecting pair-sharing.

5.1   Sharing and Groundness

In this paper, we consider a finite set of variables of interest $VI \subset \mathcal{V}$, which are the relevant variables. According to this, abstract domains are restricted to have variables in VI and do not explicitly show the set of relevant variables they refer to. Let us recall the definitions of the abstract domains Sh, Sh^+ and Def, in order to fix the notation. All domains refer to the (finite) set of variables VI. For the definition of Sh we follow the notation in [2] and define an element of Sh as a collection of nonempty sets of variables. The domain Sh is defined as follows:

$$Sh \overset{\text{def}}{=} \wp(\wp(VI) \setminus \{\emptyset\}).$$

For the abstraction function $\alpha_{Sh} : \wp(Sub) \mapsto Sh$ from the concrete domain of substitutions to Sh and the corresponding closure $\rho_{Sh} \in uco(\wp(Sub))$ we refer to [12,13]. We briefly recall the definitions of the operations on Sh. The *closure*

---

[1] Note that, in general, given $A, B, \pi \in \wp(Sub)$, it does not hold that $(A \sqcap B)^{\pi} = A^{\pi} \sqcap B^{\pi}$.

under union function $\cdot^* : \mathsf{Sh} \mapsto \mathsf{Sh}$ is defined as follows, for any $A \in \mathsf{Sh}$:

$$A^* \stackrel{\text{def}}{=} \{T \subseteq VI \mid \exists n \geq 1, \exists T_1, \ldots, T_n \in A, T = \bigcup_{1 \leq i \leq n} T_i\}.$$

The *extraction of the relevant components* $rel : \wp(VI) \times \mathsf{Sh} \mapsto \mathsf{Sh}$, for $V \subseteq VI$ and $A \in \mathsf{Sh}$ is given by:

$$rel(V, A) \stackrel{\text{def}}{=} \{T \in A \mid T \cap V \neq \emptyset\}.$$

For $A, B \in \mathsf{Sh}$, the *binary union* $bin : \mathsf{Sh} \times \mathsf{Sh} \mapsto \mathsf{Sh}$ is defined as:

$$bin(A, B) \stackrel{\text{def}}{=} \{T_1 \cup T_2 \mid T_1 \in A, T_2 \in B\}.$$

Finally, the *unification* operation $\mathbf{amgu} : \mathsf{Sh} \times Sub \mapsto \mathsf{Sh}$ is inductively given, for $A \in \mathsf{Sh}$ and $\{x \mapsto t\}, \theta \in Sub$, by:

$$\mathbf{amgu}(A, \{x \mapsto t\}) \stackrel{\text{def}}{=} (A \setminus rel(vars(t) \cup \{x\}))$$
$$\cup \; bin(rel(\{x\}, B)^*, rel(vars(t), B)^*)$$

$$\mathbf{amgu}(A, \{x \mapsto t\} \circ \theta) \stackrel{\text{def}}{=} \mathbf{amgu}(\mathbf{amgu}(A, \{x \mapsto t\}), \theta).$$

It is well-known that the domain Sh can be decomposed into two parts, namely Sh^+ and Def ([4]). The abstract domain Sh^+ is defined as the subset of Sh whose elements contain all the singletons.

$$\mathsf{Sh}^+ \stackrel{\text{def}}{=} \{A \in \mathsf{Sh} \mid \forall x \in VI \; \{x\} \in A\}.$$

The corresponding closure operator $\alpha_{\mathsf{Sh}^+} \in uco(\mathsf{Sh})$ is given by $\alpha_{\mathsf{Sh}^+}(A) \stackrel{\text{def}}{=} A \cup \{\{x\} \mid x \in VI\}$. Moreover, we denote by $\rho_{\mathsf{Sh}^+} \in uco(\wp(Sub))$ the closure on the concrete domain $\wp(Sub)$ corresponding to Sh^+.

The domain PSD has been recently proposed in [2] for capturing pair-sharing dependency. As we will see in the following, PSD is strictly related to our construction. We briefly recall the definition of PSD (see [2,22] for details). PSD is defined by a closure operator on the domain Sh in the following way. For any $T \subseteq VI$, let $pairs(T) = \{P \in \wp(T) \mid |P| = 2\}$. We say that T is *redundant* for an abstract object $A \in \mathsf{Sh}$ if and only if $|T| > 2$ and $pairs(T) = \cup\{pairs(S) \mid S \in A, S \subset T\}$. In other words, T is redundant for A if all its pairs can be recovered from the sets $S \in A$ which are contained in T. The closure operator $\alpha_{\mathsf{PSD}} \in uco(\mathsf{Sh})$ is defined as follows:

$$\alpha_{\mathsf{PSD}}(A) \stackrel{\text{def}}{=} A \cup \{T \subseteq VI \mid T \text{ is redundant for } A\}.$$

We denote by $\mathsf{G} \stackrel{\text{def}}{=} \wp(VI)$ the basic domain for groundness analysis by Jones and Søndergaard ([14]), where each $V \subseteq VI$ denotes the set of substitutions which ground every variable in V. We denote by $\rho_{\mathsf{G}} : \wp(Sub) \mapsto \mathsf{G}$ the abstraction function from the concrete domain of substitutions to G. The domains Def [1] and Pos [16,6,1] can be characterized, starting from G, in the following way ([20]):

$$\mathsf{Def} \stackrel{\text{def}}{=} \bigwedge(\{a \multimap b \mid a, b \in \gamma(\mathsf{G})\})$$

$$\text{Pos} \stackrel{\text{def}}{=} \bigwedge (\{a \multimap b \mid a \in \text{Def}, b \in \gamma(\text{G})\}).$$

Let us denote, respectively, by $\rho_{\text{Def}}, \rho_{\text{Pos}} \in uco(\wp(Sub))$ the closure operators corresponding to the domains Def and Pos. It is well-known that Def induces a Galois insertion on Sh [3]. We denote by $\rho_{\text{ShDef}} \in uco(\text{Sh})$ the closure operator on Sh corresponding to Def, thus $\rho_{\text{ShDef}}(\text{Sh})$ is isomorphic to Def (see [3]). Intuitively, an element $\cap X \multimap x \in \text{Def}$ corresponds to the element in Sh $\{T \subseteq VI \mid x \in T \Rightarrow X \cap T \neq \emptyset\}$. In the following, we shall abuse the notation and call Def its isomorphic image $\rho_{\text{ShDef}}(\text{Sh})$. This does not give rise to ambiguity, since one can distinguish the domains according to the context.

The next result summarizes the behavior of PSD on the two components of Sh, i.e., Sh^+ and Def.

Proposition 4.

1. $\alpha_{\text{PSD}}(\text{Def}) = \text{Def}$
2. $\alpha_{\text{PSD}} \circ \alpha_{\text{Sh}^+} = \alpha_{\text{Sh}^+} \circ \alpha_{\text{PSD}}$
3. $\text{PSD} = \alpha_{\text{PSD}}(\text{Sh}^+) \sqcap \text{Def}.$

Note that, by Point 2 above, $\alpha_{\text{PSD}}(\text{Sh}^+)$ turns out to be an abstract domain. Therefore, the reduced product in Point 3 is well-defined.

5.2   Pair-Sharing

We say that two variables x and y are *independent* for the substitution θ when $vars(\theta(x)) \cap vars(\theta(y)) = \emptyset$. Let us denote by I_{xy} the set of substitutions for which x and y are independent:

$$I_{xy} \stackrel{\text{def}}{=} \{\theta \in Sub \mid vars(\theta(x)) \cap vars(\theta(y)) = \emptyset\}.$$

Our basic domain PSh for pair-sharing is given by the most abstract domain which contains all the objects I_{xy}, for any $x, y \in VI$, with $x \neq y$. In the following, we shall assume that $|VI| \geq 2$.

$$\text{PSh} \stackrel{\text{def}}{=} \bigwedge (\{I_{xy} \mid x, y \in VI, x \neq y\}).$$

It is immediate to see that it holds $I_{xy} = \gamma_{\text{Sh}}(\{T \subseteq VI \mid \{x, y\} \nsubseteq T\})$. Therefore, PSh induces a Galois insertion $(\alpha_{\text{PSh}}, \text{Sh}, \text{PSh}, \gamma_{\text{PSh}})$ defined as follows, for any $A \in \text{Sh}$ and $B \in \text{PSh}$:

$$\alpha_{\text{PSh}}(A) \stackrel{\text{def}}{=} \cap \{I_{xy} \mid x, y \in VI, x \neq y, \forall T \in A \: \{x, y\} \nsubseteq T\}$$

$$\gamma_{\text{PSh}}(B) \stackrel{\text{def}}{=} \{T \subseteq VI \mid x, y \in VI, x \neq y, T \neq \emptyset, B \subseteq I_{xy} \Rightarrow \{x, y\} \nsubseteq T\}.$$

6 Optimal Semantics for PSh

Now that we have formally defined the basic domain encoding the pair-sharing property, we are ready to compute $\mathsf{Sh}^{\mathsf{PSh}} = \curlywedge(\sigma^{\mathsf{PSh}}(\mathsf{Sh}))$. We proceed modularly on the two parts of Sh, namely Sh^+ and Def. We start by computing $\sigma^{\mathsf{PSh}}(\mathsf{Sh}^+)$. The next theorem states that, for any $c \in \wp(Sub)$, the object $\sigma^{\mathsf{PSh}}(\rho_{\mathsf{Sh}+}(c))$ coincides with the abstraction α_{PSD} on $\rho_{\mathsf{Sh}+}(c)$.

Theorem 3.

$$\sigma^{\mathsf{PSh}} \circ \rho_{\mathsf{Sh}+} = \rho_{\mathsf{PSD}} \circ \rho_{\mathsf{Sh}+}.$$

In order to better understand the behavior of the optimal semantics on the elements of Def, let us first characterize the bottom element $\bot_{\sigma^{\mathsf{PSh}}}$ of σ^{PSh}, given by $\sigma^{\mathsf{PSh}}(\emptyset)$. Since the domain $\mathsf{Sh}^{\mathsf{PSh}}$ is an abstraction of σ^{PSh}, it is clear that any object $c \in \mathsf{Sh}^{\mathsf{PSh}}$ must approximate the bottom of σ^{PSh}.

Proposition 5. $\bot_{\sigma^{\mathsf{PSh}}} = \bigcap \{\gamma_{\mathsf{G}}(x) \cup \gamma_{\mathsf{G}}(y) \mid x, y \in VI, x \neq y\}.$

The previous proposition shows that the least element of σ^{PSh} is given by the intersection of all the possible disjunctions $\gamma_{\mathsf{G}}(x) \cup \gamma_{\mathsf{G}}(y)$, where $\gamma_{\mathsf{G}}(x)$ is the set of substitutions which ground x. This result is quite surprising, since it implies that the optimal semantics for detecting pair-sharing does not need to take into account the information given by the groundness of a single variable. By exploiting the distributive property of the concrete domain, the object $\bot_{\sigma^{\mathsf{PSh}}}$ can be equivalently characterized as follows:

$$\bot_{\sigma^{\mathsf{PSh}}} = \bigcup_{x \in VI} \bigcap_{v \in VI \setminus \{x\}} \gamma_{\mathsf{G}}(v).$$

Note that, for any $x \in VI$, the object $\bigcap_{v \in VI \setminus \{x\}} \gamma_{\mathsf{G}}(v)$ is the set of substitutions which ground every variable but x. It is clear that this information suffices for proving that x is independent form any other variable. Therefore, the disjunction of all these objects is the least amount of information which we need in order to observe pair-independence. In other words, from the pair-sharing point of view, it is equivalent to know either that a variable x is ground or that every variable but x is ground. In both cases, x does not share with any other variable. Finally, note that $\bot_{\sigma^{\mathsf{PSh}}}$ does not belong to Sh, and therefore nor to Def (but it is easily seen that $\bot_{\sigma^{\mathsf{PSh}}} \in \mathsf{Pos}$). Hence, we expect that the domain $\mathsf{Sh}^{\mathsf{PSh}}$ will be incomparable to Sh, as we will see in the following.

Since any object in $\mathsf{Sh}^{\mathsf{PSh}}$ approximates $\bot_{\sigma^{\mathsf{PSh}}}$, it follows that for any object $a \in \mathsf{Def}$, $\sigma^{\mathsf{PSh}}(a)$ must approximate $a \cup \bot_{\sigma^{\mathsf{PSh}}}$. The next result proves that $\sigma^{\mathsf{PSh}}(\rho_{\mathsf{Def}}(a))$ coincides with the abstraction in Pos of the object $a \cup \bot_{\sigma^{\mathsf{PSh}}}$.

Theorem 4. Let $d \in \wp(Sub)$.

$$\sigma^{\mathsf{PSh}}(\rho_{\mathsf{Def}}(d)) = \rho_{\mathsf{Pos}}(\rho_{\mathsf{Def}}(d) \cup \bot_{\sigma^{\mathsf{PSh}}}).$$

The next theorem proves that the result of the application of σ^{PSh} to an element of Sh can be computed modularly on the two components of Sh, i.e., Sh^+ and Def.

Theorem 5. *Let* $A \in \gamma(\mathsf{Sh})$. $\sigma^{\mathsf{PSh}}(A) = \rho_{\mathsf{PSD}}(\rho_{\mathsf{Sh}^+}(A)) \cap \rho_{\mathsf{Pos}}(\rho_{\mathsf{Def}}(A) \cup \bot_{\sigma^{\mathsf{PSh}}})$.

As a consequence, the domain $\mathsf{Sh}^{\mathsf{PSh}}$ can be specified as the reduced product of the two parts.

Corollary 1. $\mathsf{Sh}^{\mathsf{PSh}} = \rho_{\mathsf{PSD}}(\mathsf{Sh}^+) \sqcap \{\rho_{\mathsf{Pos}}(A \cup \bot_{\sigma^{\mathsf{PSh}}}) \mid A \in \mathsf{Def}\}$.

6.1   Comparing Sh to $\mathsf{Sh}^{\mathsf{PSh}}$

Since pair-sharing is clearly a decidable domain, from Section 3 we immediately inherits the following results for $\mathsf{Sh}^{\mathsf{PSh}}$.

Corollary 2.

- $\mathsf{Sh}^{\mathsf{PSh}} \sqsubseteq \mathsf{PSh}$
- $\mathsf{Sh}^{\mathsf{PSh}}$ *is complete for* $\otimes$ *w.r.t.* Sh, *i.e., for all* $A, B \in \gamma_{\mathsf{Sh}}(\mathsf{Sh})$, *it holds:*

$$\rho_{\mathsf{Sh}^{\mathsf{PSh}}}(A \otimes B) = \rho_{\mathsf{Sh}^{\mathsf{PSh}}}(\rho_{\mathsf{Sh}^{\mathsf{PSh}}}(A) \otimes \rho_{\mathsf{Sh}^{\mathsf{PSh}}}(B))$$

- *For any* $\beta \in C(\mathsf{Sh}, \mathsf{PSh})$, *it holds:*

$$\beta \text{ is complete for } \otimes \text{ w.r.t. } \mathsf{Sh}^{\mathsf{PSh}} \iff \beta \sqsubseteq \mathsf{Sh}^{\mathsf{PSh}}.$$

This corollary summarizes the properties of the domain $\mathsf{Sh}^{\mathsf{PSh}}$ which are straightforwardly inherited by construction. In particular, $\mathsf{Sh}^{\mathsf{PSh}}$ turns out to be a concretization of PSh and, at least, as precise as Sh in computing the abstract unification. Moreover, the last property ensures us that, among all domains which are as precise as Sh, it does not exist any domain β which is precise as $\mathsf{Sh}^{\mathsf{PSh}}$ and that does not contain $\mathsf{Sh}^{\mathsf{PSh}}$. The importance of this result relies on the fact that $\mathsf{Sh}^{\mathsf{PSh}}$ is compared to all possible domains candidate to improving Sh, including those which are incomparable to Sh. A similar result as been shown in [2]. The authors proved that $\mathsf{PSD} \in C(\mathsf{Sh}, \mathsf{PSh})$ and that it does not exist any proper abstraction of PSD which is as precise as PSD. Note that in [2] the domain PSD is compared to its proper abstractions only, which is a rather restrictive hypothesis and, in general, it does not suffice in order to ensure the optimality of a given domain.

The next example shows that $\mathsf{Sh}^{\mathsf{PSh}}$ is strictly more precise than Sh under the hypothesis that $|VI| \geq 2$.

Example 1. Let $VI = \{x_1, ..., x_n\}$, with $n \geq 2$. Let $\theta, \delta \in Sub$ defined as follows:

$$\theta = \{x_1 \leftarrow a\} \qquad \delta = \{x_2 \leftarrow a, \dots, x_n \leftarrow a\}$$

where a is a constant of the language. Let us unify the concrete object $c = \{\theta, \delta\}$ with the substitution $\{x_1 \leftarrow x_2\}$. On the concrete domain of substitutions we obtain:

$$c \otimes \{x_1 \leftarrow x_2\} = \{\theta \otimes \{x_1 \leftarrow x_2\}, \delta \otimes \{x_1 \leftarrow x_2\}\}$$
$$= \{\{x_1 \leftarrow a, x_2 \leftarrow a\}, \{x_1 \leftarrow a, \dots, x_n \leftarrow a\}\} \subseteq I_{x_1, x_2}.$$

Instead, when computing on Sh, we obtain:

$$\mathbf{amgu}(\alpha_{\mathsf{Sh}}(c), \{x_1 \leftarrow x_2\}) = \mathbf{amgu}(\{\{x_i\} \mid x_i \in VI\}, \{x_1 \leftarrow x_2\})$$
$$= \{\{x_1, x_2\}, \{x_3\}, \dots, \{x_n\}\}.$$

Therefore, $\gamma_{\mathsf{Sh}}(\mathbf{amgu}(\alpha_{\mathsf{Sh}}(c), \{x_1 \leftarrow x_2\})) \nsubseteq I_{x_1, x_2}$.

Note that, by definition of $\mathsf{Sh}^{\mathsf{PSh}}$, it holds $\rho_{\mathsf{Sh}^{\mathsf{PSh}}}(\theta) = \rho_{\mathsf{Pos}}(\rho_{\mathsf{Def}}(\theta) \cup \perp_{\sigma^{\mathsf{PSh}}}) = \rho_{\mathsf{Pos}}(x_1 \cup \perp_{\sigma^{\mathsf{PSh}}}) = x_1 \cup (x_2 \cap \dots \cap x_n)$ which stands for all the substitutions for which either x_1 is ground or all the variables but x_1 are ground. Hence $\delta \in \rho_{\mathsf{Sh}^{\mathsf{PSh}}}(\{\theta\})$ and therefore $\rho_{\mathsf{Sh}^{\mathsf{PSh}}}(\{\theta, \delta\}) = \rho_{\mathsf{Sh}^{\mathsf{PSh}}}(\{\theta\}) = x_1 \cup (x_2 \cap \dots \cap x_n)$. As a consequence, we have the following computation:

$$\rho_{\mathsf{Sh}^{\mathsf{PSh}}}(\rho_{\mathsf{Sh}^{\mathsf{PSh}}}(c) \otimes \{x_1 \leftarrow x_2\})$$
$$= \rho_{\mathsf{Sh}^{\mathsf{PSh}}}(x_1 \cup (x_2 \cap \dots \cap x_n) \otimes \{x_1 \leftarrow x_2\})$$
$$= \rho_{\mathsf{Sh}^{\mathsf{PSh}}}((x_1 \otimes \{x_1 \leftarrow x_2\}) \cup (x_2 \cap \dots \cap x_n) \otimes \{x_1 \leftarrow x_2\}))$$
$$= \rho_{\mathsf{Sh}^{\mathsf{PSh}}}((x_1 \cap x_2) \cup (x_1 \cap \dots \cap x_n))$$
$$= \rho_{\mathsf{Sh}^{\mathsf{PSh}}}(x_1 \cap x_2) \subseteq I_{x_1, x_2}.$$

Therefore, the domain $\mathsf{Sh}^{\mathsf{PSh}}$ is precise enough to detect that x_1 and x_2 are independent, while Sh is not able to detect it.   □

It is worth noting that, being PSD an abstraction of Sh, it is as precise as Sh, and therefore, according to the above example, PSD is strictly less precise than $\mathsf{Sh}^{\mathsf{PSh}}$. Surprisingly, the increasing precision of $\mathsf{Sh}^{\mathsf{PSh}}$ w.r.t. Sh is not due to an enlargement of the domain. On the contrary, if we compare the size of $\mathsf{Sh}^{\mathsf{PSh}}$ to the sizes of Sh and PSD, we find out that the cardinality of $\mathsf{Sh}^{\mathsf{PSh}}$ is strictly smaller than the cardinality of PSD, and therefore of Sh.

Proposition 6. $|\mathsf{Sh}^{\mathsf{PSh}}| < |\mathsf{PSD}|$

As an example of two abstract objects in PSD which are identified by $\mathsf{Sh}^{\mathsf{PSh}}$, consider a variable $x \in VI$ and the objects $A = \emptyset$ and $B = \{\{x\}\}$ of PSD. Note that A is the bottom of Sh and B denotes the set of substitutions which ground all variables in VI but x. From the characterization of $\perp_{\sigma^{\mathsf{PSh}}}$ given in Proposition 5, it is immediate to see that $\gamma_{\mathsf{Sh}}(A) \subseteq \gamma_{\mathsf{Sh}}(B) \subseteq \perp_{\sigma^{\mathsf{PSh}}}$, and thus $\sigma^{\mathsf{PSh}}(A) = \sigma^{\mathsf{PSh}}(B) = \perp_{\sigma^{\mathsf{PSh}}}$.

For $VI = \{x, y\}$, the domains Sh, PSD and $\mathsf{Sh}^{\mathsf{PSh}}$ are depicted in Figure 1, where $x \cup y$ denotes the object $\gamma_G(x) \cup \gamma_G(y)$ (note that, in this particular case, the domains Sh and PSD do coincide). As a further example of objects which are identified by $\mathsf{Sh}^{\mathsf{PSh}}$, from Figure 1 it is easy to see that the objects $\emptyset, \{\{y\}\}, \{\{x, y\}\}, \{\{x\}\} \in \mathsf{Sh}$ all collapse in the same object $x \cup y \in \mathsf{Sh}^{\mathsf{PSh}}$ and $\{\{y\}, \{x, y\}\}, \{\{x\}, \{x, y\}\}$ collapse in $\top$.

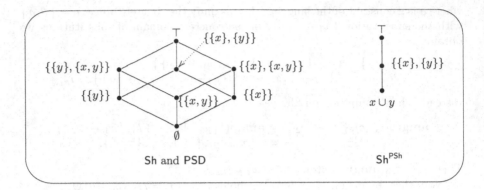

Fig. 1. Sh, PSD and Sh^{PSh}

7 Groundness Analysis

In this section we apply our construction to the property of groundness. We consider as basic domain of groundness the domain G by Jones and Søndergaard ([14]). The next theorem shows that both domains Def and Pos are not further transformed by our construction.

Theorem 6.

- Def^G = Def
- Pos^G = Pos

This result is a consequence of the fact that Def and Pos are both abstractions of the optimal semantics for G (see [20]).

8 Conclusion

We have proposed a new technique for transforming abstract domains for logic program analysis. The basic idea is to exploit the optimal semantics of a given property in order to set up an enriched abstract domain, which improves the precision of the analysis. The main point of this construction is that the new domain is, at least, as precise as the original one. It is important to remark that the transformation we propose is not a refinement operator. In fact, given a domain α, the resulting domain α^π can be incomparable to the original one (e.g., this is the case for the domains Sh and Sh^{PSh}).

As an application, we have fixed the property of pair-sharing and we have instantiated our construction to the well-known domain Sh. The new domain Sh^{PSh} obtained by transforming Sh, turns out to be more precise than Sh and, at the same time, smaller in size. A refining of the domain Sh for observing pair-sharing was first presented in [2]. The authors propose the domain PSD, proving that it is as precise as Sh and that no proper abstraction of PSD is as precise as PSD. The weak point of the construction in [2] is that the domain PSD is compared to its proper abstractions only. On the contrary, by using our optimal semantic-based transformation, we can set up abstract domains which are incomparable to the original ones. Up to our knowledge, this is the first method which allows us to construct domains which are strictly more precise and, at the same time, smaller in size than the original ones.

References

1. T. Armstrong, K. Marriott, P. Schachte, and H. Søndergaard. Two classes of Boolean functions for dependency analysis. *Science of Computer Programming*, 31(1):3–45, 1998. 398, 401, 405

2. R. Bagnara, P.M. Hill, and E. Zaffanella. Set-sharing is redundant for pair-sharing. *Theoretical Computer Science*, 2000. To appear. 398, 404, 405, 408, 410, 411

3. A. Cortesi, G. Filé, , and W. Winsborough. The quotient of an abstract interpretation. *Theor. Comput. Sci.*, 202(1-2):163–192, 1998. 406

4. A. Cortesi, G. Filé, R. Giacobazzi, C. Palamidessi, and F. Ranzato. Complementation in abstract interpretation. *ACM Trans. Program. Lang. Syst.*, 19(1):7–47, 1997. 404, 405

5. A. Cortesi, G. Filè, and W. Winsborough. *Prop* revisited: Propositional formula as abstract domain for groundness analysis. In *Proc. Sixth IEEE Symp. on Logic In Computer Science*, pages 322–327, Los Alamitos, Calif., 1991. IEEE Computer Society Press. 398, 401

6. A. Cortesi, G. Filé, and W. Winsborough. Optimal groundness analysis using propositional logic. *J. Logic Program.*, 27(2):137–167, 1996. 405

7. P. Cousot and R. Cousot. Abstract interpretation: A unified lattice model for static analysis of programs by construction or approximation of fixpoints. In *Conference Record of the 4th ACM Symposium on Principles of Programming Languages (POPL '77)*, pages 238–252, New York, 1977. ACM Press. 397, 398

8. P. Cousot and R. Cousot. Systematic design of program analysis frameworks. In *Conference Record of the 6th ACM Symposium on Principles of Programming Languages (POPL '79)*, pages 269–282, New York, 1979. ACM Press. 398

9. M. Falaschi, G. Levi, M. Martelli, and C. Palamidessi. Declarative modeling of the operational behavior of logic languages. *Theoretical Computer Science*, 69(3):289–318, 1989. 397, 400

10. R. Giacobazzi. "Optimal" collecting semantics for analysis in a hierarchy of logic program semantics. In C. Puech and R. Reischuk, editors, *Proc. of the 13th Int'l Symposium on Theoretical Aspects of Computer Science (STACS '96)*, volume 1046 of *Lecture Notes in Computer Science*, pages 503–514, Berlin, 1996. Springer-Verlag. 397

11. R. Giacobazzi, F. Ranzato, and F. Scozzari. Building complete abstract interpretations in a linear logic-based setting. In G. Levi, editor, *Static Analysis, Proceedings of the Fifth International Static Analysis Symposium SAS 98*, volume 1503 of *Lecture Notes in Computer Science*, pages 215–229, Berlin, 1998. Springer-Verlag. 397, 400, 401

12. D. Jacobs and A. Langen. Accurate and efficient approximation of variable aliasing in logic programs. In E.L. Lusk and R.A. Overbeek, editors, *Proc. of the 1989 North American Conference on Logic Programming (NACLP '89)*, Workshops in Computing, pages 154–165, Cambridge, Mass., 1989. The MIT Press. 398, 404

13. D. Jacobs and A. Langen. Static analysis of logic programs for independent AND-parallelism. *J. Logic Program.*, 13(2-3):154–165, 1992. 398, 403, 404

14. N. D. Jones and H. Søndergaard. A semantics-based framework for the abstract interpretation of Prolog. In S. Abramsky and C. Hankin, editors, *Abstract Interpretation of Declarative Languages*, pages 123–142. Ellis Horwood Ltd, Chichester, UK, 1987. 398, 401, 405, 410

15. J.-L. Lassez, M. J. Maher, and K. Marriott. Unification revisited. In J. Minker, editor, *Foundations of Deductive Databases and Logic Programming*, pages 587–625. Morgan Kaufmann, Los Altos, 1988. 399

16. K. Marriott and H. Søndergaard. Abstract interpretation of logic programs: the denotational approach. In A. Bossi, editor, *Proc. GULP '90*, pages 399–425, Padova, 1990. 398, 401, 405

17. K. Muthukumar and M. Hermenegildo. Compile-time derivation of variable dependency using abstract interpretation. *Journal of Logic Programming*, 13(2-3):315–347, 1992. 403

18. C. Palamidessi. Algebraic properties of idempotent substitutions. In M. S. Paterson, editor, *Proc. of the 17th International Colloquium on Automata, Languages and Programming*, volume 443 of *Lecture Notes in Computer Science*, pages 386–399, Berlin, 1990. Springer-Verlag. 399

19. F. Scozzari. *Domain theory in abstract interpretation: equations, completeness and logic.* PhD thesis, Dipartimento di Matematica, Univ. di Siena, 1999. Available at http://www.di.unipi.it/~scozzari/. 400

20. F. Scozzari. Logical optimality of groundness analysis. *Theoretical Computer Science*, 2000. To appear. 405, 410

21. H. Søndergaard. An application of abstract interpretation of logic programs: occur check reduction. In *Proc. ESOP '86*, volume 213 of *Lecture Notes in Computer Science*, pages 327–338, Berlin, 1986. Springer-Verlag. 403, 404

22. E. Zaffanella, P.M. Hill, and R. Bagnara. Decomposing non-redundant sharing by complementation. In A. Cortesi and G. Filé, editors, *Proceedings of the 6th International Symposium on Static Analysis (SAS'99)*, volume 1694 of *Lecture Notes in Computer Science*, pages 69–84, Berlin, 1999. Springer-Verlag. 405

Concurrency Analysis for Java

Cristian Ungureanu and Suresh Jagannathan

NEC Research Institute
4 Independence Way, Princeton NJ 08540, USA
{cristian,suresh}@research.nj.nec.com

Abstract. Concurrency is an integral feature of Java. While there has been recent research [CGS+99,BH99,WR99,Bla99] on devising analyses to eliminate the overhead imposed by synchronization, these analyses do not explicitly track multiple threads of control, nor do they appear particularly well-suited to facilitate other concurrency-related optimizations that may be applicable in a parallel or distributed environment.

In this paper, we develop a novel program analysis for Java, which explicitly incorporates an abstract (semantic) notion of threads. Our analysis framework is distinguished from related efforts in three important respects:

1. It employs a whole-program flow analysis adapted from a simple sequential analysis framework that formally defines a notion of an *abstract* thread of control. Our initial approximation defines for each thread the set of objects potentially locked or accessed by that thread.

2. The approximation imposes no restriction on the lifetime of objects involved in a synchronization event. Thus, objects may freely escape from the context in which they are created without necessarily being regarded as shared by multiple threads.

3. To provide added precision, the analysis is subsequently refined to use a per program-point abstract heap. The use of such a heap allows thread-specific flow-sensitive optimizations to be selectively applied in different program contexts, but requires a more sophisticated notion of reachability. One immediate consequence of this framework is its ability to support strong-updates [CWZ90] of global shared data.

Our analysis has been implemented as part of a native-code optimizing compiler for Java currently under development. Benchmark results indicate the analyses have relatively small computation cost, but can lead to significant improvements in the quality of generated code.

1 Introduction

An important reason for Java's growing popularity is its integral support for concurrency. Java's simple thread semantics coupled with various extensions for distributed and parallel computing [Jav98,Jav99] are likely to make it increasingly attractive as a vehicle for expressing parallel and distributed applications.

In this paper, we define a novel flow analysis framework that deals explicitly with Java's concurrency features. Our starting point is a monovariant analysis for

J. Palsberg (Ed.): SAS 2000, LNCS 1824, pp. 413–432, 2000.
© Springer-Verlag Berlin Heidelberg 2000

Java's sequential core extended with support for threads. The analysis defines an approximate notion of an exact thread, and uses this approximation to associate with each object o, the set of threads that lock or access o during execution of the program. The analysis also imposes constraints to allow it to identify potentially multiple (active) exact instances of the same abstract thread.

To improve precision, we subsequently develop a flow-sensitive refinement of this analysis which introduces a per program-point abstract heap. For many concurrent programs, an object that is not initially shared by multiple threads, may *eventually* become shared. By using a per program-point heap, the analysis can effectively capture this intuition; the structure of the heap at a given program point reveals the sharing properties of an object with respect to the threads which reference it at that point. By incorporating a notion of data reachability at method call and return points, unreachable paths can be filtered, further improving the precision. One immediate consequence of this analysis is its ability to support strong-update [CWZ90] of globally shared data.

We envision a number of optimizations facilitated by our analysis framework. Synchronization elimination is one obvious candidate. Researchers have recently focussed on eliminating synchronization overhead in Java programs because of its negative impact on sequential programs [BKMS98]. Because Java's thread semantics implicitly associates a lock with every object, many instances whose state is not actually accessed simultaneously by multiple threads will nonetheless incur synchronization penalties. Some implementations, including ours, reserve space in each object for a lock. By knowing which objects will never be involved in a synchronization event, this space overhead can be eliminated. Moreover, synchronization operations on objects that cannot be locked by other threads can be eliminated. Instances of the same type but allocated at different program points, and calls to the same synchronized method made at different call points, may have different synchronization requirements. The flow analysis framework proposed here allows optimizations to *selectively* eliminate both kinds of synchronization overhead.

For distributed programs, our analysis can also help improve locality. For example, an object known to be local to a given thread can be allocated on the same processor as that thread. An object shared among multiple threads can be allocated on a heap accessible to just these threads. By explicitly tracking the relation between objects and the threads which reference them, locality-specific optimizations that improve memory layout are more easily expressed.

We have implemented the analysis as part of an optimizing native-code Java compiler under development. Experimental results for both sequential and multi-threaded Java programs are encouraging.

The remainder of the paper is organized as follows. Sections 2 and 3 introduce a core language and its semantics. Section 4 presents the control-flow analysis for this language. Section 5 extends this analysis with a notion of heap reachability, leading to an analysis that yields a collection of heaps, indexed by program points. Experimental results are described in Section 6, and related work is discussed in Section 7.

2 Syntax

We describe our analysis using a small kernel typed intermediate language (*IL*) shown in Figure 1. A program in this language consists of a collection of type, class, and static definitions. The expression $\mu f.fn$ defines a local recursive function; $x.i$ selects field i from instance x; $x \Leftarrow m$ extracts m from x and binds *self* in m to x; $x \Leftarrow c.m$ extracts method m from class c and binds *self* to x; $r \cdot \underline{i}$ and $r \cdot \underline{m}$ extract static fields and methods respectively; $\mathtt{spawn}\,(c,m)$ allocates a new thread object and creates a new thread of control to run method m defined in class c; $\mathtt{synch}\,(x)$ blocks execution if x is already locked by a different thread; $y \rightarrow [\iota_i \Rightarrow exp_i]^*\,\mathtt{else}\,exp_n$ defines a case statement that dispatches on y; $\mathtt{store}$ and $\mathtt{fetch}$ have the obvious meaning. To make the presentation tractable, we have omitted many important features found in Java that must be expressed within a realistic intermediate language; exceptions, mutable local variables, type-casting, and arrays are some notable examples. Adapting these features into the analysis is straightforward.

3 *IL* Exact Semantics

We present an exact semantics for our IL as a small-step operational semantics. The semantic domain of values is given in Figure 2. Methods evaluate to closures, which are pairs consisting of expressions and environments; local recursive functions are defined in the obvious way [MTHM97]. A class value is a record, containing the definition of method bodies; the static fields and static methods of a class are collected in a separate record. The elaboration of declarations produces an initial environment, $\rho_\perp$, containing bindings for these records. Every instance is represented as a triple consisting of the instance's class, the variable to which the instance is bound, and an integer used to distinguish multiple incarnations of the instance from the same program point. A location is either

---

$$
\begin{array}{lll}
P ::= T^*\ C^*\ S^*\ exp & & \text{program}\\
T ::= \mathtt{type}\ ot\ \big[\ <:\ ot_j\ \big]\ \mathtt{fields}\ \{(i:\ t)^*\}\ \mathtt{methods}\ \{(m:mt)^*\} & & \text{types}\\
C ::= \mathtt{class}\ c\ \mathtt{implements}\ ot\ \big[\mathtt{inherits}\ \{c'\}\big]\ \mathtt{with}\ \{(m=\lambda self.fn)^*\} & & \text{classes}\\
S ::= \mathtt{record}\ r\ \{(\underline{i}:\ t)^*\}\ \{(\underline{m}:t=fn)^*\} & & \text{statics}
\end{array}
$$

$$
\begin{array}{lll}
fn & ::= & \lambda x.exp \hspace{4cm} \text{functions}\\
exp & ::= & x\ \mid\ \mathtt{let}\ x = ntExp\ \mathtt{in}\ exp\ \mathtt{end} \hspace{1cm} \text{expressions}\\
ntExp & ::= & \iota\ \mid\ \mu f.fn\ \mid\ x.i\ \mid\ x \Leftarrow m\ \mid\ x \Leftarrow c.m\ \mid\ r \cdot \underline{i}\ \mid\ r \cdot \underline{m}\ \mid\\
& & x(x^*)\ \mid\ \mathtt{new}\ c\ \mid\ \mathtt{spawn}\,(c,m)\ \mid\ \mathtt{synch}\,(x)\ \mid\\
& & y \rightarrow [\iota_i \Rightarrow exp_i]^*\,\mathtt{else}\ exp_n\ \mid\ \mathtt{store}\,(x,y)\ \mid\ \mathtt{fetch}\,(y)
\end{array}
$$

Fig. 1. The Language.

an instance, a static field, or an instance field. An executing thread consists of an identifier, the expression currently being evaluated by the thread, an environment, and a continuation stack which is a list of continuation frames. There are only three kinds of frames in the semantics: *return* frames are used to pass control from return points at non-tail calls; *unlock* frames are used to handle synchronization; and *halt* frames are used to mark terminated threads.

$$
\begin{aligned}
v \in &\quad Value = Loc + Clos + Record + Const \\
\texttt{Closure}\langle exp, \rho \rangle \in &\quad Clos = LambdaExp \times Env \\
\texttt{Rec}\,\langle f, exp, \rho \rangle \in &\quad Rec = Var \times LambdaExp \times Env \\
\rho \in &\quad Env = Name \stackrel{fin}{\to} Value \\
\sigma \in &\quad Store = Loc \stackrel{fin}{\to} Value \\
l \in &\quad Loc = Inst + (ClassName + Inst) \times FieldName \\
r \in &\quad Record = Name \stackrel{fin}{\to} Value \\
o \in &\quad Inst = ClassName \times Var \times Integer \\
t \in &\quad Thread = ThreadID \times Exp \times Env \times Kont^* \\
tid \in &\quad ThreadID = \{Main\} + Inst \\
TM \in &\quad ThreadMap = ThreadID \stackrel{fin}{\to} Thread \\
LM \in &\quad LockMap = Inst \stackrel{fin}{\to} \mathcal{P}(ThreadID \times N) \\
k \in &\quad Kont = \mathsf{Return}\langle y, \rho, e \rangle + \mathsf{Unlock}\langle y \rangle + \mathsf{Halt}
\end{aligned}
$$

Fig. 2. Semantic Domains.

A program *configuration* consists of a *thread map*, a *store*, and a *lock map*. A thread map binds thread identifiers to thread states. A lock map binds instances to pairs $\langle tid, n \rangle$ consisting of a thread identifier tid for the thread that has locked it and the number n of times it has been locked by that thread. The transition rules are shown in Figure 3; we omit the rules for declarations. In presenting the rules, we also omit unneeded components of a configuration.

The rules make use of auxiliary functions ($CheckLock$, $CheckUnlock$, $Lock$ and $Unlock$) that track how locks are acquired and released. Their definitions are obvious and omitted here.

We define the semantics via an evaluation relation, $Eval \subseteq Prog \times Value$:

$$Eval(T^*C^* exp) = \rho_0(last(exp)), \text{if}\{\langle Main, exp, \rho_0, \mathsf{Halt}\rangle\}, \phi, \phi \Longrightarrow^* \ TM, \sigma, LM$$

where $\begin{cases} \text{for all } tid \in Dom(TM), TM(tid) = \langle tid, x, \rho, \mathsf{Halt} : k \rangle. \\ Main \text{ is the main thread's id.} \end{cases}$

The transition relation, written as $\to_T$, is a relation on configurations,

$$\to_T \ \subseteq \ (TM \times Store \times LM) \ \times \ (TM \times Store \times LM).$$

Thus,

$$TM, \sigma, LM \to_T TM - \{t_i\} \bullet S, \sigma', LM'$$

$$\boxed{Thread \times Store \times LockMap \;\rightarrow\; \mathcal{P}(\,Thread) \times Store \times LockMap}$$

$\langle tid, x, \rho, \mathsf{Halt} : k^* \rangle \;\rightarrow\; \{\}$

$\langle tid, x, \rho, \mathsf{Return}\langle y, \rho', e\rangle : k^* \rangle \;\rightarrow\; \{\langle tid, e, \rho'[y \mapsto \rho(x)], k^* \rangle\}$

$\langle tid, x, \rho, \mathsf{Unlock}\langle y \rangle : k^* \rangle, \sigma, LM \;\rightarrow\; \{\langle tid, x, \rho, k^* \rangle\}, \sigma, LM'$
        if $CheckUnlock(\rho(y), tid, LM)$ and $LM' = Unlock(\rho(y), tid, LM)$

$\langle tid, \mathsf{let}\ x = \iota\ \mathsf{in}\ e\ \mathsf{end}, \rho, k^* \rangle \;\rightarrow\; \{\langle tid, e, \rho[x \mapsto \iota], k^* \rangle\}$

$\langle tid, \mathsf{let}\ x = r \cdot \underline{i}\ \mathsf{in}\ e\ \mathsf{end}, \rho, k^* \rangle \;\rightarrow\; \{\langle tid, e, \rho[x \mapsto \rho(r).\underline{i}], k^* \rangle\}$

$\langle tid, \mathsf{let}\ x = r \cdot \underline{m}\ \mathsf{in}\ e\ \mathsf{end}, \rho, k^* \rangle \;\rightarrow\; \{\langle tid, e, \rho[x \mapsto \rho(r).\underline{m}], k^* \rangle\}$

$\langle tid, \mathsf{let}\ x = \mathtt{new}(c)\ \mathsf{in}\ e\ \mathsf{end}, \rho, k^* \rangle, \sigma \;\rightarrow\; \{\langle tid, e, \rho[x \mapsto \langle c, x, n\rangle], k^* \rangle\}, \sigma'$
        where $\sigma' = \sigma[\langle c, x, n\rangle \mapsto NewObject(c)]$ and n is fresh

$\langle tid, \mathsf{let}\ x = y.i\ \mathsf{in}\ e\ \mathsf{end}, \rho, k^* \rangle \;\rightarrow\; \{\langle tid, e, \rho[x \mapsto \sigma(\rho(y)).i], k^* \rangle\}$

$\langle tid, \mathsf{let}\ x = y \Leftarrow m\ \mathsf{in}\ e\ \mathsf{end}, \rho, k^* \rangle \;\rightarrow\; \{\langle tid, e, \rho', k^* \rangle\},$
        where $\sigma(\rho(y)).m = \mathtt{Closure}\langle \lambda self.\lambda z.e', \rho_\perp \rangle$
        and $\rho' = \rho[x \mapsto \mathtt{Closure}\langle \lambda z.e', \rho_\perp[self \mapsto \rho(y)] \rangle]$

$\langle tid, \mathsf{let}\ x = y \Leftarrow c.m\ \mathsf{in}\ c\ \mathsf{end}, \rho, k^* \rangle \;\rightarrow\; \{\langle tid, e, \rho', k^* \rangle\}$
        where $\rho(c).m = \mathtt{Closure}\langle \lambda self.\lambda z.e', \rho_\perp \rangle$
        and $\rho' = \rho[x \mapsto \mathtt{Closure}\langle \lambda z.e', \rho_\perp[self \mapsto \rho(y)] \rangle]$

$\langle tid, \mathsf{let}\ x = y(z)\ \mathsf{in}\ e\ \mathsf{end}, \rho, k^* \rangle \;\rightarrow\; \{\langle tid, e', \rho'[w \mapsto \rho(z)], \mathsf{Return}\langle x, \rho, e\rangle : k^* \rangle$
        where $\rho(y) = \mathtt{Closure}\langle \lambda w.e', \rho' \rangle$

$\langle tid, \mathsf{let}\ x = \mu f.fn\ \mathsf{in}\ e\ \mathsf{end}, \rho, k^* \rangle \;\rightarrow\; \{\langle tid, e, \rho[x \mapsto \mathtt{Rec}\ \langle f, fn, \rho\rangle], k^* \rangle\}$

$\langle tid, \mathsf{let}\ x = y(z)\ \mathsf{in}\ e\ \mathsf{end}, \rho, k^* \rangle \;\rightarrow\; \{\langle tid, e', \rho'', \mathsf{Return}\langle x, \rho, e\rangle : k^* \rangle\}$
        where $\rho(y) = \mathtt{Rec}\ \langle f, \lambda w.e', \rho' \rangle, \rho'' = \rho'[w \mapsto \rho(z), f \mapsto \mathtt{Rec}\ \langle f, \lambda w.e', \rho' \rangle]$

$\langle tid, \mathsf{let}\ x = \mathtt{store}\ (y, z)\ \mathsf{in}\ e\ \mathsf{end}, \rho, k^* \rangle, \sigma \;\rightarrow\; \{\langle tid, e, \rho, k^* \rangle, \sigma[\rho(y) \mapsto \rho(z)]\}$

$\langle tid, \mathsf{let}\ x = \mathtt{fetch}\ (y)\ \mathsf{in}\ e\ \mathsf{end}, \rho, k^* \rangle, \sigma \;\rightarrow\; \{\langle tid, e, \rho[x \mapsto \sigma(\rho(y))], k^* \rangle\}$

$\langle tid, \mathsf{let}\ x = \mathtt{spawn}\ (c, m)\ \mathsf{in}\ e\ \mathsf{end}, \rho, k^* \rangle, \sigma \;\rightarrow\;$
        $\{\langle tid, e, \rho[x \mapsto \langle c, x, n\rangle], k^* \rangle, \langle tid', e', \rho_0[self_i \mapsto \langle c, x, n\rangle], \mathsf{Halt}\rangle\}, \sigma'$
        where tid' is fresh and $\sigma' = \sigma[\langle c, x, n\rangle \mapsto NewObject(c)]$ and $m = \lambda self_i.\lambda().e'$

$\langle tid, \mathsf{let}\ x = \mathtt{synch}\ (y)\ \mathsf{in}\ e\ \mathsf{end}, \rho, k^* \rangle, \sigma, LM \;\rightarrow\; \{\langle tid, e, \rho', \mathsf{Unlock}\langle y \rangle : k^* \rangle\}, \sigma, LM'$
        if $CheckLock(\rho(y), tid, LM) = \mathtt{true}, \rho' = \rho[x \mapsto \{\}], LM' = Lock(\rho(y), tid, LM)$

$\langle tid, \mathsf{let}\ x = y \rightarrow [\iota_i \Rightarrow e_i]^*\ \mathsf{else}\ e_n\ \mathsf{in}\ e\ \mathsf{end}, \rho, k^* \rangle \;\rightarrow\; \{\langle tid, \mathsf{let}\ x = e'\ \mathsf{in}\ e\ \mathsf{end}, \rho, k^* \rangle\}$
        where $e' = e_i$ if $\rho(y) = \iota_i$, and $e' = e_n$ otherwise

Fig. 3. Exact semantics

if $t_i, \sigma, LM \;\rightarrow\; S, \sigma', LM'$ where t_i is some thread in TM, and S is the set of new threads created during the one-step transition of t_i. We write $F \bullet S$ to mean $F[tid \mapsto \langle tid, e, \rho, k\rangle]$ for all $\langle tid, e, \rho, k\rangle \in S$.

4   Abstract Semantics

Our initial specification is a monovariant analysis similar in spirit to other flow systems developed for object-based languages [PC94,DGC98,PS91]. We differ primarily in our support for concurrency. We subsequently refine the analysis to derive a more precise heap reachability map. The analysis is given as a triple

$\langle F_{env}, F_{cell}, F_{lock} \rangle$ consisting of an abstract environment, an abstract store, and an abstract lock map. We call this triple an *abstract configuration*; unlike the exact semantics, the analysis computes a single abstract configuration for a given program. An abstract environment maps variables to abstract values, *i.e.*, a finite approximation of the set of values to which a variable may be bound during program execution. An abstract store maps abstract locations to abstract values. An abstract location approximates a set of locations. An abstract lock map approximates the set of threads that synchronize on a particular instance. Unlike the exact semantics, all abstract threads share a single abstract environment, F_{env}. Since the analysis models the collection of exact states in a program's evaluation by a single abstract configuration, the only relevant information about a thread is its identity, making an abstract thread map unnecessary. Thread identifiers are represented by abstract thread instances.

$$
\begin{array}{lll}
F_{env} & \in Flow & = Var \rightarrow Aval \\
F_{cell} & \in FStore & = Aloc \rightarrow Aval \\
F_{lock} & \in FLock & = Ainst \rightarrow \mathcal{P}(AThreadId) \\
\hat{v} & \in Aval & = \mathcal{P}(Aloc + ARecord + LambdaExp + \{\mathbf{ground}\}) \\
\hat{l} & \in Aloc & = Ainst + (ClassName \times FieldName) + (Ainst \times FieldName) \\
\hat{o} & \in Ainst & = ClassName \times Var \\
\hat{r} & \in ARecord & = Name \rightarrow Aval \\
\hat{tid} & \in AThreadId & = \{Main\} + Ainst
\end{array}
$$

Fig. 4. Domains for the flow analysis.

One useful approximation is to regard the abstract value of an instance as a set of class names. If o is an object instantiated from a class named c and bound to variable x, and if the flow analysis associates abstract value $\hat{v}$ with o, it must be the case that $\langle c, x \rangle \in \hat{v}$. Similarly, the abstract value of a method selection of the form "$o \Leftarrow m$" is the set of λ-expressions named m occurring in the classes denoted by o's abstract value. Ground values are used to approximate values of primitive type. Abstract cells approximate exact locations. Abstract values and cells are partially ordered by ordinary set inclusion.

To formally specify the meaning of an analysis, we define a relation between exact and abstract configurations:

Definition 1. *An exact configuration $\langle TM, \sigma, LM \rangle$ agrees with an abstract configuration, $\langle F_{env}, F_{cell}, F_{lock} \rangle$ written $\langle TM, \sigma, LM \rangle \sqsubseteq \langle F_{env}, F_{cell}, F_{lock} \rangle$ if $TM \sqsubseteq F_{env}$, $\sigma \sqsubseteq F_{cell}$, and $LM \sqsubseteq F_{lock}$.*

The agreement relation is defined inductively over terms and values in the exact semantics. Its definition is given in Figure 5.

1. $TM \sqsubseteq F_{env}$ if for all $tid \in Dom(TM)$ such that $TM(tid) = \langle tid, exp, \rho, k^* \rangle$, $\rho \sqsubseteq F_{env}$ and $k^* \sqsubseteq F_{env}$.
2. $\rho \sqsubseteq F_{env}$ if for all $x \in Dom(\rho)$, $\rho(x) \sqsubseteq F_{env}(x)$.
3. $\sigma \sqsubseteq F_{cell}$ if for all $l \in Dom(\sigma)$ there exists $\hat{l} \in Dom(F_{cell})$ such that $l \sqsubseteq \hat{l}$.
4. $LM \sqsubseteq F_{lock}$ if for every $o \in Dom(LM)$, there exists $\hat{o} \in Dom(F_{lock})$ such that for all $tid \in LM(o)$ there exists $\hat{tid} \in F_{lock}(\hat{o})$ such that $tid \sqsubseteq \hat{tid}$.
5. $l \sqsubseteq \hat{l}$ if $\sigma(l) \sqsubseteq F_{cell}(\hat{l})$.
6. $k^* \sqsubseteq F_{env}$ if for every $\mathsf{Return}\langle y, \rho, e \rangle \in k^*$, $\rho \sqsubseteq F_{env}$.
7. $\iota \sqsubseteq \hat{v}$ if $\mathbf{ground} \in \hat{v}$.
8. $\langle c, x, n \rangle \sqsubseteq \langle c, x \rangle$.
9. $\langle o, f \rangle \sqsubseteq \langle \hat{o}, f \rangle$ if $o \sqsubseteq \hat{o}$.
10. $\mathsf{Closure}\langle \lambda x . e, \rho \rangle \sqsubseteq \hat{v}$ if $\lambda x . e \in \hat{v}$ and $\rho \sqsubseteq F_{env}$.
11. $\mathsf{Rec} \langle f, fn, \rho \rangle \sqsubseteq \hat{v}$ if $fn \in \hat{v}$ and $\rho \sqsubseteq F_{env}$.
12. $r \sqsubseteq \hat{r}$ if for every $x \in Dom(r), r(x) \sqsubseteq \hat{r}(x)$.

Fig. 5. Agreement relation.

For a specific program, there may be many flow functions which satisfy the constraints shown in Figure 6. The following theorem states that any flow satisfying the safety constraints conservatively approximates the exact semantics.

Theorem 1 (Safety $\Rightarrow$ Soundness). *If* $\langle TM, \sigma, LM \rangle \sqsubseteq \langle F_{env}, F_{cell}, F_{lock} \rangle$, $\langle F_{env}, F_{cell}, F_{lock} \rangle$ *is safe and* $\langle TM, \sigma, LM \rangle \to_\top \langle TM', \sigma', LM' \rangle$ *then* $\langle TM', \sigma', LM' \rangle \sqsubseteq \langle F_{env}, F_{cell}, F_{lock} \rangle$

Proof. By induction on exact transition sequences.

4.1 Multiplicity

To improve precision, the constraints incorporate a simple liveness property among methods and threads. Recall that the flow analysis computes for every instance an approximation to the set of exact threads that synchronize on that instance. Because an abstract thread is represented by a birthplace, this information is insufficient to distinguish between one or multiple invocations of a thread created at a given **spawn** point. Consequently, the effectiveness of optimizations such as synchronization elimination, that rely crucially on knowing if there exists a *unique* thread accessing an instance, would be weakened.

To alleviate this problem, we fold a simple liveness calculation into the flow analysis to reveal multiplicity properties of threads and methods. Given a method m, we compute a conservative approximation of the number of times m is invoked. To do so, we first define a *multiplicity* map that associates with every method an element in a flat lattice:

$$\mathcal{M} : LambdaExp \to M + CallSite + \top$$

Definition 2. Let R be an indexed set, whose indices are drawn from the set of abstract threads. Each element in the set is itself a set of expressions *reachable* from the representative thread. Let $P = T^* \, C^* \, S^* \, exp$ where $exp \in R_{Main}$. Define for each $x \in P$, $\top \geq \mathcal{M}(x)$. Then, a flow analysis $\langle F_{env}, F_{cell}, F_{lock} \rangle$ is safe if the following conditions hold:

For all $exp \in R_{tid}$
  if $exp = $ **let** $(x = b)$ **in** exp' **end**, then $exp' \in R_{t\hat{i}d}$ and
  (a) if $b = \iota$, then $\{\textbf{ground}\} \leq F_{env}(x)$ if $PrimType(c)$;
  (b) if $b = \mu f.fn$ then $\{fn\} \leq F_{env}(f)$ and $\{fn\} \leq F_{env}(x)$;
  (c) if $b = y.i$, then $\forall \hat{o} \in F_{env}(y)$, $F_{cell}(\hat{o}).i \leq F_{env}(x)$;
  (d) if $b = r.\underline{i}$ then $\forall \hat{r} \in F_{env}(r)$, $\hat{r}(i) \leq F_{env}(x)$
  (e) if $b = r.\underline{m}$ then $\forall \hat{r} \in F_{env}(r)$, $\hat{r}(m) \leq F_{env}(x)$
  (f) if $b = y \Leftarrow m$, then $\forall \hat{o} = \langle c, z \rangle \in F_{env}(y)$, $GetMethod(c, m) = \lambda self_i . f$,
      1. $\{f\} \leq F_{env}(x)$
      2. $F_{env}(y) \leq F_{env}(self_i)$;
  (g) if $b = y \Leftarrow c.m$ and $GetMethod(c, m) = \lambda self_i . f$, then
      1. $\{f\} \leq F_{env}(x)$
      2. $F_{env}(y) \leq F_{env}(self_i)$;
  (h) if $b = f(y_1, \ldots, y_n)$ then $\forall \lambda_c = \lambda w_1, \ldots, w_n . exp'' \in F_{env}(f)$,
      1. for $i = 1, \ldots, n$, $F_{env}(y_i) \leq F_{env}(w_i)$
      2. $F_{env}(last(exp'')) \leq F_{env}(x)$
      3. $\mathcal{M}(\lambda_c) = \mathcal{M}(\lambda_c) \sqcap (\langle \lambda_c, x \rangle \bowtie \langle \lambda_r, \mathcal{M}(\lambda_r) \rangle)$ where λ_r encloses b.
      4. $exp'' \in R_{t\hat{i}d}$;
  (i) if $b = $ **store** (y, z) then $\forall \hat{l} \in F_{env}(y)$, $F_{env}(z) \leq F_{cell}(\hat{l})$;
  (j) if $b = $ **fetch** (y) then $\forall \hat{l} \in F_{env}(y)$, $F_{cell}(\hat{l}) \leq F_{env}(x)$
  (k) if $b = y \rightarrow [k_i \Rightarrow exp_i]^*$ **else** exp_n then
      1. for $i = 1, \ldots, n$, $exp_i \in R_{t\hat{i}d}$
      2. for $i = 1, \ldots, n$, $F_{env}(last(exp_i)) \leq F_{env}(x)$;
  (l) if $b = $ **new** (c) then $\{\langle c, x \rangle\} \leq F_{env}(x)$;
  (m) if $b = $ **spawn** (c, m) and $GetMethod(c, m) = \lambda self_i . f$, then
      1. $\{\langle c, x \rangle\} \leq F_{env}(x)$
      2. $\{\langle c, x \rangle\} \leq F_{env}(self_i)$
      3. $exp'' \in R_{\langle c, x \rangle}$, where $f = \lambda z. exp''$
      4. $\mathcal{M}(f) = \mathcal{M}(f) \sqcap (\langle f, x \rangle \bowtie \langle \lambda_r, \mathcal{M}(\lambda_r) \rangle)$ where λ_r encloses b;
  (n) if $b = $ **synch** (y) then $\forall \hat{o} \in F_{env}(y)$, $t\hat{i}d \leq F_{lock}(\hat{o})$.

Fig. 6. Safety constraints on flows.

where $M \leq CallSite \leq \top$, and $CallSite$ ranges over variables bound to call expressions in the program. The bottom element of the lattice is M, indicating the method is invoked multiple times. Initially, $\mathcal{M}$ maps all methods to $\top$, indicating that there are no calls to any method. The other elements of the lattice are call-sites; if a method has at least two different call sites, then it is considered multiple: $p \sqcap q = M$ if $p \neq q$.

However, a method can be multiple even if it has a single call site, if that site is located in a method which is itself *multiple*. Thus, in stating the safety rules for our flow analysis, we must take into account the multiplicity of the caller as well as that of the callee. For this, we define a join operation, ($\bowtie$), on tuples of methods and multiplicities:

$$(\langle m_1, p \rangle \bowtie \langle m_2, q \rangle) = \begin{cases} p & \text{if } m_1 \neq m_2 \text{ and } q \neq M \\ M & \text{otherwise} \end{cases}$$

Then, the multiplicity of a method m_1 called at site p in method m_2 with multiplicity q, is obtained from joining $\langle m_1, p \rangle$ with $\langle m_2, q \rangle$, and then doing a meet operation with the previous value of m_1's multiplicity.

4.2   Constraints

We specify the analysis as a collection of constraints (see Figure 6). We regard these constraints as *safety* rules that specify the structure of abstract value sets. These constraints must ensure that the abstract values computed by an implementation of the analysis can be interpreted as a conservative approximation of a program's exact behavior. The rules specify a monovariant flow analysis akin to 0CFA [Shi91] for expressions.

The rules refer to several auxiliary functions. The function *getMethod*, when given a class name and a method name, returns the definition of the method found in the class; and, *last* returns the variable bound to the last sub-term of an expression. The rules are sensitive to *reachable* expressions. Informally, an expression is reachable if its abstract value set is not empty. To express reachability in the presence of threads, we define an index set of reachable expressions, with each element in the set corresponding to the set of expressions reachable from a particular thread. We express reachability in the rules in several places. Obviously, the main expression of a program is reachable. Second, if a **let** expression is reachable, then its body is also reachable. Third, when a new thread is spawned, the body of the thread is reachable, *i.e.*, as in **spawn** (c, m) the body of m is reachable. Finally, the body of a method is reachable if there is an application of the method that is reachable (i.e., the λ-expression corresponding to the method occurs as an abstract value element in the flow).

Of particular interest are the rules for application and thread creation. Condition (3) in the rule for function application reflects the multiplicity constraints described in the previous section. The multiplicity of a function at a call point is computed as $\mathcal{M}(\lambda_c) \sqcap (\langle \lambda_c, x \rangle \bowtie \langle \lambda_r, \mathcal{M}(\lambda_r) \rangle)$.

The $\bowtie$ operator returns a multiplicity based on the multiplicities of the caller (λ_r) and of the callee (λ_c). The callee is marked M if it has been applied at some other call-site, or if the caller is itself M. The rule for thread creation also uses the multiplicity map to record the multiplicity of the function being spawned.

```
class Container {                          class CThread extends Thread {
  static Container container;                Vector vec;
  Vector leftV;                              CThread( Vector v) { vec = v;  }
  Vector rightV;                             public void run() {
  Container() {                                vec.addElement( new Integer(1));
    leftV = new Vector();  // p3            }
    rightV = new Vector(); // p4          }
  }

  static void main() {
    container = new Container(); // p0
    CThread leftT =  new CThread( container.leftV); // p1
    CThread rightT = new CThread( container.rightV); // p2
    leftT.start();
    rightT.start();
  }
}
```

F_{env}
container $\mapsto$ $\langle$ Container, $p0$ $\rangle$
leftV $\mapsto$ $\langle$ Vector, $p3$ $\rangle$
rightV $\mapsto$ $\langle$ Vector, $p4$ $\rangle$
leftT $\mapsto$ $\langle$ CThread, $p1$ $\rangle$
rightT $\mapsto$ $\langle$ CThread, $p2$ $\rangle$

F_{cell}
Container.container $\mapsto$ $\langle$ Container, $p0$ $\rangle$
$\langle$ Container, $p0$ $\rangle$.leftV $\mapsto$ $\langle$ Vector, $p3$ $\rangle$
$\langle$ Container, $p0$ $\rangle$.rightV $\mapsto$ $\langle$ Vector, $p4$ $\rangle$
$\langle$ CThread, $p1$ $\rangle$.vec $\mapsto$ $\langle$ Vector, $p3$ $\rangle$
$\langle$ CThread, $p2$ $\rangle$.vec $\mapsto$ $\langle$ Vector, $p4$ $\rangle$

F_{lock}
$\langle$ Vector, $p3$ $\rangle$ $\mapsto$ $\langle$ CThread, $p1$ $\rangle$
$\langle$ Vector, $p4$ $\rangle$ $\mapsto$ $\langle$ CThread, $p2$ $\rangle$
$\langle$ CThread, $p1$ $\rangle$ $\mapsto$ $Main$
$\langle$ CThread, $p2$ $\rangle$ $\mapsto$ $Main$

$\mathcal{M}$
$\langle$ CThread, $p1$ $\rangle$ $\mapsto$ $p1$ (single)
$\langle$ CThread, $p2$ $\rangle$ $\mapsto$ $p2$ (single)
$Main$ (single)

Fig. 7. A simple multithreaded program and the result of its flow analysis.

4.3   Example

Figure 7 presents an example to illustrate the analysis. Objects of type Container have two fields, left and right, each of type Vector. The main method allocates a container and stores it in a static field, and then starts two threads each of which operates on only one of the fields. Even though both vectors are reachable from a (global) static field, and also from the thread instances themselves, neither vector is accessed by multiple threads. The bottom of Figure 7 shows the relevant maps produced by the analysis. The program points $p0$ to $p4$ are the birthplaces of the respective instances. Note that because of the start method, both thread objects must be **synchronized** in the main method. The results obtained by the analysis enable the removal of *all* synchronization operations on `rightV` and `leftV` in the program, since no object is locked by two different threads.

5 Flow-Sensitive Extensions

The analysis presented in the previous section tells us the objects for which contention among various threads in the program is possible. However, even objects manipulated by multiple threads are not always shared during their entire lifetime. An analysis that tracks sharing properties of threads and instances at different program points can lead to further optimization opportunities.

Conceptually, the refined analysis builds for each program point an approximation of the heap *that is relevant at that program point*. For efficiency and precision, it is important that we do not build an approximation of the entire heap at every program point. For example, the interesting portion of the heap to a leaf procedure that does not have any `synchronized` operations, and does not refer to any static field, is limited to its arguments and what is reachable from them. Since only a few operations affect the heap, abstract heaps can often be shared among many program points.

For every heap at every program point, there is a set of roots that is considered *shared*; any other node that is reachable in the heap from these roots is potentially *shared* as well. The root set must include: (1) any thread object (because it is accessible to both the new thread of control and the thread that created it); and (2) static fields whose contents consists of objects touched by more than one thread.

5.1 Computing a Reachability Map

Prior to computing the structure of the per program-point heap, we must first compute a transitive closure of the static fields accessed by a method. To compute the closure we need:

1. some approximation of the control flow graph. In our case, this approximation is given by the earlier analysis;
2. the set of static fields accessed by each method

From (1) and (2) we compute the transitive closure of the static field accesses for a method and all the methods it calls.

$$FreeVarMap : \qquad\qquad\qquad Method \rightarrow \mathcal{P}(Aval)$$
$$FreeVarMap(\lambda self.\lambda x.exp) \qquad = FreeVarMap(exp)$$

$$FreeVarMap : \qquad\qquad\qquad Exp \rightarrow \mathcal{P}(Aval)$$
$$FreeVarMap(x) \qquad\qquad\qquad = \{\}$$
$$FreeVarMap(\text{let } (x = b) \text{ in } exp' \text{ end}) = FreeVarMap(exp') \bigcup$$
$$\begin{cases} \langle r, \underline{i} \rangle & \text{if } b \equiv r.\underline{i} \\ \bigcup_j FreeVarMap(\lambda_j) & \text{if } b \equiv f(y_1, \ldots, y_n), \text{ where } \lambda_j \in F_{env}(f) \\ \{\} & \text{otherwise} \end{cases}$$

5.2   Abstract Domains

The refined analysis computes an *abstract heap* at every program point. A heap is a map from nodes to sets of nodes. For our purposes, a node is represented as an abstract value. Given node n, $AH(n)$ denotes the set of nodes immediately reachable from n.

$$AH \in AHeap = Node \rightarrow \mathcal{P}(Node)$$
$$n \in Node \ \ = Aval$$
$$e \in Edge \ \ = Node \times Node$$

The function *Reach* computes the part of the abstract heap that is reachable starting from the roots (a set of abstract values) given as arguments:

$$Reach : AHeap \times \mathcal{P}(Aval) \rightarrow AHeap$$

It is used to propagate heaps from caller to callee at method call points, and from callee to caller at method return points.

Single is a function from abstract cells to Booleans: $Single : \mathcal{P}(Aloc) \rightarrow Boolean$. *Single* returns true if a *strong update* is possible on the argument. Strong update is a property of an analysis that allows the contents of an abstract cell to be overwritten if it is known that the cell corresponds to one exact cell. Thus, the function returns true in the following cases:

- the cell corresponds to a local variable of a function called only once as defined by the function's multiplicity.
- the cell corresponds to a *clean* static field (*i.e.*, a static field which contains objects touched by only one thread).
- the cell corresponds to an instance field, and the instance is clean and single (*i.e.*, the instance is allocated in a function called only once)

Figure 8 contains the rules to compute the abstract heaps. Since most of the expressions do not change the heap, the heap at the program point succeeding the expression is the same as that of the preceding program point. The notable exceptions are instance allocation, cell update, control flow join points and function calls. To build new heaps, the analysis uses two functions, *Node* and *Edge* to inject nodes (respectively edges) into heaps, and a join operation, $\oplus$ to merge two heaps. Their definitions are obvious, and are omitted here.

5.3   Filtering Environments

This analysis uses the results of monovariant analysis presented in the previous section which provides safe flow and cell environments. Because the results of the flow analysis are valid at any program point (due to the safety rules), there are cases when values are added to the environment because of merging induced by the constraint satisfaction algorithm [JW95]. Since the second analysis computes a solution per program point, we could compute a tighter approximation

---

Definition 3.
For all $exp \in R_{t\hat{\imath}d}$

1. if $exp = \mathbf{let}\ (x = b)\ \mathbf{in}\ exp'\ \mathbf{end}$, then $exp' \in R_{t\hat{\imath}d}$ and
   (a) if $b = f(y_1, \ldots, y_n)$ then $\forall \lambda_j = \lambda w_1, \ldots, w_n . exp_j \in F_{env}(f)$, let
      - $F = FreeVarMap(\lambda_j)$
      - $S = \{\hat{o} \in F_{env}(y_i) | \hat{o} \in AH_{exp}\}$.
      Then,
      i. $AH_{exp_j} = Reach(AH_{exp}, F \cup S)$
      ii. $AH_{exp'} = \oplus_j Reach(AH_{last(exp_j)}, F \cup S \cup \{F_{env}(last(exp_j))\})$
      iii. $exp_j \in R_{t\hat{\imath}d}$
   (b) if $b = \mathbf{new}(c)$, then $AH_{exp'} = AH_{exp} \oplus Node(\langle c, x \rangle)$;
   (c) if $b = \mathbf{store}(y, z)$ then $\forall \hat{l} \in F_{env}(y)|_{AH_{exp}}$,
      let $S = \{Edge(\hat{l}, \hat{o}) \mid \hat{o} \in F_{env}(z)|_{AH_{exp}}\}$; then
      i. if $Single(\hat{l})$, $AH_{exp'} = (AH_{exp} - D) \oplus S$,
         where $D = \{e = Edge(\hat{l}, \hat{v}) | e \in AH_{exp}\}$
      ii. otherwise, $AH_{exp'} = AH_{exp} \oplus S$.
   (d) if $b = y \rightarrow [k_i \Rightarrow exp_i]^* \ \mathbf{else}\ exp_n$ then
      i. for $i = 1, \ldots, n$, $AH_{exp_i} = AH_{exp}$
      ii. $AH_{exp'} = \oplus_i AH_{last(exp_i)}$
      iii. $exp_i \in R_{t\hat{\imath}d}$
   (e) if $b = \mathbf{spawn}(c, m)$, and $GetMethod(\langle c, m \rangle) = \lambda self . \lambda() . exp''$
      i. $AH_{exp'} = AH_{exp''} = AH_{exp} \oplus Node(\langle c, x \rangle)$,
      ii. $exp'' \in R_{\langle c, x \rangle}$
   (f) $AH_{exp'} = AH_{exp}$ otherwise

Fig. 8. Safety constraints on abstract heaps.

---

as follows. Initially, the starting heap contains only the (empty) cells corresponding to the static fields. Whenever an allocation expression is encountered, the abstract values corresponding to the new object is added as a new node in the heap at that program point. Now, when we use the flow environment of some variable, we can restrict the set of values to those that actually exist in the heap at that program point. The result is an analysis whose implementation has slower convergence, but improved precision.

The filtering of the environment explains why the rules for allocation of instances (**new** and **spawn**) introduce new nodes. Edges are added by the **store** expression which augments the contents of a node with a new abstract value. As mentioned above, some of these updates can be *strong* if the cell that is updated is *single*.

5.4 Thread Local Objects

The results of the flow analysis can be used to eliminate runtime overhead incurred by unnecessary synchronization in two ways. First, we can eliminate any lock operations performed on objects that are locked by a *single* abstract thread.

Second, we can eliminate synchronization on *local objects*. A local object is any non-thread object that is accessible only from stack or from other local objects. Thread instances and objects that are stored in static fields are *non-local* (or *global*). Because an abstract thread that is multiple might correspond to many exact threads, these two optimizations are complementary.

Local objects are obtained from a data dependency graph built from the flow and cell environment as follows; any distinct abstract value used during the analysis is represented by a node in the graph. Edges are introduced between: (i) an abstract instance and its abstract instance fields, (ii) an abstract cell `cell` and the abstract values in $F_{cell}(\texttt{cell})$. Starting from static fields and thread instances, we compute the transitive closure of global objects. Any remain nodes represent *local objects*. Note that we can have data-paths of arbitrary length composed entirely of local objects. This gives us a first-order approximation of the set of local objects, an approximation improved upon by the second analysis. By refining the construction of abstract heaps on a per program point basis, we obtain heaps with fewer edges, thus decreasing the number of nodes that become *global*.

5.5   Abstract Heaps Example

Figure 9 contains an example for our second analysis: a tree whose nodes are implemented by vectors of successor nodes. The class `Node` defines the data type used for implementing the nodes of the tree; the class `Main` contains code to build the tree, store its root in a static field, and then start a thread to read the values stored in the nodes. Since the nodes of the tree are eventually accessed by more than one thread (in this case the main thread and an instance of `TreeThread`), our earlier analysis would be unable to reveal any opportunities for optimization. However, note that during the construction of the tree, its nodes are only accessible from one thread. By using a per program-point heap, this information is revealed. Figure 10 presents the results of the analysis at the program points shown inside comments. For the purposes of synchronization elimination, synchronization overhead can be eliminated at program point `p4`, (just before the call to `addElement`), and for the call to `addChild` at program point `p5`.

6   Experiments

We have applied our analysis on the applications presented in Table 11. `JLex` and `JCup` are a lexer and parser generator; `Zothello` is a program playing the game Othello; `Dhry` is a numeric benchmark. The other two programs are multithreaded: `_224_richards` creates a number of threads running multiple versions of OS simulator, and `_233_tmix` is a mix of applications (fibonacci, sort, producer-consumer, etc.) each run in its own thread.

Since synchronization costs depend greatly on machine hardware, lock allocation strategy used, etc., measuring interesting dynamic counts presents a more

```
                        class Node {
                     Vector successors ;
            Node() { successors = new Vector(); }
           synchronized void addChild( Node child) {
              /* p4 */  successors.addElement( child);
                             }
        synchronized Enumeration getChildren( Node n) { ... }
                             }
                        class Main {
                     static Node root;
                  Node buildTree( int max) {
                     Node n = new Node();
                        if( max > 0 )
                     while( randomBool()) {
                       Node t = buildTree( max - 1 );
                   /* p5 */  n.addChild( t);   }
                          return n;
                             }
                     static void main() {
               /* p1 */  root = buildTree( 5);
           /* p2 */  TreeThread thread = new TreeThread();
                       thread.start();
               /* p3 */  // ... more code here ...
                             }
                             }
```

Fig. 9. Tree example

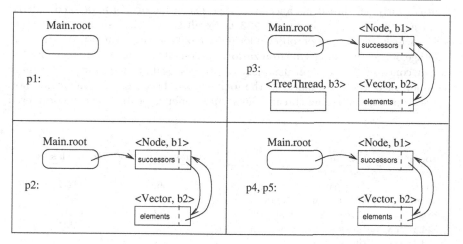

Fig. 10. Abstract heaps

objective view of the analyses' utility. Table 12 shows the dynamic counts for the number of instances allocated in both the program and libraries, the number of locks acquired, and the total number of calls made. To quantify the utility of our analyses, we present results focused on synchronization overhead; these results are easily extrapolated to other kinds of concurrency optimizations discussed in the earlier sections. Table 13 gives percentages based on the baseline numbers for the total number of allocations that were marked local by our analyses, the total number of locks acquired on objects deemed local by our analyses, and the total number of lock operations on objects (either local or global) that were synchronized by only one thread. Synchronization overhead on local objects or synchronization on an object accessed by only a single thread can be eliminated.

Note that our thread analysis reveals that no synchronization overhead must be incurred by any of the sequential programs; however, as an ancillary benefit, flow-sensitive heap analysis can also be used to reveal useful information about object locality and lifetime. For example, an overwhelming majority of locks can be removed from jcup, zothello, and dhry simply because the objects on which these operations are performed have been identified as local. However, using just reachability information leads to less convincing results for jlex because many instances are referenced via static fields. For this program, it was critical that we analyzed the structure of the global lock map computed by the thread analysis. This map indicates that no object is shared by multiple threads, even though many of these objects are accessible via static fields.

Whereas in the first four applications our initial monovariant thread analysis gave perfect information, it alone wasn't precise enough on the multi-threaded benchmarks. In _224_richards it found that only 5% of the lock operations are performed on objects locked by only one thread. This was caused by the fact that the program spawns a number of identical threads from the same program point; consequently, all thread instances with the exception of *Main* were considered *multiple*. On the other hand, in _233_tmix all threads are *single*, and 40% of all synchronizations are on objects locked by only a single thread. A large percentage of the remaining synchronizations are on StringBuffer objects used in string concatenation and on the queue of objects used in the producer-consumer component of the benchmark. In the former case, because the concat method is used in more than one thread, the string buffer allocated in it is considered

Program	Description	Number of methods	size of classes
jlex	Java lexer generator	136	101K
jcup	Java parser generator	362	142K
zothello	Othello game program	132	36K
dhry	Dhrystone benchmark	22	6.5K
_224_richards	threads running OS simulator	394	143K
_233_tmix	thread mix	140	53K

Fig. 11. Benchmark description

Program	Allocations		Number of locks		Total number
	application	libraries	application	libraries	of calls
jlex	23231	20094	1379642	1141876	8263281
jcup	26225	80414	34013	156831	1142196
zothello	83782	5179	14462	3350	32389270
dhry	600141	227	0	145	5405595
_224_richards	2317	5077	66	4156	63604540
_233_tmix	94825	245585	708917	841336	8699788

Fig. 12. Dynamic counts

Program	Local Allocations		Synchronizations locks on local objects		Synchronizations on single threaded objects	% Locks unoptimized
	app.	app. + lib.	app.	app + lib.		
jlex	47%	36%	13%	39%	100%	0%
jcup	55%	67%	78%	93%	100%	0%
zothello	89%	86%	100%	99%	100%	0%
dhry	99%	99%	–	80%	100%	0%
_224_richards	20%	26%	53%	83%	5%	17%
_233_tmix	45%	84%	85%	93%	40%	7%

Fig. 13. Percentages of local objects and locks removed

locked on by all these threads. In the latter case, the queue of objects is indeed shared by two threads; for correctness, synchronization overhead cannot be removed here. For both these programs, the precision of the analysis was greatly enhanced by employing our flow-sensitive heap analysis, which discovered that many of the objects synchronized on were local, thus enabling the optimization of 83% (respectively 93%) of lock operations.

The compilation overhead incurred by our analysis has two components. The first component is constraint generation, and is about 3% of the compilation time; the constraints that are generated can be reused as long as the source code of the respective class does not change (such is the case of libraries, for example). The second component is constraint solving; for the six benchmarks presented, it took between 8% and 27% of the compilation time of the application only, with an average of 19%. These percentages are likely to go down as we fine-tune the implementation, and as more optimizations are added to the compiler.

7 Related Work

There have been many algorithms proposed for analyzing object-oriented programs with varying precision and costs [PS91,PC94,Age95,DGC98]. Many of these analyses are variants or extensions of monovariant control-flow analyses [Hei94,JM79,Shi91]. Extensions of control-flow analyses to handle concurrency have been explored in [CI92,Mer91,JW94]. While these efforts have influenced our design, there are numerous technical differences in the development. Most notably, none of these efforts consider analysis of monitor-style concurrency in an object-oriented language, nor justify the practicality of their approach with a realistic implementation.

There is a large body of work on analyzing reachability and computing shapes over an abstract representation of a program's memory; none of these efforts have considered the applicability of such analyses for optimizing concurrent programs. Ruggieri and Murtagh [RM88] compute sets of objects passed to and returned from procedures for lifetime analysis to enable stack allocation of objects on frames with greater lifetimes. Serrano and Feeley [SF96] present a similar idea for a higher-order language. Deutsch [Deu90] uses abstract reachability to enable stack allocation and to determine when objects can be destructively updated. Chase et al. [CWZ90] use a per-program point "storage shape graph" to analyze a language with mutable cons cells. They introduce the notion of "strong update" in this context. Sagiv, Reps, and Wilhelm [SRW96] present an abstract interpretation of a simple imperative language with heap-allocated data structures. Like [CWZ90], they compute a per-program point static storage graph that approximates the heaps at each point. Rather than using a notion of birthplace (or allocation point) to partition exact cells into abstract cells, their analysis keeps track of cells immediately pointed to by program variables. Abstract heap nodes are represented by sets of variables that must all point to the same runtime location, for some execution reaching that point.

More recently, there has been increased interest in exploring optimization opportunities for Java, especially in the context of its concurrency features. Bogda and Holzle developed an analysis which identifies unnecessary synchronizations [BH99] based on the observation that objects that are only reachable from the stack can not possibly be accessed by two different threads. They employ a flow-insensitive analysis that separates objects which can be stack allocated from those that cannot; stack allocated objects require no synchronization to access. Choi et al. [CGS+99] describe an escape analysis for Java that can be used to facilitate synchronization elimination. They introduce an abstraction, called *connection graph*, used to establish reachability constraints among objects and object references. Their analysis takes into account thread objects, but not threads of control. If the connection graph reveals that an object does not escape, its methods require no synchronization. Like [CGS+99], Whaley and Rinard [WR99] present a pointer and escape analysis for Java using an abstraction of a points-to graph that describes how objects refer to one another. Blanchet [Bla99] describes another escape analysis for Java using a type-based abstract interpretation rather than a dataflow graph framework. Aldrich et al. [ACSE99] describe a static analysis for eliminating unnecessary synchronization in Java programs, which discovers locking relationships between instances. For example, no synchronization is necessary on a method that is always invoked at call points where the corresponding receiver object is already locked.

Our framework is distinguished from these efforts insofar as it deals explicitly with threads. In contrast to analyses that indirectly compute sharing properties of objects via their lifetime (escape) properties, our analysis defines an approximation in terms of how threads access objects. In particular, it derives perfect information about synchronization requirements for single-threaded programs. Our second analysis provides a flow-sensitive characterization of object reachability, and, like [WR99], supports strong-updates on assignment to global data. Using a per program-point heap abstraction in conjunction with a thread-aware analysis leads to a refined approximation useful in optimizing a program's heap and stack layout. Our refined analysis may still find a number of program points where an object is local, even though that object may eventually escape into the heap. By tracking object reachability through threads, our analyses provide a more refined approximation of the concurrency properties of a program.

References

ACSE99.   Jonathan Aldrich, Craig Chambers, Emin Sirer, and Susan Eggers. Static analysis for eliminating unnecessary synchronization in Java programs. In *International Static Analysis Symposium*, pages 19–38, September 1999. 430

Age95.   Ole Agesen. The cartesian product algorithm: simple and precise type inference of parametric polymorphism. *ECOOP'95 Conference Proceedings*, pages 2–26, 1995. 429

BH99.   Jeff Bogda and Urs Holzle. Removing unnecessary synchronization in Java. In *Conference on Object-Oriented Programming Systems, Languages, and Applications*, pages 35–47, November 1999. 413, 430

BKMS98.   David Bacon, Ravi Konru, Chet Murthy, and Mauricio Serrano. Thin locks: featherweight synchronization for Java. In *ACM Conference on Programming Language Design and Implementation*, pages 258–268, June 1998. 414

Bla99.   Bruno Blanchet. Escape analysis for object-oriented languages: application to Java. In *Conference on Object-Oriented Programming Systems, Languages, and Applications*, pages 20–35, November 1999. 413, 430

CGS+99.   Jong-Deok Choi, Manish Gupta, Mauricio Serrano, Vugranam Sreedhar, and Sam Midkiff. Escape analysis for Java. In *Conference on Object-Oriented Programming Systems, Languages, and Applications*, pages 1–19, November 1999. 413, 430

CI92.   Jyh-Herng Chow and Williams Ludwell Harrison III. Compile time analysis of parallel programs that share memory. In *19th ACM Symposium on Principles of Programming Languages*, January 1992. 430

CWZ90.   David. R. Chase, M. Wegman, and F.K. Zadeck. Analysis of pointers and structures. In *ACM Conference on Programming Language Design and Implementation*, pages 296–310, June 1990. 413, 414, 430

Deu90.   Alain Deutsch. On determining lifetime and aliasing of dynamically allocated data in higher-order functional specifications. In *17th ACM Symposium on Principles of Programming Languages*, pages 157–168, January 1990. 430

DGC98.   Greg DeFouw, David Grove, and Craig Chambers. Fast interprocedural class analysis. In *25th ACM Symposium on Principles of Programming Languages*, pages 222–236, January 1998. 417, 429

Hei94.   Nevin Heintze. Set-based analysis of ML programs. In *ACM International Conference on Lisp and Functional Programming*, pages 306–317, June 1994. 429

Jav98.   *ACM Workshop on Java for High-Performance Network Computing*, 1998. 413

Jav99.   *Java Grande 99*. ACM, June 1999. 413

JM79.   Neil Jones and Stephen Muchnick. Flow analysis and optimization of Lisp-like structures. In *6th ACM Symposium on Principles of Programming Languages*, pages 244–256, January 1979. 429

JW94.   Suresh Jagannathan and Stephen T. Weeks. Analyzing stores and references in a parallel symbolic language. In *ACM International Conference on Lisp and Functional Programming*, pages 294–305, 1994. 430

JW95.   Suresh Jagannathan and Stephen T. Weeks. A unified treatment of flow analysis in higher-order languages. In *22nd ACM Symposium on Principles of Programming Languages*, pages 393–407, January 1995. 424

Mer91.   N. Mercouroff. An algorithm for analyzing communicating processes. In *Mathematical Foundations of Programming Semantics*. Springer-Verlag, 1991. 430

MTHM97.   Robin Milner, Mads Tofte, Robert Harper, and David B. Macqueen. *The Definition of Standard ML (Revised)*. MIT Press, 1997. 415

PC94.   John Plevyak and Andrew A. Chien. Precise concrete type inference for object-oriented languages. *Conference on Object-Oriented Programming Systems, Language, and Applications*, pages 324–340, October 1994. 417, 429

PS91.   Jens Palsberg and Michael I. Schwartzbach. Object-oriented type inference. *Conference on Object-Oriented Programming Systems, Languages, and Applications*, pages 146–161, October 1991. 417, 429

RM88.   Cristina Ruggieri and Thomas P. Murtagh. Lifetime analysis of dynamically allocated objects. In *ACM Symposium on Principles of Programming Languages*, pages 285–293, January 1988. 430

SF96.   Manuel Serrano and Marc Feeley. Storage use analysis and its applications. In *International Conference on Functional Programming*, May 1996. 430

Shi91.   Olin Shivers. *Control-Flow Analysis of Higher-Order Languages or Taming Lambda*. PhD thesis, School of Computer Science, Carnegie-Mellon University, 1991. 421, 429

SRW96.   Mooly Sagiv, Thomas Reps, and Reinhard Wilhelm. Solving shape analysis problems in languages with destructive updating. *ACM Transactions on Programming Languages and Systems*, 20(1):1–50, 1996. 430

WR99.   John Whaley and Martin Rinard. Compositional pointer and escape analysis for Java programs. In *Conference on Object-Oriented Programming Systems, Languages, and Applications*, pages 187–207, November 1999. 413, 430, 431

Author Index

Lecture Notes in Computer Science

For information about Vols. 1–1741
please contact your bookseller or Springer-Verlag